PEARSON

Principles of Finance
FIN 3000

Fifth Custom Edition for Baruch College of CUNY

Taken from:
Fundamentals of Investing, Thirteenth Edition
by Scott B. Smart, Lawrence J. Gitman, and Michael D. Joehnk

Financial Management: Principles and Applications, Twelfth Edition
by Sheridan Titman, Arthur J. Keown, and John D. Martin

Cover art: Courtesy of Getty/Photodisc

Taken from:

Fundamentals of Investing, Thirteenth Edition
by Scott B. Smart, Lawrence J. Gitman, and Michael D. Joehnk
Copyright © 2017, 2014, 2011 by Pearson Education, Inc.
New York, NY 10013

Financial Management: Principles and Applications, Twelfth Edition
by Sheridan Titman, Arthur J. Keown, and John D. Martin
Copyright © 2014, 2011, 2008 by Pearson Education, Inc.
New York, NY 10013

This special edition published in cooperation with Pearson Education, Inc.

All trademarks, service marks, registered trademarks, and registered service marks are the
property of their respective owners and are used herein for identification purposes only.

Pearson Education, Inc., 330 Hudson Street, New York, New York 10013
A Pearson Education Company
www.pearsoned.com

Printed in the United States of America

1   16

000200010272057132
000200010272057410

NH

ISBN 10: 1-323-41210-7   ISBN 10: 1-323-50357-9
ISBN 13: 978-1-323-41210-7   ISBN 13: 978-1-323-50357-7

Dedicated To
Susan R. Smart,
Robin F. Gitman, and
Charlene W. Joehnk

Brief Contents

Chapters 1-3, 7-11 and 13 are taken from *Fundamentals of Investing*, Thirteenth Edition, by Scott B. Smart, Lawrence J. Gitman, and Michael D. Joehnk.

Chapters 4-6 and 12 are taken from *Financial Management: Principles and Applications*, Twelfth Edition, by Sheridan Titman, Arthur J. Keown, and John D. Martin.

Contents

Chapters 1-3, 7-11 and 13 are taken from *Fundamentals of Investing*, Thirteenth Edition, by Scott B. Smart, Lawrence J. Gitman, and Michael D. Joehnk.

Chapters 4-6 and 12 are taken from *Financial Management: Principles and Applications*, Twelfth Edition, by Sheridan Titman, Arthur J. Keown, and John D. Martin.

Chapter 1
Common Stocks 1

Chapter 2
Fixed-Income Securities 40

Chapter 3
Securities Markets and Transactions 87

Chapter 4
Firms and the Financial Market 124

Chapter 5
Time Value of Money—The Basics 147

Chapter 6
The Time Value of Money—Annuities and Other Topics 180

Chapter 7
Market Efficiency and Behavioral Finance 217

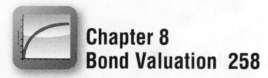

Chapter 8
Bond Valuation 258

Chapter 9
Stock Valuation 299

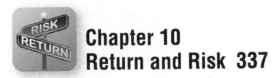

Chapter 10
Return and Risk 337

Chapter 11
Modern Portfolio Concepts 373

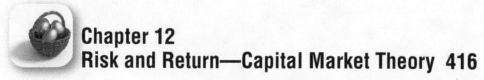

Chapter 12
Risk and Return—Capital Market Theory 416

Chapter 13
Options: Puts and Calls 449

■ **FAMOUS FAILURES IN FINANCE**
Ethical Lapse or Extraordinarily Good
Timing? 461

■ **FAMOUS FAILURES IN FINANCE**
The Volatility Index 466

Preface

"Great firms aren't great investments unless the price is right." Those words of wisdom come from none other than Warren Buffett, who is, without question, one of the greatest investors ever. The words of Mr. Buffett sum up very nicely the essence of this book—namely, to help students learn to make informed investment decisions, not only when buying stocks but also when investing in bonds, mutual funds, or any other type of investment.

The fact is, investing may sound simple, but it's not. Investors in today's turbulent financial markets confront many challenges when deciding how to invest their money. Nearly a decade after the 2008 meltdown in financial markets, investors are still more wary of risk than they were before the crisis. This book is designed to help students understand the risks inherent in investing and to give them the tools they need to answer the fundamental questions that help shape a sound investment strategy. For example, students want to know, what are the best investments for me? Should I buy individual securities, mutual funds, or exchange-traded funds? How do I make judgments about risk? Do I need professional help with my investments, and can I afford it? Clearly, investors need answers to questions like these to make informed decisions.

The language, concepts, and strategies of investing are foreign to many. In order to become informed investors, students must first become conversant with the many aspects of investing. Building on that foundation, they can learn how to make informed decisions in the highly dynamic investment environment. This thirteenth edition of *Fundamentals of Investing* provides the information and guidance needed by individual investors to make such informed decisions and to achieve their investment goals.

This book meets the needs of professors and students in the first investments course offered at colleges and universities, junior and community colleges, professional certification programs, and continuing education courses. Focusing on both individual securities and portfolios, *Fundamentals of Investing* explains how to develop, implement, and monitor investment goals after considering the risk and return of different types of investments. A conversational tone and liberal use of examples guide students through the material and demonstrate important points.

New for the Thirteenth Edition

Our many adopters are interested in how we have changed the content from the twelfth to the thirteenth edition. We hope that this information will also interest potential adopters because it indicates our mandate to stay current in the field of investments and to continue to craft a book that will truly meet the needs of students and professors.

Some of the major changes made in the thirteenth edition are the following:

- Updated all real-world data through 2015 (or 2014 if 2015 numbers were not yet available), including text, tables, and figures.

- Created new videos of worked-out solutions to in-text examples that students can see on MyFinanceLab and use as a guide for the end-of-chapter problems as well as related assignments made by their professors.

- Revised many end-of-chapter problems.

- Expanded coverage of mutual funds, ETFs, and hedge funds in Chapter 1, and introduced new coverage on formulating a personal investment policy statement.

- Replaced the previous Markets in Crisis feature, which focused on various causes and consequences of the 2007 to 2008 financial crisis and recession, with a new Famous Failures in Finance boxed item. Famous Failures shares some lessons from the financial crisis, but it also highlights other "problem areas" in the investments world such as market crashes, ethical scandals, and failures of financial service providers to act in their clients' best interests.

- Updated QR codes in the margins of each chapter. Students can scan these codes with their smart phones to gain access to videos and other web content that enhance the topical coverage of each chapter.

- Added a new feature called Watch Your Behavior. These boxes appear in the margins of most chapters and highlight investment lessons gleaned from the behavioral finance literature.

- Updated numerous Investor Facts boxes from the twelfth edition and incorporated entirely new ones in most chapters.

- Expanded the use of real-world data in examples.

- Added new coverage of the free-cash-flow-to-equity stock valuation model in Chapter 8.

- Expanded and updated coverage of behavioral finance, particularly but not exclusively in Chapter 9. Also added new content on the role of arbitrage in moving financial markets toward efficiency.

- Included new historical data on interest rates and bond returns in Chapter 10, highlighting the link between changes in interest rates and total returns earned on bonds.

- Revised or replaced every chapter opener, and in many chapters, included an end-of-chapter problem that ties back to the chapter opener.

- Created a new feature called Excel@Investing, which provides students with online access to electronic copies of most tables in the text that involve calculations. Students can explore these Excel files to better understand the calculations embedded in the printed tables, and students make the textbook's tables dynamic by using these spreadsheets to change key assumptions to see how doing so affects the key results.

Hallmarks of *Fundamentals of Investing*

Using information gathered from academicians and practicing investment professionals, plus feedback from adopters, the thirteenth edition reflects the realities of today's investment environment. At the same time, the following characteristics provide a structured framework for successful teaching and learning.

Clear Focus on the Individual Investor

According to a Gallup poll, today about 55% of all U.S. households own stock either directly or indirectly through mutual funds or participation in 401(k)s. That percentage peaked at 65% in 2008 but if fell for six consecutive years in the aftermath of the financial crisis and has only recently started rising again. The focus of *Fundamentals of*

Investing has always been on the individual investor. This focus gives students the information they need to develop, implement, and monitor a successful investment program. It also provides students with a solid foundation of basic concepts, tools, and techniques. Subsequent courses can build on that foundation by presenting the advanced concepts, tools, and techniques used by institutional investors and money managers.

Comprehensive Yet Flexible Organization

The text provides a firm foundation for learning by first describing the overall investment environment, including the various investment markets, information, and transactions. Next, it presents conceptual tools needed by investors—the concepts of return and risk and the basic approaches to portfolio management. It then examines the most popular types of investments—common stocks, bonds, and mutual funds. Following this series of chapters on investment vehicles is a chapter on how to construct and administer one's own portfolio. The final section of the book focuses on derivative securities—options and futures—which require more expertise. Although the first two parts of the textbook are best covered at the start of the course, instructors can cover particular investment types in just about any sequence. The comprehensive yet flexible nature of the book enables instructors to customize it to their own course structure and teaching objectives.

We have organized each chapter according to a decision-making perspective, and we have been careful always to point out the pros and cons of the various investments and strategies we present. With this information, individual investors can select the investment actions that are most consistent with their objectives. In addition, we have presented the various investments and strategies in such a way that students learn the decision-making implications and consequences of each investment action they contemplate.

Timely Topics

Various issues and developments constantly reshape financial markets and investment vehicles. Virtually all topics in this book take into account changes in the investment environment. For example, in every chapter we've added a new feature called Famous Failures in Finance. This feature highlights various aspects of the recent and historic financial crisis, as well as other "failures" in financial markets such as bank runs and ethical lapses by corporate managers and rogue traders. Fundamentally, investing is about the tradeoff between risk and return, and the Famous Failures in Finance feature serves as a reminder to students that they should not focus exclusively on an investment's returns.

In addition, the thirteenth edition provides students access to short video clips from professional investment advisors. In these clips, which are carefully integrated into the content of each chapter, students will hear professionals sharing the lessons that they have learned through years of experience working as advisors to individual investors.

Globalization

One issue that is reshaping the world of investing is the growing globalization of securities markets. As a result, *Fundamentals of Investing* continues to stress the global aspects of investing. We initially look at the growing importance of international markets, investing in foreign securities (directly or indirectly), international investment performance, and the risks of international investing. In later chapters, we describe popular international investment opportunities and strategies as part of the coverage of each specific type of investment vehicle. This integration of international topics helps students understand the importance of maintaining a global focus when planning, building, and managing an investment portfolio. Global topics are highlighted by a globe icon in the margin.

Comprehensive, Integrated Learning System

Another feature of the thirteenth edition is its comprehensive and integrated learning system, which makes clear to students what they need to learn in the chapter and helps them focus their study efforts as they progress through the chapter. For more detailed discussion of the learning system, see the feature walkthrough later in the preface (beginning on page xxi).

CFA Exam Questions

We are pleased to include CFA exam questions in the thirteenth edition, both in the written text and in MyFinanceLab. CFA exam questions appear in the text at the end of five of the book's six parts. Due to the nature of the material in some of the early chapters, the CFA questions for Parts One and Two are combined and appear at the end of Part Two. These questions offer students an opportunity to test their investment knowledge against that required for the CFA Level-I exam.

In MyFinanceLab on the Course Home page, there are three Sample CFA Exams. Each of these exams is patterned after the CFA Level-I exam and comes with detailed guideline answers. The exams deal only with topics that are actually covered in the thirteenth edition of *Fundamentals of Investing* and are meant to replicate as closely as possible the types of questions that appear on the standard Level-I Exam. The Sample CFA Exams on MyFinanceLab come in three lengths: 30 questions, 40 questions, and 50 questions. Each exam is unique and consists of a different set of questions, so students can take any one or all of the exams without running into any duplicate questions. For the most part, these questions are adapted from past editions of the CFA Candidate Study Notes. Answers are included for immediate reinforcement.

MyFinanceLab

MyFinanceLab is a fully integrated online homework and tutorial system that offers flexible instructor tools like the easy-to-use homework manager for test, quiz, and homework assignments, automatic grading, and a powerful online Gradebook. Students can take preloaded Sample Tests for each chapter and their results generate an individualized Study Plan that helps focus and maximize their study time. Please visit http://www.myfinancelab.com for more information or to register.

The Smart, Gitman & Joehnk

PROVEN TEACHING/LEARNING/MOTIVATIONAL SYSTEM

Users of *Fundamentals of Investing* have praised the effectiveness of the Smart/Gitman/Joehnk teaching and learning system, which has been hailed as one of its hallmarks. In the thirteenth edition we have retained and polished the system, which is driven by a set of carefully developed learning goals. Users have also praised the rich motivational framework that underpins each chapter. Key elements of the pedagogical and motivational features are illustrated and described below.

THE LEARNING GOAL SYSTEM

The Learning Goal system begins each chapter with **six Learning Goals**, labeled with numbered icons. These goals anchor the most important concepts and techniques to be learned. The Learning Goal icons are then tied to key points in the chapter's structure, including:

- First-level headings
- Summary
- Discussion Questions
- Problems
- Cases

This tightly knit structure provides a clear road map for students—they know what they need to learn, where they can find it, and whether they've mastered it by the end of the chapter.

An **opening story** sets the stage for the content that follows by focusing on an investment situation involving a real company or real event, which is in turn linked to the chapter topics. Students see the relevance of the vignette to the world of investments.

In many cases, an end-of-chapter problem draws students back to the chapter opener and asks them to use the data in the opener to make a calculation or draw a conclusion to demonstrate what they learned in the chapter.

What Is Inflation?

In the margins of each chapter students will find **QR codes**. By scanning these codes with their smart phones, students will be taken to websites with useful information to enhance their understanding of the topics covered in the textbook. For example, many of these QR codes link students with free online video tutorials covering a range of topics.

Also new to this edition, **Watch Your Behavior** boxes appear in the margins of most chapters and highlight investment lessons gleaned from the behavioral finance literature.

WATCH YOUR BEHAVIOR

Short-Lived Growth So-called value stocks are stocks that have low price-to-book ratios, and growth stocks are stocks that have relatively high price-to-book ratios. Many studies demonstrate that value stocks outperform growth stocks, perhaps because investors overestimate the odds that a firm that has grown rapidly in the past will continue to do so.

Each chapter contains a handful of **Investor Facts**—brief sidebar items that give an interesting statistic or cite an unusual investment experience. These facts add a bit of seasoning to the concepts under review and capture a real-world flavor. The Investor Facts sidebars include material focused on topics such as art as an investment, the downgrade of the U.S. government's credit rating, the use of financial statements to detect accounting fraud, and recent issues of unusual securities such as bonds with 100-year maturities.

An Advisor's Perspective consists of short video clips of professional investment advisers discussing the investments topics covered in each chapter. Students can access the video clips on MyFinanceLab.

AN ADVISOR'S PERSPECTIVE

Ed Slott
CEO, Ed Slott and Company

"The greatest money making asset any individual can possess is time."

MyFinanceLab

INVESTOR FACTS

A Steady Stream York Water Company raised its dividend for the 17th consecutive year in February 2015. That's an impressive run, but it's not the most notable fact about York's dividend stream. The company paid dividends without missing a single year since 1816, the year that Indiana was admitted as the 19th U.S. state! No other U.S. company can match York's record of nearly two centuries of uninterrupted dividend payments.

FAMOUS FAILURES IN FINANCE

Fears of Deflation Worry Investors

For most of your lifetime, prices of most goods and services have been rising. There are important exceptions, such as the prices of consumer electronics and computers, but from one year to the next, the overall price level rose continuously in the United States from 1955 through 2007. However, as the recession deepened in 2008, consumer prices in the United States began to decline, falling in each of the last five months that year. Countries in the European Union experienced a brief deflationary period around the same time. The news raised fears among some investors that the recession might turn into a depression like the one that had brought about

a price decline of −27% from November 1929 to March 1933. Although prices began to rise again, fears of deflation resurfaced again in late 2014 and early 2015. Prices in the United States were flat or down in the first three months of 2015, while countries in the European Union experienced falling prices for four consecutive months starting in December 2015.

Critical Thinking Question Suppose you own an investment that pays a fixed return in dollars year after year. How do you think inflation (rising prices) or deflation (falling prices) would influence the value of this type of investment?

Famous Failures in Finance boxes— short, boxed discussions of real-life scenarios in the investments world, many of which focus on ethics— appear in selected chapters and on the book's website. Many of these boxes contain a Critical Thinking Question for class discussion, with guideline answers given in the Instructor's Manual.

WITHIN THE CHAPTER

Key Equations are screened in yellow throughout the text to help readers identify the most important mathematical relationships. Select key equations also appear in the text's rear endpapers.

Equation 8.4	$$\text{Estimated dividends per share in year } t = \text{Estimated EPS for year } t \times \text{Estimated payout ratio}$$

Calculator Keystrokes At appropriate spots in the text the student will find sections on the use of financial calculators, with marginal calculator graphics that show the inputs and functions to be used.

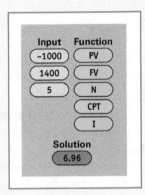

Input	Function
−1000	PV
1400	FV
5	N
	CPT
	I
Solution	
6.96	

CONCEPTS IN REVIEW
Answers available at
http://www.pearsonhighered
.com/smart

3.1 Discuss the impact of the Internet on the individual investor and summarize the types of resources it provides.

3.2 Identify the four main types of online investment tools. How can they help you become a better investor?

3.3 What are the pros and cons of using the Internet to choose and manage your investments?

Concepts in Review questions appear at the end of each section of the chapter. These review questions allow students to test their understanding of each section before moving on to the next section of the chapter. Answers for these questions are available in the Multimedia Library of MyFinanceLab, at the book's website, and by review of the preceding text.

The **end-of-chapter summary** makes *Fundamentals of Investing* an efficient study tool by integrating chapter contents with online learning resources available in **MyFinanceLab**. A thorough summary of the key concepts— What You Should Know—is directly linked with the text and online resources—Where to Practice. **Learning Goal** icons precede each summary item, which begins with a boldfaced restatement of the learning goal.

Discussion Questions, keyed to Learning Goals, guide students to integrate, investigate, and analyze the key concepts presented in the chapter. Many questions require that students apply the tools and techniques of the chapter to investment information they have obtained and then make a recommendation with regard to a specific investment strategy or vehicle. These project-type questions are far broader than the Concepts in Review questions within the chapter. Answers to odd-numbered questions are available to students in MyFinanceLab and on the book's website.

Expanded and Revised Problem Sets offer additional review and homework opportunities and are keyed to Learning Goals. Answers to odd-numbered Problems are available to students in MyFinanceLab and on the book's website, while all answers/solutions are available for instructors in the Instructor's Manual.

MyFinanceLab

Here is what you should know after reading this chapter. MyFinanceLab will help you identify what you know and where to go when you need to practice.

What You Should Know	Key Terms	Where to Practice
LG1 **Explain the behavior of market interest rates and identify the forces that cause interest rates to change.** The behavior of interest rates is the most important force in the bond market. It determines not only the amount of current income an investor will receive but also the investor's capital gains (or losses). Changes in market interest rates can have a dramatic impact on the total returns obtained from bonds over time.	yield spreads, p. 426	MyFinanceLab Study Plan 11.1
LG2 **Describe the term structure of interest rates and note how investors can use yield curves.** Many forces drive the behavior of interest rates over time, including inflation, the cost and availability of funds, and the level of interest rates in major foreign markets. One particularly important force is the term structure of interest rates, which relates yield to maturity to term to maturity. Yield curves essentially plot the term structure and are often used by investors as a way to get a handle on the future behavior of interest rates.	expectations hypothesis, p. 432 liquidity preference theory, p. 433 market segmentation theory, p. 433 term structure of interest rates, p. 429 yield curve, p. 429	MyFinanceLab Study Plan 11.2
LG3 **Understand how investors value bonds in the marketplace.** Bonds are valued (priced) in the	accrued interest, p. 438 clean price, p. 439	MyFinanceLab Study Plan 11.3

Discussion Questions

LG1 **Q11.1** Briefly describe each of the following theories of the term structure of interest rates.
 a. Expectations hypothesis
 b. Liquidity preference theory
 c. Market segmentation theory

According to these theories, what conditions would result in a downward-sloping yield curve? What conditions would result in an upward-sloping yield curve? Which theory do you think is most valid, and why?

LG2 **Q11.2** Using the *Wall Street Journal*, *Barron's*, or an online source, find the bond yields for Treasury securities with the following maturities: 3 months, 6 months, 1 year, 3 years, 5 years, 10 years, 15 years, and 20 years. Construct a yield curve based on these reported yields, putting term to maturity on the horizontal (x) axis and yield to maturity on the vertical (y) axis. Briefly discuss the general shape of your yield curve. What conclusions might you draw about future interest rate movements from this yield curve?

LG5 **Q11.3** Briefly explain what will happen to a bond's duration measure if each of the following events occur.
 a. The yield to maturity on the bond falls from 8.5% to 8%.
 b. The bond gets 1 year closer to its maturity.

Problems

All problems are available on http://www.myfinancelab.com

LG3 **P11.1** You are considering the purchase of a $1,000 par value bond with an 6.5% coupon rate (with interest paid semiannually) that matures in 12 years. If the bond is priced to provide a required return of 8%, what is the bond's current price?

LG3 **P11.2** Two bonds have par values of $1,000. One is a 5%, 15-year bond priced to yield 8%. The other is a 7.5%, 20-year bond priced to yield 6%. Which of these has the lower price? (Assume annual compounding in both cases.)

LG3 **P11.3** Using semiannual compounding, find the prices of the following bonds.
 a. A 10.5%, 15-year bond priced to yield 8%
 b. A 7%, 10-year bond priced to yield 8%
 c. A 12%, 20-year bond priced at 10%

Repeat the problem using annual compounding. Then comment on the differences you found in the prices of the bonds.

LG3 **P11.4** You have the opportunity to purchase a 25-year, $1,000 par value bond that has an annual coupon rate of 9%. If you require a YTM of 7.6%, how much is the bond worth to you?

LG3 **P11.5** A $1,000 par value bond has a current price of $800 and a maturity value of $1,000 and matures in five years. If interest is paid semiannually and the bond is priced to yield 8%, what is the bond's annual coupon rate?

LG3 **P11.6** A 20-year bond has a coupon of 10% and is priced to yield 8%. Calculate the price per $1,000 par value using semiannual compounding. If an investor purchases this bond two months before a scheduled coupon payment, how much accrued interest must be paid to the seller?

Case Problem 4.2   The Risk-Return Tradeoff: Molly O'Rourke's Stock Purchase Decision

LG3 LG6   Over the past 10 years, Molly O'Rourke has slowly built a diversified portfolio of common stock. Currently her portfolio includes 20 different common stock issues and has a total market value of $82,500.

Molly is at present considering the addition of 50 shares of either of two common stock issues—X or Y. To assess the return and risk of each of these issues, she has gathered dividend income and share price data for both over the last 10 years (2007–2016). Molly's investigation of the outlook for these issues suggests that each will, on average, tend to behave in the future just as it has in the past. She therefore believes that the expected return can be estimated by finding the average HPR over the past 10 years for each of the stocks. The historical dividend income and stock price data collected by Molly are given in the accompanying table.

Two **Case Problems**, keyed to the Learning Goals, encourage students to use higher-level critical thinking skills: to apply techniques presented in the chapter, to evaluate alternatives, and to recommend how an investor might solve a specific problem. Again, Learning Goals show the student the chapter topics on which the case problems focus.

Excel@Investing problems, appearing at the end of all chapters, challenge students to solve financial problems and make decisions through the creation of spreadsheets. In addition, in this edition we provide electronic versions of many in-text tables so students can see how the calculations in the tables work, and they can alter the baseline assumption in the printed tables to see how changing assumptions affects the main results of each table. In Chapter 1 students are directed to the website http://www.myfinancelab.com, where they can complete a spreadsheet tutorial, if needed. In addition, this tutorial and selected tables within the text carrying a spreadsheet icon are available in spreadsheet form on the text's website.

Excel@Investing

Excel@Investing

The cash flow component of bond investments is made up of the annual interest payments and the future redemption value or its par value. Just like other time-value-of-money considerations, the bond cash flows are discounted back in order to determine their present value.

In comparing bonds to stocks, many investors look at the respective returns. The total returns in the bond market are made up of both current income and capital gains. Bond investment analysis should include the determination of the current yield as well as a specific holding period return.

On January 13, 2016, you gather the following information on three corporate bonds issued by the General Pineapple Corporation (GPC). Remember that corporate bonds are quoted as a percentage of their par value. Assume the par value of each bond to be $1,000. These debentures are quoted in eighths of a point. Create a spreadsheet that will model and answer the following bond investment problems.

Bonds	Current Yield	Volume	Close
GPC 5.3 13	?	25	$105^7/_8$
GPC 6.65s 20	?	45	103
GPC 7.4 22	?	37	$104^6/_8$

CFA Exam Questions from the 2010 Level One Curriculum and the *CFA Candidate Study Notes, Level 1, Volume 4* are now at the end of each part of the book, starting at Part Two. These questions are also assignable in MyFinanceLab.

CFA Exam Questions

Investing in Common Stocks

Following is a sample of 11 Level-I CFA exam questions that deal with many topics covered in Chapters 6, 7, 8, and 9 of this text, including the use of financial ratios, various stock valuation models, and efficient market concepts. (*Note:* When answering some of the questions, remember: "Forward P/E" is the same as a P/E based on estimated earnings one year out.) When answering the questions, give yourself 1½ minutes for each question; the objective is to correctly answer 8 of the 11 questions in a period of 16½ minutes.

1. Holding constant all other variables and excluding any interactions among the determinants of value, which of the following would most likely increase a firm's price-to-earnings multiple?
   a. The risk premium increases.
   b. The retention rate increases.
   c. The beta of the stock increases.

2. A rationale for the use of the price-to-sales (P/S) approach is:
   a. Sales are more volatile than earnings.
   b. P/S ratios assess cost structures accurately.
   c. Revenues are less subject to accounting manipulation than earnings.

3. A cyclical company tends to
   a. have earnings that track the overall economy.
   b. have a high price-to-earnings ratio.
   c. have less volatile earnings than the overall market.

4. Consider a company that earned $4.00 per share last year and paid a dividend of $1.00. The firm has maintained a consistent payout ratio over the years and analysts expect this to continue. The firm is expected to earn $4.40 per share next year, and the stock is expected to sell for $30.00. The required rate of return is 12%. What is the best estimate of the stock's current value?
   a. $44.00
   b. $22.67
   c. $27.77

5. A stock's current dividend is $1 and its expected dividend is $1.10 next year. If the investor's required rate of return is 15% and the stock is currently trading at $20.00, what is the implied expected price in one year?
   a. $21.90
   b. $22.00
   c. $23.00

6. A firm has total revenues of $187,500, net income of $15,000, total current liabilities of $50,000, total common equity of $75,000, and total assets of $150,000. What is the firm's ROE?
   a. 15%
   b. 20%
   c. 24%

INTERACTIVE LEARNING

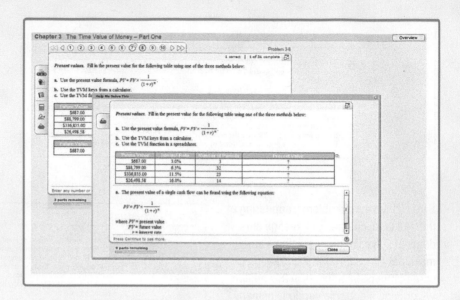

MyFinanceLab is a fully integrated homework and tutorial system which solves one of the biggest teaching problems in finance courses—students learn better with lots of practice, but grading complex multipart problems is time-consuming for the instructor. In MyFinanceLab, students can work the end-of-chapter problems with algorithmically generated values for unlimited practice and instructors can create assignments that are automatically graded and recorded in an online Gradebook.

MyFinanceLab also contains brief videos of author Scott Smart walking students through step-by-step solutions of select problems.

MyFinanceLab: hands-on practice, hands-off grading.

Supplemental Materials

We recognize the key role of a complete and creative package of materials to supplement a basic textbook. We believe that the following materials, offered with the thirteenth edition, will enrich the investments course for both students and instructors.

Fundamentals of Investing Companion Website

The book's Companion Website offers students and professors an up-to-date source of supplemental materials. This resource is located at http://www.pearsonhighered.com /smart. Visitors will find answers to Concepts in Review questions and answers to odd-numbered Discussion Questions and Problems and spreadsheets of selected tables within the text carrying the Excel@Investing icon.

Instructor's Manual

Revised by Robert J. Hartwig of Worcester State College, the *Instructor's Manual* contains chapter outlines; lists of key concepts discussed in each chapter; detailed chapter overviews; answers/suggested answers to all Concepts in Review and Discussion Questions, Problems, and Critical Thinking Questions to Famous Failures in Finance boxes; solutions to the Case Problems; and ideas for outside projects.

Test Bank

Revised for the thirteenth edition, also by Robert J. Hartwig of Worcester State College, the *Test Bank* includes a substantial number of questions. Each chapter features true-false and multiple-choice questions, as well as several problems and short-essay questions. The *Test Bank* is also available in Test Generator Software (TestGen with QuizMaster). Fully networkable, this software is available for Windows and Macintosh. TestGen's graphical interface enables instructors to easily view, edit, and add questions; export questions to create tests; and print tests in a variety of fonts and forms. Search and sort features let the instructor quickly locate questions and arrange them in a preferred order. QuizMaster, working with your school's computer network, automatically grades the exams, saves results, and allows the instructor to view or print a variety of reports.

PowerPoint Lecture Slides

To facilitate classroom presentations, PowerPoint slides of all text images and classroom lecture notes are available for Windows and Macintosh. The slides were revised by textbook author Scott Smart.

Acknowledgments

Many people gave their generous assistance during the initial development and revisions of *Fundamentals of Investing*. The expertise, classroom experience, and general advice of both colleagues and practitioners have been invaluable. Reactions and suggestions from students throughout the country—comments we especially enjoy receiving—sustained our belief in the need for a fresh, informative, and teachable investments text.

A few individuals provided significant subject matter expertise in the initial development of the book. They are Terry S. Maness of Baylor University, Arthur L. Schwartz, Jr., of the University of South Florida at St. Petersburg, and Gary W. Eldred. Their contributions are greatly appreciated. In addition, Pearson obtained the advice of a large group of experienced reviewers. We appreciate their many suggestions and criticisms, which have had a strong influence on various aspects of this volume. Our special thanks go to the following people, who reviewed all or part of the manuscript for the previous twelve editions of the book.

Kevin Ahlgrim	Albert J. Fredman	Wendy Ku	Rathin Rathinasamy
M. Fall Ainina	John Gerlach	George Kutner	William A. Richard
Joan Anderssen	Tom Geurts	Blake LeBaron	Linda R. Richardson
Felix O. Ayadi	Chaim Ginsberg	Robert T. LeClair	William A. Rini
Gary Baker	Joel Gold	Chun I. Lee	Roy A. Roberson
Harisha Batra	Terry Grieb	William Lepley	Tammy Rogers
Anand K. Bhattacharya	Frank Griggs	Steven Lifland	Edward Rozalewicz
Richard B. Bellinfante	Brian Grinder	Ralph Lim	William J. Ruckstuhl
Cecil C. Bigelow	Arthur S. Guarino	James Lock	David Russo
Robert J. Boldin	Harry P. Guenther	Larry A. Lynch	Arthur L. Schwartz, Jr.
Paul Bolster	Tom Guerts	Barry Marchman	William Scroggins
Denis O. Boudreaux	John Guess	Weston A. McCormac	Daniel Singer
A. David Brummett	Robert Hartwig	David J. McLaughlin	Keith V. Smith
Gary P. Cain	Mahboubul Hassan	Anne Macy	Pat R. Stout
Gary Carman	Gay Hatfield	James Mallett	Nancy E. Strickler
Daniel J. Cartell	Dan Hess	Keith Manko	Glenn T. Sweeney
P. R. Chandy	Robert D. Hollinger	Timothy Manuel	Amir Tavakkol
Steven P. Clark	Sue Beck Howard	Kathy Milligan	Phillip D. Taylor
William Compton	Ping Hsiao	Warren E. Moeller	Wenyuh Tsay
David M. Cordell	Roland Hudson, Jr.	Homer Mohr	Robert C. Tueting
Timothy Cowling	Raad Jassim	Majed R. Muhtaseb	Howard E. Van Auken
Robert M. Crowe	Donald W. Johnson	Joseph Newhouse	P. V. Viswanath
Richard F. DeMong	Samuel Kyle Jones	Michael Nugent	Doug Waggle
Clifford A. Diebold	Rajiv Kalra	Joseph F. Ollivier	Hsinrong Wei
Steven Dolvin	Ravindra R. Kamath	Michael Palermo	John R. Weigel
James Dunn	Bill Kane	John Palffy	Sally Wells
Betty Marie Dyatt	Daniel J. Kaufmann, Jr.	John Park	Peter M. Wichert
Scott Ehrhorn	Burhan Kawosa	Thomas Patrick	John C. Woods
Steven J. Elbert	Nancy Kegelman	Michael Polakoff	Michael D. Woodworth
Robert Eldridge	Phillip T. Kolbe	Barbara Poole	Robert J. Wright
Imad Elhaj	Sheri Kole	Ronald S. Pretekin	Richard H. Yanow
Thomas Eyssell	Christopher M. Korth	Stephen W. Pruitt	Ali E. Zadeh
Frank J. Fabozzi	Marie A. Kratochvil	Mark Pyles	Edward Zajicek
Robert A. Ford	Thomas M. Krueger	S. P. Umamaheswar Rao	

The following people provided extremely useful reviews and input to the thirteenth edition:

James DeMello, Western Michigan University
Matthew Haertzen, Northern Arizona University
Jeffrey Jones, College of Southern Nevada
Lynn Kugele, University of Mississippi
Michael G. Nugent, Stony Brook University
James Pandjiris, University of Missouri-St. Louis
Daniel Wolman, Nassau Community College
Dazhi Zheng, West Chester University

Because of the wide variety of topics covered in the book, we called upon many experts for advice. We thank them and their firms for allowing us to draw on their insights and awareness of recent developments to ensure that the text is as current as possible. In particular, we want to mention Bill Bachrach, Bachrach & Associates, San Diego, CA; John Markese, President, American Association of Individual Investors, Chicago, IL; Frank Hatheway, CFA, Chief Economist, Nasdaq, New York, NY; George Ebenhack, Oppenheimer & Co., Los Angeles, CA; Mark D. Erwin, ChFC, Commonwealth Financial Network, San Diego, CA; David M. Love, C. P. Eaton and Associates, La Jolla, CA; Michael R. Murphy, Sceptre Investment Counsel, Toronto, Ontario, Canada; Mark S. Nussbaum, CFP®, Wells Fargo Advisors, Inc., La Jolla, CA; Richard Russell, Dow Theory Letters, La Jolla, CA; and Michael J. Steelman, Merrill Lynch, Bonsall, CA.

To create the video feature An Advisor's Perspective, we relied on the generosity of many investment professionals from around the country. We are especially thankful to David Hays of CFCI and Ed Slott of Ed Slott and Company for helping us to do a great deal of the videotaping for this feature at the Ed Slott conference in Phoenix, Arizona. We are thankful to all of the investment professionals who participated in this project on video:

Catherine Censullo, Founder, CMC Wealth Management
Joseph A. Clark, Managing Partner, Financial Enhancement Group
Ron Courser, CFO, Ron Courser and Associates
Bob Grace, President, Grace Tax Advisory Group
James Grant, Founder, Grant's Interest Rate Observer
Bill Harris, Founder, WH Cornerstone Investments
James Johnson, President, All Mark Insurance Services
Mary Kusske, President, Kusske Financial Management
Rick Loek, CEO, Calrima Financial and Insurance Agency
Ryan McKeown, Senior VP, Wealth Enhancement Group
Thomas O'Connell, President, International Financial Advisory Group
Phil Putney, Owner, AFS Wealth Management
Tom Riquier, Owner, The Retirement Center
Rob Russell, CEO, Russell and Company
Carol Schmidlin, President, Franklin Planning
Ed Slott, CEO, Ed Slott and Company
Bryan Sweet, Owner, Sweet Financial Services
Steve Wright, Managing Member, The Wright Legacy Group

Special thanks to Robert Hartwig of Worcester State College for revising and updating the *Test Bank* and *Instructor's Manual*.

The staff at Pearson, particularly Donna Battista, contributed their creativity, enthusiasm, and commitment to this textbook. Pearson Program Manager Kathryn Dinovo and Project Manager Alison Kalil managed and pulled together the various strands of the project. Other dedicated Pearson staff, including Acquisitions Editor Kate Fernandes, Digital Studios Project Managers Melissa Honig and Andra Skaalrud, Digital Content Team Lead for MyFinanceLab Miguel Leonarte, Senior Product Marketing Manager Alison Haskins, warrant special thanks for shepherding the project through the development, production, marketing, and website construction stages. Without their care and concern, this text would not have evolved into the teachable and interesting text and package we believe it to be.

Finally, our wives, Susan, Robin, and Charlene, played important roles by providing support and understanding during the book's development, revision, and production. We are forever grateful to them, and we hope that this edition will justify the sacrifices required during the many hours we were away from them working on this book.

SCOTT B. SMART
LAWRENCE J. GITMAN
MICHAEL D. JOEHNK

FAMOUS FAILURES IN FINANCE

Beware of the Lumbering Bear

Bear markets occur when stock prices are falling. But not all falling markets end up as bears. A drop of 5% or more in one of the major market indexes, like the Dow Jones Industrial Average, is called a "routine decline." Such declines are considered routine because they typically occur several times a year. A "correction" is a drop of 10% or more in an index, whereas the term *bear market* is reserved for severe market declines of 20% or more. Bear markets occur every three to four years on average, although that pattern does not make it easy to predict bear markets. For example, the 1990s were totally bear-free. The most recent bear market began in October 2007 when the S&P 500 peaked a little shy of 1,600. The next 20 months witnessed one of the worst bear markets in U.S. history, with the S&P 500 falling almost 57% by March 2009.

course, reflect the general behavior of the market as a whole, not necessarily that of individual stocks. Think of them as the return behavior on a well-balanced portfolio of common stocks.

The table shows several interesting patterns. First, the returns from capital gains range from an average of 16.5% during the booming 1990s to −1.4% in the 1930s. Returns from dividends vary too, but not nearly as much, ranging from 5.8% in the 1940s to 1.8% in the 2000–2009 period. Breaking down the returns into dividends and capital gains reveals, not surprisingly, that the big returns (or losses) come from capital gains.

Second, stocks generally earn positive total returns over long time periods. From 1930 to 2014, the average annual total return on the S&P 500 was 11.4% per year. At that rate, you could double your money every six or seven years. To look at the figures another way, if you had invested $10,000 in the S&P 500 at the beginning of 1930,

Excel@Investing

TABLE 1.1   HISTORICAL AVERAGE ANNUAL RETURNS ON THE STANDARD AND POOR'S 500, 1930–2014

	Rate of Return from Dividends	Rate of Return from Capital Gains	Average Annual Total Return
1930s	5.7%	−1.4%	4.3%
1940s	5.8%	3.8%	9.6%
1950s	4.7%	16.2%	20.9%
1960s	3.2%	5.4%	8.6%
1970s	4.2%	3.3%	7.5%
1980s	4.1%	13.8%	17.9%
1990s	2.4%	16.5%	18.9%
2000–2009	1.8%	−0.7%	1.1%
1900–2014	3.9%	7.5%	11.4%

Note: The S&P 500 annual total returns come from Damodaran Online and the S&P 500 annual dividend returns come from multpl.com. The S&P 500 annual capital gain returns are approximations, imputed by the authors by subtracting the annual dividend return from the annual total return.

(Sources: Data from http://pages.stern.nyu.edu/~adamodar/New_Home_Page/datafile/histretSP.html and http://www.multpl.com)

then based on the yearly annual returns, your investment would have grown to more than $21.9 million over the next 85 years. You can get rich by investing in the stock market, as long as you are patient!

Third, investing in stocks is clearly not without risk. Although during the first seven decades shown in Table 1.1 the average annual return on stocks was 12.5%, the beginning of the 21st century witnessed several years with double-digit negative returns. In 2008 alone, the S&P 500 lost roughly 36% of its value. From 2000 through 2009, the U.S. stock market's average annual return was only 1.1% per year! If you had invested $10,000 in stocks in 1930, your portfolio would have grown to more than $16 million by the end of 2007, but one year later your portfolio would have fallen to approximately $10 million, before rising again to just over $26 million by the end of 2014. These figures suggest that stocks may be a very good investment in the long run, but that was little consolation to investors who saw their wealth fall dramatically in the early years of the 21st century.

Now keep in mind that the numbers here represent market performance. Individual stocks can and often do perform quite differently. But at least the averages give us a benchmark against which we can assess current stock returns and our own expectations. For example, if a return of about 11% can be considered a good long-term estimate for stocks, then sustained returns of 16% to 18% should definitely be viewed as extraordinary. (These higher returns are possible, of course, but to get them, you very likely will have to take on more risk.) Likewise, long-run stock returns of only 4% to 6% should probably be viewed as substandard. If that's the best you think you can do, then you may want to consider sticking with bonds, where you'll earn almost as much, but with less risk.

A Real Estate Bubble Goes Bust and So Does the Market

An old investment tip is, "Buy land because they aren't making any more of it." For many years, it appeared that this advice applied to housing in the United States, as home prices enjoyed a long, upward march. According to the Standard and Poor's Case-Shiller Home Price Index, a measure of the average value of a single-family home in the United States, the average home price peaked in July 2006. Over the next three years, home prices fell sharply, falling 31% by the summer of 2009. As prices fell, some homeowners realized that they owed more on their mortgages than their homes were worth, and mortgage defaults began to rise. Unfortunately, some of the biggest investors in home mortgages were U.S. commercial and investment banks. As homeowners fell behind on their mortgage payments, the stock prices of financial institutions began to drop, raising serious concerns about the health of the entire U.S. financial system. Those fears seemed to have been realized when a top-tier investment bank, Lehman Brothers, filed for bankruptcy in September 2008. That event sparked a free fall in the stock market.

Figure 1.1 shows that U.S. stocks rose along with housing prices for many years, but when weakness in the housing sector spilled over into banking, stock prices plummeted. Over the same three-year period the S&P 500 Index lost 28% of its value, and the U.S. economy fell into a deep recession. In the spring of 2009 the stock and housing markets signaled that a recovery might be on the horizon. Indeed, the recession officially ended in June 2009, but by historical standards the economic recovery was somewhat anemic and the housing market continued to languish for another three years. In early 2012 the housing market began a sustained recovery and by the end of 2014 values had climbed back to 84% of their peak values.

The House Price Puzzle

WATCH YOUR BEHAVIOR

Not Cutting Their Losses Research has shown that homeowners are very reluctant to sell their houses at a loss. During a period of falling home prices, homeowners who put their homes up for sale tend to set asking prices that are too high to avoid taking a loss, and as a result homes remain unsold for a very long time.

FIGURE 1.1   **A Snapshot of U.S. Stock and Housing Indexes (2003 through 2014)**

From the start of 2003 until the summer of 2006, U.S. stocks rose along with housing prices, but when crumbling U.S. housing prices began to spill over into banking, stock prices plummeted, wiping out all the gains accumulated over the prior six years. Three years after the stock market hit bottom, it had still not reached its precrisis peak, nor had house prices rebounded from their crisis lows to any significant degree. In the summer of 2012 the housing market began a sustained appreciation, and in early 2013 the stock market surged past its precrisis peak.
(Source: Data from S&P Dow Jones Indices LLC.)

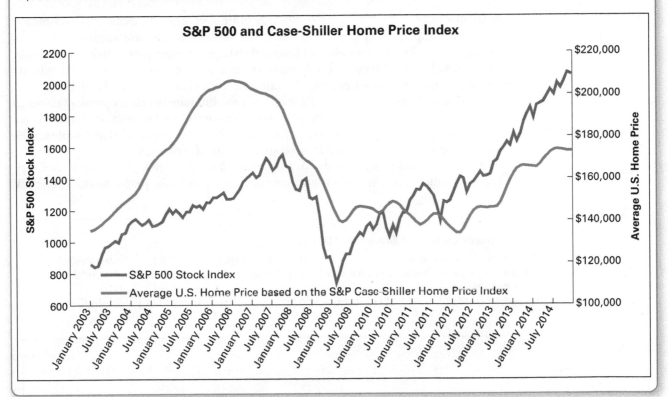

The Pros and Cons of Stock Ownership

Investors own stocks for all sorts of reasons. Some buy stock for the potential for capital gains, while others seek dividend income. Still others appreciate the high degree of liquidity in the stock market. But as with any investment, there are pros and cons to these securities.

The Advantages of Stock Ownership One reason stocks are so appealing is the possibility for substantial returns that they offer. As we just saw, stocks generally provide relatively high returns over the long haul. Indeed, common stock returns compare very favorably to other investments such as long-term corporate bonds and U.S. Treasury securities. For example, over the last century, high-grade corporate bonds earned annual returns that were about half as large as the returns on common stocks. Although long-term bonds outperform stocks in some years, the opposite is true more often than not. Stocks typically outperform bonds, and usually by a wide margin. Stocks also provide protection from inflation because over time their returns exceed the inflation rate. In other words, by purchasing stocks, you gradually increase your purchasing power.

Stocks offer other benefits as well. They are easy to buy and sell, and the costs associated with trading stocks are modest. Moreover, information about stock prices and the stock market is widely disseminated in the news and financial media. A final advantage is that the unit cost of a share of common stock is typically fairly low. Unlike bonds, which normally carry minimum denominations of at least $1,000, and some mutual funds that have fairly hefty minimum investments, common stocks don't have such minimums. Instead, most stocks today are priced at less than $50 or $60 a share—and you can buy any number of shares that you want.

The Disadvantages of Stock Ownership There are also some disadvantages to common stock ownership. Risk is perhaps the most significant. Stocks are subject to various types of risk, including business and financial risk, purchasing power risk, market risk, and event risk. All of these can adversely affect a stock's earnings and dividends, its price appreciation, and, of course, the rate of return that you earn. Even the best of stocks possess elements of risk that are difficult to eliminate because company earnings are subject to many factors, including government control and regulation, foreign competition, and the state of the economy. Because such factors affect sales and profits, they also affect stock prices and (to a lesser degree) dividend payments.

All of this leads to another disadvantage. Stock returns are highly volatile and very hard to predict, so it is difficult to consistently select top performers. The stock

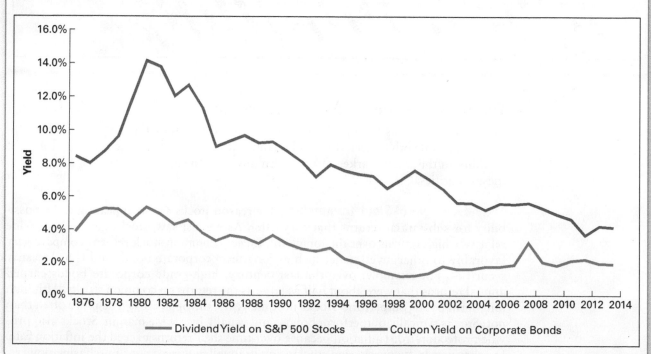

FIGURE 1.2   **The Current Income of Stocks and Bonds**

The current income (dividends) paid to stockholders falls far short of interest income paid to bondholders. The dividend yield is the average dividend yield for stocks in the S&P 500 Index, and the bond yield is for high-quality corporate bonds.
(Source: Data from Federal Reserve Board of Governors and http://www.multpl.com/s-p-500-dividend-yield/table.)

selection process is complex because so many elements affect how a company will perform. In addition, the price of a company's stock today reflects investors' expectations about how the company will perform. In other words, identifying a stock that will earn high returns requires that you not only identify a company that will exhibit strong future financial performance (in terms of sales and earnings) but also that you can spot that opportunity before other investors do and bid up the stock price.

A final disadvantage is that stocks generally distribute less current income than some other investments. Several types of investments—bonds, for instance—pay more current income and do so with much greater certainty. Figure 1.2 compares the dividend yield on common stocks with the coupon yield on high-grade corporate bonds. It shows the degree of sacrifice common stock investors make in terms of current income. Clearly, even though the yield gap has narrowed a great deal in the past few years, common stocks still have a long way to go before they catch up with the current income levels available from bonds and most other types of fixed-income securities.

CONCEPTS IN REVIEW

Answers available at
http://www.pearsonhighered.com/smart

1.1 What is a common stock? What is meant by the statement that holders of common stock are the residual owners of the firm?

1.2 What are two or three of the major investment attributes of common stocks?

1.3 Briefly describe the behavior of the U.S. stock market over the last half of the 20th century and the early part of the 21st century.

1.4 How important are dividends as a source of return to common stock? What about capital gains? Which is more important to total return? Which causes wider swings in total return?

1.5 What are some of the advantages and disadvantages of owning common stock? What are the major types of risks to which stockholders are exposed?

Basic Characteristics of Common Stock

LG3 LG4 Each share of common stock represents an equity (or ownership) position in a company. It's this equity position that explains why common stocks are often referred to as *equity securities* or **equity capital**. Every share entitles the holder to an equal ownership position and participation in the corporation's earnings and dividends, an equal vote (usually), and an equal voice in management. Together the common stockholders own the company. The more shares an investor owns, the bigger his or her ownership position. Common stock has no maturity date—it remains outstanding indefinitely.

Common Stock as a Corporate Security

All corporations issue common stock of one type or another. But the shares of many, if not most, corporations are never traded because the firms either are too small or are family controlled. The stocks of interest to us in this book are **publicly traded issues**— the shares that are readily available to the general public and that are bought and sold in the open market. The firms issuing such shares range from giants like Apple Inc. and Exxon Mobil Corporation to much smaller regional and local firms. The market for publicly traded stocks is enormous. According to the World Federation of Exchanges, the value of all U.S. stocks in early 2015 was more than $26.6 trillion.

Issuing New Shares Companies can issue shares of common stock in several ways. The most widely used procedure is the **public offering**. When using this procedure, the corporation offers the investing public a certain number of shares of its stock at a certain price. Figure 1.3 shows an announcement for such an offering. In this case Box is offering 12,500,000 shares of its Class A stock at a price of $14 per share. At $14 per share, the offering will raise $175 million and after underwriting fees Box will receive $162.75 million. Notice that each of the newly issued shares of Class A stock sold by the company to public investors will be entitled to one vote, whereas the Class B shares that remain in the hands of the Box's founders have 10 votes per share. The result of this dual-class stock structure is that following the IPO the new investors will control fewer than 2% of the votes compared to the founders, who will control more than 98% of the votes.

Companies also can issue new shares of stock using what is known as a **rights offering**. In a rights offering, existing stockholders are given the first opportunity to buy the new issue. In essence, a stock right gives a shareholder the right (but not the obligation) to purchase new shares of the company's stock in proportion to his or her current ownership position.

For instance, if a stockholder currently owns 1% of a firm's stock and the firm issues 10,000 additional shares, the rights offering will give that stockholder the opportunity to purchase 1% (100 shares) of the new issue. If the investor does not want to use the rights, he or she can sell them to someone who does. The net result of a rights offering is the same as that of a public offering. The firm ends up with more equity in its capital structure, and the number of shares outstanding increases.

Stock Spin-Offs Perhaps one of the most creative ways of bringing a new issue to the market is through a **stock spin-off**. Basically, a spin-off occurs when a company gets rid of one of its subsidiaries or divisions. For example, Time Warner did this when it spun off its Time Inc. subsidiary in June 2014. The company doesn't just sell the subsidiary to some other firm. Rather, it creates a new stand-alone company and then distributes stock in that company to its existing stockholders. Thus, every Time Warner shareholder received 1 share in the newly created, and now publicly traded, Time Inc. for every 8 shares of Time Warner stock that he or she held.

There have been hundreds of stock spin-offs in the last 10 to 15 years. Some of the more notable recent ones are the spin-off of Land's End by Sears Holdings, News Corporation by 21st Century Fox, and TripAdvisor by Expedia. Normally, companies execute stock spin-offs if they believe the subsidiary is no longer a good fit or if they feel they've become too diversified and want to focus on their core products. The good news is that such spin-offs often work very well for investors, too.

Stock Splits Companies can also increase the number of shares outstanding by executing a **stock split**. In declaring a split, a firm merely announces that it will increase the number of shares outstanding by exchanging a specified number of new shares for each outstanding share of stock. For example, in a two-for-one stock split, two new shares of stock are exchanged for each old share. In a three-for-two split, three new shares are exchanged for every two old shares outstanding. Thus, a stockholder who owned 200 shares of stock before a two-for-one split becomes the owner of 400 shares; the same investor would hold 300 shares if there had been a three-for-two split.

A company uses a stock split when it wants to enhance its stock's trading appeal by lowering its market price. Normally, the price of the stock falls roughly in proportion to the terms of the split (unless the stock split is accompanied by a big increase in the level of dividends). For example, using the ratio of the number of old shares to new, we

FIGURE 1.3 An Announcement of a New Stock Issue

This announcement indicates that the company—Box—is issuing 12,500,000 shares of stock at a price of $14 per share. For this cloud-based file-sharing and document-management company, the new issue will mean $162.75 million in fresh capital.

(Source: *Box Inc.*, Initial Public Offer prospectus, http://www.nasdaq.com/markets/ipos/filing .ashx?filingid=9961051.)

PROSPECTUS

12,500,000 Shares

CLASS A COMMON STOCK

Box, Inc. is offering 12,500,000 shares of its Class A common stock. This is our initial public offering and no public market currently exists for shares of our Class A common stock. The initial public offering price is $14.00 per share.

Following this offering, we will have two classes of authorized common stock, Class A common stock and Class B common stock. The rights of the holders of our Class A common stock and Class B common stock will be identical, except with respect to voting and conversion rights. Each share of our Class A common stock will be entitled to one vote. Each share of our Class B common stock will be entitled to 10 votes and will be convertible at any time into one share of our Class A common stock. The holders of our outstanding Class B common stock will hold approximately 98.8% of the voting power of our outstanding capital stock following this offering.

Our Class A common stock has been approved for listing on the New York Stock Exchange under the symbol "BOX."

We are an "emerging growth company" as defined under the federal securities laws and, as such, may elect to comply with certain reduced public company reporting requirements for future filings. Investing in our Class A common stock involves risks. See **"Risk Factors"** beginning on page 16.

Price $14.00 A Share

	Price to Public	Underwriting Discounts and Commissions [1]	Proceeds to Box, Inc.
Per Share	$14.00	$0.98	$13.02
Total	$175,000,000	$12,250,000	$162,750,000

[1] See the section titled "Underwriters" for a description of the compensation payable to the underwriters.

We have granted the underwriters the right to purchase up to an additional 1,875,000 shares of our Class A common stock to cover over-allotments.

Entities affiliated with Coatue Management, L.L.C. (Coatue Entities), an affiliate of certain of our existing stockholders, may purchase less than 1,250,000 shares of our Class A common stock in this offering at the initial public offering price. The Coatue Entities may ultimately elect not to purchase shares in this offering or the underwriters may elect not to sell any shares in this offering to the Coatue Entities. The underwriters will receive the same discount from any shares sold to the Coatue Entities as they will from any other shares sold to the public in this offering.

The Securities and Exchange Commission and state securities regulators have not approved or disapproved of these securities, or determined if this prospectus is truthful or complete. Any representation to the contrary is a criminal offense.

The underwriters expect to deliver the shares of our Class A common stock to purchasers on January 28, 2015.

Morgan Stanley   **Credit Suisse**   **J.P. Morgan**

BMO Capital Markets

Canaccord Genuity   Pacific Crest Securities   Raymond James   Wells Fargo Securities

January 22, 2015

can expect a $100 stock to trade at or close to $50 a share after a two-for-one split. Specifically, we divide the original price per share by the ratio of new shares to old. That same $100 stock would trade at about $67 after a three-for-two split—that is, $100 \div 3/2 = \$100 \div 1.5 = \$67$.

Example

> On April 9, 2015, Starbucks Corporation split its shares two-for-one. On the day before the split, Starbucks shares closed at $95.23. Theoretically, after the split the stock price should fall by half to $47.62. In fact, once the split went into effect on April 9th, the opening price of 1 Starbucks share fell to $47.65.

Treasury Stock Instead of increasing the number of outstanding shares, corporations sometimes find it desirable to reduce the number of shares by buying back their own stock. Firms may repurchase their own stock when they view it as undervalued in the marketplace. When that happens, the company's own stock becomes an attractive investment candidate. Firms also repurchase shares as an alternative to paying dividends. Paying dividends may force some shareholders to pay taxes on the income they receive, while repurchasing shares may have different tax consequences for shareholders.

Firms usually purchase their stock in the open market, like any other individual or institution. When acquired, these shares become known as **treasury stock**. Technically, treasury stocks are simply shares of stock that have been issued and subsequently repurchased by the issuing firm. Treasury stocks are kept by the corporation and can be used at a later date for several purposes. For example, they could be used to pay for mergers and acquisitions, to meet employee stock option plans, or as a means of paying stock dividends. Or the shares can simply be held in treasury for an indefinite time.

The short-term impact of these share repurchases—or *buybacks*, as they're sometimes called—is generally positive, meaning that stock prices generally go up when firms announce their intentions to conduct share repurchases. The long-term impact is less settled, with some research indicating that share repurchases are followed by periods of above-average stock returns and other research contesting that conclusion.

Classified Common Stock For the most part, all the stockholders in a corporation enjoy the same benefits of ownership. Occasionally, however, a company will issue different classes of common stock, each of which entitles holders to different privileges and benefits. These issues are known as **classified common stock**. Hundreds of publicly traded firms, including well-known tech companies such as Google and Facebook, have created such stock classes. Although issued by the same company, each class of common stock may have unique characteristics.

Firms that issue multiple classes of stock usually do so to grant different voting rights to different groups of investors. For instance, when Facebook conducted its 2012 IPO, it issued Class A and Class B shares. The Class A shares, available for purchase by the public, were entitled to 1 vote per share. Class B shares, held by Facebook CEO and founder Mark Zuckerberg (and other Facebook insiders) were entitled to 10 votes per share. This ensured that Zuckerberg would have voting control of the company even if Facebook issued many more Class A shares over time in subsequent stock offerings. On rare occasions firms may use classified stock to grant different dividend rights to different investors.

Regardless of the specifics, whenever there is more than one class of common stock outstanding, you should take the time to determine the privileges, benefits, and limitations of each class.

Buying and Selling Stocks

To be an informed stock trader, you need a basic awareness of how to read stock-price quotes. You also need to understand the transaction costs associated with buying and selling stock. Certainly, keeping track of current prices is an essential element in buy-and-sell decisions. Prices help you monitor the market performance of your security holdings. Similarly, transaction costs are important because of the impact they have on investment returns. Indeed, the costs of executing stock transactions can sometimes consume most (or all) of the profits from an investment. You should not take these costs lightly.

Reading the Quotes Investors in the stock market have come to rely on a highly efficient information system that quickly disseminates market prices to the public. The stock quotes that appear daily in the financial press and online are a vital part of that information system. To see how to read and interpret stock price quotations, consider the quotes that appear at Yahoo! Finance. These quotes give not only the most recent price of each stock but also a great deal of additional information.

Figure 1.4 illustrates a basic quote for Abercrombie & Fitch Co. stock, which trades under the ticker symbol ANF. The quote was taken after trading hours on Friday, May 15, 2015. On that day, the price of Abercrombie common stock closed at $21.42 per share, up $0.17 (or 0.8%) from the previous day's close of $21.25. Notice that the stock opened on Friday at $21.27, reaching an intraday high of $21.55 and an intraday low of $21.17 (see "Day's Range"). Figure 1.4 also reveals that during the preceding 52 weeks Abercrombie stock traded as high as $45.50 and as low as $19.34 (see "52wk Range"). Trading volume for the stock on May 15 was 1.245 million shares, considerably less than the average daily volume over the previous three months of just under three million shares.

A few other items from Figure 1.4 are noteworthy. Abercrombie's stock has a beta of 2.2, meaning that it is more than twice as risky (i.e., has more than twice as much systematic risk) as the average stock in the market (as the very wide trading range over the past year would also indicate). Abercrombie's total *market capitalization* (or market cap) is $1.49 billion. Remember, a company's market cap is simply its share price times

FIGURE 1.4 **A Stock Quote for Abercrombie & Fitch**

This figure shows a stock quote for Abercrombie & Fitch on May 15, 2015.
(Source: Yahoo! Finance, http://finance.yahoo.com/q?uhb=uh3_finance_vert&fr=&type=2button&s=anf.)

the number of shares outstanding. In its most recent reporting period, the company earned $0.71 per share, and given the closing price of $21.42, the price-to-earnings ratio of Abercrombie stock was just over 30.

Transaction Costs Investors can buy and sell common stock in round or odd lots. A *round lot* is 100 shares of stock or multiples thereof. An *odd lot* is a transaction involving fewer than 100 shares. For example, the sale of 400 shares of stock would be a round-lot transaction, and the sale of 75 shares would be an odd-lot transaction. Trading 250 shares of stock would involve a combination of two round lots and an odd lot.

An investor incurs certain transaction costs when buying or selling stock. In addition to some modest transfer fees and taxes paid by the seller, the major cost is the brokerage fee paid—by both buyer and seller—at the time of the transaction. As a rule, brokerage fees can amount to just a fraction of 1% to as much as 2% or more, depending on whether you use the services of a discount broker or full-service broker. But they can go even higher, particularly for very small trades. Historically, transactions involving odd lots required a specialist called an *odd-lot dealer* and triggered an extra cost called an *odd-lot differential*. Today, electronic trading systems make it easier to process odd-lot transactions, so these trades do not increase trading costs as much as they once did. Not surprisingly, odd-lot trades have become more common in recent years. For example, roughly one-third of all trades of Google shares involve odd lots.

Another type of transaction cost is the *bid-ask spread*, the difference between the bid and ask prices for a stock. In Figure 1.4, you can see that the last quoted ask price for Abercrombie stock was $21.42 and the bid price was $21.41, so the spread between these two prices was $0.01. Remember that the ask price represents what you would pay to buy the stock and the bid price is what you receive if you sell the stock, so the difference between them is a kind of transaction cost that you incur when you make a roundtrip (i.e., a purchase and then later a sale) trade. Of course, these prices change throughout the trading day, as does the spread between them, but the current bid-ask spread gives you at least a rough idea of the transaction cost that you pay to the market maker or dealer who makes a living buying and selling shares every day.

Common Stock Values

The worth of a share of common stock can be described in a number of ways. Terms such as *par value*, *book value*, *market value*, and *investment value* are all found in the financial media. Each designates some accounting, investment, or monetary attribute of a stock.

Par Value A stock's **par value** is an arbitrary amount assigned to the stock when it is first issued. It has nothing to do with the stock's market price, but instead represents a minimum value below which the corporate charter does not allow a company to sell shares. Because par value establishes a kind of floor for the value of a stock, companies set par values very low. For example, in Facebook's IPO, the par value of its shares was set at $0.000006. Except for accounting purposes, par value is of little consequence. Par value is a throwback to the early days of corporate law, when it was used as a basis for assessing the extent of a stockholder's legal liability. Because the term has little or no significance for investors, many stocks today are issued without a par value.

Book Value Another accounting measure, **book value** is the stockholders' equity in the firm as reported on the balance sheet (and sometimes expressed on a per share basis). Remember that on the balance sheet, stockholders' equity is just the difference between the value of the firm's assets and its liabilities (less any preferred stock). The book value represents the amount of capital that shareholders contributed to the firm when it initially sold shares as well as any profits that have been reinvested in the company over time.

Example

> Social Networks Incorporated (SNI) lists assets worth $100 million on its balance sheet along with $60 million in liabilities. There is no preferred stock, but the company has 10 million common shares outstanding. The book value of SNI's stockholders' equity is $40 million, or $4 per common share. Of the $40 million in stockholders' equity, $30 million was raised in the company's initial public offering of common stock and the other $10 million represents profits that the company earned and reinvested in the business since its IPO.

A stock's book value is inherently a backward-looking estimate of its value because it focuses on things that happened in the past (like the original sale of stock and profits earned and reinvested in earlier periods). In contrast, a stock's market value is forward-looking and reflects investors' expectations about how the company will perform in the future.

Market Value A stock's **market value** is simply its prevailing market price. It reflects what investors are willing to pay to acquire the company today, and it is essentially independent of the book value. In fact, stocks usually trade at market prices that exceed their book values, sometimes to a very great degree.

As you have already learned, by multiplying the market price of the stock by the number of shares outstanding, you can calculate a firm's market capitalization, which represents the total market value of claims held by shareholders. A firm's market capitalization is somewhat analogous to the stockholders' equity figure on the balance sheet, except that the market capitalization represents what the firm's equity is actually worth in today's market, whereas the stockholders' equity balance is a backward-looking assessment of shareholders' claims.

Example

> Investors believe that prospects for Social Networks Incorporated are very bright and that the company will rapidly increase its revenues and earnings for the next several years. As a result, investors have bid up the market price of SNI's stock to $20, which is five times greater than the company's book value per share. With 10 million common shares outstanding, SNI's market capitalization is $200 million compared to the book value of stockholders' equity of just $40 million.

When a stock's market value drops below its book value, it is usually because the firm is dealing with some kind of financial distress and does not have good prospects for growth. Some investors like to seek out stocks that are trading below book value in the hope that the stocks will recover and earn very high returns in the process. While such a strategy may offer the prospect of high returns, it also entails significant risks.

Investment Value **Investment value** is probably the most important measure for a stockholder. It indicates the worth investors place on the stock—in effect, what they think the stock should be trading for. Determining a security's investment value is a complex process based on expectations of the return and risk characteristics of a stock. Any stock has two potential sources of return: dividend payments and capital gains. In establishing investment value, investors try to determine how much money they will make from these two sources. They then use those estimates as the basis for formulating the return potential of the stock. At the same time, they try to assess the amount of risk to which they will be exposed by holding the stock. Such return and risk information helps them place an investment value on the stock. This value represents the maximum price an investor should be willing to pay for the issue.

**CONCEPTS
IN REVIEW**

Answers available at
http://www.pearsonhighered
.com/smart

1.6   What is a stock split? How does a stock split affect the market value of a share of stock? Do you think it would make any difference (in price behavior) if the company also changed the dividend rate on the stock? Explain.

1.7   What is a stock spin-off? In very general terms, explain how a stock spin-off works. Are these spin-offs of any value to investors? Explain.

1.8   Define and differentiate between the following pairs of terms.

   a. Treasury stock versus classified stock
   b. Round lot versus odd lot
   c. Par value versus market value
   d. Book value versus investment value

1.9   What is an odd-lot differential? How can you avoid odd-lot differentials? Which of the following transactions would involve an odd-lot differential?

   a. Buy 90 shares of stock
   b. Sell 200 shares of stock
   c. Sell 125 shares of stock

Common Stock Dividends

LG5   In 2014, U.S. corporations paid out billions in dividends. Counting only the companies included in the S&P 500 stock index, dividends that year totaled more than $375 billion. Yet, in spite of these numbers, dividends still don't get much attention. Many investors, particularly younger ones, often put very little value on dividends. To a large extent, that's because capital gains provide a much bigger source of return than dividends—at least over the long haul.

But attitudes toward dividends are changing. The protracted bear market of 2007 through 2009 revealed just how uncertain capital gains can be and, indeed, that all those potential profits can turn into substantial capital losses. Dividend payments do not fluctuate as much as stock prices do. Plus, dividends provide a nice cushion when the market stumbles (or falls flat on its face). Moreover, current tax laws put dividends on the same plane as capital gains. Both now are taxed at the same tax rate. Dividends are tax-free for taxpayers in the 10% and 15% brackets, taxed at a 15% rate for the 25% to 35% tax brackets, and taxed at a 20% rate for taxpayers whose income surpasses the 35% tax bracket. Single taxpayers with modified adjusted gross income of $200,000 and married couples exceeding $250,000 are also subject to a 3.8% Medicare surtax on investment income, including dividend income.

INVESTOR FACTS

A Steady Stream York Water Company raised its dividend for the 17th consecutive year in February 2015. That's an impressive run, but it's not the most notable fact about York's dividend stream. The company paid dividends without missing a single year since 1816, the year that Indiana was admitted as the 19th U.S. state! No other U.S. company can match York's record of nearly two centuries of uninterrupted dividend payments.

The Dividend Decision

By paying out dividends, typically on a quarterly basis, companies share some of their profits with stockholders. Actually, a firm's board of directors decides how much to pay in dividends. The directors evaluate the firm's operating results and financial condition to determine whether dividends should be paid and, if so, in what amount. They also consider whether the firm should distribute some of its cash to investors by paying a dividend or by repurchasing some of the firm's outstanding stock. If the directors decide to pay dividends, they also establish several important payment dates. In this section we'll look at the corporate and market factors that go into the dividend decision. Then we'll briefly examine some of the key payment dates.

Corporate versus Market Factors When the board of directors assembles to consider the question of paying dividends, it weighs a variety of factors. First, the board looks at the firm's earnings. Even though a company does not have to show a profit to pay dividends, profits are still considered a vital link in the dividend decision.

With common stocks, the annual earnings of a firm are usually measured and reported in terms of **earnings per share** (**EPS**). Basically, EPS translates aggregate corporate profits into profits per share. It provides a convenient measure of the amount of earnings available to stockholders. Earnings per share is found by using the following formula.

Equation 1.1

$$EPS = \frac{\text{Net profit after taxes} - \text{Preferred dividends}}{\text{Number of shares of common stock outstanding}}$$

For example, if a firm reports a net profit of $1.25 million, pays $250,000 in dividends to preferred stockholders, and has 500,000 shares of common stock outstanding, it has an EPS of $2 (($1,250,000 − $250,000)/500,000). Note in Equation 1.1 that preferred dividends are subtracted from profits because they must be paid before any funds can be made available to common stockholders.

While assessing profits, the board also looks at the firm's growth prospects. It's very likely that the firm will need some of its earnings for investment purposes and to help finance future growth. In addition, the board will take a close look at the firm's cash position, making sure that paying dividends will not lead to a cash shortfall. Furthermore, the firm may be subject to a loan agreement that legally limits the amount of dividends it can pay.

After looking at internal matters, the board will consider certain market effects and responses. Most investors feel that if a company is going to retain earnings rather than pay them out in dividends, it should reinvest those funds to achieve faster growth and higher profits. If the company retains earnings but cannot reinvest them at a favorable rate of return, investors begin to clamor for the firm to distribute those earnings through dividends.

Moreover, to the extent that different types of investors tend to be attracted to different types of firms, the board must make every effort to meet the dividend expectations of its shareholders. For example, income-oriented investors are attracted to firms that generally pay high dividends. Failure to meet those expectations might prompt some investors to sell their shares, putting downward pressure on the stock price. In addition, some institutional investors (e.g., certain mutual funds and pension funds) are restricted to investing only in companies that pay a dividend. This is a factor in some companies' decisions to initiate a dividend payment.

Some Important Dates Let's assume the directors decide to declare a dividend. Once that's done, they must indicate the date of payment and other important dates associated with the dividend. Three dates are particularly important to the stockholders: date of record, payment date, and ex-dividend date. The **date of record** is the date on which the investor must be a registered shareholder of the firm to be entitled to a dividend. All investors who are official stockholders as of the close of business on that date will receive the dividends that have just been declared. These stockholders are often referred to as *holders of record*. The **payment date**, also set by the board of directors, generally follows the date of record by a week or two. It is the actual date on which the company will mail dividend checks to holders of record (and is also known as the *payable date*).

Because of the time needed to make bookkeeping entries after a stock is traded, the stock will sell without the dividend (ex-dividend) for three business days up to and including the date of record. The **ex-dividend date** will dictate whether you were an official shareholder and therefore eligible to receive the declared dividend. If you sell a stock on or after the ex-dividend date, you receive the dividend. The reason is that the buyer of the stock (the new shareholder) will not have held the stock on the date of record. Instead, you (the seller) will still be the holder of record. Just the opposite will occur if you sell the stock before the ex-dividend date. In this case, the new shareholder (the buyer of the stock) will receive the dividend because he or she will be the holder of record.

To see how this works, consider the following sequence of events. On June 3, the board of directors of Cash Cow, Inc., declares a quarterly dividend of 50 cents per share to holders of record on June 18. Checks will be mailed out on the payment date, June 30. The calendar below shows these dividend dates. In this case, if you bought 200 shares of the stock on June 15, you would receive a check in the mail sometime after June 30 in the amount of $100. On the other hand, if you purchased the stock on June 16, the seller of the stock would receive the check because he or she, not you, would be recognized as the holder of record.

June

S	M	T	W	T	F	S	
	1	2	③	4	5	6	— Declaration date
7	8	9	10	11	12	13	
14	15	⑯	17	⑱	19	20	— Date of record
21	22	23	24	25	26	27	— Ex-dividend date
28	29	㉚					— Payment date

Types of Dividends

Normally, companies pay dividends in the form of cash. Sometimes they pay dividends by issuing additional shares of stock. The first type of distribution is known as a **cash dividend**, and the second is a **stock dividend**. Occasionally, companies pay dividends in other forms, such as a stock spin-off (discussed earlier) or perhaps even samples of the company's products. But these other forms of dividend payments are relatively rare compared to cash dividends.

Cash Dividends More firms pay cash dividends than any other type of dividend. A nice feature of cash dividends is that they tend to increase over time, as companies' earnings grow. In fact, for companies that pay cash dividends, the average annual increase in dividends is around 3% to 5%. This trend represents good news for investors because a steadily increasing stream of dividends tends to shore up stock returns in soft markets.

A convenient way of assessing the amount of dividends received is to measure the stock's **dividend yield**. Basically, this is a measure of dividends on a relative (percentage) basis rather than on an absolute (dollar) basis. A stock's dividend yield measures its current income as a percentage of its price. The dividend yield is computed as follows:

Equation 1.2

$$\text{Dividend yield} = \frac{\text{Annual dividends received per share}}{\text{Current market price of the stock}}$$

Thus, a company that annually pays $2 per share in dividends to its stockholders, and whose stock is trading at $40, has a dividend yield of 5%.

Example

> In May 2015 Nordic American Tankers (NAT) paid its quarterly dividend of $0.38 per share, which translates into an annual dividend of $1.52. At that time, NAT's share price was $11.40, so its dividend yield was 13.3% ($1.52 ÷ $11.40), which is an unusually high level for common stock.

Firms generally do not pay out all of their earnings as dividends. Instead, they distribute some of their earnings as dividends and retain some to reinvest in the business. The **dividend payout ratio** measures the percentage of earnings that a firm pays in dividends. It is computed as follows:

Equation 1.3

$$\text{Dividend payout ratio} = \frac{\text{Dividends per share}}{\text{Earnings per share}}$$

A company would have a payout ratio of 50% if it had earnings of $4 a share and paid annual dividends of $2 a share. Although stockholders like to receive dividends, they normally do not like to see extremely high payout ratios. Such high payout ratios are difficult to maintain and may lead the company into trouble.

Example

> In the 12 months ending in May 2015, Pepsico Inc. paid dividends of $2.81 per share to investors. Over the same period, the company's earnings per share were $4.30, so Pepsico's dividend payout ratio was about 65%. In other words, Pepsico used almost two-thirds of its earnings to pay dividends and it reinvested the other third.

The appeal of cash dividends took a giant leap forward in 2003 when the federal tax code changed to reduce the tax on dividends. Prior to this time, cash dividends were taxed as ordinary income, meaning at that time they could be taxed at rates as high as 35%. For that reason, many investors viewed cash dividends as a relatively unattractive source of income, especially because capital gains (when realized) were taxed at much lower preferential rates. After 2003 both dividends and capital gains were taxed at the same rate. That, of course, makes dividend-paying stocks far more attractive, even to investors in higher tax brackets. Firms responded to the tax change in two ways. First, firms that already paid dividends increased them. Total dividends paid by U.S. companies increased by 30% from 2003 to 2005. Second, many firms that had never paid dividends began paying them. In the year leading up to the tax cut, about four firms per quarter announced plans to initiate dividend payments. In the following year, the number of firms initiating dividends surged to 29 companies per quarter, an increase of roughly 700%! The dividend paying trend resumed as the economy began to recover from the most recent recession. In 2010 U.S. companies paid out $197 billion worth of dividends and for 2013 the amount grew to $302 billion, a 50% increase. Paying dividends is fashionable not only in the United States but around the world as well. In 2013 publicly traded companies worldwide paid over $1 trillion in dividends for the first time and between 2009 and 2013 companies worldwide paid about $4.4 trillion in cash dividends.

Stock Dividends Occasionally, a firm may declare a stock dividend. A stock dividend simply means that the firm pays its dividend by distributing additional shares of stock. For instance, if the board declares a 10% stock dividend, then you will receive 1 new share of stock for each 10 shares that you currently own.

Stock dividends are similar to stock splits in the sense that when you receive a stock dividend, you receive no cash. As the number of shares outstanding increases due to the dividend, the share price falls, leaving the total value of your holdings in the company basically unchanged. As with a stock split, a stock dividend represents primarily a cosmetic change because the market responds to such dividends by adjusting share prices downward according to the terms of the stock dividend. Thus, in the example above, a 10% stock dividend normally leads to a decline of around 10% in the stock's share price. If you owned 200 shares of stock that were trading at $100 per share, the total market value of your investment would be $20,000. After a 10% stock dividend, you would own 220 shares of stock (i.e., 200 shares × 1.10), but each share would be worth about $90.91. You would own more shares, but they would be trading at lower prices, so the total market value of your investment would remain about the same (i.e., 220 × $90.91 = $20,000.20). There is, however, one bright spot in all this. Unlike cash dividends, stock dividends are not taxed until you actually sell the stocks.

Dividend Reinvestment Plans

For investors who plan to reinvest any dividends that they receive, a **dividend reinvestment plan (DRIP)** may be attractive. In these corporate-sponsored programs, shareholders can have their cash dividends automatically reinvested into additional shares of the company's common stock. (Similar reinvestment programs are offered by mutual funds and by some brokerage houses such as Bank of America and Fidelity.) The basic investment philosophy is that *if the company is good enough to invest in, it's good enough to reinvest in.* As Table 1.2 demonstrates, such an approach can have a tremendous impact on your investment position over time.

Today more than 1,000 companies (including most major corporations) offer dividend reinvestment plans. These plans provide investors with a convenient and inexpensive way to accumulate capital. Stocks in most DRIPs are acquired free of brokerage commissions, and most plans allow partial participation. That is, participants may specify a portion of their shares for dividend reinvestment and receive cash dividends

TABLE 1.2 CASH OR REINVESTED DIVIDENDS?

Situation: You buy 100 shares of stock at $25 a share (total investment, $2,500); the stock currently pays $1 a share in annual dividends. The price of the stock increases at 8% per year; dividends grow at 5% per year.

Investment Period (yr.)	Number of Shares Held	Market Value of Stock Holdings ($)	Total Cash Dividends Received ($)
Take Dividends in Cash			
5	100	$ 3,672	$ 552
10	100	$ 5,397	$1,258
15	100	$ 7,930	$2,158
20	100	$11,652	$3,307
Full Participation in Dividend Reinvestment Plan (100% of cash dividends reinvested)			
5	115.59	$ 4,245	0
10	135.66	$ 7,322	0
15	155.92	$12,364	0
20	176.00	$20,508	0

on the rest. Some plans even sell stocks to their DRIP investors at below-market prices—often at discounts of 3% to 5%. In addition, most plans will credit fractional shares to the investor's account, and many will even allow investors to buy additional shares of the company's stock. For example, once enrolled in the General Mills plan, investors can purchase up to $3,000 worth of the company's stock each quarter, free of commissions.

Shareholders can join dividend reinvestment plans by simply sending a completed authorization form to the company. Once you're enrolled, the number of shares you hold will begin to grow with each dividend. There is a catch, however. Even though these dividends take the form of additional shares of stock, you must still pay taxes on them as though they were cash dividends. Don't confuse these dividends with stock dividends—reinvested dividends are treated as taxable income in the year they're received, just as though they had been received in cash. But as long as the preferential tax rate on dividends remains in effect, paying taxes on stock dividends, will be much less of a burden than it used to be.

CONCEPTS IN REVIEW

Answers available at
http://www.pearsonhighered.com/smart

1.10 Briefly explain how the dividend decision is made. What corporate and market factors are important in deciding whether, and in what amount, to pay dividends?

1.11 Why is the ex-dividend date important to stockholders? If a stock is sold on the ex-dividend date, who receives the dividend—the buyer or the seller? Explain.

1.12 What is the difference between a cash dividend and a stock dividend? Which would be more valuable to you? How does a stock dividend compare to a stock split? Is a 200% stock dividend the same as a two-for-one stock split? Explain.

1.13 What are dividend reinvestment plans, and what benefits do they offer to investors? Are there any disadvantages?

Types and Uses of Common Stock

 Common stocks appeal to investors because they offer the potential for everything from current income and stability of capital to attractive capital gains. The market contains a wide range of stocks, from the most conservative to the highly speculative. Generally, the kinds of stocks that investors seek depend on their investment objectives and investment programs. We will examine several of the more popular types of common stocks here, as well as the various ways such securities can be used in different types of investment programs.

Types of Stocks

Not all stocks are alike, and the risk and return profile of each stock depends on the characteristics of the company that issued it. Some of the characteristics include whether the company pays a dividend, the company's size, how rapidly the company is growing, and how susceptible its earnings are to changes in the business cycle. Over time, investors have developed a classification scheme that helps them place a particular stock into one of several categories. Investors use these categories to help design their portfolios to achieve a good balance of risk and return. Some of the categories that you hear about most often are blue chip stocks, income stocks, growth stocks, tech stocks, cyclical stocks, defensive stocks, large-cap stocks, mid-cap stocks, and small-cap stocks.

Blue-Chip Stocks   Blue chips are the cream of the common stock crop. They are stocks issued by companies that have a long track record of earning profits and paying dividends. **Blue-chip stocks** are issued by large, well-established firms that have impeccable financial credentials. These companies are often the leaders in their industries.

Not all blue chips are alike, however. Some provide consistently high dividend yields; others are more growth-oriented. Good examples of blue-chip growth stocks are Nike, Procter & Gamble, Home Depot, Walgreen's, Lowe's Companies, and United Parcel Service. Figure 1.5 shows some basic operating and market information about P&G's stock, as obtained from the introductory part of a typical Zacks Investment Research report. Notice that in addition to a real-time quotation and hold recommendation, the Zacks report provides a company summary, price chart, consensus recommendations, EPS information, and more for P&G. Examples of high-yielding blue chips include such companies as AT&T, Chevron, Merck, Johnson & Johnson, McDonald's, and Pfizer.

While blue-chip stocks are not immune from bear markets, they are less risky than most stocks. They tend to appeal to investors who are looking for quality, dividend-paying investments with some growth potential. Blue chips appeal to investors who want to earn higher returns than bonds typically offer without taking a great deal of risk.

Income Stocks   Some stocks are appealing simply because of the dividends they pay. This is the case with **income stocks**. These issues have a long history of regularly paying higher-than-average dividends. Income stocks are ideal for those who seek a relatively safe and high level of current income from their investment capital. Holders of income stocks (unlike bonds and preferred stocks) can expect the dividends they receive to increase regularly over time. Thus, a company that paid, say, $1.00 a share in dividends in 2000 would be paying just over $1.80 a share in 2015, if dividends had been

FIGURE 1.5 A Blue-Chip Stock

growing at around 4% per year. Dividends that grow over time provide investors with some protection from the effects of inflation.

The major disadvantage of income stocks is that some of them may be paying high dividends because of limited growth potential. Indeed, it's not unusual for income securities to exhibit relatively low earnings growth. This does not mean that such firms are unprofitable or lack future prospects. Quite the contrary: Most firms whose shares qualify as income stocks are highly profitable organizations with excellent prospects. A number of income stocks are among the giants of U.S. industry, and many are also classified as quality blue chips. Many public utilities, such as American Electric Power, Duke Energy, Oneok, Scana, DTE Energy, and Southern Company, are in this group. Also in this group are selected industrial and financial issues like Conagra Foods, General Mills, and Altria Group. By their very nature, income stocks are not exposed to a great deal of business and market risk. They are, however, subject to a fair amount of interest rate risk.

Growth Stocks Shares issued by companies that are experiencing rapid growth in revenues and earnings are known as **growth stocks**. A good growth stock might exhibit a sustained earnings growth of 15% to 18% when most common stocks are growing at 6% to 8% per year. Generally speaking, established growth companies combine steady earnings growth with high returns on equity. They also have high operating margins and plenty of cash flow to service their debt. Amazon.com, Apple, Google, eBay, Berkshire Hathaway, and Starbucks are all prime examples of growth stocks. As this list suggests, some growth stocks also rate as blue chips and provide quality growth, whereas others represent higher levels of speculation.

Growth stocks normally pay little or no dividends. Their payout ratios seldom exceed 10% to 15% of earnings. Instead, these companies reinvest most of their profits to help finance additional growth. Thus, investors in growth stocks earn their returns through price appreciation rather than dividends—and that can have both a good side and a bad side. When the economy is strong and the stock market is generally rising, these stocks are particularly hot. When the markets turn down, so do these stocks, often in a big way. Growth shares generally appeal to investors who are looking for attractive capital gains rather than dividends and who are willing to bear more risk.

Tech Stocks Over the past 20 years or so, tech stocks have become such a dominant force in the market (both positive and negative) that they deserve to be put in a class all their own. **Tech stocks** basically represent the technology sector of the market. They include companies that produce computers, semiconductors, data storage devices, and software. They also include companies that provide Internet services, networking equipment, and wireless communications. Some of these stocks are listed on the NYSE, although the vast majority of them are traded on the Nasdaq. Tech stocks, in fact, dominate the Nasdaq market and, thus, the Nasdaq Composite Index.

These stocks would probably fall into either the growth stock category or the speculative stock class, although some of them are legitimate blue chips. Tech stocks may offer the potential for very high returns, but they also involve considerable risk and are probably most suitable for the more risk-tolerant investor. Included in the tech-stock category you'll find some big names, like Apple, Cisco Systems, Google, and Intel. You'll also find many not-so-big names, like NVIDIA, Marvell Technology, LinkedIn, SanDisk, Advantest, L-3 Communications, and Electronic Arts.

Speculative Stocks Shares that lack sustained records of success but still offer the potential for substantial price appreciation are known as **speculative stocks**. Perhaps investors' hopes are spurred by a new management team that has taken over a troubled company or by the introduction of a promising new product. Other times, it's the hint that some new information, discovery, or production technique will favorably affect the growth prospects of the firm. Speculative stocks are a special breed of securities, and they enjoy a wide following, particularly when the market is bullish.

Generally speaking, the earnings of speculative stocks are uncertain and highly unstable. These stocks are subject to wide swings in price, and they usually pay little or nothing in dividends. On the plus side, speculative stocks such as Sirius XM Radio, Bona Film Group, Destination Maternity, Global Power Equipment Group, and Iridium Communications offer attractive growth prospects and the chance to "hit it big" in the market. To be successful, however, an investor has to identify the big-money winners before the rest of the market does. Speculative stocks are highly risky; they require not only a strong stomach but also a considerable amount of investor know-how. They are used to seek capital gains, and investors will often aggressively trade in and out of these securities as the situation demands.

Cyclical Stocks **Cyclical stocks** are issued by companies whose earnings are closely linked to the overall economy. They tend to move up and down with the business cycle. Companies that serve markets tied to capital equipment spending by business or to consumer spending for big-ticket, durable items like houses and cars typically head the list of cyclical stocks. Examples include Alcoa, Caterpillar, Genuine Parts, Lennar, Brunswick, and Timken.

Cyclical stocks generally do well when the economy is moving ahead, but they tend to do especially well when the country is in the early stages of economic recovery. Likewise, they perform poorly when the economy begins to weaken. Cyclical stocks are probably most suitable for investors who are willing to trade in and out of these stocks as the economic outlook dictates and who can tolerate the accompanying exposure to risk.

Defensive Stocks Sometimes it is possible to find stocks whose prices remain stable or even increase when general economic activity is tapering off. These securities are known as **defensive stocks**. They tend to be less susceptible to downswings in the business cycle than the average stock.

Defensive stocks include the shares of many public utilities, as well as industrial and consumer goods companies that produce or market such staples as beverages, foods, and drugs. An excellent example of a defensive stock is Walmart. This recession-resistant company is the world's leading retailer. Other examples are Checkpoint Systems, a manufacturer of antitheft clothing security clips, WD-40, the maker of that famous all-purpose lubricant, and Extendicare, a leading provider of long-term care and assisted-living facilities. Defensive shares are commonly used by more aggressive investors, who tend to "park" their funds temporarily in defensive stocks while the economy remains soft or until the investment atmosphere improves.

Market-Cap Stocks A stock's size is based on its market value—or, more commonly, its market capitalization. This value is calculated as the market price of the stock times the number of shares outstanding. Generally speaking, the U.S. stock market can be broken into three segments, as measured by a stock's market cap:

Small-cap	less than $2 billion
Mid-cap	$2 billion up to $10 billion
Large-cap	more than $10 billion

The **large-cap stocks** are the corporate giants such as Walmart, Exxon Mobil, and Apple. Although large-cap stocks are few in number, these companies account for more than 75% of the market value of all U.S. equities. But as the saying goes, bigger isn't necessarily better. Nowhere is that statement more accurate than in the stock market. On average, small-cap stocks tend to earn higher returns than do large-caps.

Mid-cap stocks offer investors some attractive return opportunities. They provide much of the sizzle of small-stock returns, without as much price volatility. At the same time, because mid-caps are fairly good-sized companies and many of them have been around for a long time, they offer some of the safety of the big, established stocks. Among the ranks of the mid-caps are such well-known companies as Dick's Sporting Goods, Hasbro, Wendy's, and Williams-Sonoma. Although these securities offer a nice alternative to large stocks without the uncertainties of small-caps, they probably are most appropriate for investors who are willing to tolerate a bit more risk and price volatility than large-caps have.

One type of mid-cap stock of particular interest is the so-called baby blue chip. Also known as "baby blues," these companies have all the characteristics of a regular blue chip except size. Like their larger counterparts, baby blues have rock-solid balance sheets, modest levels of debt, and several years of steady profit growth. Baby blues normally pay a modest level of dividends, but like most mid-caps, they tend to emphasize growth. Thus, they're considered ideal for investors seeking quality long-term growth. Some well-known baby blues are Logitech, American Eagle Outfitters, and Garmin Ltd.

Some investors consider small companies to be in a class by themselves in terms of attractive return opportunities. In many cases, this has turned out to be true. Known as **small-cap stocks**, these companies generally have annual revenues of less than $250 million. But because of their size, spurts of growth can have dramatic effects on their earnings and stock prices. Callaway Golf, MannKind, and Shoe Carnival are some of the better-known small-cap stocks.

Although some small-caps are solid companies with equally solid financials, that's not the case with most of them. Indeed, because many of these companies are so small, they don't have a lot of stock outstanding, and their shares are not widely traded. In addition, small-cap stocks have a tendency to be "here today and gone tomorrow." Although some of these stocks may hold the potential for high returns, investors should also be aware of the very high-risk exposure that comes with many of them.

A special category of small-cap stocks is the initial public offering (IPO). Most IPOs are small, relatively new companies that are going public for the first time. (Prior to their public offering, these stocks were privately held and not publicly traded.) Like other small-company stocks, IPOs are attractive because of the substantial capital gains that investors can earn. Of course, there's a catch: To stand a chance of buying some of the better, more attractive IPOs, you need to be either an active trader or a preferred client of the broker. Otherwise, the only IPOs you're likely to hear of will be the ones these investors don't want. Without a doubt, IPOs are high-risk investments, with the odds stacked against the investor. Because there's no market record to rely on, only investors who know what to look for in a company and who can tolerate substantial risk should buy these stocks.

Investing in Foreign Stocks

One of the most dramatic changes to occur in U.S. financial markets in the past 25 years was the trend toward globalization. Indeed, globalization became the buzzword of the 1990s, and nowhere was that more evident than in the world's equity markets. Consider, for example, that in 1970 the U.S. stock market accounted for fully two-thirds of the world market. In essence, the U.S. stock market was twice as big as all the rest of the world's stock markets combined. That's no longer true: According to the World Federation of Exchanges in 2015, the U.S. share of the world equity market value had dropped to 40%.

Today the world equity markets are dominated by just six markets, which together account for about 75% of the global total. The United States, by far, has the biggest equity market, which in 2015 had a total value approaching $27 trillion. China is in second place with nearly $8 trillion in total equity market value, and if you include the Hong Kong Exchanges, then China's total is more than $11 trillion. Japan is in third place with nearly $5 trillion and is followed by Euronext, which includes exchanges in Belgium, France, the Netherlands, Portugal, and the United Kingdom. The last of the markets valued above $3 trillion is India with its two major exchanges. Other equity markets worth more than $1 trillion can be found in Canada, Germany, Switzerland, Australia, and Korea.

Comparative Returns The United States still dominates the world equity markets in terms of sheer size. But that leaves unanswered an important question: How has the U.S. equity market performed in comparison to the rest of the world's major stock markets? In 2014, which was generally a good year for stock returns, the U.S. market earned more than 13.5% (as measured by the S&P 500 Index). One year is probably not the best way to judge the performance of a country's stock market, so Figure 1.6 plots the average annual return on stocks from 1900 to 2014 for 19 countries. Over that period the U.S. stock market earned an average annual return of 9.6%, a performance equal to the average for the countries listed. In other words, over a long period of time, stock returns in the United States have been unremarkable relative to stock

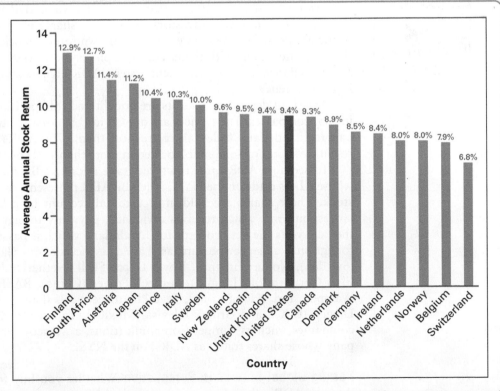

FIGURE 1.6

Average Annual Stock Returns around the World (1900 to 2014)

(Source: Elroy Dimson, Paul Marsh, and Mike Staunton, Credit Suisse Global Investment Returns Sourcebook 2015, https://www.credit-suisse.com/investment_banking/doc/cs_global_investment_returns_yearbook.pdf.)

returns in other markets around the world. If we looked on a year-by-year basis, we would see that U.S. stocks rarely earn the highest returns in any given year. Translated, that means there definitely are attractive returns awaiting those investors who are willing to venture beyond our borders.

Going Global: Direct Investments Basically, there are two ways to invest in foreign stocks: through direct investments or through ADRs.

Without a doubt, the most adventuresome way is to buy shares directly in foreign markets. Investing directly is *not* for the uninitiated, however. You have to know what you're doing and be prepared to tolerate a good deal of market risk. Although most major U.S. brokerage houses are set up to accommodate investors interested in buying foreign securities, there are still many logistical problems to face. To begin with, you have to cope with currency fluctuations that can have a dramatic impact on your returns. But that's just the start. You also have to deal with different regulatory and accounting standards. The fact is that most foreign markets, even the bigger ones, are not as closely regulated as U.S. exchanges. Investors in foreign markets, therefore, may have to put up with insider trading and other practices that can create disadvantages for foreign investors. Finally, there are the obvious language barriers, tax issues, and general "red tape" that all too often plague international transactions. The returns from direct foreign investments can be substantial, but so can the obstacles.

Going Global with ADRs Fortunately, there is an easier way to invest in foreign stocks, and that is to buy American Depositary Receipts (ADRs). ADRs are dollar-denominated instruments (or certificates) that represent ownership interest in American Depositary Shares (ADSs). ADSs, in turn, represent a certain number of shares in a non-U.S. company that have been deposited with a U.S. bank (the number of shares can range from a fraction of a share to 20 shares or more). The first ADR was created in 1927 by a U.S. bank to allow U.S. investors to invest in shares of a British department store. ADRs are great for investors who want to own foreign stocks but don't want the hassles that often come with them. For example, because ADRs trade in U.S. dollars and are cleared through U.S. settlement system, ADR holders avoid having to transact in a foreign currency.

How Do ADRs Work?

American depositary receipts are bought and sold on U.S. markets just like stocks in U.S. companies. Their prices are quoted in U.S. dollars. Furthermore, dividends are paid in U.S. dollars. Today, there are more than 3,700 ADRs available in the U.S. representing shares of companies located in more than 100 countries around the world.

To see how ADRs are structured, take a look at BP, the British oil and gas firm whose ADRs trade on the NYSE. Each BP ADR represents ownership of 6 shares of BP stock. These shares are held in a custodial account by a U.S. bank (or its foreign correspondent), which receives dividends, pays any foreign withholding taxes, and then converts the net proceeds to U.S. dollars, which it passes on to investors. Other foreign stocks that can be purchased as ADRs include Sony (Japan), Ericsson Telephone (Sweden), Nokia (Finland), Royal Dutch Shell (Netherlands), Nestle (Switzerland), Elan Corporation (Ireland), Suntech Power (China), BASF (Germany), Hutchison Wampoa, Ltd. (Hong Kong), Teva Pharmaceuticals (Israel), Norsk Hydro (Norway), Diageo (U.K.), and Grupo Televisa (Mexico). You can even buy ADRs on Russian companies, such as Vimpel-Communications, a Moscow-based cellular phone company whose shares trade (as ADRs) on the NYSE.

Putting Global Returns in Perspective Whether you buy foreign stocks directly or through ADRs, the whole process of global investing is a bit more complicated and more risky than domestic investing. When investing globally, you have to pick both the right stock and the right market. Basically, foreign stocks are valued much the same way as U.S. stocks. Indeed, the same variables that drive U.S. share prices (earnings, dividends, and so on) also drive stock values in foreign markets. On top of this, each market reacts to its own set of economic forces (inflation, interest rates, level of economic activity), which set the tone of the market. At any given time, some markets are performing better than others. The challenge facing global investors is to be in the right market at the right time.

As with U.S. stocks, foreign shares produce the same two basic sources of returns: dividends and capital gains (or losses). But with global investing, there is a third variable—currency exchange rates—that affects returns to U.S. investors. In particular, as the U.S. dollar weakens or strengthens relative to a foreign currency, the returns to U.S. investors from foreign stocks increase or decrease accordingly. In a global context, total return to U.S. investors in foreign securities is defined as follows:

Equation 1.4

$$\begin{matrix} \text{Total returns} \\ \text{(in U.S. dollars)} \end{matrix} = \begin{matrix} \text{Current income} \\ \text{(dividends)} \end{matrix} + \begin{matrix} \text{Capital gains} \\ \text{(or losses)} \end{matrix} \pm \begin{matrix} \text{Changes in currency} \\ \text{exchange rates} \end{matrix}$$

Because current income and capital gains are in the "local currency" (the currency in which the foreign stock is denominated, such as the euro or the Japanese yen), we can shorten the total return formula to:

Equation 1.5

$$\begin{matrix} \text{Total return} \\ \text{(in U.S. dollars)} \end{matrix} = \begin{matrix} \text{Returns from current} \\ \text{income and capital gains} \\ \text{(in local currency)} \end{matrix} + \begin{matrix} \text{Returns from} \\ \text{changes in currency} \\ \text{exchange rates} \end{matrix}$$

Thus, the two basic components of total return are those generated by the stocks themselves (dividends plus change in share prices) and those derived from movements in currency exchange rates.

Measuring Global Returns Employing the same two basic components noted in Equation 1.5, we can compute total return in U.S. dollars by using the following holding period return (HPR) formula, as modified for changes in currency exchange rates.

Equation 1.6

$$\begin{matrix} \text{Total return} \\ \text{(in U.S. dollars)} \end{matrix} = \left[\frac{\begin{matrix} \text{Ending value of} & \text{Amount of dividends} \\ \text{stock in foreign} + & \text{received in} \\ \text{currency} & \text{foreign currency} \end{matrix}}{\begin{matrix} \text{Beginning value of stock} \\ \text{in foreign currency} \end{matrix}} \times \frac{\begin{matrix} \text{Exchange rate} \\ \text{at end of} \\ \text{holding period} \end{matrix}}{\begin{matrix} \text{Exchange rate} \\ \text{at beginning of} \\ \text{holding period} \end{matrix}} \right] - 1$$

In Equation 1.6, the "exchange rate" represents the value of the foreign currency in U.S. dollars—that is, how much one unit of the foreign currency is worth in U.S. money.

This modified HPR formula is best used over investment periods of one year or less. Essentially, the first component of Equation 1.6 provides returns on the stock in local currency, and the second element accounts for the impact of changes in currency exchange rates.

To see how this formula works, consider a U.S. investor who buys several hundred shares of Siemens AG, the German electrical engineering and electronics company that trades on the Frankfurt Stock Exchange. Since Germany is part of the European Community (EC), its currency is the euro. Let's assume that the investor paid a price per share of 90.48 euros for the stock, at a time when the exchange rate between the U.S. dollar and the euro (US\$/€) was \$0.945, meaning one euro was worth almost 95 (U.S.) cents. The stock paid annual dividends of 5 euros per share. Twelve months later, the stock was trading at 94.00 euros, when the US\$/€ exchange rate was \$1.083. Clearly, the stock went up in price and so did the euro, so the investor must have done all right. To find out just what kind of return this investment generated (in U.S. dollars), we'll have to use Equation 1.6.

$$\begin{aligned}\text{Total return}\atop\text{(in U.S. dollars)} &= \left[\frac{€94.00 + €5.00}{€90.48} \times \frac{\$1.083}{\$0.945}\right] - 1\\ &= [1.0942 \times 1.1460] - 1\\ &= [1.2540] - 1\\ &= 25.4\%\end{aligned}$$

With a return of 25.4%, the investor obviously did quite well. However, most of this return was due to currency movements, not to the behavior of the stock. Look at just the first part of the equation, which shows the return (in local currency) earned on the stock from dividends and capital gains: $1.0942 - 1 = 9.42\%$. Thus, the stock itself produced a return of less than 9.50%. All the rest of the return—about 16% (i.e., $25.40\% - 9.42\%$)—came from the change in currency values. In this case, the value of the U.S. dollar went down relative to the euro and thus added to the return.

Currency Exchange Rates As we've just seen, exchange rates can have a dramatic impact on investor returns. They can convert mediocre returns or even losses into very attractive returns—and vice versa. Only one thing determines whether the so-called currency effect is going to be positive or negative: the behavior of the U.S. dollar relative to the currency in which the security is denominated. In essence, a stronger dollar has a negative impact on total returns to U.S. investors, and a weaker dollar has a positive impact. Thus, other things being equal, the best time to be in foreign securities is when the dollar is falling.

Of course, the greater the amount of fluctuation in the currency exchange rate, the greater the impact on total returns. The challenge facing global investors is to find not only the best-performing foreign stock(s) but also the best-performing foreign currencies. You want the value of both the foreign stock and the foreign currency to go up over your investment horizon. And note that this rule applies both to direct investment in foreign stocks and to the purchase of ADRs. (Even though ADRs are denominated in dollars, their quoted prices vary with ongoing changes in currency exchange rates.)

Alternative Investment Strategies

Basically, common stocks can be used as (1) a "storehouse" of value, (2) a way to accumulate capital, and (3) a source of income. Storage of value is important to all investors, as nobody likes to lose money. However, some investors are more concerned than others about losses. They rank safety of principal as their most important stock selection criterion. These investors are more quality-conscious and tend to gravitate toward blue chips and other nonspeculative shares.

Accumulation of capital, in contrast, is generally an important goal to those with long-term investment horizons. These investors use the capital gains and/or dividends that stocks provide to build up their wealth. Some use growth stocks for this purpose, while others do it with income shares, and still others use a little of both.

Finally, some investors use stocks as a source of income. To them, a dependable flow of dividends is essential. High-yielding, good-quality income shares are usually their preferred investment vehicle.

Individual investors can use various investment strategies to reach their investment goals. These include buy-and-hold, current income, quality long-term growth, aggressive stock management, and speculation and short-term trading. The first three strategies appeal to investors who consider storage of value important. Depending on the temperament of the investor and the time he or she has to devote to an investment program, any of these strategies might be used to accumulate capital. In contrast, the current-income strategy is the logical choice for those using stocks as a source of income.

We discuss these strategies in more detail below. You should understand these strategies so that you can choose which one suits your needs.

Buy-and-Hold Buy-and-hold is the most basic of all investment strategies and certainly one of the most conservative. The objective is to place money in a secure investment (safety of principal is vital) and watch it grow over time. In this strategy, investors select high-quality stocks that offer attractive current income and/or capital gains and hold them for extended periods—perhaps as long as 10 to 15 years. This strategy is often used to finance retirement funds, to meet the educational needs of children, or simply to accumulate capital over the long haul. Generally, investors pick a portfolio of good stocks and invest in them on a regular basis for long periods of time—until either the investment climate or corporate conditions change dramatically.

Buy-and-hold investors regularly add fresh capital to their portfolios (many treat them like savings plans). Most also plow the income from annual dividends back into the portfolio and reinvest in additional shares (often through dividend reinvestment plans). Long popular with so-called value-oriented investors, this approach is used by quality-conscious individuals who are looking for competitive returns over the long haul.

Current Income Some investors use common stocks to seek high current income. Common stocks are desirable for this purpose, not so much for their high dividend yields but because their dividends tend to increase over time. In this strategy, safety of principal and stability of income are vital; capital gains are of secondary importance. Quality income shares are the obvious choice for this strategy. Some investors adopt it simply as a way of earning high (and relatively safe) returns on their investment capital. More often, however, the current-income strategy is used by those who are trying to supplement their income. Indeed, many of these investors plan to use the added income for consumption purposes, such as a retired couple supplementing their retirement benefits.

Quality Long-Term Growth This strategy is less conservative than either of the first two in that it seeks capital gains as the primary source of return. A fair amount of trading takes place with this approach. Most of the trading is confined to quality growth stocks (including some of the better tech stocks, as well as baby blues and other mid-caps). These stocks offer attractive growth prospects and the chance for considerable price appreciation. Although a number of growth stocks also pay dividends, this strategy emphasizes capital gains as the principal way to earn big returns.

This approach involves greater risk because of its heavy reliance on capital gains. Therefore, a good deal of diversification is often used. Long-term accumulation of capital is the most common reason for using this approach, but compared to the buy-and-hold tactic, the investor aggressively seeks a bigger payoff by doing considerably more trading and assuming more market risk.

A variation of this investment strategy combines quality long-term growth with high income. This is the total-return approach to investing. Although solidly anchored in long-term growth, this approach also considers dividend income as a source of return. Investors who use the total-return approach seek attractive long-term returns from both dividend income and capital gains by holding both income stocks and growth stocks in their portfolios. Or they may hold stocks that provide both dividends and capital gains. In the latter case, the investor doesn't necessarily look for high-yielding stocks but for stocks that offer the potential for high rates of growth in their dividend streams.

Total-return investors are very concerned about quality. Indeed, about the only thing that separates them from current-income and quality long-term growth investors is that total-return investors care more about the amount of return than about the source of return. For this reason, total-return investors seek the most attractive returns wherever they can find them, be it from a growing stream of dividends or from appreciation in the price of a stock.

Aggressive Stock Management Aggressive stock management also seeks attractive rates of return through a fully managed portfolio. An investor using this strategy aggressively trades in and out of stocks to achieve eye-catching returns, primarily from capital gains. Blue chips, growth stocks, big-name tech stocks, mid-caps, and cyclical issues are the primary investments. More aggressive investors might even consider small-cap stocks, including some of the more speculative tech stocks, foreign shares, and ADRs.

This approach is similar to the quality long-term growth strategy. However, it involves considerably more trading, and the investment horizon is generally much shorter. For example, rather than waiting 2 or 3 years for a stock to move, an aggressive stock trader would go after the same investment payoff in 6 to 12 months. Timing security transactions and turning investment capital over fairly rapidly are both key elements of this strategy. These investors try to stay fully invested in stocks when the market is bullish. When the market weakens, they put a big chunk of their money into defensive stocks or even into cash and other short-term debt instruments.

This aggressive strategy has substantial risks and trading costs. It also places real demands on the individual's time and investment skills. But the rewards can be substantial.

Speculation and Short-Term Trading Speculation and short-term trading characterize the least conservative of all investment strategies. The sole objective of this strategy is capital gains. The shorter the time in which the objective can be achieved, the better. Although investors who use this strategy confine most of their attention to speculative or small-cap stocks and tech stocks, they are not averse to using foreign shares (especially those in so-called emerging markets) or other forms of common stock if they offer attractive short-term opportunities. Many speculators feel that information about the industry or company is less important than market psychology or the general tone of the market. It is a process of constantly switching from one position to another, as new opportunities appear.

Because the strategy involves so much risk, many transactions yield little or no profit, or even substantial losses. The hope is, of course, that when one does hit, it will be in a big way, and returns will be more than sufficient to offset losses. This strategy obviously requires considerable knowledge and time. Perhaps most important, it also requires the psychological and financial fortitude to withstand the shock of financial losses.

CONCEPTS IN REVIEW

Answers available at
http://www.pearsonhighered.com/smart

1.14 Define and briefly discuss the investment merits of each of the following.

a. Blue chips
b. Income stocks
c. Mid-cap stocks
d. American depositary receipts
e. IPOs
f. Tech stocks

1.15 Why do most income stocks offer only limited capital gains potential? Does this mean the outlook for continued profitability is also limited? Explain.

1.16 With all the securities available in the United States, why would a U.S. investor want to buy foreign stocks? Describe the two ways in which a U.S. investor can buy stocks in a foreign company. As a U.S. investor, which approach would you prefer? Explain.

1.17 Which investment approach (or approaches) do you feel would be most appropriate for a quality-conscious investor? What kind of investment approach do you think you'd be most comfortable with? Explain.

MyFinanceLab

Here is what you should know after reading this chapter. MyFinanceLab will help you identify what you know and where to go when you need to practice.

What You Should Know	Key Terms	Where to Practice
LG1 **Explain the investment appeal of common stocks and why individuals like to invest in them.** Common stocks have long been a popular investment vehicle, largely because of the attractive return opportunities they provide. From current income to capital gains, there are common stocks available to fit any investment need.	residual owners, *p. 2*	MyFinanceLab Study Plan 1.1
LG2 **Describe stock returns from a historical perspective and understand how current returns measure up to historical standards of performance.** Stock returns consist of both dividends and capital gains, although price appreciation is the key component. Over the long run, stocks have provided investors with annual returns of around 10% to 12%. The decade of the 1990s was especially rewarding, as stocks generated returns of anywhere from around 20% (on the Dow) to nearly 30% in the tech-heavy Nasdaq market. That situation changed in early 2000, when one of the biggest bull markets in history came to an abrupt end. From 2000 through late 2002, the S&P 500 fell nearly 50%, but it moved to an all-time high in October 2007. With the onset of the financial crises and economic recession the S&P 500 again lost half of its value between 2007 and 2009, nearly doubling over the next two years to a post-recession high in early 2011. After giving back 17% during 2011, the market surged in value 88% to set a new all-time high in early 2015.		MyFinanceLab Study Plan 1.2

What You Should Know	Key Terms	Where to Practice
LG3 Discuss the basic features of common stocks, including issue characteristics, stock quotations, and transaction costs. Common stocks are a form of equity capital, with each share representing partial ownership of a company. Publicly traded stock can be issued via a public offering or through a rights offering to existing stockholders. Companies can also increase the number of shares outstanding through a stock split. To reduce the number of shares in circulation, companies can buy back shares, which are then held as treasury stock. Occasionally, a company issues different classes of common stock, known as classified common stock.	classified common stock, *p. 10* equity capital, *p. 7* public offering, *p. 8* publicly traded issues, *p. 7* rights offering, *p. 8* stock spin-off, *p. 8* stock split, *p. 8* treasury stock, *p. 10*	MyFinanceLab Study Plan 1.3 Video Learning Aid for Problem P1.1
LG4 Understand the different kinds of common stock values. There are several ways to calculate the value of a share of stock. Book value represents accounting value. Market value is a security's prevailing market price. Investment value is the amount that investors think the stock should be worth.	book value, *p. 13* investment value, *p. 13* market value, *p. 13* par value, *p. 12*	MyFinanceLab Study Plan 1.4
LG5 Discuss common stock dividends, types of dividends, and dividend reinvestment plans. Companies often share their profits by paying out cash dividends to stockholders. Companies pay dividends only after carefully considering a variety of corporate and market factors. Sometimes companies declare stock dividends rather than, or in addition to, cash dividends. Many firms that pay cash dividends have dividend reinvestment plans, through which shareholders can automatically reinvest cash dividends in the company's stock.	cash dividend, *p. 16* date of record, *p. 16* dividend payout ratio, *p. 17* dividend reinvestment plan (DRIP), *p. 18* dividend yield, *p. 17* earnings per share (EPS), *p. 15* ex-dividend date, *p. 16* payment date, *p. 16* stock dividend, *p. 16*	MyFinanceLab Study Plan 1.5
LG6 Describe various types of common stocks, including foreign stocks, and note how stocks can be used as investment vehicles. Depending on their needs and preferences, investors can choose blue chips, income stocks, growth stocks, tech stocks, speculative issues, cyclicals, defensive shares, large-cap, mid-cap stocks, small-cap stocks, and initial public offerings. Also, U.S. investors can buy common stock of foreign companies either directly on foreign exchanges or on U.S. markets as American depositary Receipts (ADRs). Generally, common stocks can be used as a storehouse of value, as a way to accumulate capital, or as a source of income. Investors can follow different investment strategies (buy-and-hold, current income, quality long-term growth, aggressive stock management, and speculation and short-term trading) to achieve these objectives.	blue-chip stocks, *p. 20* cyclical stocks, *p. 23* defensive stocks, *p. 23* growth stocks, *p. 22* income stocks, *p. 20* mid-cap stocks, *p. 24* small-cap stocks, *p. 24* speculative stocks, *p. 26* tech stocks, *p. 26*	MyFinanceLab Study Plan 1.6 Video Learning Aid for Problem P1.14

Log into MyFinanceLab, take a chapter test, and get a personalized Study Plan that tells you which concepts you understand and which ones you need to review. From there, MyFinanceLab will give you further practice, tutorials, animations, videos, and guided solutions.
Log into http://www.myfinancelab.com

Discussion Questions

LG1 **Q1.1** Look at the record of stock returns in Table 1.1.
a. How would you compare the average annual returns for the various decades?
b. Considering the average annual returns that have been generated over holding periods of 10 years or more, what rate of return do you feel is typical for the stock market in general? Is it unreasonable to expect this kind of return, on average, in the future? Explain.

LG2 **Q1.2** Given the information in Figure 1.4, answer the following questions for Abercrombie & Fitch Co.
a. On what day did the trading activity occur?
b. At what price did the stock sell when the market closed?
c. What is the firm's price-to-earnings ratio? What does that indicate?
d. What is the first price at which the stock traded on the date quoted?
e. What was the dividend paid per share for the previous year?
f. What are the highest and lowest prices at which the stock traded during the latest 52-week period?
g. How many shares of stock were traded on the day quoted?
h. How much, if any, of a change in price took place between the day quoted and the immediately preceding day? At what price did the stock close on the immediately preceding day?

LG4 **Q1.3** Listed below are three pairs of stocks. Look at each pair and select the security you would like to own, given that you want to select the one that's worth more money. Then, after you make all three of your selections, use the *Wall Street Journal* or some other source to find the latest market value of the securities in each pair.
a. 50 shares of Berkshire Hathaway (stock symbol BRKA) or 150 shares of Coca-Cola (stock symbol KO). (Both are listed on the NYSE.)
b. 100 shares of WD-40 (symbol WDFC—a Nasdaq National Market issue) or 100 shares of Nike (symbol NKE—a NYSE stock).
c. 150 shares of Walmart (symbol WMT) or 50 shares of Sprint Nextel Corp. (symbol S). (Both are listed on the NYSE.)
How many times did you pick the one that was worth more money? Did the price of any of these stocks surprise you? If so, which one(s)? Does the price of a stock represent its value? Explain.

LG6 **Q1.4** Assume that a wealthy woman comes to you looking for some investment advice. She is in her early forties and has $250,000 to put into stocks. She wants to build up as much capital as she can over a 15-year period and is willing to tolerate a "fair amount" of risk.
a. What types of stocks do you think would be most suitable for this investor? Come up with at least three types of stocks, and briefly explain the rationale for each.
b. Would your recommendations change if you were dealing with a smaller amount of money—say, $50,000? What if the investor were more risk-averse? Explain.

LG6 **Q1.5** Identify and briefly describe the three sources of return to U.S. investors in foreign stocks. How important are currency exchange rates? With regard to currency exchange rates, when is the best time to be in foreign securities?
a. Listed below are exchange rates (for the beginning and end of a hypothetical one-year investment horizon) for the British pound (B£), the Australian dollar (A$), and the Mexican peso (Mp).

Currency Exchange Rates		
Currency	Beginning of Investment Horizon	End of 1-Year Investment Horizon
British pound (B£)	1.55 U.S.$ per B£	1.75 U.S.$ per B£
Australian dollar (A$)	1.35 A$ per U.S.$	1.25 A$ per U.S.$
Mexican peso (Mp)	0.10 U.S.$ per Mp	0.08 U.S.$ per Mp

From the perspective of a U.S. investor holding a foreign (British, Australian, or Mexican) stock, which of the above changes in currency exchange rates would have a positive effect on returns (in U.S. dollars)? Which would have a negative effect?

b. ADRs are denominated in U.S. dollars. Are their returns affected by currency exchange rates? Explain.

LG6   Q1.6 Briefly define each of the following types of investment programs and note the kinds of stock (blue chips, speculative stocks, etc.) that would best fit with each.
a. A buy-and-hold strategy
b. A current-income portfolio
c. Long-term total return
d. Aggressive stock management

Problems

All problems are available on http://www.myfinancelab.com

LG3   P1.1 An investor owns some stock in Harry's Pottery Inc. The stock recently underwent a 5-for-3 stock split. If the stock was trading at $40 per share just before the split, how much is each share most likely selling for after the split? If the investor owned 200 shares of the stock before the split, how many shares would she own afterward?

LG3   P1.2 An investor deposits $20,000 into a new brokerage account. The investor buys 1,000 shares of Tipco stock for $19 per share. Two weeks later, the investor sells the Tipco stock for $20 per share. When the investor receives his brokerage account statement, he sees that there is a balance of $20,900 in his account:

Item	Number of Shares	Price per Share ($)	Total Transaction ($)	Account Balance ($)
1. Deposit			$20,000	$20,000
2. Tipco purchase	1,000	$19	($19,000)	$20,000
3. Tipco sale	1,000	$20	$20,000	$21,000
4.				
5. Balance				$20,900

What belongs in item 4 on this statement?

LG4   P1.3 Ron's Rodents Co. has total assets of $5 million, total short- and long-term debt of $2.8 million, and $400,000 worth of 8% preferred stock outstanding. What is the firm's total book value? What would its book value per share be if the firm had 50,000 shares of common stock outstanding?

LG4   P1.4 Lockhart's Bookstores is trading at $45 per share. There are 280 million shares outstanding. What is the market capitalization of this company?

LG5 **P1.5** The MedTech Company recently reported net profits after taxes of $15.8 million. It has 2.5 million shares of common stock outstanding and pays preferred dividends of $1 million per year.
 a. Compute the firm's earnings per share (EPS).
 b. Assuming that the stock currently trades at $60 per share, determine what the firm's dividend yield would be if it paid $2 per share to common stockholders.
 c. What would the firm's dividend payout ratio be if it paid $2 per share in dividends?

LG5 **P1.6** On January 1, 2013, an investor bought 200 shares of Gottahavit, Inc., for $50 per share. On January 3, 2014, the investor sold the stock for $55 per share. The stock paid a quarterly dividend of $0.25 per share. How much (in $) did the investor earn on this investment and, assuming the investor is in the 33% tax bracket, how much will she pay in income taxes on this transaction?

LG4 **LG5** **P1.7** Consider the following information about Truly Good Coffee, Inc.

Total assets	$240 million
Total debt	$115 million
Preferred stock	$ 25 million
Common stockholders' equity	$100 million
Net profits after taxes	$22.5 million
Number of preferred stock outstanding	1 million shares
Number of common stock outstanding	10 million shares
Preferred dividends paid	$2 per share
Common dividends paid	$0.75 per share
Market price of the preferred stock	$30.75 per share
Market price of the common stock	$25.00 per share

Use the information above to find the following.
 a. The company's book value
 b. Its book value per share
 c. The stock's earnings per share (EPS)
 d. The dividend payout ratio
 e. The dividend yield on the common stock
 f. The dividend yield on the preferred stock

LG5 **P1.8** East Coast Utilities is currently trading at $28 per share. The company pays a quarterly dividend of $0.28 per share. What is the dividend yield?

LG5 **P1.9** West Coast Utilities had a net profit of $900 million. It has 900 million shares outstanding and paid annual dividends of $0.90 per share. What is the dividend payout ratio?

LG5 **P1.10** Wilfred Nadeau owns 200 shares of Consolidated Glue. The company's board of directors recently declared a cash dividend of 50 cents a share payable April 18 (a Wednesday) to shareholders of record on March 22 (a Thursday).
 a. How much in dividends, if any, will Wilfred receive if he sells his stock on March 20?
 b. Assume Wilfred decides to hold on to the stock rather than sell it. If he belongs to the company's dividend reinvestment plan, how many new shares of stock will he receive if the stock is currently trading at $40 and the plan offers a 5% discount on the share price of the stock? (Assume that all of Wilfred's dividends are diverted to the plan.) Will Wilfred have to pay any taxes on these dividends, given that he is taking them in stock rather than cash?

LG5   **P1.11** Southern Cities Trucking Company has the following five-year record of earnings per share.

Year	EPS
2012	$1.40
2013	$2.10
2014	$1.00
2015	$3.25
2016	$0.80

Which of the following procedures would produce higher dividends to stockholders over this five-year period?
   a. Paying out dividends at a fixed ratio of 40% of EPS
   b. Paying out dividends at a fixed rate of $1 per share

LG4 LG5   **P1.12** Using the resources at your campus or public library or on the Internet, select any three common stocks you like and determine the latest book value per share, earnings per share, dividend payout ratio, and dividend yield for each. (Show all your calculations.)

LG4 LG5   **P1.13** In January 2012 an investor purchased 800 shares of Engulf & Devour, a rapidly growing high-tech conglomerate. From 2012 through 2016, the stock turned in the following dividend and share price performance.

Year	Share Price Beginning of Year	Dividends Paid during Year	Share Price End of Year
2012	$42.50*	$0.82	$ 54.00
2013	$54.00	$1.28	$ 74.25
2014	$74.25	$1.64	$ 81.00
2015	$81.00	$1.91	$ 91.25
2016	$91.25	$2.30	$128.75

*Investor purchased stock in 2012 at this price.

On the basis of this information, find the annual holding period returns for 2012 through 2016.

LG4   **P1.14** George Robbins considers himself an aggressive investor. He's thinking about investing in some foreign securities and is looking at stocks in (1) Bayer AG, the big German chemical and health-care firm, and (2) Swisscom AG, the Swiss telecommunications company.
   Bayer AG, which trades on the Frankfurt Exchange, is currently priced at 53.25 euros per share. It pays annual dividends of 1.50 euros per share. Robbins expects the stock to climb to 60.00 euros per share over the next 12 months. The current exchange rate is 0.9025€/US$, but that's expected to rise to 1.015€/US$. The other company, Swisscom, trades on the Zurich Exchange and is currently priced at 71.5 Swiss francs (Sf) per share. The stock pays annual dividends of 1.5 Sf per share. Its share price is expected to go up to 76.0 Sf within a year. At current exchange rates, 1 Sf is worth $0.75 U.S., but that's expected to go to $0.85 by the end of the one-year holding period.
   a. Ignoring the currency effect, which of the two stocks promises the higher total return (in its local currency)? Based on this information, which looks like the better investment?
   b. Which of the two stocks has the better total return in U.S. dollars? Did currency exchange rates affect their returns in any way? Do you still want to stick with the same stock you selected in part **a**? Explain.

LG6 **P1.15** Bruce buys $25,000 of UH-OH Corporation stock. Unfortunately, a major newspaper reveals the very next day that the company is being investigated for accounting fraud, and the stock price falls by 50%. What is the percentage increase now required for Bruce to get back to $25,000 of value?

Visit http://www.myfinancelab.com for web exercises, spreadsheets, and other online resources.

Case Problem 1.1   Sara Decides to Take the Plunge

LG1 LG6 Sara Thomas is a child psychologist who has built a thriving practice in her hometown of Boise, Idaho. Over the past several years she has been able to accumulate a substantial sum of money. She has worked long and hard to be successful, but she never imagined anything like this. Even so, success has not spoiled Sara. Still single, she keeps to her old circle of friends. One of her closest friends is Terry Jenkins, who happens to be a stockbroker and who acts as Sara's financial advisor.

Not long ago Sara attended a seminar on investing in the stock market, and since then she's been doing some reading about the market. She has concluded that keeping all of her money in low-yielding savings accounts doesn't make sense. As a result, Sara has decided to move part of her money to stocks. One evening, Sara told Terry about her decision and explained that she had found several stocks that she thought looked "sort of interesting." She described them as follows:

• *North Atlantic Swim Suit Company.* This highly speculative stock pays no dividends. Although the earnings of NASS have been a bit erratic, Sara feels that its growth prospects have never been brighter—"what with more people than ever going to the beaches the way they are these days," she says.

• *Town and Country Computer.* This is a long-established computer firm that pays a modest dividend yield (of about 1.50%). It is considered a quality growth stock. From one of the stock reports she read, Sara understands that T&C offers excellent long-term growth and capital gains potential.

• *Southeastern Public Utility Company.* This income stock pays a dividend yield of around 5%. Although it's a solid company, it has limited growth prospects because of its location.

• *International Gold Mines, Inc.* This stock has performed quite well in the past, especially when inflation has become a problem. Sara feels that if it can do so well in inflationary times, it will do even better in a strong economy. Unfortunately, the stock has experienced wide price swings in the past. It pays almost no dividends.

Questions

a. What do you think of the idea of Sara keeping "substantial sums" of money in savings accounts? Would common stocks make better investments for her than savings accounts? Explain.

b. What is your opinion of the four stocks Sara has described? Do you think they are suitable for her investment needs? Explain.

c. What kind of common stock investment program would you recommend for Sara? What investment objectives do you think she should set for herself, and how can common stocks help her achieve her goals?

Case Problem 1.2   Wally Wonders Whether There's a Place for Dividends

LG5 LG6   Wally Wilson is a commercial artist who makes a good living by doing freelance work—mostly layouts and illustrations—for local ad agencies and major institutional clients (such as large department stores). Wally has been investing in the stock market for some time, buying mostly high-quality growth stocks as a way to achieve long-term growth and capital appreciation. He feels that with the limited time he has to devote to his security holdings, high-quality issues are his best bet. He has become a bit perplexed lately with the market, disturbed that some of his growth stocks aren't doing even as well as many good-grade income shares. He therefore decides to have a chat with his broker, Al Fried.

During their conversation, it becomes clear that both Al and Wally are thinking along the same lines. Al points out that dividend yields on income shares are indeed way up and that, because of the state of the economy, the outlook for growth stocks is not particularly bright. He suggests that Wally seriously consider putting some of his money into income shares to capture the high dividend yields that are available. After all, as Al says, "the bottom line is not so much where the payoff comes from as how much it amounts to!" They then talk about a high-yield public utility stock, Hydro-Electric Light and Power. Al digs up some forecast information about Hydro-Electric and presents it to Wally for his consideration:

Year	Expected EPS ($)	Expected Dividend Payout Ratio (%)
2016	$3.25	40%
2017	$3.40	40%
2018	$3.90	45%
2019	$4.40	45%
2020	$5.00	45%

The stock currently trades at $60 per share. Al thinks that within five years it should be trading at $75 to $80 a share. Wally realizes that to buy the Hydro-Electric stock, he will have to sell his holdings of CapCo Industries—a highly regarded growth stock that Wally is disenchanted with because of recent substandard performance.

Questions

a. How would you describe Wally's present investment program? How do you think it fits him and his investment objectives?

b. Consider the Hydro-Electric stock.

1. Determine the amount of annual dividends Hydro-Electric can be expected to pay over the years 2016 to 2020.
2. Compute the total dollar return that Wally will make from Hydro-Electric if he invests $6,000 in the stock and all the dividend and price expectations are realized.
3. If Wally participates in the company's dividend reinvestment plan, how many shares of stock will he have by the end of 2020? What will they be worth if the stock trades at $80 on December 31, 2020? Assume that the stock can be purchased through the dividend reinvestment plan at a net price of $50 a share in 2016, $55 in 2017, $60 in 2018, $65 in 2019, and $70 in 2020. Use fractional shares, to 2 decimals, in your computations. Also, assume that, as in part b, Wally starts with 100 shares of stock and all dividend expectations are realized.

c. Would Wally be going to a different investment strategy if he decided to buy shares in Hydro-Electric? If the switch is made, how would you describe his new investment program? What do you think of this new approach? Is it likely to lead to more trading on Wally's behalf? If so, can you reconcile that with the limited amount of time he has to devote to his portfolio?

Excel@Investing

Build a spreadsheet containing the following quoted information. Based on the information given, what is the firm's current market cap? What was the firm's net income?

Apple Inc. (AAPL) - NasdaqGS ★ Watchlist				Add to Portfolio
130.49 ↑1.72(1.33%) 3:41PM EDT - Nasdaq Real Time Price				

Prev Close:	128.77	Day's Range:	128.36 - 130.72
Open:	128.36	52wk Range:	85.33 - 134.54
Bid:	130.50 x 1200	Volume:	42,775,652
Ask:	130.51 x 900	Avg Vol (3m):	51,361,400
1y Target Est:	148.18	Market Cap:	751.74B
Beta:	0.91	P/E (ttm):	16.21
Earnings Date:	Jul 20 - Jul 24 (Est.)	EPS (ttm):	8.05
		Div & Yield:	2.08 (1.60%)

(Source: Courtesy of Yahoo! Finance.)

2 | Fixed-Income Securities

LEARNING GOALS

After studying this chapter, you should be able to:

LG1 Explain the basic investment attributes of bonds and their use as investment vehicles.

LG2 Describe the essential features of a bond, note the role that bond ratings play in the market, and distinguish among different types of call, refunding, and sinking-fund provisions.

LG3 Explain how bond prices are quoted in the market and why some bonds are more volatile than others.

LG4 Identify the different types of bonds and the kinds of investment objectives these securities can fulfill.

LG5 Discuss the global nature of the bond market and the difference between dollar-denominated and non-dollar-denominated foreign bonds.

LG6 Describe the basic features and characteristics of convertible securities and measure the value of a convertible security.

When investors lend money to corporations or governments by purchasing bonds, they are very focused on the likelihood that their loans will be paid back. One way to assess that likelihood is to examine a borrower's credit rating. On April 10, 2014, the credit rating arm of Standard & Poor's downgraded Automated Data Processing (ADP) from the top triple-A (AAA) credit rating to double-A (AA). This move was significant not only because ADP had held the AAA rating for years but also because it left only three U.S. companies holding the coveted AAA rating: Johnson & Johnson, Microsoft, and Exxon-Mobil. As recently as 1980, the AAA rating was held by 60 U.S. firms, but that number had been dwindling for years. ADP joined the likes of General Electric and Pfizer, who also lost their AAA ratings after the recession.

Despite some high-profile downgrades, as the world economy slowly recovered from the 2008 recession, fewer companies received downgrades and more earned upgrades. It wasn't until 2014 that upgrades outnumbered downgrades on a global basis, and even then the margin was slim, with roughly nine companies receiving a downgrade for every ten companies whose credit ratings were upgraded. Still, the improving economy meant that most firms were more likely to generate the cash that would enable them to repay their debts, so credit ratings were on the rise.

Before you invest in debt securities, whether issued by corporations or countries, it is important that you consider credit quality, interest rates, maturity, and other relevant factors. Chapters 2 and 8 will provide the background you need to make wise choices in the bond market.

(Sources: "Fitch: Corporate Downgrades Trailed Upgrades in 2014," Reuters, March 16, 2015, http://www.reuters.com/article/2015/03/16/idUSFit91529120150316; "ADP Downgraded by Moody's, S&P after Spin-off News," MarketWatch, April 10, 2014, http://www.marketwatch.com/story/adp-downgraded-by-moodys-sp-after-spin-off-news-2014-04-10.)

Why Invest in Bonds?

LG1 In contrast to stocks, bonds are liabilities—publicly traded IOUs where the bond-holders are actually lending money to the issuer. **Bonds** are publicly traded, long-term debt securities. They are issued in various denominations, by a variety of borrowing organizations, including the U.S. Treasury, agencies of the U.S. government, state and local governments, and corporations. Bonds are often referred to as *fixed-income securities* because the payments made by bond issuers are usually fixed. That is, in most cases the issuing organization agrees to pay a fixed amount of interest periodically and to repay a fixed amount of principal at maturity.

Like stocks, bonds can provide two kinds of income: (1) current income and (2) capital gains. The current income comes from the periodic interest payments paid over the bond's life. The capital gains component is a little different. Because the companies issuing bonds promise to repay a fixed amount when the bonds mature, the interest payments that bonds make do not typically rise in step with a firm's profits the way that stock dividends often do, which is another reason bonds are known as fixed-income securities. By the same token, a company's stock price tends to rise and fall dramatically with changes in the firm's financial performance, but bond prices are less sensitive to changes in a company's profits. However, bond prices do rise and fall as market interest rates change. A basic relationship that you must keep in mind is that interest rates and bond prices move in opposite directions. When interest rates rise, bond prices fall, and when rates drop, bond prices move up. We'll have more to say about this relation later in the chapter, but here's the intuition behind it. Imagine that you buy a brand-new bond, issued by a company like GE, paying 5% interest. Suppose that a month later market rates have risen, and new bonds pay investors 6% interest. If you want to sell your GE bond, you're likely to experience a capital loss because investors will not want to buy a bond paying 5% interest when the going rate in the market is 6%. With fewer buyers interested in them, GE bonds will decline in value. Happily, the opposite outcome can occur if market rates fall. When the going rate on bonds is 4%, your GE bond paying 5% would command a premium in the market. Taken together, the current income and capital gains earned from bonds can lead to attractive returns.

A wide variety of bonds are available in the market, from relatively safe issues (e.g., General Electric bonds) sought by conservative investors to highly speculative securities (e.g., Sirius XM bonds) appropriate for investors who can tolerate a great deal of risk. In addition, the risks and returns offered by all types of bonds depend in part upon the volatility of interest rates. Because interest rate movements cause bond prices to change, higher interest rate volatility makes bond returns less predictable.

Other bonds have special features designed to appeal to certain types of investors. Investors in high tax brackets who want to shelter income from taxes find tax-exempt bonds appealing. Bonds issued by state and local government entities, called municipal bonds, pay interest that is not subject to federal income taxation, so these bonds have special appeal to investors in high tax brackets. Interest on U.S. Treasury bonds is exempt from state income tax, so taxpayers from states with high income tax rates may have particular interest in these bonds. Despite the term *fixed income*, some bonds make interest payments that vary through time according to a formula. In a sense, the term *fixed income* is still appropriate for these bonds because the formula that determines their interest payments is contractually fixed. For example, governments in the United States and many other countries issue inflation-indexed bonds with interest payments that rise with inflation. As the inflation rate changes, the payments on these bonds will change, but investors know in advance exactly how the interest payments will adjust as inflation occurs. Those bonds appeal to investors who want some protection from the risk of rising inflation.

A Brief History of Bond Prices, Returns, and Interest Rates

Interest rates drive the bond market. In fact, the behavior of interest rates is the most important influence on bond returns. Interest rates determine not only the current income investors will receive but also the capital gains (or losses) they will incur. It's not surprising, therefore, that bond-market participants follow interest rates closely. When commentators in the news media describe how the market has performed on a particular day, they usually speak in terms of what happened to bond yields (i.e., what happened to interest rates) that day rather than what happened to bond prices.

Figure 2.1 provides a look at interest rates on bonds issued by U.S. corporations and the U.S. government from 1963 through 2014. It shows that rates on both types of bonds rose steadily through the 1960s and 1970s, peaking in 1982 at more than three times their 1963 levels. Rates then began a long downward slide, and by 2014 the rates were not that different from their 1963 levels. Keep in mind that rising interest rates lead to falling bond prices, so prior to the 1980s investors who held bonds that had been issued in the 60s and 70s realized capital losses if they sold their bonds after

FIGURE 2.1

The Behavior of Interest Rates over Time, 1963 through 2014

Interest rates rose dramatically from 1963 to 1982 before starting a long-term decline that continued through 2014. Rates on corporate bonds tend to mirror rates on government bonds, although corporate rates are higher due to the risk of default by the issuing corporation. Note that the gap, or "spread," between U.S. corporate bond and U.S. Treasury bond yields has been particularly wide following the 2008 financial crisis. (Source: Board of Governors of the Federal Reserve System (US), Moody's Seasoned Aaa Corporate Bond Yield© [AAA], retrieved from FRED, Federal Reserve Bank of St. Louis **https://research .stlouisfed.org/fred2/series/AAA/**, May 20, 2015. Board of Governors of the Federal Reserve System (US), 10-Year Treasury Constant Maturity Rate [DGS10], retrieved from FRED, Federal Reserve Bank of St. Louis **https://research.stlouisfed.org/fred2/series/DGS10/**, May 20, 2015.)

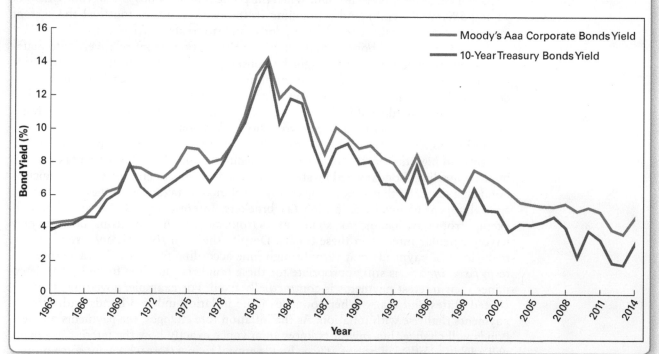

interest rates had risen. By the same token, investors who purchased bonds when interest rates were high earned capital gains from selling their bonds after market interest rates had declined.

Figure 2.1 shows that rates on corporate and government bonds tend to move together, but corporate bond rates are higher. Higher rates on corporate bonds provide compensation for the risk that corporations might default on their debts. The difference between the rate on corporate bonds and the rate on government bonds is called the *yield spread*, or the *credit spread*. When the risk of defaults on corporate bonds increases, the yield spread widens, as it did in 2008. The average annual yield spread for triple-A corporate bonds over the 52 years shown in Figure 2.1 was about 1%, the average from 1987 through 2014 was nearly 1.4%, and the average from 2008 through 2014 was 1.8%. Because changes in the credit spread are tied to the risk of default on corporate bonds, prices of these bonds are not completely insensitive to a company's financial performance. When a company's performance improves, investors recognize the default risk is falling, so the credit spread falls and the company's bond prices rise. When a firm's financial results deteriorate, default risk rises, the credit spread increases, and the company's bond prices fall. Even so, bond prices are nowhere near as sensitive to a firm's financial results as are stock prices.

Historical Returns As with stocks, total returns in the bond market are made up of both current income from the bond's interest payments and capital gains (or losses) from changes in the bond's value. Table 2.1 lists beginning-of-year and end-of-year bond yields and the total returns for 10-year U.S. government bonds from 1963 through 2014. The beginning-of-year yield represents the return that investors buying 10-year Treasury bonds require at the start of each year, and likewise the end-of-year yield represents the interest rate required by purchasers of 10-year bonds at the end of the year. Note how different the beginning-of-year yields can be from the end-of-year yields. For example, the year 2009 began with 10-year bond investors requiring a 2.3% return, but by the end of that year the required return on 10-year bonds had gone up to 3.9%. Notice the effect that this increase in interest rates had on the total return that investors earned on 10-year bonds in 2009. An investor who purchased a bond in January of 2009 received interest payments based on the bond's 2.3% yield, but they also experienced a capital loss during the year because 10-year bond yields increased (remember, bond prices go down when interest rates go up). The total return on 10-year bond in 2009 was −10.8%, which simply means that the capital loss on bonds that year far exceed the 2.3% in interest income that bondholders received.

During a period of rising rates, total returns on bonds include capital losses that can sometimes exceed the bonds' current interest income, resulting in a negative total return. Total returns on U.S. Treasury bonds were negative in 10 out of 52 years, and as Table 2.1 shows, the years with negative total returns on bonds were years in which bond yields rose: That is, the end-of-year yield was higher than the beginning-of-year yield.

Fortunately the inverse relationship between bond prices and yields can work in favor of investors too. Consider 2008. At the beginning of that year, the required return on bonds was 4.0%, but by the end of the year the required return had fallen to 2.3%. Notice that the total return earned by bond investors that year was 19.9%. In other words, bondholders earned about 4% in interest income, but they also earned a large capital gain (almost 16%) because interest rates fell during the year. As Table 2.1 shows, the years with the highest total returns on bonds are almost always years in which bond yields fell during the year.

TABLE 2.1   HISTORICAL ANNUAL YIELDS AND TOTAL RETURNS FOR TREASURY BONDS

Year	Beginning-of-Year T-Bond Yield	End-of-Year T-Bond Yield	T-Bond Total Return	Year	Beginning-of-Year T-Bond Yield	End-of-Year T-Bond Yield	T-Bond Total Return
1963	3.9%	4.1%	1.5%	1989	9.1%	7.9%	17.3%
1964	4.1%	4.2%	3.6%	1990	7.9%	8.1%	6.9%
1965	4.2%	4.7%	0.8%	1991	8.1%	6.7%	17.8%
1966	4.7%	4.6%	4.7%	1992	6.7%	6.7%	6.8%
1967	4.6%	5.7%	−3.3%	1993	6.7%	5.8%	13.2%
1968	5.7%	6.2%	2.3%	1994	5.8%	7.8%	−7.8%
1969	6.2%	7.9%	−5.4%	1995	7.8%	5.6%	24.8%
1970	7.9%	6.5%	17.8%	1996	5.6%	6.4%	−0.6%
1971	6.5%	5.9%	11.0%	1997	6.4%	5.8%	11.5%
1972	5.9%	6.4%	2.1%	1998	5.8%	4.7%	14.4%
1973	6.4%	6.9%	3.0%	1999	4.7%	6.5%	−8.3%
1974	6.9%	7.4%	3.5%	2000	6.5%	5.1%	16.7%
1975	7.4%	7.8%	5.0%	2001	5.1%	5.1%	5.5%
1976	7.8%	6.8%	14.5%	2002	5.1%	3.8%	15.2%
1977	6.8%	7.8%	0.2%	2003	3.8%	4.3%	0.3%
1978	7.8%	9.2%	−1.0%	2004	4.3%	4.2%	4.5%
1979	9.2%	10.3%	2.0%	2005	4.2%	4.4%	3.0%
1980	10.3%	12.4%	−1.3%	2006	4.4%	4.7%	1.9%
1981	12.4%	14.0%	4.3%	2007	4.7%	4.0%	10.1%
1982	14.0%	10.4%	35.9%	2008	4.0%	2.3%	19.9%
1983	10.4%	11.8%	2.0%	2009	2.3%	3.9%	−10.8%
1984	11.8%	11.6%	13.4%	2010	3.9%	3.3%	8.5%
1985	11.6%	9.0%	27.9%	2011	3.3%	1.9%	16.0%
1986	9.0%	7.2%	21.3%	2012	1.9%	1.8%	2.9%
1987	7.2%	8.8%	−3.1%	2013	1.8%	3.0%	−8.9%
1988	8.8%	9.1%	6.9%	2014	3.0%	2.2%	10.8%

(Source: Board of Governors of the Federal Reserve System (US), 10-Year Treasury Constant Maturity Rate [DGS10], retrieved from FRED, Federal Reserve Bank of St. Louis https://research.stlouisfed.org/fred2/series/DGS10/, May 20, 2015.)

We can use the return data from Table 2.1 to look at average bond returns over different periods, as shown below:

Period	Average Annual Total Returns
5 years: 2010–2014	5.9%
10 years: 2005–2014	5.3%
20 years: 1995–2014	6.9%
30 years: 1985–2014	8.5%

These figures show that the last 30 years were generally good to bond investors. This was mostly due to the fact that the U.S. economy was in a sustained period of declining interest rates, which in turn produced hefty capital gains and above-average returns. In fact, in 14 of the last 30 years, bonds earned double-digit total returns. Whether market interest rates will (or even can) continue on that path is, of course, the big question. Given the current record low yields, most market observers expect yields to begin rising over the next several years, leading to capital losses and below-average returns on bonds.

Bonds versus Stocks Compared to stocks, bonds are generally less risky and provide higher current income. Bonds, like stocks, are issued by a wide range of companies as well as various governmental bodies, so investors can construct well-diversified portfolios with bonds, just as they do with stocks. On the other hand, compared to stocks, the potential for very high returns on bonds is much more limited, even though the last two decades have been exceptional for bonds.

Figure 2.2 illustrates some of the performance differences between stocks and bonds by showing how a $10,000 investment in either stocks or bonds would have grown from 1990 through 2014. Although the investment in bonds slightly outpaced stocks in the early 1990s, investors in stocks were far better off in the late 1990s as the equity market boomed. Stocks peaked in August 2000 and then fell sharply. Stocks fell even more after the terrorist attacks on September 11, 2001, and they eventually hit bottom in September 2002. By the end of 2002, the bond investment was back in front, but only for a brief time. Stocks quickly recovered much of the ground that they had lost, peaking again in October 2007, only to have the U.S. housing bubble burst and the financial crisis begin. With the stock market in free fall in 2008 the bond market investment again took over the lead, and it would remain there for more than four years. After the financial crisis began to ease, stocks began a rocky rebound, and by the end of 2014, the $10,000 investment in stocks had grown to more than $60,000, whereas the money invested in bonds had grown to just over $48,000.

Figure 2.2 illustrates that over the last 25 years, stocks have outperformed bonds, but it also illustrates that stock returns are much more volatile than bond returns. If stocks are riskier, then investors should, on average, earn higher returns on stocks than on bonds, and we know from the historical evidence that stocks have outperformed bonds over long horizons. Still, Figure 2.2 shows that bonds can outperform stocks for a long time. For example, the cumulative returns on bonds far outpaced returns on stocks from July 2000 all the way through 2014. An investor who purchased $10,000 in bonds in July 2000 would have accumulated more than $21,200 by the end of 2014, whereas a $10,000 investment in stocks would have grown to just $13,900 over the same period.

The biggest differences in returns between stocks and bonds usually come during bear markets when stock returns are negative. In part, this reflects a phenomenon called "flight to quality" in which investors pull their funds out of the stock market to invest in less risky securities such as bonds. For example, while Figure 2.2 shows that investors in stocks lost roughly 40% of their money in 2008, Table 2.1 shows that government bond investors made about 20% that year.

Many investors argue that even if bonds earn lower returns than stocks on average, that's a low price to pay for the stability that bonds bring to a portfolio. The fact is, bond returns are far more stable than stock returns, plus they possess excellent portfolio diversification properties. As a general rule, adding bonds to a portfolio will, up to a point, reduce the portfolio's risk without dramatically reducing its return. Investors don't buy bonds for their high returns, except when they think interest rates are heading down. Rather, investors buy them for their current income and for the stability they bring to a portfolio.

FIGURE 2.2

Comparative Performance of Stocks and Bonds, 1990 through 2014

This graph shows what happened to $10,000 invested in bonds and $10,000 invested in stocks over the 25-year period from January 1990 through December 2014. Clearly, while stocks held a commanding lead going into the 21st century, the ensuing bear market more than erased that advantage. That pattern repeated itself as stocks outperformed bonds from early 2003 to late 2007, only to fall sharply through the end of 2008. From early 2009 through the end of 2012, stocks took a bumpy path toward rebounding, and from there stocks continued to climb at a rapid pace through 2014.

Note: Performance figures and graphs are based on rates of return and include reinvested current income (dividends and interest) as well as capital gains (or losses); taxes have been ignored in all calculations.

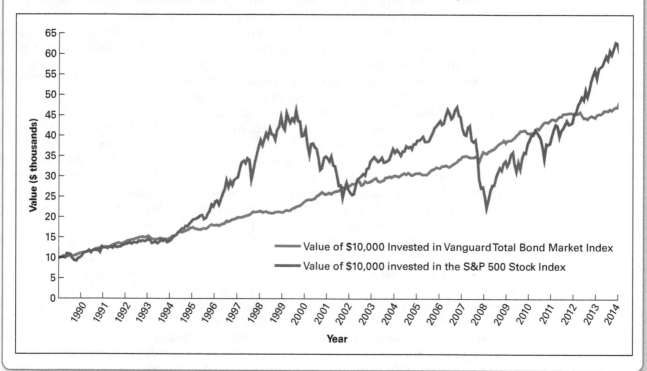

Exposure to Risk

Like all other investments, bonds are subject to a variety of risks. Generally speaking, bonds are exposed to five major types of risk: interest rate risk, purchasing power risk, business/financial risk, liquidity risk, and call risk.

- *Interest Rate Risk.* Interest rate risk is the most important risk that fixed-income investors face because it's the major cause of price volatility in the bond market. For bonds, interest rate risk translates into market risk, meaning that the behavior of interest rates affects nearly all bonds and cuts across all sectors of the market, even the U.S. Treasury market. When market interest rates rise, bond prices fall, and vice versa. As interest rates become more volatile, so do bond prices.

- *Purchasing Power Risk.* Inflation erodes the purchasing power of money, and that creates purchasing power risk. Naturally, investors are aware of this, so market interest rates on bonds compensate investors for the rate of inflation that they expect over a bond's life. When inflation is low and predictable, bonds do pretty well because their returns exceed the inflation rate by an amount sufficient to provide investors with a positive return, even after accounting for inflation's effect on purchasing power. When inflation takes off unexpectedly, as it did in the late 1970s, bond yields start to lag behind inflation rates, and the interest payments made by bonds fail to keep up. The end result is that the purchasing power of the money that bond investors receive falls faster than they anticipated. That's what the term *purchasing power risk* means. Of course, risk cuts both ways, so when the inflation rate falls unexpectedly, bonds do exceptionally well.

- *Business/Financial Risk.* This is basically the risk that the issuer will default on interest or principal payments. Also known as *credit risk*, or *default risk*, business/financial risk has to do with the quality and financial health of the issuer. The stronger the financial position of the issuer, the less business/financial risk there is to worry about. Default risk is negligible for some securities. Historically, investors have viewed U.S. Treasury securities as being free of default risk, although the growing debt of the United States has raised some concern about the potential for a default. For other types of bonds, such as corporate and municipal bonds, default risk is a much more important consideration.

- *Liquidity Risk.* Liquidity risk is the risk that a bond will be difficult to sell quickly without cutting the price if the investor wants to sell it. In some market sectors, this can be a big problem. Even though the bond market is enormous, many bonds do not trade actively once they are issued. U.S. Treasury bonds are the exception to the rule, but most corporate and municipal bonds are relatively illiquid.

- *Call Risk.* Call risk, or *prepayment risk*, is the risk that a bond will be "called" (retired) long before its scheduled maturity date. Issuers often prepay their bonds when interest rates fall. (We'll examine call features later.) When issuers call their bonds, the bondholders get their cash back and have to find another place for their funds, but because rates have fallen, bondholders have to reinvest their money at lower rates. Thus, investors have to replace high-yielding bonds with much lower-yielding bonds.

The returns on bonds are, of course, related to risk. Other things being equal, the more risk embedded in a bond, the greater the expected return. The risks of investing in bonds depend upon the characteristics of the bond and the entity that issued it. For example, as we'll see later in the chapter, there's more interest rate risk with a long-term bond than with a short-term bond. In addition, for particular bonds, the characteristics that affect risk may have offsetting effects, and that makes risk comparisons of bonds difficult. That is, one issue could have more interest rate and call risk but less credit and liquidity risk than another issue. We'll examine the various features that affect a bond's risk exposure as we work our way through this chapter.

WATCH YOUR BEHAVIOR

Buffet's Bonds Bomb Even the most savvy investors make mistakes. Warren Buffett recently acknowledged that one of his biggest mistakes was purchasing $2 billion in bonds issued by Energy Future Holdings Corporation. A prolonged drop in natural gas prices hurt the company's prospects, and in 2012 the value of Buffett's bonds was less than $900 million.

CONCEPTS IN REVIEW

Answers available at
http://www.pearsonhighered.com/smart

2.1 What appeal do bonds hold for investors? Give several reasons why bonds make attractive investment outlets.

2.2 How would you describe the behavior of market interest rates and bond returns over the last 50 years? Do swings in market interest rates have any bearing on bond returns? Explain.

2.3 Identify and briefly describe the five types of risk to which bonds are exposed. What is the most important source of risk for bonds in general? Explain.

Essential Features of a Bond

LG2 LG3 A bond is a long-term debt instrument that carries certain obligations (the payment of interest and the repayment of principal) on the part of the issuer. Bondholders are lenders, not owners, so they are not entitled to any of the rights and privileges associated with common stock, such as the right to vote at shareholders' meetings. But bondholders do have a number of well-defined rights and obligations that together define the essential features of a bond. We'll now take a look at some of these features. When it comes to bonds, it's especially important for investors to know what they're getting into, for many seemingly insignificant features can have dramatic effects on a bond's return.

Bond Interest and Principal

Bonds make periodic interest and principal payments. Most bonds pay interest every six months, although some make monthly interest payments, and some pay interest annually. A bond's **coupon** is the annual interest income that the issuer will pay to the bondholder, and its **par value, principal,** or **face value** is the amount of capital that the borrower must repay at maturity. For instance, if a bond with a par value of $1,000 pays $60 in interest each year, we say that $60 is the coupon. The **coupon rate** is the dollar coupon divided by the bond's par value, and it simply expresses the interest payment that the bond issuer makes as a percentage of the bond's par value. In the case of the $1,000 par value bond paying an annual $60 coupon, the coupon rate is 6% (i.e., $60 ÷ $1,000). If the bond makes semiannual payments, there would be a $30 interest payment every six months. Likewise, if the bond made monthly payments, the $60 coupon would be paid as 12 equal monthly interest payments of $5. The bond's **current yield** measures the interest component of a bond's return relative to the bond's market price. The current yield equals the annual coupon divided by the bond's current market price.

Example

Suppose that a 6% bond with a $1,000 par value is currently priced in the market at $950. You can calculate the bond's current yield as follows:

$$\frac{\$1,000 \times 0.06}{\$950} = 0.0632 = 6.32\%$$

Notice that the 6.32% current yield is greater than the bond's coupon rate. That's because the bond's market price is below its par value. Note that a bond's market price need not, and usually does not, equal its par value. As we have discussed, bond prices fluctuate as interest rates move, yet a bond's par value remains fixed over its life.

Maturity Date

Unlike common stock, all debt securities have limited lives and will mature on some future date, the issue's **maturity date**. Whereas bond issuers may make interest payments annually or semiannually over the life of the issue, they repay principal only at maturity. The maturity date on a bond is fixed. It not only defines the life of a new issue but also denotes the amount of time remaining for older, outstanding bonds. Such a life span is known as an issue's *term to maturity*. For example, a new issue may come out as a 25-year bond; five years later, it will have 20 years remaining to maturity.

We can distinguish two types of bond offerings based on the issuer's plans to mature the debt: term and serial bond issues. A **term bond** issue has a single, fairly lengthy maturity date for all of the bonds being issued and is the most common type of bond issue. A **serial bond** issue, in contrast, has a series of bonds with different maturity dates, perhaps as many as 15 or 20, within a single bond offering. For example, in an offering of 20-year term bonds issued in 2015, all the bonds have a single maturity date of 2035. If the bonds were offered as serial bonds, they might have different maturity dates, extending from 2016 through 2035. At each of these maturity dates, a certain portion of the issue (i.e., a certain number of bonds) would mature.

Debt instruments with different maturities go by different names. A debt security that's originally issued with a maturity of 2 to 10 years is known as a **note**, whereas a bond technically has an initial term to maturity of more than 10 years. In practice, notes are often issued with maturities of 5 to 7 years, whereas bonds normally carry maturities of 20 to 30 years, or more.

Practice Pricing Bonds

Principles of Bond Price Behavior

The price of a bond is a function of the bond's coupon, its maturity, and the level of market interest rates. Figure 2.3 captures the relationship of bond prices to market interest rates. Basically, the graph reinforces the *inverse relationship* that exists between bond prices and market rates: Lower rates lead to higher bond prices.

Figure 2.3 also shows the difference between premium and discount bonds. A **premium bond** is one that sells for more than its par value. A premium results when market interest rates drop below the bond's coupon rate. A **discount bond**, in contrast, sells for less than par value. The discount is the result of market interest rates being greater than the issue's coupon rate. Thus, the 10% bond in Figure 2.3 trades at a premium when the market requires 8% but at a discount when the market rate is 12%.

When a bond is first issued, it usually sells at a price that equals or is very close to par value because bond issuers generally set the coupon rate equal or close to the market's required interest rate at the time of the issue. Likewise, when the bond matures—some 15, 20, or 30 years later—it will once again be priced at its par value. What happens to the price of the bond in between is of considerable interest to most bond investors. In this regard, the extent to which bond prices move depends not only on the direction of change in market interest rates but also on the magnitude of such change. The greater the moves in interest rates, the greater the swings in bond prices.

However, bond price volatility also varies according to an issue's coupon and maturity. Bonds with lower coupons and/or longer maturities have more price volatility and are more responsive to changes in market interest rates. (Note in Figure 2.3 that for a given change in interest rates—for example, from 10% to 8%—the largest change in price occurs when the bond has the greatest number of years to maturity.) Therefore, if investors expect a decline in interest rates, they should buy bonds with lower coupons and longer maturities to maximize capital gains. When interest rates move up, they should do just the opposite: Purchase bonds with high coupons and short maturities. This choice will minimize the price decline and act to preserve as much capital as possible.

The maturity of an issue has a greater impact on price volatility than the coupon does. For example, suppose there are two bonds that both pay an 8% coupon rate and currently sell at par value. One bond matures in 5 years while the other matures in 25 years. Look what happens to the bond prices when market rates change:

Interest Rate Change	Percentage Change in the Price of an 8% Coupon Bond When Market Interest Rates Change					
	−3%	−2%	−1%	+1%	+2%	+3%
Bond Maturity (yr)						
5	13.0%	8.4%	4.1%	−3.9%	−7.6%	−11.1%
25	42.3%	25.6%	11.7%	−9.8%	−18.2%	−25.3%

The prices of both bonds rise when interest rates fall, but the effect is much larger for the 25-year bond. Similarly, both bonds fall in value when rates rise, but the 25-year bond falls a lot more than the 5-year bond does. Such behavior is universal with all fixed-income securities and is very important. It means that if investors want to reduce their exposure to capital losses or, more to the point, to lower the price volatility in their bond holdings, then they should buy bonds with shorter maturities.

FIGURE 2.3

The Price Behavior of a Bond

A bond will sell at its par value so long as the prevailing market interest rate remains the same as the bond's coupon—in this case, 10%. However, even when the market rate does not equal the coupon rate, as a bond approaches its maturity, the price of the issue moves toward its par value.

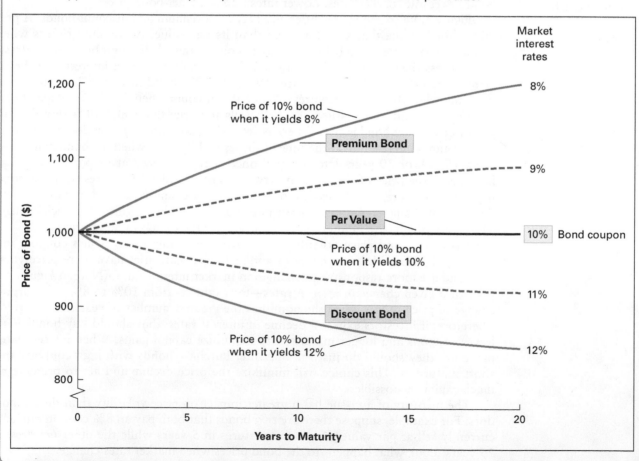

Quoting Bond Prices

Unlike stocks, the vast majority of bonds—especially corporate and municipal bonds—rarely change hands in the secondary markets. As a result, with the exception of U.S. Treasury and some agency issues, bonds are not widely quoted in the financial press, not even in the *Wall Street Journal*. Prices of all types of bonds are usually expressed as a percent of par, meaning that a quote of, say, 85 translates into a price of 85% of the bond's par value or $850 for a bond with a $1,000 par value (most corporate and municipal bonds have $1,000 par values). Also, the price of any bond depends on its coupon and maturity, so those two features are always a part of any price quote.

In the corporate and municipal markets, bond prices are expressed in decimals, using three places to the right of the decimal. Thus, a quote of 87.562, as a percent of a $1,000 par bond, converts to a price of $875.62. Similarly, a quote of 121.683 translates into a price of $1,216.83. In contrast, U.S. Treasury and agency bond quotes are stated in thirty-seconds of a point (where 1 point equals $10). For example, a website might list the price of a T-bond at 94:16. Translated, that means the bond is priced at 94 16/32, or 94.5% of par—in other words, at $945.00. With government bonds, the figures to the right of the colon show the number of thirty-seconds embedded in the price. Consider another bond that's trading at 141:08. This bond is being priced at 141 8/32, or 141.25% of par. Thus, the price of this bond in dollars is $1,412.50.

Call Features—Let the Buyer Beware!

Consider the following situation: You've just made an investment in a newly issued 25-year bond with a high coupon rate. Now you can sit back and let the cash flow in, right? Well, perhaps. Certainly, that will happen for the first several years. But if market interest rates drop, it's also likely that you'll receive a notice from the issuer that the bond is being called—that the issue is being retired before its maturity date. There's really nothing you can do but turn in the bond and invest your money elsewhere. Every bond is issued with a **call feature**, which stipulates whether and under what conditions a bond can be called in for retirement prior to maturity.

Basically, there are three types of call features:

1. A bond can be *freely callable*, which means the issuer can prematurely retire the bond at any time.

2. A bond can be *noncallable*, which means the issuer is prohibited from retiring the bond prior to maturity.

3. The issue could carry a *deferred call*, which means the issue cannot be called until after a certain length of time has passed from the date of issue. In essence, the issue is noncallable during the deferment period and then becomes freely callable thereafter.

Call features allow bond issuers to take advantage of declines in market interest rates. Companies usually call outstanding bonds paying high rates and then reissue new bonds at lower rates. In other words, call features work for the benefit of the issuers. When a bond is called, the net result is that the investor is left with a much lower rate of return than would be the case if the bond could not be called.

Investors who find their bonds called away from them often receive a small amount of extra compensation called the **call premium**. If the issue is called, the issuer will pay the call premium to investors, along with the issue's par value. The sum of the par value plus the call premium represents the issue's **call price**. This is the amount the issuer must pay to retire the bond prematurely. Call premiums often amount to as much as a year's worth of interest payments, at least if the bond is called at the earliest possible date. As the bond gets closer to maturity, the call premium gets smaller. Using this rule, the initial call price of a 5% bond could be as high as $1,050, where $50 represents the call premium.

In addition to call features, some bonds may carry **refunding provisions**. These are much like call features except that they prohibit the premature retirement of an issue from the proceeds of a lower-coupon bond. For example, a bond could come out as freely callable but nonrefundable for five years. In this case, brokers would probably sell the bond as a *deferred refunding issue*, with little or nothing said about its call feature. The distinction between nonrefundable and noncallable is important. A nonrefundable bond can still be called at any time as long as the money that the company uses to retire the bond prematurely comes from a source other than a new, lower-coupon bond issue.

Sinking Funds

Another provision that's important to investors is the **sinking fund**, which stipulates how the issuer will pay off the bond over time. This provision applies only to term bonds, of course, because serial issues already have a predetermined repayment schedule. Not all (term) bonds have sinking-fund requirements, but for those that do, the sinking fund specifies the annual repayment schedule that will be used to pay off the issue. It indicates how much principal will be retired each year.

Sinking-fund requirements generally begin one to five years after the date of issue and continue annually thereafter until all or most of the issue is paid off. Any amount not repaid (which might equal 10% to 25% of the issue) would then be retired with a single "balloon" payment at maturity. Unlike a call or refunding provision, the issuer generally does not have to pay a call premium with sinking-fund calls. Instead, the bonds are normally called at par for sinking-fund purposes.

There's another difference between sinking-fund provisions and call or refunding features. That is, whereas a call or refunding provision gives the issuer the right to retire a bond prematurely, a sinking-fund provision obligates the issuer to pay off the bond systematically over time. The issuer has no choice. It must make sinking-fund payments in a prompt and timely fashion or run the risk of being in default.

Secured or Unsecured Debt

A single issuer may have a number of different bonds outstanding at any given time. In addition to coupon and maturity, one bond can be differentiated from another by the type of collateral behind the issue. Bonds can be either junior or senior. **Senior bonds** are secured obligations, which are backed by a legal claim on some specific property of the issuer. Such issues include the following:

- **Mortgage bonds,** which are secured by real estate
- **Collateral trust bonds,** which are backed by financial assets owned by the issuer but held in trust by a third party
- **Equipment trust certificates,** which are secured by specific pieces of equipment (e.g., boxcars and airplanes) and are popular with railroads and airlines
- **First and refunding bonds,** which are basically a combination of first mortgage and junior lien bonds (i.e., the bonds are secured in part by a first mortgage on

some of the issuer's property and in part by second or third mortgages on other properties).

Note that first and refunding bonds are less secure than, and should not be confused with, straight first-mortgage bonds.

Junior bonds, on the other hand, are backed only by the promise of the issuer to pay interest and principal on a timely basis. There are several classes of unsecured bonds, the most popular of which is a **debenture**. For example, a major company like Hewlett-Packard could issue $500 million worth of 20-year debenture bonds. Being a debenture, the bond would be totally unsecured, meaning there is no collateral backing up the obligation, other than the good name of the issuer. For that reason, highly regarded firms have no trouble selling billion-dollar debenture bond issues at competitive rates.

Subordinated debentures can also be found in the market. These issues have a claim on income secondary to other debenture bonds. **Income bonds**, the most junior of all bonds, are unsecured debts requiring that interest be paid only after a certain amount of income is earned. With these bonds, there is no legally binding requirement to meet interest payments on a timely or regular basis so long as a specified amount of income has not been earned. These issues are similar in many respects to revenue bonds found in the municipal market.

Bond Ratings

To many investors, an issue's *agency rating* is just as important in defining the characteristics of a bond as are its coupon, maturity, and call features. **Bond rating agencies** are institutions that perform extensive financial analysis on companies issuing bonds to assess the credit risk associated with a particular bond issue. The ratings that these agencies publish indicate the amount of credit risk embedded in a bond, and they are widely used by fixed-income investors. **Bond ratings** are essentially the grades that rating agencies give to new bond issues, where the letter grade corresponds to a certain level of credit risk. Ratings are an important part of the municipal and corporate bond markets, where issues are regularly evaluated and rated by one or more of the rating agencies. The three largest and best-known rating agencies are Moody's, Standard & Poor's, and Fitch.

How Ratings Work When a new bond issue comes to the market, a staff of professional credit analysts from the rating agencies estimates the likelihood that the bond issuer will default on its obligations to pay principal and interest. The rating agency studies the financial records of the issuing organization and assesses its prospects. As you might expect, the firm's financial strength and stability are very important in determining the appropriate bond rating. Although there is far more to setting a rating than cranking out a few financial ratios, a strong relationship does exist between the operating results and financial condition of the firm and the rating its bonds receive. Generally, higher ratings are associated with more profitable companies that rely less on debt as a form of financing, are more liquid, have stronger cash flows, and have no trouble servicing their debt in a prompt and timely fashion.

Table 2.2 lists the various ratings assigned to bonds by two of the three major services. In addition to the standard rating categories noted in the table, Moody's uses numerical modifiers (1, 2, or 3) on bonds rated Aa to Caa, while S&P uses plus (+) and minus (−) signs on the same rating classes to show relative standing within a major

TABLE 2.2   **BOND RATINGS**

Moody's	S&P	Definition
Aaa	AAA	High-grade investment bonds. The highest rating assigned, denoting extremely strong capacity to pay principal and interest. Often called "gilt-edge" securities.
Aa	AA	High-grade investment bonds. High quality but rated lower primarily because the margins of protection are not quite as strong as AAA bonds.
A	A	Medium-grade investment bonds. Many favorable investment attributes, but elements may be present that suggest susceptibility to adverse economic changes.
Baa	BBB	Medium-grade investment bonds. Adequate capacity to pay principal and interest but possibly lacking certain protective elements against adverse economic conditions.
Ba	BB	Speculative issues. Only moderate protection of principal and interest in varied economic times.
B	B	Speculative issues. Generally lacking desirable characteristics of investment bonds. Assurance of principal and interest may be small.
Caa	CCC	Default. Poor-quality issues that may be in default or in danger of default.
Ca	CC	Default. Highly speculative issues, often in default or possessing other market shortcomings.
C		Default. These issues may be regarded as extremely poor in investment quality.
	C	Default. Rating given to income bonds on which no interest is paid.
	D	Default. Issues actually in default, with principal or interest in arrears.

(Source: Moody's Investors Service and Standard & Poor's Ratings Services.)

rating category. For example, A+ (or A1) means a strong, high A rating, whereas A− (or A3) indicates that the issue is on the low end of the A rating scale.

Note that the top four ratings (Aaa through Baa, or AAA through BBB) designate **investment-grade bonds.** Such ratings are highly coveted by issuers because they indicate financially strong, well-run companies. Companies and governmental bodies that want to raise money by issuing bonds save money if they have an investment-grade rating because investors will accept lower yields on these bonds. Bonds with below-investment-grade ratings are called **high-yield bonds,** or **junk bonds.** The issuers of these bonds generally lack the financial strength that backs investment-grade issues. Most of the time, when the rating agencies assign ratings to a particular bond issue, their ratings agree. Sometimes, however, an issue carries different ratings from different rating agencies, and in that case the bond issue is said to have a **split rating.** For example, an issue might be rated Aa by Moody's but A or A+ by S&P. These split ratings are viewed simply as "shading" the quality of an issue one way or another.

Also, just because a bond receives a certain rating at the time of issue doesn't mean it will keep that rating for the rest of its life. Ratings change as the financial condition of the issuer changes, as the example involving Automated Data Processing at the start of this chapter illustrates. In fact, all rated issues are reviewed regularly to ensure that the assigned rating is still valid. Many issues do carry a single rating to maturity, but it

INVESTOR FACTS

Some Big-Name Junk Junk bonds are low-rated debt securities that carry a relatively high risk of default. You'd expect to find a bunch of no-name companies issuing junk bonds, but that's not always the case. Here's a list of some of the familiar companies (and their Moody's rating) whose bonds were rated as junk in the summer of 2015:

- General Motors (Ba)
- JC Penney (Ba1)
- Sprint Corp (B)
- Toys R Us (Caa)
- Sears (Caa)
- Clear Channel Communications (Ca)

These fallen angels are still promptly servicing their debt. The reason they've been slapped with low ratings is that their operating earnings lack the quality and consistency of high-grade bonds. Why invest in these bonds? For their high returns!

is not uncommon for ratings to be revised up or down, and the market responds to rating revisions by adjusting bond yields accordingly. For example, an upward revision (e.g., from A to AA) causes the market yield on the bond to drop, reflecting the bond's improved quality. By the same token, if a company's financial condition deteriorates, ratings on its bonds may be downgraded. In fact, there is a special name given to junk bonds that once had investment-grade ratings—fallen angels. Although it may appear that the firm is receiving the rating, it is actually the issue that receives it. As a result, a firm's different issues can have different ratings. The senior securities, for example, might carry one rating and the junior issues another, lower rating.

What Ratings Mean Investors pay close attention to agency ratings because ratings are tied to bond yields. Specifically, the higher the rating the lower the yield, other things being equal. For example, whereas an A-rated bond might offer a 6.5% yield, a comparable AAA issue would probably yield something like 6%. Furthermore, a bond's rating has an impact on how sensitive its price is to interest rate movements as well as to changes in the company's financial performance. Junk bond prices tend to respond more when a company's financial position improves (or deteriorates) than prices of investment-grade bonds do.

Perhaps most important, bond ratings serve to relieve individual investors of the drudgery of evaluating the investment quality of an issue on their own. Large institutional investors often have their own staff of credit analysts who independently assess the creditworthiness of various corporate and municipal issuers. Individual investors, in contrast, have little if anything to gain from conducting their own credit analysis. After all, credit analysis is time-consuming and costly, and it demands a good deal more expertise than the average individual investor possesses. Two words of caution are in order, however. First, bear in mind that bond ratings are intended to measure only an issue's default risk, which has no bearing whatsoever on an issue's exposure to interest rate risk. Thus, if interest rates increase, even the highest-quality issues go down in price, subjecting investors to capital losses. Second, ratings agencies do make mistakes, and during the recent financial crisis, their mistakes made headlines.

FAMOUS FAILURES IN FINANCE

Rating Agencies Miss a Big One

Mortgage-backed securities, essentially debt instruments with returns that depended upon payments on an underlying pool of residential real estate mortgages, played a central role in the financial crisis that began in 2007 and the Great Recession that followed. Moody's and Standard & Poor's provided ratings on these instruments, just as they did with corporate bonds. Rating these securities was much more complex than rating corporate bonds for a variety of reasons, among them the fact that rating agencies knew relatively little about the creditworthiness of the individual homeowners whose mortgages were in the pool. The rating agencies gave many mortgage-backed securities investment-grade ratings, and those ratings prompted investors of all kinds, including large financial institutions, to pour money into those assets. As real estate prices began to decline, the values of "toxic" mortgage-backed securities plummeted. That led to the failure of Lehman Brothers and bailouts of other large financial institutions.

2.4 Can issue characteristics (such as coupon and call features) affect the yield and price behavior of bonds? Explain.

2.5 What is the difference between a call feature and a sinking-fund provision? Briefly describe the three types of call features. Can a bond be freely callable but nonrefundable?

2.6 What is the difference between a premium bond and a discount bond? What three attributes are most important in determining an issue's price volatility?

2.7 Bonds are said to be quoted "as a percent of par." What does that mean? What is one point worth in the bond market?

2.8 What are bond ratings, and how can they affect investor returns? What are split ratings?

2.9 From the perspective of an individual investor, what good are bond ratings? Do bond ratings indicate the amount of market risk embedded in a bond? Explain.

The Market for Debt Securities

LG4 LG5 Thus far, our discussion has dealt with basic bond features. We now shift our attention to a review of the market in which these securities are traded. To begin with, the bond market is chiefly over-the-counter in nature, as listed bonds represent only a small portion of total outstanding obligations. In addition, this market is far more stable than the stock market. Indeed, although interest rates—and therefore bond prices—do move up and down over time, when bond price activity is measured daily, it is remarkably stable. Two other things that stand out about the bond market are its size and its growth rate. From a $250 billion market in 1950, it has grown to the point where, at the end of 2014, the amount of bonds outstanding in the United States totaled $39 trillion! That makes the U.S. bond market quite a bit larger than the size of the U.S. stock market.

Here's what the U.S. bond market looked like at the end of 2014:

	Amount Outstanding ($ trillions)
Treasury bonds	12.5
Agency bonds	2.0
Municipal bonds	3.7
Corporate bonds	7.8
Mortgage-backed bonds	8.7
Asset-backed bonds	1.3
Other	2.9
Total	39.0

(Source: Securities Industry and Financial Markets Association, "U.S. Bond Market Issuance and Outstanding," 2014.)

Major Market Segments

There are bonds available in today's market to meet almost any investment objective and to suit just about any type of investor. As a matter of convenience, the domestic bond market is normally separated into four major segments, according to type of

More about
Treasury Bills

issuer: Treasury, agency, municipal, and corporate. As we shall see, each
sector has developed its own features, as well as its own trading
characteristics.

Treasury Bonds "Treasuries" (or "governments," as they are sometimes
called) are a dominant force in the fixed-income market. If not the most
popular type of bond, they certainly are the best known. In addition to
T-bills (a popular short-term debt security), the U.S. Treasury issues notes
and bonds. It also issues *inflation-indexed securities*.

All Treasury obligations are of the highest quality because they are all
backed by the "full faith and credit" of the U.S. government. This backing,
along with their liquidity, makes them very popular with individual and institutional
investors both in the United States and abroad. Indeed, U.S. Treasury securities are traded
in all the major markets of the world, from New York to London to Sydney and Tokyo.

Treasury notes are issued with maturities of 2, 3, 5, 7, and 10 years, whereas
Treasury bonds carry 30-year maturities. All Treasury notes and bonds pay interest
semiannually. Interest income from these securities is subject to normal federal income
tax but is exempt from state and local taxes. The Treasury today issues only noncallable securities; the last time it issued callable debt was in 1984. It issues its securities at
regularly scheduled auctions, the results of which are widely reported by the financial
media (see Figure 2.4). The Treasury establishes the initial yields and coupons on the
securities it issues through this auction process.

Investors participating in an auction have a choice of two bidding options—
competitive and noncompetitive. Investors who place competitive bids specify the yield
that they are willing to accept (and hence, the price that they are willing to pay).
Investors submitting competitive bids may be allocated securities in any given auction
depending on how their bids compare to bids submitted by others. In a noncompetitive
bid, investors agree to accept securities at the yield established in the auction. To conduct an auction, the Treasury first accepts all noncompetitive bids and then accepts
competitive bids in ascending order in terms of their yield (i.e., descending order in
terms of price) until the quantity of accepted bids reaches the full offering amount. All
bidders receive the same yield as the highest accepted bid.

FIGURE 2.4

Auction Results for a 30-Year Treasury Bond

Treasury auctions are closely followed by the financial media. The number of competitive bids submitted
generally far exceeds the number accepted; in this case only 45% of the competitive bids were accepted and
issued bonds. (Source: Department of the Treasury, Bureau of Public Debt, Washington, DC 20239, May 14,
2015.)

U.S. Treasury Auction Results February 15, 2012	
Type of security	30-Year Bond
Interest rate	3%
High yield[1]	3.044%
Price	99.138514
Competitive	$15,980,095,000
Total	**$35,551,052,800**

[1] All tenders at lower yields were accepted in full.

FAMOUS FAILURES IN FINANCE

Yield Spreads Approach Records

One interesting indicator of the state of the economy is the yield spread between low-risk government bonds and high-risk junk bonds issued by corporations. During the 1990–1991 recession, this yield spread set a record of 10.5%. That means that if investors require a 3% interest rate on government bonds, then they will demand a 13.5% rate on the most risky corporate bonds. In 2008 the junk bond credit spread widened again, reaching a new high of 14.68%, eclipsing the 1990s record. Interestingly, both of these episodes corresponded with a major crisis in the investment banking industry.

In 1990 it was the failure of Drexel Burnham Lambert and the fall of junk-bond king Michael Milken that led to wide spreads on junk bonds. In 2008 the yield spreads reflected investors' concerns following the 2007 failure of Lehman Brothers and bailouts of several other large financial institutions. In part due to the growing crisis in Europe, junk bond credit spreads began climbing again in 2011. Although the spread topped 7% in October of 2011, as of early 2015 it has remained below this level.

(Source: New York University Salomon Center and FRED Economic Data, St. Louis Fed.)

Inflation-Protected Securities The newest form of Treasury security (first issued in 1997) is the **Treasury Inflation-Protected Securities**, also known as **TIPS**. They are issued with 5-, 10-, and 30-year maturities, and they pay interest semiannually. They offer investors the opportunity to stay ahead of inflation by periodically adjusting their returns for any inflation that has occurred. The adjustment occurs through the bond's principal or par value. That is, the par value rises over time at a pace that matches the inflation rate. Coupon payments rise, too, because the coupon rate is paid on the inflation-adjusted principal.

Example

Suppose you purchased a 30-year TIPS with a par value of $1,000 and a 2% coupon rate. If there is no inflation, you expect to receive $20 in interest per year (i.e., $1,000 × 0.020), paid in two $10 semiannual installments. However, one year after you purchased the bond, inflation has caused the prices of goods and services to increase by 3%. The par value of your bond will increase by 3% to $1,030, and your interest payments will rise to $20.60 per year (i.e., $1,030 × 0.02). Notice that your interest payments have increased by 3%, thus compensating you for the inflation that occurred while you held the bond.

Because this type of bond offers payments that automatically adjust with inflation, investors do not have to guess what the inflation rate will be over the bond's life. In other words, TIPS eliminate purchasing power risk. Because they are less risky than ordinary bonds, TIPS generally offer lower returns than ordinary Treasury bonds do.

Agency Bonds **Agency bonds** are debt securities issued by various agencies and organizations of the U.S. government, such as the Federal Home Loan Bank, the Federal Farm Credit Systems, the Small Business Administration, the Student Loan Marketing Association, and the Federal National Mortgage Association. Although these securities are the closest things to Treasuries, they are not obligations of the U.S. Treasury and technically should not be considered the same as Treasury bonds. Even so, they are very high-quality securities that have almost no risk of default. In spite of the similar default risk, however, these securities usually provide yields that are slightly above the market rates for Treasuries. Thus, they offer a way to increase returns with little or no real difference in risk.

FAMOUS FAILURES IN FINANCE

Implicit Guarantee Becomes Explicit

Debt securities issued by agencies such as the Federal National Mortgage Association (Fannie Mae) and the Federal Home Loan Mortgage Corporation (Freddie Mac) have generally had an implicit guarantee from the federal government, meaning that investors believed that the government would not allow a default on any of these instruments even if they were not "officially" backed by the full faith and credit of the U.S. government as Treasury bills, notes, and bonds are. In 2007 as residential mortgage defaults began to rise, Fannie Mae and Freddie Mac came under severe financial distress. On

September 7, 2008, the federal government effectively took over these institutions, injecting $100 billion of new capital into each to stabilize them and to reassure investors that these giants of the mortgage industry, who held or guaranteed about $5.5 trillion in residential mortgage debt, would not disappear. Although the capital infusion helped initially, investor confidence in the two government-sponsored enterprises was rocked again on August 8, 2011, when their credit ratings were downgraded. Standard & Poor's said that the downgrade reflected their "direct reliance on the U.S. government," which had seen its own credit rating downgraded three days earlier.

There are basically two types of agency issues: government-sponsored and federal agencies. Six government-sponsored organizations and more than two dozen federal agencies offer agency bonds. To overcome some of the problems in the marketing of many relatively small federal agency securities, Congress established the Federal Financing Bank to consolidate the financing activities of all federal agencies. (As a rule, the generic term *agency* is used to denote both government-sponsored and federal agency obligations.)

Table 2.3 presents selected characteristics of some of the more popular agency bonds. As the list of issuers shows, most of the government agencies support either agriculture or housing. Although agency issues are not direct liabilities of the U.S. government, a few of them do carry government guarantees and therefore represent the full faith and credit of the U.S. Treasury. Even those issues that do not carry such guarantees are viewed as moral obligations of the U.S. government, implying it's highly unlikely that Congress would allow one of them to default. Agency issues are normally noncallable or carry lengthy call deferment features.

Municipal Bonds **Municipal bonds** (also called munis) are issued by states, counties, cities, and other political subdivisions (such as school districts and water and sewer districts). This is a $3.7 trillion market today, and it's the only segment of the bond market where the individual investor plays a major role: More than 40% of municipal bonds are directly held by individuals. These bonds are often issued as *serial obligations*, which means the issue is broken into a series of smaller bonds, each with its own maturity date and coupon.

Municipal bonds ("munis") are brought to the market as either general obligation or revenue bonds. **General obligation bonds** are backed by the full faith, credit, and taxing power of the issuer. **Revenue bonds**, in contrast, are serviced by the income generated from specific income-producing projects (e.g., toll roads). The vast majority of munis today come out as revenue bonds, accounting for about 75% to 80% of the new-issue volume. Municipal bonds are customarily issued in $5,000 denominations.

The distinction between a general obligation bond and a revenue bond is important because the issuer of a revenue bond is obligated to pay principal and interest only if a sufficient level of revenue is generated. If the funds aren't there, the issuer does not have to make payment on the bond. General obligation bonds, however, must be

TABLE 2.3   CHARACTERISTICS OF SOME POPULAR AGENCY ISSUES

Type of Issue	Minimum Denomination	Initial Maturity	Tax Status* Federal	State	Local
Federal Farm Credit System	$ 1,000	13 months to 15 years	T	E	E
Federal Home Loan Bank	$10,000	1 to 20 years	T	E	E
Federal Land Banks	$ 1,000	1 to 10 years	T	E	E
Farmers Home Administration	$25,000	1 to 25 years	T	T	T
Federal Housing Administration	$50,000	1 to 40 years	T	T	T
Federal Home Loan Mortgage Corp.** ("Freddie Mac")	$25,000	18 to 30 years	T	T	T
Federal National Mortgage Association** ("Fannie Mae")	$25,000	1 to 30 years	T	T	T
Government National Mortgage Association** (GNMA— "Ginnie Mae")	$25,000	12 to 40 years	T	T	T
Student Loan Marketing Association ("Sallie Mae")	$10,000	3 to 10 years	T	E	E
Tennessee Valley Authority (TVA)	$ 1,000	5 to 50 years	T	E	E
U.S. Postal Service	$10,000	25 years	T	E	E
Federal Financing Corp.	$ 1,000	1 to 20 years	T	E	E

*T = taxable; E = tax-exempt.
**Mortgage-backed securities.

serviced in a timely fashion irrespective of the level of tax income generated by the municipality. Obviously, revenue bonds involve more risk than general obligations, and because of that, they provide higher yields.

Some municipal bonds are backed by **municipal bond guarantees**, though these have become much less common than they once were. With these guarantees, a party other than the issuer assures the bondholder that payments will be made in a timely manner. The third party, in essence, provides an additional source of collateral in the form of insurance, placed on the bond at the date of issue, which is nonrevocable over the life of the obligation. This additional collateral improves the quality of the bond. The three principal insurers are the Assured Guaranty Corp., Municipal Bond Investors Assurance Corporation, and the American Municipal Bond Assurance Corporation. These guarantors will normally insure any general obligation or revenue bond as long as it carries an S&P rating of BBB or better. Municipal bond insurance results in higher ratings and improved liquidity for these bonds, which are generally more actively traded in the secondary markets. Insured bonds are more common in the revenue market, where the insurance markedly boosts their attractiveness. That is, whereas an uninsured revenue bond lacks certainty of payment, a guaranteed issue is very much like a general obligation bond because the investor knows that principal and interest payments will be made on time.

Tax Advantages   The most important unique feature of municipal securities is that, in most cases, their interest income is exempt from federal income taxes. That's why these issues are known as tax-free, or tax-exempt, bonds.

Normally, municipal bonds are also exempt from state and local taxes in the state in which they were issued. For example, a California issue is free of California tax if the bondholder lives in California, but its interest income is subject to state tax if the investor resides in Arizona. Note that capital gains on municipal bonds are not exempt from taxes.

Individual investors are the biggest buyers of municipal bonds, and the tax-free interest that these bonds offer is a major draw. When investors think about buying municipal bonds, they compare the tax-free yield offered by the municipal bond and compare it to the after-tax yield that they could earn on a similar taxable bond.

Example

Suppose you are in the 25% tax bracket, so each dollar of interest that you earn triggers $0.25 in taxes, allowing you to keep $0.75. Suppose a tax-free municipal bond offers a yield of 6%. What yield would a taxable bond have to offer to give you the same 6% return after taxes that you could earn on the municipal bond? The after-tax yield on a taxable bond is just the stated yield times one minus the tax rate:

$$\text{After-tax yield} = \text{Yield on taxable bond} \times (1 - \text{tax rate})$$

If you desire an after-tax yield of 6% (because that's what the municipal bond offers) and your tax rate is 25%, then we can calculate the yield that you would need to earn on a taxable bond as follows:

$$0.06 = \text{Yield on taxable bond} \times (1 - 0.25)$$
$$\text{Yield on taxable bond} = 0.06 \div (1 - 0.25)$$
$$= 0.08$$

If the taxable bond offers 8% and the municipal bond offers 6%, then you are essentially indifferent to the choice between the two securities as long as they are similar in terms of risk (and not counting any tax benefit on your state income taxes). Notice that this value is highlighted in Table 2.4.

Table 2.4 shows how the yield that a taxable bond would have to offer to remain competitive with a municipal bond depends on the investor's *marginal tax rate*. Intuitively, the tax break that municipal bonds offer is more appealing to investors in higher tax brackets who face higher marginal tax rates. For these investors, taxable bonds are not very attractive unless their yields are much higher than the yields on municipal bonds. To put it another way, investors facing high tax rates will gladly purchase municipal bonds even if they offer yields that are somewhat lower than yields on taxable bonds. For example, Table 2.4 shows that an investor in the 10% tax bracket would be indifferent to the choice between a municipal bond offering a 6% yield and a taxable bond offering a slightly higher 6.67% yield. In contrast, an investor in the 35% tax bracket would prefer the 6% municipal bond unless the yield on the taxable bond was much higher at 9.23%. Not surprisingly, investors subject to high tax rates are the main purchasers of municipal bonds. Individuals in lower tax brackets generally do not

TABLE 2.4   TAXABLE EQUIVALENT YIELDS FOR VARIOUS TAX-EXEMPT RETURNS

Federal Tax Bracket	Tax-Free Yield					
	5%	6%	7%	8%	9%	10%
10%	5.56%	6.67%	7.78%	8.89%	10.00%	11.11%
15%	5.88%	7.06%	8.24%	9.41%	10.59%	11.76%
25%	6.67%	8.00%	9.33%	10.67%	12.00%	13.33%
28%	6.94%	8.33%	9.72%	11.11%	12.50%	13.89%
33%	7.46%	8.96%	10.45%	11.94%	13.43%	14.93%
35%	7.69%	9.23%	10.77%	12.31%	13.85%	15.38%
39.6%	8.28%	9.93%	11.59%	13.25%	14.90%	16.56%

invest as heavily in municipal bonds because for them, the higher yield on taxable bonds more than offsets the benefit of earning tax-free income. The favorable tax status given to municipal bonds allows state and local governments to borrow money at lower rates than they would otherwise be able to obtain in the market.

Taxable Equivalent Yields   As you can see from the previous example and from Table 2.4, it is possible to determine the return that a fully taxable bond would have to provide in order to match the return provided by a tax-free bond. The taxable yield that is equivalent to a municipal bond's lower, tax-free yield is called the municipal's **taxable equivalent yield.** The taxable equivalent yield allows an investor to quickly compare the yield on a municipal bond with the yield offered by any number of taxable issues. The following formula shows how to calculate the taxable equivalent yield given the yield on the municipal bond and the investor's tax rate.

Equation 2.1

$$\text{Taxable equivalent yield} = \frac{\text{Yield on municipal bond}}{1 - \text{Marginal federal tax rate}}$$

For example, if a municipal offered a yield of 6.5%, then an individual in the 35% tax bracket would have to find a fully taxable bond with a yield of 10.0% (i.e., 6.5% ÷ (1 − 0.35) = 10.0%) to reap the same after-tax returns as the municipal.

Note, however, that Equation 2.1 considers federal income taxes only. As a result, the computed taxable equivalent yield applies only to certain situations: (1) to states that have no state income tax; (2) to the investor who is looking at an out-of-state bond (which would be taxable by the investor's state of residence); or (3) to the investor who is comparing a municipal bond to a Treasury (or agency) bond—in which case both the Treasury and the municipal bonds are free from state income tax; (4) to taxpayers with income levels low enough such that they are not subject to the 3.8% tax on net investment income that was passed as part of the Affordable Care Act. Under any of these conditions, the only tax that's relevant is federal income tax, so using Equation 2.1 is appropriate.

But what if you are comparing an in-state bond to a corporate bond? In this case, the in-state bond would be free from both federal and state taxes, but the corporate bond would not. As a result, Equation 2.1 would not calculate the correct taxable equivalent yield. Instead, you should use a form of the equivalent yield formula that considers both federal and state income taxes:

Equation 2.2 $$\text{Taxable equivalent yield for both federal and state taxes} = \frac{\text{Municipal bond yield}}{1 - [\text{Federal tax rate} + \text{State tax rate}(1 - \text{Federal tax rate})]}$$

Notice that the inclusion of state taxes means that the denominator of Equation 2.2 is slightly smaller than the denominator of Equation 2.1, which in turn means that the taxable equivalent yield will be higher with state taxes as part of the analysis. Intuitively this makes sense because if municipal bonds offer tax advantages at both the federal and state levels, then taxable yields must be even higher to remain competitive.

Example

Suppose your marginal federal tax rate is 35% and your state income tax rate is 3%. There is a municipal bond issued by your state that offers a yield of 6.305%. According to Equation 2.2, the taxable-equivalent yield is 10%:

$$\frac{0.06305}{1 - [0.35 + 0.03(1 - 0.35)]} = 0.10$$

Just to confirm that this is correct, suppose you purchased a $1,000 bond paying a 10% coupon rate. In the first year, you would receive $100 in interest income that is fully taxable at both the state and federal levels. Remember that taxes paid to state governments may be deducted from income before you pay federal taxes. How much of the $100 coupon payment will you have to pay in combined federal and state taxes?

Income	$100.00
State taxes (3%)	−$3.00
Taxable income (federal)	$97.00
Federal taxes (35%)	−$33.95
Net	$ 63.05

After paying $3 in state taxes and $33.95 in federal taxes, you get to keep $63.05 of the bond's $100 coupon payment. Given that you paid $1,000 for the bond, your return is 6.305%. In other words, as you found by using Equation 2.2, a 6.305% yield on a tax-free bond is equivalent to a 10% yield on a taxable bond.

Notice that if there had been no state tax in this example, the taxable equivalent yield would have been 9.7%. That's not a huge difference, but the difference would be higher for a higher state tax rate, and some U.S. states have tax rates as high as 11%.

Corporate Bonds Corporations are the major nongovernmental issuers of bonds. The market for corporate bonds is customarily subdivided into four segments based on the types of companies that issue bonds: *industrials* (the most diverse of the groups), *public utilities* (the dominant group in terms of volume of new issues), *transportation*, and *financial services* (e.g., banks, finance companies). In the corporate sector of the bond market investors can find bonds from high-quality AAA-rated issues to junk bonds in or near default, and there is also a wide assortment of bonds with many different features. These range from first-mortgage obligations to convertible bonds (which we'll examine later in this chapter), debentures, subordinated debentures, senior subordinated issues, capital notes (a type of unsecured debt issued by banks and other financial institutions), and income bonds. Companies pay interest on corporate bonds semiannually, and sinking funds are fairly common. The bonds usually come in $1,000 denominations and are issued on a term basis with a single maturity date of 10 years or more. Many corporate bonds, especially the longer ones, carry call deferment provisions that prohibit prepayment for the first 5 to 10 years. Corporate issues are popular with individuals because of the steady, predictable income that they provide.

While most corporate issues fit the general description above, one that does not is the *equipment trust certificate*, a security issued by railroads, airlines, and other transportation concerns. The proceeds from equipment trust certificates are used to purchase equipment (e.g., jumbo jets and railroad engines) that serves as the collateral for the issue. These bonds are usually issued in serial form and carry uniform annual installments throughout. They normally carry maturities that range up to about 15 years, with the maturity reflecting the useful life of the equipment. Despite a near-perfect payment record that dates back to pre-Depression days, these issues generally offer above-average yields to investors.

Specialty Issues

In addition to the basic bonds described above, investors can choose from a number of specialty issues—bonds that possess unusual issue characteristics. These bonds have coupon or repayment provisions that are out of the ordinary. Most of them are issued by corporations, although they are being used increasingly by other issuers as well. Four of the most actively traded specialty issues today are zero-coupon bonds, mortgage-backed securities, asset-backed securities, and high-yield junk bonds. All of these rank as some of the more popular bonds on Wall Street.

Zero-Coupon Bonds As the name implies, **zero-coupon bonds** have no coupons. Rather, these securities are sold at a discount from their par values and then increase in value over time at a compound rate of return. Thus, at maturity, they are worth more than their initial cost, and this difference represents the bond's return. Other things being equal, the cheaper the zero-coupon bond, the greater the return an investor can earn: For example, a bond with a 6% yield might cost $420, but one with a 10% yield might cost only $240.

Because they do not have coupons, these bonds do not pay interest semiannually. In fact, they pay nothing at all until the issue matures. As strange as it might seem, this feature is the main attraction of zero-coupon bonds. Because there are no coupon payments, there is no need to worry about reinvesting interest income twice a year. Instead, the rate of return on a zero-coupon bond is virtually guaranteed to be the yield that existed at the time of purchase as long as the investor holds the bond to maturity. For example, in mid-2015, U.S. Treasury zero-coupon bonds with 10-year maturities were available at yields of around 2.5%. For around $780, investors could buy a bond that would be worth $1,000 at maturity in 10 years. That 2.5% yield is a rate of return that's locked in for the life of the issue.

The foregoing advantages notwithstanding, zeros do have some serious disadvantages. One is that if market interest rates move up, investors won't be able to participate in the higher return. (They'll have no interest income to reinvest.) In addition, zero-coupon bonds are subject to tremendous price volatility. If market rates climb, investors will experience a sizable capital loss as the prices of zero-coupons plunge. (Of course, if interest rates drop, investors who hold long-term zeros will reap enormous capital gains.) A final disadvantage is that the IRS has ruled that zero-coupon bondholders must pay tax on interest as it accrues, even though investors holding these bonds don't actually receive interest payments.

Zeros are issued by corporations, municipalities, and federal agencies. Actually, the Treasury does not issue zero-coupon bonds. Instead, it allows government securities dealers to sell regular coupon-bearing notes and bonds in the form of zero-coupon securities known as **Treasury strips**. Essentially, the interest and principal payments are stripped from a Treasury bond and then sold separately as zero-coupon bonds. For example, a 10-year Treasury note has 20 semiannual interest payments, plus 1 principal payment. These 21 cash flows can be sold as 21 different zero-coupon securities, with maturities that range from 6 months to 10 years. The minimum par value needed to strip a Treasury note or bond is $100 and any par value to be stripped above $100 must be in a multiple of $100. Treasury strips with the same maturity are often bundled and sold in minimum denominations (par values) of $10,000. Because there's an active secondary market for Treasury strips, investors can get in and out of these securities with ease just about anytime they want. Strips offer the maximum in issue quality, a wide array of maturities, and an active secondary market—all of which explains why they are so popular.

Mortgage-Backed Securities Simply put, a **mortgage-backed bond** is a debt issue that is secured by a pool of residential mortgages. An issuer, such as the Government National Mortgage Association (GNMA), puts together a pool of home mortgages and then issues securities in the amount of the total mortgage pool. These securities, also known as *pass-through securities* or *participation certificates*, are usually sold in minimum denominations of $25,000. Although their maturities can go out as far as 30 years, the average life is generally much shorter (perhaps as short as 8 years) because many of the mortgages are paid off early.

As an investor in one of these securities, you hold an undivided interest in the pool of mortgages. When a homeowner makes a monthly mortgage payment, that payment is essentially passed through to you, the bondholder, to pay off the mortgage-backed bond you hold. Although these securities come with normal coupons, the interest is paid monthly rather than semiannually. Actually, the monthly payments received by bondholders are, like mortgage payments, made up of both principal and interest. Because the principal portion of the payment represents return of capital, it is considered tax-free. The interest portion, however, is subject to ordinary state and federal income taxes.

Mortgage-backed securities (MBSs) are issued primarily by three federal agencies. Although there are some state and private issuers (mainly big banks and S&Ls), agency issues dominate the market and account for 90% to 95% of the activity. The major agency issuers of mortgage-backed securities (MBSs) are:

- *Government National Mortgage Association (GNMA)*. Known as Ginnie Mae, it is the oldest and largest issuer of MBSs.

- *Federal Home Loan Mortgage Corporation (FHLMC)*. Known as Freddie Mac, it was the first to issue pools containing conventional mortgages.

- *Federal National Mortgage Association (FNMA)*. Known as Fannie Mae, it's the leader in marketing seasoned/older mortgages.

One feature of mortgage-backed securities is that they are self-liquidating investments; that is, a portion of the monthly cash flow to the investor is repayment of principal. Thus, investors are always receiving back part of the original investment capital, so that at maturity, there is no big principal payment. To counter this effect, a number of mutual funds invest in mortgage-backed securities but automatically reinvest the capital/principal portion of the cash flows. Mutual fund investors therefore receive only the interest from their investments and their capital remains fully invested.

Collateralized Mortgage Obligations Loan prepayments are another problem with mortgage-backed securities. In fact, it was in part an effort to diffuse some of the prepayment uncertainty in standard mortgage-backed securities that led to the creation of **collateralized mortgage obligations (CMOs)**. Normally, as pooled mortgages are prepaid, all bondholders receive a prorated share of the prepayments. The net effect is to sharply reduce the life of the bond. A CMO, in contrast, divides investors into classes (called *tranches*, which is French for "slice"), depending on whether they want a short-, intermediate-, or long-term investment. Although interest is paid to all bondholders, all principal payments go first to the shortest tranche until it is fully retired. Then the next class in the sequence becomes the sole recipient of principal, and so on, until the last tranche is retired.

Basically, CMOs are *derivative securities* created from traditional mortgage-backed bonds, which are placed in a trust. Participation in this trust is then sold to the investing public in the form of CMOs. The net effect of this transformation is that CMOs look and behave very much like any other bond. They offer predictable interest payments and have (relatively) predictable maturities. However, although they carry the same AAA ratings and implicit U.S. government backing as the mortgage-backed bonds that underlie them, CMOs represent a quantum leap in complexity. Some types of CMOs can be as simple and safe as Treasury bonds. Others can be far more volatile— and risky—than the standard MBSs they're made from. That's because when putting CMOs together, Wall Street performs the financial equivalent of gene splicing. Investment bankers isolate the interest and principal payments from the underlying MBSs and rechannel them to the different tranches. It's not issue quality or risk of default that's the problem here, but rather prepayment, or call, risk. Even if all of the bonds are ultimately paid off, investors don't know exactly when those payments will arrive. Different types of CMO tranches have different levels of prepayment risk. The overall risk in a CMO cannot, of course, exceed that of the underlying mortgage-backed bonds, so in order for there to be some tranches with very little (or no) prepayment risk, others have to endure a lot more. The net effect is that while some CMO tranches are low in risk, others are loaded with it.

Investors discovered just how complex and how risky these securities could be as the financial crisis unfolded in 2007 and 2008. As homeowner defaults on residential mortgages began to rise, the values of CMOs plummeted. Trading in the secondary market dried up, so it was difficult to know what the underlying values of some CMOs really were. Investment and commercial banks that had invested heavily in these securities came under intense pressure as doubts about their solvency grew into a near panic. Everyone wanted to know which institutions held these "toxic assets" on their balance sheets and how large their losses were on these instruments. Lehman Brothers, Bear Stearns, Merrill Lynch, and many other financial institutions went bankrupt or were acquired under distress by other institutions, and the federal government poured hundreds of billions of dollars into the banking system to try to prevent total collapse.

Asset-Backed Securities The creation of mortgage-backed securities and CMOs quickly led to the development of a new market technology—the process of **securitization,** whereby various lending vehicles are transformed into marketable securities, much like a mortgage-backed security. In recent years, investment bankers sold billions of dollars' worth of pass-through securities, known as **asset-backed securities (ABS),** which are backed by pools of auto loans, credit card bills, and home equity lines of credit (three of the principal types of collateral), as well as computer leases, hospital receivables, small business loans, truck rentals, and even royalty fees.

These securities, first introduced in the mid-1980s, are created when an investment bank bundles some type of debt-linked asset (such as loans or receivables) and then sells to investors—via asset-backed securities—the right to receive all or part of the future payments made on that debt. For example, GMAC, the financing arm of General Motors, is a regular issuer of collateralized auto loan securities. When it wants to get some of its car loans off its books, GMAC takes the monthly cash flow from a pool of auto loans and pledges them to a new issue of bonds, which are then sold to investors. In similar fashion, credit card receivables are regularly used as collateral for these bonds (indeed, they represent the biggest segment of the ABS market), as are home equity loans, the second-biggest type of ABS.

Investors are drawn to ABSs for a number of reasons. These securities offer relatively high yields, and they typically have short maturities, which often extend out no more than five years. A third reason that investors like ABSs is the monthly, rather than semiannual, principal/interest payments that accompany many of these securities. Also important to investors is their high credit quality. That's due to the fact that most of these deals are backed by generous credit protection. For example, the securities are often overcollateralized: the pool of assets backing the bonds may be 25% to 50% larger than the bond issue itself. A large fraction of ABSs receive the highest credit rating possible (AAA) from the leading rating agencies.

Junk Bonds Junk bonds (or high-yield bonds, as they're also called) are highly speculative securities that have received low, sub-investment-grade ratings (typically Ba or B). These bonds are issued primarily by corporations and also by municipalities. Junk bonds often take the form of *subordinated debentures*, which means the debt is unsecured and has a low claim on assets. These bonds are called "junk" because of their high risk of default. The companies that issue them generally have excessive amounts of debt in their capital structures and their ability to service that debt is subject to considerable doubt.

Probably the most unusual type of junk bond is something called a **PIK bond.** PIK stands for *payment in kind* and means that rather than paying the bond's coupon in cash, the issuer can make annual interest payments in the form of additional debt. This "financial printing press" usually goes on for five or six years, after which time the issuer is supposed to start making interest payments in real money.

Why would any rational investor be drawn to junk bonds? The answer is simple: They offer very high yields. Indeed, in a typical market, relative to investment-grade bonds, investors can expect to pick up anywhere from two to five percentage points in added yield. For example, in June of 2015, investors were getting roughly 6.5% yields on junk bonds, compared to just under 4% on investment-grade corporates. Obviously, such yields are available only because of the correspondingly higher exposure to risk. Junk bonds are subject to a good deal of risk, and their prices are unstable. Indeed, unlike investment-grade bonds, whose prices are closely linked to the behavior of market interest rates, junk bonds tend to behave more like stocks. As a result, the returns are highly unpredictable. Accordingly, only investors who are thoroughly familiar with the risks involved, and who are comfortable with such risk exposure, should purchase these securities.

A Global View of the Bond Market

Globalization has hit the bond market, just as it has the stock market. Foreign bonds have caught on with U.S. investors because of their high yields and attractive returns. There are risks with foreign bonds, of course, but high risk of default is not always one of them. Instead, the big risk with foreign bonds has to do with the impact that currency fluctuations can have on returns in U.S. dollars.

The United States has the world's biggest bond market, accounting for a little less than half of the global market. Following the United States is Japan, China, and several countries in the European Union (principally Germany, Italy, and France). Together these countries account for more than 90% of the world bond market. Worldwide, various forms of government bonds (e.g., Treasuries, agencies, and munis) dominate the market.

U.S.-Pay versus Foreign-Pay Bonds   There are several ways to invest in foreign bonds. From the perspective of a U.S. investor, we can divide foreign bonds into two broad categories on the basis of the currency in which the bond is denominated: *U.S.-pay* (or dollar-denominated) bonds and *foreign-pay* (or non-dollar-denominated) bonds. All the cash flows—including purchase price, maturity value, and coupon income—from dollar-denominated foreign bonds are in U.S. dollars. The cash flows from non-dollar bonds are designated in a foreign currency, such as the euro, British pound, or Swiss franc.

Dollar-Denominated Bonds   Dollar-denominated foreign bonds are of two types: Yankee bonds and Eurodollar bonds. **Yankee bonds** are issued by foreign governments or corporations or by so-called supranational agencies, like the World Bank and the InterAmerican Bank. These bonds are issued and traded in the United States; they're registered with the SEC, and all transactions are in U.S. dollars. Not surprisingly, Canadian issuers dominate the Yankee-bond market. Buying a Yankee bond is really no different from buying any other U.S. bond. These bonds are traded on U.S. exchanges and the OTC market, and because everything is in dollars, there's no currency exchange risk to deal with. The bonds are generally very high in quality (which is not surprising, given the quality of the issuers) and offer highly competitive yields to investors.

Eurodollar bonds, in contrast, are issued and traded outside the United States. They are denominated in U.S. dollars, but they are not registered with the SEC, which means underwriters are legally prohibited from selling new issues to the U.S. public. (Only "seasoned" Eurodollar issues can be sold in this country.) The Eurodollar market today is dominated by foreign-based investors (though that is changing) and is primarily aimed at institutional investors.

Foreign-Pay Bonds   From the standpoint of U.S. investors, foreign-pay international bonds encompass all those issues denominated in a currency other than dollars. These bonds are issued and traded overseas and are not registered with the SEC. Examples are

German government bonds, which are payable in euros; Japanese bonds, issued in yen; and so forth. When investors speak of foreign bonds, it's this segment of the market that most of them have in mind.

Foreign-pay bonds are subject to changes in currency exchange rates, which can dramatically affect total returns to U.S. investors. The returns on foreign-pay bonds depend on three things: (1) the level of coupon (interest) income earned on the bonds; (2) the change in market interest rates, which determines the level of capital gains (or losses); and (3) the behavior of currency exchange rates. The first two variables are the same as those that drive U.S. bond returns. They are, of course, just as important to foreign bonds as they are to domestic bonds. Thus, if individuals are investing overseas, they still want to know what the yields are today and where they're headed. It's the third variable that separates the return behavior of dollar-denominated from foreign-pay bonds.

We can assess returns from foreign-pay bonds by employing the following equation:

Equation 2.3

$$\text{Total return (in U.S. dollars)} = \left[\frac{\text{Ending value of bond in foreign currency} + \text{Amount of interest received in foreign currency}}{\text{Beginning value of bond in foreign currency}} \times \frac{\text{Exchange rate at end of holding period}}{\text{Exchange rate at beginning of holding period}} \right] - 1.00$$

For example, assume a U.S. investor purchased a Swedish government bond, in large part because of the attractive 7.5% coupon it carried. If the bond was bought at par and market rates fell over the course of the year, the security itself would have provided a return in excess of 7.5% (because the decline in rates would provide some capital gains). However, if the Swedish krona (SEK) fell relative to the dollar, the total return (in U.S. dollars) could have actually ended up at a lot less than 7.5%, depending on what happened to the U.S.$/SEK exchange rate. To find out exactly how this investment performed, you could use the equation above. Like foreign stocks, foreign-pay bonds can pay off from both the behavior of the security and the behavior of the currency. That combination, in many cases, means superior returns to U.S. investors. Knowledgeable investors find these bonds attractive not only because of their competitive returns but also because of the positive diversification effects they have on bond portfolios.

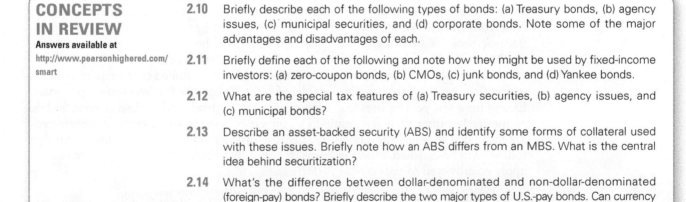

CONCEPTS IN REVIEW
Answers available at
http://www.pearsonhighered.com/smart

2.10 Briefly describe each of the following types of bonds: (a) Treasury bonds, (b) agency issues, (c) municipal securities, and (d) corporate bonds. Note some of the major advantages and disadvantages of each.

2.11 Briefly define each of the following and note how they might be used by fixed-income investors: (a) zero-coupon bonds, (b) CMOs, (c) junk bonds, and (d) Yankee bonds.

2.12 What are the special tax features of (a) Treasury securities, (b) agency issues, and (c) municipal bonds?

2.13 Describe an asset-backed security (ABS) and identify some forms of collateral used with these issues. Briefly note how an ABS differs from an MBS. What is the central idea behind securitization?

2.14 What's the difference between dollar-denominated and non-dollar-denominated (foreign-pay) bonds? Briefly describe the two major types of U.S.-pay bonds. Can currency exchange rates affect the total return of U.S.-pay bonds? Of foreign-pay bonds? Explain.

Convertible Securities

 In addition to the many types of bonds covered in the preceding material, there is still another type of fixed-income security that merits discussion at this point—namely, **convertible bonds.** Issued only by corporations, convertibles are different from most other types of corporate debt because even though these securities may start out as bonds, they usually end up as shares of common stock. That is, while these securities are originally issued as bonds (or even preferred stock), they contain a provision that gives investors the option to convert their bonds into shares of the issuing firm's stock. Convertibles are *hybrid securities* because they contain attributes of both debt and equity. But even though they possess the features and performance characteristics of both fixed-income and equity securities, convertibles should be viewed primarily as a form of equity. That's because most investors commit their capital to such obligations not for the yields they provide but rather for the potential price performance of the stock side of the issue. In fact, it is always a good idea to determine whether a corporation has convertible issues outstanding whenever you are considering a common stock investment. In some circumstances, the convertible may be a better investment than the firm's common stock. (Preferred stocks represent another type of hybrid security because they too have features and characteristics of both equity and fixed-income securities.)

Convertibles as Investment Outlets

Convertible securities are popular with investors because of their **equity kicker**—the right to convert these bonds into shares of the company's common stock. Because of this feature, the market price of a convertible has a tendency to behave very much like the price of its underlying common stock. Convertibles are used by all types of companies and are issued either as convertible bonds (by far the most common type) or as convertible *preferreds*. Convertibles enable firms to raise equity capital at fairly attractive prices. That is, when a company issues stock in the normal way (by selling more shares in the company), it does so by setting a price on the stock that's slightly below prevailing market prices. For example, it might be able to get $25 for a stock that's currently priced in the market at, say, $27 a share. In contrast, when it issues the stock indirectly through a convertible issue, the firm can set a price that's above the prevailing market—for example, it might be able to get $35 for the same stock. In this case, convertible bond investors will only choose to convert their bonds into shares if the market price of the shares subsequently increases above $35. As a result, the company can raise the same amount of money by issuing a lot less stock. Thus, companies issue convertibles not as a way of raising debt capital but as a way of raising equity. Because they are eventually converted into shares of the issuing company's common stock, convertibles are usually viewed as a form of **deferred equity.**

Convertible bonds and convertible preferreds are both linked to the equity position of the firm, so they are usually considered interchangeable for investment purposes. Except for a few peculiarities (e.g., preferreds pay dividends rather than interest and do so quarterly rather than semiannually), convertible bonds and convertible preferreds are evaluated in much the same way. Because of their similarities, the discussion that follows will be couched largely in terms of bonds, but the information and implications apply equally well to convertible preferreds.

Convertible Notes and Bonds Firms usually issue convertible bonds as subordinated debentures attached with the provision that within a stipulated time period, the bond may be converted into a certain number of shares of the issuing company's common stock. Convertible notes are just like convertible bonds except that the debt portion of the security carries a shorter maturity—usually of 5 to 10 years. Other than the life of the debt, there is no real difference between the convertible notes and bonds. They're both unsecured debt obligations, and they're usually subordinated to other forms of debt.

Generally speaking, little or no cash is exchanged between investors and issuing firms at the time of conversion. Convertible bondholders merely trade in the convertible bond (or note) for a stipulated number of shares of common stock. For example, assume that a certain convertible security recently came to the market, and it carried the provision that each $1,000 note could be converted into shares of the issuing company's stock at $50 a share. Thus, regardless of what happens to the market price of the stock, investors can redeem each note for 20 shares of the company's stock ($1,000 ÷ $50 = 20 shares). So, if the company's stock is trading in the market at, say, $65 a share at the time of conversion, then an investor could convert a $1,000 debt obligation into $1,300 worth of stock (20 × $65 = $1,300). Not surprisingly, this conversion privilege comes at a price: the low coupon (or dividend) that convertibles usually carry. That is, when new convertible issues come to the market, their coupons are normally just a fraction of those on comparable straight (nonconvertible) bonds. Indeed, the more attractive the conversion feature, the lower the coupon.

Actually, while it's the bondholder who has the right to convert the bond at any time, more often than not, the issuing firm initiates conversion by calling the bonds—a practice known as **forced conversion**. To provide the corporation with the flexibility to retire the debt and force conversion, most convertibles come out as freely callable issues, or they carry very short call deferment periods. To force conversion, the corporation would call for the retirement of the bond and give the bondholder two options: Either convert the bond into common stock or redeem it for cash at the stipulated call price (which, in the case of convertibles, contains very little call premium). As long as the convertible is called when the market value of the stock exceeds the call price of the bond (which is almost always the case), seasoned investors would never choose the second option. Instead, they would opt to convert the bond, as the firm wants them to. Then they can hold the stocks if they want to or they can sell their new shares in the market (and end up with more cash than they would have received by taking the call price). After the conversion is complete, the bonds no longer exist; instead, there is additional common stock in their place.

Conversion Privilege The key element of any convertible is its **conversion privilege**, which stipulates the conditions and specific nature of the conversion feature. To begin with, it states exactly when the debenture can be converted. With some issues, there may be an initial waiting period of six months to perhaps two years after the date of issue, during which time the security cannot be converted. The **conversion period** then begins, and the issue can be converted at any time. The conversion period typically extends for the remaining life of the debenture, but in some instances, it may exist for only a certain number of years. This is done to give the issuing firm more control over its capital structure. If the issue has not been converted by the end of its conversion period, it reverts to a straight-debt issue with no conversion privileges.

From the investor's point of view, the most important piece of information is the conversion price or the conversion ratio. These terms are used interchangeably and specify, either directly or indirectly, the number of shares of stock into which the bond can be converted. The **conversion ratio** denotes the number of common shares into which the bond can be converted. The **conversion price** indicates the stated value per share at which the common stock will be delivered to the investor in exchange for the bond. When you stop to think about these two measures, it becomes clear that a given conversion ratio implies a certain conversion price, and vice versa.

Example

> Suppose that a certain $1,000 convertible bond stipulates a conversion ratio of 40, which means that the bond can be converted into 40 shares of common stock. In effect, if you give up your $1,000 bond in exchange for 40 shares, you are essentially buying 40 shares of stock for $1,000, or $25 per share. In other words, the conversation ratio of 40 is equivalent to a conversion price of $25. (One basic difference between a convertible debenture and a convertible preferred relates to conversion ratio: The conversion ratio of a debenture generally deals with large multiples of common stock, such as 15, 20, or 30 shares. In contrast, the conversion ratio of a preferred is generally very small, often less than one share of common and seldom more than three or four shares.)

The conversion ratio is normally adjusted for stock splits and significant stock dividends. As a result, if a firm declares, say, a 2-for-1 stock split, the conversion ratio of any of its outstanding convertible issues also doubles. And when the conversion ratio includes a fraction, such as 33.5 shares of common, the conversion privilege specifies how any fractional shares are to be handled. Usually, the investor can either put up the additional funds necessary to purchase another full share of stock at the conversion price or receive the cash equivalent of the fractional share (at the conversion price).

LYONs Leave it to Wall Street to take a basic investment product and turn it into a sophisticated investment vehicle. That's the story behind LYONs, which some refer to as "zeros on steroids." Start with a zero-coupon bond, throw in a conversion feature and a put option, and you have a **LYON** (the acronym stands for **liquid yield option note**). LYONs are zero-coupon convertible bonds that are convertible, at a fixed conversion ratio, for the life of the issue. Thus, they offer the built-in increase in value over time that accompanies any zero-coupon bond (as it moves toward its par value at maturity), plus full participation in the equity side of the issue via the equity kicker. Unlike most convertibles, there's no current income with a LYON (because it is a zero-coupon bond). On the other hand, however, it does carry an option feature that enables investors to "put" or sell the bonds back to the issuer (at specified values). That is, the put option gives investors the right to redeem their bonds periodically at prespecified prices. Thus, investors know they can get out of these securities, at set prices, if they want to.

Although LYONs may appear to provide the best of all worlds, they do have some negative aspects. It is true that LYONs provide downside protection (via the put option feature) and full participation in the equity kicker. But like all zero-coupon bonds, they don't generate current income. And investors have to watch out for the put option. Depending on the type of put option, the payout does not have to be in cash—it can be in stocks or bonds. One other important issue to be aware of is that because the conversion ratio on the LYON is fixed, the conversion price on the stock increases over time. This occurs because the value of the zero-coupon bond increases as it reaches maturity. Thus, the market price of the stock had better go up by more than the bond's rate of appreciation or investors will never be able to convert their LYONs.

Sources of Value

Because convertibles are fixed-income securities linked to the equity position of the firm, they are normally valued in terms of both the stock and the bond dimensions of the issue. Thus, it is important to both analyze the underlying common stock and formulate interest rate expectations when considering convertibles as an investment outlet. Let's look first at the stock dimension.

Convertible securities trade much like common stock whenever the market price of the stock starts getting close to (or exceeds) the stated conversion price. When that happens, the convertible will exhibit price behavior that closely matches that of the underlying common stock. If the stock goes up in price, so does the convertible, and vice versa. In fact, the absolute price change of the convertible will exceed that of the common because of the conversion ratio, which will define the convertible's rate of change in price. For example, if a convertible carries a conversion ratio of, say, 20, then for every dollar the common stock goes up (or down) in price, the price of the convertible will move in the same direction by roughly that same multiple (in this case, $20). In essence, whenever a convertible trades as a stock, its market price will approximate a multiple of the share price of the common, with the size of the multiple being defined by the conversion ratio.

When the market price of the common is well below the conversion price, the convertible loses its tie to the underlying common stock and begins to trade as a bond. When that happens, the convertible becomes linked to prevailing bond yields, and investors focus their attention on market rates of interest. However, because of the equity kicker and their relatively low agency ratings, convertibles generally do not possess high interest rate sensitivity. Gaining more than a rough idea of what the prevailing yield of a convertible obligation ought to be is often difficult. For example, if the issue is rated Baa and the market rate for this quality range is 9%, then the convertible should be priced to yield something around 9%, plus or minus perhaps half a percentage point. Because of the interest and principal payments that they offer, convertible bonds essentially have a price floor, meaning that convertible values generally cannot drop as much as the underlying stock can. If a company experiences financial problems that cause its stock price to drop dramatically, the firm's convertible bonds will retain much of their value because investors are still entitled to receive interest and principal payments. That is, the price of the convertible will not fall to much less than its price floor because at that point, the issue's bond value will kick in.

Measuring the Value of a Convertible

In order to evaluate the investment merits of convertible securities, investors should consider both the bond and the stock dimensions of the issue. Fundamental security analysis of the equity position is, of course, especially important in light of the key role the equity kicker plays in defining the price behavior of a convertible. In contrast, market yields and agency ratings are used in evaluating the bond side of the issue. But there's more: In addition to analyzing the bond and stock dimensions of the issue, it is essential to evaluate the conversion feature itself. The two critical areas in this regard are conversion value and investment value. These measures have a vital bearing on a convertible's price behavior and therefore can have a dramatic effect on an issue's holding period return.

Conversion Value In essence, **conversion value** indicates what a convertible issue would trade for if it were priced to sell on the basis of its stock value. Conversion value is easy to find:

Equation 2.4   Conversion value = Conversion ratio × Current market price of the stock

> **Example**
>
> Suppose that a particular convertible bond has a conversion ratio of 20. If the price of the company's stock is $60 per share, then the conversion value of the bond is $1,200 (i.e., 20 × $60).

Sometimes analysts use an alternative measure that computes the **conversion equivalent**, also known as **conversion parity**. The conversion equivalent indicates the price at which the common stock would have to sell in order to make the convertible security worth its present market price. The conversion equivalent is calculated as follows:

Equation 2.5 $$\text{Conversion equivalent} = \frac{\text{Current market price of the convertible bond}}{\text{Conversion ratio}}$$

> **Example**
>
> If a convertible bond has a current market price of $1,400 and a conversion ratio of 20, the conversion equivalent of the common stock would be $70 per share (i.e., $1,400 ÷ 20). Although convertible bonds can trade above par value simply because of a decline in interest rates, as a practical matter, it would be unusual for a bond to trade as high as $1,400 based only on an interest rate drop. Accordingly, you would expect the current market price of the common stock in this example to be at or near $70 per share in order to support a convertible trading at $1,400.

Conversion Premium   Convertible issues seldom trade precisely at their conversion values. Rather, they usually trade at prices that exceed the bond's underlying conversion value. The extent to which the market price of the convertible exceeds its conversion value is known as the *conversion premium*. The absolute size of an issue's conversion premium is found by taking the difference between the convertible's market price and its conversion value (per Equation 2.4). To place the premium on a relative basis, simply divide the dollar amount of the conversion premium by the issue's conversion value. That is,

Equation 2.6 $$\text{Conversion premium (in \$)} = \begin{matrix}\text{Current market price}\\\text{of the convertible bond}\end{matrix} - \begin{matrix}\text{Conversion}\\\text{value}\end{matrix}$$

where conversion value is found according to Equation 2.4.
Then

Equation 2.7 $$\text{Conversion premium (in \%)} = \frac{\text{Conversion premium (in \$)}}{\text{Conversion value}}$$

> **Example**
>
> Suppose that a convertible bond trades at $1,400 and its conversion value equals $1,200. This bond has a conversion premium of $200 (i.e., $1,400 − $1,200). That $200 represents a conversion premium of 16.7% relative to the bond's conversion value.

Conversion premiums are common in the market and can often amount to 30% to 40% (or more) of an issue's conversion value. Investors are willing to pay a premium because of the added current income that a convertible provides relative to the underlying common stock and because of the convertible's upside potential. An investor can recover this premium either through the added current income or by selling the issue at a premium equal to or greater than that which existed at the time of purchase. Unfortunately, the latter source of recovery is tough to come by because conversion premiums tend to fade away as the price of the convertible goes up. That means that if an investor purchases a convertible for its potential price appreciation, then he must accept the fact that all or a major portion of the price premium is very likely to disappear as the convertible appreciates over time and moves closer to its true conversion value. Thus, if he hopes to recover any conversion premium, it will probably have to come from the added current income that the convertible provides.

Payback Period   The size of the conversion premium can obviously have a major impact on investor return. When picking convertibles, one of the major questions investors should ask is whether the premium is justified. One way to assess conversion premium is to compute the issue's **payback period**, a measure of the length of time it will take to recover the conversion premium from the extra interest income earned on the convertible. Because this added income is a principal reason for the conversion premium, it makes sense to use it to assess the premium. The payback period can be found as follows:

Equation 2.8

$$\text{Payback period} = \frac{\text{Conversion premium (in \$)}}{\begin{array}{c}\text{Annual interest} \\ \text{income from the} \\ \text{convertible bond}\end{array} - \begin{array}{c}\text{Annual dividend} \\ \text{income from the} \\ \text{underlying common stock}\end{array}}$$

In this equation, annual dividends are found by multiplying the stock's latest annual dividends per share by the bond's conversion ratio.

Example

In the previous example, the bond had a conversion premium of $200. Assume this bond (which carries a conversion ratio of 20) has an 8.5% coupon ($85 per year), and the underlying stock paid dividends this past year of 50 cents a share. Given this information, you can use Equation 2.8 to find the payback period.

$$\begin{aligned}\text{Payback period} &= \frac{\$200}{\$85 - (20 \times \$0.50)} \\ &= \frac{\$200}{\$85 - (\$10.00)} = 2.7 \text{ years}\end{aligned}$$

In essence, you would recover the premium in 2.7 years (a fairly short payback period).

As a rule, everything else being equal, the shorter the payback period, the better. Also, watch out for excessively high premiums (of 50% or more). Indeed, to avoid such premiums, which are difficult to recover, most experts recommend that investors look for convertibles that have payback periods of five to seven years, or less. Be careful when using this measure, however. Some convertibles will have very high payback periods simply because they carry very low coupons (of 1% to 2%, or less).

Investment Value   The price floor of a convertible is defined by its bond properties and is the focus of the investment value measure. It's the point within the valuation process where we focus on current and expected market interest rates. **Investment value** is the price at which the bond would trade if it were nonconvertible and if it were priced at or near the prevailing market yields of comparable nonconvertible bonds.

We will cover the mechanics of bond pricing in more detail later, but suffice it to say at this point that the investment value of a convertible is found by discounting the issue's coupon stream and its par value back to the present, using a discount rate equal to the prevailing yield on comparable nonconvertible issues. In other words, using the yields on comparable nonconvertible bonds as the discount rate, find the present value of the convertible's coupon stream, add that to the present value of its par value, and you have the issue's investment value. In practice, because the convertible's coupon and maturity are known, the only additional piece of information needed is the market yield of comparably rated issues.

For example, if comparable nonconvertible bonds were trading at 9% yields, we could use that 9% return as the discount rate in finding the present value (i.e., "investment value") of a convertible. Thus, if a particular 20-year, $1,000 par value convertible bond carried a 6% annual coupon rate, its investment value (using a 9% discount rate) can be found using a financial calculator as shown in the margin.

Input	Function
60	PMT
1000	FV
20	N
9	I
	CPT
	PV

Solution
−726.14

CALCULATOR USE   Based on the information given, $60 is entered as the interest payment amount, PMT; the $1,000 par value is entered as the future value, FV; the time till maturity, 20 years, is entered, N; and the yield of 9% is entered for the discount rate, I. Push the compute key, CPT, and then the present value key, PV, to find that the resulting value of the convertible would be about $726. This figure indicates how far the convertible will have to fall before it hits its price floor and begins trading as a straight-debt instrument.

Other things being equal, the greater the distance between the current market price of a convertible and its investment value, the farther the issue can fall in price and, as a result, the greater the downside risk exposure.

CONCEPTS IN REVIEW

Answers available at
http://www.pearsonhighered.com/ smart

2.15   What is a convertible debenture? How does a convertible bond differ from a convertible preferred?

2.16   Identify the equity kicker of a convertible security and explain how it affects the value and price behavior of convertibles.

2.17   Explain why it is necessary to examine both the bond and stock properties of a convertible debenture when determining its investment appeal.

2.18   What is the difference between conversion parity and conversion value? How would you describe the payback period on a convertible? What is the investment value of a convertible, and what does it reveal?

MyFinanceLab	Here is what you should know after reading this chapter. MyFinanceLab will help you identify what you know and where to go when you need to practice.

What You Should Know	Key Terms	Where to Practice
LG1 **Explain the basic investment attributes of bonds and their use as investment vehicles.** Bonds are publicly traded debt securities that provide investors with 2 basic sources of return: (1) current income and (2) capital gains. Current income is derived from the coupon (interest) payments received over the life of the issue. Capital gains can be earned whenever market interest rates fall. Bonds also can be used to shelter income from taxes and for the preservation and long-term accumulation of capital. The diversification properties of bonds are such that they can greatly enhance portfolio stability.	bonds, *p. 41*	MyFinanceLab Study Plan 2.1
LG2 **Describe the essential features of a bond, note the role that bond ratings play in the market, and distinguish among different types of call, refunding, and sinking-fund provisions.** All bonds carry some type of coupon, which specifies the annual rate of interest the issuer will pay. Bonds also have predetermined maturity dates: Term bonds carry a single maturity date, and serial bonds have a series of maturity dates. Municipal and corporate issues are rated for bond quality by independent rating agencies. These ratings indicate a bond's risk of default: The lower the rating, the higher the risk and the higher the expected return.	bond ratings, *p. 53*	MyFinanceLab Study Plan 2.2
	bond rating agencies, *p. 53*	
	call feature, *p. 51*	Video Learning Aid for Problem P2.8
	call premium, *p. 51*	
	call price, *p. 51*	
	collateral trust bonds, *p. 52*	
	coupon, *p. 48*	
	coupon rate, *p. 48*	
	current yield, *p. 48*	
	debenture, *p. 53*	
	discount bond, *p. 49*	
	equipment trust certificates, *p. 52*	
Every bond is issued with some type of call feature, be it freely callable, noncallable, or deferred callable. Call features spell out whether an issue can be prematurely retired and, if so, when. Some bonds (temporarily) prohibit the issuer from paying off one bond with the proceeds from another by including a refunding provision. Others are issued with sinking-fund provisions, which specify how a bond is to be paid off over time.	face value, *p. 58*	
	first and refunding bonds, *p. 52*	
	high-yield bonds, *p. 54*	
	income bonds, *p. 53*	
	investment-grade bonds, *p. 54*	
	junior bonds, *p. 53*	
	junk bonds, *p. 54*	
	maturity date, *p. 48*	
	mortgage bonds, *p. 52*	
	note, *p. 49*	
	par value, *p. 48*	
	premium bond, *p. 49*	
	principal, *p. 48*	
	refunding provisions, *p. 52*	
	senior bonds, *p. 52*	
	serial bond, *p. 49*	
	sinking fund, *p. 52*	
	split ratings, *p. 54*	
	subordinated debentures, *p. 53*	
	term bond, *p. 49*	

What You Should Know	Key Terms	Where to Practice
LG3 **Explain how bond prices are quoted in the market and why some bonds are more volatile than others.** In the bond market prices are quoted as a percentage of par and are driven by the issue's coupon and maturity, along with prevailing market yields. When interest rates go down, bond prices go up, and vice versa. The extent to which bond prices move up or down depends on the coupon and maturity of an issue. Bonds with lower coupons and/or longer maturities generate larger price swings.		MyFinanceLab Study Plan 2.3
LG4 **Identify the different types of bonds and the kinds of investment objectives these securities can fulfill.** The bond market is divided into four major segments: Treasuries, agencies, municipals, and corporates. Treasury bonds are issued by the U.S. Treasury and are virtually default-free. Agency bonds are issued by various subdivisions of the U.S. government and make up an increasingly important segment of the bond market. Municipal bonds are issued by state and local governments in the form of either general obligation or revenue bonds. Corporate bonds make up the major nongovernment sector of the market and are backed by the assets and profitability of the issuing companies. Generally speaking, Treasuries are attractive because of their high quality; agencies and corporates, because of the added returns they provide; and munis, because of the tax shelter they offer.	agency bonds, *p. 58* asset-backed securities (ABS), *p. 67* collateralized mortgage obligation (CMO), *p. 66* Eurodollar bonds, *p. 68* general obligation bonds, *p. 59* mortgage-backed bond, *p. 65* municipal bond guarantees, *p. 60* municipal bonds, *p. 59* PIK bond, *p. 67* revenue bonds, *p. 59* securitization, *p. 67* taxable equivalent yield, *p. 62* Treasury bonds, *p. 57* Treasury Inflation-Protected Securities (TIPS), *p. 58* Treasury notes, *p. 57* Treasury strips, *p. 65* Yankee bonds, *p. 68* zero-coupon bonds, *p. 64*	MyFinanceLab Study Plan 2.4
LG5 **Discuss the global nature of the bond market and the difference between dollar-denominated and non-dollar-denominated foreign bonds.** Foreign bonds, particularly foreign-pay securities, offer highly competitive yields and returns. Foreign-pay bonds cover all issues that are denominated in some currency other than U.S. dollars. These bonds have an added source of return: currency exchange rates. In addition, there are dollar-denominated foreign bonds—Yankee bonds and Eurodollar bonds—which have no currency exchange risk because they are issued in U.S. dollars.		MyFinanceLab Study Plan 2.5

What You Should Know	Key Terms	Where to Practice
LG6 Describe the basic features and characteristics of convertible securities, and measure the value of a convertible. Convertible securities are initially issued as bonds (or preferreds) but can subsequently be converted into shares of common stock. These securities offer investors a stream of fixed income (annual coupon payments) plus an equity kicker (a conversion feature). The value of a convertible is driven by the price behavior of the underlying common stock (when the stock price is at or above its conversion price) or by market interest rates and the behavior of bonds (when the stock's price is well below its conversion price). The key values of a convertible are (1) its conversion (stock) value and (2) its investment (bond) value.	conversion equivalent (conversion parity), p. 74 conversion period, p. 71 conversion price, p. 71 conversion privilege, p. 71 conversion ratio, p. 71 conversion value, p. 73 convertible bonds, p. 70 deferred equity, p. 70 equity kicker, p. 70 forced conversion, p. 71 investment value, p. 76 LYON (liquid yield option note), p. 72 payback period, p. 75	MyFinanceLab Study Plan 2.6 Video Learning Aid for Problem P2.20

Log into MyFinanceLab, take a chapter test, and get a personalized Study Plan that tells you which concepts you understand and which ones you need to review. From there, MyFinanceLab will give you further practice, tutorials, animations, videos, and guided solutions.
Log into http://www.myfinancelab.com

Discussion Questions

LG1 **Q2.1** Using the bond returns in Table 2.1 as a basis of discussion:
a. Compare the total returns on Treasury bonds during the 1970s to those produced in the 1980s. How do you explain the differences?
b. How did the bond market do in the 1990s? How does the performance in this decade compare to that in the 1980s? Explain.
c. What do you think would be a reasonable rate of return from bonds in the future? Explain.
d. Assume that you're out of school and hold a promising, well-paying job. How much of your portfolio (in percentage terms) would you want to hold in bonds? Explain. What role do you see bonds playing in your portfolio, particularly as you go farther and farther into the future?

LG4 **LG5** **Q2.2** Identify and briefly describe each of the following types of bonds.
a. Agency bonds
b. Municipal bonds
c. Zero-coupon bonds
d. Junk bonds
e. Foreign bonds
f. Collateralized mortgage obligations (CMOs)

What type of investor do you think would be most attracted to each?

LG1 **LG4** **Q2.3** "Treasury securities are guaranteed by the U.S. government. Therefore, there is no risk in the ownership of such bonds." Briefly discuss the wisdom (or folly) of this statement.

LG4 **LG5** **Q2.4** Select the security in the left-hand column that best fits the investor's desire described in the right-hand column.

a. 5-year Treasury note	1. Lock in a high-coupon yield
b. A bond with a low coupon and a long maturity	2. Accumulate capital over a long period of time
c. Yankee bond	3. Generate a monthly income
d. Insured revenue bond	4. Avoid a lot of price volatility
e. Long-term Treasury strips	5. Generate tax-free income
f. Noncallable bond	6. Invest in a foreign bond
g. CMO	7. Go for the highest yield available
h. Junk bond	8. Invest in a pool of credit card receivables
i. ABS receivables	9. Go for maximum price appreciation

LG6 **Q2.5** Why do companies like to issue convertible securities? What's in it for them?

LG6 **Q2.6** Describe LYONs, and note how they differ from conventional convertible securities. Are there any similarities between LYONs and conventional convertibles? Explain.

LG6 **Q2.7** Using the resources at your campus or public library or on the Internet, find the information requested below.
a. Select any two convertible debentures (notes or bonds) and determine the conversion ratio, conversion parity, conversion value, conversion premium, and payback period for each.
b. Select any two convertible preferreds and determine the conversion ratio, conversion parity, conversion value, conversion premium, and payback period for each.
c. In what way(s) are the two convertible bonds and the two convertible preferreds you selected similar? Are there any differences? Explain.

Problems

All problems are available on http://www.myfinancelab.com

LG2 **P2.1** A 9%, 20-year bond is callable in 12 years at a call price of $1,090. The bond is currently priced in the market at $923.68. What is the issue's current yield?

LG2 **P2.2** A certain bond has a current yield of 6.5% and a market price of $846.15. What is the bond's coupon rate?

LG2 **P2.3** Buck buys a 7.5% corporate bond with a current yield of 4.8%. How much did he pay for the bond?

LG4 **P2.4** An investor is in the 28% tax bracket and lives in a state with no income tax. He is trying to decide which of two bonds to purchase. One is a 7.5% corporate bond that is selling at par. The other is a municipal bond with a 5.25% coupon that is also selling at par. If all other features of these bonds are comparable, which should the investor select? Why? Would your answer change if this were an in-state municipal bond and the investor lived in a place with high state income taxes? Explain.

LG4 **P2.5** An investor lives in a state with a 3% income tax rate. Her federal income tax bracket is 35%. She wants to invest in one of two bonds that are similar in terms of risk (and both bonds currently sell at par value). The first bond is fully taxable and offers a yield of 10%. The second bond is exempt from both state and federal taxes and offers a yield of 7%. In which bond should she invest?

LG4 **P2.6** Maria Lopez is a wealthy investor who's looking for a tax shelter. Maria is in the maximum (35%) federal tax bracket and lives in a state with a very high state income tax. (She pays the maximum of 11½% in state income tax.) Maria is currently looking at two municipal bonds, both of which are selling at par. One is a AA-rated, in-state bond that carries a coupon of 6⅜%. The other is a AA-rated, out-of-state bond that carries a 7⅛% coupon. Her broker has informed her that comparable fully taxable corporate bonds are currently available with yields of 9¾%. Alternatively, long Treasuries are now available at yields of 9%. She has $100,000 to invest, and because all the bonds are high-quality issues, she wants to select the one that will give her maximum after-tax returns.
a. Which one of the four bonds should she buy?
b. Rank the four bonds (from best to worst) in terms of their taxable equivalent yields.

LG4 **P2.7** Sara Nixon is looking for a fixed-income investment. She is considering two bond issues:
a. A Treasury with a yield of 5%
b. An in-state municipal bond with a yield of 4%
Sara is in the 33% federal tax bracket and the 8% state tax bracket. Which bond would provide Sara with a higher tax-adjusted yield?

LG2 **P2.8** Which of the following bonds offers the highest current yield?
a. A 9½%, 20-year bond quoted at 97¾
b. A 16%, 15-year bond quoted at 164⅝
c. A 5¼%, 18-year bond quoted at 54

LG2 **P2.9** Assume that you pay $850 for a long-term bond that carries a 7½% coupon. Over the course of the next 12 months, interest rates drop sharply. As a result, you sell the bond at a price of $962.50.
a. Find the current yield that existed on this bond at the beginning of the year. What was it by the end of the 1-year holding period?
b. Determine the holding period return on this investment. (See Chapter 11 for the HPR formula.)

LG3 **P2.10** Caleb buys an 8.75% corporate bond with a current yield of 5.6%. When he sells the bond 1 year later, the current yield on the bond is 6.6%. How much did Caleb make on this investment?

LG1 **P2.11** In early January 2010, you purchased $30,000 worth of some high-grade corporate bonds. The bonds carried a coupon of 8⅛% and mature in 2024. You paid a price of 94.125 when you bought the bonds. Over the five years from 2010 through 2014, the bonds were priced in the market as follows:

| | Quoted Prices (% of $1,000 par value) | |
Year	Beginning of the Year	End of the Year
2010	94.125	100.625
2011	100.625	102.000
2012	102.000	104.625
2013	104.625	110.125
2014	110.125	121.250

Coupon payments were made on schedule throughout the five-year period.
a. Find the annual holding period returns for 2010 through 2014. (See Chapter 11 for the HPR formula.)
b. Use the return information in Table 2.1 to evaluate the investment performance of this bond. How do you think it stacks up against the market? Explain.

LG4 P2.12 Rhett purchased a 13%, zero-coupon bond with a 15-year maturity and a $20,000 par value 15 years ago. The bond matures tomorrow. How much will Rhett receive in total from this investment, assuming all payments were made on these bonds as expected?

LG4 P2.13 Nate purchased an interest-bearing security last year, planning to hold it until maturity. He received interest payments and, to his surprise, a sizable amount of the principal was paid back in the first year. This happened again in year two. What type of security did Nate purchase?

LG5 P2.14 Letticia Garcia, an aggressive bond investor, is currently thinking about investing in a foreign (non-dollar-denominated) government bond. In particular, she's looking at a Swiss government bond that matures in 15 years and carries a 9½% coupon. The bond has a par value of 10,000 Swiss francs (CHF) and is currently trading at 110 (i.e., at 110% of par).

Letticia plans to hold the bond for one year, at which time she thinks it will be trading at 117½—she's anticipating a sharp decline in Swiss interest rates, which explains why she expects bond prices to move up. The current exchange rate is 1.58 CHF/U.S.$, but she expects that to fall to 1.25 CHF/U.S.$. Use the foreign investment total return formula (Equation 2.3) to find the following information.

a. Ignoring the currency effect, find the bond's total return (in its local currency).
b. Now find the total return on this bond in U.S. dollars. Did currency exchange rates affect the return in any way? Do you think this bond would make a good investment? Explain.

LG5 P2.15 Red Electrica España SA (E.REE) is refinancing its bank loans by issuing Eurobonds to investors. You are considering buying $10,000 of these bonds, which will yield 6%. You are also looking at a U.S. bond with similar risk that will yield 5%. You expect that interest rates will not change over the course of the next year, after which time you will sell the bonds you purchase.

a. How much will you make on each bond if you buy it, hold it for one year, and then sell it for $10,000 (or the Eurodollar equivalent)?
b. Assume the dollar/euro exchange rate goes from 1.11 to 0.98. How much will this currency change affect the proceeds from the Eurobond? (Assume you receive annual interest at the same time you sell the Eurobond.)

LG6 P2.16 A certain convertible bond has a conversion ratio of 21 and a conversion premium of 20%. The current market price of the underlying common stock is $40. What is the bond's conversion equivalent?

LG6 P2.17 You are considering investing $800 in Higgs B. Technology Inc. You can buy common stock at $25 per share; this stock pays no dividends. You can also buy a convertible bond ($1,000 par value) that is currently trading at $790 and has a conversion ratio of 30. It pays $40 per year in interest. If you expect the price of the stock to rise to $33 per share in one year, which instrument should you purchase?

LG6 P2.18 A certain 6% annual coupon rate convertible bond (maturing in 20 years) is convertible at the holder's option into 20 shares of common stock. The bond is currently trading at $800. The stock (which pays 75¢ a share in annual dividends) is currently priced in the market at $35 a share.

a. What is the bond's conversion price?
b. What is its conversion ratio?
c. What is the conversion value of this issue? What is its conversion parity?
d. What is the conversion premium, in dollars and as a percentage?
e. What is the bond's payback period?
f. If comparably rated nonconvertible bonds sell to yield 8%, what is the investment value of the convertible?

LG6 **P2.19** An 8% convertible bond carries a par value of $1,000 and a conversion ratio of 20. Assume that an investor has $5,000 to invest and that the convertible sells at a price of $1,000 (which includes a 25% conversion premium). How much total income (coupon plus capital gains) will this investment offer if, over the course of the next 12 months, the price of the stock moves to $75 per share and the convertible trades at a price that includes a conversion premium of 10%? What is the holding period return on this investment? Finally, given the information in the problem, determine what the underlying common stock is currently selling for.

LG6 **P2.20** Assume you just paid $1,200 for a convertible bond that carries a 7½% coupon and has 15 years to maturity. The bond can be converted into 24 shares of stock, which are now trading at $50 a share. Find the bond investment value of this issue, given that comparable nonconvertible bonds are currently selling to yield 9%.

LG1 **P2.21** Find the conversion value of a convertible preferred stock that carries a conversion ratio of 1.8, given that the market price of the underlying common stock is $40 a share. Would there be any conversion premium if the convertible preferred were selling at $90 a share? If so, how much (in dollar and percentage terms)? Also, explain the concept of conversion parity, and then find the conversion parity of this issue, given that the preferred trades at $90 per share.

Visit **http://www.myfinancelab.com** for web exercises, spreadsheets, and other online resources.

Case Problem 2.1 Max and Veronica Develop a Bond Investment Program

LG1 **LG4** Max and Veronica Shuman, along with their teenage sons, Terry and Thomas, live in Portland, Oregon. Max is a sales rep for a major medical firm, and Veronica is a personnel officer at a local bank. Together they earn an annual income of around $100,000. Max has just learned that his recently departed rich uncle has named him in his will to the tune of some $250,000 after taxes. Needless to say, the family is elated. Max intends to spend $50,000 of his inheritance on a number of long-overdue family items (like some badly needed remodeling of their kitchen and family room, the down payment on a new Porsche Boxster, and braces to correct Tom's overbite). Max wants to invest the remaining $200,000 in various types of fixed-income securities.

Max and Veronica have no unusual income requirements or health problems. Their only investment objectives are that they want to achieve some capital appreciation, and they want to keep their funds fully invested for at least 20 years. They would rather not have to rely on their investments as a source of current income but want to maintain some liquidity in their portfolio just in case.

Questions

a. Describe the type of bond investment program you think the Shuman family should follow. In answering this question, give appropriate consideration to both return and risk factors.

b. List several types of bonds that you would recommend for their portfolio and briefly indicate why you would recommend each.

c. Using a recent issue of the *Wall Street Journal, Barron's*, or an online source, construct a $200,000 bond portfolio for the Shuman family. Use real securities and select any bonds (or notes) you like, given the following ground rules:

1. The portfolio must include at least one Treasury, one agency, and one corporate bond; also, in total, the portfolio must hold at least five but no more than eight bonds or notes.
2. No more than 5% of the portfolio can be in short-term U.S. Treasury bills (but note that if you hold a T-bill, that limits your selections to just seven other notes/bonds).
3. Ignore all transaction costs (i.e., invest the full $200,000) and assume all securities have par values of $1,000 (although they can be trading in the market at something other than par).
4. Use the latest available quotes to determine how many bonds/notes/bills you can buy.

d. Prepare a schedule listing all the securities in your recommended portfolio. Use a form like the one shown below and include the information it calls for on each security in the portfolio.

e. In one brief paragraph, note the key investment attributes of your recommended portfolio and the investment objectives you hope to achieve with it.

Security Issuer-Coupon-Maturity	Latest Quoted Price	Number of Bonds Purchased	Amount Invested	Annual Coupon Income	Current Yield
Example: U.S. Treas - 8½%-'18	146⁸/₃₂	15	$21,937.50	$1,275	5.81%
1.					
2.					
3.					
4.					
5.					
6.					
7.					
8.					
Totals	—		$200,000.00	$	%

Case Problem 2.2 The Case of the Missing Bond Ratings

LG2

It's probably safe to say that there's nothing more important in determining a bond's rating than the underlying financial condition and operating results of the company issuing the bond. Just as financial ratios can be used in the analysis of common stocks, they can also be used in the analysis of bonds—a process we refer to as credit analysis. In credit analysis, attention is directed toward the basic liquidity and profitability of the firm, the extent to which the firm employs debt, and the ability of the firm to service its debt.

A TABLE OF FINANCIAL RATIOS
(All ratios are real and pertain to real companies.)

Financial Ratio	Company 1	Company 2	Company 3	Company 4	Company 5	Company 6
1. Current ratio	1.13	1.39	1.78	1.32	1.03	1.41
2. Quick ratio	0.48	0.84	0.93	0.33	0.50	0.75
3. Net profit margin	4.6%	12.9%	14.5%	2.8%	5.9%	10.0%
4. Return on total capital	15.0%	25.9%	29.4%	11.5%	16.8%	28.4%
5. Long-term debt to total capital	63.3%	52.7%	23.9%	97.0%	88.6%	42.1%

(Continued)

A TABLE OF FINANCIAL RATIOS (*Continued*)
(All ratios are real and pertain to real companies.)

Financial Ratio	Company 1	Company 2	Company 3	Company 4	Company 5	Company 6
6. Owners' equity ratio	18.6%	18.9%	44.1%	1.5%	5.1%	21.2%
7. Pretax interest coverage	2.3	4.5	8.9	1.7	2.4	6.4
8. Cash flow to total debt	34.7%	48.8%	71.2%	20.4%	30.2%	42.7%

Notes:
1. Current ratio = current assets / current liabilities
2. Quick ratio = (current assets − inventory) / current liabilities
3. Net profit margin = net profit / sales
4. Return on total capital = pretax income / (equity + long-term debt)
5. Long-term debt to total capital = long-term debt / (long-term debt + equity)
6. Owner's equity ratio = stockholders' equity / total assets
7. Pretax interest coverage = earnings before interest and taxes / interest expense
8. Cash flow to total debt = (net profit + depreciation) / total liabilities

The financial ratios shown in the preceding table are often helpful in carrying out such analysis. The first two ratios measure the liquidity of the firm; the next two, its profitability; the following two, the debt load; and the final two, the ability of the firm to service its debt load. (For ratio 5, the lower the ratio, the better. For all the others, the higher the ratio, the better.) The table lists each of these ratios for six companies.

Questions

a. Three of these companies have bonds that carry investment-grade ratings. The other three companies carry junk-bond ratings. Judging by the information in the table, which three companies have the investment-grade bonds and which three have the junk bonds? Briefly explain your selections.

b. One of these six companies is an AAA-rated firm and one is B-rated. Identify those companies. Briefly explain your selections.

c. Of the remaining four companies, one carries an AA rating, one carries an A rating, and two have BB ratings. Which companies are they?

Excel@Investing

Excel@Investing

The cash flow component of bond investments is made up of the annual interest payments and the future redemption value or its par value. Just like other time-value-of-money considerations, the bond cash flows are discounted back in order to determine their present value.

In comparing bonds to stocks, many investors look at the respective returns. The total returns in the bond market are made up of both current income and capital gains. Bond investment analysis should include the determination of the current yield as well as a specific holding period return.

On January 13, 2016, you gather the following information on three corporate bonds issued by the General Pineapple Corporation (GPC). Remember that corporate bonds are quoted as a percentage of their par value. Assume the par value of each bond to be $1,000. These debentures are quoted in eighths of a point. Create a spreadsheet that will model and answer the following bond investment problems.

Bonds	Current Yield	Volume	Close
GPC 5.3 13	?	25	$105^7/_8$
GPC 6.65s 20	?	45	103
GPC 7.4 22	?	37	$104^6/_8$

Questions

a. Calculate the current yields for these 3 GPC corporate debentures.

b. Calculate the holding period returns under the following scenarios.
    1. Purchased the 5.3 bonds for $990 on January 13, 2015
    2. Purchased the 6.65s for $988 on January 13, 2015
    3. Purchased the 7.4 bonds for $985 on January 13, 2013

c. As of January 13, 2016, GPC common stock had a close price of $26.20. The price of GPC stock in January 2013 was $25.25. The stock paid a 2013 dividend of $0.46, a 2014 dividend of $0.46, and a 2015 dividend of $0.46.
    1. Calculate the current (January 13, 2016) dividend yield for this security.
    2. Assuming you purchased the stock in January 2013, what is the holding period return as of January 2015?

Chapter-Opening Problem

The chart shows the number of global corporate bond issues for which Standard & Poor's issued ratings upgrades or downgrades every year from 1981 to 2014.

a. What is the trend in the number of ratings changes (both upgrades and downgrades) over time? Why?

b. Which type of ratings change, upgrade or downgrade, is most common in most years? Why do you think that is so?

c. In what years does the ratio of downgrades/upgrades appear to be particularly high? Why?

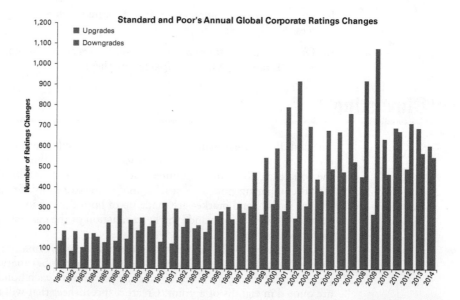

3

Securities Markets and Transactions

LEARNING GOALS

After studying this chapter, you should be able to:

LG1 Identify the basic types of securities markets and describe their characteristics.

LG2 Explain the initial public offering (IPO) process.

LG3 Describe broker markets and dealer markets, and discuss how they differ from alternative trading systems.

LG4 Review the key aspects of the globalization of securities markets and discuss the importance of international markets.

LG5 Discuss trading hours and the regulation of securities markets.

LG6 Explain long purchases, margin transactions, and short sales.

"**Wall Street**" is an early 17th-century testament to the global beginnings of U.S. financial markets. Wall Street was originally the northern boundary of a Dutch colonial settlement founded in 1625 called New Amsterdam, which after coming under English rule in 1664 became New York City. The U.S. financial markets that we know today began to take shape in the late 18th century as stockbrokers and speculators informally gathered on Wall Street under a buttonwood tree to trade. In 1792 twenty-four stockbrokers signed the Buttonwood Agreement, agreeing to trade securities on a commission basis, thus becoming the first organized American securities exchange. In 1817 the Buttonwood organization renamed itself the New York Stock & Exchange Board (and later became known simply as "The Big Board") and rented rooms on Wall Street to establish the first centralized exchange location of what in 1863 became known as the New York Stock Exchange (NYSE). Jumping ahead 144 years, NYSE Euronext was formed in 2007 through a merger of NYSE Group, Inc., and Euronext N.V., thus creating the first global stock exchange. Euronext brought a consortium of European exchanges to the merger, including the Paris, Brussels, Lisbon, and Amsterdam stock exchanges and the London-based electronic derivatives market Euronext.liffe, which is known now as NYSE Liffe. In 2008 NYSE Liffe U.S. was launched, offering a wide range of U.S. derivatives contracts. Further expansion occurred in 2008 when NYSE Euronext acquired the American Stock Exchange. As a result of the acquisition, more than 500 Amex-listed companies joined NYSE Euronext. Through a series of acquisitions and mergers, the Buttonwood Agreement had become the world's largest and most liquid exchange group.

In November 2013 the Atlanta-based Intercontinental Exchange, Inc., acquired NYSE Euronext, paying NYSE Euronext shareholders stock in cash worth about $11 billion. The combined entity controlled 11 exchanges that traded common stocks as well as more exotic securities such as options, interest rate and credit derivatives, foreign exchange, and futures contracts on commodities and financial contracts. The transaction reflected the growing importance of derivatives trading (an Intercontinental Exchange specialty) and the declining influence of the 220-year-old Big Board. For years NYSE Euronext's share of trading volume had been on the decline, squeezing its profit margins.

From trading under a buttonwood tree in a Dutch colonial settlement in 1792 to the combination of NYSE Euronext with Intercontinental Exchange, Wall Street remains a truly global marketplace.

(Sources: "Who We Are," http://www.nyx.com, accessed April 12, 2012; "Wall Street," http://en.wikipedia.org/wiki/Wall_street, accessed April 12, 2012; "NYSE Group and Euronext N.V. Agree to a Merger of Equals," NYSE press release, June 2, 2006, http://www.euronext.com/fic/000/001/891/18919.pdf, accessed April 12, 2012; and "Intercontinental Exchange Completes Acquisition of NYSE Euronext," NYSE press release, November 13, 2013, http://www1.nyse.com/press/1388665271901.html, accessed February 27, 2015)

Securities Markets

LG1 LG2 LG3   **Securities markets** are markets that allow buyers and sellers of securities to make financial transactions. Their goal is to permit such transactions to be made quickly and at a fair price. In this section we will look at the various types of securities markets and their general characteristics.

Types of Securities Markets

In general, securities markets are broadly classified as either **money markets** or **capital markets**. The money market is the market where *short-term* debt securities (with maturities less than one year) are bought and sold. Investors use the money market for short-term borrowing and lending. Investors turn to the capital market to buy and sell *long-term* securities (with maturities of more than one year), such as stocks and bonds. In this text we will devote most of our attention to the capital market. There investors can make transactions in a wide variety of financial securities, including stocks, bonds, mutual funds, exchange-traded funds, options, and futures. Capital markets are classified as either *primary* or *secondary*, depending on whether securities are being sold initially to investors by the issuer (primary market) or resold among investors (secondary market).

Before offering its securities for public sale, the issuer must register them with and obtain approval from the **Securities and Exchange Commission (SEC)**. This federal regulatory agency must confirm both the adequacy and the accuracy of the information provided to potential investors. In addition, the SEC regulates the securities markets.

The Primary Market   The market in which *new issues* of securities are sold to investors is the **primary market**. In the primary market, the issuer of the equity or debt securities receives the proceeds of sales. The most significant transaction in the primary market is the **initial public offering (IPO)**, which marks the first public sale of a company's stock and results in the company's taking on a public status. The primary markets also provide a forum for the sale of additional stock, called *seasoned equity issues*, by already public companies.

Table 3.1 shows that only 21 operating companies sold stock to the public for the first time in the primary market in the United States during 2008, the first full year of the Great Recession, a period considered by many economists to be the worst economic downturn since the Great Depression of the 1930s. That number is less than one-twentieth the number of IPOs in 1999, the end of the technology-stock-driven bull market. When recovery from the Great Recession began in 2009, the number of IPOs per year also began to rebound, producing nearly twice as many IPOs relative to the previous year. Over the next five years, as the economy continued to rebound, so did IPO volume, reaching 206 IPOs in 2014. Seasoned equity offerings (SEOs) follow a similar pattern. The low point for SEO volume also occurred in 2008, though SEO deals have picked up since then.

Hear about Shake Shack's IPO

To sell its securities in the primary market, a firm has three choices. It may make (1) a **public offering**, in which the firm offers its securities for sale to public investors; (2) a **rights offering**, in which the firm offers shares to existing stockholders on a pro rata basis (each outstanding share gets an equal proportion of new shares); or (3) a **private placement**, in which the firm sells securities directly without SEC registration to select groups of private investors such as insurance companies, investment management funds, and pension funds.

Going Public: The IPO Process Most companies that go public are small, fast-growing companies that require additional capital to continue expanding. For example, Shake Shack, a company that originated from a hot dog cart setup in 2001 to support the rejuvenation of New York City's Madison Square Park, raised about $98 million when it went public on January 30, 2015, at $21 per share. But not every IPO fits the typical start-up profile. Large companies may decide to spin off a unit into a separate public corporation. The media and entertainment company Time Warner did this when it spun off its magazine business, Time, Inc., in June 2014.

When a company decides to go public, it first must obtain the approval of its current shareholders, the investors who own its privately issued stock. Next, the company's auditors and lawyers must certify that all financial disclosure documents for the company are legitimate. The company then finds an investment bank willing to *underwrite* the offering. This bank is the lead underwriter and is responsible for promoting the company's stock and facilitating the sale of the company's IPO shares. The lead underwriter often brings in other investment banking firms to help underwrite and market the company's stock. We'll discuss the role of the investment banker in more detail in the next section.

The underwriter also assists the company in filing a registration statement with the SEC. One portion of this statement is the **prospectus**. It describes the key aspects of the securities to be issued, the issuer's management, and the issuer's financial position. Once a firm files a prospectus with the SEC, a *quiet period* begins, during which the firm faces a variety of restrictions on what it can communicate to investors. While waiting for the registration statement's SEC approval, prospective investors may receive a preliminary prospectus. This preliminary version is called a **red herring** because a notice printed in red on the front cover indicates the tentative nature of the offer. The purpose of the quiet period is to make sure that all potential investors have access to the same information about the company—that which is presented in the preliminary prospectus—but not to any unpublished data that might provide an unfair advantage. The quiet period ends when the SEC declares the firm's prospectus to be effective. The cover of the preliminary prospectus describing the 2015 stock issue of Shake Shack, Inc., appears in Figure 3.1. Notice that the preliminary prospectus has a blank where the offering price of the stock should be, just under the header that has the company name. Note also the warning, often referred to as the red herring, printed across the top of the front page.

During the registration period and before the IPO date, the investment bankers and company executives promote the company's stock offering through a *road show*, which consists of a series of presentations to potential investors—typically institutional investors—around the country and sometimes overseas. In addition to providing investors with information about the new issue, road shows help the investment bankers gauge the demand for the offering and set an expected price range. Once all of the issue terms have been set, including the price, the SEC must approve the offering before the IPO can take place.

Table 3.1 highlights several interesting features of the IPO market over the last 16 years. First, the table shows the number of IPOs each year. As mentioned earlier, the number of IPOs per year moves dramatically as economic conditions change and as the stock market moves up and down. Generally speaking, more companies go public when the economy is strong and stock prices are rising. Second, the table shows the average *first-day return* for IPOs each year. An IPO's first-day return is simply the percentage change from the price of the IPO in the prospectus to the closing price of the stock on its first day of trading. For example, when the details of Shake Shack's IPO were finalized, shares were offered to investors in the final prospectus at $21 per share.

FIGURE 3.1

Cover of a Preliminary Prospectus for a Stock Issue

Some of the key factors related to the 2015 common stock issue by Shake Shack Inc., are summarized on the cover of the prospectus. The disclaimer statement across the top of the page is normally printed in red, which explains its name, "red herring."

(Source: Shake Shack Inc., "Form S-1 Registration Statement," December 29, 2014, p. 2.)

The information in this preliminary prospectus is not complete and may be changed. We may not sell these securities until the registration statement filed with the Securities and Exchange Commission is effective. This preliminary prospectus is not an offer to sell these securities and it is not soliciting an offer to buy these securities in any state where the offer or sale is not permitted.

Subject to completion, dated December 29, 2014

PRELIMINARY PROSPECTUS

Shares

Class A Common Stock

This is an initial public offering of Shake Shack Inc. We anticipate that the initial public offering price will be between $ and $ per share of our Class A common stock.

Prior to this offering, there has been no public market for our Class A common stock. We have applied to have our Class A common stock listed on the New York Stock Exchange under the symbol "SHAK."

We will use the net proceeds that we receive from this offering to purchase from SSE Holdings, LLC, which we refer to as "SSE Holdings," newly-issued common membership interests of SSE Holdings, which we refer to as the "LLC Interests." There is no public market for the LLC Interests. The purchase price for the newly-issued LLC Interests will be equal to the public offering price of our Class A common stock, less the underwriting discount referred to below. We intend to cause SSE Holdings to use the net proceeds it receives from us in connection with this offering as described in "Use of Proceeds." In connection with the closing of this offering, certain of the holders of LLC Interests received in exchange for existing membership interests in SSE Holdings, whom we refer to as "Former SSE Equity Owners," will exchange their indirect ownership of LLC Interests for shares of Class A common stock and certain other holders of LLC Interests received in exchange for existing membership interests in SSE Holdings, whom we refer to as "Continuing SSE Equity Owners," will continue to own their LLC Interests. In addition, certain individuals who hold existing awards under our Unit Appreciation Rights Plan, whom we refer to as the "Former UAR Plan Participants," will receive shares of Class A common stock in settlement of their awards.

We will have two classes of common stock outstanding after this offering: Class A common stock and Class B common stock. Each share of Class A common stock and Class B common stock entitles its holder to one vote on all matters presented to our stockholders generally. All of our Class B common stock will be held by the Continuing SSE Equity Owners, on a one-to-one basis with the number of LLC Interests they own. Immediately following this offering, the holders of our Class A common stock issued in this offering collectively will hold   % of the economic interests in us and   % of the voting power in us, the Former SSE Equity Owners and the Former UAR Plan Participants, through their ownership of Class A common stock, collectively will hold   % of the economic interests in us and   % of the voting power in us, and the Continuing SSE Equity Owners, through their ownership of all of the outstanding Class B common stock, collectively will hold no economic interest in us and the remaining   % of the voting power in us. We will be a holding company, and upon consummation of this offering and the application of proceeds therefrom, our principal asset will be the LLC Interests we purchase from SSE Holdings and acquire from the Former SSE Equity Owners, representing an aggregate   % economic interest in SSE Holdings. The remaining   % economic interest in SSE Holdings will be owned by the Continuing SSE Equity Owners through their ownership of LLC Interests.

Although we will have a minority economic interest in SSE Holdings, because we will be the sole managing member of SSE Holdings, we will operate and control all of the business and affairs of SSE Holdings and, through SSE Holdings and its subsidiaries, conduct our business.

Following this offering, we will be a "controlled company" within the meaning of the corporate governance rules of the New York Stock Exchange. See "The Transactions" and "Management—Corporate Governance."

We are an "emerging growth company," as defined in Section 2(a) of the Securities Act of 1933, as amended, and will be subject to reduced public reporting requirements. This prospectus complies with the requirements that apply to an issuer that is an emerging growth company.

Investing in our Class A common stock involves risks. See "Risk Factors" beginning on page 22.

	Per Share	Total
Initial public offering price	$	$
Underwriting discounts and commissions(1)	$	$
Proceeds to us, before expenses	$	$

(1) See "Underwriting (Conflicts of Interest)" for additional information regarding underwriting compensation.

We have granted the underwriters an option for a period of 30 days to purchase up to an additional   shares of Class A common stock solely to cover over-allotments.

Neither the Securities and Exchange Commission nor any other regulatory body has approved or disapproved of these securities or passed upon the accuracy or adequacy of this prospectus. Any representation to the contrary is a criminal offense.

Delivery of the shares will be made on or about

J.P. Morgan   **Morgan Stanley**

Goldman,
Barclays   **Sachs & Co.**   **Jefferies**
William Blair   **Stifel**

The date of this prospectus is   , 2015.

At the end of the stock's first trading day, its price had risen to $45.90, a one-day return of 118%! You can see in Table 3.1 that the average first-day return for all IPOs is positive in every year from 1999 to 2014, ranging from 6.4% in 2008 to 71.1% in 1999. Because IPO shares typically go up in value as soon as they start trading, we say that IPOs are *underpriced* on average. IPO shares are underpriced if they are sold to investors at a price that is lower than what the market will bear. In the Shake Shack offering, investors were apparently willing to pay $45.90 per share (based on the value of the shares once trading began), but shares were initially offered at just $21. We could say then that Shake Shack shares (say that three times fast) were underpriced by $24.90. Table 3.1 indicates that the average first-day return is closely connected to the number of IPOs. Average first-day returns are higher in years when many firms choose to go public (as in 1999), and first-day returns are lower in years when few firms conduct IPOs (as in 2008).

Shake Shack sold 5.75 million shares in its IPO for $21 per share, so the *gross proceeds* from the offer were $120.7 million, which equals 5.75 million shares times $21 per share. This is the third feature of the IPO market highlighted in Table 3.1. Total gross proceeds from IPOs ranged from $9.5 billion in 2003 to $65 billion in 1999. The last column in Table 3.1 lists total "money left on the table." *Money left on the table* represents a cost that companies bear when they go public if their shares are underpriced (as most IPOs are). For example, Shake Shack underpriced its offering by $143.2 million, which comes from multiplying 5.75 million shares sold times $24.90 underpricing per share. It shouldn't be a surprise that in the IPO market, aggregate money left on the table peaked at the same time that underpricing did. In 1999 the 477 companies that went public left $37.1 billion on the table by underpricing their shares. Given that the gross proceeds of IPOs that year (i.e., the total money paid by investors in the primary market to acquire IPO shares) were $65 billion, it seems that companies left more than half as much money on the table as they raised by going public in the first place. Put differently, if shares had not been underpriced at all in 1999, companies would have raised $102.1 billion rather than $65.0 billion, a difference of 57%.

Investing in IPOs is risky business, particularly for individual investors who can't easily acquire shares at the offering price. Most of those shares go to institutional investors and brokerage firms' best clients. Although news stories may chronicle huge first-day gains, IPO stocks are not necessarily good long-term investments.

The Investment Banker's Role Most public offerings are made with the assistance of an investment banker. The **investment banker** is a financial intermediary that specializes in assisting companies issuing new securities and advising firms with regard to major financial transactions. In the context of IPOs, the main activity of the investment banker is **underwriting**. This process involves purchasing the securities from the issuing firm at an agreed-on price and bearing the risk of reselling them to the public. The investment banker also provides the issuer with advice about pricing and other important aspects of the issue.

In the case of large security issues, the lead or originating investment banker brings in other bankers as partners to form an **underwriting syndicate**. The syndicate shares the financial risk associated with buying the entire issue from the issuer and reselling the new securities to the public. The lead investment banker and the syndicate members put together a **selling group**, normally made up of themselves and a large number of brokerage firms. Each member of the selling group is responsible for selling a certain portion of the issue and is paid a commission on the securities it sells. The selling process for a large security issue is depicted in Figure 3.2.

TABLE 3.1   U.S. ANNUAL IPO DATA, 1999–2014

Year	Number of IPOs	Average First-Day Return	Aggregate Gross Proceeds (billions)	Aggregate Money Left on the Table (billions)
1999	477	71.1%	$65.0	$37.1
2000	381	56.3%	$64.9	$29.8
2001	79	14.2%	$34.2	$ 3.0
2002	66	9.1%	$22.0	$ 1.1
2003	63	11.7%	$ 9.5	$ 1.0
2004	173	12.3%	$31.2	$ 3.9
2005	159	10.3%	$28.2	$ 2.6
2006	157	12.1%	$30.5	$ 4.0
2007	159	14.0%	$35.7	$ 5.0
2008	21	6.4%	$22.8	$ 5.7
2009	41	9.8%	$13.2	$ 1.5
2010	91	9.4%	$29.8	$ 1.8
2011	81	13.3%	$ 27.0	$ 3.2
2012	93	17.9%	$31.1	$ 2.8
2013	157	21.1%	$38.8	$ 8.6
2014	206	15.5%	$42.2	$ 5.4

(Source: "Initial Public Offerings: Updated Statistics," http://bear.warrington.ufl.edu/ritter/ IPOs2014Statistics.pdf, Table 1, accessed February 26, 2015.)

The relationships among the participants in this process can also be seen on the cover of the December 29, 2014, preliminary prospectus for the common stock offering for Shake Shack, Inc., in Figure 3.1. The layout of the prospectus cover indicates the roles of the various participating firms. Placement and larger typefaces differentiate the originating underwriters (J.P. Morgan and Morgan Stanley) from the underwriting syndicate members (Goldman, Sachs & Co., Barclays, Jefferies, William Blair, and Stifel), whose names appear in a smaller font below. J.P. Morgan and Morgan Stanley are acting as joint-lead investment banks for Shake Shack's IPO.

Compensation for underwriting and selling services typically comes in the form of a discount on the sale price of the securities. For example, in the Shake Shack IPO, the investment bank, acting as a lead underwriter (say J.P. Morgan), might pay Shake Shack $19.50 for stock that investors will ultimately purchase for $21. Having guaranteed the issuer $19.50 per share, the lead underwriter may then sell the shares to the underwriting syndicate members for $19.75 per share. The additional 25 cents per share represents the lead underwriter's management fee. Next the underwriting syndicate members sell the shares to members of the selling group for 85 cents more, or $20.60 per share. That 85 cent difference represents the underwriters' discount, which is their profit per share. Finally, members of the selling group earn a selling concession of 40 cents per share when they sell shares to investors at $21 per share. The $1.50 difference between the price per share paid to Shake Shack ($19.50) and that paid by the investor ($21) is the *gross spread*, which comprises the lead underwriter's management fee ($0.25), the syndicate underwriters' discounts ($0.85), and the selling group's selling concession ($0.40). Although the issuer places (or sells) some primary security offerings directly, the majority of new issues are sold through public offering via the process just described.

FIGURE 3.2   **The Selling Process for a Large Security Issue**

The lead investment banker hired by the issuing firm may form an underwriting syndicate. The underwriting syndicate buys the entire security issue from the issuing corporation at an agreed-on discount to the public offering price. The investment banks in the underwriting syndicate then bear the risk of reselling the issue to the public at a public offering price. The investment banks' profit is the difference between the price they guaranteed the issuer and the public offering price. Both the lead investment bank and the other syndicate members put together a selling group to sell the issue on a commission basis to investors.

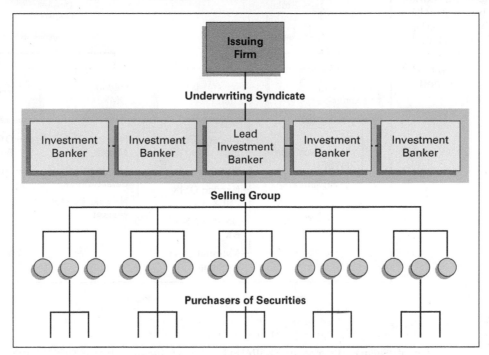

The Secondary Market   The **secondary market,** or the *aftermarket,* is the market in which securities are traded *after they have been issued.* Unlike the primary market, secondary-market transactions do not involve the corporation that issued the securities. Instead, the secondary market permits an investor to sell his or her holdings to another investor. The secondary market provides an environment for continuous pricing of securities that helps to ensure that security prices reflect the securities' true values on the basis of the best available information at any time. The ability to make securities transactions quickly and at a fair price in the secondary market provides securities traders with *liquidity.*

One major segment of the secondary market consists of various *national securities exchanges,* which are markets, registered with the SEC, in which the buyers and sellers of *listed securities* come together to execute trades. There are 18 national securities exchanges registered with the SEC under Section 6(a) of the Exchange Act. The **over-the-counter (OTC) market,** which involves trading in smaller, *unlisted securities,* represents the other major segment of the secondary market. The Financial Industry Regulatory Authority (FINRA) regulates securities transactions in the OTC market. FINRA is the largest independent regulator of securities firms doing business in the United States. FINRA's mission is to protect investors by making sure that the thousands of brokerage firms, tens of thousands of branch offices, and hundreds of thousands of registered securities representatives it oversees operate fairly and honestly.

FIGURE 3.3

Broker and Dealer Markets

On a typical trading day, the secondary market is a beehive of activity, where literally billions of shares change hands. The market consists of two distinct parts—the broker market and the dealer market. As shown, each of these markets is made up of various exchanges and trading venues.

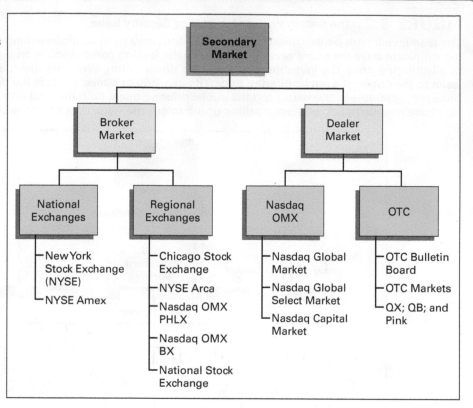

Broker Markets and Dealer Markets

Historically, the secondary market has been divided into two segments on the basis of how securities are traded: broker markets and dealer markets. Figure 3.3 depicts the makeup of the secondary market in terms of broker or dealer markets. As you can see, the **broker market** consists of national and regional securities exchanges, whereas the **dealer market** is made up of the Nasdaq OMX and OTC trading venues.

Before we look at these markets in more detail, it's important to understand that probably the biggest difference in the two markets is a technical point dealing with the way trades are executed. That is, when a trade occurs in a broker market, the two sides to the transaction, the buyer and the seller, are brought together—the seller sells his or her securities directly to the buyer. With the help of a *broker*, the securities effectively change hands on the floor of the exchange.

In contrast, when trades are made in a dealer market, buyers' orders and sellers' orders are never brought together directly. Instead, their buy/sell orders are executed by **market makers**, who are *securities dealers* that "make markets" by offering to buy or sell a certain amount of securities at stated prices. Essentially, two separate trades are made: The seller sells his or her securities (for example, in Intel Corp.) to a dealer, and the buyer buys his or her securities (in Intel Corp.) from another, or possibly even the same, dealer. Thus, there is always a dealer (*market maker*) on one side of a dealer-market transaction.

As the secondary market continues to evolve, the distinction between broker and dealer markets continues to fade. In fact, since the 21st century began there has been unprecedented consolidation of trading venues and their respective trading technologies to the point where most exchanges in existence today function as broker-dealer markets. Broker-dealer markets seamlessly facilitate both broker and dealer functions as necessary to provide liquidity for investors in the secondary market.

Broker Markets If you're like most people, when you think of the stock market, the first thing that comes to mind is the New York Stock Exchange (NYSE), which is a national securities exchange. Known as "the Big Board," the NYSE is, in fact, the largest stock exchange in the world. In 2015 more than 2,400 firms with an aggregate market value of greater than $19 trillion listed on the NYSE. Actually, the NYSE has historically been the dominant broker market. Also included in broker markets are the NYSE Amex (formally the American Stock Exchange), another national securities exchange, and several so-called regional exchanges. Regional exchanges are actually national securities exchanges, but they reside outside New York City. The number of securities listed on each of these exchanges is typically in the range of 100 to 500 companies. As a group, they handle a very small fraction (and a declining fraction) of the shares traded on organized exchanges. The best known of these are the Chicago Stock Exchange, NYSE Arca (formally the Pacific Stock Exchange), Nasdaq OMX PHLX (formally the Philadelphia Stock Exchange), Nasdaq OMX BX (formally the Boston Stock Exchange), and National Stock Exchange. These exchanges deal primarily in securities with local and regional appeal. Most are modeled after the NYSE, but their membership and listing requirements are considerably more lenient. To enhance their trading activity, regional exchanges often list securities that are also listed on the NYSE.

Other broker markets include foreign stock exchanges that list and trade shares of firms in their own foreign markets (we'll say more about these exchanges later in this chapter). Also, separate domestic exchanges exist for trading in options and in futures. Next we consider the basic structure, rules, and operations of each of the major exchanges in the broker markets.

The New York Stock Exchange Most organized securities exchanges were originally modeled after the New York Stock Exchange. Before the NYSE became a for-profit, publicly traded company in 2006, an individual or firm had to own or lease 1 of the 1,366 "seats" on the exchange to become a member of the exchange. The word *seat* comes from the fact that until the 1870s, members sat in chairs while trading. On December 30, 2005, in anticipation of becoming a publicly held company, the NYSE ceased having member seats. Now part of the NYSE Euronext group of exchanges, the NYSE sells one-year trading licenses to trade directly on the exchange. As of January 1, 2015, a one-year trading license cost $40,000 per license for the first two licenses and $25,000 per additional license held by a member organization. Investment banks and brokerage firms comprise the majority of trading license holders, and each typically holds more than one trading license.

Firms such as Merrill Lynch designate officers to hold trading licenses. Only such designated individuals can make transactions on the floor of the exchange. The two main types of floor broker are the commission broker and the independent broker. *Commission brokers* execute orders for their firm's customers. An *independent broker* works for herself and handles orders on a fee basis, typically for smaller brokerage firms or large firms that are too busy to handle their own orders.

Trading Activity The floor of the NYSE is an area about the size of a football field. It was once a hub of trading activity, and in some respects it looks the same today as it did years ago. The NYSE floor has trading posts, and certain stocks trade at each post.

See the NYSE's
iPad App

Electronic gear around the perimeter transmits buy and sell orders from brokers' offices to the exchange floor and back again after members execute the orders. Transactions on the floor of the exchange occur through an auction process that takes place at the post where the particular security trades. Members interested in purchasing a given security publicly negotiate a transaction with members interested in selling that security. The job of the **designated market maker (DMM)**—an exchange member who specializes in making transactions in one or more stocks—is to manage the auction process. The DMM buys or sells (at specified prices) to provide a continuous, fair, and orderly market in those securities assigned to her. Despite the activity that still occurs on the NYSE trading floor, the trades that happen there account for a tiny fraction of trading volume. Most trading now occurs through electronic networks off the floor.

Listing Policies To list its shares on a stock exchange, a domestic firm must file an application and meet minimum listing requirements. Some firms have **dual listings**, or listings on more than one exchange. Listing requirements have evolved over time, and as the NYSE has come under competitive pressure, it has relaxed many of its listing standards. Companies that sought a listing on the NYSE were once required to have millions in pretax earnings. Today, the NYSE will list companies with $750,000 in pretax earnings, or in some cases, with no pretax earnings at all. The NYSE does require that a listed firm have a minimum stock price of $2 to $3, and usually the market value of a company's public float (the value of shares available for trading on the exchange) must be $15 million or more. Still, an NYSE listing does not have the prestige that it once did.

Regional Stock Exchanges Most regional exchanges are modeled after the NYSE, but their membership and listing requirements are more lenient. Trading costs are also lower. The majority of securities listed on regional exchanges are also listed on the NYSE. About 100 million NYSE shares pass through one of the regional exchanges on a typical trading day. This dual listing may enhance a security's trading activity.

Options Exchanges *Options* allow their holders to sell or to buy another security at a specified price over a given period of time. The dominant options exchange is the Chicago Board Options Exchange (CBOE). Options are also traded on the NYSE, on Nasdaq OMX BX, NYSE Arca, and Nasdaq OMX PHLX exchanges, and on the International Securities Exchange (ISE). Usually an option to sell or buy a given security is listed on many of the exchanges.

Futures Exchanges *Futures* are contracts that guarantee the delivery of a specified commodity or financial instrument at a specific future date at an agreed-on price. The dominant player in the futures trading business is the CME Group, a company comprised of four exchanges (CME, CBOT, NYMEX, and COMEX) known as designated contract markets. Some futures exchanges specialize in certain commodities and financial instruments rather than handling the broad spectrum of products.

Dealer Markets One of the key features of the *dealer market* is that it has no centralized trading floors. Instead it is made up of a large number of market makers who are linked via a mass electronic network. Each market maker is actually a securities dealer who makes a market in one or more securities by offering to buy or sell them at stated bid/ask prices. The **bid price** and **ask price** represent, respectively, the highest price offered to purchase a given security and the lowest price offered to sell a given security. An investor pays the ask price when *buying* securities and receives the bid price when *selling* them. The dealer market is made up of both the Nasdaq OMX and the OTC markets. As an aside, the *primary market* is also a dealer market because all new issues—IPOs and **secondary distributions**, which involve the public sale of large blocks of previously issued securities held by large investors—are sold to the investing public by securities dealers acting on behalf of the investment banker.

Nasdaq The largest dealer market is made up of a large list of stocks that are listed and traded on the National Association of Securities Dealers Automated Quotation System, typically referred to as Nasdaq. Founded in 1971, Nasdaq had its origins in the OTC market but is today considered a totally separate entity that's no longer a part of the OTC market. In fact, in 2006 Nasdaq was formally recognized by the SEC as a national securities exchange, giving it pretty much the same stature and prestige as the NYSE.

To be traded on Nasdaq, all stocks must have at least two market makers, although the bigger, more actively traded stocks, like Cisco Systems, have many more than that. These dealers electronically post all their bid/ask prices so that when investors place market orders, they are immediately filled at the best available price.

The Nasdaq listing standards vary depending on the Nasdaq listing market. The 1,200 or so stocks traded on the Nasdaq Global Select Market meet the world's highest listing standards. Created in 2006, the Global Select Market is reserved for the biggest and the "bluest"—highest quality—of the Nasdaq stocks. In 2012 Facebook elected to list on Nasdaq Global Select rather than on the NYSE, further cementing Nasdaq's position as the preferred listing exchange for leading technology companies.

The listing requirements are also fairly comprehensive for the roughly 1,450 stocks traded on the Nasdaq Global Market. Stocks included on these two markets are all widely quoted, actively traded, and, in general, have a national following. The big-name stocks traded on the Nasdaq Global Select Market, and to some extent, on the Nasdaq Global Market, receive as much national visibility and are as liquid as those traded on the NYSE. As a result, just as the NYSE has its list of big-name players (e.g., ExxonMobil, GE, Citigroup, Walmart, Pfizer, IBM, Procter & Gamble, Coca-Cola, Home Depot, and UPS), so too does Nasdaq. Its list includes companies like Microsoft, Intel, Cisco Systems, eBay, Google, Yahoo!, Apple, Starbucks, and Staples. Make no mistake: Nasdaq competes head-to-head with the NYSE for listings. In 2015, 13 companies with a combined market capitalization of $82 billion moved their listings from the NYSE to Nasdaq. Some well-known companies that moved to Nasdaq include Viacom, Kraft Foods, and Texas Instruments. The Nasdaq Capital Market is still another Nasdaq market; it makes a market in about 600 or 700 stocks that, for one reason or another, are not eligible for the Nasdaq Global Market. In total, 48 countries are represented by approximately 3,000 securities listed on Nasdaq as of 2015.

The Over-the-Counter Market The other part of the dealer market is made up of securities that trade in the over-the-counter (OTC) market. These non-Nasdaq issues include mostly small companies that either cannot or do not wish to comply with Nasdaq's listing requirements. They trade on either the OTC Bulletin Board (OTCBB) or OTC Markets Group. The OTCBB is an electronic quotation system that links the market makers who trade the shares of small companies. The OTCBB provides access to more than 3,300 securities, includes more than 230 participating market makers, and electronically transmits real-time quote, price, and volume information in traded securities. The Bulletin Board is regulated by the FINRA, which, among other things, requires all companies traded on this market to file audited financial statements and comply with federal securities law.

The OTC Markets is an unregulated segment of the market, where the companies are not even required to file with the SEC. This market is broken into three tiers. The biggest is OTC Pink, which is populated by many small and often questionable companies that provide little or no information about their operations. Securities in the OTC QB tier must provide SEC, bank, or insurance reporting and be current in their disclosures. The top tier, OTC QX, albeit the smallest, is reserved for companies that choose to provide audited financial statements and other required information. If a security has been the subject of promotional activities and adequate current information concerning the issuer is not publicly available, OTC Markets will label the security "Caveat Emptor" (buyers beware). Promotional activities, whether they are published by the issuer or a third party, may include spam e-mail or unsolicited faxes or news releases.

Alternative Trading Systems

Some individual and institutional traders now make direct transactions outside of the broker and dealer markets in the third and fourth markets. The **third market** consists of over-the-counter transactions made in securities listed on the NYSE, the NYSE Amex, or one of the other exchanges. These transactions are typically handled by market makers that are not members of a securities exchange. They charge lower commissions than the exchanges and bring together large buyers and sellers. Institutional investors, such as mutual funds, pension funds, and life insurance companies, are thus often able to realize sizable savings in brokerage commissions and to have minimal impact on the price of the transaction.

The **fourth market** consists of transactions made through a computer network, rather than on an exchange, directly between large institutional buyers and sellers of securities. Unlike third-market transactions, fourth-market transactions bypass the market maker. **Electronic communications networks** (ECNs) are at the heart of the fourth market. Archipelago (part of the NYSE Arca), Bloomberg Tradebook, Island, Instinet, and MarketXT are some of the many ECNs that handle these trades. As with the exchanges, ECNs have undergone much consolidation. For example, in 2002 Island was merged with Instinet, and then in 2005 Instinet was acquired by Nasdaq.

ECNs are most effective for high-volume, actively traded securities, and they play a key role in after-hours trading, discussed later in this chapter. They automatically match buy and sell orders that customers place electronically. If there is no immediate match, the ECN, acting like a broker, posts its request under its own name on an exchange or with a market maker. The trade will be executed if another trader is willing to make the transaction at the posted price.

ECNs can save customers money because they charge only a transaction fee, either per share or based on order size. For this reason, money managers and institutions such as pension funds and mutual funds with large amounts of money to invest favor ECNs. Many also use ECNs or trade directly with each other to find the best prices for their clients.

General Market Conditions: Bull or Bear

Conditions in the securities markets are commonly classified as "bull" or "bear," depending on whether securities prices are rising or falling over time. Changing market conditions generally stem from changes in investor attitudes, changes in economic activity, and government actions aimed at stimulating or slowing down economic activity. **Bull markets** are normally associated with rising prices, investor optimism, economic recovery, and government stimulus. **Bear markets** are normally associated with falling prices, investor pessimism, economic slowdown, and government restraint. The beginning of 2003 marked the start of a generally bullish market cycle that peaked before turning sharply bearish in October 2007. The bearish market bottomed out in March 2009 and was generally bullish for the next several years. Since posting a return of almost –37% in 2008, the Standard and Poor's 500 Stock Index earned a positive return in each year from 2009 to 2014.

In general, investors experience higher (or positive) returns on common stock investments during a bull market. However, some securities perform well in a bear market and fare poorly in a bull market. Market conditions are notoriously difficult to predict, and it is nearly impossible to identify the bottom of a bear market or the top of a bull market until months after the fact.

CONCEPTS IN REVIEW

Answers available at
http://www.pearsonhighered.com/smart

3.1 Differentiate between each of the following pairs of terms.

    a. *Money market* and *capital market*
    b. *Primary market* and *secondary market*
    c. *Broker market* and *dealer market*

3.2 Briefly describe the IPO process and the role of the investment banker in underwriting a public offering. Differentiate among the terms *public offering*, *rights offering*, and *private placement*.

3.3 For each of the items in the left-hand column, select the most appropriate item in the right-hand column.

a. Prospectus	1. Trades unlisted securities
b. Underwriting	2. Buying securities from firms and reselling them to investors
c. NYSE	3. Conditions a firm must meet before its stock can be traded on an exchange
d. Nasdaq OMX BX	4. A regional stock exchange
e. Listing requirements	5. Describes the key aspects of a security offering
f. OTC	6. The largest stock exchange in the world

3.4 Explain how the dealer market works. Be sure to mention market makers, bid and ask prices, the Nasdaq market, and the OTC market. What role does the dealer market play in initial public offerings (IPOs) and secondary distributions?

3.5 What are the third and fourth markets?

3.6 Differentiate between a bull market and a bear market.

Globalization of Securities Markets

 LG4 Today investors, issuers of securities, and securities firms look beyond the markets of their home countries to find the best returns, lowest costs, and best international business opportunities. The basic goal of most investors is to earn the highest return with the lowest risk. This outcome is achieved through **diversification**—the inclusion of a number of different securities in a portfolio to increase returns and reduce risk. An investor can greatly increase the potential for diversification by holding (1) a wider range of industries and securities, (2) securities traded in a larger number of markets, and (3) securities denominated in different currencies, and the diversification is even greater if the investor does these things for a mix of domestic and foreign securities. The smaller and less diversified an investor's home market is, the greater the potential benefit

from prudent international diversification. However, even investors in the United States and other highly developed markets can benefit from global diversification.

In short, globalization of the securities markets enables investors to seek out opportunities to profit from rapidly expanding economies throughout the world. Here we consider the growing importance of international markets, international investment performance, ways to invest in foreign securities, and the risks of investing internationally.

Growing Importance of International Markets

Securities exchanges now operate in over 100 countries worldwide. Both large (Tokyo Stock Exchange) and small (South Pacific Stock Exchange), they are located not only in the major industrialized nations such as Japan, Great Britain, Canada, and Germany but also in emerging economies such as Brazil, Chile, India, South Korea, Malaysia, Mexico, Poland, Russia, and Thailand. The top four securities markets worldwide (based on dollar volume) are the NYSE, Nasdaq, London Stock Exchange, and Tokyo Stock Exchange. Other important foreign exchanges include the Shanghai Stock Exchange, Osaka Securities Exchange, Toronto Stock Exchange, Montreal Exchange, Australian Securities Exchange, Hong Kong Exchanges and Clearing Ltd., Swiss Exchange, and Taiwan Stock Exchange Corp.

The economic integration of the European Monetary Union (EMU), along with pressure from financial institutions that want an efficient process for trading shares across borders, is changing the European securities market environment. Instead of many small national exchanges, countries are banding together to create cross-border markets and to compete more effectively in the pan-European equity-trading markets. The Paris, Amsterdam, Brussels, and Lisbon exchanges, plus a derivatives exchange in London, merged to form Euronext, and the Scandinavian markets formed Norex. In mid-2006 Euronext and the NYSE Group—the NYSE parent—signed an agreement to combine their businesses in a merger of equals. Some stock exchanges—for example, Tokyo and Australian—are forming cooperative agreements. Others are discussing forming a 24-hour global market alliance, trading the stocks of selected large international companies via an electronic order-matching system. Nasdaq, with joint ventures in Japan, Hong Kong, Canada, and Australia, plans to expand into Latin America and the Middle East. The increasing number of mergers and cooperative arrangements represent steps toward a worldwide stock exchange.

Bond markets, too, have become global, and more investors than ever before regularly purchase government and corporate fixed-income securities in foreign markets. The United States dominates the international government bond market, followed by Japan, Germany, and Great Britain.

International Investment Performance

A motive for investing overseas is the lure of high returns. In fact, only once since 1980 did the United States stock market post the world's highest rate of return. For example, in 2014, a good year for U.S stocks, investors would have earned higher returns in many foreign markets. During that year the Standard and Poor's Global Index reported returns (translated into U.S. dollars) of 32% in India, 26% in Egypt, 20% in Indonesia, and 14% in Turkey. By comparison, the U.S. stock price index increased about 11%. Of course, foreign securities markets tend to be riskier than U.S. markets. A market with high returns in one year may not do so well in the next. However, even in 2008, one of the worst years on record for stock market investors, more than a dozen foreign exchanges earned returns higher than the NYSE Euronext.

Investors can compare activity on U.S. and foreign exchanges by following market indexes that track the performance of those exchanges. For instance, the Dow Jones averages and the Standard & Poor's indexes are popular measures of the U.S. markets, and indexes for dozens of different stock markets are available.

Ways to Invest in Foreign Securities

Investors can make foreign security transactions either indirectly or directly. One form of *indirect* investment is to purchase shares of a U.S.-based multinational corporation with substantial foreign operations. Many U.S.-based multinational firms, such as Accenture, Facebook, Google, IBM, Intel, McDonald's, Dow Chemical, Coca-Cola, and Nike, receive more than 50% of their revenues from overseas operations. By investing in the securities of such firms, an investor can achieve a degree of international diversification. Purchasing shares in a mutual fund or exchange-traded fund that invests primarily in foreign securities is another way to invest indirectly. Investors can make both of these indirect foreign securities investment transactions through a stockbroker.

To make *direct* investments in foreign companies, investors have three options. They can purchase securities on foreign exchanges, buy securities of foreign companies that trade on U.S. exchanges, or buy American Depositary Shares (ADSs).

The first way—purchasing securities on foreign exchanges—involves additional risks because foreign securities do not trade in U.S. dollars and, thus, investors must cope with currency fluctuations. This approach is not for the timid or inexperienced investor. Investors also encounter different securities exchange rules, transaction procedures, accounting standards, and tax laws in different countries. Direct transactions are best handled either through brokers at major Wall Street firms with large international operations or through major banks, such as JPMorgan Chase and Citibank, that have special units to handle foreign securities transactions. Alternatively, investors can deal with foreign broker-dealers, but such an approach is more complicated and riskier.

The second form of direct investment is to buy the securities of foreign companies that trade on both organized and over-the-counter U.S. exchanges. Transactions in foreign securities that trade on U.S. exchanges are handled in the same way as exchange-traded domestic securities. These securities are issued by large, well-known foreign companies. Stocks of companies such as Barrick Gold Corporation (Canada), General Steel Holdings (China), Cosan Ltd. (Brazil), Paragon Shipping (Greece), Manchester United (United Kingdom), and Tyco International (Switzerland) trade directly on U.S. exchanges. In addition, **Yankee bonds**, U.S. dollar–denominated debt securities issued by foreign governments or corporations and traded in U.S. securities markets, trade in both broker and dealer markets.

Finally, foreign stocks also trade on U.S. exchanges in the form of **American depositary shares (ADSs)**. These securities have been created to permit U.S. investors to hold shares of non-U.S. companies and trade them on U.S. stock exchanges. They are backed by **American depositary receipts (ADRs)**, which are U.S dollar–denominated receipts for the stocks of foreign companies that are held in the vaults of banks in the companies' home countries. Today more than 3,700 ADRs representing more than 100 home countries are traded on U.S. exchanges. About one-fourth of them are actively traded. Included are well-known companies such as Daimler, Fujitsu, LG Electronics, Mitsubishi, Nestle, and Royal Dutch Shell.

Risks of Investing Internationally

Investing abroad is not without pitfalls. In addition to the usual risks involved in any security transaction, investors must consider the risks of doing business in a particular foreign country. Changes in trade policies, labor laws, and taxation may affect operating conditions for the country's firms. The government itself may not be stable. You must track similar environmental factors in each foreign market in which you invest. This is clearly more difficult than following your home market.

U.S. securities markets are generally viewed as highly regulated and reliable. Foreign markets, on the other hand, may lag substantially behind the United States in both operations and regulation. Additionally, some countries place various restrictions on foreign investment. Saudi Arabia and China only recently opened their stock markets to foreign investors, and even then only to a limited extent. Mexico has a two-tier market, with certain securities restricted from foreigners. Some countries make it difficult for foreigners to get their funds out, and many impose taxes on dividends. For example, Swiss taxes are about 35% on dividends paid to foreigners. Other difficulties include illiquid markets and an inability to obtain reliable investment information because of a lack of reporting requirements.

Furthermore, accounting standards vary from country to country. Differences in accounting practices can affect a company's apparent profitability, conceal assets (such as the hidden reserves and undervalued assets that are permitted in many countries), and facilitate failure to disclose other risks. As a result, it is difficult to compare the financial performance of firms operating in different countries. Although the accounting profession has agreed on a set of international accounting standards, it will be years until all countries have adopted them and even longer until all companies apply them.

Another concern stems from the fact that international investing involves securities denominated in foreign currencies. Trading profits and losses are affected not only by a security's price changes but also by fluctuations in currency values. The price of one currency in terms of another is called the **currency exchange rate**. The values of the world's major currencies fluctuate with respect to each other daily, and these price movements can have a significant positive or negative impact on the return that you earn on an investment in foreign securities.

For example, on January 2, 2015, the exchange rate for the European Monetary Union euro (€) and the U.S. dollar (US$) was expressed as follows:

$$\text{US\$} = €0.8324 \qquad € = \text{US\$}1.2013$$

This means that 1 U.S. dollar was worth 0.8324 euros, or equivalently, 1 euro was worth 1.2013 U.S. dollars. On that day, if you had purchased 100 shares of Heineken, which was trading for €57.72 per share on Euronext Amsterdam, it would have cost you $6,933.90 (i.e., 100 × 57.72 × 1.2013).

Four months later, the value of the euro had fallen relative to the dollar. On April 14, 2015, the euro/US$ exchange rate was 0.9386, which meant that during the first four months of 2015, the euro *depreciated* relative to the dollar (and therefore the dollar *appreciated* relative to the euro). On April 14 it took more euros to buy $1 (€0.9386 in April versus €0.8324 in January), so each euro was worth less in dollar terms (one euro was worth $1.0654 in April versus $1.2013 in January). Had the European Monetary Union euro instead *appreciated* (and the dollar *depreciated* relative to the euro), each euro would have been worth more in dollar terms.

Currency exchange risk is the risk caused by the varying exchange rates between the currencies of two countries. For example, assume that on April 14, 2015, you sold your 100 shares of Heineken, which was trading for €75.82 per share on Euronext Amsterdam; sale proceeds would have been $8,077.86 (i.e., 75.82 × 100 × 1.0654).

In this example you had a win-lose outcome. The price of Heineken stock rose 31.4% (from €57.72 to €75.82), but the value of the euro declined 11.3% (falling from 1.2013 to 1.0654). You made money on the investment in Heineken, but to purchase Heineken shares, you also had to purchase euros. Because the euro depreciated from January to April, you lost money on that part of the transaction. On net you realized a gain of 16.5% because you invested $6,933.90 in January and you received $8,077.86 in April. Put another way, the increase in the value of Heineken shares more than offset the currency loss that you experienced, so your overall return was positive. If the depreciation in the euro had been greater, it could have swamped the increase in Heineken shares, resulting in an overall negative rate of return. Similarly, if the euro had appreciated, that would have magnified the return on Heineken stock. Investors in foreign securities must be aware that the value of the foreign currency in relation to the dollar can have a profound effect on returns from foreign security transactions.

CONCEPTS IN REVIEW	
CONCEPTS IN REVIEW Answers available at http://www .pearsonhighered.com/smart	**3.7** Why is globalization of securities markets an important issue today? How have international investments performed in recent years?
	3.8 Describe how foreign security investments can be made, both indirectly and directly.
	3.9 Describe the risks of investing internationally, particularly currency exchange risk.

Trading Hours and Regulation of Securities Markets

LG5 Understanding the structure of domestic and international securities markets is an important foundation for developing a sound investment program. We'll begin with an overview of the trading hours and regulations that apply to U.S. securities markets.

WATCH YOUR BEHAVIOR

Overreacting to News A recent study found that when the prices of exchange-traded funds (ETFs) moved sharply during normal trading hours, those movements were often quickly reversed, suggesting that the initial move might have been caused by investors overreacting to news. During after-hours trading, the same pattern was not evident, suggesting that the traders who buy and sell after regular trading hours are less prone to overreaction.

MyFinanceLab

Trading Hours of Securities Markets

Traditionally, the regular trading session for organized U.S. exchanges ran from 9:30 A.M. to 4:00 P.M. eastern time. However, trading is no longer limited to these hours. Most securities exchanges and ECNs offer extended trading sessions before and after regular hours. Most of the after-hours markets are **crossing markets,** in which orders are filled only if they can be matched. That is, buy and sell orders are filled only if they can be matched with identical opposing sell and buy orders at the desired price. If an investor submits an order to buy shares but no matching sell order is posted, then the buy order is not filled. As you might expect, the liquidity of the market during extended hours is less than it is during the day. On the other hand, extended hours allow traders to respond to information that they receive after the official 4:00 P.M. market close. Extended hours allow U.S. securities markets to compete more effectively with foreign securities markets, in which investors can execute trades when U.S. markets are closed. ECNs were off limits to individual investors until 2003, but now both individuals and institutions can trade shares outside the traditional 9:30 to 4:00 trading day. For example, Nasdaq has its own extended-hours electronic-trading sessions from 4:00 A.M. to 9:30 A.M. and from 4:00 P.M. to 8:00 P.M.

Regulation of Securities Markets

U.S. securities laws protect investors and participants in the financial marketplace. A number of state and federal laws require that investors receive adequate and accurate disclosure of information. Such laws also regulate the activities of participants in the securities markets. State laws that control the sale of securities within state borders are

TABLE 3.2   IMPORTANT FEDERAL SECURITIES LAWS

Act	Brief Description
Securities Act of 1933	Passed to ensure full disclosure of information about new security issues. Requires the issuer of a new security to file a registration statement with the Securities and Exchange Commission (SEC) containing information about the new issue. The firm cannot sell the security until the SEC approves the registration statement, which usually takes about 20 days. Approval of the registration statement by the SEC merely indicates that the facts presented in the statement appear to reflect the firm's true position.
Securities Exchange Act of 1934	Formally established the SEC as the agency in charge of administering federal securities laws. The act gave the SEC the power to regulate the organized exchanges and the OTC market; their members, brokers, and dealers; and the securities traded in these markets.
Maloney Act of 1938	An amendment to the Securities Exchange Act of 1934, it provided for the establishment of trade associations to self-regulate the securities industry and led to the creation of the National Association of Securities Dealers (NASD). Today the Financial Industry Regulatory Authority (FINRA) has replaced the NASD as the industry's only self-regulatory body.
Investment Company Act of 1940	Established rules and regulations for investment companies (e.g., mutual funds) and authorized the SEC to regulate their practices. It required investment companies to register with the SEC and to fulfill certain disclosure requirements.
Investment Advisors Act of 1940	Requires investment advisors, persons hired by investors to advise them about security investments, to disclose all relevant information about their backgrounds, conflicts of interest, and any investments they recommend. Advisors must register and file periodic reports with the SEC.
Securities Acts Amendments of 1975	Requires the SEC and the securities industry to develop a competitive national system for trading securities. First, the SEC abolished fixed-commission schedules, thereby providing for negotiated commissions. Second, it established the Intermarket Trading System (ITS), an electronic communications network linking 9 markets and trading over 4,000 eligible issues, which allowed trades to be made across these markets wherever the network shows a better price for a given issue.
Insider Trading and Act of 1988	Established penalties for insider trading. Insiders include anyone who obtains nonpublic information, typically a company's directors, officers, major shareholders, bankers, investment bankers, accountants, and attorneys. The SEC requires corporate insiders to file monthly reports detailing all transactions made in the company's stock. Recent legislation substantially increased the penalties for insider trading and gave the SEC greater power to investigate and prosecute claims of illegal insider-trading activity.
Regulation Fair Disclosure (2000)	Reg FD required companies to disclosure material information to all investors at the same time.
Sarbanes-Oxley Act of 2002	Passed to protect investors against corporate fraud, particularly accounting fraud. It created an oversight board to monitor the accounting industry, tightened audit regulations and controls, toughened penalties against executives who commit corporate fraud, strengthened accounting disclosure requirements and ethical guidelines for financial officers, established corporate board structure and membership guidelines, established guidelines for analyst conflicts of interest, and increased the SEC's authority and budgets for auditors and investigators. The act also mandated instant disclosure of stock sales by corporate executives.
Dodd-Frank Wall Street Reform and Consumer Protection Act of 2010	Passed in the wake of the 2007–2008 financial crisis. Its stated aim was to promote the financial stability of the United States by improving accountability and transparency. It created the Bureau of Consumer Financial Protection and other new agencies.

commonly called *blue sky laws* because they are intended to prevent investors from being sold nothing but "blue sky." These laws typically establish procedures for regulating both security issues and sellers of securities doing business within the state. Most states have a regulatory body, such as a state securities commission, that is charged with enforcing the related state statutes. Table 3.2 summarizes the most important securities laws enacted by the federal government (listed in chronological order).

The intent of these federal securities laws is to protect investors. Most of these laws were passed in response to some type of crisis or scandal in the financial markets. In recent decades, Congress passed two major laws in response to public concern over corporate financial scandals: The *Sarbanes-Oxley Act of 2002* focuses on eliminating corporate fraud related to accounting and other information releases. The Dodd-Frank Wall Street Reform and Consumer Protection Act was passed in the wake of the 2007–2008 financial crisis. It sought to improve the financial stability of the U.S. economy through improved accountability and transparency in the financial system. The act created new financial regulatory agencies and merged or eliminated some existing agencies. Both of these acts heightened the public's awareness of **ethics**—standards of conduct or moral judgment—in business. The government and the financial community are continuing to develop and enforce ethical standards that will motivate market participants to adhere to laws and regulations. Ensuring that market participants adhere to ethical standards, whether through law enforcement or incentives, remains an ongoing challenge.

CONCEPTS IN REVIEW
Answers available at
http://www.pearsonhighered
.com/smart

3.10 How are after-hours trades typically handled? What is the outlook for after-hours trading?

3.11 Briefly describe the key requirements of the following federal securities laws:

    a. Securities Act of 1933
    b. Investment Company Act of 1940
    c. Investment Advisors Act of 1940
    d. Insider Trading and Fraud Act of 1988
    e. Regulation Fair Disclosure (2000)
    f . Sarbanes-Oxley Act of 2002
    g. Dodd-Frank Wall Street Reform and Consumer Protection Act of 2010

Basic Types of Securities Transactions

 An investor can make a number of basic types of security transactions. Each type is available to those who meet the requirements established by government agencies as well as by brokerage firms. Although investors can use the various types of transactions in a number of ways to meet investment objectives, we describe only the most popular use of each transaction here, as we consider the long purchase, margin trading, and short selling.

Long Purchase

The **long purchase** is a transaction in which investors buy securities, usually in the hope that they will increase in value and can be sold at a later date for profit. The object, then, is to *buy low and sell high*. A long purchase is the most common type of transaction. Because investors generally expect the price of a security to rise over the period of time they plan to hold it, their return comes from any dividends or interest received during the ownership period, plus the difference (capital gain or loss) between the purchase and selling prices. Transaction costs, of course, reduce this return.

Ignoring dividends and transaction costs, we can illustrate the long purchase by a simple example. After studying Varner Industries, you are convinced that its common stock, which currently sells for $20 per share, will increase in value over the next few years. You expect the stock price to rise to $30 per share within two years. You place an order and buy 100 shares of Varner for $20 per share. If the stock price rises to, say, $40 per share, you will profit from your long purchase. If it drops below $20 per share, you will experience a loss on the transaction. Obviously, one of the major motivating factors in making a long purchase is an expected rise in the price of the security.

Margin Trading

Security purchases do not have to be made on a cash basis; investors can use funds borrowed from brokerage firms instead. This activity is referred to as **margin trading**. It is used for one basic reason: to magnify returns. As peculiar as it may sound, the term *margin* refers to the amount of equity (stated as a percentage) in an investment, or the amount that is *not* borrowed. If an investor uses 75% margin, for example, it means that 75% of the investment position is being financed with the person's own funds and the balance (25%) with borrowed money.

The Federal Reserve Board (the "Fed") sets the **margin requirement,** specifying the minimum amount of equity that must be the margin investor's own funds. The margin requirement for stocks has been at 50% for some time. By raising and lowering the margin requirement, the Fed can depress or stimulate activity in the securities markets. Brokers must approve margin purchases. The brokerage firm then lends the purchaser the needed funds and retains the purchased securities as collateral. It is important to recognize that margin purchasers must pay interest on the amount they borrow.

With the use of margin, you can purchase more securities than you could afford on a strictly cash basis and, thus, magnify your returns. However, the use of margin also presents substantial risks. Margin trading can only magnify returns, not produce them. One of the biggest risks is that the security may not perform as expected. If the security's return is negative, margin trading magnifies the loss. Because the security being margined is always the ultimate source of return, choosing the right securities is critical to this trading strategy. In the next section, we will look at how margin trading can magnify returns and losses.

Essentials of Margin Trading Investors can use margin trading with most kinds of securities. They regularly use it, for example, to buy common and preferred stocks, most types of bonds, options, warrants, and futures. It is not normally used with tax-exempt municipal bonds because the interest paid on such margin loans is not deductible for income tax purposes. It is also possible to use margin on certain foreign stocks and bonds that meet prescribed criteria. Foreign stocks eligible for margin trading must trade on an exchange located in a FTSE Global Index recognized country (there are roughly 50 such countries), and the companies issuing the shares must have a market capitalization of at least $500 million. These stocks must have daily price quotations that are made available to a U.S. broker continuously via an electronic quote system, and they must have median daily trading volume of 100,000 shares or $500,000.

Magnified Profits and Losses The idea of margin trading is to employ **financial leverage**—the use of debt financing to magnify investment returns. Here is how it works: Suppose you have $5,000 to invest and are considering the purchase of 100 shares of stock at $50 per share. If you do not margin, you can buy exactly 100 shares of the

TABLE 3.3   THE EFFECT OF MARGIN TRADING ON SECURITY RETURNS

	Without Margin (100% Equity)	With Margins of		
		80%	65%	50%
Number of $50 shares purchased	100	100	100	100
Cost of investment	$5,000	$5,000	$5,000	$5,000
Less: Borrowed money	–$ 0	–$1,000	–$1,750	–$2,500
Equity in investment	$5,000	$4,000	$3,250	$2,500
A. Investor's position if price rises by $30 to $80/share				
Value of stock	$8,000	$8,000	$8,000	$8,000
Less: Cost of investment	–$5,000	–$5,000	–$5,000	–$5,000
Capital gain	$3,000	$3,000	$3,000	$3,000
Return on investor's equity (capital gain/equity in investment)	60%	75%	92.3%	120%
B. Investor's position if price falls by $30 to $20/share				
Value of stock	$2,000	$2,000	$2,000	$2,000
Less: Cost of investment	–$5,000	–$5,000	–$5,000	–$5,000
Capital loss*	–$3,000	–$3,000	–$3,000	–$3,000
Return on investor's equity (capital loss/equity in investment)*	(60%)	(75%)	(92.3%)	(120%)

*Both the capital loss and the return on investor's equity are negative, as noted by the parentheses.

stock (ignoring brokerage commissions). If you margin the transaction—for example, at 50%—you can acquire the same $5,000 position with only $2,500 of your own money. This leaves you with $2,500 to use for other investments or to buy on margin another 100 shares of the same stock. Either way, by margining you will reap greater benefits from the stock's price appreciation.

Table 3.3 illustrates the concept of margin trading. It shows a nonmargined (100% equity) transaction, along with the same transaction using various margins. For simplicity, we assume here that the investor pays no interest on borrowed funds, but in reality investors do pay interest, and that would lower returns throughout Table 3.3. Remember that the margin rates indicate the investor's equity in the investment. When the investment is not margined and the price of the stock goes up by $30 per share (see Table 3.3, part A), the investor enjoys a very respectable 60% rate of return. However, observe how the rate of return goes up when margin is used. For example, consider an investor who buys 100 shares using 80% margin. This means that to pay for the $5,000 cost of the shares, the investor uses 80% of her own money ($4,000) and borrows 20% ($1,000) to pay for the rest. Now suppose that the stock price rises from $50 to $80 per share. The shares are worth $8,000, so the investor earns a $3,000 capital gain. The gain, relative to the investor's initial investment of $4,000, represents a 75% rate of return. In other words, margin allowed the investor to earn 75% when the underlying stock only increased by 60%. It is in this sense that margin magnifies an investor's rate of return. In part A of Table 3.3, the rate of return ranges from 75% to 120%, depending on the amount of equity in the investment. The more the investor borrows, the greater her rate of return. This occurs because the dollar gain is the same ($3,000) *regardless of how the investor finances the transaction.* Clearly, as the investor's equity in the investment declines (with lower margins), the rate of return increases accordingly. Given this example, you might ask why an investor would ever buy a stock without borrowing money. The answer is that trading on margin also magnifies losses. Look at part B of Table 3.3. Suppose the investor uses 80% margin to buy 100 shares of the stock at $50 per share, but then the price of the stock falls to $20. In that case, the investor experiences a $3,000 capital loss. Relative to the initial $4,000 investment, the investor earns a −75% rate of return, whereas the decline in the stock price was just 60%.

Three important lessons about margin trading emerge from the table:

- Movements in the stock's price are not influenced by the method used to purchase the stock.

- The lower the amount of the investor's equity in the position, the *greater the rate of return* the investor will enjoy when the price of the security rises.

- The *loss is also magnified* when the price of the security falls (see Table 3.3, part B).

Note that Table 3.3 has an Excel@Investing icon. Throughout the text, tables with this icon indicate that the spreadsheet is available on http://www.myfinancelab.com. The use of electronic spreadsheets in finance and investments, as well as in all functional areas of business, is pervasive. We use spreadsheets from time to time throughout the text to demonstrate how the content has been constructed or calculated. As you know, we include Excel spreadsheet exercises at the end of most chapters to give you practice with spreadsheets and help you develop the ability to clearly set out the logic needed to solve investment problems.

Advantages and Disadvantages of Margin Trading A magnified return is the major advantage of margin trading. The size of the magnified return depends on both the price behavior of the security and the amount of margin used. Another, more modest benefit of margin trading is that it allows for greater diversification of security holdings because investors can spread their limited capital over a larger number of investments.

The major disadvantage of margin trading, of course, is the potential for magnified losses if the price of the security falls. Another disadvantage is the cost of the margin loans themselves. A **margin loan** is the official vehicle through which the borrowed funds are made available in a margin transaction. All margin loans are made at a stated interest rate, which depends on prevailing market rates and the amount of money being borrowed. This rate is usually 1% to 3% above the **prime rate**—the interest rate charged to creditworthy business borrowers. For large accounts, the margin loan rate may be at the prime rate. The loan cost, which investors pay, will increase daily, reducing the level of profits (or increasing losses) accordingly.

Making Margin Transactions To execute a margin transaction, an investor must establish a **margin account** with a minimum of $2,000 in equity or 100% of the purchase price, whichever is less, in the form of either cash or securities. The broker will retain any securities purchased on margin as collateral for the loan.

The margin requirement established by the Federal Reserve Board sets the minimum amount of equity for margin transactions. Investors need not execute all margin transactions by using exactly the minimum amount of margin; they can use more than the minimum if they wish. Moreover, it is not unusual for brokerage firms and the major exchanges to establish their own margin requirements, which are more restrictive than those of the Federal Reserve. Brokerage firms also may have their own lists of especially volatile stocks for which the margin requirements are higher. There are basically two types of margin requirement: initial margin and maintenance margin.

TABLE 3.4   INITIAL MARGIN REQUIREMENTS FOR VARIOUS TYPES OF SECURITIES

Security	Minimum Initial Margin (Equity) Required
Listed common and preferred stock	50%
Nasdaq OMX stocks	50%
Convertible bonds	50%
Corporate bonds	30%
U.S. government bills, notes, and bonds	10% of principal
U.S. government agencies	24% of principal
Options	Option premium plus 20% of market value of underlying stock
Futures	2% to 10% of the value of the contract

Initial Margin   The minimum amount of equity that must be provided by the investor at the time of purchase is the **initial margin**. Because margin refers to the amount of equity in a trade, establishing a minimum margin requirement is equivalent to establishing a maximum borrowing limit. Initial margin requirements therefore place some restraint on how much risk investors can take through margin trading. All securities that can be margined have specific initial requirements, which the governing authorities can change at their discretion. Table 3.4 shows initial margin requirements for various types of securities. The more stable investments, such as U.S. government issues, generally have substantially lower margin requirements and thus offer greater opportunities to magnify returns. Stocks traded on the Nasdaq OMX markets can be margined like listed securities.

As long as the margin in an account remains at a level equal to or higher than prevailing initial requirements, the investor may use the account in any way he or she wants. However, if the value of the investor's holdings declines, the margin in his or her account will also drop. In this case, the investor will have what is known as a **restricted account**, one whose equity is less than the initial margin requirement. It does not mean that the investor must put up additional cash or equity. However, as long as the account is restricted, the investor may not make further margin purchases and must bring the margin back to the initial level when securities are sold.

Maintenance Margin   The absolute minimum amount of margin (equity) that an investor must maintain in the margin account at all times is the **maintenance margin**. When an insufficient amount of maintenance margin exists, an investor will receive a **margin call**. This call gives the investor a short period of time, ranging from a few hours to a few days, to bring the equity up above the maintenance margin. If this doesn't happen, the broker is authorized to sell enough of the investor's margined holdings to bring the equity in the account up to this standard.

Margin investors can be in for a surprise if markets are volatile. When the Nasdaq stock market fell 14% in one day in early April 2000, brokerages made many more margin calls than usual. Investors rushed to sell shares, often at a loss, to cover their margin calls—only to watch the market bounce back a few days later.

The maintenance margin protects both the brokerage house and investors. Brokers avoid having to absorb excessive investor losses, and investors avoid being wiped out. The maintenance margin on equity securities is currently 25%. It rarely changes, although it is often set slightly higher by brokerage firms for the added protection of brokers and customers. For straight debt securities such as government bonds, there is no official maintenance margin except that set by the brokerage firms themselves.

The Basic Margin Formula The amount of margin is always measured in terms of its relative amount of equity, which is considered the investor's collateral. A simple formula can be used with all types of long purchases to determine the amount of margin in the transaction at any given time. Basically, only two pieces of information are required: (1) the prevailing market value of the securities being margined and (2) the **debit balance**, which is the amount of money being borrowed in the margin loan. Given this information, we can compute margin according to Equation 3.1.

Equation 3.1

$$\text{Margin} = \frac{\text{Value of securities} - \text{Debit balance}}{\text{Value of securities}}$$

Equation 3.1a

$$= \frac{V - D}{V}$$

To illustrate, consider the following example. Assume you want to purchase 100 shares of stock at $40 per share at a time when the initial margin requirement is 70%. Because 70% of the transaction must be financed with equity, you can finance the (30%) balance with a margin loan. Therefore, you will borrow $0.30 \times \$4,000$, or $1,200. This amount, of course, is the *debit balance*. The remaining $2,800 needed to buy the securities represents your equity in the transaction. In other words, equity is represented by the numerator $(V - D)$ in the margin formula.

What happens to the margin as the value of the security changes? If over time the price of the stock moves to $65, the margin is then

$$\text{Margin} = \frac{V - D}{V} = \frac{\$6,500 - \$1,200}{\$6,500} = 0.815 = \underline{81.5\%}$$

Note that the margin (equity) in this investment position has risen from 70% to 81.5%. *When the price of the security goes up, your margin also increases.*

On the other hand, *when the price of the security goes down, so does the amount of margin.* For instance, if the price of the stock in our illustration drops to $30 per share, the new margin is only 60% [i.e., ($3,000 − $1,200) ÷ $3,000]. In that case, we would be dealing with a *restricted account* because the margin level would have dropped below the prevailing initial margin of 70%.

Finally, note that although our discussion has been couched largely in terms of individual transactions, the same margin formula applies to margin accounts. The only difference is that we would be dealing with input that applies to the account *as a whole*—the value of all securities held in the account and the total amount of margin loans.

Return on Invested Capital When assessing the return on margin transactions, you must take into account the fact that you put up only part of the funds. Therefore, you are concerned with the *rate of return* earned on only the portion of the funds that you provided. Using both current income received from dividends or interest and total interest paid on the margin loan, we can apply Equation 3.2 to determine the return on invested capital from a margin transaction.

Equation 3.2

$$\text{Return on invested capital from a margin transaction} = \frac{\begin{matrix}\text{Total} \\ \text{current} \\ \text{income} \\ \text{received}\end{matrix} - \begin{matrix}\text{Total} \\ \text{interest} \\ \text{paid on} \\ \text{margin loan}\end{matrix} + \begin{matrix}\text{Market} \\ \text{value of} \\ \text{securities} \\ \text{at sale}\end{matrix} - \begin{matrix}\text{Market} \\ \text{value of} \\ \text{securities} \\ \text{at purchase}\end{matrix}}{\text{Amount of equity at purchase}}$$

We can use this equation to compute either the expected or the actual return from a margin transaction. To illustrate: Assume you want to buy 100 shares of stock at $50 per share because you feel it will rise to $75 within six months. The stock pays $2 per share in annual dividends, and during your 6-month holding period, you will receive half of that amount, or $1 per share. You are going to buy the stock with 50% margin and will pay 10% interest on the margin loan. Therefore, you are going to put up $2,500 equity to buy $5,000 worth of stock that you hope will increase to $7,500 in six months. Because you will have a $2,500 margin loan outstanding at 10% for six months, the interest cost that you will pay is calculated as $2,500 × 0.10 × 6 ÷ 12 which is $125. We can substitute this information into Equation 3.2 to find the expected return on invested capital from this margin transaction:

$$\text{Return on invested capital from a margin transaction} = \frac{\$100 - \$125 + \$7,500 - \$5,000}{\$2,500} = \frac{\$2,475}{\$2,500} = 0.99 = \underline{\underline{99\%}}$$

Keep in mind that the 99% figure represents the rate of return earned over a 6-month holding period. If you wanted to compare this rate of return to other investment opportunities, you could determine the transaction's annualized rate of return by multiplying by 2 (the number of six-month periods in a year). This would amount to an annual rate of return of 198% (i.e., 99 × 2 = 198).

Uses of Margin Trading Investors most often use margin trading in one of two ways. As we have seen, one of its uses is to magnify transaction returns. The other major margin tactic is called pyramiding, which takes the concept of magnified returns to its limits. **Pyramiding** uses the paper profits in margin accounts to partly or fully finance the acquisition of additional securities. This allows investors to make such transactions at margins below prevailing initial margin levels, sometimes substantially so. In fact, with this technique it is even possible to buy securities with no new cash at all. Rather, they can all be financed entirely with margin loans. The reason is that the paper profits in the account lead to **excess margin**—more equity in the account than required. For instance, if a margin account holds $60,000 worth of securities and has a debit balance of $20,000, it is at a margin level of 66.6% [i.e., ($60,000 − $20,000) ÷ $60,000]. This account would hold a substantial amount of excess margin if the prevailing initial margin requirement were only 50%.

The principle of pyramiding is to use the excess margin in the account to purchase additional securities. The only constraint—and the key to pyramiding—is that when the additional securities are purchased, your margin account must be at or above the prevailing required initial margin level. Remember that it is the account, not the individual transactions, that must meet the minimum standards. If the account has excess margin, you can use it to build up security holdings. Pyramiding can continue as long as there are additional paper profits in the margin account and as long as the margin level exceeds the initial requirement that prevailed when purchases were made. The tactic is somewhat complex but is also profitable, especially because it minimizes the amount of new capital required in the investor's account.

In general, margin trading is simple, but it is also risky. Risk is primarily associated with possible price declines in the margined securities. A decline in prices can result in a restricted account. If prices fall enough to cause the actual margin to drop below the maintenance margin, the resulting margin call will force you to deposit additional equity into the account almost immediately. In addition, losses (resulting from the price decline) are magnified in a fashion similar to that demonstrated in Table 3.3, part B. Clearly, the chance of a margin call and the magnification of losses make margin trading riskier than nonmargined transactions. Only investors who fully understand its operation and appreciate its pitfalls should use margin.

Short Selling

In most cases, investors buy stock hoping that the price will rise. What if you expect the price of a particular security to fall? By using short selling, you may be able to profit from falling security prices. Almost any type of security can be "shorted," including common and preferred stocks, all types of bonds, convertible securities, listed mutual funds, options, and warrants. In practice, though, the short-selling activities of most investors are limited almost exclusively to common stocks and to options. (However, investors are prohibited from using short-selling securities that they already own to defer taxes, a strategy called *shorting-against-the-box*.)

The Basics of Short Selling Explained

Essentials of Short Selling **Short selling** is generally defined as the practice of selling borrowed securities. Unusual as it may sound, selling borrowed securities is (in most cases) legal and quite common. Short sales start when an investor borrows securities from a broker and sells these securities in the marketplace. Later, when the price of the issue has declined, the short seller buys back the securities and then returns them to the lender. A short seller must make an initial equity deposit with the broker, subject to rules similar to those for margin trading. The deposit plus the proceeds from sale of the borrowed shares assure the broker that sufficient funds are available to buy back the shorted securities at a later date, even if their price increases. Short sales, like margin transactions, require investors to work through a broker.

Making Money When Prices Fall Making money when security prices fall is what short selling is all about. Like their colleagues in the rest of the investment world, short sellers are trying to make money by buying low and selling high. The only difference is that they reverse the investment process: *They start the transaction with a sale and end it with a purchase.*

Table 3.5 shows how a short sale works and how investors can profit from such transactions. (For simplicity, we ignore transaction costs.) The transaction results in a net profit of $2,000 as a result of an initial sale of 100 shares of stock at $50 per share (step 1) and subsequent covering (purchase) of the 100 shares for $30 per share (step 2). The amount of profit or loss generated in a short sale depends on the price at which the short seller can buy back the stock. Short sellers earn profits when the proceeds from the sale of the stock are higher than the cost of buying it back.

Who Lends the Securities? Acting through their brokers, short sellers obtain securities from the brokerage firm or from other investors. (Brokers are the principal source of

Excel@Investing

TABLE 3.5   THE MECHANICS OF A SHORT SALE

Step 1. Short sale initiated	
100 shares of borrowed stock are sold at $50/share:	
Proceeds from sale to investor	$5,000
Step 2. Short sale covered	
Later, 100 shares of the stock are purchased at $30/share and returned to broker from whom stock was borrowed:	
Cost to investor	–$3,000
Net profit	$2,000

borrowed securities.) As a service to their customers, brokers lend securities held in their portfolios or in *street-name* accounts. It is important to recognize that when the brokerage firm lends street-name securities, it is lending the short seller the securities of other investors. Individual investors typically do not pay fees to the broker for the privilege of borrowing the shares; in exchange, investors do not earn interest on the funds they leave on deposit with the broker.

Margin Requirements and Short Selling To make a short sale, the investor must make a deposit with the broker that is equal to the initial margin requirement (currently 50%) applied to the short-sale proceeds. In addition, the broker retains the proceeds from the short sale.

To demonstrate, assume that you sell short 100 shares of Smart, Inc., at $50 per share at a time when the initial margin requirement is 50% and the maintenance margin on short sales is 30%. The values in lines 1 through 4 in column A in Table 3.6 indicate that your broker would hold a total deposit of $7,500 on this transaction. Note in columns B and C that regardless of subsequent changes in Smart's stock price, your deposit with the broker would remain at $7,500 (line 4).

By subtracting the cost of buying back the shorted stock at the given share price (line 5), you can find your equity in the account (line 6) for the current (column A) and two subsequent share prices (columns B and C). We see that at the initial short sale price of $50 per share, your equity would equal $2,500 (column A). If the share price subsequently drops to $30, your equity would rise to $4,500 (column B). If the share price subsequently rises to $70, your equity would fall to $500 (column C). Dividing these account equity values (line 6) by the then-current cost of buying back the stock

FAMOUS FAILURES IN FINANCE

Short Sellers Tip 60 Minutes

On March 1, 2015, the television news program, *60 Minutes*, ran a story alleging that Lumber Liquidators, a retail purveyor of home flooring products, was selling Chinese-made flooring that contained formaldehyde in concentrations that were up to 20 times greater than the legal limit in California. The day after the story was aired, Lumber Liquidators stock fell by 25%. Where did the producers at *60 Minutes* get the idea to investigate

Lumber Liquidators? Apparently Whitney Tilson, manager of the hedge fund Kase Capital, approached *60 Minutes* after he had conducted his own investigation and concluded that Lumber Liquidators was indeed selling flooring products that did not meet regulatory standards. Prior to giving *60 Minutes* the idea for the story, Tilson shorted 44,676 shares of Lumber Liquidators. Within days of the *60 Minutes* program being aired, Tilson had earned a profit on his short sale of $1.4 million.

TABLE 3.6   MARGIN POSITIONS ON SHORT SALES

Line	Item	A Initial Short Sale Price	B Subsequent Share Prices	C
1	Price per share	$ 50	$ 30	$ 70
2	Proceeds from initial short sale [(1) × 100 shares]	$5,000		
3	Initial margin deposit [0.50 × (2)]	$2,500		
4	Total deposit with broker [(2) + (3)]	$7,500	$ 7,500	$ 7,500
5	Current cost of buying back stock [(1) × 100 shares]	$5,000	$3,000	$7,000
6	Account equity [(4) − (5)]	$2,500	$4,500	$ 500
7	Actual margin [(6) ÷ (5)]	50%	150%	7.14%
8	Maintenance margin position [(7) > 30%?]	OK	OK	Margin call*

*Investor must either (a) deposit at least an additional $1,600 with the broker to bring the total deposit to $9,100 (i.e., $7,500 + $1,600), which would equal the current value of the 100 shares of $7,000 plus a 30% maintenance margin deposit of $2,100 (i.e., 0.30 × $7,000) or (b) buy back the 100 shares of stock and return them to the broker.

(line 5), we can calculate the actual margins at each share price (line 7). We see that at the current $50 price the actual margin is 50%, whereas at the $30 share price it is 150%, and at the $70 share price it is 7.14%.

As indicated in line 8, given the 30% maintenance margin requirement, your margin would be okay at the current price of $50 (column A) or lower (column B). But at the $70 share price, the 7.14% actual margin would be below the 30% maintenance margin, thereby resulting in a margin call. In that case (or whenever the actual margin on a short sale falls below the maintenance margin), you must respond to the margin call either by depositing additional funds with the broker or by buying the stock and covering (i.e., closing out) the short position.

If you wished to maintain the short position when the share price has risen to $70, you would have to deposit an additional $1,600 with the broker. Those funds would increase your total deposit to $9,100 (i.e., $7,500 + $1,600)—an amount equal to the $7,000 value of the shorted stock plus the 30% maintenance margin, or $2,100. Buying back the stock to cover the short position would cost $7,000, thereby resulting in the return of the $500 of equity in your account from your broker. Clearly, margin requirements tend to complicate the short-sale transaction and the impact of an increase in the shorted stock's share price on required deposits with the broker.

Advantages and Disadvantages The major advantage of selling short is, of course, the chance to profit from a price decline. The key disadvantage of many short-sale transactions is that the investor faces limited return opportunities along with high-risk exposure. The price of a security can fall only so far (to zero or near zero), yet there is really no limit to how far such securities can rise in price. (Remember, a short seller is hoping for a price decline; when a security goes up in price, a short seller loses.) For example, note in Table 3.5 that the stock in question cannot possibly fall by more than $50, yet who is to say how high its price can go?

A less serious disadvantage is that short sellers never earn dividend (or interest) income. In fact, short sellers owe the lender of the shorted security any dividends (or interest) paid while the transaction is outstanding. That is, if a dividend is paid during the course of a short-sale transaction, the short seller must pay an equal amount to the lender of the stock. (The mechanics of these payments are taken care of automatically by the short seller's broker.)

Uses of Short Selling Investors sell short primarily to seek speculative profits when they expect the price of a security to drop. Because the short seller is betting against the market, this approach is subject to a considerable amount of risk. The actual procedure works as demonstrated in Table 3.5. Note that had you been able to sell the stock at $50 per share and later repurchase it at $30 per share, you would have generated a profit of $2,000 (ignoring dividends and brokerage commissions). However, if the market had instead moved against you, all or most of your $5,000 investment could have been lost.

CONCEPTS IN REVIEW

Answers available at
http://www.pearsonhighered.com/smart

3.12 What is a long purchase? What expectation underlies such a purchase? What is margin trading, and what is the key reason why investors sometimes use it as part of a long purchase?

3.13 How does margin trading magnify profits and losses? What are the key advantages and disadvantages of margin trading?

3.14 Describe the procedures and regulations associated with margin trading. Be sure to explain restricted accounts, the maintenance margin, and the margin call. Define the term *debit balance*, and describe the common uses of margin trading.

3.15 What is the primary motive for short selling? Describe the basic short-sale procedure. Why must the short seller make an initial equity deposit?

3.16 What relevance do margin requirements have in the short-selling process? What would have to happen to experience a margin call on a short-sale transaction? What two actions could be used to remedy such a call?

3.17 Describe the key advantages and disadvantages of short selling. How are short sales used to earn speculative profits?

MyFinanceLab

Here is what you should know after reading this chapter. MyFinanceLab will help you identify what you know and where to go when you need to practice.

What You Should Know	Key Terms	Where to Practice
LG1 Identify the basic types of securities markets and describe their characteristics. Short-term investments trade in the money market; longer-term securities, such as stocks and bonds, trade in the capital market. New security issues are sold in the primary market. Investors buy and sell existing securities in the secondary markets.	ask price, *p. 96* bear markets, *p. 98* bid price, *p. 96* broker market, *p. 94* bull markets, *p. 98* capital market, *p. 88* dealer market, *p. 94* designated market maker (DMM), *p. 96* dual listing, *p. 96* electronic communications network (ECN), *p. 98* fourth market, *p. 98* initial public offering (IPO), *p. 88* investment banker, *p. 91* market makers, *p. 94* money market, *p. 88*	MyFinanceLab Study Plan 3.1

What You Should Know	Key Terms	Where to Practice
LG2 **Explain the initial public offering process.** The first public issue of a company's common stock is an IPO. The company selects an investment banker to sell the IPO. The lead investment banker may form a syndicate with other investment bankers and then create a selling group to sell the issue. The IPO process includes filing a registration statement with the Securities and Exchange Commission, getting SEC approval, promoting the offering to investors, pricing the issue, and selling the shares.		MyFinanceLab Study Plan 3.2
LG3 **Describe broker markets and dealer markets, and discuss how they differ from alternative trading systems.** In dealer markets, buy/sell orders are executed by market makers. The market makers are securities dealers who "make markets" by offering to buy or sell certain securities at stated bid/ask prices. Dealer markets also serve as primary markets for both IPOs and secondary distributions. Over-the-counter transactions in listed securities take place in the third market. Direct transactions between buyers and sellers are made in the fourth market. Market conditions are commonly classified as "bull" or "bear," depending on whether securities prices are generally rising or falling. Broker markets bring together buyers and sellers to make trades. Included are the New York Stock Exchange, the NYSE Amex, regional stock exchanges, foreign stock exchanges, options exchanges, and futures exchanges. In these markets the forces of supply and demand drive transactions and determine prices. These securities exchanges are secondary markets where existing securities trade.	over-the-counter (OTC) market, *p. 93* primary market, *p. 88* private placement, *p. 88* prospectus, *p. 89* public offering, *p. 88* red herring, *p. 89* rights offering, *p. 88* secondary distributions, *p. 97* secondary market, *p. 93* Securities and Exchange Commission (SEC), *p. 88* securities markets, *p. 88* selling group, *p. 91* third market, *p. 98* underwriting, *p. 91* underwriting syndicate, *p. 91*	MyFinanceLab Study Plan 3.3
LG4 **Review the key aspects of the globalization of securities markets, and discuss the importance of international markets.** Securities exchanges operate in over 100 countries—both large and small. Foreign security investments can be made indirectly by buying shares of a U.S.-based multinational with substantial foreign operations or by purchasing shares of a mutual fund that invests primarily in foreign securities. Direct foreign investment can be achieved by purchasing securities on foreign exchanges, by buying securities of foreign companies that are traded on U.S. exchanges, or by buying American depositary shares. International investments can enhance returns, but they entail added risk, particularly currency exchange risk.	American depositary receipts (ADRs), *p. 101* American depositary shares (ADSs), *p. 101* currency exchange rate, *p. 102* currency exchange risk, *p. 102* diversification, *p. 99* Yankee bonds, *p. 101*	MyFinanceLab Study Plan 3.4 Video Learning Aid for Problem P3.3

What You Should Know	Key Terms	Where to Practice
LG5 **Discuss trading hours and the regulation of securities markets.** Investors now can trade securities outside regular market hours (9:30 A.M. to 4:00 P.M., eastern time). Most after-hours markets are crossing markets, in which orders are filled only if they can be matched. Trading activity during these sessions can be quite risky. The securities markets are regulated by the federal Securities and Exchange Commission and by state commissions. The key federal laws regulating the securities industry are the Securities Act of 1933, the Securities Exchange Act of 1934, the Maloney Act of 1938, the Investment Company Act of 1940, the Investment Advisors Act of 1940, the Securities Acts Amendments of 1975, the Insider Trading and Fraud Act of 1988, the Sarbanes-Oxley Act of 2002, and the Dodd-Frank Wall Street Reform and Consumer Protection Act of 2010.	crossing markets, *p. 103* ethics, *p. 105* insider trading, *p. 104*	MyFinanceLab Study Plan 3.5
LG6 **Explain long purchases, margin transactions, and short sales.** Most investors make long purchases—that is, they buy securities—in expectation of price increases. Many investors establish margin accounts to use borrowed funds to enhance their buying power. The Federal Reserve Board establishes the margin requirement—the minimum investor equity in a margin transaction. The return on capital in a margin transaction is magnified for both positive returns and negative returns. Paper profits can be used to pyramid a margin account by investing its excess margin. The risks of margin trading are the chance of a restricted account or margin call and the consequences of magnified losses due to price declines. Short selling is used when a decline in security prices is anticipated. It involves selling securities, typically borrowed from the broker, to earn a profit by repurchasing them at a lower price in the future. The short seller makes an initial equity deposit with the broker. If the price of a shorted stock rises, the investor may receive a margin call and must then either increase the deposit with the broker or buy back the stock to cover the short position. The major advantage of selling short is the chance to profit from a price decline. The disadvantages of selling short are the unlimited potential for loss and the fact that short sellers never earn dividend (or interest) income. Short selling is used primarily to seek speculative profits.	debit balance, *p. 110* excess margin, *p. 111* financial leverage, *p. 106* initial margin, *p. 109* maintenance margin, *p. 109* long purchase, *p. 105* margin account, *p. 108* margin call, *p. 109* margin loan, *p. 108* margin requirement, *p. 106* margin trading, *p. 106* prime rate, *p. 108* pyramiding, *p. 111* restricted account, *p. 109* short selling, *p. 112*	MyFinanceLab Study Plan 3.6 Excel Tables 3.3, 3.5 Video Learning Aid for Problem P3.19

Log into MyFinanceLab, take a chapter test, and get a personalized Study Plan
that tells you which concepts you understand and which ones you need to
review. From there, MyFinanceLab will give you further practice, tutorials,
animations, videos, and guided solutions.
Log into http://www.myfinancelab.com

Discussion Questions

LG2   **Q3.1**   From 1999 to 2014, the average IPO rose by 19% in its first day of trading. In 1999, 117 deals doubled in price on the first day. What factors might contribute to the huge first-day returns on IPOs? Some critics of the current IPO system claim that underwriters may knowingly underprice an issue. Why might they do this? Why might issuing companies accept lower IPO prices? What impact do institutional investors have on IPO pricing?

LG1 LG3   **Q3.2**   Why do you think some large, well-known companies such as Cisco Systems, Intel, and Microsoft prefer to trade on the Nasdaq OMX markets rather than on an organized securities exchange such as the NYSE (for which they easily meet the listing requirements)? Discuss the pros and cons of listing on an organized securities exchange.

LG1 LG2 LG4   **Q3.3**   On the basis of the current structure of the world's financial markets and your knowledge of the NYSE and Nasdaq OMX markets, describe the key features, functions, and problems that would be faced by a single global market (exchange) on which transactions can be made in all securities of all of the world's major companies. Discuss the likelihood of such a market developing.

LG5   **Q3.4**   Critics of longer trading hours believe that expanded trading sessions turn the stock market into a casino and place the emphasis more on short-term gains than on long-term investment. Do you agree? Why or why not? Is it important to have a "breathing period" to reflect on the day's market activity? Why are smaller brokerages and ECNs, more than the NYSE and Nasdaq, pushing for longer trading hours?

LG6   **Q3.5**   Describe how, if at all, conservative and aggressive investors might use each of the following types of transactions as part of their investment programs. Contrast these two types of investors in view of these preferences.
a. Long purchase
b. Margin trading
c. Short selling

Problems   All problems are available on http://www.myfinancelab.com

LG4   **P3.1**   The current exchange rate between the U.S. dollar and the Japanese yen is 120 (yen/$). That is, 1 dollar can buy 120 yen. How many dollars would you get for 1,000 Japanese yen?

LG4   **P3.2**   An investor recently sold some stock in a European company that was worth 20,000 euros. The U.S.$/euro exchange rate is currently 1.300, meaning that 1 euro buys 1.3 dollars. How many U.S. dollars will the investor receive?

LG4   **P3.3**   In each of the following cases, calculate the price of one share of the foreign stock measured in United States dollars (US$).
a. A Belgian stock priced at 103.2 euros (€) when the exchange rate is 0.93€/US$.
b. A Swiss stock priced at 93.3 Swiss francs (Sf) when the exchange rate is 0.96Sf/US$.
c. A Japanese stock priced at 1,350 yen (¥) when the exchange rate is 110¥/US$.

LG4   **P3.4**   Erin McQueen purchased 50 shares of BMW, a German stock traded on the Frankfurt Exchange, for €64.5 (euros) per share exactly one year ago when the exchange rate was €0.67/US$1. Today the stock is trading at €71.8 per share, and the exchange rate is €0.75/US$1.

    a. Did the € depreciate or appreciate relative to the US$ during the past year? Explain.

    b. How much in US$ did Erin pay for her 50 shares of BMW when she purchased them a year ago?

    c. For how much in US$ can Erin sell her BMW shares today?

    d. Ignoring brokerage fees and taxes, how much profit (or loss) in US$ will Erin realize on her BMW stock if she sells it today?

LG4   **P3.5**   Harold Perto purchased 100 shares of Barclays, a U.K. financial services firm, when they were trading for £260 (pounds sterling) and the exchange rate between British pounds and U.S. dollars was $1.50 per pound. A few months later, Harold sold his Barclays shares at a price of £280, converting the proceeds back into dollars at an exchange rate of $1.25 per pound. How much money did Harold spend (in U.S. dollars) to purchase the shares, and how much did he receive when he sold them?

LG5   **P3.6**   An investor believes that the U.S. dollar will rise in value relative to the Japanese yen. The same investor is considering two investments with identical risk and return characteristics: One is a Japanese yen investment and the other is a U.S. dollar investment. Should the investor purchase the Japanese yen investment?

LG6   **P3.7**   Elmo Inc.'s stock is currently selling at $60 per share. For each of the following situations (ignoring brokerage commissions), calculate the gain or loss that Courtney Schinke realizes if she makes a 100-share transaction.

    a. She sells short and repurchases the borrowed shares at $70 per share.

    b. She takes a long position and sells the stock at $75 per share.

    c. She sells short and repurchases the borrowed shares at $45 per share.

    d. She takes a long position and sells the stock at $60 per share.

LG6   **P3.8**   Assume that an investor buys 100 shares of stock at $50 per share, putting up a 60% margin.

    a. What is the debit balance in this transaction?

    b. How much equity capital must the investor provide to make this margin transaction?

LG6   **P3.9**   Assume that an investor buys 100 shares of stock at $50 per share, putting up a 60% margin. If the stock rises to $60 per share, what is the investor's new margin position?

LG6   **P3.10**   Assume that an investor buys 100 shares of stock at $35 per share, putting up a 75% margin.

    a. What is the debit balance in this transaction?

    b. How much equity funds must the investor provide to make this margin transaction?

    c. If the stock rises to $55 per share, what is the investor's new margin position?

LG6   **P3.11**   Miguel Torres purchased 100 shares of CantWin.com.com for $50 per share, using as little of his own money as he could. His broker has a 50% initial margin requirement and a 30% maintenance margin requirement. The price of the stock falls to $30 per share. What does Miguel need to do?

LG6   **P3.12**   Jerri Kingston bought 100 shares of stock at $80 per share using an initial margin of 50%. Given a maintenance margin of 25%, how far does the stock have to drop before Jerri faces a margin call? (Assume that there are no other securities in the margin account.)

LG6   **P3.13**   An investor buys 200 shares of stock selling at $80 per share using a margin of 60%. The stock pays annual dividends of $1 per share. A margin loan can be obtained at an annual interest cost of 8%. Determine what return on invested capital the investor will realize if the price of the stock increases to $104 within six months. What is the annualized rate of return on this transaction?

LG6 **P3.14** Marlene Bellamy purchased 300 shares of Writeline Communications stock at $55 per share using the prevailing minimum initial margin requirement of 50%. She held the stock for exactly four months and sold it without brokerage costs at the end of that period. During the 4-month holding period, the stock paid $1.50 per share in cash dividends. Marlene was charged 9% annual interest on the margin loan. The minimum maintenance margin was 25%.

    a. Calculate the initial value of the transaction, the debit balance, and the equity position on Marlene's transaction.

    b. For each of the following share prices, calculate the actual margin percentage, and indicate whether Marlene's margin account would have excess equity, would be restricted, or would be subject to a margin call.

       1. $45

       2. $70

       3. $35

    c. Calculate the dollar amount of (1) dividends received and (2) interest paid on the margin loan during the 4-month holding period.

    d. Use each of the following sale prices at the end of the 4-month holding period to calculate Marlene's annualized rate of return on the Writeline Communications stock transaction.

       1. $50

       2. $60

       3. $70

LG6 **P3.15** Not long ago, Jack Edwards bought 200 shares of Almost Anything Inc. at $45 per share; he bought the stock on margin of 60%. The stock is now trading at $60 per share, and the Federal Reserve has recently lowered *initial margin* requirements to 50%. Jack now wants to do a little pyramiding and buy another 300 shares of the stock. What is the minimum amount of equity that he'll have to put up in this transaction?

LG6 **P3.16** An investor short sells 100 shares of a stock for $20 per share. The initial margin is 50%. How much equity will be required in the account to complete this transaction?

LG6 **P3.17** An investor short sells 100 shares of a stock for $20 per share. The initial margin is 50%. Ignoring transaction costs, how much will be in the investor's account after this transaction if this is the only transaction the investor has undertaken and the investor has deposited only the required amount?

LG6 **P3.18** An investor short sells 100 shares of a stock for $20 per share. The initial margin is 50%, and the maintenance margin is 30%. The price of the stock falls to $12 per share. What is the margin, and will there be a *margin call*?

LG6 **P3.19** An investor short sells 100 shares of a stock for $20 per share. The *initial margin* is 50%, and the maintenance margin is 30%. The price of the stock rises to $28 per share. What is the margin, and will there be a margin call?

LG6 **P3.20** Calculate the profit or loss per share realized on each of the following short-sale transactions.

Transaction	Stock Sold Short at Price/Share	Stock Purchased to Cover Short at Price/Share
A	$75	$83
B	$30	$24
C	$18	$15
D	$27	$32
E	$53	$45

LG6 **P3.21** Charlene Hickman expected the price of Bio International shares to drop in the near future in response to the expected failure of its new drug to pass FDA tests. As a result, she sold short 200 shares of Bio International at $27.50. How much would Charlene earn or lose on this transaction if she repurchased the 200 shares four months later at each of the following prices per share?

  a. $24.75
  b. $25.13
  c. $31.25
  d. $27.00

Visit http://www.myfinancelab.com for web exercises,
spreadsheets, and other online resources.

Case Problem 3.1   Dara's Dilemma: What to Buy?

LG6 Dara Simmons, a 40-year-old financial analyst and divorced mother of two teenage children, considers herself a savvy investor. She has increased her investment portfolio considerably over the past five years. Although she has been fairly conservative with her investments, she now feels more confident in her investment knowledge and would like to branch out into some new areas that could bring higher returns. She has between $20,000 and $25,000 to invest.

Attracted to the hot market for technology stocks, Dara was interested in purchasing a tech IPO stock and identified NewestHighTech.com, a company that makes sophisticated computer chips for wireless Internet connections, as a likely prospect. The 1-year-old company had received some favorable press when it got early-stage financing and again when its chip was accepted by a major cell phone manufacturer.

Dara also was considering an investment in 400 shares of Casinos International common stock, currently selling for $54 per share. After a discussion with a friend who is an economist with a major commercial bank, Dara believes that the long-running bull market is due to cool off and that economic activity will slow down. With the aid of her stockbroker, Dara researches Casinos International's current financial situation and finds that the future success of the company may hinge on the outcome of pending court proceedings on the firm's application to open a new floating casino on a nearby river. If the permit is granted, it seems likely that the firm's stock will experience a rapid increase in value, regardless of economic conditions. On the other hand, if the company fails to get the permit, the falling stock price will make it a good candidate for a short sale.

Dara felt that the following alternatives were open to her:

Alternative 1: Invest $20,000 in NewestHighTech.com when it goes public.

Alternative 2: Buy Casinos International now at $54 per share and follow the company closely.

Alternative 3: Sell Casinos short at $54 in anticipation that the company's fortunes will change for the worse.

Alternative 4: Wait to see what happens with the casino permit and then decide whether to buy or short sell the Casinos International stock.

Questions

a. Evaluate each of these alternatives. On the basis of the limited information presented, recommend the one you feel is best.

b. If Casinos International's stock price rises to $60, what will happen under alternatives 2 and 3? Evaluate the pros and cons of these outcomes.

c. If the stock price drops to $45, what will happen under alternatives 2 and 3? Evaluate the pros and cons of these outcomes.

Case Problem 3.2   Ravi Dumar's High-Flying Margin Account

Ravi Dumar is a stockbroker who lives with his wife, Sasha, and their five children in Milwaukee, Wisconsin. Ravi firmly believes that the only way to make money in the market is to follow an aggressive investment posture—for example, to use margin trading. In fact, Ravi has built himself a substantial margin account over the years. He currently holds $75,000 worth of stock in his margin account, though the debit balance in the account amounts to only $30,000. Recently Ravi uncovered a stock that, on the basis of extensive analysis, he feels is about to take off. The stock, Running Shoes (RS), currently trades at $20 per share. Ravi feels it should soar to at least $50 within a year. RS pays no dividends, the prevailing initial margin requirement is 50%, and margin loans are now carrying an annual interest charge of 10%. Because Ravi feels so strongly about RS, he wants to do some pyramiding by using his margin account to purchase 1,000 shares of the stock.

Questions

a. Discuss the concept of pyramiding as it applies to this investment situation.

b. What is the present margin position (in percent) of Ravi's account?

c. Ravi buys the 1,000 shares of RS through his margin account (bear in mind that this is a $20,000 transaction).

    1. What will the margin position of the account be after the RS transaction if Ravi follows the prevailing initial margin (50%) and uses $10,000 of his money to buy the stock?

    2. What if he uses only $2,500 equity and obtains a margin loan for the balance ($17,500)?

    3. How do you explain the fact that the stock can be purchased with only 12.5% margin when the prevailing initial margin requirement is 50%?

d. Assume that Ravi buys 1,000 shares of RS stock at $20 per share with a minimum cash investment of $2,500 and that the stock does take off and its price rises to $40 per share in one year.

    1. What is the return on invested capital for this transaction?

    2. What return would Ravi have earned if he had bought the stock without margin—that is, if he had used all his own money?

e. What do you think of Ravi's idea to pyramid? What are the risks and rewards of this strategy?

Excel@Investing

Excel@Investing

You have just learned about the mechanics of margin trading and want to take advantage of the potential benefits of financial leverage. You have decided to open a margin account with your broker and to secure a margin loan. The specifics of the account are as follows:

- Initial margin requirement is 70%.

- Maintenance margin is 30%.

- You are informed that if the value of your account falls below the maintenance margin, your account will be subject to a margin call.

You have been following the price movements of a stock over the past year and believe that it is currently undervalued and that the price will rise in the near future. You feel that opening a margin account is a good investment strategy. You have decided to purchase three round lots (i.e., 300 shares) of the stock at its current price of $25 per share.

Create a spreadsheet similar to the spreadsheet for Table 3.3, which can be viewed at http://www.myfinancelab.com, to model and analyze the following market transactions.

Questions

a. Calculate the value of your investment in the stock if you did not make use of margin trading. In other words, how much must you invest if you fund your purchase with 100% cash equity?

b. Calculate the debit balance and the cash equity in the investment at the time of opening a margin account, adhering to the initial margin requirement.

c. If you use margin and the price of the stock rises by $15 to $40/share, calculate the capital gain earned and the return on investor's equity.

d. What is the current margin percentage based on item **c**?

e. If you use margin and the price of the stock falls by $15 to $10/share, calculate the capital loss and the respective return on investor's equity.

f. What is the new margin percentage based on item **e**, and what is the implication for you, the investor?

4

Firms and the Financial Market

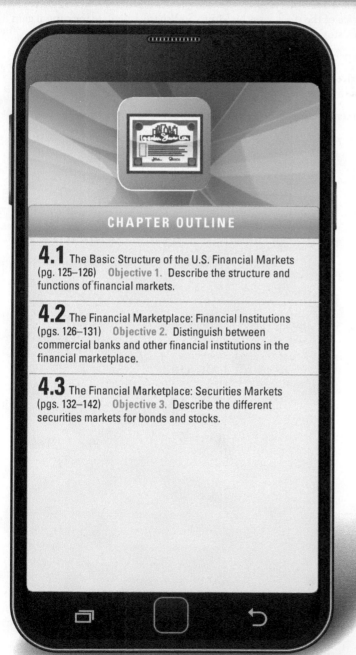

CHAPTER OUTLINE

Principles P2, P4, and P5 Applied

When hen reading this chapter, you should keep in mind three of the basic principles of finance: P Principle 2: **There Is a Risk-Return Tradeoff**, P Principle 4: **Market Prices Reflect Information**, and P Principle 5: **Individuals Respond to Incentives**. Financial markets are organized to offer investors a wide range of investment opportunities that have different risks and different expected rates of return that reflect those risks. The goal of these markets is to provide investors with opportunities that best fit their risk and return objectives, while at the same time to provide businesses with opportunities to raise funds—to train employees, do research, and build new plants—at prices that appropriately reflect the prospects of the business.

If you have a student loan or a car loan, you have already been introduced to financial markets. You are spending more than you currently earn and have borrowed money through the financial markets to make ends meet. But once you graduate and enter the workforce, you may earn more than you spend and therefore be able to save. Once again, you will become involved in the financial markets, but this time as a saver rather than a borrower. This pattern of borrowing and saving also holds true for businesses, as they borrow money to finance their investments and as they invest their savings in the hopes of generating even more money in the future.

In this chapter we provide a preliminary overview of the U.S. financial markets. We first review some of the primary institutions that facilitate the transfer of money from investors to companies and individuals. Next, we discuss the securities markets in which different securities issued by businesses are bought and sold. The primary objective of this chapter is to provide a sense of the richness of the financial marketplace, the critical role that it plays in each of our lives, and how corporations use the financial markets to raise capital.

REGARDLESS OF YOUR MAJOR...

"Defined Benefit vs. Defined Contribution Retirement Plans"

When you start your first job after graduating, your employer will probably give you the option of automatically investing part of your paycheck each pay period for your retirement. Learning about the financial markets will help you analyze your options and make good selections. Twenty years ago, retirement plans were typically **defined benefit plans**. You would work for only one company, and the company would reward your loyalty and hard work by paying you a pension during your retirement based on your years of employment and the level of pay that you earned. In other words, the company set aside money to pay your pension benefit and invested it for you. Today, people change jobs often, and pension plans like the one just described are very rare. Instead, most employers now offer their employees defined **contribution plans**, such as a 401(k) savings plan. With a defined contribution pension plan, you, the employee, and your employer make periodic cash contributions to your retirement fund that you must take responsibility for investing. So, it doesn't matter whether you're a doctor, lawyer, truck driver, or salesperson, you are going to be a pension fund manager.

Your Turn: See Study Question 4–1.

4.1   The Basic Structure of the U.S. Financial Markets

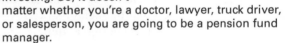

We have showed that businesses typically opt to take on the form of a corporation when they need to raise large amounts of capital. In this chapter, we will demonstrate how a corporation raises capital using the U.S. financial markets.

A financial market is any place where money and credit are exchanged. When you take out a car loan from your bank, you participate in the financial markets. Within the financial markets there are three principal sets of players that interact:

1. **Borrowers.** Those who need money to finance their purchases. This includes businesses that need money to finance their investments or to expand their inventories as well as individuals who borrow money to purchase a new automobile or a new home.

2. **Savers (Investors).** Those who have money to invest. These are principally individuals who save money for a variety of reasons, such as accumulating a down payment for a home or saving for a return to graduate school. Firms also save when they have excess cash.

3. **Financial Institutions (Intermediaries).** The financial institutions and markets that help bring borrowers and savers together. The financial institution you are probably most familiar with is the **commercial bank,** a financial institution that accepts deposits and makes loans, such as Bank of America or Citibank, where you might have a checking account. However, as we discuss in the next section, there are many other types of financial institutions that bring together borrowers and savers.

4.2 The Financial Marketplace: Financial Institutions

The financial markets facilitate the movement of money from savers, who tend to be individuals, to borrowers, who tend to be businesses. In return for the use of the savers' money, borrowers provide the savers with a return on their investment.

As shown in Figure 4.1, the institutions that make up the financial marketplace consist of commercial banks, finance companies, insurance companies, investment banks, and investment companies. We call these institutions that help bring together individuals and businesses **financial intermediaries,** because these institutions stand between those who have money to invest and those who need money. Financial markets are often described by the maturities of the securities traded in them. For example, the **money markets** are markets for short-term debt instruments, with "short-term" meaning maturities of one year or less. On the other hand, **capital markets** are markets for long-term financial instruments. "Long-term" here means having maturities that extend beyond one year.

There are no national boundaries on financial markets. A borrower in Brazil, for example, might borrow money from a bank in London to finance a plant expansion. Furthermore, it's not just individuals and companies that raise money and invest in the global financial markets. Governments can enter the financial markets when they are experiencing a deficit and need to raise money to finance their expenditures. Governments can also enter financial markets when they have more money than they plan to spend and want to invest the surplus. For example, the Chinese government invests huge sums of money in U.S. Treasury bonds, which are long-term debt securities issued by the U.S. government.

Commercial Banks: Everyone's Financial Marketplace

As previously mentioned, the commercial bank is probably the first financial intermediary each of us has dealt with in the financial marketplace. And, because they provide many firms with their initial funding, commercial banks also tend to be one of the first financial intermediaries that businesses deal with. Banks collect the savings of individuals as well as businesses and then lend these pooled savings to other individuals and businesses. They make money by charging a rate of interest to borrowers that exceeds the rate they pay to savers. They are also one of the major lenders to businesses.

In the United States, although banks can loan money to industrial corporations, banks are prohibited by law from owning them. This restriction prevents banks from loaning money to the industrial firms that they own; however, this restriction is not universal around the world. For instance, in countries such as Japan and Germany,

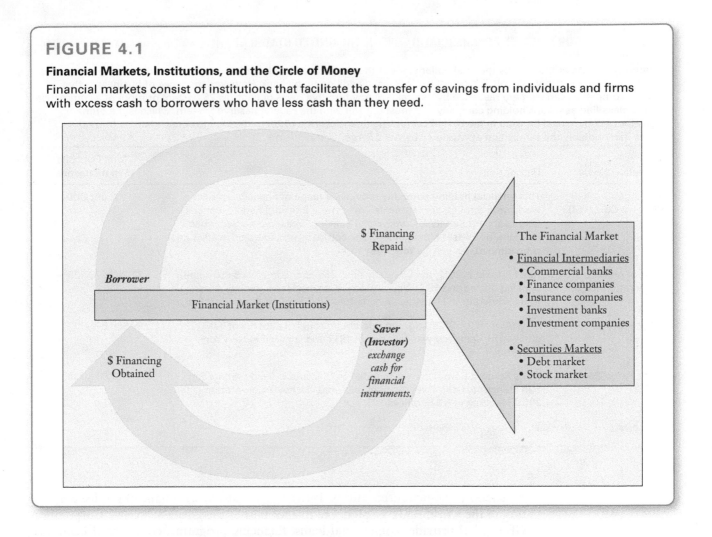

FIGURE 4.1

Financial Markets, Institutions, and the Circle of Money

Financial markets consist of institutions that facilitate the transfer of savings from individuals and firms with excess cash to borrowers who have less cash than they need.

$ Financing
Repaid

Borrower

Financial Market (Institutions)

*Saver
(Investor)
exchange
cash for
financial
instruments.*

$ Financing
Obtained

The Financial Market

• Financial Intermediaries
  • Commercial banks
  • Finance companies
  • Insurance companies
  • Investment banks
  • Investment companies

• Securities Markets
  • Debt market
  • Stock market

banks are among the largest owners of industrial firms. Table 4.1 lists the four largest banks in the United States and their total deposits. It is very possible that you will recognize your personal bank among this list because the very largest banks operate throughout the entire United States, and the 25 largest banks hold more than 50 percent of total deposits.

Non-Bank Financial Intermediaries

In addition to commercial banks, there are a number of highly specialized financial intermediaries that also provide financial services to businesses. These include:

- financial services corporations, such as General Electric's (GE) GE Capital division and CIT Corporation (CIT);

- insurance companies, such as American International Group, Inc. (AIG), and Prudential (PRU);

- investment banks, such as Goldman Sachs (GS) and Morgan Stanley (MS); and

- investment companies, including mutual funds, hedge funds, and private equity firms.

TABLE 4.1   FOUR LARGEST COMMERCIAL BANKS IN THE UNITED STATES AT THE END OF THIRD QUARTER 2009

Commercial banks are ranked by the total dollar value of their deposits. Most large banks are owned by holding companies, which are companies that own other types of businesses in addition to the bank. However, the types of businesses that holding companies can own are restricted by federal law. Any firm that owns or controls 25 percent or more of a commercial bank is classified as a bank holding company and must register with the Federal Reserve System, which is the primary regulator of commercial banking in the United States. The financial crisis of 2008–2009 led to consolidations of weaker banks, most notably the acquisition of Wachovia by Wells Fargo.

Institution Name	Description	Total Deposits ($ in thousands)
JPMorgan Chase & Co. (JPM)	This financial holding company provides a range of financial services worldwide through six segments: Investment Banking, Retail Financial Services, Card Services, Commercial Banking, Treasury and Securities Services, and Asset Management. The company was founded in 1823 and is headquartered in New York, New York.	$1,162,998,000
Bank of America Corporation (BAC)	As of August 2, 2012, the company operated approximately 5,693 retail banking offices and 18,000 automated teller machines. Bank of America was founded in 1874 and is headquartered in Charlotte, North Carolina.	$1,062,273,625
Citigroup, Inc. (C)	As of August 3, 2012, Citigroup operated through a network of 1,036 offices. The company was founded in 1812 and is based in New York, New York.	$ 950,510,000
Wells Fargo Bank (WFC)	Wells Fargo & Company was founded in 1852 and is headquartered in San Francisco, California. The bank acquired Wachovia Corporation in 2008, resulting in 6,345 offices.	$ 921,071,000

(Source: http://www.ibanknet.com/scripts/callreports/fiList.aspx?type=031)

Financial Services Corporations Perhaps the best-known financial service corporation in the world is GE Capital, the finance unit of the General Electric Corporation. GE Capital provides commercial loans, financing programs, commercial insurance, equipment leasing of every kind, and other services, in over 35 countries around the world. GE provides credit services to more than 130 million customers, including consumers, retailers, auto dealers, and mortgage lenders, offering products and services ranging from credit cards to debt consolidation to home equity loans. CIT Group, Inc. is another commercial finance company that offers a wide range of financing services to businesses. The important thing to note here is that although financial services corporations are in the lending or financing business, they are not commercial banks.

Insurance Companies Insurance companies are by definition in the business of selling insurance to individuals and businesses to protect their investments. This means that they collect premiums, hold the premiums in reserves until there is an insured loss, and then pay out claims to the holders of the insurance contracts. Note that in the course of collecting and holding premiums, the insurance companies build up huge pools of reserves to pay these claims. These reserves are then used in various types of investments, including loans to individuals and businesses. American International Group, Inc. (AIG) is now a household name because of the debt market crisis of 2008 and the ensuing government bailout. However, the company's business activities serve as an example of the degree to which insurance companies have become involved in business finance. AIG not only sells insurance products but also provides financial services, including aircraft and equipment leasing, consumer finance, insurance premium financing, and debt and loan insurance. Of particular note in this listing of services is debt and loan insurance, which includes selling guarantees to lenders that reimburse them should the loans they made go into default. This type of transaction is called a **credit default swap.**

Investment Banks **Investment banks** are specialized financial intermediaries that help companies and governments raise money and provide advisory services to client firms when they enter into major transactions such as buying or merging with other firms. When we look at raising funds, we will take an in-depth look at investment banking. Prominent firms that provide investment banking services include Bank of America, Merrill Lynch, Barclays, Citigroup, Credit Suisse, Deutsche Bank, Goldman Sachs, HSBC, JPMorgan Chase, Morgan Stanley, and UBS AG.

Investment Companies

Investment companies are financial institutions that pool the savings of individual savers and invest the money, purely for investment purposes, in the securities issued by other companies.

Mutual Funds and Exchange-Traded Funds (ETFs) Perhaps the most widely known type of investment company is the **mutual fund,** a special type of intermediary through which individuals can invest in virtually all of the securities offered in the financial markets.[1] When individuals invest in a mutual fund, they receive shares in a fund that is professionally managed according to a stated investment objective or goal—for example, investing only in international stocks. Shares in the mutual fund grant ownership claim to a proportion of the mutual fund's portfolio.

A share in a mutual fund is not really like a share of stock because you can only buy and sell shares in the mutual fund directly from the mutual fund itself. The price that you pay when you buy your shares and the price you receive when you sell your shares is called the mutual fund's **net asset value (NAV),** which is calculated daily based on the total value of the fund divided by the number of mutual fund shares outstanding. In effect, as the value of the mutual fund investments goes up, so does the price of the mutual fund's shares.

Mutual funds can either be *load* or *no-load* funds. A **load fund** is a mutual fund that is sold through a broker, financial advisor, or financial planner who earns a commission in the form of the load fee when he or she sells shares of the mutual fund. The term *load* refers to the sales commission you pay when acquiring ownership shares. These commissions can be quite large, typically in the 3.0 to 6.0 percent range, but in some cases they can run as high as 8.5 percent. A mutual fund that doesn't charge a commission is referred to as a **no-load fund.** When you purchase a no-load mutual fund, you generally don't deal with a broker or advisor. Instead, you deal directly with the mutual fund investment company via its website, by direct mail, or through an 800 telephone number.

An **exchange-traded fund** (or **ETF**) is very much like a mutual fund except for the fact that the ownership shares in the ETF can be bought and sold on the stock exchanges. Most ETFs track an index, such as the Dow Jones Industrial Average or the S&P 500, and generally have relatively low expenses.

[1]For a more in-depth discussion of mutual funds go to http://www.sec.gov/answers/mutfund.htm.

Controlling Costs in Mutual Funds

In choosing the right mutual fund, one thing is clear—costs kill. You will want to pick your fund with an eye toward keeping expenses down.

In fact, the Securities and Exchange Commission has put together a website (www.sec.gov/investor/tools/mfcc/mfcc-int.htm) to show you how much damage mutual fund expenses will do to your investment. If you start with $10,000 and invest it for 30 years, achieving gross returns (before expenses) of 10.2 percent (the market average for the last three-quarters of a century), and assuming fund operating expenses of 1.4 percent (the average expense on a U.S. domestic stock fund), your $10,000 will grow to $120,713. That sounds pretty good until you notice that the cost of that 1.4 percent operating expense plus foregone earnings on your investment totals $63,554! That's over 34 percent of the gross earnings of the fund. If you knock expenses down to 0.18 percent, your investment grows to $174,572 and your expenses drop down to $9,695!

It is possible to cut your expenses down to as little as 0.10 percent by investing in an index fund (i.e., a fund that tries to track a market index, such as the S&P 500, by buying the stocks that make up that

index). In general, index funds perform better than the actively managed funds. In fact, from 1985 to 2000, 84.5 percent of U.S. actively managed stock mutual funds (as opposed to index funds) underperformed the S&P 500 index, with 77.5 percent underperforming over the entire 10 years and 81.6 percent underperforming in the most recent 5 years. According to a study from Jeremy J. Siegel's book *Stocks for the Long Run*, between 1982 and 2003, there were only three years in which more than 50 percent of mutual funds beat the S&P 500.

Your Turn: See Study Question 4–9

Mutual funds and ETFs provide a cost-effective way to diversify, which reduces risk—a great benefit for the small investor. If you only have $10,000 to invest, it would be difficult to diversify by purchasing shares of individual companies, as you would have to pay a brokerage commission for each individual stock you purchase. For example, buying 50 different stocks is likely to cost you $500 or more in commissions, which would be 5 percent of the amount invested. By buying a mutual fund or ETF you can indirectly purchase a portfolio of 50 or more stocks with just one transaction.

Hedge Funds A **hedge fund** is very much like a mutual fund, but hedge funds are less regulated and tend to take more risk. They also tend to more actively influence the managers of the corporations that they invest in. Because of the higher risk, hedge funds are open to a limited range of investors who are deemed to be sufficiently savvy. Only an **accredited investor,** which means an individual with a net worth that exceeds $1 million, can invest in a hedge fund.

Management fees are also quite a bit higher for hedge funds; they typically run at about 2 percent of the assets and include an incentive fee (typically 20 percent of profits) based on the fund's overall performance.

Private Equity Firms A **private equity firm** is a financial intermediary that invests in equities that are not traded on the public capital markets. Two types of private equity firms dominate this group: venture capital (VC) firms and leveraged buyout (LBO) firms. **Venture capital firms** raise money from investors (wealthy people and other financial institutions), which they then use to provide financing for private start-up companies when they are first founded. For example, Sevin Rosen Funds, established in 1980, has provided venture financing to Cypress Semiconductor (CY) and Silicon Graphics (SGIC). Kleiner Perkins Caufield & Byers, or KPCB as it is commonly called, is a venture capital firm located in Silicon Valley. KPCB is perhaps best known today for its involvement in the initial financing of Google (GOOG). It has also partnered with Apple to found the iFund™, a $100 million investment initiative that will fund market-changing ideas and products that extend the iPhone and iPod Touch platform.

The second major category of private equity firms is the **leveraged buyout fund**. These funds acquire established firms that typically have not been performing very well with the objective of making them profitable again and then selling them. LBO funds have been the subject of a number of movies, including *Barbarians at the Gate, Other People's Money,* and *Wall Street.*

Prominent LBO private equity firms include Cerberus Capital Management, L.P., which purchased the Chrysler Corporation from Daimler Benz, and TPG (formerly Texas Pacific Group), which has invested in a number of prominent firms, including Continental Airlines (CAL), Ducati (DMH.BE), Neiman Marcus, Burger King (BKC), MGM (MGM), Harrah's (HAG.HM), and Freescale Semiconductor (FSL-B). A third well-known LBO private equity firm is KKR (Kohlberg, Kravis, and Roberts), whose investment in the likes of RJR Nabisco provided the storyline for the popular movie *Barbarians at the Gate.*

The amount of money managed by private equity firms has grown dramatically over the last three decades, with new funds raised surpassing $262 billion in 2011. Three-quarters of the total is raised in North America; the majority of the remainder is raised in Europe. Of the total amount of money managed by private equity firms, roughly two-thirds is invested in the buyout or LBO category. In fact, LBO transactions grew from $7.5 billion in 1991 to $500 billion in 2006! But as you might expect, the number of deals dropped dramatically in the fourth quarter of 2008 and 2009, and is still not up to the 2006 level. However, the dollar amount of capital invested by the private equity intermediaries understates their importance to the economy. Private equity funding is largely responsible for financing the birth of new businesses and underwriting the renovation of old and faltering businesses.

CONCEPT CHECK: 4.2 Before you move on to 4.3	
1.	Explain how individuals and firms use financial intermediaries to raise money in the financial markets.
2.	How do commercial banks differ from other non-bank financial intermediaries?
3.	What are examples of investment companies?
4.	What is a hedge fund, and how does it differ from a mutual fund?
5.	What are the two principal types of private equity firms?

4.3 The Financial Marketplace: Securities Markets

A **security** is a negotiable instrument that represents a financial claim. It can take the form of ownership (stocks) or a debt agreement. The securities markets allow businesses and individual investors to trade the securities issued by public corporations. Public corporations are those whose debt and equity are traded in public markets. Securities markets are typically discussed in terms of the primary and secondary markets.

A **primary market** is a market in which new, as opposed to previously issued, securities are bought and sold for the first time. In this market, firms issue new securities to raise money that they can then use to help finance their businesses. The key feature of the primary market is that the firms selling securities actually receive the money raised.

The **secondary market** is where all subsequent trading of previously issued securities takes place. In this market the issuing firm does not receive any new financing, as the securities it has sold are simply being transferred from one investor to another. The principal benefit of the secondary market for the shareholders of firms that sell their securities to the public is liquidity. That is, if you purchased some of the shares of Google when it went public, you could easily sell those shares in the secondary market if you decided you no longer wanted to hold them. This ability to sell when you want to means that your Google stock is a very liquid investment. As a result, investors are more willing to invest in these securities, which benefits the issuing firm.

How Securities Markets Bring Corporations and Investors Together

Figure 4.2 describes the role of securities markets in bringing investors together with businesses looking for financing. In this regard, the securities markets are just another component of the financial marketplace. They are unique, however, in that investors in securities markets provide money directly to the firms that need it, as opposed to making deposits in commercial banks that then loan money to those firms.

We can think of the process of raising money in the securities markets in terms of the four-step process highlighted in Figure 4.2:

Step 1. **The firm sells securities to investors.** Corporations raise money in the securities markets by selling either debt or equity. When the firm initially sells the securities to the public, it is considered to take place in the primary markets. This is the only time the firm receives money in return for its securities.

Step 2. **The firm invests the funds it raises in its business.** The corporation invests the cash raised in the security market in hopes that it will generate cash flows—for example, it may invest in a new restaurant, a new hotel, a factory expansion, or a new product line.

Step 3. **The firm distributes the cash earned from its investments.** The cash flow from the firm's investments is reinvested in the corporation, paid to the government in taxes, or distributed to the investors who own the securities issued in Step 1. In the latter case, the cash is distributed to the investors who loaned the firm money (that is, bought the firm's debt securities) through the payment of interest and principal. Cash is paid to the investors who bought equity (stock) through the payment of cash dividends or the repurchase of the shares of the firm's previously issued stock.

Step 4. **Securities trading in the secondary market.** Immediately after the securities are sold to the public, the investors who purchased them are free to resell them to other investors. These subsequent transactions take place in the secondary market.

FIGURE 4.2

Security Markets Provide a Link between the Corporation and Investors

Step 1: Initially, the corporation raises funds in the financial markets by selling securities (a primary market transaction). **Step 2:** The corporation then invests this cash in return-generating assets—new projects.
Step 3: The cash flow from those assets is either reinvested in the corporation, given back to the investors, or paid to the government in the form of taxes. **Step 4**: Immediately after the securities have been issued, they are traded among investors in the secondary market, thereby setting their market price.

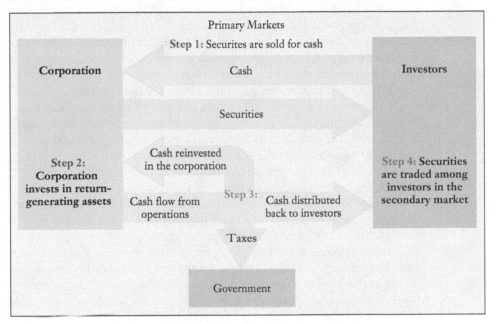

Types of Securities

If you read the financial section of your newspaper or watch financial TV channels such as CNBC, you are already aware of the wide variety of investment alternatives to choose from. These choices fall into one of two basic categories: debt and equity.

Debt Securities Firms borrow money by selling **debt securities** in the debt market. If the debt must be repaid in less than a year, these securities are sold in the short-term debt market, also called the money market. If the debt has a **maturity** (the length of time until the debt is due) between 1 and 10 years, it is often referred to as a **note,** and if longer than 10 years it is called a **bond** and is sold in the capital market. The capital market refers to the market for long-term financial instruments. The vast majority of these bonds pay a fixed interest rate, which means that the interest the owner of the bond receives never changes over its lifetime. Bonds are generally described using fairly exotic terminology. For example, we might say that a bond has a **face** or **par value** of $1,000 and that it pays an 8 percent **coupon rate** with two payments per year. What this means is that when the bond matures and the issuer (borrower) has to repay it, the owner of the bond (the lender) will receive a payment of $1,000. In the meantime, the holder will receive an interest payment every six months equal to $40, or $80 per year, which is 8 percent of $1,000.

Equity Securities Equity securities represent ownership of the corporation. There are two major types of equity securities: *common stock* and *preferred stock*. When you buy equity security you are making an investment that you expect will generate a return. However, unlike a bond, which provides a promised set of interest payments and a schedule for the repayment of principal, the returns earned from an equity security are less certain. To further explore this topic, let's take a brief look at both types of equity securities.

Common Stock Common stock is a security that represents equity ownership in a corporation, provides voting rights, and entitles the holder to a share of the company's success in the form of dividends and any capital appreciation in the value of the security. Investors who purchase common stock are the residual owners of the firm. This means that the common stockholder's return is earned only after all other security-holder claims (debt and preferred equity) have been satisfied in full.

If you were to purchase 100 shares of Disney's common stock, you would be a part-owner in the company. In essence, you would own an interest in the firm's studios, a piece of its movies, and a piece of its theme parks, including the new park in Shanghai. The more shares you buy, the bigger the portion of Disney you own. What do you get as an owner of Disney's stock? Don't count on free tickets to Disney World or a copy of the latest *Pirates of the Caribbean* movie. As an owner of the firm, you will have voting rights that entitle you to vote for the members of the firm's board of directors who oversee the selection of the management team. But as a small-time investor, you will have limited voting rights—your 100 shares of Disney's stock give you about 0.00000556 percent of Disney's shares. So, you aren't going to have much say about who gets elected to the Disney board of directors. Nonetheless, if Disney earns a profit, you will probably receive a portion of those profits in the form of a dividend payment. *It should be noted that unlike bond payments, firms don't have to pay dividends.* For example, if a company needs money to invest in a new product or project, it can choose to retain all of its earnings within the firm and pay no dividends.

Generally, firms that earn higher profits can pay higher dividends, and this often means that investors place a higher value on that firm's stock. For example, in 1999 the stock price of Qualcomm, a high-tech communications firm, went up 2,621 percent! However, when Qualcomm's profits and dividends, and people's expectations about its future prospects, deteriorated, its stock price fell by 50 percent in 2000, another 26 percent in 2001, and then by another drop of 30 percent in 2002. Since the end of 2002 there have been ups and downs, but by 2013 the price of Qualcomm rose almost three-fold from its 2003 level. This all goes to show that stock prices can fluctuate dramatically.

Preferred Stock Preferred stock, like common stock, is an equity security. However, as the name implies, preferred stockholders take a "preferred" position relative to common shareholders. This means that preferred shareholders receive their dividends before any dividends are distributed to the common stockholders, who receive their dividends from whatever is left over. Note, however, that if the company does not earn enough to pay its interest expenses, neither preferred nor common stockholders will be paid a dividend. However, the dividends promised to the preferred stockholders will generally accrue and must be paid in full before common shareholders can receive any dividends. This feature is oftentimes referred to as a cumulative feature, and preferred stock with this feature is often referred to as cumulative preferred stock. In addition, preferred stockholders have a preferred claim on the distribution of assets of the firm in the event that the firm goes bankrupt and sells or liquidates its assets. Very simply, the firm's creditors (bondholders) get paid first, followed by the preferred stockholders, and anything left goes to the common stockholders. Of interest is that not all firms issue preferred stock.

Preferred stock is sometimes referred to as a hybrid security because it has many characteristics of both common stock and bonds. Preferred stock is similar to common stock in that (i) it has no fixed maturity date, (ii) the nonpayment of dividends does not bring on bankruptcy for the firm, and (iii) the dividends paid on these securities are not deductible for tax purposes. However, preferred stock is similar to corporate bonds in that (i) the dividends paid on the stock, like the interest payments made on bonds, are typically a fixed amount, and (ii) it does not come with any voting rights.

Stock Markets A stock market is a public market in which the stock of companies is traded. Traditionally, the stock markets are classified as either organized security exchanges or the over-the-counter markets. **Organized security exchanges** are tangible entities; that is, they physically occupy space (such as a building or part of a building), and financial instruments are traded on their premises. The **over-the-counter markets** include all security markets except the organized exchanges. In the United States, the largest public market is the New York Stock Exchange (NYSE), whose history is traced back to 1792. Because it occupies a physical space (it is located at 11 Wall Street in Manhattan), it is considered an organized exchange. The common stock of more than 4,000 listed companies is traded on this exchange, which has monthly trading volume that exceeds 20 billion shares! In addition, the total value of the shares of stock listed on the NYSE at the beginning of 2013 reached just over $14.5 trillion. As you might expect, the dramatic stock market slide in 2008 took a toll on this figure; in fact, it was down from its peak of over $18 trillion in 2007.

Today, the NYSE is a hybrid market, having qualities of both an organized exchange and an over-the-counter market, allowing for face-to-face trading between individuals on the floor of the stock exchange in addition to automated electronic trading. As a result, during times of extreme flux in the market, at the opening or close of the market, or on large trades, human judgment can be called upon to make sure that the trade is properly executed.

NASDAQ, which stands for National Association of Securities Dealers Automated Quotations, is an over-the-counter market and describes itself as a "screen-based, floorless market." NASDAQ was formed in 1971 and is actually home to the securities of more companies than the NYSE. In 2013 some 3,200 companies were listed on NASDAQ, after reaching a peak of 5,556 in 1996. It has become highly popular as the trading mechanism of choice of several fast-growth sectors in the United States, including the high-technology sector. The common stock of computer chip maker Intel (INTC), for example, is traded via the NASDAQ, as is that of Dell (DELL), Starbucks (SBUX), Whole Foods Market (WFM), and Google (GOOG).

Reading Stock Price Quotes Figure 4.3 illustrates how to read stock price quotes from www.google.com/finance. This is just a bit of the information available on Google Finance. You'll also find stock price charts, any news items, Internet discussions, information on related companies, and analyst estimates along with the firm's financial statements and key statistics and ratios. Similar information is given at finance.yahoo. com and *Wall Street Journal Online* (*www.wsj.com*) in the "Market Data Center" under the "U.S. Stocks" link.

Other Financial Instruments So far we have touched on only the tip of the iceberg in terms of the variety of different types of financial instruments that are available to investors and firms. Table 4.2 provides a listing of a number of different financial

FIGURE 4.3

Common Stock Price Quotes

The following is typical of what you would see if you looked at www.google.com/finance.

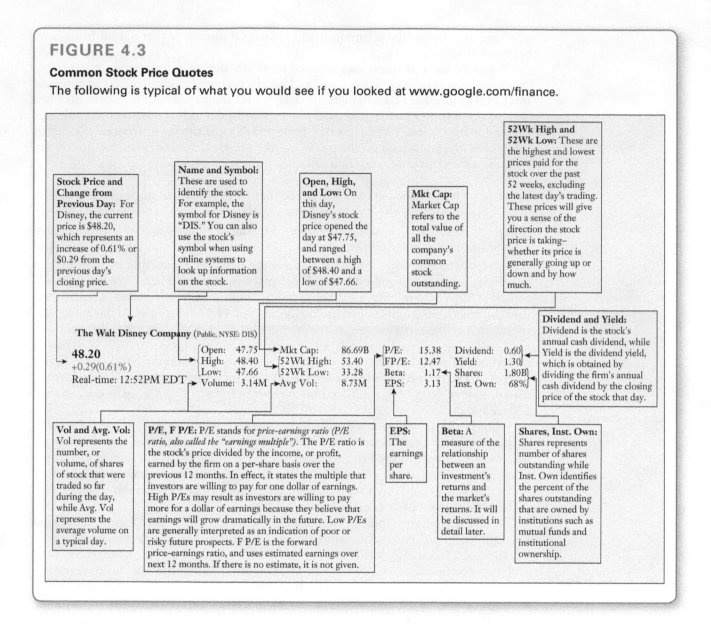

instruments used by firms to raise money, beginning with the shortest-maturity instruments that are traded in the money market and moving through the longest-maturity securities that are traded in the capital market.

Financial Markets and the Financial Crisis   Beginning in 2007 the United States experienced its most severe financial crisis since the Great Depression of the 1930s. As a result, some financial institutions collapsed while the government bailed others out, unemployment skyrocketed, the stock market plummeted, and the United States entered into a recession. Although the recession is now officially over, the economy still faces the lingering effects of the financial crisis that continue in the form of both a high rate of unemployment and a dramatic rise in our country's debt.

TABLE 4.2   CHARACTERISTICS OF DIFFERENT FINANCIAL INSTRUMENTS

Money Market Debt

For the Borrower:
- Good way of inexpensively raising money for short periods of time.
- Rates tend to be lower than long-term rates.
- Can borrow money to match short-term needs.
- If interest rates rise, the cost of borrowing will immediately rise accordingly.

For the Investor:
- Very liquid—you have access to your money when you need it.
- Safe—generally invested in high-quality investments for brief periods.
- Low returns—rates tend to be close to the rate of inflation.

Instrument	Market	Major Participants	Riskiness	Original Maturity	Interest Rates*
U.S. Treasury bills	Money— Debt	Issued by U.S. Treasury	Default-free	4 weeks to 1 year	0.09% to 0.14%
Bankers' acceptances	Money— Debt	A firm's promise to pay, guaranteed by a bank	Low risk of default, dependent on the risk of the guaranteeing bank	Up to 180 days	0.23% to 0.38%
Commercial paper	Money— Debt	Issued by financially secure firms to fund operating expenses or current assets (e.g., inventories and receivables)	Low default risk	Up to 270 days	0.14% to 0.25%
Negotiable certificates of deposit (CDs)	Money— Debt	Issued by major money-center commercial banks with a denomination of at least $100,000 to large investors	Default risk depends on the strength of the issuing bank	2 weeks to 1 year	National average 0.30%
Money market mutual funds	Money— Debt	Issued by mutual funds and invested in debt obligations such as Treasury bills, CDs, and commercial paper; held by individuals and businesses	Low degree of risk	No specific maturity date (can be redeemed any time)	0.02% to 0.19%
Consumer credit, including credit card debt	Money— Debt	Non-mortgage consumer debt issued by banks/credit unions/finance companies	Risk is variable	Varies	Variable depending upon the risk level

Continued

TABLE 4.2 CHARACTERISTICS OF DIFFERENT FINANCIAL INSTRUMENTS (*Continued*)

Long-Term Debt and Fixed Income Securities Market	**For the Borrower:** • Interest rates are locked in over the entire life of the debt. • Has a tax advantage over common stock in that interest payments are tax deductible, whereas dividend payments are not. **For the Investor:** • Can be used to generate dependable current income. • Some bonds produce tax-free income. • Long-term debt tends to produce higher returns than short-term debt. • Less risky than common stock. • Investor can lock in an interest rate and know the future returns (assuming the issuer does not default on its payments).

Instrument	Market	Major Participants	Riskiness	Original Maturity	Interest Rates*
U.S. Treasury notes and bonds	Capital—Debt	Issued by the U.S. government to mutual funds, businesses, individuals, and foreign countries	No default risk but price will decline if interest rates rise	Notes have original maturities of 2, 5, and 10 years; bonds have original maturities greater than 10 years	0.17% to 2.31%
Federal agency debt	Capital—Debt	Issued by federal agencies (Fannie Mae, Ginnie Mae, and others) to businesses, individuals, and foreign countries	Close to Treasury debt, but not obligations of the federal government, still very low risk	Up to 30 years	0.14% to 2.74%
Mortgages	Capital—Debt	Borrowings from commercial banks and savings and loans (S&Ls) by individuals	Risk is variable, with subprime mortgages having a good deal of risk	Up to 30 years	2.83% (15-year fixed) to 3.41% (30-year fixed)
Municipal bonds (state and local government bonds)	Capital—Debt	Issued by state and local governments to individuals, institutional investors, and foreign countries	Riskier than U.S. government securities, with the level of risk dependent upon the issuer, but exempt from most taxes	Up to 30 years	3.41% (30-year, AAA-rated bonds)
Corporate bonds	Capital—Debt	Issued by corporations to individuals and institutional investors	Risk is dependent upon the financial strength of the issuer; riskier than U.S. government securities but less risky than preferred and common stocks	In general up to 40 years, however Walt Disney and Coca-Cola have issued 100-year bonds	2.11% (10-year, AAA bonds), 3.85% (20-year AAA bonds)

Continued

Preferred Stock

For the Insurer:

- Dividends can be omitted without the risk of bankruptcy.
- Has the disadvantage that dividends are not tax deductible for the issuer, whereas interest payments from debt are tax deductible.

For the Investor:

- To corporate investors, it has a tax advantage because at minimum, 70 percent of dividends received are tax free.

Instrument	Market	Major Participants	Riskiness	Original Maturity	Interest Rates*
Preferred stocks	Capital—Equity (Preferred Stock)	Issued by corporations to individuals, other corporations, and institutional investors	Riskier than corporate bonds, but less risky than common stock	No maturity date	Dependent upon risk, generally ranging from 4.03% to 8.47%

Common Stock

For the Issuer:

- The issuing firm is not legally obligated to make payments.
- Does not have a maturity date.
- Issuance of common stock increases creditworthiness because the firm has more investor money to cushion the firm in the case of a loss.
- Has a tax disadvantage relative to debt; whereas debt interest payments are deductible for tax purposes, common stock dividends are not.

For the Investor:

- Over the long run, common stock has outperformed debt-based financial assets.
- Along with the increased expected return comes increased risk.

Instrument	Market	Major Participants	Riskiness	Original Maturity	Interest Rates
Common stocks	Capital—Equity (Common Stock)	Issued by corporations to individuals, other corporations, and institutional investors	Risky, with dividends only paid when they are declared	No maturity date	Do not pay interest

*The yields were taken from http://online.wsj.com, http://www.bloomberg.com, http://research.stlouisfed.org, http://finance.yahoo.com, and http://www.bankrate.com, retrieved November 21, 2012.

Although many factors contributed to the financial crisis, the most immediate cause has been attributed to the collapse of the real estate market and the resulting real estate loan (mortgage) defaults—in particular, what are commonly referred to as subprime mortgages. These were loans made to borrowers whose ability to repay them was highly doubtful. When the market for real estate began to falter in 2006, many of the homebuyers with subprime mortgages began to default. As the economy contracted during the recession, people lost their jobs and could no longer make their mortgage loan payments, resulting in even more defaults.

To complicate the problem, most real estate mortgages were packaged in portfolios and resold to investors around the world. This process of packaging mortgages is called securitization, because it takes loans that cannot be publicly traded and turns them into

FINANCE IN A FLAT WORLD

Where's the Money around the World

The figure below describes the total value of financial assets (bonds, equities, and bank assets) in the financial markets for each of the major regions of the world at the end of 2010. Although the totals change from year to year, these data provide some insight into the distribution of the value of financial assets around the world. When it comes to stock market capitalization—that is, the value of all equities—the United States clearly dominates, being the home for about one-third of equities.

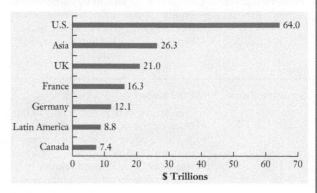

Source: International Monetary Fund, Global Financial Stability Report Statistical Appendix, April 2012, http://www.imf.org/external/pubs/ft/gfsr/2012/01/pdf/statapp.pdf

Your Turn: See Study Question 4–10

securities that can be freely bought and sold by financial institutions. Here's how mortgages are securitized:

1. First, homebuyers borrow money by taking out a mortgage to finance a home purchase.

2. Second, the lender, generally a bank, savings and loan institution, or mortgage broker that made the loan, then sells the mortgage to another firm or financial institution.

3. Third, that financial institution pools together a portfolio of many different mortgages, and the purchase of that pool of mortgages is financed through the sale of securities called mortgage-backed securities, or MBSs.

4. Fourth, these MBSs are sold to investors who can hold them as an investment or resell them to other investors.

This process allows the mortgage bank or other financial institution that made the original mortgage loan to get its money back out of the loan and lend it to someone else. Thus, securitization provides liquidity to the mortgage market and makes it possible for banks to loan more money to homebuyers.

Okay, so what's the catch? As long as lenders properly screen the mortgages to make sure the borrowers are willing and able to repay their home loans and real estate values remain higher than the amount owed, everything works fine. However, if the financial institution that originates the mortgage plans on selling it rather than holding it, it may have less incentive to properly screen the borrower. Why would lenders do this? It all goes back to ▣ Principle 5: **Individuals Respond to Incentives;** the lenders made their money by making the loans, and sold them almost immediately. As a result, some lenders were not concerned with whether or not the borrower could repay the loan; they were only concerned with making the loan—to them, repayment was someone else's problem.

As a result, starting around 2006, homeowners began to default on their mortgage loans. These defaults triggered losses at major banks, which in turn triggered a recession, causing people to lose their jobs and, correspondingly, the ability to make their mortgage payments. This was the scenario that played out at least through 2009. In essence, this was a perfect storm of bad loans, falling housing prices, and a contracting economy.

Unfortunately, these problems did not stay in the United States, as banks in Europe also held many of these mortgage-backed securities (MBSs), triggering a world-wide banking crisis. On top of this, European banks hold a lot of the European sovereign debt, so if countries such as Greece default on their debt, the European banking system will be in trouble. The recession that was originally sparked by the banking crisis revealed that the government budget situation in countries such as Greece was unsustainable, leading to the current European debt crisis. Many members of the European Union (EU) are experiencing severe budget problems, including Greece, Italy, Ireland, Portugal, and Spain. These nations are all unable to balance their budgets and face a very real prospect of defaulting on payments tied to government loans.

As a further result of the financial crisis, the stand-alone investment banking industry in the United States is no more. From the time of George Washington until the Great Depression in the 1930s, the U.S. economy experienced financial panics and banking crises about every 15 years. In response to the Great Depression and the failures of 4,004 banks in 1933, Congress enacted the National Banking Act of 1933, of which several sections are commonly referred to as the Glass–Steagall Act. An important component of the Glass–Steagall Act was the separation of commercial banking and the investment industry. Specifically, the act prohibited commercial banks from entering the investment industry in order to limit risks to banks. As a result, a "stand-alone" investment banking industry was created with firms like Lehman Brothers, Bear Stearns, Merrill Lynch, Goldman Sachs, and Morgan Stanley. However, in 1999 Glass–Steagall was repealed, and many commercial banks acquired investment banks, whereas others, such as JPMorgan Chase & Co. (JPM), entered the investment banking business. The advantage of this combination was that it gave investment banks access to stable funding through bank deposits along with the ability to borrow from the Federal Reserve in the case of an emergency, while the commercial bank gained access to the more lucrative, albeit more risky, investment industry.

In the wake of the 2008 financial crisis, the financial industry was again transformed. During the crisis, the major stand-alone investment banks either failed (Lehman Brothers), were acquired by commercial banks (Bear Stearns and Merrill Lynch), or were converted to commercial banks (Morgan Stanley and Goldman Sachs). Indeed, by the end of 2008, there were no major stand-alone investment banking firms left.

Then in 2010 the Dodd–Frank Wall Street Reform and Consumer Protection Act was passed. Under Dodd–Frank, banks as well as non-bank financial institutions are subject to considerably more oversight and are required to be more transparent. Another important feature of this legislation is what is known as the "Volker" rule, which prohibits banks that take deposits from **proprietary trading**, which is using the bank's capital to make speculative bets on derivatives and securities.

The hope is that these changes will increase the stability of the U.S. financial system and ensure that we will no longer be subject to financial crises that throw our economy into a severe recession. However, critics have argued that on one hand the recent legislation has not done enough to protect consumers as well as the safety of the financial system, and on the other hand that it adds unnecessary bureaucracy to our financial institutions.

CONCEPT CHECK: 4.3
Before you begin end of chapter material

1. What are debt and equity securities, and how do they differ?
2. How is a primary market different from a secondary market?
3. How does common stock differ from preferred stock?

Applying the Principles of Finance to Chapter 4

P Principle 2: **There Is a Risk-Return Tradeoff** Financial markets are organized to offer investors a wide range of investment opportunities that have different risks and different expected rates of return that reflect those risks.

P Principle 4: **Market Prices Reflect Information** It is through the operations of the financial markets that new information is efficiently impounded in security prices.

P Principle 5: **Individuals Respond to Incentives** One of the reasons for the recent subprime mortgage crisis may have been in improper incentives to screen borrowers.

Chapter Summaries

Summary	Key Terms
4.1 Describe the structure and functions of financial markets. (pg. 125)	
Financial markets allocate the supply of savings in the economy to the individuals and companies that need the money. A primary market is a market in which new, as opposed to previously issued, securities are bought and sold for the first time. In this market firms issue new securities to raise money that they can then use to help finance their businesses. The key feature of the primary market is that the firms that raise money by selling securities actually receive the money. The secondary market is where all subsequent trading of previously issued securities takes place. In this market the issuing firm does not receive any new financing, as the securities it has sold are simply being transferred from one investor to another. The principal benefit to investors of having a secondary market is the ease with which the investor can sell or liquidate investments.	**Commercial bank, page 126** A financial institution that accepts demand deposits, makes loans, and provides other services to the public. **Defined benefit plans, page 125** A company retirement plan, such as a pension plan, in which a retired employee receives a specific amount based on his or her salary history and years of service. **Defined contribution plans, page 125** A company retirement plan, such as a 401(k) plan, in which the employee elects to contribute some amount of his or her salary to the plan and the employee takes responsibility for the investment decisions.

Summary	Key Terms

4.2 Distinguish between commercial banks and other financial institutions in the financial marketplace. (pgs. 126–131)

Financial institutions are intermediaries that stand in the middle between borrowers who need money and savers who have money to invest. Widely varying financial institutions have evolved over time to meet special needs for intermediation, including commercial banks that accept deposits from savers and lend to borrowers, investment banks that help companies sell their securities to investors in order to raise the money they need, and many other institutions. Of particular interest are mutual funds that collect the investments of many small investors and invest the pool of funds in stocks, bonds, and other types of securities that are issued by businesses. In recent years, two types of investment companies have captured the headlines: hedge funds and private equity funds. Both of these types of investment companies accept investments from other financial institutions or wealthy individuals and invest in speculative and risky ventures.

Accredited investor, page 130 Investor who is permitted to invest in certain types of higher-risk investments. These investors include wealthy individuals, corporations, endowments, and retirement plans.

Capital market, page 126 The market for long-term financial instruments.

Credit default swap, page 129 An insurance contract that pays off in the event of a credit event such as default or bankruptcy.

Exchange-traded fund (ETF), page 129 An investment vehicle traded on stock exchanges much like a share of stock. The entity holds investments in assets that meet the investment objective of the entity (e.g., shares of stock of companies from emerging markets).

Financial intermediaries, page 126 Institutions whose business is to bring together individuals and institutions with money to invest or lend with other firms or individuals in need of money.

Hedge fund, page 130 An investment fund that is open to a limited range of investors (accredited investors) and that can undertake a wider range of investment and trading activities than other types of investment funds that are open to the general public (e.g., mutual funds).

Investment bank, page 129 A financial institution that raises capital, trades in securities, and manages corporate mergers and acquisitions.

Investment company, page 129 A firm that invests the pooled funds of retail investors for a fee.

Leveraged buyout fund, page 131 A private equity firm that raises capital from individual investors and uses these funds along with significant amounts of debt to acquire controlling interests in operating companies.

Load fund, page 129 A mutual fund that charges investors a sales commission called a "load."

Money market, page 126 The financial market for short-term debt securities (maturing in one year or less).

Mutual fund, page 129 A professionally managed investment company that pools the investments of many individuals and invests it in stocks, bonds, and other types of securities.

Net asset value (NAV), page 129 The difference between the current market value of an entity's (such as a mutual fund) assets and the value of its liabilities.

No-load fund, page 129 A mutual fund that doesn't charge a commission.

Private equity firm, page 131 A financial intermediary that invests in equities that are not traded on the public capital markets.

Venture capital firm, page 131 An investment company that raises money from accredited investors and uses the proceeds to invest in new start-up companies.

Concept Check: 4.2

1. Explain how individuals and firms use financial intermediaries to raise money in the financial markets.
2. How do commercial banks differ from other non-bank financial intermediaries?
3. What are examples of investment companies?
4. What is a hedge fund, and how does it differ from a mutual fund?
5. What are the two principal types of private equity firms?

Summary	Key Terms

4.3 Describe the different securities markets for bonds and stocks. (pgs. 132–142)

When a corporation needs to raise large sums of money, it generally turns to the public market for bonds if it borrows or equity if it seeks funds from new owners. The buyers of these securities include individual investors and investment companies such as mutual funds. The U.S. stock and bond markets are the largest and most active in the world. In some instances these markets are physical locations where buyers and sellers interact, such as the New York Stock Exchange at 11 Wall Street, or they consist of an electronic market of interconnected computers, such as NASDAQ. Beginning in 2007, the United States experienced its most severe financial crisis since the Great Depression of the 1930s. Although there is not a single cause for the crisis, the collapse of the real estate market certainly contributed to this event.

Bond, page 133 A long-term (10-year or more) promissory note issued by a borrower, promising to pay the owner of the security a predetermined amount of interest each year.

Common stock, page 134 A form of equity security that represents the residual ownership of the firm.

Coupon rate, page 133 The amount of interest paid per year expressed as a percent of the face value of the bond.

Debt securities, page 133 Financial instruments that represent loans to corporations. Long-term debt securities are called bonds and can be bought and sold in the bond market.

Equity securities, page 134 Financial instruments that represent ownership claims on a business. Equity securities for corporations are called shares of stock and can be bought and sold in the stock market.

Face, or par value, page 133 On the face of a bond, the stated amount that the firm is to repay on the maturity date.

Maturity, page 133 The date when a debt must be repaid.

Note, page 133 Another term used to refer to indebtedness. Notes generally have a maturity between 1 and 10 years when originally issued.

Organized security exchanges, page 135 Security exchanges that physically occupy space (such as a building or part of a building) and trade financial instruments on their premises.

Over-the-counter markets, page 135 All security markets except the organized exchanges.

Proprietary trading, page 141 Using the bank's capital to make speculative bets on derivatives and securities.

Preferred stock, page 134 An equity security that holds preference over common stock in terms of the right to the distribution of cash (dividends) and the right to the distribution of proceeds in the event of the liquidation and sale of the issuing firm.

Primary market, page 132 A part of the financial market where new security issues are initially bought and sold.

Secondary market, page 132 The financial market where previously issued securities such as stocks and bonds are bought and sold.

Security, page 132 A negotiable instrument that represents a financial claim that has value. Securities are broadly classified as debt securities (bonds) and equity securities (shares of common stock).

Concept Check: 4.3

1. What are debt and equity securities, and how do they differ?
2. How is a primary market different from a secondary market?
3. How does common stock differ from preferred stock?

Study Questions

Q4.1 (Related to Regardless of Your Major: Defined Benefit vs. Defined Contribution Retirement Plans on page 125) In the *Regardless of Your Major* box feature, two types of pension plans are discussed. Describe each. Which type is now the dominant type in use?

Q4.2 What are the three principal sets of players that interact in the financial markets?

Q4.3 What is a financial intermediary? List and describe the principal types of financial intermediaries in the U.S. financial markets.

Q4.4 What do investment banks do in the financial markets?

Q4.5 Describe the difference between the primary market and the secondary market.

Q4.6 What is a mutual fund, and how does it differ from an exchange-traded fund (ETF)?

Q4.7 What is the difference between a debt security and an equity security?

Q4.8 What makes preferred stock "preferred"?

Q4.9 (Related to The Business of Life: Controlling Costs in Mutual Funds on page 130) In *The Business of Life: Controlling Costs in Mutual Funds* feature, the importance of keeping expenses down is discussed. The Financial Industry Regulatory Authority website provides an easy way to compare two mutual funds. Go to the website, http://apps.finra.org/ fundanalyzer/1/fa.aspx, then enter Vanguard 500 Index Fund Investor Class (you will enter the ticker symbol VFINX), American Beacon Balanced Fund Class A (ABFAX), and Quantitative Futures Strategy Fund Class C Shares (QMFCX). Now, click on "show results." Set your investment at $10,000, your return at 8%, and your period at 10 years. What is your profit or loss? Why do you think there is such a big difference? (Think expenses and fees.)

Q4.10 (Related to Finance in a Flat World: Where's the Money around the World on page 140) The distribution of financial assets around the world is described in the *Finance in a "Flat" World* box feature. What country dominates in terms of the stock market and total financial assets? Of the UK, Germany, and France, which country has the most in the way of financial assets and which country has the least?

Q4.11 What is a hedge fund, and how is it different from a mutual fund?

Q4.12 What are the two types of private equity funds? What does each do with the money it raises from investors?

Q4.13 Go to Yahoo! Finance (http://finance.yahoo.com) and enter the symbol for Google (GOOG) in the "Enter Symbol(s)" box at the top of the page. What price did it last trade at? What is the last trade time, and how long ago was that? What is the day's price range for the stock? What is the closing change in the price of the stock, both in dollar and percentage terms? What is the stock's 52-week price range? Now check out some of the links on the left-hand side of the page. What kind of information listed there do you find interesting?

Q4.14 Go to the CNN-Money website (http://money.cnn.com) and visit the retirement section by clicking on "Personal Finance" on the top banner. From there, click on "Retirement." You'll find all kinds of interesting articles under this link. (But be forewarned: Some are a bit scary. Saving for retirement is not an easy task.) Write up a summary of any one of the articles listed there.

Q4.15 Go to the Market Watch website (www.marketwatch.com) Personal Finance section by clicking on "Personal Finance" on the top banner. This is a great website for information and help in managing your personal finances. Find an article you like, read it, and write a summary of it. Also, consider bookmarking this website—it's one you might want to start visiting on a regular basis.

Q4.16 Calculate the value of the total shareholder wealth for Google, Inc., using the number of common shares outstanding and the current price of the firm's shares. You can obtain the necessary information from the Yahoo! Finance website.

Q4.17 Go to the Smartmoney.com website (www.smartmoney.com) and select one of the listed stories for the day; read it and prepare a brief summary to share with the class.

Q4.18 Go to the Motley Fool website (www.fool.com) and select the Retirement tab. Describe the information available here for planning for your retirement.

5

Time Value of Money
The Basics

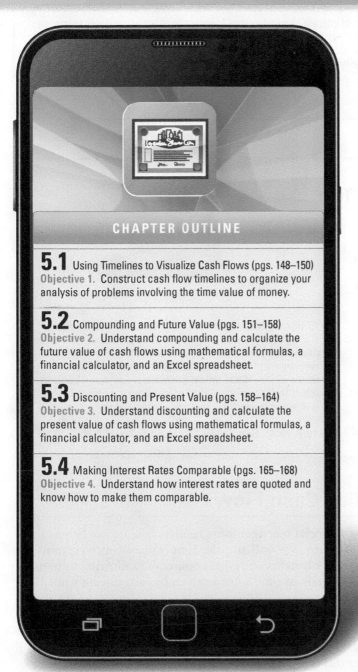

CHAPTER OUTLINE

5.1 Using Timelines to Visualize Cash Flows (pgs. 148–150)
Objective 1. Construct cash flow timelines to organize your analysis of problems involving the time value of money.

5.2 Compounding and Future Value (pgs. 151–158)
Objective 2. Understand compounding and calculate the future value of cash flows using mathematical formulas, a financial calculator, and an Excel spreadsheet.

5.3 Discounting and Present Value (pgs. 158–164)
Objective 3. Understand discounting and calculate the present value of cash flows using mathematical formulas, a financial calculator, and an Excel spreadsheet.

5.4 Making Interest Rates Comparable (pgs. 165–168)
Objective 4. Understand how interest rates are quoted and know how to make them comparable.

Principles P 1 Applied

hapters 5 and 6 are dedicated to P Principle 1: **Money Has a Time Value.** This basic idea—a dollar received today, other things being the same, is worth more than a dollar received a year from now—underlies many financial decisions faced in business. In this chapter, we learn how to calculate the value today of money you will receive in the future, as well as the future value of money you have today. In Chapter 6 we extend our analysis to multiple cash flows spread out over time.

Payday Loans

Sometimes marketed to college students as quick relief for urgent expenses, a payday loan is a short-term loan to cover expenses until the next payday. As some borrowers turn to these loans during times of financial desperation, lenders can charge them extremely high rates of interest. For example, in 2012, one payday lender advertised that you could borrow $500 and repay $626.37 in eight days. This might not sound like a bad deal on the surface, but if we apply some basic rules of finance to analyze this loan, we see quite a different story. The annual interest rate for this payday loan is a whopping 2,916,780 percent! (We will examine this later in the chapter on pages 144–145.)

The very high rates of interest charged by these lenders have led some states to impose limits on the interest rates payday lenders can charge. Even so, the cost of this type of loan can be extremely high. Understanding the time value of money is an essential tool to analyzing the cost of this and other types of financing.

REGARDLESS OF YOUR MAJOR...

"A Dollar Saved Is Two Dollars Earned"

Suppose that you and your classmate each receive a gift of $10,000 from grandparents, but choose different ways to invest the newfound money. You immediately invest your gift until retirement, whereas your classmate carries around his gift in his wallet in the form of 100 crisp $100 bills. Then, after 15 years of carrying around a fat wallet, your classmate decides to invest his $10,000 for retirement.

If you invest your $10,000 for 46 years and earn 10 percent per year until you retire, you'll end up with over $800,000. If your classmate invests his $10,000 for 31 years (remember that he carried his money around for 15 years in his wallet) and earns the same

10 percent per year, he'll only end up with about $192,000. Knowing about the power of the time value of money provided you with an additional $600,000 at retirement. In this chapter we'll learn more about these kinds of valuation problems. For now, keep in mind that the time value of money is a concept you will want to understand, regardless of your major.

Your Turn: See Study Question 5–7 and 5–8.

5.1 Using Timelines to Visualize Cash Flows

To evaluate a new project, a financial manager must be able to compare benefits and costs that occur at different times. We will use the time-value-of-money tools we develop in this chapter to make the benefits and costs comparable, allowing us to make logical decisions. We begin our study of time value analysis by introducing some basic tools. As a first step, we can construct a **timeline**, a linear representation of the timing of cash flows. A timeline identifies the timing and amount of a stream of payments—both cash received and cash spent—along with the interest rate earned. Timelines are a critical first step that financial analysts use to solve financial problems, and we will refer to timelines throughout this text.

To learn how to construct a timeline, consider the following example, where we have annual cash inflows and outflows over the course of four years. The following timeline illustrates these cash inflows and outflows from time Period 0 (the present) until the end of Year 4:

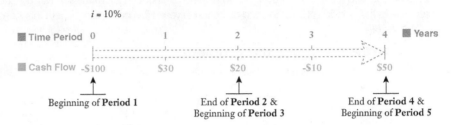

For our purposes, time periods are identified on the top of the timeline. In this example, the time periods are measured in years, indicated on the far right of the timeline. For example, time Period 0 in this example is the current year. The dollar amount of the cash flow received or spent during each time period is shown below the timeline. Positive values represent *cash inflows*. Negative values represent *cash outflows*. For example, in the timeline shown, a $100 cash outflow occurs at the beginning of the first year (at Time 0), followed by cash inflows of $30 and $20 in Years 1 and 2, a cash outflow (a negative cash flow) of $10 in Year 3, and finally a cash inflow of $50 in Year 4.

Timelines are typically expressed in years, but could be expressed in months, days, or, for that matter, any unit of time. For now, let's assume we're looking at cash flows that occur annually, so the distance between 0 and 1 represents the time period between today and the end of the first year. The interest rate, 10 percent in this example, is listed above the timeline.

5.2 Compounding and Future Value

If we assume that an investment will only earn interest on the original principal, we call this **simple interest**. Suppose that you put $100 in a savings account earning 6 percent interest annually. How much will your savings grow after one year? If you invest for one year at an interest rate of 6 percent, you will earn 6 percent simple interest on your initial deposit of $100, giving you a total of $106 in your account. What if you left your $100 in the bank for two years? In this case, you will earn interest not only on your original $100 deposit but also on the $6 in interest you earned during the first year. This process of accumulating interest on an investment over multiple time periods is called **compounding**. And, when interest is earned on both the initial principal and the reinvested interest during prior periods, the result is called **compound interest**.

Time-value-of-money calculations are essentially comparisons between what we will refer to as **present value**, what a cash flow would be worth to you today, and **future value**, what a cash flow will be worth in the future. The following is a mathematical formula that shows how these concepts relate to each other when the future value is in one year:

Equation 5.1   Future Value in 1 Year = Present Value × (1 + Interest Rate)

In the earlier example, you began with a $100 investment, so the present value is $100. The future value in one year is then given by the equation

$$\$100 \times (1 + .06) = \$106.00$$

Checkpoint 5.1

Creating a Timeline

Suppose you lend a friend $10,000 today to help him finance a new Jimmy John's Sub Shop franchise and in return he promises to give you $12,155 at the end of the fourth year. How can one represent this as a timeline? Note that the interest rate is 5%.

STEP 1: Picture the problem

A timeline provides a tool for visualizing cash flows and time:

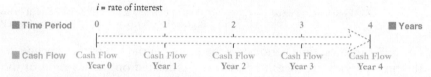

STEP 2: Decide on a solution strategy

To complete the timeline we simply record the cash flows onto the template.

STEP 3: Solve

We can input the cash flows for this investment on the timeline as shown below. Time period zero (the present) is shown at the left end of the timeline, and future time periods are shown above the timeline, moving from left to right, with the year that each cash flow occurs shown above the timeline.

Keep in mind that Year 1 represents the end of the first year as well as the beginning of the second year.

STEP 4: Analyze

Using timelines to visualize cash flows is useful in financial problem solving. From analyzing the timeline, we can see that there are two cash flows, an initial $10,000 cash outflow, and a $12,155 cash inflow at the end of Year 4.

STEP 5: Check yourself

Draw a timeline for an investment of $40,000 today that returns nothing in one year, $20,000 at the end of Year 2, nothing in Year 3, and $40,000 at the end of Year 4, where the interest rate is 13.17 percent.

ANSWER:

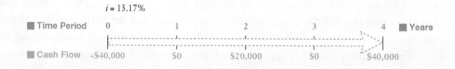

Before you move on to 4.2
CONCEPT
CHECK: 5.1

1. What is a timeline, and how does it help you solve problems involving the time value of money?

2. Does Year 5 represent the end of the fifth year, the beginning of the sixth year, or both?

To see how to calculate the future value in two years, let's do a timeline and a few calculations:

During the first year, your $100 deposit earns $6 in interest. Summing the interest and the original deposit gives you a balance of $106 at the end of the first year. In the second year, you earn $6.36 in interest, giving you a future value of $112.36. Why do you earn $0.36 more in interest during the second year than during the first? Because in the second year, you earn an additional 6 percent on the $6 in interest you earned in the first year. This amounts to $0.36 (or $6 × .06). Again, this result is an example of compound interest. Anyone who has ever had a savings account or purchased a government savings bond has received compound interest.

What happens to the value of your investment at the end of the third year, assuming the same interest rate of 6 percent? We can follow the same approach to calculate the future value in three years.

Using a timeline, we can calculate the future value of your $100 as follows:

Note that every time we extend the analysis for one more period, we just multiply the previous balance by *(1 + Interest Rate)*. Consequently, the future value of any amount of money for any number of periods can be expressed with the following equation, where *n* = the number of periods during which the compounding occurs:

$$\underset{\text{Period } n}{\text{Future}} \text{Value} = \underset{\text{Value (Deposit)}}{\text{Present}} \times \left(1 + \frac{\text{Interest}}{\text{Rate } (i)}\right)^{n}$$

or

Equation 5.1a

$$\underset{(FV_n)}{\underset{\text{in Year } n}{\text{Future Value}}} = \underset{\text{Value } (PV)}{\text{Present}} \left(1 + \frac{\text{Annual}}{\text{Interest Rate } (i)}\right)^{\text{Number of Years } (n)}$$

Important Definitions and Concepts:

- FV_n = the future value of the investment at the end of n periods.
- i = the interest (or growth) rate per period.
- PV = the present value, or original amount invested at the beginning of the first period.

We also refer to $(1 + i)^n$ as the **future value interest factor**. To find the future value of a dollar amount, simply multiply that dollar amount by the appropriate future value interest factor,

$$FV_n = PV(1 + i)^n$$

$$FV_n = PV \times \text{Future Value Interest Factor}$$

$$\text{where, Future Value Interest Factor} = (1 + i)^n$$

Panel A in Figure 5.1 shows what your investment of $100 would grow to in four years if it continues to earn an annual compound interest rate of 6 percent. Notice how the amount of interest earned increases each year. In the first year, you earn only $6, but by Year 4, you earn $7.15 in interest.

Prior to the introduction of inexpensive financial calculators and Excel, future values were commonly calculated using time-value-of-money tables containing future value interest factors for different combinations of i and n. Table 5.1 provides an abbreviated future value interest factor table; you can find the expanded future value interest factor tables in Appendix B in MyFinanceLab. So, to find the value of $100 invested for four years at 6 percent, we would simply look at the intersection of the $n = 4$ row and the 6% column, finding a future value interest factor of 1.262. We would then multiply this value by $100 to find that our investment of $100 at 6 percent for four years would grow to $126.20.

Compound Interest and Time

As Panel C of Figure 5.1 shows, the future value of an investment grows with the number of periods we let it compound. For example, after five years, the future value of $100 earning 10 percent interest each year will be $161.05. However, after 25 years, the future value of that investment will be $1,083.47. Note that although we increased the number of years threefold, the future value increases by more than sixfold ($1,083.47/$161.05 = 6.7 fold). This illustrates an important point: Future value is not directly proportional to time. Instead, future value grows exponentially. This means it grows by a fixed percentage each year, which means that the dollar value grows by an increasing amount each year.

Compound Interest and the Interest Rate

Panel C of Figure 5.1 illustrates that future value increases dramatically with the level of the rate of interest. For example, the future value of $100 in 25 years, given a 10 percent interest rate, compounded annually, is $1,083.47. However, if we double the rate of interest to 20 percent, the future value increases almost ninefold in 25 years to equal $9,539.62. This illustrates another important point: The increase in future value is not directly proportional to the increase in the rate of interest. We doubled the rate of interest, and the future value of the investment increased by 8.80 times. Why did the future value jump by so much? Because there is a lot of time over 25 years for the higher interest rate to result in more interest being earned on interest.

Techniques for Moving Money through Time

In this book, we will refer to three methods for solving problems involving the time value of money: mathematical formulas, financial calculators, and spreadsheets.

- **Do the math.** You can use the mathematical formulas just as we have done in this chapter. You simply substitute the values that you know into the appropriate time-value-of-money equation to find the answer.

FIGURE 5.1 Future Value and Compound Interest Illustrated

(Panel A) Calculating Compound Interest

This panel shows how interest compounds annually. During the first year, $100 invested at a 6% interest rate earns only $6. Because we earn 6% on the ending value for Year 1 (or $106), in Year 2 we earn $6.36 in interest. This increase in the amount of interest results from interest being earned on both the initial deposit of $100 plus the $6.00 in interest earned during Year 1. The fact that we earn interest on both principal and interest is why we refer to this as compound interest. Simple interest, on the other hand, would be earning only $6.00 in interest each and every year.

$$\text{Interest Earned} = \text{Beginning Value} \times \text{Interest Rate}$$

Year	Beginning Value	Interest Earned	Ending Value
1	$ 100.00	**$ 6.00**	$ 106.00
2	$ 106.00	**$ 6.36**	$ 112.36
3	$ 112.36	**$ 6.74**	$ 119.10
4	$ 119.10	**$ 7.15**	$ 126.25

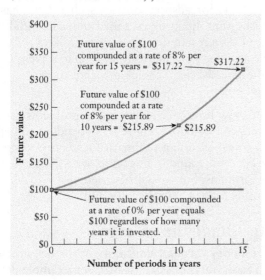

(Panel B) The Power of Time

This figure illustrates the importance of time when it comes to compounding. Because interest is earned on past interest, the future value of $100 deposited in an account that earns 8% compounded annually grows over threefold in 15 years. If we were to expand this figure to 45 years (which is about how long you have until you retire, assuming you're around 20 years old right now), it would grow to over 31 times its initial value.

(Panel C) The Power of the Rate of Interest

This figure illustrates the importance of the interest rate in the power of compounding. As the interest rate climbs, so does the future value. In fact, when we change the interest rate from 10% to 20%, the future value in 25 years increases by over 8 times, jumping from $1,083.47 to $9,539.62.

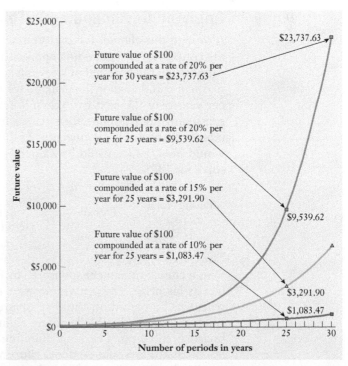

TABLE 5.1   FUTURE VALUE INTEREST FACTORS

Number of Periods (n)	i = 3%	i = 6%	i = 9%	i = 12%
1	1.030	1.060	1.090	1.120
2	1.061	1.124	1.188	1.254
3	1.093	1.191	1.295	1.405
4	1.126	1.262	1.412	1.574

- **Use financial calculators.** Financial calculators have preprogrammed functions that make time-value-of-money calculations simple.

- **Use a spreadsheet on your personal computer.** Spreadsheet software such as Excel has preprogrammed functions built into it. The same inputs that are used with a financial calculator are also used as inputs to Excel. As a result, if you can correctly set a problem up to solve on your financial calculator, you can easily set it up to solve using Excel. In the business world, Excel is the spreadsheet of choice and is the most common way of moving money through time.

In Appendix A in MyFinanceLab, we will show how to solve valuation problems using each of these methods. Because the authors of this book believe that spending enough time solving problems the old-fashioned way—by doing the math—leads to a deeper understanding and better retention of the concepts found in this book, we will first demonstrate how to solve problems using the formulas; but we will also demonstrate, whenever possible, how to derive the solution using a financial calculator and Excel.

Applying Compounding to Things Other Than Money

Although this chapter focuses on moving money through time at a given interest rate, the concept of compounding applies to almost anything that grows. For example, let's suppose we're interested in knowing how big the market for wireless printers will be in five years, and assume the demand for them is expected to grow at a rate of 25 percent per year over the next five years. We can calculate the future value of the market for printers using the same formula we used to calculate the future value for a sum of money. If the market is currently 25,000 printers per year, then 25,000 would be *PV*, *n* would be 5, and *i* would be 25 percent. Substituting into Equation (5–1a) we would solve for *FV*,

$$\text{Future Value in Year } n\ (FV_n) = \text{Present Value } (PV)\left(1 + \text{Annual Interest Rate } (i)\right)^{\text{Number of Years } (n)} = 25,000\,(1 + .25)^5 = 76,293$$

The power of compounding can also be illustrated through the story of a peasant who wins a chess tournament sponsored by the king. The king then asks him what he would like as his prize. The peasant answers that, for his village, he would like one grain of wheat to be placed on the first square of his chessboard, two pieces on the second square, four on the third square, eight on the fourth square, and so forth, until the board is filled up. The king, thinking he was getting off easy, pledged his word of honor that this would be done. Unfortunately for the king, by the time all 64 squares on the chessboard were filled, there were 18.5 million trillion grains of wheat on the

Checkpoint 5.2

Calculating the Future Value of a Cash Flow

You are put in charge of managing your firm's working capital. Your firm has $100,000 in extra cash on hand and decides to put it in a savings account paying 7 percent interest compounded annually. How much will you have in your account in 10 years?

STEP 1: Picture the problem

We can set up a timeline to identify the cash flows from the investment as follows:

$i = 7\%$

| Time Period | 0 | 1 | 2 | 3 | 4 | 5 | 6 | 7 | 8 | 9 | 10 | Years |

Cash Flow -$100,000   Future Value = ?

STEP 2: Decide on a solution strategy

This is a simple future value problem. We can find the future value using Equation (5–1a).

STEP 3: Solve

Using the Mathematical Formulas. Substituting $PV = \$100,000$, $i = 7\%$, and $n = 10$ years into Equation (5–1a), we get

$$\begin{array}{c}\text{Future Value}\\\text{in Year } n\\(FV_n)\end{array} = \begin{array}{c}\text{Present}\\\text{Value } (PV)\end{array}\left(1 + \begin{array}{c}\text{Annual}\\\text{Interest Rate } (i)\end{array}\right)^{\begin{array}{c}\text{Number of}\\\text{Years } (n)\end{array}} \qquad (5\text{–}1a)$$

$$FV_n = \$100,000(1 + .07)^{10}$$

$$= \$100,000(1.96715)$$

$$= \$196,715$$

At the end of 10 years, you will have $196,715 in the savings account.

Using a Financial Calculator.

Enter	10	7.0	–100,000	0	
	N	I/Y	PV	PMT	FV
Solve for					196,715

Using an Excel Spreadsheet.

= FV(rate,nper,pmt,pv) or with values entered = FV(0.07,10,0,–100000)

STEP 4: Analyze

Notice that you input the present value with a negative sign because present value represents a cash outflow. In effect, the money leaves your firm when it's first invested. In this problem your firm invested $100,000 at 7 percent and found that it will grow to $196,715 after 10 years. Put another way, given a 7 percent compound rate, your $100,000 today will be worth $196,715 in 10 years.

STEP 5: Check yourself

What is the future value of $10,000 compounded at 12 percent annually for 20 years?

ANSWER: $96,462.93.

Your Turn: For more practice, do related **Study Problems** 5–1, 5–2, 5–4, 5–6, and 5–8 through 5–11 at the end of this chapter.

>> END Checkpoint 5.2

board, because the kernels were compounding at a rate of 100 percent over the 64 squares of the chessboard. In fact, if the kernels were one-quarter inch long, they would have stretched, if laid end to end, to the sun and back 391,320 times! Needless to say, no one in the village ever went hungry. What can we conclude from this story? There is incredible power in compounding.

Compound Interest with Shorter Compounding Periods

So far, we have assumed that the compounding period is always a year in length. However, this isn't always the case. For example, banks often offer savings accounts that compound interest every day, month, or quarter. Savers prefer more frequent compounding because they earn interest on their interest sooner and more frequently. Fortunately, it's easy to adjust for different compounding periods, and later in the chapter we will examine how to compare two loans with different compounding periods in more detail.

Consider the following example: You invest $100 for five years to earn a rate of 8 percent, and the investment is compounded semiannually (twice a year). This means that interest is calculated every six months. Essentially, you are investing your money for 10 six-month periods, and in each period, you will receive 4 percent interest. In effect, we divide the annual interest rate (i) by the number of compounding periods per year (m), and we multiply the number of years (n) times the number of compounding periods per year (m) to convert the number of years into the number of periods. So, our future value formula found in Equation (5–1a) must be adjusted as follows:

Equation 5.1b

$$\text{Future Value in Year } n \; (FV_n) = \text{Present Value } (PV) \left(1 + \frac{\text{Interest Rate } (i)}{\text{Compounding}}\right)^{m \times (\text{Number of Years } (n))}$$

Substituting into Equation (5–1b) gives us the following estimate of the future value in five years:

$$FV_n = \$100 \, (1 + .08/2)^{2\times5}$$
$$= \$100(1.4802)$$
$$= \$148.02$$

But if the compounding had been annual rather than semiannual, the future value of the investment would have been only $146.93. Although the difference here seems modest, it can be significant when large sums of money are involved and the number of years and the number of compounding periods within those years are both large. For example, for your $100 investment, the difference is only $1.09. But if the amount were $50 million (not an unusually large bank balance for a major company), the difference would be $545,810.41.

Table 5.2 shows how shorter compounding periods lead to higher future values. For example, if you invested $100 at 15 percent for one year, and the investment was compounded daily rather than annually, you would end up with $1.18 ($116.18 − $115.00) more. However, if the period were extended to 10 years, then the difference grows to $43.47 ($448.03 − $404.56).

TABLE 5.2   THE VALUE OF $100 COMPOUNDED AT VARIOUS NON-ANNUAL PERIODS AND VARIOUS RATES

Notice that the impact of shorter compounding periods is heightened by both higher interest rates and compounding over longer time periods.

For 1 Year at i Percent	i 5 2%	5%	10%	15%	
Compounded annually	$102.00	$105.00	$110.00	**$115.00**	
Compounded semiannually	102.01	105.06	110.25	115.56	
Compounded quarterly	102.02	105.09	110.38	115.87	$1.18
Compounded monthly	102.02	105.12	110.47	116.08	
Compounded weekly (52)	102.02	105.12	110.51	116.16	
Compounded daily (365)	102.02	105.13	110.52	**116.18**	
For 10 Years at i Percent	i 5 2%	5%	10%	15%	
Compounded annually	$121.90	$162.89	$259.37	**$404.56**	
Compounded semiannually	122.02	163.86	265.33	424.79	
Compounded quarterly	122.08	164.36	268.51	436.04	$43.47
Compounded monthly	122.12	164.70	270.70	444.02	
Compounded weekly (52)	122.14	164.83	271.57	447.20	
Compounded daily (365)	122.14	164.87	271.79	**448.03**	

Checkpoint 5.3

Calculating Future Values Using Non-Annual Compounding Periods

You have been put in charge of managing your firm's cash position and noticed that the Plaza National Bank of Portland, Oregon, has recently decided to begin paying interest compounded semiannually instead of annually. If you deposit $1,000 with Plaza National Bank at an interest rate of 12 percent, what will your account balance be in five years?

STEP 1: Picture the problem

If you earn a 12 percent annual rate compounded semiannually for five years, you really earn 6 percent every six months for 10 six-month periods. Expressed as a timeline, this problem would look like the following:

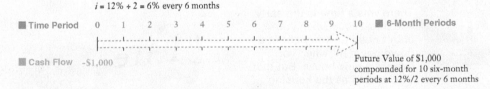

STEP 2: Decide on a solution strategy

In this instance we are simply solving for the future value of $1,000. The only twist is that interest is calculated on a semiannual basis. Thus, if you earn 12 percent compounded semiannually for five years, you really earn 6 percent every six months for 10 six-month periods. We can calculate the future value of the $1,000 investment using Equation (5–1b).

STEP 3: Solve

Using the Mathematical Formulas. Substituting number of years (n) = 5, number of compounding periods per year (m) = 2, annual interest rate (i) = 12%, and PV = $1,000 into Equation (5–1b):

$$\begin{matrix}\text{Future Value} \\ \text{in Year } n \\ (FV_n)\end{matrix} = \begin{matrix}\text{Present} \\ \text{Value } (PV)\end{matrix} \left(1 + \dfrac{\begin{matrix}\text{Annual} \\ \text{Interest Rate } (i)\end{matrix}}{\begin{matrix}\text{Compounding} \\ \text{Periods per Year } (m)\end{matrix}}\right)^{m \times \text{(Number of Years } (n))}$$

$$\text{Future Value in Year } n\ (FV_n) = \$1,000\left(1 + \frac{.12}{2}\right)^{2\times 5} = \$1,000 \times 1.79085 = \$1,790.85$$

Using a Financial Calculator.

Enter	10	6.0	-1,000	0	
	N	I/Y	PV	PMT	FV
Solve for					1,790.85

You will have $1,790.85 at the end of five years.

Using an Excel Spreadsheet.

= FV(rate,nper,pmt,pv) or with values entered = FV(0.06,10,0,−1000)

STEP 4: Analyze

The more often interest is compounded per year—that is, the larger m is, resulting in a larger value of *nper*—the larger the future value will be. That's because you are earning interest more often on the interest you've previously earned.

STEP 5: Check yourself

If you deposit $50,000 in an account that pays an annual interest rate of 10 percent compounded monthly, what will your account balance be in 10 years?

ANSWER: $135,352.07.

Your Turn: For more practice, do related **Study Problems** 5–5 and 5–7 at the end of this chapter. **>> END Checkpoint 5.3**

THE BUSINESS OF LIFE

Saving for Your First House

There was a time in the early and mid-2000s when you didn't need to worry about a down payment when you bought a new house. But that all changed as the housing bubble burst and home prices fell. Today you may be able to get away with only putting down around 10 percent, but the rate on your mortgage will be lower if you can come up with 20 percent. To buy a median-priced home, which was just over $180,000 at the beginning of 2013, you'd have to come up with a

Saving for Your First House (continued)

10 percent down payment of $18,000 or a 20 percent down payment of $36,000. On top of that, you'll need to furnish your new home, and that costs money too.

Putting into practice what you have learned in this chapter, you know that the sooner you start to save for your first home, the easier it will be. Once you estimate how much you'll need for that new house, you can easily calculate how much you'll need to save annually to reach your goal. All you need to do is look at two variables: n (the number of years you'll be saving the money) and i (the interest rate at which the savings will grow). You can start saving earlier, which gives you a larger value for n. Or, you can earn more on your investments—that is, invest at a higher value for i. Of course, you always prefer getting a higher i on your savings, but this is not something you can control.

First, let's take a look at a higher value for i, which translates into a higher return. For example, let's say you've just inherited $10,000, and you invest it at 6

percent annually for 10 years—after which you want to buy your first house. The calculation is easy. At the end of 10 years, you will have accumulated $17,908 on this investment. But suppose you are able to earn 12 percent annually for 10 years. What would the value of your investment be then? In this case, your investment would be worth $31,058. Needless to say, the rate of interest that you earn plays a major role in determining how quickly your investment will grow.

Now consider what happens if you wait five years before investing your $10,000. The value of n drops from 10 to 5, and, as a result, the amount you've saved also drops. In fact, if you invested your $10,000 for five years at 6 percent, you'd end up with $13,382, and even at 12 percent you'd end up with only $17,623.

The bottom line is the earlier you begin saving, the more impact every dollar you save will have.

Your Turn: See Study Question 5–3.

Before you move on to 5.3
CONCEPT CHECK: 5.2

1. What is compound interest, and how is it calculated?

2. Describe the three basic approaches that can be used to move money through time.

3. How does increasing the number of compounding periods affect the future value of a cash sum?

5.3   Discounting and Present Value

So far we have only been moving money forward in time; that is, we have taken a known present value of money and determined how much it will be worth at some point in the future. Financial decisions often require calculating the future value of an investment made today. However, there are many instances where we want to look at the reverse question: What is the value today of a sum of money to be received in the future? To answer this question, we now turn our attention to the analysis of a present value—the value today of a future cash flow—and the process of **discounting**, determining the present value of an expected future cash flow.

The Mechanics of Discounting Future Cash Flows

Discounting is actually the reverse of compounding. We can demonstrate the similarity between compounding and discounting by referring back to the future value formula found in Equation (5–1a):

Equation 5.1a

$$\text{Future Value in Year } n \; (FV_n) = \text{Present Value } (PV)\left(1 + \text{Annual Interest Rate } (i)\right)^{\text{Number of Years } (n)}$$

To determine the present value of a known future cash flow, we simply take Equation (5–1a) and solve for PV:

Equation 5.2

$$\text{Present Value } (PV) = \begin{matrix}\text{Future Value} \\ \text{in Year } n \\ (FV_n)\end{matrix} \left[\frac{1}{\left(1 + \begin{matrix}\text{Annual} \\ \text{Interest Rate } (i)\end{matrix}\right)^{\text{Number of Years } (n)}} \right]$$

We also refer to the term in the brackets as the **present value interest factor**, which is the value that multiples the future value to calculate the present value. Thus, to find the present value of a future cash flow, we multiply the future cash flow by the present value interest factor.[1]

$$\text{Present Value } (PV) = \begin{matrix}\text{Future Value} \\ \text{in year } n \\ (FV_n)\end{matrix} \times \left(\begin{matrix}\text{Present Value} \\ \text{Interest Factor} \\ (PVIF)\end{matrix} \right)$$

where Present Value Interest Factor $(PVIF) = \dfrac{1}{(1 + i)^n}$

Note that the present value of a future sum of money decreases as we increase the number of periods, n, until the payment is received, or as we increase the interest rate, i. That, of course, only makes sense because the present value interest factor is the *inverse* of the future value interest factor. Graphically, this relationship can be seen in Figure 5.2.

Thus, given a **discount rate**, or interest rate at which money is being brought back to present, of 10 percent, $100 received in 10 years would be worth only $38.55 today. By contrast, if the discount rate is 5 percent, the present value would be $61.39. If the discount rate is 10 percent, but the $100 is received in 5 years instead of 10 years, the present value would be $62.09. This concept of present value plays a central role in the valuation of stocks, bonds, and new proposals. You can easily verify this calculation using any of the discounting methods we describe next.

FIGURE 5.2

The Present Value of $100 Compounded at Different Rates and for Different Time Periods

The present value of $100 to be received in the future becomes smaller as both the interest rate and number of years rise. At i = 10%, notice that when the number of years goes up from 5 to 10, the present value drops from $62.09 to $38.55.

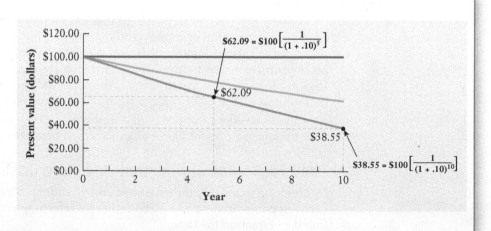

$$\$62.09 = \$100\left[\frac{1}{(1+.10)^5}\right]$$

$62.09

$38.55

$$\$38.55 = \$100\left[\frac{1}{(1+.10)^{10}}\right]$$

Year

---

[1]Related tables appear in Appendix C in MyFinanceLab.

Checkpoint 5.4

Solving for the Present Value of a Future Cash Flow

Your firm has just sold a piece of property for $500,000, but under the sales agreement, it won't receive the $500,000 until 10 years from today. What is the present value of $500,000 to be received 10 years from today if the discount rate is 6 percent annually?

STEP 1: Picture the problem

Expressed as a timeline, this problem would look like the following:

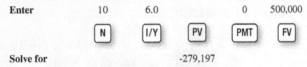

STEP 2: Decide on a solution strategy

In this instance we are simply solving for the present value of $500,000 to be received at the end of 10 years. We can calculate the present value of the $500,000 using Equation (5–2).

STEP 3: Solve

Using the Mathematical Formulas. Substituting $FV_{10} = \$500,000$, $n = 10$, and $i = 6\%$ into Equation (5–2), we find

$$PV = \$500,000 \left[\frac{1}{(1 + .06)^{10}} \right]$$
$$= \$500,000 \left[\frac{1}{1.79085} \right]$$
$$= \$500,000 [.558394]$$
$$= \$279,197$$

The present value of the $500,000 to be received in 10 years is $279,197. Earlier we noted that discounting is the reverse of compounding. We can easily test this calculation by considering this problem in reverse: What is the future value in 10 years of $279,197 today if the rate of interest is 6 percent? Using our *FV* Equation (5–1a), we can see that the answer is $500,000.

Using a Financial Calculator.

Enter	10	6.0		0	500,000
	N	I/Y	PV	PMT	FV
Solve for			-279,197		

Using an Excel Spreadsheet.

= PV(rate,nper,pmt,fv) or with values entered = PV(0.06,10,0,500000)

STEP 4: Analyze

Once you've found the present value of any future cash flow, that present value is in today's dollars and can be compared to other present values. The underlying point of this exercise is to make cash flows that occur in different time periods comparable so that we can make good decisions. Also notice that regardless of which method we use to calculate the future value—computing the formula by hand, with a calculator, or with Excel—we always arrive at the same answer.

STEP 5: Check yourself

What is the present value of $100,000 to be received at the end of 25 years given a 5 percent discount rate?

ANSWER: $29,530.

Your Turn: For more practice, do related **Study Problems** 5–12, 5–15, 5–19, and 5–28 at the end of this chapter.

>> **END Checkpoint 5.4**

Two Additional Types of Discounting Problems

Time-value-of-money problems do not always involve calculating either the present value or future value of a series of cash flows. There are a number problems that require that you solve for either the number of periods in the future, n, or the rate of interest, i. For example, to answer the following questions you will need to calculate the value for n:

- How many years will it be before the money I have saved will be enough to buy a second home?

- How long will it take to accumulate enough money for a down payment on a new retail outlet?

And to answer the following questions you must solve for the interest rate, i:

- What rate do I need to earn on my investment to have enough money for my newborn child's college education ($n = 18$ years)?

- If our firm introduces a new product line, what interest rate will this investment earn?

Fortunately, with the help of the mathematical formulas, a financial calculator, or an Excel spreadsheet, you can easily solve for i or n in any of these or similar situations.

Solving for the Number of Periods Suppose you want to know how many years it will take for an investment of $9,330 to grow to $20,000 if it's invested at 10 percent annually. Let's take a look at how to solve this using the mathematical formulas, a financial calculator, and an Excel spreadsheet.

Using Mathematical Formulas.   Substituting for FV, PV, and i in Equation (5–1a),

Equation 5.1a

$$\underset{(FV_n)}{\overset{\text{Future Value}}{\text{in Year } n}} = \underset{\text{Value } (PV)}{\text{Present}} \left(1 + \frac{\text{Annual}}{\text{Interest Rate } (i)}\right)^{\overset{\text{Number of}}{\text{Years } (n)}}$$

$$\$20,000 = \$9,330(1.10)^n$$

Solving for n mathematically is tough. One way is to solve for n using a trial-and-error approach. That is, you could substitute different values of n into the equation—either increasing the value of n to make the right-hand side of the equation larger, or decreasing the value of n to make it smaller, until the two sides of the equation are equal—but that will be a bit tedious. Using the time-value-of-money features on a financial calculator or in Excel is much easier and faster.

Using a Financial Calculator.   Using a financial calculator or an Excel spreadsheet, this problem becomes much easier. With a financial calculator, all you do is substitute in the values for i, PV, and FV, and solve for n:

Enter		10.0	-9,330	0	20,000
	N	I/Y	PV	PMT	FV
Solve for	8.0

You'll notice that PV is input with a negative sign. In effect the financial calculator is programmed to assume that the $9,330 is a cash outflow (the money leaving your hands), whereas the $20,000 is money that you will receive. If you don't give one of these values a negative sign, you can't solve the problem.

Using an Excel Spreadsheet. With Excel, solving for *n* is straightforward. You simply use the =NPER(rate,pmt,pv,fv) or with variables entered, =NPER(0.10,0,–9330,20000).

The Rule of 72

Now you know how to determine the future value of any investment. What if all you want to know is how long it will take to double your money in that investment? One simple way to approximate how long it will take for a given sum to double in value is called the **Rule of 72**. This "rule" states that you can determine how many years it will take for a given sum to double by dividing the investment's annual growth or interest rate into 72. For example, if an investment grows at an annual rate of 9 percent per year, according to the Rule of 72 it should take 72/9 = 8 years for that sum to double.

Checkpoint 5.5

Solving for the Number of Periods, *n*

Let's assume that the Toyota Corporation has guaranteed that the price of a new Prius will always be $20,000, and you'd like to buy one but currently have only $7,752. How many years will it take for your initial investment of $7,752 to grow to $20,000 if it is invested so that it earns 9 percent compounded annually?

STEP 1: Picture the problem

In this case we are solving for the number of periods:

STEP 2: Decide on a solution strategy

In this problem we know the interest rate, the present value, and the future value, and we want to know how many years it will take for $7,752 to grow to $20,000 at 9 percent per year. We are solving for *n*, and we can calculate it using Equation (5–1a).

STEP 3: Solve

Using a Financial Calculator.

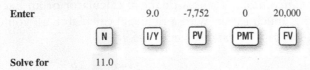

Enter   9.0   –7,752   0   20,000

| N | I/Y | PV | PMT | FV |

Solve for   11.0

Using an Excel Spreadsheet.

= NPER(rate,pmt,pv,fv) or with values entered = NPER(0.09,0,–7752,20000)

STEP 4: Analyze

It will take about 11 years for $7,752 to grow to $20,000 at 9 percent compound interest. This is the kind of calculation that both individuals and business make in trying to plan for major expenditures.

STEP 5: Check yourself

How many years will it take for $10,000 to grow to $200,000 given a 15 percent compound growth rate?

ANSWER: 21.4 years.

Your Turn: For more practice, do related **Study Problems** 5–13 and 5–18 at the end of this chapter.   **>> END Checkpoint 5.5**

Keep in mind that this is not a hard-and-fast rule, just an approximation—but it's a pretty good approximation. For example, the *future value interest factor* of $(1 + i)^n$ for 8 years ($n = 8$) at 9 percent ($i = 9\%$) is 1.993, which is pretty close to the Rule of 72's approximation of 2.0.

Solving for the Rate of Interest You have just inherited $34,946 and want to use it to fund your retirement in 30 years. If you have estimated that you will need $800,000 to fund your retirement, what rate of interest would you have to earn on your $34,946 investment? Let's take a look at solving this using the mathematical formulas, a financial calculator, and an Excel spreadsheet to calculate i.

Using Mathematical Formulas. If you write this problem using our time value of money formula you get,

Equation 5.1a

$$\underset{(FV_n)}{\overset{\text{Future Value}}{\text{in Year } n}} = \underset{\text{Value } (PV)}{\text{Present}} \left(1 + \underset{\text{Interest Rate } (i)}{\text{Annual}}\right)^{\overset{\text{Number of}}{\text{Years } (n)}}$$

$$\$800{,}000 = \$34{,}946(1+i)^{30}$$

Once again, you could resort to a trial-and-error approach by substituting different values of i into the equation and calculating the value on the right-hand side of the equation to see if it is equal to $800,000. However, again, this would be quite cumbersome and unnecessary. Alternatively, you can solve for i directly by dividing both sides of the equation above by $34,946,

$$(1+i)^{30} = \$800{,}000/\$34{,}946 = 22.8925$$

and then taking the 30th root of this equation to find the value of $(1 + i)$. Because taking the 30th root of something is the same as taking something to the 1/30 (or 0.033333) power, this is a relatively easy process if you have a financial calculator with a "y^n" key. In this case, you (1) enter 22.8925, (2) press the "y^n" key, (3) enter 0.033333, and (4) press the "=" key. The answer should be 1.109999, indicating that $(1 + i) = 1.109999$, and $i = 10.9999\%$ or 11%. As you might expect, it's faster and easier to use the time-value-of-money functions on a financial calculator or in Excel.

Using a Financial Calculator. Using a financial calculator or an Excel spreadsheet, this problem becomes much easier. With a financial calculator, all you do is substitute in the values for n, PV, and FV, and solve for i:

Enter	30		-34,946	0	800,000
	N	I/Y	PV	PMT	FV
Solve for		11.0			

Using an Excel Spreadsheet.

= RATE(nper,pmt,pv,fv) or with values entered = RATE(30,0,−34946,800000)

Before you move on to 5.4

CONCEPT CHECK: 5.3

1. What does the term *discounting* mean with respect to the time value of money?

2. How is discounting related to compounding?

Solving for the Interest Rate, *i*

Let's go back to that Prius example in Checkpoint 5.5. Recall that the Prius always costs $20,000. In 10 years, you'd really like to have $20,000 to buy a new Prius, but you only have $11,167 now. At what rate must your $11,167 be compounded annually for it to grow to $20,000 in 10 years?

STEP 1: Picture the problem

* We can visualize the problem using a timeline as follows:

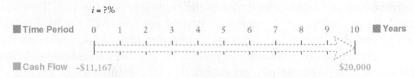

STEP 2: Decide on a solution strategy

Here we know the number of years, the present value, and the future value, and we are solving for the interest rate. We'll use Equation (5–1a) to solve this problem.

STEP 3: Solve

Using the Mathematical Formulas.

$20,000 = $11,167 $(1 + i)^{10}$,
or $1.7910 = (1 + i)^{10}$

We then take the 10th root of this equation to find the value of $(1 + i)$. Because taking the 10th root of something is the same as taking something to the 1/10 (or 0.10) power, this can be done if you have a financial calculator with a "y^x" key. In this case, you (1) enter 1.7910, (2) press the "y^x" key, (3) enter 0.10, and (4) press the "=" key. The answer should be 1.06, indicating that $(1 + i) = 1.06$, and $i = 6\%$.

Using a Financial Calculator.

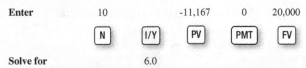

Enter	10		-11,167	0	20,000
	N	I/Y	PV	PMT	FV
Solve for		6.0			

Using an Excel Spreadsheet.

= RATE(nper,pmt,pv,fv) or with values entered = RATE(10,0,−11167,20000)

STEP 4: Analyze

You can increase your future value by growing your money at a higher interest rate or by letting your money grow for a longer period of time. For most of you, when it comes to planning for your retirement, a large *n* is a real positive for you. Also, if you can earn a slightly higher return on your retirement savings, or any savings for that matter, it can make a big difference.

STEP 5: Check yourself

At what rate will $50,000 have to grow to reach $1,000,000 in 30 years?

ANSWER: 10.5 percent.

Your Turn: For more practice, do related **Study Problems** 5–14, 5–16, 5–17, 5–20 to 5–22, 5–26, and 5–27 at the end of this chapter.

>> **END Checkpoint 5.6**

5.4 Making Interest Rates Comparable

Sometimes it's difficult to determine exactly how much you are paying or earning on a loan. That's because the loan might not be quoted as compounding annually, but rather as compounding quarterly or daily. To illustrate, let's look at two loans, one that is quoted as 8.084 percent compounded annually and another quoted as 7.85 percent compounded quarterly. Unfortunately, because on one the interest is compounded annually (you pay interest just once a year) but on the other, interest is compounded quarterly (you pay interest four times a year), they are difficult to compare. To allow borrowers to compare rates between different lenders, the U.S. Truth-in-Lending Act requires what is known as the annual percentage rate (APR) to be displayed on all consumer loan documents. The **annual percentage rate (APR)** indicates the interest rate paid or earned in one year without compounding. We can calculate APR as the interest rate per period (for example, per month or week) multiplied by the number of periods during which compounding occurs during the year (m):

Equation 5.3

$$\begin{array}{c} \text{Annual Percentage} \\ \text{Rate } (APR) \\ \text{or Simple Interest} \end{array} = \begin{pmatrix} \text{Interest Rate per} \\ \text{Period (for example} \\ \text{per month or week)} \end{pmatrix} \times \begin{array}{c} \text{Compounding} \\ \text{Periods per} \\ \text{Year } (m) \end{array}$$

Thus, if you are paying 2 percent per month, m, the number of compounding periods per year, would be 12, and the APR would be:

$$APR = 2\%/\text{month} \times 12 \text{ months/year} = 24\%$$

Unfortunately, the APR does not help much when the rates being compared are not compounded for the same number of periods per year. In fact, the APR is also called the **nominal or quoted (stated) interest rate** because it is the rate that the lender states you are paying. In our example, both 8.084 percent and 7.85 percent are the annual percentage rates (APRs), but they aren't comparable because the loans have different compounding periods.

To make them comparable, we calculate their equivalent rate using an annual compounding period. We do this by calculating the **effective annual rate (EAR)**, the annual compounded rate that produces the same return as the nominal, or stated, rate. The EAR can be calculated using the following equation:

Equation 5.4

$$\text{Effective Annual Rate } (EAR) = \left(1 + \frac{\begin{array}{c}\text{Quoted} \\ \text{Annual Rate}\end{array}}{\begin{array}{c}\text{Compounding Periods} \\ \text{per Year } (m)\end{array}} \right)^m - 1$$

We calculate the EAR for the loan that has a 7.85 percent quoted annual rate of interest compounded quarterly (i.e., $m = 4$ times per year) using Equation (5–4) as follows:

$$EAR = \left[1 + \frac{0.0785}{4} \right]^4 - 1 = .08084 \text{ or } 8.084\%$$

So if your banker offers you a loan with a 7.85 percent rate that is compounded quarterly or an 8.084 percent rate with annual compounding, which should you prefer?

Checkpoint 5.7

Calculating an Effective Annual Rate or EAR

Assume that you just received your first credit card statement and the APR, or annual percentage rate, listed on the statement is 21.7 percent. When you look closer you notice that the interest is compounded daily. What is the EAR, or effective annual rate, on your credit card?

STEP 1: Picture the problem

We can visualize the problem using a timeline as follows:

If i = an annual rate of 21.7% which is compounded on a daily basis, what is the EAR?

| ■ Time Period | 0 | 1 | 2 | 3 | 4 | 5 | 6 | 7 | 8 | 9 | 10 | ■ Daily Periods |

■ Cash Flow   –$ Amount

STEP 2: Decide on a solution strategy

We'll use Equation (5–4) to solve this problem:

$$\text{Effective Annual Rate } (EAR) = \left(1 + \frac{\text{Quoted Annual Rate}}{\text{Compounding Periods per year } (m)}\right)^m - 1 \tag{5–4}$$

STEP 3: Solve

To calculate the EAR we can use Equation (5–4), where the quoted annual rate is 21.7 percent, or 0.217, and m is 365. Substituting in these values, we get

$$EAR = \left[1 + \frac{0.217}{365}\right]^{365} - 1$$
$$EAR = 1.242264 - 1 = 0.242264 \text{ or } 24.2264\%$$

You were right in thinking that the amount of interest you owed seemed high. In reality, the EAR, or effective annual rate, is actually 24.2264 percent. Recall that whenever interest is compounded more frequently, it accumulates faster.

STEP 4: Analyze

When you invest in a certificate of deposit, or CD, at a bank, the rate the bank will quote you is the EAR—that's because it actually is the rate that you will earn on your money—and it's also higher than the simple APR. It's important to make sure when you compare different interest rates that they are truly comparable, and the EAR allows you to make them comparable. For example, if you're talking about borrowing money at 9 percent compounded daily, although the APR is 9 percent, the EAR is actually 9.426 percent. That's a pretty big difference when you're paying the interest.

STEP 5: Check yourself

What is the EAR on a quoted or stated rate of 13 percent that is compounded monthly?

ANSWER: 13.80 percent.

Your Turn: For more practice, do related **Study Problems** 5–35 through 5–38 at the end of this chapter.   **>> END Checkpoint 5.7**

If you didn't know how the time value of money is affected by compounding, you would have chosen the 7.85 percent rate because, on the surface, it looked like the loan with the lower cost. However, you should be indifferent because these two offers have the same cost to you—that is to say, they have the same EAR. The key point here is that to compare the two loan terms you need to convert them to the same number of compounding periods (annual in this case). Given the wide variety of compounding periods used by businesses and banks, it is important to know how to make these rates comparable so you can make logical decisions.

Now let's return to that payday loan we introduced at the chapter opening. What is its EAR? In that example, we looked at a payday lender that advertised that you could borrow $500 and repay $626.37 eight days later. On the surface, that looks like you are paying 25.274 percent ($626.37/$500 = 1.25274), but that's really what you are paying every eight days. To find the quoted annual rate we multiply the eight-day rate of 25.274 percent times the number of eight-day periods in a year (in effect, you are paying 25.274 percent every eight days, or 25.274% × 45.625 = 1,153.13%). In this case m is 45.625 because there are 45.625 eight-day periods in a year (365 days), and the annual rate is 0.25274 × 45.625 = 11.5313 (the eight-day rate times the number of eight-day periods in a year). Substituting into Equation (5–4), we get

$$EAR = \left[1 + \frac{11.5315}{45.625}\right]^{45.625} - 1$$

$$EAR = 29,168.80 - 1 = 29,167.80, \text{ or } 2,916,780\%$$

Needless to say, you'll want to stay away from payday loans.

Calculating the Interest Rate and Converting It to an EAR

When you have non-annual compounding and you calculate a value for i using your financial calculator or Excel, you're calculating the rate per non-annual compounding period, which is referred to as the periodic rate:

$$\text{Periodic Rate} = \frac{\text{Quoted Annual Rate}}{\text{Compounding Periods per Year} (m)}$$

You can easily convert the periodic rate into an APR by multiplying it by the number of times that compounding occurs per year (m). However, if you're interested in the EAR, you'll have to subsequently convert the value you just calculated into an EAR. Let's look at an example.

Suppose that you've just taken out a two-year, $100,000 loan with monthly compounding and that at the end of two years you will pay $126,973 to pay the loan off. How can we find the quoted interest rate on this loan and convert it to an EAR? This problem can be solved using either a financial calculator or Excel.[2] Because the problem involves monthly compounding, m, the number of compounding periods per year is 12; n, the number of periods, becomes 24 (number of years times m, or 2 times 12); and the solution, i, will be expressed as the *monthly rate*.

Financial Calculator.   Substituting in a financial calculator we find

Enter	24		-100,000	0	126,973
	N	I/Y	PV	PMT	FV
Solve for		1.0			

To determine the APR you're paying on this loan, you need to multiply the value you just calculated for i times 12—thus the APR on this loan is 12 percent—but that is *not* the loan's EAR. It's merely the APR. To convert the APR to an EAR, we can use Equation (5–4):

Equation 5.4

$$\text{Effective Annual Rate } (EAR) = \left(1 + \frac{\text{Quoted Annual Rate}}{\text{Compounding Periods per Year } (m)}\right)^m - 1$$

where the quoted annual rate is 0.12, and m is 12. Substituting these values into the above equation we get

$$EAR = \left[1 + \frac{0.12}{12}\right]^{12} - 1$$

$$EAR = 1.1268 - 1 = 0.126825, \text{ or } 12.6825\%$$

In reality, the EAR, or effective annual rate, is actually 12.6825 percent. In effect, if you took out a two-year loan for $100,000 at 12.6825 percent compounded annually, your payment at the end of two years would be $126,973, the same payment you had when you borrowed $100,000 at 12 percent compounded monthly.

To the Extreme: Continuous Compounding

As m (the number of compounding periods per year) increases, so does the EAR. That only makes sense because the greater the number of compounding periods, the more often interest is earned on interest. As you just saw, we can easily compute the EAR when interest is compounded daily ($m = 365$). We can just as easily calculate EAR if the interest, i, is compounded hourly ($m = 8,760$), compounded every minute ($m = 525,600$), or every second ($m = 31,536,000$). We can even calculate the EAR when interest is continuously compounded; that is, when the time intervals between interest payments are infinitely small, as

Equation 5.5

$$EAR = \left(e^{quoted\ annual\ rate}\right) - 1$$

where e is the number 2.71828, with the corresponding calculator key generally appearing as "e^x." This number e is an irrational number that is used in applications that involve things that grow continuously over time. It is similar to the number Π in geometry.[3]

Let's take another look at the credit card example we looked at in Checkpoint 5.7, but with continuous compounding. Again, the APR, or annual percentage rate, is listed at 21.7 percent. With continuous compounding, what's the EAR, or effective annual rate, on your credit card?

$$EAR = e^{.217} - 1 = 1.2423 - 1 = 0.2423, \text{ or } 24.23\%$$

---

[2] Using either a TI BAII-Plus or an HP 10BII calculator, there is a shortcut key that allows you to enter the number of compounding periods and the nominal rate to calculate the EAR. Those keystrokes are shown in Appendix A in MyFinanceLab.

Finance in a **Flat World**
Financial Access at Birth

Approximately half the world's population has no access to financial services such as savings, credit, and insurance. Inspired by the One-Laptop-Per-Child campaign, UCLA finance professor Bhagwan Chowdhry has a plan to take this number to zero by 2030, called the Financial Access at Birth (FAB) Campaign.

This is how FAB could work. Each child would have an online bank account opened at birth with an initial deposit of $100. The bank account would be opened together with the child's birth registration, and the deposit plus interest could be withdrawn when the child reaches 16 years of age. If the program were launched in 2011, in just 20 short years every child and young adult in the world would have access to financial services. Assuming a 5 percent annual rate of interest on the deposit, the $100 deposit would grow to about $218 when the child reaches 16. If we wait until the child reaches 21 before turning over the account, it will have grown to about $279. In many parts of the world this would be a princely sum of money. Moreover, the recipient would have a bank account!

So what's the cost of implementing FAB? Currently there are about 134 million children born annually, and assuming that a quarter of these children would not need the service, this leaves 100 million children that otherwise would not have access to a bank account. The cost of the program would then be just $10 billion per year, which is less than the amount spent per week on military expenditures around the world. If 100 million individuals would contribute just $100 per year the dream of the FAB could become a reality. Every person in the world would have access to financial services in just 20 years!

Want to learn more? Go to http://tr.im/fabcam.

Before you begin end-of-chapter material
CONCEPT CHECK: 5.4

1. How does an EAR differ from an APR?

2. What is the effect of having multiple compounding periods within a year on future values?

---

[3] Like the number Π, it goes on forever. In fact, if you're interested, you can find the first 5 million digits of *e* at http://antwrp.gsfc.nasa.gov/htmltest/gifcity/e.5mil

Applying the Principles of Finance to Chapter 5

P Principle 1: **Money Has a Time Value** This chapter begins our study of the time value of money—a dollar received today, other things being the same, is worth more than a dollar received a year from now. The concept of time value of money underlies many financial decisions faced in business. In this chapter, we learn how to calculate the value today of a sum of money received in the future and the future value of a present sum.

Chapter Summaries

Summary	Key Terms

5.1 Construct cash flow timelines to organize your analysis of problems involving time value of money. (pgs. 150–151)

Timelines can help you visualize and then solve time-value-of-money problems. Time periods—with 0 representing today, 1 the end of Period 1, and so forth—are listed on top of the timeline. Note that Period 1 represents the end of Period 1 and the beginning of Period 2. The periods can consist of years, months, days, or any unit of time. However, in general, when people analyze cash flows, they are looking at yearly periods. The cash flows appear below the timeline. Cash inflows are labeled with positive signs. Cash outflows are labeled with negative signs.	**Timeline, page 150** A linear representation of the timing of cash flows.

Concept Check: 5.1

1. What is a timeline, and how does it help you solve problems involving the time value of money?

2. Does Year 5 represent the end of the fifth year, the beginning of the sixth year, or both?

5.2 Understand compounding and calculate the future value of cash flows using mathematical formulas, a financial calculator, and an Excel spreadsheet. (pgs. 152–159)

Compounding begins when the interest earned on an investment during a past period begins earning interest in the current period. Financial managers must compare the costs and benefits of alternatives that do not occur during the same time period. Calculating the time value of money makes all dollar values comparable; because money has a time value, it moves all dollar flows either back to the present or out to a common future date. All time value formulas presented in this chapter actually stem from the single compounding formula $FV_n = PV(1 + i)^n$. The formulas are used to deal simply with common financial situations, for example, discounting single flows or moving single flows out into the future. Financial calculators are a handy and inexpensive alternative to doing the math. However, most professionals today use spreadsheet software, such as Excel.	**Compounding, page 152** The process of determining the future value of a payment or series of payments when applying the concept of compound interest. **Compound interest, page 152** The situation in which interest paid on the investment during the first period is added to the principal and, during the second period, interest is earned on the original principal plus the interest earned during the first period. **Future value, page 152** What a cash flow will be worth in the future. **Future value interest factor, page 153** The value $(1 + i)^n$ used as a multiplier to calculate an amount's future value.

Summary	Key Terms

Concept Check: 5.2

1. What is compound interest, and how is it calculated?
2. Describe the three basic approaches that can be used to move money through time.
3. How does increasing the number of compounding periods affect the future value of a cash sum?

Present value, page 152 The value in today's dollars of a future payment discounted back to the present at the required rate of return.

Simple interest, page 152 The interest earned on the principal.

Key Equations

$$\text{Future Value in Year } n\ (FV_n) = \text{Present Value } (PV)\left(1 + \frac{\text{Annual}}{\text{Interest Rate } (i)}\right)^{\text{Number of Years } (n)}$$

Equation 5.1a

$$\text{Future Value in Year } n\ (FV_n) = \text{Present Value } (PV)\left(1 + \frac{\text{Interest Rate } (i)}{\text{Compounding}}\right)^{m \times (\text{Number of Years } (n))}$$

Equation 5.1b

where m is the number of compounding periods per year.

5.3 Understand discounting and calculate the present value of cash flows using mathematical formulas, a financial calculator, and an Excel spreadsheet. (pgs. 159–167)

Previously we were solving for the future value (FV_n) of the present value (PV) of a sum of money. When we are solving for the present value, we are simply doing the reverse of solving for the future value. We can find the present value by solving for PV,

$$PV = FV_n\left[\frac{1}{(1 + i)^n}\right]$$

In addition, increasing the number of compounding periods within the year, while holding the rate of interest constant, will magnify the effects of compounding. That is, even though the rate of interest does not change, increasing the number of compounding periods means that interest gets compounded sooner than it would otherwise. This magnifies the effects of compounding.

Discount rate, page 160 The interest rate used in the discounting process.

Discounting, page 159 The inverse of compounding. This process is used to determine the present value of a future cash flow.

Present value interest factor, page 160 The value $[1/(1 + i)^n]$ used as a multiplier to calculate a future payment's present value.

Rule of 72, page 163 A method for estimating the time it takes for an amount to double in value. To determine the approximate time it takes for an amount to double in value, 72 is divided by the annual interest rate.

Concept Check: 5.3

1. What does the term discounting mean with respect to the time value of money?
2. How is discounting related to compounding?

Summary	Key Terms

Key Equations

$$\text{Present Value } (PV) = \frac{\text{Future Value in Year } n \ (FV_n)}{\left(1 + \frac{\text{Annual Interest Rate } (i)}{}\right)^{\text{Number of Years } (n)}}$$

$$\text{Present Value } (PV) = \text{Future Value in Year } n \ (FV_n) \left[\frac{1}{\left(1 + \frac{\text{Annual Interest Rate } (i)}{\text{Compounding}}\right)^{m \times (\text{Number of Years } (n))}}\right]$$ **Equation 5.2**

where m is the number of compounding periods per year.

5.4 Understand how interest rates are quoted and know how to make them comparable. (pgs. 165–168)

One way to compare different interest rates is to use the annual percentage rate (APR), which indicates the amount of interest earned in one year without compounding. The APR is the simple interest rate and is calculated as the interest rate per period multiplied by the number of periods in the year:

$$APR = \text{Interest Rate per Period} \times \text{Periods per Year}$$ **Equation 5.3**

The problem with the APR is that if compounding occurs more than once a year—for example, if the interest you owe is calculated every month, then in the second month, and from then on, you will end up paying interest from the first month. The end result of this is that the actual interest rate you are paying is greater than the APR. To find out the actual amount of interest we would pay over the course of one time period, we must convert the quoted APR rate to an effective annual rate (EAR). The EAR is the annual compounded rate that produces the same cash flow as the nominal interest rate:

$$EAR = \left(1 + \frac{\text{Quoted Annual Rate}}{m}\right)^m - 1$$ **Equation 5.4**

where EAR is the effective annual rate, and m is the number of compounding periods within a year

Annual percentage rate (APR), page 165
The interest rate paid or earned in one year without compounding. It is calculated as the interest rate per period (for example, per month or week) multiplied by the number of periods during which compounding occurs during the year (m).

Effective annual rate (EAR), page 165
The annual compounded rate that produces the same return as the nominal, or stated, rate.

Nominal or quoted (stated) interest rate, page 165 The interest rate paid on debt securities without an adjustment for any loss in purchasing power.

Concept Check: 5.4

1. How does an EAR differ from an APR?
2. What is the effect of having multiple compounding periods within a year on future values?

Summary	Key Terms

Key Equations

$$\begin{matrix} \text{Annual Percentage} \\ \text{Rate } (APR) \\ \text{or simple interest} \end{matrix} = \begin{pmatrix} \text{Interest} \\ \text{Rate per} \\ \text{Period} \end{pmatrix} \times \begin{matrix} \text{Compounding} \\ \text{Periods per} \\ \text{Year} \end{matrix}$$

Equation 5.3

$$\text{Effective Annual Rate } (EAR) = \left(1 + \frac{\text{Quoted}}{\text{Compounding Periods}} \atop \text{per Year } (m) \right)^{m} - 1$$

Equation 5.4

where EAR = the effective annual rate.

Study Questions

Q5.1. What is the time value of money? Give three examples of how the time value of money might take on importance in business decisions.

Q5.2. The processes of discounting and compounding are related. Explain this relationship.

Q5.3. What is the relationship between the number of times interest is compounded per year on an investment and the future value of that investment? What is the relationship between the number of times compounding occurs per year and the EAR?

Q5.4. How would an increase in the interest rate (i) or a decrease in the number of periods (n) affect the future value (FV_n) of a sum of money?

Q5.5. How would an increase in the interest rate (i) or a decrease in the number of periods until the payment is received (n) affect the present value (PV) of a sum of money?

Q5.6. Compare some of the different financial calculators that are available on the Internet. Look at Kiplinger Online calculators (www.kiplinger.com/tools/index.html), which include saving and investing, mutual funds, bonds, stocks, home, auto, credit cards, and budgeting online calculators. Also go to www.dinkytown.net, www.bankrate.com/calculators.aspx, and www.interest.com and click on the "Calculators" links. Which financial calculators do you find to be the most useful? Why?

Q5.7. (Related to Chapter Introduction: Payday Loans on page 127) The introduction to this chapter examined payday loans. Recently, Congress passed legislation limiting the interest rate charged to active military to 36 percent. Go to the Predatory Lending Association website at www.predatorylendingassociation.com and find the military base closest to you and identify the payday lenders that surround that base. Also, identify any payday lenders near you.

Q5.8. (Related to Chapter Introduction: Payday Loans on page 127) In the introduction to this chapter, payday loans were examined. Go to the Responsible Lending Organization website at www.responsiblelending.org/payday-lending/. How does the "debt trap" (www.responsiblelending.org/payday-lending/tools-resources/debttrap.html) associated with payday loans work?

Study Problems Compound Interest

P5.1 (Related to Checkpoint 5.2 on page 134) (**Future value**) To what amount will the following investments accumulate?
  a. $5,000 invested for 10 years at 10 percent compounded annually
  b. $8,000 invested for 7 years at 8 percent compounded annually
  c. $775 invested for 12 years at 12 percent compounded annually
  d. $21,000 invested for 5 years at 5 percent compounded annually

P5.2 (Related to Checkpoint 5.2 on page 134) (**Future value**) Leslie Mosallam, who recently sold her Porsche, placed $10,000 in a savings account paying annual compound interest of 6 percent.
  a. Calculate the amount of money that will accumulate if Leslie leaves the money in the bank for 1, 5, and 15 years.
  b. Suppose Leslie moves her money into an account that pays 8 percent or one that pays 10 percent. Rework part (a) using 8 percent and 10 percent.
  c. What conclusions can you draw about the relationship between interest rates, time, and future sums from the calculations you just did?

P5.3 (Related to The Business of Life: Saving for Your First House on page 137) (**Future value**) You are hoping to buy a house in the future and recently received an inheritance of $20,000. You intend to use your inheritance as a down payment on your house.
  a. If you put your inheritance in an account that earns a 7 percent interest rate compounded annually, how many years will it be before your inheritance grows to $30,000?
  b. If you let your money grow for 10.25 years at 7 percent, how much will you have?
  c. How long will it take your money to grow to $30,000 if you move it into an account that pays 3 percent compounded annually? How long will it take your money to grow to $30,000 if you move it into an account that pays 11 percent?
  d. What does all of this tell you about the relationship among interest rates, time, and future sums?

P5.4 (Related to Checkpoint 5.2 on page 134) (**Future value**) Bob Terwilliger received $12,345 for his services as financial consultant to the mayor's office of his hometown of Springfield. Bob says that his consulting work was his civic duty and that he should not receive any compensation. So, he has invested his paycheck into an account paying 3.98 percent annual interest and left the account in his will to the city of Springfield on the condition that the city could not collect any money from the account for 200 years. How much money will the city receive from Bob's generosity in 200 years?

P5.5 (Related to Checkpoint 5.3 on page 136) (**Compound interest with non-annual periods**) Calculate the amount of money that will be in each of the following accounts at the end of the given deposit period:

Account Holder	Amount Deposited	Annual Interest Rate	Compounding Periods per Year (M)	Compounding Periods (Years)
Theodore Logan III	$ 1,000	10%	1	10
Vernell Coles	95,000	12	12	1
Tina Elliott	8,000	12	6	2
Wayne Robinson	120,000	8	4	2
Eunice Chung	30,000	10	2	4
Kelly Cravens	15,000	12	3	3

P5.6 (Related to Checkpoint 5.2 on page 134) (**Compound interest with non-annual periods**) You just received a $5,000 bonus.

    a. Calculate the future value of $5,000, given that it will be held in the bank for five years and earn an annual interest rate of 6 percent.

    b. **Recalculate** part (a) using a compounding period that is (1) semiannual and (2) bimonthly.

    c. **Recalculate** parts (a) and (b) using a 12 percent annual interest rate.

    d. **Recalculate** part (a) using a time horizon of 12 years at a 6 percent interest rate.

    c. What conclusions can you draw when you compare the answers in parts (c) and (d) with the answers in parts (a) and (b)?

P5.7 (Related to Checkpoint 5.3 on page 136) (**Compound interest with non-annual periods**) Your grandmother just gave you $6,000. You'd like to see what it might grow to if you invest it.

    a. Calculate the future value of $6,000, given that it will be invested for five years at an annual interest rate of 6 percent.

    b. **Recalculate** part (a) using a compounding period that is (1) semiannual and (2) bimonthly.

    c. Now let's look at what might happen if you can invest the money at a 12 percent rate rather than 6 percent rate; recalculate parts (a) and (b) for a 12 percent annual interest rate.

    d. Now let's see what might happen if you invest the money for 12 years rather than 5 years; recalculate part (a) using a time horizon of 12 years (annual interest rate is still 6 percent).

    e. With respect to the changes in the stated interest rate and length of time the money is invested in parts (c) and (d), what conclusions can you draw?

P5.8 (Related to Checkpoint 5.2 on page 134) (**Future value**) A new finance book sold 15,000 copies following the first year of its release, and was expected to increase by 20 percent per year. What sales are expected during Years 2, 3, and 4? Graph this sales trend and explain.

P5.9 (Related to Checkpoint 5.2 on page 134) (**Future value**) You have just introduced "must-have" headphones for the iPod. Sales of the new product are expected to be 10,000 units this year and are expected to increase by 15 percent per year in the future. What are expected sales during each of the next three years? Graph this sales trend and explain why the number of additional units sold increases every year.

P5.10 (Related to Checkpoint 5.2 on page 134) (**Future value**) If you deposit $3,500 today into an account earning an 11 percent annual rate of return, what would your account be worth in 35 years (assuming no further deposits)? In 40 years?

P5.11 (Related to Checkpoint 5.2 on page 134) (**Future value**) (**Simple and compound interest**) If you deposit $10,000 today into an account earning an 11 percent annual rate of return, in the third year how much interest would be earned? How much of the total is simple interest and how much results from compounding of interest?

Discounting and Present Value

P5.12 (Related to Checkpoint 5.4 on page 139) (**Present value**) Sarah Wiggum would like to make a single investment and have $2 million at the time of her retirement in 35 years. She has found a mutual fund that will earn 4 percent annually. How much will Sarah have to invest today? What if Sarah were a finance major and learned how to earn a 14 percent annual return? How soon could she then retire?

P5.13 (Related to Checkpoint 5.5 on page 141) (**Solving for *n***) How many years will the following take?

    a. $500 to grow to $1,039.50 if it's invested at 5 percent compounded annually

    b. $35 to grow to $53.87 if it's invested at 9 percent compounded annually

    c. $100 to grow to $298.60 if it's invested at 20 percent compounded annually

    d. $53 to grow to $78.76 if it's invested at 2 percent compounded annually

P5.14 (Related to Checkpoint 5.6 on page 143) (**Solving for *i***) At what annual interest rate would the following have to be invested?
  a. $500 to grow to $1,948.00 in 12 years
  b. $300 to grow to $422.10 in 7 years
  c. $50 to grow to $280.20 in 20 years
  d. $200 to grow to $497.60 in 5 years

P5.15 (Related to Checkpoint 5.4 on page 139) (**Present value**) What is the present value of the following future amounts?
  a. $800 to be received 10 years from now discounted back to the present at 10 percent
  b. $300 to be received 5 years from now discounted back to the present at 5 percent
  c. $1,000 to be received 8 years from now discounted back to the present at 3 percent
  d. $1,000 to be received 8 years from now discounted back to the present at 20 percent

P5.16 (Related to Checkpoint 5.6 on page 143) (**Solving for *i***) Kirk Van Houten, who has been married for 23 years, would like to buy his wife an expensive diamond ring with a platinum setting on their 30-year wedding anniversary. Assume that the cost of the ring will be $12,000 in seven years. Kirk currently has $4,510 to invest. What annual rate of return must Kirk earn on his investment to accumulate enough money to pay for the ring?

P5.17 (Related to Checkpoint 5.6 on page 143) (**Solving for *i***) You are considering investing in a security that will pay you $1,000 in 30 years.
  a. If the appropriate discount rate is 10 percent, what is the present value of this investment?
  b. Assume these investments sell for $365, in return for which you receive $1,000 in 30 years; what is the rate of return investors earn on this investment if they buy it for $365?

P5.18 (Related to Checkpoint 5.5 on page 141) (**Solving for *n***) Jack asked Jill to marry him, and she has accepted under one condition: Jack must buy her a new $330,000 Rolls-Royce Phantom. Jack currently has $45,530 that he may invest. He has found a mutual fund that pays 4.5 percent annual interest in which he will place the money. How long will it take Jack to win Jill's hand in marriage?

P5.19 (Related to Checkpoint 5.4 on page 139) (**Present value**) Ronen Consulting has just realized an accounting error that has resulted in an unfunded liability of $398,930 due in 28 years. In other words, the company will need $398,930 in 28 years. Toni Flanders, the company's CEO, is scrambling to discount the liability to the present to assist in valuing the firm's stock. If the appropriate discount rate is 7 percent, what is the present value of the liability?

P5.20 (Related to Checkpoint 5.6 on page 143) (**Solving for *i***) Seven years ago, Lance Murdock purchased a wooden statue of a Conquistador for $7,600 to put in his home office. Lance has recently married, and his home office is being converted into a sewing room. His new wife, who has far better taste than Lance, thinks the Conquistador is hideous and must go immediately. Lance decided to sell it on e-Bay and only received $5,200 for it, and so he took a loss on the investment. What was his rate of return, that is, the value of *i*?

P5.21 (Related to Checkpoint 5.6 on page 143) (**Solving for *i***) Springfield Learning sold zero-coupon bonds (bonds that don't pay any interest—instead the bondholder gets just one payment, coming when the bond matures, from the issuer) and received $900 for each bond that will pay $20,000 when it matures in 30 years.
  a. At what rate is Springfield Learning borrowing the money from investors?
  b. If Nancy Muntz purchased a bond at the offering for $900 and sold it 10 years later for the market price of $3,500, what annual rate of return did she earn?
  c. If Barney Gumble purchased Muntz's bond at the market price of $3,500 and held it 20 years until maturity, what annual rate of return would he have earned?

P5.22 Related to Checkpoint 5.6 on page 143) (**Solving for *i***) If you were offered $1,079.50 ten years from now in return for an investment of $500 currently, what annual rate of interest would you earn if you took the offer?

P5.23 Solving for *i*) An insurance agent just offered you a new insurance product that will provide you with $2,376.50 ten years from now if you invest $700 today. What annual rate of interest would you earn if you invested in this product?

P5.24 (Solving for *n* with non-annual periods) Approximately how many years would it take for an investment to grow fourfold if it were invested at 16 percent compounded semiannually?

P5.25 Solving for *n* with non-annual periods) Approximately how many years would it take for an investment to grow by sevenfold if it were invested at 10 percent compounded semiannually?

P5.26 (Related to Checkpoint 5.6 on page 143) (Solving for *i*) You lend a friend $10,000, for which your friend will repay you $27,027 at the end of five years. What interest rate are you charging your "friend"?

P5.27 (Related to Checkpoint 5.6 on page 143) (Solving for *i*) You've run out of money for college, and your college roommate has an idea for you. He offers to lend you $15,000, for which you will repay him $37,313 at the end of five years. If you took this loan, what interest rate would you be paying on it?

P5.28 (Related to Checkpoint 5.4 on page 139) (Present-value comparison) You are offered $100,000 today or $300,000 in 13 years. Assuming that you can earn 11 percent on your money, which should you choose?

P5.29 Present-value comparison) Much to your surprise, you were selected to appear on the TV show "The Price Is Right." As a result of your prowess in identifying how many rolls of toilet paper a typical American family keeps on hand, you win the opportunity to choose one of the following: $1,000 today, $10,000 in 12 years, or $25,000 in 25 years. Assuming that you can earn 11 percent on your money, which should you choose?

P5.30 (Related to Checkpoint 5.6 on page 143) (Solving for *i*) In September 1963, the first issue of the comic book *X-MEN* was issued. The original price for the issue was 12 cents. By September 2013, 50 years later, the value of this comic book had risen to $9,500. What annual rate of interest would you have earned if you had bought the comic in 1963 and sold it in 2013?

P5.31 (Solving for *i*) In March 1963, Ironman was first introduced in issue number 39 of the comic book *Tales of Suspense*. The original price for that issue was 12 cents. By March of 2013, 50 years later, the value of this comic book had risen to $9,000. What annual rate of interest would you have earned if you had bought the comic in 1963 and sold it in 2013?

P5.32 (Solving for *i*) A financial planner just offered you a new investment product that would require an initial investment on your part of $35,000, and then 25 years from now will be worth $250,000. What annual rate of interest would you earn if you invested in this product?

P5.33 (Spreadsheet problem) If you invest $900 in a bank where it will earn 8 percent compounded annually, how much will it be worth at the end of seven years? Use a spreadsheet to calculate your answer.

P5.34 (Spreadsheet problem) In 20 years, you would like to have $250,000 to buy a vacation home. If you have only $30,000, at what rate must it be compounded annually for it to grow to $250,000 in 20 years? Use a spreadsheet to calculate your answer.

Making Interest Rates Comparable

P5.35 (Related to Checkpoint 5.7 on page 145) (Calculating an EAR) After examining the various personal loan rates available to you, you find that you can borrow funds from a finance company at 12 percent compounded monthly or from a bank at 13 percent compounded annually. Which alternative is the most attractive?

P5.36 (Related to Checkpoint 5.7 on page 145) (**Calculating an EAR**) You have a choice of borrowing money from a finance company at 24 percent compounded monthly or borrowing money from a bank at 26 percent compounded annually. Which alternative is the most attractive?

P5.37 (Related to Checkpoint 5.7 on page 145) (**Calculating an EAR**) Your grandmother asks for your help in choosing a certificate of deposit (CD) from a bank with a one-year maturity and a fixed interest rate. The first certificate of deposit, CD #1, pays 4.95 percent APR compounded daily, and the second certificate of deposit, CD #2, pays 5.0 percent APR compounded monthly. What is the effective annual rate (the EAR) of each CD, and which CD do you recommend to your grandmother?

P5.38 (Related to Checkpoint 5.7 on page 145) (**Calculating an EAR**) Based on effective interest rates, would you prefer to deposit your money into Springfield National Bank, which pays 8.0 percent interest compounded annually, or into Burns National Bank, which pays 7.8 percent compounded monthly? (Hint: Calculate the EAR on each account.)

P5.39 (**Calculating an EAR**) Payday loans issued by banks are often referred to as "direct deposit advances." In early 2013, the average direct deposit advance charged $10 for a $100 advance and was due in 10 days. What is the effective annual rate on this type of loan?

P5.40 (**Calculating an EAR**) In early 2013, typical terms on a payday loan involved a $15 charge for a two-week payday loan of $100. Assuming there are twenty-six 14-day periods in a year, what is the effective annual rate on such a loan?

Mini-Case

Emily Dao, 27, just received a promotion at work that increased her annual salary to $37,000. She is eligible to participate in her employer's 401(k) retirement plan to which the employer matches, dollar for dollar, workers' contributions up to 5 percent of salary. However, Emily wants to buy a new $25,000 car in three years, and she wants to have enough money to make a $7,000 down payment on the car and finance the balance. Fortunately, she expects a sizable bonus this year that she hopes will cover that down payment in three years.

A wedding is also in her plans. Emily and her boyfriend, Paul, have set a wedding date two years in the future, after he finishes medical school. In addition, Emily and Paul want to buy a home of their own as soon as possible. This might be possible because at age 30, Emily will be eligible to access a $50,000 trust fund left to her as an inheritance by her late grandfather. Her trust fund is invested in 7 percent government bonds.

Questions

1. Justify Emily's participation in her employer's 401(k) plan using the time-value-of-money concepts by explaining how much an investment of $10,000 will grow to in 40 years if it earns 10 percent.

2. Calculate the amount of money that Emily needs to set aside from her bonus this year to cover the down payment on a new car, assuming she can earn 6 percent on her savings. What if she could earn 10 percent on her savings?

3. What will be the value of Emily's trust fund at age 60, assuming she takes possession of half of the money ($25,000 of the $50,000 trust fund) at age 30 for a house down payment, and leaves the other half of the money untouched where it is currently invested?

4. What is the relationship between discounting and compounding?

5. List at least two actions that Emily and Paul could take to accumulate more for their retirement (think about i and n).

6

The Time Value of Money
Annuities and Other Topics

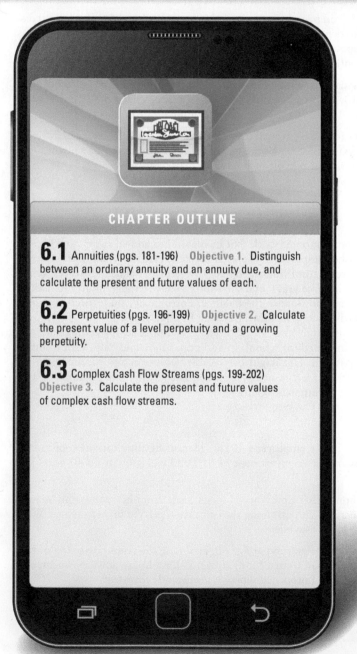

CHAPTER OUTLINE

6.1 Annuities (pgs. 181-196) Objective 1. Distinguish between an ordinary annuity and an annuity due, and calculate the present and future values of each.

6.2 Perpetuities (pgs. 196-199) Objective 2. Calculate the present value of a level perpetuity and a growing perpetuity.

6.3 Complex Cash Flow Streams (pgs. 199-202) Objective 3. Calculate the present and future values of complex cash flow streams.

Principles P1 and P3 Applied

n this chapter we provide tools that allow you to determine the value of a stream of cash flows, both with a limited life as well as those that continue forever and have no maturity date. Once you've mastered these tools, you'll be applying them to the valuation of stocks, bonds, and other investment opportunities, in addition to using them to determine your mortgage and car loan payments. In doing so, we will continue our examination of the first principle of finance— P Principle 1: **Money Has a Time Value**. In moving money through time, we will focus on cash flows because as we learned in P Principle 3: **Cash Flows Are the Source of Value**.

Many of you have bought a car that was financed by a bank. To repay such a loan, you make payments to the bank of a certain fixed amount each month for 48 or 60 months. Similarly, if you buy a house that you finance with a conventional mortgage, you will again face a schedule of payments due over a fixed period of time. Just like individuals, firms make loan payments that are due at regular intervals. In addition, they pay a fixed amount over a set period of time to lease equipment. And they often have investments that generate regular payments of cash. These examples all have one thing in common—they each require a fixed cash flow stream over a set period of time. As we'll see in this chapter, we call this type of cash flow stream an *annuity*.

REGARDLESS OF YOUR MAJOR...

"Annuities We All Know"""

We encounter annuities often in our day-to-day lives. An annuity, as defined in this chapter, is simply a series of equal payments, each payable at the end of each period (month or year) and over multiple periods. For example, if you're paying off a student loan, you're paying off an annuity. In this case, the annuity represents the payment of principal and interest on your student loan. So if you have $30,000 in student loans outstanding at a 6.8 percent interest rate that you plan to repay in 10 years, you'll be making monthly payments of $345.24 over the next 10 years. We sometimes encounter annuities in which the payments are made to us. For example, if your grandparents leave you $30,000 to help pay your college expenses, you might purchase a 6 percent annuity that provides you with monthly payments of $704.55 over the next four years.

6.1 Annuities

In Chapter 5 we learned how to move single cash flows through time, calculating their future and present values. We will now extend these formulas to find the future and present values of a constant stream of cash flows. Together with what we learned in Chapter 5, the material in this chapter provides the tools to implement **P** Principle 1: **Money Has a Time Value.** Later in the book, we will see that this principle, along with **P** Principle 3: **Cash Flows Are the Source of Value,** provides the logic behind the valuation of stocks, bonds, and other investment opportunities.

Ordinary Annuities

We define an **annuity** as a series of *equal* dollar payments that are made at the end of equidistant points in time, such as monthly, quarterly, or annually, over a finite period of time, such as three years. Payments for an annuity can be made at either the beginning or the end of each period. If payments are made at the end of each period, the annuity is often referred to as an **ordinary annuity**. An ordinary annuity is the most common form of annuity and is oftentimes referred to simply as an annuity, without the term *ordinary* preceding it. However, some annuities have payments that are made at the beginning of each period, such as apartment rent. We'll discuss this type of annuity later in this chapter. For now, when we refer to an annuity, you should assume we are referring to an ordinary annuity where the payments are made:

- at the end of each period,
- at equidistant periods of time, such as monthly or annually, and
- for a finite period of time, such as three years.

The present and future values of an ordinary annuity can be computed using the methods described in Chapter 5 and illustrated in Figure 6.1. However, this process can be time consuming, especially for longer annuities, so next we will discuss some simple time-value-of-money formulas for easily calculating the present value and future value of an annuity.

The Future Value of an Ordinary Annuity Let's assume that you are saving money to go to graduate school. You've taken your first job and you plan to save $5,000 each year for the next five years for your grad school fund. How much money will you accumulate by the end of Year 5?

This scenario presents a common annuity valuation problem, one we can solve by finding the future value. To answer this question, we first need to know two things: first, the rate of interest you earn on your savings, and second, for how long each of your savings deposits (the annuity payments) will earn interest. For our purposes, let's assume you save $5,000 each year for five years and that you deposit that amount in an account that earns 6 percent interest per year. A timeline depicting this is shown in Figure 6.1. We can use Equation (5–1a) from the last chapter to find the future value of each of the deposits. The future value at the end of Year 5 of the deposit made at the end of Year 1 (growing for four years) can be calculated as follows:

Equation 5.1a

$$FV_n = PV(1 + i)^n$$

$$FV_{year\ 4} = \$5,000(1 + .06)^4 = \$6,312.38$$

Note that the deposit made at the end of Year 1 has only four years to earn interest until the end of Year 5. Similarly, the deposit made at the end of Year 2 will have only three years to earn interest, and so forth. The future value of the first- through fifth-year deposits is as follows:

FIGURE 6.1

Future Value of a Five-Year Annuity—Saving for Grad School

The five annual annuity payments consist of $5,000 in savings that are placed in an account that earns 6% interest. This is a five-year ordinary annuity such that the first cash flow occurs at the *end* of the first year. This, in turn, means that this payment is only compounded until the end of year five (or for four years).

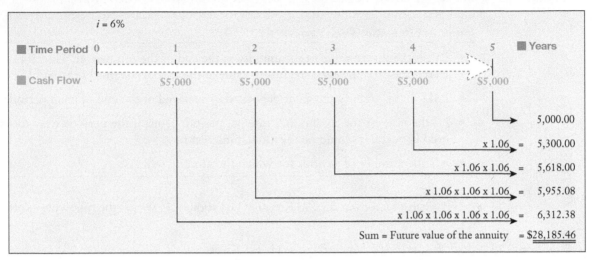

Interest Rate 5 6%
Annuity Payment 5 $5,000

Year	Payment	Future Value at the End of Year 5
1	$5,000	$ 6,312.38
2	$5,000	$ 5,955.08
3	$5,000	$ 5,618.00
4	$5,000	$ 5,300.00
5	$5,000	$ 5,000.00
Sum = Future Value of Annuity =		$28,185.46

What this calculation tells us is that by the end of five years you should, if all goes as planned, have saved a total of $28,185.47 to help fund graduate school.

Figure 6.1 illustrates the computation of a future value of an annuity using a timeline. It's important to note that the future value of an annuity is simply the sum of the future values of each of the annuity payments compounded out to the end of the annuity's life—in this case the end of Year 5.

The Formula for the Future Value of an Ordinary Annuity We can solve for the future value of an ordinary annuity using the following equation:

Future value of an annuity = The sum of the future value of the individual cash flows that make up the annuity

$$\text{Future value of an annuity, } FV_n = \text{Annuity Payment}\left(1 + \frac{\text{Interest Rate}}{}\right)^{n-1} + \text{Annuity Payment}\left(1 + \frac{\text{Interest Rate}}{}\right)^{n-2} + \cdots + \text{Annuity Payment}\left(1 + \frac{\text{Interest Rate}}{}\right)^{0}$$

Note that there are n payments in the ordinary annuity. However, because the first payment is received at the end of the first period, it is compounded for only $n - 1$ periods until the end of the nth period. In addition, the last payment is received at the end of the nth period so it is compounded for $n - n$, or zero periods. Using symbols:

Equation 6.1

$$FV_n = PMT(1 + i)^{n-1} + PMT(1 + i)^{n-2} + \cdots + PMT(1 + i)^1 + PMT(1 + i)^0$$

Important Definitions and Concepts:

- FV_n is the future value of the annuity at the end of the nth period. Thus if periods were measured in years, the future value at the end of the third year would be FV_3.

- PMT is the annuity payment deposited or received at the end of each period.

- i is the interest (or compound) rate per period. Thus, if the periods were measured in years, it would be the annual interest rate.

- n is the number of periods for which the annuity will last.

If we just factor out the PMT term in Equation (6.1) we get the following expression:

Equation 6.1a

$$FV_n = PMT \left[(1 + i)^{n-1} + (1 + i)^{n-2} + \cdots (1 + i)^1 + (1 + i)^0 \right]$$

The sum found in brackets is commonly referred to as the **annuity future value interest factor.**[1] This sum can be reduced to the following expression:

Equation 6.1b

$$\text{Annuity Future Value Factor} = \left[\frac{(1 + i)^n - 1}{i} \right]$$

So to calculate the future value of an ordinary annuity of n years where the individual payments are compounded at a rate i, we simply multiply the payment by the annuity future value interest factor:

Equation 6.1c

$$FV_n = PMT \left[\frac{(1 + i)^n - 1}{i} \right]$$

USING MATHEMATICAL FORMULAS. Continuing with our saving-for-grad-school example, we note that PMT is $5,000 per year, the rate of interest, i, is 6 percent annually, and n is five years. Thus,

$$FV_n = PMT \left[\frac{(1 + i)^n - 1}{i} \right] = \$5,000 \left[\frac{(1 + .06)^5 - 1}{.06} \right] = \$5,000(5.63709296) = \$28,185.46$$

By simply substituting the values given above for PMT, n, and i into Equation (6.1c), we compute the future value of the level payment annuity with one computation rather than five separate future value computations that must then be summed.

[1]Annuity future value interest factors can be found in Appendix D in MyFinanceLab.

Using a Financial Calculator.

Enter	5	6.0	0	-5,000	
	N	I/Y	PV	PMT	FV
Solve for					28,185.46

Using an Excel Spreadsheet.

$= FV$(rate,nper,pmt,pv) or with values entered $= FV(.06, 5, -5000, 0)$

Solving for the PMT in an Ordinary Annuity Instead of figuring out how much money you will accumulate if you deposit a steady amount of money in a savings account each year, perhaps you would like to know how much money you *need to save* each year to accumulate a certain amount by the end of n years. In this case, we know the values of n, i, and FVn in Equation (6–1c); what we do not know is the value of PMT, the annuity payment deposited each period.

Let's look at an example where you are trying to find out how much you must deposit annually in an account in order to reach a set goal. Suppose that you would like to have $50,000 saved 10 years from now to finance your goal of getting an MBA. If you are going to make equal annual end-of-year payments to an investment account that pays 8 percent, how big do these annual payments need to be?

Here, using Equation (6–1c), we know that $n = 10$, $i = 8$, and $FV_{10} = \$50,000$, but what we do not know is the value of PMT, the annuity payment deposited each year. Substituting into Equation (6–1c), we get

Equation 6.1c

$$FV_n = PMT\left[\frac{(1 + i)^n - 1}{i}\right]$$

$$\$50,000 = PMT\left[\frac{(1 + .08)^{10} - 1}{.08}\right]$$

$$\$50,000 = PMT(14.4866)$$

$$\frac{\$50,000}{14.4866} = PMT = \$3,451$$

Checkpoint 6.1 demonstrates the calculation of an annuity payment using the mathematical formulas, a financial calculator, and Excel.

Solving for the Interest Rate in an Ordinary Annuity You may also want to calculate the *interest rate* you must earn on your investment that will allow your savings to grow to a certain amount of money by a certain future date. In this case, you will be solving for i. Consider the following example: In 15 years you hope to have $30,000 saved to buy a sports car. You are able to save $1,022 at the end of each year for the next 15 years. What rate of return must you earn on your investments in order to achieve your goal?

It is easy to solve this problem with either a financial calculator or with Excel; but, as we describe next, solving it with the mathematical formula can be somewhat difficult.

USING THE MATHEMATICAL FORMULA. Substituting the numbers into Equation (6.1c) we get

Equation 6.1c

$$FV_n = PMT\left[\frac{(1+i)^n - 1}{i}\right]$$

$$\$30,000 = \$1,022\left[\frac{(1+i)^{15} - 1}{i}\right]$$

$$\frac{\$30,000}{\$1,022} = \left[\frac{(1+i)^{15} - 1}{i}\right]$$

$$29.354 = \left[\frac{(1+i)^{15} - 1}{i}\right]$$

The only way to solve for the interest rate at this point is by trial and error. Specifically, we substitute different numbers for i until we find the value of i that makes the right-hand side of the expression equal to 29.354.

USING A FINANCIAL CALCULATOR. We can use a financial calculator to solve for i directly as follows:

Enter	15		0	-1,022	30,000
	N	I/Y	PV	PMT	FV
Solve for		9.0			

Using an Excel Spreadsheet.

= RATE(nper,pmt,pv,fv) or with values entered = RATE(15,−1022,0,30000).

Solving for the Number of Periods in an Ordinary Annuity You may also want to calculate the *number of periods* it will take for an annuity to reach a certain future value. Just as with the calculation of the interest rate in an ordinary annuity, the easiest way to do this is with a financial calculator or with a spreadsheet. For example, suppose you are investing $5,000 at the end of each year in an account that pays 7 percent. How long will it be before your account is worth $51,300?

USING A FINANCIAL CALCULATOR. We can use a financial calculator to solve for n directly as follows:

Enter		7.0	0	-5,000	51,300
	N	I/Y	PV	PMT	FV
Solve for	8.0				

Thus, it will take eight years for end-of-year deposits of $5,000 every year to grow to $51,300.

Using an Excel Spreadsheet.

= NPER(rate,pmt,pv,fv) or with values entered = NPER(7%,−5000,0,51300).

The Present Value of an Ordinary Annuity Let's say you just won a radio contest, and the prize is $2,500. The only catch is that you are to receive the $2,500 in the form of five $500 payments at the end of each of the next five years. Alternatively, the radio station has offered to pay you a total of $2,000 today. Which alternative should you choose?

Checkpoint 6.1

Solving for an Ordinary Annuity Payment

How much must you deposit at the end of each year in a savings account earning 8 percent annual interest in order to accumulate $5,000 at the end of 10 years? Let's solve this problem using the mathematical formulas, a financial calculator, and an Excel spreadsheet.

STEP 1: Picture the problem

We can use a timeline to identify the annual payments earning 8 percent that must be made in order to accumulate $5,000 at the end of 10 years as follows:

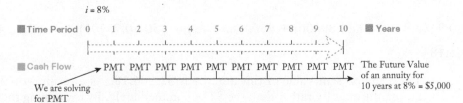

STEP 2: Decide on a solution strategy

This is a future-value-of-an-annuity problem where we know the values for n, i, and FV; and we are solving for PMT (PV is zero because there is no cash flow at time period 0). We'll use Equation (6–1c) to solve the problem.

STEP 3: Solution

Using the Mathematical Formulas. Substituting these example values in Equation (6–1c), we find

$$\$5,000 = PMT\left[\frac{(1 + .08)^{10} - 1}{.08}\right]$$

$$\$5,000 = PMT(14.4866)$$

$$PMT = \$5,000 \div 14.4866 = \$345.15$$

Thus, you must deposit $345.15 in the bank at the end of each year for 10 years at 8 percent interest to accumulate $5,000.

Using a Financial Calculator.

Enter	10	8.0	0		5,000
	N	I/Y	PV	PMT	FV
Solve for				-345.15	

Using an Excel Spreadsheet.

= PMT(rate,nper,pv,fv) or with values entered = PMT(.08,10,0,5000)

STEP 4: Analyze

Notice that in a problem involving the future value of an ordinary annuity, the last payment actually occurs at the time the future value occurs. In this case, the last payment occurs at the end of Year 10, and the end of Year 10 is when you want the future value of the annuity to equal $5,000. In effect, the final payment does not have a chance to earn any interest.

STEP 5: Check yourself

If you can earn 12 percent on your investments, and you would like to accumulate $100,000 for your newborn child's education at the end of 18 years, how much must you invest annually to reach your goal?

ANSWER: $1,793.73 at the end of each year.

Your Turn: For more practice, do related **Study Problems** 6–5, 6–17, 6–19, and 6–34 at the end of this chapter.   **>> END Checkpoint 6.1**

To make this decision, you will need to calculate the present value of the $500 annuity and compare it to the $2,000 lump sum. You can do this by discounting each of the individual future cash flows back to the present and then adding all the present values together. This can be a time-consuming task, particularly when the annuity lasts for several years. Nonetheless, it can be done. If you want to know what $500 received at the end of each of the next five years is worth today, assuming you can earn 6 percent interest on your investment, you simply substitute the appropriate values into Equation (5–2), such that

$$PV = \$500\left[\frac{1}{(1 + .06)^1}\right] + \$500\left[\frac{1}{(1 + .06)^2}\right] + \$500\left[\frac{1}{(1 + .06)^3}\right] + \$500\left[\frac{1}{(1 + .06)^4}\right] + \$500\left[\frac{1}{(1 + .06)^5}\right]$$

$$= \$500(0.94340) + \$500(0.89000) + \$500(0.83962) + \$500(0.79209) + \$500(0.74726)$$

$$= \$2,106.18$$

Thus, the present value of this annuity is $2,106.18. As a result, you'd be better off taking the annuity rather than the $2,000 immediately. By examining the math and the timeline presented in Figure 6.2, you can see that the present values of each cash flow are simply summed. However, many times we will be faced with a situation where n, the number of cash flows in the annuity, is very large. For example, a 15-year mortgage involves 180 equal monthly payments, and a 30-year mortgage involves 360 equal monthly payments—that's just too many individual cash flows to work with. For this reason, we will want to use a financial calculator, Excel, or a mathematical shortcut. Let's examine a mathematical shortcut for valuing the present value of an annuity.

In this method for finding the present value of an annuity, we discount each cash flow separately and then add them up, as represented by the following equation:

Equation 6.2

$$PV = PMT\left[\left(\frac{1}{(1 + i)^1}\right) + \left(\frac{1}{(1 + i)^2}\right) + \cdots + \left(\frac{1}{(1 + i)^n}\right)\right]$$

The term in brackets is commonly referred to as the **annuity present value interest factor**. We can simplify the present value interest factor for an annuity formula as follows:

Equation 6.2a

$$\text{Annuity Present Value Interest Factor} = \frac{1 - \dfrac{1}{(1 + i)^n}}{i}$$

Thus, we can rewrite Equation (6–2) as follows:

Equation 6.2b

$$\text{Present Value} = PMT\left[\frac{1 - \dfrac{1}{(1 + i)^n}}{i}\right]$$

Important Definitions and Concepts:

- PV is the present value of the annuity.

- PMT is the annuity payment deposited or received at the end of each period.

- i is the discount (or interest) rate on a per-period basis. For example, if annuity

FIGURE 6.2

Timeline of a Five-Year, $500 Annuity Discounted Back to the Present at 6 Percent

To find the present value of an annuity, discount each cash flow back to the present separately and then add them. In this example, we simply add up the present value of five future cash flows of $500 each to find a present value of $2,106.18.

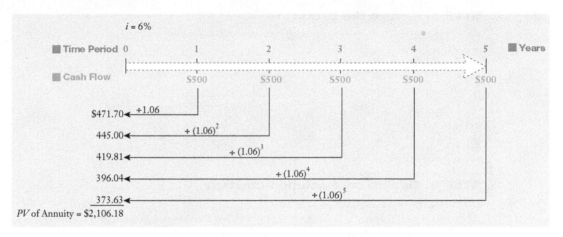

payments were received annually, i would be expressed as an annual rate; if the payments were received monthly, it would be the monthly rate.

- n is the number of periods for which the annuity will last. If the annuity payments were received annually, n would be the number of years; if the payments were received monthly, it would be the number of months.

Notice that the frequency of the payment, that is, whether payments are made on an annual, semiannual, or monthly basis, will play a role in determining the values of n and i. Moreover, it is important that n and i match; that is, if periods are expressed in terms of number of monthly payments, the interest rate must be expressed in terms of the interest rate per month. To find the present value of an annuity, all we need to do is multiply the annuity payment by the annuity present value interest factor.[2] Checkpoint 6.2 demonstrates the use of this formula along with the other techniques for calculating the present value of an annuity.

Amortized Loans

An **amortized loan** is a loan paid off in equal payments—consequently, the loan payments are an annuity. The present value can be thought of as the amount that has been borrowed, n is the number of periods the loan lasts, i is the interest rate per period, *future value* takes on a value of zero because the loan will be paid off after n periods, and *payment* is the loan payment that is made. Generally, the payments are made monthly, but sometimes they are made yearly. Most mortgages are amortized loans, as are almost all car loans. Suppose you plan to get a $6,000 car loan at 15 percent annual

---

[2] Related tables appear in Appendices B through E in MyFinanceLab.

Checkpoint 6.2

The Present Value of an Ordinary Annuity

Your grandmother has offered to give you $1,000 per year for the next 10 years. What is the present value of this 10-year, $1,000 annuity discounted back to the present at 5 percent? Let's solve this using the mathematical formula, a financial calculator, and an Excel spreadsheet.

STEP 1: Picture the problem

We can use a timeline to identify the cash flows from the investment as follows:

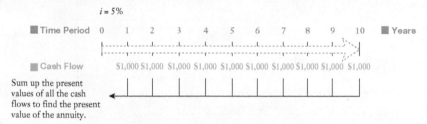

$i = 5\%$

| Time Period | 0 | 1 | 2 | 3 | 4 | 5 | 6 | 7 | 8 | 9 | 10 | Years |

Cash Flow: $1,000 $1,000 $1,000 $1,000 $1,000 $1,000 $1,000 $1,000 $1,000 $1,000

Sum up the present values of all the cash flows to find the present value of the annuity.

STEP 2: Decide on a solution strategy

In this case we are trying to determine the present value of an annuity, and we know the dollar value that is received at the end of each year, and the number of years the annuity lasts. We also know that the discount rate is 5 percent. We can use Equation (6–2b) to solve this problem.

STEP 3: Solution

Using the Mathematical Formulas. Substituting these example values in Equation (6–2b), we find that

$$PV = \$1,000 \left[\frac{1 - \dfrac{1}{(1 + .05)^{10}}}{.05} \right] = \$1,000[(1 - .6139)/.05] = \$1,000(7.722) = \$7,721.73$$

Using a Financial Calculator.

Enter	10	5.0		1,000	0
	N	I/Y	PV	PMT	FV

Solve for   -7,721.73

Using an Excel Spreadsheet.

= PV(rate,nper,pmt,fv) or with values entered = PV(0.05,10,1000,0)

STEP 4: Analyze

We will see this formula at work a bit later when we look at the value of a bond. When you buy a bond, you get the same amount of interest every year on either an annual or semiannual basis, and then at maturity you get the repayment of the bond's principal. Part of calculating the value of a bond involves calculating the present value of the bond's interest payments, which is an annuity.

STEP 5: Check yourself

What is the present value of an annuity of $10,000 to be received at the end of each year for 10 years given a 10 percent discount rate?

ANSWER: $61,446.

Your Turn: For more practice, do related **Study Problems** 6–2, 6–4, 6–28, and 6–35 at the end of this chapter.   **>> END Checkpoint 6.2**

interest with annual payments that you will pay off over four years. What will your annual payments be on this loan? Let's solve this using a financial calculator.

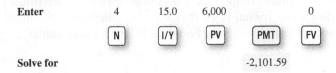

	Enter	4	15.0	6,000		0
		N	I/Y	PV	PMT	FV
	Solve for				-2,101.59	

The above calculation implies that you would make annual payments of $2,101.59. Table 6.1 shows the breakdown of interest and principal over the life of the loan, which is commonly referred to as a **loan amortization schedule**.

As you can see, the interest payment declines each year as the amount owed declines and more of the principal is repaid. This is because a loan payment is made up of two parts: interest and principal. With each payment that goes toward the principal, the size of the outstanding balance goes down. And as the size of the outstanding balance goes down, the amount of interest that is due in the next period declines. Because the size of each payment remains the same and the amount of the next payment that goes toward interest declines, the amount of the next payment that goes toward principal must increase. You can see this clearly in Table 6.1. Also, if you look at Table 6.1, you'll see that the interest portion of the annuity (column 3) is calculated by multiplying the outstanding loan balance at the beginning of the year (column 1) by the interest rate of 15 percent. Thus, for the first year, the interest portion of the first year's payment is $6,000.00 × .15 = $900.00; for Year 2 it is $4,798.41 × .15 = $719.76, and so on. Of course, the amount that isn't the interest portion must be the principal portion. Thus, the repayment of the principal portion of the annuity is calculated by subtracting the interest portion of the annuity (column 3) from the annuity payment (column 2).

Amortized Loans with Monthly Payments Many loans—for example, auto and home loans—require monthly payments. As we saw before, dealing with monthly, as opposed to yearly, payments is easy. All we do is multiply the number of years by *m,* the number of times compounding occurs during the year, to determine *n,* the number of periods. Then we divide the annual interest rate, or APR, by *m* to find the interest rate per period.

Let's look at an example. You've just found the perfect home. However, in order to buy it, you'll need to take out a $150,000, 30-year mortgage with monthly payments at an annual rate of 6 percent. What will your monthly mortgage payments be?

TABLE 6.1   THE LOAN AMORTIZATION SCHEDULE FOR A $6,000 LOAN AT 15% TO BE REPAID

Year	Amount Owed on the Principal at the Beginning of the Year (1)	Annuity Payment (2)	Interest Portion of the Annuity = (1) × 15% = (3)	Repayment of the Principal Portion of the Annuity = (2) − (3) = (4)	Outstanding Loan Balance at Year End, after the Annuity Payment = (1) − (4) = (5)
1	$6,000.00	$2,101.59	$900.00	$1,201.59	$4,798.41
2	4,798.41	2,101.59	719.76	1,381.83	3,416.58
3	3,416.58	2,101.59	512.49	1,589.10	1,827.48
4	1,827.48	2,101.59	274.12	1,827.48	0.00

MATHEMATICAL FORMULAS. As we saw in the previous chapter in Equation (5–1b), in order to determine n, the number of periods, we multiply the number of years by m, where m is the number of times compounding occurs each year. To determine the interest rate per period, we divide the annual interest rate by m, where m is the number of times compounding occurs per year. Modifying Equation (6.2b) for non-annual compounding, we find

Equation 6.2c

$$PV = PMT \left[\frac{1 - \dfrac{1}{(1 + \text{annual interest rate}/m)^{\# \text{ years} \times m}}}{\text{annual interest rate}/m} \right]$$

Substituting *annual interest rate* = .06, *number of years* = 30, $m = 12$, and $PV = \$150{,}000$ into Equation (6–2c), we get

$$\$150{,}000 = PMT \left[\frac{1 - \dfrac{1}{(1 + .06/12)^{30 \times 12}}}{.06/12} \right]$$

Notice that when you convert the annual rate of 6 percent to a monthly rate (by dividing it by 12), the monthly rate drops to 0.005, or 0.5 percent.

$$\$150{,}000 = PMT \left[\frac{1 - \dfrac{1}{(1 + .005)^{360}}}{.005} \right]$$

$$\$150{,}000 = PMT(166.7916144)$$

$$PMT = \$150{,}000/166.7916144 = \$899.33$$

USING A FINANCIAL CALCULATOR. Because there are 360 monthly periods in 30 years, 360 is entered for $\boxed{\text{N}}$, and $\boxed{\text{I/Y}}$ becomes 0.5 (annual interest rate of 6% divided by m, which is 12).

Enter	360	0.5	150,000		0
	$\boxed{\text{N}}$	$\boxed{\text{I/Y}}$	$\boxed{\text{PV}}$	$\boxed{\text{PMT}}$	$\boxed{\text{FV}}$
Solve for				-899.33	

Using an Excel Spreadsheet.

$= \text{PMT}(\text{rate,nper,pv,fv})$ or with values entered $= \text{PMT}(0.005,360,150000,0)$

COMPUTING YOUR OUTSTANDING BALANCE. Let's take a look at how you might use your understanding of annuities to calculate the outstanding balance on a home mortgage loan, which is equal to the present value of your future loan payments. Remember, when you solve for your payment, the final future value of the loan is zero because after your last payment is made, the loan is paid off. The present value of the loan represents how much you originally borrowed—that is, it is the initial outstanding loan balance. What all that means is that the *remaining outstanding balance on a loan must be equal to the present value of the remaining payments on that loan.* An example of this calculation is provided in Checkpoint 6.3.

Checkpoint 6.3

Determining the Outstanding Balance of a Loan

Let's say that exactly 10 years ago you took out a $200,000, 30-year mortgage with an annual interest rate of 9 percent and monthly payments of $1,609.25. But since you took out that loan, interest rates have dropped. You now have the opportunity to refinance your loan at an annual rate of 7 percent over 20 years. You need to know what the outstanding balance on your current loan is so you can take out a lower-interest-rate loan and pay it off. If you just made the 120th payment and have 240 payments remaining, what's your current loan balance?

STEP 1: Picture the problem

Because we are trying to determine how much you still owe on your loan, we need to determine the present value of your remaining payments. In this case, because we are dealing with a 30-year loan, with 240 remaining monthly payments, it's a bit difficult to draw a timeline that shows all the monthly cash flows. Still, we can mentally visualize the problem, which involves calculating the present value of 240 payments of $1,609.25 using a discount rate of 9%/12.

STEP 2: Decide on a solution strategy

Initially you took out a $200,000, 30-year mortgage with an interest rate of 9 percent, and monthly payments of $1,609.25. Because you have made 10 years worth of payments—that's 120 monthly payments—there are only 240 payments left before your mortgage will be totally paid off. We know that the outstanding balance is the present value of all the future monthly payments. To find the present value of these future monthly payments, we'll use Equation (6–2c).

STEP 3: Solve

Using the Mathematical Formulas.

Using Equation (6–2c), we'll solve for the present value of the remaining monthly payment. To find n, we multiply the number of years left until the mortgage is paid off (20) times the number of months in a year (12). Thus n becomes 240. The future value will be equal to zero because the loan will be fully paid off in 20 years. The payment will be $1,609.25, as given above. In effect, the present value of the payments you still need to make is how much you still owe.

$$PV = PMT \left[\frac{1 - \dfrac{1}{(1 + \text{annual rate of interest}/m)^{\text{\# years} \times m}}}{\text{annual rate of interest}/m} \right]$$ (6–2c)

where m = number of times compounding occurs per year and # years is the number of years.

Substituting annual interest rate = .09, number of years = 20, m = 12, and PMT = $1,609.25 into Equation (6–2c), we get,

$$PV = \$1,609.25 \left[\frac{1 - \dfrac{1}{(1 + .09/12)^{20 \times 12}}}{.09/12} \right]$$

$$PV = \$1,609.25(111.145)$$

$$PV = \$178,860.02$$

Using a Financial Calculator.

Enter	240	9.0÷12		-1,609.25	0
	N	I/Y	PV	PMT	FV
Solve for			178,860.02		

Using an Excel Spreadsheet.

= PV(rate,nper,pmt,fv) or with values entered = PV((9/12)%, 240,-1609.25,0)

STEP 4: Analyze

To solve this problem, we began with our monthly payments. Then we determined what the present value was of the remaining payments—this is how much you still owe. Thus, after making 10 years of monthly payments on your $200,000 mortgage that originally had a maturity of 30 years and carries a 9 percent annual rate of interest with monthly payments of $1,609.25, you still owe $178,860.02.

The logic behind what was done here is that the amount you owe on a loan should be equal to the present value of the remaining loan payments. However, if interest rates dropped and you decided to refinance your mortgage, you'd find that there are some real costs associated with refinancing that we haven't touched on here. For example, there is an application fee, an appraisal fee, legal and title search fees, an origination fee for processing the loan, and a prepayment penalty, all adding to the cost of refinancing. Once you decide on a mortgage refinancing lender, make sure that you get all of your mortgage refinancing terms written down on paper.

STEP 5: Check yourself

Let's assume you took out a $300,000, 30-year mortgage with an annual interest rate of 8 percent and monthly payments of $2,201.29. Because you have made 15 years worth of payments (that's 180 monthly payments), there are another 180 payments left before your mortgage will be totally paid off. How much do you still owe on your mortgage?

ANSWER: $230,345.

Your Turn: For more practice, do related **Study Problem** 6–38 at the end of this chapter.   **>> END Checkpoint 6.3**

Annuities Due

Thus far, we have looked only at ordinary annuities, annuities in which payments are made at equidistant points in time at the end of a period. Now we turn our attention to valuing an **annuity due**, an annuity in which all the cash flows occur at the beginning of each period. For example, rent payments on apartments are typically annuities due because the payment for the month's rent occurs at the beginning of the month. Fortunately, compounding annuities due and determining their future and present value is actually quite simple. Let's look at how this affects our compounding calculations.

Because an annuity due merely shifts the payments from the end of the period to the beginning of the period, we can calculate its future value by compounding the cash flows for one additional period. Specifically, the compound sum, or future value, of an annuity due is simply

Equation 6.3
$$FV_n(\text{annuity due}) = PMT\left[\frac{(1 + i)^n - 1}{i}\right](1 + i)$$

Recall that earlier we calculated the future value of a five-year ordinary annuity of $5,000 earning 6 percent interest to be $28,185.46. If we now assume this is a five-year annuity due, its future value increases from $28,185.46 to $29,876.59:

$$= \$5,000\left[\frac{(1 + .06)^5 - 1}{.06}\right](1 + .06) = \$28,185.46(1 + .06) = \$29,876.59$$

Because each cash flow is received one year earlier with an annuity due, its present value will be discounted back for one less period. To determine the present value of the annuity due, we merely figure out what its present value would be if it were an ordinary annuity and multiply that value by $(1 + i)$. This, in effect, cancels out one year's discounting.[3]

---

[3] Within each of the Excel functions you are given the option of identifying any cash flow as being at the beginning of a period. To solve for an annuity due in Excel, you simply change the value for "type" from 0 to 1. Recall that 0 is the default setting—the setting used to calculate an ordinary annuity. Consequently, if you don't designate a value for the variable "type," Excel will default to 0, or end-of-year payments. If you look at any of the Excel problems we have done so far, you'll notice that we have omitted entering a variable for "type," thus indicating that the cash flows occur at the end of each time period.

Equation 6.4

$$PV(\text{annuity due}) = PMT\left[\dfrac{1 - \dfrac{1}{(1 + i)^n}}{i}\right](1 + i)$$

Let's go back to our radio contest example. Suppose the radio station offered you a five-year annuity due instead of an ordinary annuity. If you were given $500 at the beginning of each of those five years and were able to invest it at an interest rate of 6 percent, its value would increase from $2,106.18 (the value of the ordinary annuity) to $2,232.55:

$$= \$500\left[\dfrac{1 - \dfrac{1}{(1 + .06)^5}}{.06}\right](1 + .06)$$

$$= \$2,106.18(1 + .06) = \$2,232.55$$

THE BUSINESS OF LIFE

Saving for Retirement

If you understand **P** Principle 1: **Money Has a Time Value**, you will have a better idea of why it's so important to begin saving for retirement as soon as possible. Putting off saving for just one year can have a big impact on the amount of money you have when you retire—in fact, it may reduce your retirement funds by over $250,000.

Individual retirement accounts, or IRAs, are personal retirement savings plans that have certain tax advantages. With a regular IRA, contributions are made on a before-tax basis. However, Roth IRA contributions are paid from earnings that have already been taxed. The difference is that after you retire and begin withdrawing money from a regular IRA, you have to pay taxes on your withdrawals. With a Roth, you don't.

Figure 6.3 assumes that at a certain age, you contribute $5,000 at the beginning of each year to a Roth IRA earning 8 percent interest per year, and you continue making contributions until age 70. For example, if at age 20 you start contributing $5,000 at the beginning of each year, you will have made 51 contributions by age 70, and you will end up with the following:

$$FV_n(\text{annuity due}) = PMT\left[\dfrac{(1 + i)^n - 1}{i}\right](1 + i)$$

Equation 6.3

$$= \$5,000\left[\dfrac{(1 + .08)^{51} - 1}{.08}\right](1 + .08)$$

$$= \$3,103,359(1 + .08) = \$3,351,628$$

But what if you wait until you're 21 to start contributing? How much money would you end up with then?

FIGURE 6.3

Skipping Just One Year Can Cost You Over a Quarter of a Million Dollars

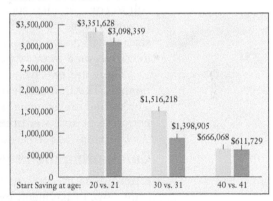

By waiting just one year longer to begin investing, you end up with $253,269 less in the account:

$$= \$5,000\left[\dfrac{(1 + .08)^{50} - 1}{.08}\right](1 + .08)$$

$$= \$2,868,850(1 + .08) = \$3,098,359$$

As you can see, instead of accumulating $3,351,628, you would accumulate only $3,098,359.

In this example, you put $5,000 into a Roth IRA each year, but if you had only put in $2,500 each year, your total accumulation would only be half of what is listed in Figure 6.3. At present the maximum you can put into your Roth IRA per year is $5,000; and, if you're over 50, you can even put more into it. Study Problem 6–3 looks at Roth IRAs.

Your Turn: See Study Question 6–3

The result of all this is that both the future value and the present value of an annuity due are larger than that of an ordinary annuity because, in each case, all payments are received or paid earlier. Thus, when *compounding* an annuity due, the cash flows come at the beginning of the period rather than the end of the period. They are, in effect, invested one period earlier, and as a result, grow to a larger future value. By contrast, when we *discount* an annuity due, the cash flows come at the beginning of each period, in effect coming one period earlier, so their present value is larger. Although annuities due are used with some frequency in accounting, their usage is less frequent in finance. Nonetheless, an understanding of annuities due can be powerful, as you can see in the box feature *Business of Life: Saving for Retirement*.

CONCEPT CHECK: 6.1
Before you move on to 6.2

1. Define the term *annuity* as it relates to cash flows.
2. Distinguish between an ordinary annuity and an annuity due.
3. Describe the adjustments necessary when annuity payments occur on a monthly basis.
4. How would you determine how much you currently owe on an outstanding loan?

6.2 Perpetuities

A **perpetuity** is simply an annuity that continues forever or has no maturity. It is difficult to conceptualize such a cash flow stream that goes on forever. One such example, however, is the dividend stream on a share of preferred stock. In theory, this dividend stream will go on as long as the firm continues to pay dividends, so technically the dividends on a share of preferred stock form an infinite annuity, or perpetuity.

There are two basic types of perpetuities that we will encounter in our study of finance. The first is a **level perpetuity** in which the payments are constant over time. The second is a **growing perpetuity** in which the payments grow at a constant rate from period to period over time. Let's consider each in turn.

Calculating the Present Value of a Level Perpetuity

Determining the present value of a perpetuity is simple—you merely divide the constant flow, or payment, by the discount rate. For example, the present value of a $100 perpetuity discounted back to the present at 5 percent is $100/.05 = $2,000. The equation representing the present value of a level perpetuity is as follows:

Equation 6.5

$$PV = \frac{PMT}{i}$$

Important Definitions and Concepts:

- PV = the present value of a level perpetuity.
- PMT = the constant dollar amount provided by the perpetuity.
- i = the interest (or discount) rate per period.

Calculating the Present Value of a Growing Perpetuity

Not all perpetuities have equal cash payments. In this text, we will encounter growing perpetuities. For example, if the first payment at the end of Year 1 is $100 and the payments are assumed to grow at a rate of 5 percent per year, then the payment for Year 2 will be $100(1.05) = $105, and the payment for Year 3 will be $100(1.05)(1.05) = $110.25, and so forth.

We can calculate the present value of a growing perpetuity as follows:

Equation 6.6 $$PV = \frac{PMT_{period}}{i-g}$$

Checkpoint 6.4

The Present Value of a Level Perpetuity

What is the present value of a perpetuity of $500 paid annually discounted back to the present at 8 percent?

STEP 1: Picture the problem

With a perpetuity, a timeline doesn't have an ending point but goes on forever, with the same cash flow occurring period after period, or in this case, year after year:

STEP 2: Decide on a solution strategy

Because calculating the present value of a perpetuity only involves simple division, we don't need to look at an Excel solution or any unique keystrokes with a financial calculator; instead, using Equation (6–5), we just divide the amount you received at the end of each period (forever) by the interest rate.

STEP 3: Solve

Substituting *PMT* = $500 and *i* = .08 into Equation (6–5), we find

$$PV = \frac{\$500}{.08} = \$6,250$$

Thus, the present value of this perpetuity is $6,250.

STEP 4: Analyze

Notice there is no symbol for the future value of a perpetuity. This is because there isn't a future time period when things end because a perpetuity goes on indefinitely. So, how much will this perpetuity be worth at the end of 2 years or 100 years? The answer is $6,250. That is because this perpetuity will always return $500 — regardless of what the time period is, the present value of a perpetuity paying $500 at 8 percent is always $6,250.

STEP 5: Check yourself

 What is the present value of stream of payments equal to $90,000 paid annually and discounted back to the present at 9 percent?

ANSWER: $1,000,000

Your Turn: For more practice, do related **Study Problem** 6–42 at the end of this chapter.   >> **END Checkpoint 6.4**

Important Definitions and Concepts:

- PV = the present value of a growing perpetuity.

- $PMT_{period\ 1}$ = the amount of the payment made at the end of the first period (e.g., this was $100 in the example used above).

- i = the rate of interest used to discount the growing perpetuity's cash flows.

- g = the rate of growth in the payment cash flows from period to period.

The growth rate, g, must be less than the rate of interest used to discount the cash flows, i. If g is greater than i, then the present value becomes infinitely large because the cash flows are growing at a faster rate than they are being discounted.

Checkpoint 6.5

The Present Value of a Growing Perpetuity

What is the present value of a perpetuity stream of cash flows that pays $500 at the end of Year 1 but grows at a rate of 4 percent per year indefinitely? The rate of interest used to discount the cash flows is 8 percent.

STEP 1: Picture the problem

With a growing perpetuity, a timeline doesn't have an ending point, but goes on forever, with the cash flow growing at a constant rate period after period, or in this case, year after year:

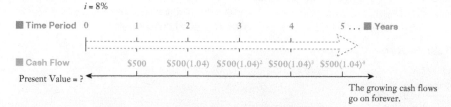

STEP 2: Decide on a solution strategy

Because calculating the present value of a growing perpetuity only involves substituting into Equation (6–6), we don't need to look at an Excel solution or any unique keystrokes with a financial calculator. Instead, we just divide the amount receive at the end of each period (forever) by the interest rate minus the growth rate.

STEP 3: Solve

Substituting $PMT_{period\ 1}$ = $500, g = .04, and i = .08 into Equation (6–6), we find

$$PV = \frac{PMT_{period\ 1}}{i - g} = \frac{\$500}{.08 - .04} = \$12{,}500$$

Thus, the present value of the growing perpetuity is $12,500.

STEP 4: Analyze

Comparing the value of the $500 level perpetuity in Checkpoint 6.5 to the $500 perpetuity that grows at 4 percent per year, we see that adding growth to the cash flows has a dramatic effect on value. To see why this occurs, consider the Year 50 payment under both the level perpetuity and growing perpetuity. For the level perpetuity, this payment is still $500; however, for the growing perpetuity, the payment for Year 50 is the following:

$$PMT_{year\ 50} = \$500(1 + .04)^{50} = \$3,553.34$$

STEP 5: Check yourself

What is the present value of a stream of payments where the Year 1 payment is $90,000 and the future payments grow at a rate of 5 percent per year? The interest rate used to discount the payments is 9 percent.

ANSWER: $2,250,000

Your Turn: For more practice, do related **Study Problem** 6–44 at the end of this chapter.   **>> END Checkpoint 6.5**

CONCEPT CHECK: 6.2
Before you move on to 6.3

1. Define the term *perpetuity* as it relates to cash flows.

2. What is a growing perpetuity, and how is it calculated?

6.3 Complex Cash Flow Streams

Actual investment cash flows are often more complicated than the examples we have considered thus far. They often consist of multiple sets of annuities or different cash flow amounts mixed in with annuities. In general they will involve spending money today in the hopes of receiving more in the future, and once we bring all the future cash flows back to the present, they can be compared. For example, Marriott recently decided to build timeshare resorts in Dubai, United Arab Emirates. The resorts are close to Dubailand, a giant entertainment complex that, when finished, will be twice the size of the entire Disneyland and Disney World resorts put together.

The resorts' cash flows are a mixture of both positive and negative cash flows, as shown in Figure 6.4. The early cash flows are negative as Marriott begins construction on the various phases of the project and later become positive as the development makes money. Because of this mixture of positive and negative cash flows, we cannot use the annuities formulas that we described earlier. Instead, we calculate the present value of the investment project by summing the present values of all the individual cash flows.

Assuming a 6 percent discount rate, we can calculate the present value of all 10 years of cash flows by discounting each back to the present and adding the positive flows and subtracting the negative ones. Note that the cash flows for Years 1 through 3 are different, so we will have to find their present values by discounting each cash flow back to the present. The present values of the payments (in millions of $) received in Years 1 through 3 are $471.70 = $500/(1 + .06), $178.00 = $200/(1 + .06)^2, and −$335.85 = −$400/(1 + .06)^3.

Next, we see that in Years 4 through 10 the cash flows correspond to an ordinary annuity of $500 per year. Because these cash flows are all equal and are received annually, they are a seven-year annuity. The unique feature of the annuity is that the first cash flow comes at the end of Year 4. To find the present value of the seven-year annuity, we follow a two-step process:

- First, we consolidate the seven-year annuity into a single cash flow that is equal to its present value. In effect, we are consolidating the $500 million payments that

FIGURE 6.4

Present Value of Single Cash Flows and an Annuity ($ value in millions)

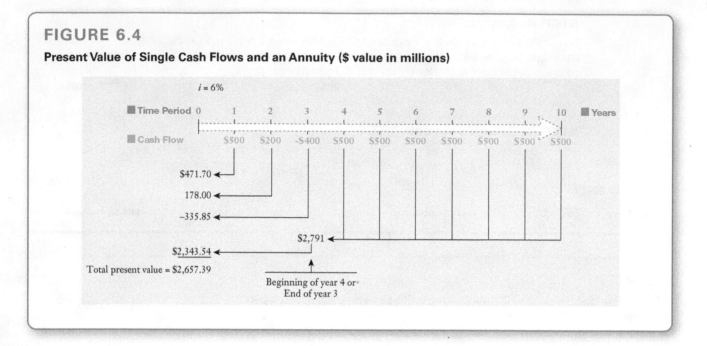

Checkpoint 6.6

The Present Value of a Complex Cash Flow Stream

What is the present value of cash flows of $500 at the end of Years 1 through 3, a cash flow of a negative $800 at the end of Year 4, and cash flows of $800 at the end of Years 5 through 10 if the appropriate discount rate is 5 percent?

STEP 1: Picture the problem

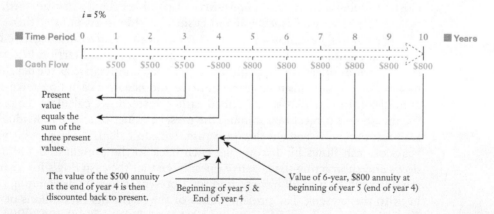

STEP 2: Decide on a solution strategy

This problem involves two annuities and the single (negative) cash flow. Once their present value is determined they will be added together. The $500 annuity over Years 1 through 3 can be discounted directly to the present using Equation (6–2b), and the $800 cash outflow at the end of Year 4 can be discounted back to present using Equation (5–2) . Because it is an outflow, it will carry a negative sign and be subtracted from the present value of the inflows. To determine the present value of the six-year, $800 annuity over Years 5 through 10, we must first consolidate the six-year annuity that runs from Years 5 through 10 into an equivalent single cash flow at the beginning of Year 5, which is the same as the end of Year 4, using Equation (6–2b). We now have an equivalent single cash flow at the end of Year 4 that we can bring directly back to the present using Equation (5–2). Once everything is in today's dollars, we simply add the values together.

STEP 3: Solve

Using the Mathematical Formulas.

Here we have two annuities. One of them, an annuity of $500 over Years 1 through 3, can be discounted directly back to the present by multiplying it by the annuity present value interest factor, or

$$\left[\frac{1 - \dfrac{1}{(1 + .05)^3}}{.05} \right]$$

for a value of $1,361.62. The second annuity, which is a six-year annuity of $800 per year over Years 5 through 10, must be discounted twice—once to find the value of the annuity at the beginning of Year 5, which is also the end of Year 4, and then again to bring that value back to the present. The value of the second annuity at the end of Year 4 is found by multiplying it ($800) by the annuity present value interest factor, or

$$\left[\frac{1 - \dfrac{1}{(1 + .05)^6}}{.05} \right]$$

resulting in a value $4,060.55. In effect, we have now consolidated the annuity into an equivalent single cash flow at the end of Year 4. This equivalent single cash flow is then discounted back to the present by multiplying it by the value of $1/(1.05)^4$, for a value of $3,340.62. Because cash flows in the same time period can be added and subtracted from each other, to arrive at the total present value of this investment, we subtract the present value of the $800 cash outflow at the end of Year 4 (which is $658.16) from the sum of the present value of the two annuities ($1,361.62 and $3,340.62). Thus, the present value of this series of cash flows is $4,044.08. Remember, once the cash flows from an investment have been brought back to the present, they can be combined by adding and subtracting to determine the project's total present value.

Using a Financial Calculator. Using a financial calculator, we can arrive at the same answer:

(a) The present value of the first annuity, Years 1 through 3 (give it a positive sign because it is an inflow) = **$1,361.62**.

Enter	3	5		500	0
	N	I/Y	PV	PMT	FV
Solve for			-1,361.62		

(b) The present value of the $800 cash **outflow** (thus it is given a negative sign because it is an outflow) = **–$658.16**.

Enter	4	5		0	-800
	N	I/Y	PV	PMT	FV
Solve for			658.16		

(c) (Part 1) The value at end of Year 4 of the second annuity (which is a six-year annuity), Years 5 through 10 (give it a positive sign because it is an inflow) = $4,060.55,

Enter	6	5		800	0
	N	I/Y	PV	PMT	FV
Solve for			-4,060.55		

and then,

(Part 2) The present value (give it a positive sign because it is an inflow) of the $4,060.55 (which was calculated in c: part 1 and is received at the end of Year 4) = **$3,340.62**.

(6.6 CONTINUED >> ON NEXT PAGE)

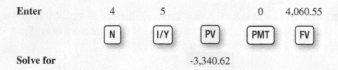

Enter   4   5   0   4,060.55

| N | I/Y | PV | PMT | FV |

Solve for   -3,340.62

(d) Summing the present values together, the total present value = **$4,044.08**.

Using an Excel Spreadsheet. Using Excel, the cash flows are brought back to the present using the =PV function, keeping in mind that inflows will take on positive signs and outflows negative signs.

STEP 4: Analyze

When cash flows from different time periods are expressed in the same time period's dollars, they can be added in the case of an inflow or subtracted in the case of an outflow to come up with a total value at some point in time. In fact, we will combine Principle 1: **Money Has a Time Value** with Principle 3: **Cash Flows Are the Source of Value** later in the book to value stocks, bonds, and investment proposals. The bottom line is that understanding the time value of money is a key to making good decisions.

STEP 5: Check yourself

What is the present value of cash flows of $300 at the end of Years 1 through 5, a cash flow of negative $600 at the end of Year 6, and cash flows of $800 at the end of Years 7 through 10 if the appropriate discount rate is 10 percent?

ANSWER: $2,230.

Your Turn: For more practice, do related **Study Problem** 6–48 at the end of this chapter.   **>> END Checkpoint 6.6**

---

occur at the end of Years 4 through 10 into an equivalent single cash flow at the beginning of Year 4 (or the end of Period 3). Recall that we can find the present value of the annuity by multiplying the annual payment of $500 by the annuity present value interest factor:

- $$\frac{1 - \dfrac{1}{(1 + i)^n}}{i}.$$ In Figure 6.4 we see that the present value of this annuity at the end of Year 3 is $2,791 million.

- Second, we discount the $2,791 million present value of the annuity cash flows back three years to the present, which is the beginning of Year 1. The present value of this sum (in millions), then, is $2,343.54 = $2,791/(1 + .06)^3$.

Finally, we can calculate the present value of the complex set of future cash flows by adding up the individual present values of each of the future cash flows. The result is a present value of $2,657.39 million. We would then compare the present value of all the future cash flows with what the project costs. It should now be apparent that drawing out a timeline is a critical first step when trying to solve any complex problem involving the time value of money.

CONCEPT CHECK: 6.3

Before you begin end-of-chapter material

1. When are cash flows comparable—that is, when can they be added together or subtracted from each other?

2. Why would you want to be able to compare cash flows that occur in different time periods with each other?

Applying the Principles of Finance to Chapter 6

P Principle 1: **Money Has a Time Value** This chapter continues our study of the time value of money—a dollar received today, other things being the same, is worth more than a dollar received a year from now. In this chapter, we expand upon what we learned in the previous chapter by applying the time value of money to annuities, perpetuities, and complex cash flows.

P Principle 3: **Cash Flows Are the Source of Value** In this chapter we introduced the idea that we will use **Principle 1** in combination with **Principle 3** to value stocks, bonds, and investment proposals.

Chapter Summaries

Summary	Key Terms

6.1 Distinguish between an ordinary annuity and an annuity due, and calculate the present and future values of each. (pgs. 181–196)

An annuity is a series of equal dollar payments, where the periods between the payments are of equal length, such as monthly or annually. An ordinary annuity involves cash payments made at the end of each period, whereas an annuity due involves payments at the beginning of each period. Appendices B through E in MyFinanceLab contain tables with future value interest factors, present value interest factors, annuity future value interest factors, and annuity present value interest factors for various combinations of i and n.

Amortized loan, page 189 A loan that is paid off in equal periodic payments.

Annuity, page 182 A series of equal dollar payments for a specified period of time.

Annuity due, page 194 An annuity in which the payments occur at the beginning of each period.

Annuity future value interest factor, page 184 The value, $\left[\dfrac{(1 + i)^n - 1}{i} \right]$, used as a multiplier to calculate the future value of an annuity.

Annuity present value interest factor, page 188 The value, $\left[\dfrac{1 - \dfrac{1}{(1 + i)^n}}{i} \right]$, used as a multiplier to calculate the present value of an annuity.

Loan amortization schedule, page 191 A breakdown of the interest and principal payments on an amortized loan.

Ordinary annuity, page 192 A series of equal dollar payments for a specified number of periods with the payments occurring at the end of each period.

Key Equations

$$FV_n = PMT \left[\frac{(1 + i)^n - 1}{i} \right]$$

(6–1c)

$$PV = PMT \left[\frac{1 - \dfrac{1}{(1 + i)^n}}{i} \right]$$

(6–2b)

Key Equations	
Concept Check: 6.1 1. Define the term *annuity* as it relates to cash flows. 2. Distinguish between an ordinary annuity and an annuity due. 3. Describe the adjustments necessary when annuity payments occur on a monthly basis. 4. How would you determine how much you currently owe on an outstanding loan?	$$PV = PMT\left[\frac{1 - \dfrac{1}{\left(1 + \text{annual interest rate}/m\right)^{\#\ years \times m}}}{\text{annual interest rate}/m}\right] \quad \text{(6–2c)}$$ $$FV_n = PMT\left[\frac{\left(1 + \text{annual interest rate}/m\right)^{\#\ years \times m} - 1}{\text{annual interest rate}/m}\right]$$ $$FV_n(\text{annuity due}) = PMT\left[\frac{(1 + i)^n - 1}{i}\right](1 + i) \quad \text{(6–3)}$$ $$PV(\text{annuity due}) = PMT\left[\frac{1 - \dfrac{1}{(1 + i)^n}}{i}\right](1 + i) \quad \text{(6–4)}$$

Summary	Key Terms

6.2 Calculate the present value of a level perpetuity and a growing perpetuity. (pgs. 194–196)

A perpetuity is an annuity that continues forever. That is, every period it pays the same dollar amount. With a growing perpetuity, rather than receiving the same amount each period, the periodic payment increases at a constant rate every period.	**Growing perpetuity, page 194** A perpetuity in which the payments grow at a constant rate from period to period over time. **Level perpetuity, page 194** An annuity with a constant level of payments with an infinite life. **Perpetuity, page 194** An annuity with an infinite life.

Key Equations	
Concept Check: 6.2 1. Define the term *perpetuity* as it relates to cash flows. 2. What is a growing perpetuity, and how is it calculated?	$$PV = \frac{PMT}{i} \quad \text{(6–5)}$$ $$PV = \frac{PMT_{period}}{i - g} \quad \text{(6–6)}$$

Summary	

6.3 Calculate the present and future values of complex cash flow streams. (pgs. 197–200)

Concept Check: 6.3 1. When are cash flows comparable—that is, when can they be added together or subtracted from each other? 2. Why would you want to be able to compare cash flows that occur in different time periods with each other?	Understanding how to make cash flows that occur in different time periods comparable is essential to understanding finance. All time value formulas presented in this chapter and in the previous chapter stem from the single compounding formula $FV_n = PV(1 + i)^n$. The formulas are used to deal simply with common financial situations, such as, for example, discounting single flows, compounding annuities, and discounting annuities.

Study Questions

Q6.1 What is an annuity? Give some examples of annuities.

Q6.2 How do you calculate the future value of an annuity?

Q6.3 What is the relationship between the present value interest factor (from Chapter 5) and the annuity present value interest factor (from Equation [6–2])?

Q6.4 Assume you bought a home and took out a 30-year mortgage on it 10 years ago. How would you determine how much principal on your mortgage you still have to pay off?

Q6.5 Distinguish between an ordinary annuity and an annuity due.

Q6.6 What is a level perpetuity? A growing perpetuity?

Q6.7 How do you calculate the present value of an annuity? A perpetuity? A growing perpetuity?

Q6.8 With an uneven stream of future cash flows, the present value is determined by discounting all of the cash flows back to the present and then adding the present values up. Is there ever a time when you can treat some of the cash flows as annuities and apply the annuity techniques you learned in this chapter?

Study Problems Annuities

P6.1 (Future value of an ordinary annuity)
What is the future value of each of the following streams of payments?

a. $500 a year for 10 years compounded annually at 5 percent
b. $100 a year for 5 years compounded annually at 10 percent
c. $35 a year for 7 years compounded annually at 7 percent
d. $25 a year for 3 years compounded annually at 2 percent

P6.2 (Related to Checkpoint 6.2 on page 165) (Present value of an ordinary annuity)
What is the present value of the following annuities?

a. $2,500 a year for 10 years discounted back to the present at 7 percent
b. $70 a year for 3 years discounted back to the present at 3 percent
c. $280 a year for 7 years discounted back to the present at 6 percent
d. $500 a year for 10 years discounted back to the present at 10 percent

P6.3 (Related to The Business of Life: Saving for Retirement on page 170) (Future value of an ordinary annuity) You are graduating from college at the end of this semester and after reading the *The Business of Life* box in this chapter, you have decided to invest $5,000 at the end of each year into a Roth IRA for the next 45 years. If you earn 8 percent compounded annually on your investment, how much will you have when you retire in 45 years? How much will you have if you wait 10 years before beginning to save and only make 35 payments into your retirement account?

P6.4   (Related to Checkpoint 6.2 on page 165) (**Present value of an ordinary annuity**) Nicki Johnson, a sophomore mechanical engineering student, received a call from an insurance agent who believes that Nicki is an older woman who is ready to retire from teaching. He talks to her about several annuities that she could buy that would guarantee her a fixed annual income. The annuities are as follows:

Annuity	Purchase Price of the Annuity	Amount of Money Received Per Year	Duration of the Annuity (Years)
A	$50,000	$8,500	12
B	$60,000	$7,000	25
C	$70,000	$8,000	20

Nicki could earn 11 percent on her money by placing it in a savings account. Alternatively, she could place it in any of the above annuities. Which annuities in the table above, if any, will earn Nicki a higher return than investing in the savings account earning 11 percent?

P6.5   (Related to Checkpoint 6.1 on page 162) (**Annuity payments**) Mr. Bill S. Preston, Esq., purchased a new house for $80,000. He paid $20,000 up front on the down payment and agreed to pay the rest over the next 25 years in 25 equal annual payments that include principal payments plus 9 percent compound interest on the unpaid balance. What will these equal payments be?

P6.6   (**Annuity payments**) Emily Morrison purchased a new house for $150,000. She paid $30,000 up front and agreed to pay the rest over the next 25 years in 25 equal annual payments that include principal payments plus 10 percent compound interest on the unpaid balance. What will these equal payments be?

P6.7   (**Annuity payments**) To pay for your education, you've taken out $25,000 in student loans. If you make monthly payments over 15 years at 7 percent compounded monthly, how much are your monthly student loan payments?

P6.8   (**Annuity payments**) To pay for your child's education, you wish to have accumulated $15,000 at the end of 15 years. To do this, you plan to deposit an equal amount into the bank at the end of each year. If the bank is willing to pay 6 percent compounded annually, how much must you deposit each year to obtain your goal?

P6.9   (**Annuity payments**) You plan to retire in 10 years and buy a house in Oviedo, Florida. The house you are looking at currently costs $100,000 and is expected to increase in value each year at a rate of 5 percent. Assuming you can earn 10 percent annually on your investments, how much must you invest at the end of each of the next 10 years to be able to buy your dream home when you retire?

P6.10   (**Annuity payments**) The Aggarwal Corporation needs to save $10 million to retire a $10 million mortgage that matures in 10 years. To retire this mortgage, the company plans to put a fixed amount into an account at the end of each year for 10 years. The Aggarwal Corporation expects to earn 9 percent annually on the money in this account. What equal annual contribution must the firm make to this account to accumulate the $10 million by the end of 10 years?

P6.11 **(Annuity payments)** The Knutson Corporation needs to save $15 million to retire a $15 million mortgage that matures in 10 years. To retire this mortgage, the company plans to put a fixed amount into an account at the end of each year for 10 years. The Knutson Corporation expects to earn 10 percent annually on the money in this account. What equal annual contribution must the firm make to this account to accumulate the $15 million by the end of 10 years?

P6.12 **(Future value of an annuity)** Upon graduating from college 35 years ago, Dr. Nick Riviera was already planning for his retirement. Since then, he has made deposits into a retirement fund on a quarterly basis in the amount of $300. Nick has just completed his final payment and is at last ready to retire. His retirement fund has earned 9 percent compounded quarterly.

    a. How much has Nick accumulated in his retirement account?
    b. In addition to this, 15 years ago Nick received an inheritance check for $20,000 from his beloved uncle. He decided to deposit the entire amount into his retirement fund. What is his current balance in the fund?

P6.13 **(Annuity number of periods)** How long will it take to pay off a loan of $50,000 at an annual rate of 10 percent compounded monthly if you make monthly payments of $600?

P6.14 **(Annuity number of periods)** Alex Karev has taken out a $200,000 loan with an annual rate of 8 percent compounded monthly to pay off hospital bills from his wife Izzy's illness. If the most Alex can afford to pay is $1,500 per month, how long will it take to pay the loan off? How long will it take for him to pay off the loan if he can pay $2,000 per month?

P6.15 **(Present value of an annuity)** What is the present value of a 10-year annuity that pays $1,000 annually, given a 10 percent discount rate?

P6.16 **(Annuity interest rate)** Your folks just called and would like some advice from you. An insurance agent just called them and offered them the opportunity to purchase an annuity for $21,074.25 that will pay them $3,000 per year for 20 years. They don't have the slightest idea what return they would be making on their investment of $21,074.25. What rate of return would they be earning?

P6.17 (Related to Checkpoint 6.1 on page 162) **(Annuity payments)** On December 31, Beth Klemkosky bought a yacht for $50,000. She paid $10,000 down and agreed to pay the balance in 10 equal annual installments that include both the principal and 10 percent interest on the declining balance. How big will the annual payments be?

P6.18 **(Annuity interest rate)** You've been offered a loan of $30,000, which you will have to repay in five equal annual payments of $10,000, with the first payment to be received one year from now. What interest rate would you be paying on that loan?

P6.19 (Related to Checkpoint 6.1 on page 162) **(Annuity payments)** A firm borrows $25,000 from the bank at 12 percent compounded annually to purchase some new machinery. This loan is to be repaid in equal annual installments at the end of each year over the next five years. How much will each annual payment be?

P6.20 (**Annuity payments**) You plan to buy some property in Florida five years from today. To do this, you estimate that you will need $20,000 at that time. You would like to accumulate these funds by making equal annual deposits in your savings account, which pays 12 vpercent annually. If you make your first deposit at the end of this year, and you would like your account to reach $20,000 when the final deposit is made, how much will you have to deposit in the account annually?

P6.21 (**Annuity number of periods**) You've just bought a new flat-screen TV for $3,000 and the store you bought it from offers to let you finance the entire purchase at an annual rate of 14 percent compounded monthly. If you take the financing and make monthly payments of $100, how long will it take to pay the loan off? How much will you pay in interest over the life of the loan?

P6.22 (**Comprehensive problem**) You would like to have $75,000 in 15 years. To accumulate this amount, you plan to deposit an equal sum in the bank each year that will earn 8 percent interest compounded annually. Your first payment will be made at the end of the year.

  a. How much must you deposit annually to accumulate this amount?
  b. If you decide to make a large lump-sum deposit today instead of the annual deposits, how large should the lump-sum deposit be? (Assume you can earn 8 percent on this deposit.)
  c. At the end of five years, you will receive $20,000 and deposit it in the bank in an effort to reach your goal of $75,000 at the end of 15 years. In addition to the deposit, how much must you deposit in equal annual deposits to reach your goal? (Again, assume you can earn 8 percent on this deposit.)

P6.23 (**Annuity payments**) You plan to buy property in Florida five years from today. To do this, you estimate that you will need $30,000 at that time for the purchase. You would like to accumulate these funds by making equal annual deposits in your savings account, which pays 10 percent annually. If you make your first deposit at the end of this year, and you would like your account to reach $30,000 when the final deposit is made, what amount do you need to deposit annually?

P6.24 (**Future value of an annuity and annuity payments**) You are trying to plan for retirement in 10 years and currently you have $150,000 in a savings account and $250,000 in stocks. In addition, you plan to deposit $8,000 per year into your savings account at the end of each of the next five years, and then $10,000 per year at the end of each year for the final five years until you retire.

  a. Assuming your savings account returns 8 percent compounded annually, and your investment in stocks will return 12 percent compounded annually, how much will you have at the end of 10 years?
  b. If you expect to live for 20 years after you retire, and at retirement you deposit all of your savings in a bank account paying 11 percent, how much can you withdraw each year after you retire (making 20 equal withdrawals beginning one year after you retire) so that you end up with a zero balance at death?

P6.25 (**Annuity payments**) On December 31, Son-Nan Chen borrowed $100,000, agreeing to repay this sum in 20 equal annual installments that include both principal and 15 percent interest on the declining balance. How large will the annual payments be?

P6.26 (**Annuity payments**) To buy a new house, you must borrow $150,000. To do this, you take out a $150,000, 30-year, 10 percent mortgage. Your mortgage payments, which are made at the end of each year (one payment each year), include both principal and 10 percent interest on the declining balance. How large will your annual payments be?

P6.27 (**Components of annuity payments**) You've just taken on a 20-year, $150,000 mortgage with a quoted interest rate of 6 percent calling for payments semiannually. How much of your first year's loan payments (the initial two payments, with the first coming after six months have passed, and the second one coming at the end of the first year) goes toward paying *interest*, rather than principal?

P6.28 (Related to Checkpoint 6.2 on page 165) (**Present value of annuity payments**) The state lottery's million-dollar payout provides for $1 million to be paid over the course of 19 years in amounts of $50,000. The first $50,000 payment is made immediately, and the 19 remaining $50,000 payments occur at the end of each of the next 19 years. If 10 percent is the discount rate, what is the present value of this stream of cash flows? If 20 percent is the discount rate, what is the present value of the cash flows?

P6.29 (**Future value of an annuity**) Find the future value at the end of Year 10 of an annuity that pays $1,000 per year for 10 years compounded annually at 10 percent. What would be the future value of this annuity if it were compounded annually at 15 percent?

P6.30 (**Present value of an annuity due**) Determine the present value of an annuity due of $1,000 per year for 10 years discounted back to the present at an annual rate of 10 percent. What would be the present value of this annuity due if it were discounted at an annual rate of 15 percent?

P6.31 (**Present value of an annuity**) Determine the present value of an ordinary annuity of $1,000 per year for 10 years, assuming it earns 10 percent. Assume that the first cash flow from the annuity comes at the end of Year 8 and the final payment at the end of Year 17. That is, no payments are made on the annuity at the end of Years 1 through 7. Instead, annual payments are made at the end of Years 8 through 17.

P6.32 (**Components of an annuity payment**) You take out a 25-year mortgage for $300,000 to buy a new house. What will your monthly payments be if the interest rate on your mortgage is 8 percent? Use a spreadsheet to calculate your answer. Now, calculate the portion of the 48th monthly payment that goes toward interest and principal.

P6.33 (**Comprehensive problem**) Over the past few years, Microsoft founder Bill Gates's net worth has fluctuated between $20 and $130 billion. In early 2006, it was about $26 billion—after he reduced his stake in Microsoft from 21 percent to around 14 percent by moving billions into his charitable foundation. Let's see what Bill Gates can do with his money in the following problems.

a. Manhattan's native tribe sold Manhattan Island to Peter Minuit for $24 in 1626. Now, 387 years later in 2013, Bill Gates wants to buy the island from the "current natives." How much would Bill have to pay for Manhattan if the "current natives" want a 6 percent annual return on the original $24 purchase price?

b. Bill Gates decides to pass on Manhattan and instead plans to buy the city of Seattle, Washington, for $50 billion in 10 years. How much would Bill have to invest today at 10 percent compounded annually in order to purchase Seattle in 10 years?

c. Now assume Bill Gates only wants to invest half his net worth today, $13 billion, in order to buy Seattle for $50 billion in 10 years. What annual rate of return would he have to earn in order to complete his purchase in 10 years?

d. Instead of buying and running large cities, Bill Gates is considering quitting the rigors of the business world and retiring to work on his golf game. To fund his retirement, Bill would invest his $20 billion fortune in safe investments with an expected annual rate of return of 7 percent. He also wants to make 40 equal annual withdrawals from this retirement fund beginning a year from today, running his retirement fund to $0 at the end of 40 years. How much can his annual withdrawal be in this case?

P6.34 (Related to Checkpoint 6.1 on page 162) (**Annuity payments**) Lisa Simpson wants to have $1,000,000 in 45 years by making equal annual end-of-the-year deposits into a tax-deferred account paying 8.75 percent annually. What must Lisa's annual deposit be?

P6.35 (Related to Checkpoint 6.2 on page 165) (**Present value of an annuity**) Imagine that Homer Simpson actually invested the $100,000 he earned providing Mr. Burns entertainment five years ago at 7.5 percent annual interest and that he starts investing an additional $1,500 a year today and at the beginning of each year for 20 years at the same 7.5 percent annual rate. How much money will Homer have 20 years from today?

P6.36 (**Annuity payments**) Prof. Finance is thinking about trading cars. She estimates she will still have to borrow $25,000 to pay for her new car. How large will Prof. Finance's monthly car loan payment be if she can get a five-year (60 equal monthly payments) car loan from the VTech Credit Union at 6.2 percent APR?

P6.37 (**Annuity payments**) Ford Motor Company's current incentives include 4.9 percent APR financing for 60 months or $1,000 cash back on a Mustang. Let's assume Suzie Student wants to buy the premium Mustang convertible, which costs $25,000, and she has no down payment other than the cash back from Ford. If she chooses the $1,000 cash back, Suzie can borrow from the VTech Credit Union at 6.9 percent APR for 60 months (Suzie's credit isn't as good as that of Prof. Finance). What will Suzie Student's monthly payment be under each option? Which option should she choose?

P6.38 (Related to Checkpoint 6.3 on page 168) (**Determining the outstanding balance of a loan**) Five years ago you took out a $300,000, 25-year mortgage with an annual interest rate of 7 percent and monthly payments of $2,120.34. What is the outstanding balance on your current loan if you just made the 60th payment?

P6.39 (**Annuity payments**) Calvin Johnson has a $5,000 debt balance on his Visa card that charges 12.9 percent APR compounded monthly. In 2005, Calvin's minimum monthly payment is 3 percent of his debt balance, which is $150. How many months (round up) will it take Calvin Johnson to pay off his credit card if he pays the current minimum payment of $150 at the end of each month? In 2006, as the result of a federal mandate, the minimum monthly payment on credit cards rose to 4 percent. If Calvin made monthly payments of $200 at the end of each month, how long would it take to pay off his credit card?

P6.40 (**Future value of an annuity**) Let's say you deposited $160,000 in a 529 plan (a tax-advantaged college savings plan) hoping to have $420,000 available 12 years later when your first child starts college. However, you didn't invest very well, and two years later the account's balance dropped to $140,000. Let's look at what you need to do to get the college savings plan back on track.

a. What was the original annual rate of return needed to reach your goal when you started the fund two years ago?

b. With only $140,000 in the fund and 10 years remaining until your first child starts college, what annual rate of return would the fund have to make to reach your $420,000 goal if you add nothing to the account?

c. Shocked by your experience of the past two years, you feel the college fund has invested too much in stocks, and you want a low-risk fund in order to ensure you have the necessary $420,000 in 10 years. You are willing to make end-of-the-month deposits to the fund as well. You find you can get a fund that promises to pay a guaranteed annual return of 6 percent that is compounded monthly. You decide to transfer the $140,000 to this new fund and make the necessary monthly deposits. How large of a monthly deposit must you make into this new fund each month?

d. After seeing how large the monthly deposit would be (in part c of this problem), you decide to invest the $140,000 today and $500 at the end of each month for the next 10 years into a fund consisting of 50 percent stock and 50 percent bonds and hope for the best. What APR would the fund have to earn in order to reach your $420,000 goal?

P6.41 (Saving for retirement—future value of an annuity) Selma and Patty Bouvier are twins and both work at the Springfield DMV. Selma and Patty Bouvier decide to save for retirement, which is 35 years away. They'll both receive an 8 percent annual return on their investment over the next 35 years. Selma invests $2,000 per year at the end of each year *only* for the first 10 years of the 35-year period—for a total of $20,000 saved. Patty doesn't start saving for 10 years and then saves $2,000 per year at the end of each year for the remaining 25 years—for a total of $50,000 saved. How much will each of them have when they retire?

Perpetuities

P6.42 (Related to Checkpoint 6.4 on page 172) (Present value of a perpetuity) What is the present value of the following?

a. A $300 perpetuity discounted back to the present at 8 percent
b. A $1,000 perpetuity discounted back to the present at 12 percent
c. A $100 perpetuity discounted back to the present at 9 percent
d. A $95 perpetuity discounted back to the present at 5 percent

P6.43 (Present value of a perpetuity) At a discount rate of 8.5 percent, find the present value of a perpetual payment of $1,000 per year. If the discount rate were lowered to half the size (4.25 percent), what would be the value of the perpetuity?

P6.44 (Related to Checkpoint 6.5 on page 173) (Present value of a growing perpetuity) What is the present value of a perpetuity stream of cash flows that pays $1,000 at the end of Year 1, and the annual cash flows grow at a rate of 4 percent per year indefinitely, if the appropriate discount rate is 8 percent? What if the appropriate discount rate is 6 percent?

P6.45 (Present value of a growing perpetuity) What is the present value of a perpetuity stream of cash flows that pays $50,000 at the end of Year 1 and then grows at a rate of 6 percent per year indefinitely? The rate of interest used to discount the cash flows is 10 percent.

P6.46 (Present value of a growing perpetuity) As a result of winning the Gates Energy Innovation Award, you are awarded a growing perpetuity. The first payment will occur in a year and will be for $20,000. You will continue receiving monetary awards annually, with each award increasing by 5 percent over the previous award, and these monetary awards will continue forever. If the appropriate interest rate is 10 percent, what is the present value of this award?

P6.47 (Present value of a growing perpetuity) Your firm has taken on cost-saving measures that will provide a benefit of $10,000 in the first year. These cost savings will decrease each year at a rate of 3 percent forever. If the appropriate interest rate is 6 percent, what is the present value of these savings?

Complex Cash Flow Streams

P6.48 (Related to Checkpoint 6.6 on page 175) (**Present value of annuities and complex cash flows**) You are given three investment alternatives to analyze. The cash flows from these three investments are as follows:

Investment Alternatives

End of Year	A	B	C
1	$10,000		$10,000
2	10,000		
3	10,000		
4	10,000		
5	10,000	$10,000	
6		10,000	50,000
7		10,000	
8		10,000	
9		10,000	
10		10,000	10,000

Assuming a 20 percent discount rate, find the present value of each investment.

P6.49 (**Present value of annuities and complex cash flows**) You are given three investment alternatives to analyze. The cash flows from these three investments are as follows:

Investment

End of Year	A	B	C
1	$15,000		$20,000
2	15,000		
3	15,000		
4	15,000		
5	15,000	$15,000	
6		15,000	60,000
7		15,000	
8		15,000	
9		15,000	
10		15,000	20,000

Assuming a 20 percent interest rate, find the present value of each investment.

P6.50 (Present value of an uneven stream of payments) You are given three investment alternatives to analyze. The cash flows from these three investments are as follows:

Investment

End of Year	A	B	C
1	$2,000	$2,000	$ 5,000
2	3,000	2,000	5,000
3	4,000	2,000	(5,000)
4	(5,000)	2,000	(5,000)
5	5,000	5,000	15,000

What is the present value of each of these three investments if the appropriate discount rate is 10 percent?

P6.51 (Present value of complex cash flows) You have an opportunity to make an investment that will pay $100 at the end of the first year, $400 at the end of the second year, $400 at the end of the third year, $400 at the end of the fourth year, and $300 at the end of the fifth year.

a. Find the present value if the interest rate is 8 percent. (Hint: You can simply bring each cash flow back to the present and then add them up. Another way to work this problem is to either use the =NPV function in Excel or to use the CF key on your financial calculator—but you'll want to check your calculator's manual before you use this key. Keep in mind that with the =NPV function in Excel, there is no initial outlay. That is, all this function does is bring all of the future cash flows back to the present. With a financial calculator, you should keep in mind that CF_0 is the initial outlay or cash flow at time 0, and, because there is no cash flow at time 0, $CF_0 = 0$.)

b. What would happen to the present value of this stream of cash flows if the interest rate were 0 percent?

P6.52 (Present value of complex cash flows) How much do you have to deposit today so that beginning 11 years from now you can withdraw $10,000 a year for the next five years (Periods 11 through 15) plus an *additional* amount of $20,000 in the last year (Period 15)? Assume an interest rate of 6 percent.

P6.53 (Comprehensive problem) You would like to have $50,000 in 15 years. To accumulate this amount, you plan to deposit an equal sum in the bank each year that will earn 7 percent interest compounded annually. Your first payment will be made at the end of the year.

a. How much must you deposit annually to accumulate this amount?

b. If you decide to make a large lump-sum deposit today instead of the annual deposits, how large should this lump-sum deposit be? (Assume you can earn 7 percent on this deposit.)

c. At the end of five years, you will receive $10,000 and deposit this in the bank toward your goal of $50,000 at the end of 15 years. In addition to this deposit, how much must you deposit in equal annual deposits to reach your goal? (Again, assume you can earn 7 percent on this deposit.)

P6.54 **(Complex annuity payments)** Milhouse, 22, is about to begin his career as a rocket scientist for a NASA contractor. Being a rocket scientist, Milhouse knows that he should begin saving for retirement immediately. Part of his inspiration came from reading an article on Social Security in *Time*. The article indicated that the ratio of workers paying taxes to retirees collecting checks will drop dramatically in the future. In fact, the number will drop to two workers for every retiree in 2040. Milhouse's retirement plan allows him to make equal yearly contributions, and it pays 9 percent interest annually. Upon retirement, Milhouse plans to buy a new boat, which he estimates will cost him $300,000 in 43 years, which is when he plans to retire (at age 65). He also estimates that in order to live comfortably he will require a yearly income of $80,000 for each year after he retires. Based on his family history, Milhouse expects to live until age 80 (that is, he would like to receive 15 payments of $80,000 at the end of each year). When he retires, Milhouse will purchase his boat in one lump sum and place the remaining balance into an account that pays 6 percent interest, from which he will withdraw his $80,000 per year. If Milhouse's first contribution is made one year from today, and his last is made the day he retires, how much money must he contribute each year to his retirement fund?

P6.55 **(Comprehensive problem)** Having just inherited a large sum of money, you are trying to determine how much you should save for retirement and how much you can spend now. For retirement, you will deposit today (January 1, 2013) a lump sum in a bank account paying 10 percent compounded annually. You don't plan on touching this deposit until you retire in five years (January 1, 2018), and you plan on living for 20 additional years. During your retirement, you would like to receive income of $50,000 per year to be received the first day of each year, with the first payment on January 1, 2018, and the last payment on January 1, 2037. Complicating this objective is your desire to have one final three-year fling during which time you'd like to track down all the original members of *Hey Dude* and *Saved by the Bell* and get their autographs. To finance this, you want to receive $250,000 on January 1, 2033, and *nothing* on January 1, 2034, and January 1, 2035, because you will be on the road. In addition, after you pass on (January 1, 2038), you would like to have a total of $100,000 to leave to your children.

a. How much must you deposit in the bank at 10 percent interest on January 1, 2013, to achieve your goal? (Use a timeline to answer this question. Keep in mind that the last second of December 31st is equivalent to the first second of January 1st.)

b. What kinds of problems are associated with this analysis and its assumptions?

P6.56 **(Future value of a complex annuity)** Springfield mogul Montgomery Burns, age 80, wants to retire at age 100 so he can steal candy from babies full time. Once Mr. Burns retires, he wants to withdraw $1 billion at the beginning of each year for 10 years from a special offshore account that will pay 20 percent annually. In order to fund his retirement, Mr. Burns will make 20 equal end-of-the-year deposits in this same special account that will pay 20 percent annually. How much money will Mr. Burns need at age 100, and how large of an annual deposit must he make to fund this retirement amount?

P6.57 **(Comprehensive problem)** Suppose that you are in the fall of your senior year and are faced with the choice of either getting a job when you graduate or going to law school. Of course, your choice is not purely financial. However, to make an informed decision you would like to know the financial implications of the two alternatives. Let's assume that your opportunities are as follows:

If you take the "get a job" route you expect to start off with a salary of $40,000 per year. There is no way to predict what will happen in the future, your best guess is that your salary will grow at 5 percent per year until you retire in 40 years. As a law student, you will be paying $25,000 per year tuition for each of the three years you are in graduate school. However, you can then expect a job with a starting salary of $70,000 per year. Moreover, you expect your salary to grow by 7 percent per year until you retire 35 years later.

Clearly, your total expected lifetime salary will be higher if you become a lawyer. However, the additional future salary is not free. You will be paying $25,000 in tuition at the beginning of each of the three years of law school. In addition, you will be giving up a little more than $126,000 in lost income over the three years of law school: $40,000 the first year, $42,000 the second year, and $44,100 the third year.

a. To start your analysis of whether to go to law school, calculate the present value of the future earnings that you will realize by going directly to work, assuming a 3 percent discount rate.

b. What is the present value today of your future earnings if you decide to attend law school, assuming a 3 percent discount rate? Remember that you will be in law school for three years before you start to work as a lawyer. (Hint: Assume that you are paid at the end of each year so that your first salary payment if you decide to go to law school occurs four years from now.)

c. If you pay your law school tuition at the beginning of each year, what is the present value of your tuition, assuming a 3 percent discount rate?

P6.58 **(Present value of a complex stream)** Don Draper has signed a contract that will pay him $80,000 at the end of each year for the next six years, plus an additional $100,000 at the end of Year 6. If 8 percent is the appropriate discount rate, what is the present value of this contract?

P6.59 **(Present value of a complex stream)** Don Draper has signed a contract that will pay him $80,000 at the *beginning* of each year for the next six years, plus an additional $100,000 at the end of Year 6. If 8 percent is the appropriate discount rate, what is the present value of this contract?

P6.60 **(Complex stream of cash flows)** Roger Sterling has decided to buy an ad agency and is going to finance the purchase with seller financing—that is, a loan from the current owners of the agency. The loan will be for $2,000,000 financed at a 7 percent nominal annual interest rate. This loan will be paid off over five years with end-of-month payments along with a $500,000 lump-sum payment at the end of Year 5. That is, the $2 million loan will be paid off with monthly payments and there will also be a final payment of $500,000 at the end of the final month. How much will the monthly payments be?

Mini-Case

Bill Petty, 56, just retired after 31 years of teaching. He is a husband and father of two children who are still dependent. He received a $150,000 lump-sum retirement bonus and will receive $2,800 per month from his retirement annuity. He has saved $150,000 in a 403(b) retirement plan and another $100,000 in other accounts. His 403(b) plan is invested in mutual funds, but most of his other investments are in bank accounts earning 2 or 3 percent annually. Bill has asked your advice in deciding where to invest his lump-sum bonus and other accounts now that he has retired. He also wants to know how much he can withdraw per month, considering he has two children and a nonworking spouse. Because he has children, his current monthly expenses total $5,800. He is not eligible for Social Security until age 62, when he will draw approximately $1,200 per month; however, he would rather defer drawing on Social Security until age 67 to increase his monthly benefit amount to $1,550.

Questions

1. Bill has an emergency fund already set aside, so he can use his $400,000 of savings for retirement. How much can he withdraw on a monthly basis to supplement his retirement annuity if his investments return 5 percent annually and he expects to live 30 more years?

2. Ignoring his Social Security benefit, is the amount determined in question 1 sufficient to meet his current monthly expenses (keep in mind that he will receive a pension of $2,800 per month)? If not, how long will his retirement last if his current expenses remain the same? What if his expenses are reduced to $4,500 per month?

3. Considering the information obtained in question 2, should Bill wait until age 67 for his Social Security benefits? If he waits until age 67, how will his monthly Social Security benefit change the answers to question 2? (*Hint:* Calculate his portfolio value as of age 67 and then calculate how long that amount will last if it earns 5 percent annually.)

4. If the inflation rate averages 3.5 percent during Bill's retirement, how old will he be when prices have doubled from current levels? How much will a soda cost when Bill dies, if he lives the full 30 years and the soda costs $1 today?

7

Market Efficiency and Behavioral Finance

LEARNING GOALS

After studying this chapter, you should be able to:

LG1 Describe the characteristics of an efficient market, explain what market anomalies are, and note some of the challenges that investors face when markets are efficient.

LG2 Summarize the evidence which indicates that the stock market is efficient.

LG3 List four "decision traps" that may lead investors to make systematic errors in their investment decisions.

LG4 Explain how behavioral finance links market anomalies to investors' cognitive biases.

LG5 Describe some of the approaches to technical analysis, including, among others, moving averages, charting, and various indicators of the technical condition of the market.

LG6 Compute and use technical trading rules for individual stocks and the market as a whole.

In 2013 the Nobel Prize in economics was awarded to three co-recipients: Eugene Fama, Robert Shiller, and Lars Peter Hanson. In giving a shared award to Fama and Shiller, the committee appeared to display a sense of humor because those two scholars are best known for holding opposing views on the efficiency of financial markets. Eugene Fama was among the first to define the term "efficient markets" in his landmark study that concluded that stock prices moved almost at random and that any attempt to earn better-than-average returns by identifying winners and losers in the stock market was a fool's errand. Fama argued that competition among rational investors resulted in stock prices that accurately reflected all information available to market participants. If market prices reflected all available information, then no single investor could consistently identify overvalued or undervalued stocks, and therefore no investor could earn a return that consistently beat the market average (on a risk-adjusted basis).

Shiller, on the other hand, gained popular notoriety through his book, *Irrational Exuberance*, which argued that the stock market had become grossly overvalued in the late 1990s due to irrational behavior by investors. Indeed, Shiller's book was published just before a stock market crash in 2000. Shiller's message was that the stock market was anything but efficient, and that smart investors could identify times when it would be wiser to sit on the sidelines than to invest in stocks. Less than a decade later, Shiller made headlines again through his warnings that the housing market was becoming overheated, a prediction that the subsequent collapse in housing prices and related financial crisis seemed to confirm.

For many years, academics and investment professionals were on opposite sides of this debate. A broad consensus existed among academics that the market was very efficient and that neither amateur nor professional investors were likely to earn better-than-average returns over time. The professional investment community mostly disagreed with this view, arguing that well-trained investors with access to sophisticated information and trading systems could deliver superior returns to their clients. Over time, the two sides have moved closer together. A growing body of academic research, generally referred to as *behavioral finance*, has found evidence that the market is not as efficient as scholars once believed and that human cognitive biases place a limit on how efficient the market can be. At the same time, members of the investment community have acknowledged that consistently identifying overvalued or undervalued securities is extremely difficult and that many investors will be better off buying and holding a diversified portfolio of securities rather than paying experts to identify mispriced stocks. Among practitioners, this view has led to the growth in low-cost investment options such as index funds and exchange-traded funds.

Efficient Markets

LG1 **LG2** To some observers, the stock market is little more than a form of legalized gambling. They argue that movements in the stock market have no real connection to what is happening in the economy or to the financial results produced by specific companies. In the eyes of people who hold this view, large swings in the market are driven by emotions like greed and fear rather than by business fundamentals. In this chapter we study the connection between prices in the stock market (and other financial markets) and real business conditions, and we ask whether and how stock prices might be affected by human emotions.

To begin, consider Figure 7.1, which shows quarterly revenues reported by Walmart from 2000 to mid 2015. A quick glance at the figure reveals two obvious patterns. First, Walmart's revenues have grown over time. In early 2015 the company reported quarterly revenues of $132 billion, more than double the quarterly revenues that they had generated in early 2000. Perhaps an even more striking pattern is that there is clearly one quarter each year in which Walmart earns higher revenues than any other quarter. Those peaks, marked by red dots in Figure 7.1, occur in Walmart's first quarter, which ends on January 31st each year. In other words, in every year since 2000, Walmart has sold more goods in November, December, and January than in any other quarter, a remarkably stable pattern. When you think about this pattern a little, it should come as no surprise. Nearly every retail company in the United States sells more near the end of the year because of the Christmas season, and Walmart is no exception. Although Figure 7.1 plots Walmart's revenues, a plot of the company's net income would show similar patterns.

Walmart is a huge corporation, and roughly 11% of U.S. retail sales (not counting automobiles) occur in Walmart stores. Partly because it is so large and partly because much of its business focuses on life's necessities, Walmart's financial results are not terribly difficult to predict. This is another lesson from Figure 7.1. The persistence of the patterns in Walmart's revenues over a long period of time suggests that forecasts of

FIGURE 7.1

Walmart Quarterly Revenues

From 2000 to mid 2015 Walmart steadily increased its quarterly revenues from $43 billion to more than $132 billion. The long-term upward trend is marked by a distinct seasonal pattern in which Walmart's revenues peak in the first quarter each year, marked by red dots in the figure. The peak in revenues is due to the Christmas shopping season and is common in retail companies.

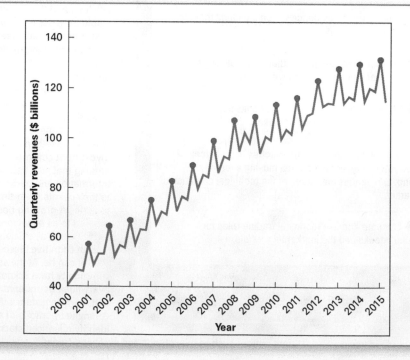

FIGURE 7.2

Walmart's Stock Price

From 2000 to mid 2015, Walmart's stock price rose, but it did not follow a predictable trend. Furthermore, the seasonal pattern in Walmart's revenues does not appear in its stock price. The stock price in the first quarter of each year is marked by a red dot, and those red dots show no discernible pattern over the past 15 years.

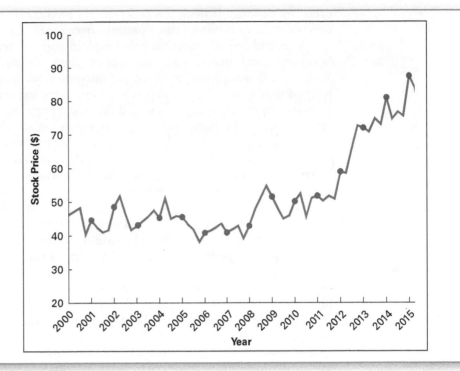

Walmart's future performance, at least in the not-too-distant future, are likely to be fairly accurate. Is Walmart's stock price just as predictable?

Figure 7.2 plots Walmart's stock price at the end of each quarter from 2000 to mid 2015, the same period covered in Figure 7.1. Like the company's revenues, Walmart's stock price was higher in 2015 than it was in 2000, but it hardly followed the relatively smooth upward trend that revenues did. The striking difference between Figures 7.1 and 7.2 is the seemingly random movements in Walmart's stock price, which stand in sharp contrast to the predictable movements in Walmart's revenues. Clearly there was no tendency for Walmart's stock to peak at the same time that its revenues did (i.e., at the end of the first quarter each year, marked by the red dots in Figure 7.2). Does this mean that there is no connection between Walmart's financial performance and the behavior of its stock?

Naturally our answer to that question is a firm no. To understand why, it may be helpful to think about what would happen if Walmart's stock price moved in sync with its revenues, showing a seasonal peak at the end of each year. Suppose that over many years, Walmart stock displayed a regular, predictable tendency to shoot up every year in the fourth quarter. If that pattern persisted and investors came to expect the pattern to continue, what would they do? Smart investors would buy Walmart's stock in the third quarter each year, hoping to profit from the fourth quarter runup. But if investors rushed to buy Walmart shares in the third quarter each year, their actions would put upward pressure on the stock price in the third quarter rather than the fourth. In other words, the pattern of fourth-quarter peaks in the stock price would change to a pattern of third-quarter peaks. Pretty soon, investors would see that pattern and begin buying even sooner, perhaps in the second quarter each year. Eventually, the actions of investors trying to buy ahead of any peak in the stock price would cause the seasonal pattern to disappear. So the lesson here is that even if a company's financial results follow a highly predictable pattern, its stock price will not follow the same pattern (or perhaps even any pattern). If stock prices do exhibit predictable patterns, the actions of investors will tend to eliminate those patterns over time.

A second line of argument helps explain why the seemingly random behavior of Walmart's stock price (or any stock price) does not imply that the stock market and Walmart's financial performance are unconnected. Remember that you previously learned that a stock's price depends on investors' expectations about the future performance of the company that issued the stock. Prices move up when investors' expectations become brighter, and prices move down when the opposite occurs. Investors who bought Walmart's stock way back in 2000 probably expected that over the next 15 years the company's revenues would grow and that they would peak in the fourth quarter every year. After all, by the year 2000, Walmart had already established a long history of growth, and the seasonal pattern in revenues was well known to the investment community. In other words, much of the performance displayed in Figure 7.1 would not have surprised investors and therefore would not have moved Walmart's stock a great deal. What would cause a sudden and potentially large change in Walmart's stock price is any sign that the firm's future financial performance would deviate from what investors expected. For example, suppose that in 2015 Walmart's revenues were not only high in the first quarter (as usual) but that they were even higher than investors had anticipated they would be. In that case, investors would likely raise their expectations about Walmart's future performance, and the company's stock price would go up as a result. If Walmart reported financial results that failed to match investors' expectations, then its stock price would probably fall as investors revised their views about how the company would perform in the future.

The main point here is that stock prices respond to *new* information. By definition, new information is something that people do not already know and that they do not anticipate. That Walmart's revenues peak at the end of each year is not new information, so when the peak occurs each year it does not tend to boost the company's stock price. Only if fourth-quarter revenues are surprising (better or worse than expected) would Walmart's stock price respond. Because new information is unpredictable, stock price movements are also largely unpredictable. This is the central idea of the **random walk hypothesis**, which says that predicting stock price movements is very difficult, if not impossible. We must emphasize here that if stock prices move at random, it is not a sign that the stock market is a casino that lacks any connection to the real business world. Just the opposite is true. The seemingly random behavior of stock prices is a sign that the stock market is processing information quickly and efficiently. In fact, economists say that a market that rapidly and fully incorporates all new information is an **efficient market**.

The Efficient Markets Hypothesis

The notion that stock prices (and prices in other financial markets) rapidly incorporate new information is known formally as the **efficient markets hypothesis (EMH)**. An implication of this idea is that it is very difficult for investors, even professional investors, to earn abnormally high returns by identifying undervalued stocks and buying them (or identifying overvalued stocks and selling them). Spotting bargains in the stock market is difficult because if the market is indeed efficient, by the time you have processed the information that leads you to believe that a stock is a good buy, the market has already incorporated that information, and the information is reflected in the stock's price.

The EMH says that investors should not expect to earn abnormal returns consistently. What constitutes an abnormal return? Previously you learned that there is a positive relation between risk and return. Investments that tend to earn higher returns also tend to be riskier. Therefore, an investment's expected return is directly related to its risk. An **abnormal return** (also known as **alpha**) is the difference between an investment's actual return and its expected return (i.e., the return that it should earn given its risk).

Equation 7.1   Abnormal return (or alpha) = Actual return − Expected return

One way that investors can estimate the expected return on a stock is to use the capital asset pricing model, or CAPM. Recall that the CAPM says that the expected return on a stock ($E(r_j)$) is equal to the risk-free rate (r_{rf}) plus the product of the stock's beta (b_j) and the risk premium on the overall market ($r_m - r_{rf}$).

Equation 7.2 $E(r_j) = r_{rf} + b_j(r_m - r_{rf})$

Example

> Suppose that a particular stock has a beta of 1.0. This means that the stock has average risk and should earn a return that is on average equal to the return on the overall market. Suppose that in a particular year the risk-free rate is 2% and the return on the overall stock market is 10%. Equation 7.2 tells us that the return that we should expect on this stock is 10%:
>
> $$E(r) = 2\% + 1.0(10\% - 2\%) = 10\%$$
>
> Suppose instead that the stock earned a 12% return. In this case it earns an abnormal positive return (alpha) of 2%:
>
> $$\text{Abnormal return} = \text{Actual return} - \text{Expected return}$$
>
> $$= 12\% - 10\%$$
>
> $$= 2\%$$
>
> The EMH says that spotting stocks like this (i.e., stocks that earn positive abnormal returns) on a consistent basis over time is nearly impossible, even for highly sophisticated investors with extensive training.

The efficient markets hypothesis focuses on the extent to which markets incorporate information into prices. The more information that is incorporated into stock prices and the more rapidly that information becomes incorporated into prices, the more efficient the market becomes. One way of characterizing the extent to which markets are efficient is to define different levels of efficiency corresponding to different types of information that prices may reflect. These levels of market efficiency are known as the weak form, the semi-strong form, and the strong form.

Weak Form The **weak form of the EMH** holds that stock prices fully reflect any relevant information that can be obtained from an analysis of past price movements. If investors study the historical record of stock prices and spot some kind of pattern that seems to repeat, their attempts to exploit that pattern through trading will cause the pattern to disappear over time. We have already described this idea to explain why Walmart's stock price does not exhibit predictable patterns, even though its revenues show distinct seasonal peaks. In short, the weak form of the EMH says that past data on stock prices are of no use in predicting future price changes. According to this hypothesis, prices follow a random walk, meaning that tomorrow's price change is unrelated to today's or yesterday's price, or that of any other day.

The earliest research on the weak form of market efficiency appeared to confirm the prediction that prices moved at random. Using databases that contained the past prices of listed stocks in the United States, researchers constructed a variety of "trading rules," such as buying a stock when it hit a 52-week low, and then tested these rules using historical information to see what returns investors following these rules might have earned. The results were encouraging to theorists but not to traders—none of the trading rules earned abnormal returns, but they did generate significant transactions costs. The researchers concluded that investors would do better by purchasing a diversified portfolio and holding it.

Semi-Strong Form The **semi-strong form of the EMH** asserts that stock prices fully reflect all relevant information that investors can obtain from any public source. This means that investors cannot consistently earn abnormally high returns using publicly available information such as annual reports and other required filings, analyst recommendations, product reviews, and so on. To illustrate the idea, suppose that you see that a particular firm has just posted its latest financial results online. You read the report and see that the company reported an unexpected surge in profits in the most recent quarter. Should you call your broker and buy some shares? The semi-strong form of the EMH says that by the time you download the annual report, read it, and call your broker, the market price of the stock will have already increased, reflecting the company's latest good news.

Figure 7.3 comes from a recent research study that tested this form of the EMH. The researchers gathered data on a large number of earnings announcements by

FIGURE 7.3 Daily Stock Price Reactions Surrounding Positive Earnings News

The figure shows that for a group of companies reporting favorable earnings, abnormal returns are close to 0 leading up to the announcement and beyond 2 days after the announcement. The market responds fully to the new information in 1 or at most 2 days. (Source: Modified from Andreas Neuhierl, Anna Scherbina, and Bernd Schlusche, "Market Reaction to Corporate Press Releases," *Journal of Financial and Quantitative Analysis*, August 2013.)

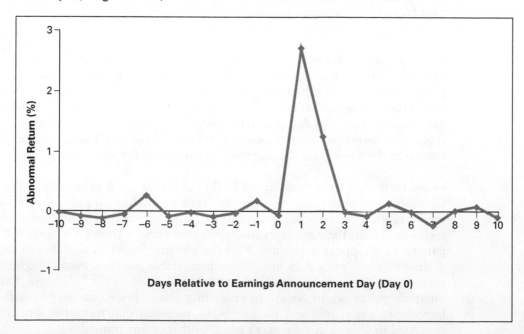

different companies and tracked the companies' stock price behavior before and after the announcements. The common factor in all of these announcements was that the companies were reporting good news that their earnings were higher than analysts had expected. In a sense, the question that the researchers were asking was, is it smart to buy the stock of a company that announces this kind of good news?

The horizontal axis of Figure 7.3 measures time relative to the earnings announcement day. The earnings announcement day is day 0, so day −1 is one day before the announcement and day +1 is one day after the announcement. Keep in mind that many firms release their financial information after the market has closed. This means that the first opportunity for the stock market to incorporate the new information occurs the day after the announcement, on day +1. The vertical axis in the figure measures the average abnormal return exhibited by companies in the sample. The behavior of stock prices exhibited in Figure 7.3 is very close to what the semi-strong form of the EMH would predict. Observe that leading up to the earnings announcements, the companies in the sample earn returns that are essentially normal (i.e., the abnormal return is 0, so the actual return matches the expected return). However, from day 0 to day +1, the average company in the sample earned an abnormal return of about 2.5%, with an additional 1% abnormal return occurring from day +1 to day +2. Beyond that point, however, abnormal returns quickly revert to 0%. In other words, the market quickly (in a day or at most two days) incorporates the good news from earnings announcements.

Many tests of semi-strong efficiency have examined how stock prices respond before and after particular types of news. One study looked at four companies that were major contractors in the space shuttle program. When the shuttle *Challenger* exploded shortly after liftoff in 1986, the stock prices of all four companies fell, but the one that fell the most was Morton Thiokol. That company made the booster rockets that lifted the shuttle into orbit, and months after the accident occurred, an investigation concluded that a problem with the O-rings in these rockets had caused the accident. In other words, the market's initial reaction within minutes of the accident seemed to point to the same conclusion as the subsequent investigation.

Numerous studies have examined the investment performance of professional investors such as mutual fund managers. Some people argue that although the stock market may be efficient enough to prevent individual investors from earning abnormally high returns, surely professional investors who have advanced training in investments and who spend their entire professional lives thinking about investments can perform better. The conclusions from research in this area are not unanimous, but most studies find that even professional investors struggle to earn abnormal returns on a consistent basis. On average, mutual fund managers do not earn returns that beat the market average by a sufficient degree to cover the fees that they charge investors. Furthermore, there is not much persistence in mutual fund returns. In other words, fund managers who have above-average returns one year do not have a very high likelihood of generating above-average returns the next year.

The overwhelming evidence indicates that stock prices react very rapidly to any important new information, which makes it very hard for investors (individuals or professionals) to "beat the market." Unless you hear about an event almost as soon as it happens, the stock price will adjust to the news before you can trade the stock.

Strong Form The **strong form of the EMH** holds that the stock market can rapidly incorporate new information even if it is not disseminated through public sources. It states that stock prices rapidly adjust to any information, even if it isn't available to every investor.

One type of private information is the kind obtained by corporate insiders, such as officers and directors of a corporation. They have access to valuable information about major strategic and tactical decisions the company makes. They also have detailed information about the financial state of the firm that may not be available to other shareholders. Insiders are generally prohibited from trading the shares of their employers prior to major news releases. However, at other times corporate insiders may legally trade shares of stock in their company, if they report the transactions to the Securities and Exchange Commission (SEC). When insiders file the required forms with the SEC, they are quickly made available to the public via the Internet. Several studies of corporate insiders find that their trades are particularly well timed, meaning that they tend to buy before significant price increases and sell prior to big declines. This, of course, is contrary to what you'd expect to find if the strong form of the EMH were true.

Insiders and other market participants occasionally have inside—nonpublic—information that they obtained or traded on illegally. With this information, they can gain an unfair advantage that permits them to earn an abnormal return. Clearly, those who violate the law when they trade have an unfair advantage. Empirical research has confirmed that those with such inside information do indeed have an opportunity to earn an abnormal return—but there might be an awfully high price attached, such as spending time in prison, if they're caught.

Arbitrage and Efficient Markets Closely linked to the notion of efficient markets is the concept of arbitrage. **Arbitrage** is a type of transaction in which an investor simultaneously buys and sells the same asset at different prices to earn an instant, risk-free profit. Let us give a simple example to illustrate the concept of arbitrage before examining the concept more closely.

Example

Suppose that banks in New York City will convert dollars into euros (or vice versa) at an exchange rate of one dollar per euro. In London, however, banks are exchanging dollars and euros at the rate of $1.25 dollars per euro. Notice that given these exchange rates, one euro is more valuable in London than in New York. Another way to say this is that euros are relatively cheap in New York and relatively expensive in London. This means that we have the identical asset (the euro) trading in different markets at different prices, so we would say that this presents an arbitrage opportunity. A trader could exploit this opportunity by buying cheap euros in New York and selling them in London as follows:

1. At a New York bank, use $1 million to buy €1 million. Remember, in New York, €1 is worth $1. Of course, if many traders begin buying euros in New York, the price of the euro will tend to rise in this market.
2. At a bank in London, sell the €1 million in exchange for $1.25 million at the prevailing exchange rate of $1.25 dollars per euro. Again, if many investors begin selling euros on the London market, then the price of the euro should begin to fall there.
3. Simply by purchasing euros in New York and selling them in London, the trader makes an instant profit of $250,000. But as the price of the euro rises in New York and falls in London, the opportunity to profit from these transactions will shrink, and ultimately vanish.

Consider how the definition of arbitrage applies to this example. First, arbitrage occurs when an investor simultaneously buys and sells the same asset. In this example, the underlying asset is just a currency, so the investor is buying euros in New York and selling them in London. The underlying asset is literally the same thing in each market. Furthermore, the purchase in New York and the sale in London can occur simultaneously through electronic transactions. The second part of the definition says that the purchase and sale must occur at different prices, and clearly that is the case here. In New York, €1 is worth $1, but in London it is worth $1.25. Finally, the definition of arbitrage says that the profit earned must be instantaneous and free of risk. Again, this example seems to satisfy those conditions because the trader earns the profit as soon as the currency trades take place, and because they take place essentially at the same time, there would appear to be no risk involved.

In the real world, naturally, we do not see large differences in currency prices in different markets. The price quoted in New York and in London will be virtually the same. If that were not true, arbitragers would exploit the price differences and, through their buying and selling transactions, push the prices closer together until no arbitrage opportunity remained. Economists refer to this as the "no arbitrage" condition, which simply means that prices in financial markets will quickly adjust to eliminate arbitrage opportunities.

Believers in efficient markets often cite arbitrage as a key mechanism that makes markets efficient. For example, suppose that the true intrinsic value of Pepsi stock is $100 per share but for some reason investors have been irrationally pessimistic about the company and have driven its price down to $80. To efficient markets advocates, this represents a kind of arbitrage opportunity. Smart investors will buy the undervalued shares of Pepsi and to hedge their bets they will simultaneously sell shares in another similar company, like Coca-Cola, for example. The buying pressure will cause Pepsi shares to move back toward their intrinsic value of $100, so in the end the market price and the intrinsic value of Pepsi are equal.

Arbitrage is a powerful force, and it plays a very important role in setting the prices of many types of securities, but there are limits to arbitrage. In the Pepsi example, the arbitrage process involves not only buying Pepsi shares but also selling something else that is very similar to Pepsi. Although Pepsi and Coca-Cola are similar stocks, one cannot really argue that they are identical investments. They are imperfect substitutes for one another, so even if Pepsi is mispriced, buying Pepsi and selling Coca-Cola may be risky. In addition, making these trades is costly, especially for an investor who wants to sell Coca-Cola but does not own any shares. That investor must engage in a short sale, which means that the investor must borrow Coca-Cola shares from someone else before selling them. Short sales often carry high transactions costs, and at times, shorting a particular stock is just not possible because there is no one willing to lend the required shares.

Another risk associated with arbitrage has to do with what created the apparent arbitrage opportunity in the first place. We presumed that some investors were irrationally pessimistic about Pepsi, and their pessimism caused Pepsi to be undervalued. It may be true that some smart investors can spot this situation, but what if other traders continue to be pessimistic or become even more pessimistic about Pepsi? In that case, there is no absolute guarantee that the actions of smart traders (who are buying Pepsi) will swamp the trades of irrational traders (who continue to sell Pepsi) and thereby move Pepsi's stock price toward its intrinsic value. Instead, Pepsi could become more undervalued, which would cause losses for the "smart" traders conducting the arbitrage trades.

To sum up, there is considerable evidence suggesting that the stock market is relatively efficient, and there are compelling reasons to expect that to be the case. Nevertheless, some contrary evidence exists, and it is to that evidence that we now turn.

Market Anomalies

Despite considerable evidence in support of the EMH, researchers have uncovered some patterns that seem inconsistent with the theory. Collectively, this body of puzzling evidence is known as **market anomalies**, a name that itself suggests that there is less evidence contradicting the EMH than there is in support of it. What all of these anomalies have in common is that they reveal patterns or trading strategies that, at least in hindsight, earned higher returns than would be expected in efficient markets.

Calendar Effects One widely cited anomaly is the *calendar effect*, which holds that stock returns may be closely tied to the time of the year or the time of the week. That is, certain months or days of the week may produce better investment results than others. The most famous of the calendar anomalies is the *January effect*, which is a tendency for small-cap stocks to outperform large-cap stocks by an unusually wide margin in the month of January. One possible explanation for this pattern has to do with taxes. Under certain conditions, investors can deduct investment losses when calculating their federal income taxes. Thus, there is an incentive for investors to sell stocks that have gone down in value during the year, and investors who recognize that incentive are particularly likely to sell in December as the tax year comes to a close. Think about what happens to the market capitalization of a firm when its stock falls during the year—the market cap gets smaller. Thus, if investors have a tax incentive to sell their loser stocks in December, and if these stocks by definition tend to be smaller than average, then their prices may be temporarily depressed due to December tax selling, and they may rebound in January. As plausible as this explanation may sound, there is at best mixed evidence that it can account for the puzzling behavior of small stocks in January.

Small-Firm Effect Another anomaly is the *small-firm effect*, or *size effect*, which states that small firms tend to earn positive abnormal returns of as much as 5% to 6% per year. Indeed, several studies have shown that small firms (or small-cap stocks) earn higher returns than large firms (or large-cap stocks), even after taking into account the higher betas typical of most small firms. This tendency has been documented in the United States as well as in many stock markets around the world and is not confined to the month of January.

Post Earnings Announcement Drift (or Momentum) Another market anomaly has to do with how stock prices react to earnings announcements. In Figure 7.3 we showed the results of a study that tracked stock returns around earnings announcements. In that study, stocks reporting good earnings exhibited abnormal returns for a day or two, but those abnormal returns quickly dissipated. However, several older studies reported a tendency for stocks to "drift" after earnings announcements in the same direction as the initial reaction. In other words, when companies reported better-than-expected earnings, their stock prices jumped immediately, earning positive abnormal returns. But surprisingly, these firms' stock prices continued to earn positive abnormal returns for weeks or even months after the earnings announcements. Similarly, firms reporting bad earnings earned negative abnormal returns that continued for several months beyond the initial announcement. This seems to indicate that investors *underreact* to the information in earnings announcements. When firms report good news, investors don't realize just how good the news is, and similarly, when bad news comes, investors don't fully appreciate how bad the news is, so stock prices take a long time to fully adjust to a new level. This pattern seems to create an opportunity for investors to earn abnormal returns by purchasing stocks that have recently issued good earnings news or by short selling stocks that have recently delivered poor earnings results.

Figure 7.4 illustrates the post earnings announcement drift pattern. The horizontal axis marks time measured in weeks relative to an earnings announcement, and the vertical axis measures the cumulative abnormal return from 52 weeks prior to the earnings announcement to 52 weeks after the announcement. The earnings announcement occurs at week 0. Two types of companies are tracked in the figure—companies that announce better-than-expected earnings and companies that announce worse-than-expected earnings. The blue line in the figure plots cumulative abnormal returns (i.e., the abnormal return over the entire period) earned by the sample of "good news" stocks, and the red line tracks abnormal returns for the "bad news" stocks. Notice that when firms announce good news, their stock prices react quickly, as indicated by the jump in the blue line at week 0. Similarly, when firms reveal that their earnings are below investors' expectations, their stock prices move down almost immediately, as shown by the drop in the red line at week 0. That rapid initial reaction is exactly the pattern that an efficient market should produce.

However, it appears that investors underreact to the news contained in earnings announcements. Observe that after the initial reaction to the earnings announcement,

FIGURE 7.4

Post Earnings Announcement Drift

When firms announce better-than-expected earnings, their stock prices jump quickly, as the EMH would predict, but contrary to the EMH, stock prices continue to drift upward at an abnormally rapid clip over the next year or so. The same thing happens in reverse when firms announce poor earnings.

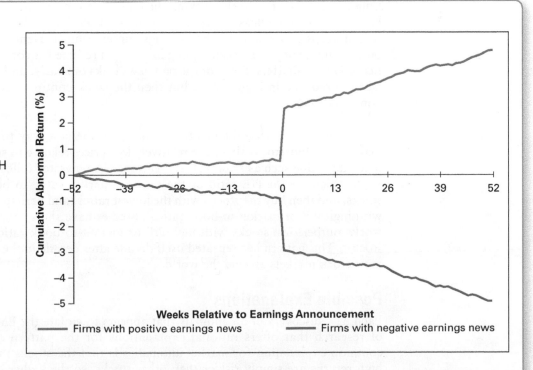

Weeks Relative to Earnings Announcement

— Firms with positive earnings news   — Firms with negative earnings news

both the blue and red lines exhibit trends, with the blue line slowly rising and the red line slowly falling. This means that the initial reaction to the earnings announcement was not large enough, and stock prices are adjusting slowly to the information contained in the earnings announcement. The slow adjustment process creates an opportunity for investors. For example, after a company announces positive earnings news (i.e., investors do not have to anticipate what the content of the announcement will be), investors who buy the stock earn significant abnormal returns. Looking at the blue line in Figure 7.4, you can see that the amount of drift is roughly 2% over the 52 weeks following the earnings announcement. In other words, Figure 7.4 suggests that investors who closely monitor earnings announcements and buy stocks after firms announce better-than-expected returns will earn a return that is about 2% above normal (i.e., 2% greater than one would expect given the risk of the stocks being purchased). Investors can also make money by short selling the shares of companies that announce poor earnings results. The drift in stock prices following the earnings announcement is not consistent with the predictions of the EMH.

A slight variation on this story is known as the momentum anomaly. In physics, *momentum* refers to the tendency of an object in motion to continue moving or the tendency of an object at rest to remain at rest. Applied to stocks, momentum refers to the tendency for stocks that have gone up recently to keep going up or the tendency for stocks that have gone down recently to continue going down. The connection to earnings announcement drift is easy to see. When a company has a particularly good quarter, it is common for some of the good news to leak out into the market before the official earnings announcement. So leading up to the earnings release, it is common to see the stock price moving up, just as the blue line in Figure 7.4 rises ahead of the earnings news. As we've already discussed, when the firm releases the news that it has had a very strong quarter, the price goes up more, but then it continues to drift up for weeks. Taking the entire pattern into account, we observe that before a company releases very good earnings news, its stock price has gone up, and then it keeps going up after the earnings announcement. Hence, these stocks display positive momentum. The same thing happens in reverse for companies that have particularly bad quarters. Some of the bad news leaks out early, and the stock goes down (see the red line in Figure 7.4), but then the stock continues to go down after the announcement.

The Value Effect According to the *value effect*, the best way to make money in the market is to buy stocks that have relatively low prices relative to some measure of fundamental value such as book value or earnings. An investor following a value strategy might calculate the P/E ratio or the ratio of market value to book value for many stocks, and then buy the stocks with the lowest ratios (and perhaps short sell the stocks with high P/E or market-to-book ratios). Studies have shown that, on average, value stocks outperform stocks with high P/E or market-to-book ratios (so-called growth stocks). This pattern has repeated itself decade after decade in the United States and in most stock markets around the world.

Possible Explanations

Each new discovery of an anomaly that appears to violate the EMH prompts a flurry of research that offers rational explanations for the pattern observed. The most common explanation for market anomalies is that the stocks that earn abnormally high returns are simply riskier than other stocks, so the higher returns reflect a risk premium rather than mispricing by the market. For example, most academics and practitioners would agree that small firms are riskier than large firms, so it is not sur-prising that small stocks earn higher returns. The real question is, how much riskier are small firms, and how large should the risk premium be on those securities? According to the CAPM, if a small stock has a beta of 2.0 and a large stock has a beta of 1.0, the small stock should earn roughly twice the risk premium (over Treasury bills) that the large stock earns. The reason that the small-firm effect is known as an anomaly is that small stocks seem to earn higher returns than their betas can justify. Believers in the EMH argue that beta is an imperfect measure of risk and that if a better risk measure were available, the difference in returns between small and large stocks could be fully attributed to differences in risk.

Another explanation for market anomalies is that even in an efficient market where prices move essentially at random, some trading rules may appear to earn abnormally high returns simply as a matter of chance. For example, one of the more amusing market anomalies is known as the Super Bowl anomaly. This anomaly says that if the team winning the Super Bowl in a particular year is one of the original National Football League teams (prior to the merger with the old American Football League), then the stock market will rise. Otherwise, the stock market will fall. This "trading rule" correctly predicted the direction of the market more than 80% of the time in the last 48 years. But should investors rely on it in the future? Most people would agree that the connection between the Super Bowl winner and the stock market is purely a matter of chance and is unlikely to exhibit a similar track record in the next 48 years. Some EMH advocates believe that most market anomalies are similarly just an artifact of random chance. However, this explanation is less persuasive in the face of evidence that anomalies such as the small-firm effect, momentum, and the value effect appear in most markets around the world.

The discovery of these and other anomalies led to the development of an entirely new way of viewing the workings of financial markets that has come to be known as **behavioral finance**. In contrast to traditional finance, which starts with the assumption that investors, managers, and other actors in financial markets are rational, behavioral finance posits that market participants make systematic mistakes and that those mis-takes are inextricably linked to cognitive biases that are hard-wired into human nature. We now turn to a discussion of the basic tenets of behavioral finance and how they may help explain market anomalies.

CONCEPTS IN REVIEW

Answers available at
http://www.pearsonhighered.com/smart

7.1 What is the random walk hypothesis, and how does it apply to stocks? What is an effi-cient market? How can a market be efficient if its prices behave in a random fashion?

7.2 Explain why it is difficult, if not impossible, to consistently outperform an efficient market.

    a. Does this mean that high rates of return are not available in the stock market?
    b. How can an investor earn a high rate of return in an efficient market?

7.3 What are market anomalies and how do they come about? Do they support or refute the EMH? Briefly describe each of the following:

    a. The January effect
    b. The size effect
    c. The value effect

Behavioral Finance: A Challenge to the Efficient Markets Hypothesis

LG3 LG4   For more than 40 years, the efficient markets hypothesis has been an influential force in financial markets. The notion that asset prices fully reflect all available information is supported by a large body of academic research. In practitioner circles, supporters of market efficiency include John Bogle of Vanguard, who helped pioneer the development of a special type of mutual fund known as an index fund. Managers of index funds don't try to pick individual stocks or bonds because they assume that the market is efficient. They recognize that any time and energy spent researching individual securities will merely serve to increase the fund's expenses, which will drag down investors' returns.

Although considerable evidence supports the concept of market efficiency, an increasing number of academic studies have begun to cast doubt on the EMH. This research documents various anomalies and draws from research on cognitive psychology to offer explanations for the anomalies. One notable event that acknowledged the importance of this field was the awarding of the 2002 Nobel Prize in economics to Daniel Kahneman, whose work integrated insights from psychology and economics. In addition to academic studies, some professional money managers are also incorporating concepts from behavioral finance into their construction and management of portfolios.

> ### INVESTOR FACTS
>
> **Behavioral Funds Underperform Too** A recent study tracked the performance of 22 U.S. mutual funds that claimed to use the findings from behavioral finance to guide their stock selections. From 2007 to 2013, these funds as a group performed slightly worse than average, generating negative abnormal returns of less than 0.20% per month.
>
> (Source: Nikolaos Philippas, "Did Behavioral Funds Exploit Market Inefficiencies during or after the Financial Crisis?" *Multinational Finance Journal* 2014, Vol. 18, Iss.1/2, pp. 85–138.)

Investor Behavior and Security Prices

Researchers in behavioral finance believe that investors' decisions are affected by a number of psychological biases that lead investors to make systematic, predictable mistakes in certain decision-making situations. These mistakes, in turn, may lead to predictable patterns in stock prices that create opportunities for other investors to earn abnormally high profits without accepting abnormally high risk. Let's now take a look at some of the behavioral factors that might influence the actions of investors.

Overconfidence and Self-Attribution Bias Research in psychology provides overwhelming evidence that, on average, people tend to exhibit **overconfidence**, putting too much faith in their own ability to perform complex tasks. Try this experiment. The next time you are in a large group, ask people to indicate whether they believe they have above average, average, or below average skill in driving a car. What you will probably find is that a majority of the group believes that they have above-average ability, and almost no one will lay claim to having below-average skill. But simply by the definition of average, some people have to be above average and some must be below average. Therefore, at least some people in the group are overconfident in their driving ability.

Closely linked to overconfidence is a phenomenon known as self-attribution bias. **Self-attribution bias** roughly means that when something good happens, individuals attribute that outcome to actions that they have taken, but when something bad happens, they attribute it to bad luck or external factors beyond their control. The connection to overconfidence is straightforward. An individual takes an action or makes a decision that leads to a favorable outcome. Self-attribution bias causes the individual to discount the role that chance may have played in determining the outcome and to put too much emphasis on his or her actions as the cause. This causes the individual to become overconfident.

Overconfidence and Acquisitions Warren Buffett summarized the role of overconfidence in acquisitions in one of his famous letters to shareholders: "Many managements apparently were overexposed in impressionable childhood years to the story in which the imprisoned handsome prince is released from a toad's body by a kiss from a beautiful princess. Consequently, they are certain their managerial kiss will do wonders for the profitability of Company Target.... We've observed many kisses but very few miracles. Nevertheless, many managerial princesses remain serenely confident about the future potency of their kisses—even after their corporate backyards are knee-deep in unresponsive toads." (Source: http://www .berkshirehathaway.com/ owners.html.)

What effects do overconfidence and self-attribution bias have in the investments realm? Consider an individual investor, or even a professional money manager, who analyzes stocks to determine which ones are overvalued and which are bargains. Suppose in a particular year the investor's portfolio earns very high returns. Perhaps the high returns are largely due to a booming stock market, but perhaps in addition the investor's stock picks performed even better than the overall market. Is this the result of good fortune or good analysis? It's not easy to separate the roles of skill and luck, but most investors would probably attribute the favorable outcome to their own investing prowess. What is the consequence if investors mistakenly attribute investment success to their own skill? One study found that investors whose portfolios had outperformed the market in the past subsequently increased their trading activity. After beating the overall market average by 2% per year for several years, these investors increased their trading activity more than 70%. The increase in trading led to much higher transactions costs and much lower returns. The same group of investors trailed the market by 3% per year after increasing their trading activity.

This tendency is not confined to individual investors. A recent study found that CEOs exhibit similar behavior when they undertake acquisitions of other firms. When a CEO acquires a firm and the acquisition target performs well, the CEO is more likely to acquire a second firm. The CEO is also more likely to buy more shares in his or her employer's stock prior to the next acquisition. But these second acquisitions actually destroy shareholder value on average. In other words, it appears that CEOs become overconfident regarding their ability to acquire other firms and run them profitably.

Loss Aversion Here's an interesting series of questions. Suppose you have just won $8,500 in a game of chance. You can walk away with your winnings or you can risk them. If you take the risk, there is a 90% chance that you will win an additional $1,500, but there is a 10% chance that you will lose everything. Would you walk away or gamble? Most people who are asked this question say that they would take the $8,500—the sure thing. They say this even though the expected value from the additional gamble is $500. That is,

Expected value = (Probability of gain) × (Amount of gain) − (Probability of loss)

$$\times (\text{Amount of loss}) = 0.90 \times \$1,500 - 0.10 \times \$8,500 = \underline{\$500}$$

In this case, the decision to take the $8,500 indicates that the individual making that choice is risk averse. The risk of losing $8,500 isn't worth the expected $500 gain.

However, if we reframe the question, most people respond differently. Suppose you have already lost $8,500 in a game of chance. You can walk away and cut your losses or you can gamble again. If you gamble, there is a 90% chance that you will lose $1,500 more, but there is a 10% chance that you will win $8,500, thus entirely reversing your initial loss. When confronted with this choice, most people say that they will take the risk to try to "get even," even though the expected value of this gamble is −$500.

$$\text{Expected value} = 0.10 \times \$8,500 - 0.90 \times \$1,500 = \underline{-\$500}$$

In this case, people are exhibiting risk-seeking behavior. They are accepting a risk that they do not have to take, and it is a risk that has a negative expected return.

FAMOUS FAILURES IN FINANCE

Loss Aversion and Trading Volume

When people are loss averse, they are reluctant to sell investments that have lost value because doing so forces them to realize the loss. But if investors are reluctant to sell when prices are falling, trading activity can dry up. That was a finding from a study of residential real estate activity over several market cycles in Boston. Researchers found that when market prices were rising, homeowners were generally willing to sell their properties at market value. But when price declines left homeowners in a position such that the market value of their home was less than what they had paid for it, homeowners exhibited a tendency to set asking prices above the true market value. For these homeowners, selling at the current market price would mean recognizing a loss, something homeowners were very averse to do. As a consequence, overpriced homes sat on the market month after month, with very few transactions taking place.

(Source: David Genesove and Christopher Mayer, "Loss Aversion and Seller Behavior: Evidence from the Housing Market," *Quarterly Journal of Economics*, 2001, Vol. 116, No. 4, pp. 1233–1260.)

In behavioral finance, the tendency to exhibit risk-averse behavior when confronting gains and risk-seeking behavior when confronting losses is called **loss aversion**. Loss aversion simply means that people feel the pain of loss more acutely than the pleasure of gain. In an investments context, loss aversion can lead people to hold onto investments that have lost money longer than they should. In fact, numerous studies have documented that when investors want to sell a stock in their portfolio, they are much more likely to sell a stock that has gone up in value than one that has fallen. Other studies have documented a tendency for the stocks that investors sell (i.e., stocks that have gone up) to perform better than the stocks that they choose to hold (i.e., stocks that have lost value).

Representativeness

Overreaction In an interesting experiment, six people were asked to flip a coin 20 times and count the number of heads that came up. Six others were asked to imagine flipping a coin 20 times and write down the sequence of heads and tails that might occur. The table below shows the results reported by each group.

Group	Subject	Number of Heads	Group	Subject	Number of Heads
A	1	10	B	1	6
	2	10		2	13
	3	8		3	7
	4	10		4	11
	5	10		5	8
	6	10		6	14
	Average	9.7		Average	9.8

Looking at the responses from individuals in each group, which group do you think actually flipped coins, and which imagined doing so?

The answer is that Group A only imagined flipping coins. Notice that almost everyone in the group said they expected to obtain 10 heads in 20 flips, but in the group that actually tossed the coins, the number of heads varied widely, from 6 to 14. What accounts for the differences between the two groups?

Representativeness refers to cognitive biases that occur because people have difficulty thinking about randomness in outcomes. Subjects in Group A assume (correctly) that the probability of obtaining a heads on any single flip of a coin is 50%, but they also assume (incorrectly) that this means that in 20 flips of a coin, it is very likely that heads will come up exactly 10 times. It is true that 10 is the average number of heads that one should expect, and notice that the average number of heads flipped by both groups was about 10. However, individual results vary quite a bit around that average. As the results of Group B's coin flips clearly show, it is rather unusual to obtain exactly 10 heads in 20 flips. Lots of other outcomes are quite likely.

Consider this analogy. Suppose picking stocks is like flipping coins in the sense that if markets are efficient, when you buy a stock there is about a 50% chance that it will do better than average (let's call that outcome heads) and a 50% chance that it will do worse than average (call that tails). Investors in Group A would appear to believe that if one buys 20 stocks, it is very likely that the outcome of that portfolio will be average because 10 stocks will do better than average and 10 will perform worse than average. However, we know from Group B that it is quite likely that a portfolio of 20 stocks could perform much better (more than 10 heads) or much worse (fewer than 10 heads) than average. In other words, even in an efficient market, some portfolios will do very well while others will lag behind.

Subjects in this experiment were also asked to report whether they obtained a "string" of five heads or five tails in a row in the course of flipping a coin 20 times. Here are their answers to that question.

Group	Subject	Five Heads or Tails in a Row?	Group	Subject	Five Heads or Tails in a Row
A	1	no	B	1	yes
	2	no		2	yes
	3	no		3	no
	4	no		4	yes
	5	no		5	no
	6	no		6	yes

Notice that among the subjects in Group B, those who actually flipped coins 20 times, obtaining a string of five flips in a row with the same outcome (either five heads or five tails in a row) was relatively common. But subjects in Group A did not imagine that they would see a string of five consecutive identical outcomes. Why not? These subjects know that there is a 50% chance of getting heads (or tails) in every flip, so they imagine that on a series of flips they will see a kind of oscillation in outcomes. That is, they appear to believe that a sequence of alternating heads and tails is more likely than a sequence that has several heads (or tails) in a row. This is representativeness at work again. Subjects in Group A dramatically underestimate the likelihood of getting the coin to come up heads or tails several times in a row because they think a 50-50 gamble is much more likely to result in alternating heads and tails.

Now consider how this feature of representativeness can influence the behavior of investors. Think about investors who are trying to decide which mutual fund to invest in. The EMH says that for a mutual fund to earn an above-average return is more a matter of luck than of skill, so any particular fund manager has roughly a

50% chance of beating the market in a particular year. There are thousands of mutual funds to choose from, so even if mutual fund performance is as much due to luck as it is to skill, there will be some fund managers who "beat the market" several years in a row, just as there were several coin flippers in Group B who flipped five heads in a row. However, if investors misinterpret randomness like the subjects in Group A did, they will believe that it is very unlikely for a fund manager to have a string of several good years in a row if the market is efficient. Put another way, these investors will interpret a string of good years as a sign that the market is not efficient, at least not for the fund manager achieving that string of good performance. Therefore, when investors see a manager who has delivered better-than-average returns for several years in a row, they may mistakenly attribute that record to skill. Research shows that investors overreact to a string of good performance and pour money into successful funds, enriching the fund managers but not necessarily themselves. Apparently, many investors see a string of good performance and overestimate the likelihood that the trend will continue. Investors overreact to the past performance of funds, even though there is little objective evidence that past performance is a good predictor of future success.

This logic may provide a behavioral explanation for the value phenomenon cited earlier. Recall that value stocks are stocks that have low prices relative to earnings or book value. These stocks generally display rather poor past performance—several years of declining prices is what puts these stocks in the value category. Similarly, growth stocks, stocks with high prices relative to earnings or book value, generally have very good past performance. One of the earliest studies of the value effect studied the results of a very simple trading rule. Each year, researchers sorted all stocks based on their cumulative performance in the previous three years. The trading rule was to buy the stocks that had performed worst (the value stocks) and sell short the stocks that had performed best (the growth stocks). Researchers discovered that this strategy earned returns that beat the market by 8% per year! Why would such a simple trading rule that anyone could follow work so well?

The researchers argued that it was due to representativeness. To be specific, they proposed that investors who watched particular stocks decline in value for three years in a row overreacted to those events by deciding that the trend would continue indefinitely, so they bid the prices of these stocks below their true values. Similarly, after watching other stocks do very well several years in a row, investors overreacted to that trend by naively assuming that this excellent performance would continue, and they bid up the prices of these stocks above their true values. Over time, the firms that had been performing poorly surprised investors by rebounding, and the firms that had been earning spectacular returns failed to sustain that performance. As a result, past price trends reversed themselves, and value investors made money.

Individual investors are not the only participants in markets likely to be affected by representativeness. Consider a firm that is looking to make an acquisition. What makes an acquisition target attractive? One criterion might be recent increases in sales and earnings. Would acquirers be wise to pay a premium to acquire a firm that has been growing faster than its competitors in recent years? The research evidence says no. There is almost no correlation between how fast firms have grown in the past and how fast they will grow in the future. In fact, that is a fundamental prediction of basic economic theory. When one firm enjoys great success in a particular market, other firms will enter the industry. Competition makes it more difficult for firms to sustain the high growth that

FAMOUS FAILURES IN FINANCE

Buying High and Selling Low

Research by the Federal Reserve and the University of Michigan suggests that individual investors, particularly those with lower incomes and wealth, displayed particularly poor timing with their investment decisions before, during, and after the sharp market downturn in 2008. Data from the Fed's triennial Survey of Consumer Finance shows that as the stock market rose from 2004 to 2007, the percentage of lower-income households who owned stocks climbed. However, from 2007 to 2010, a period containing a steep drop in stock values, the percentage of households owning stocks dropped, and that drop was steepest among households with lower incomes and wealth. The percentage of lower-income households owning stocks continued to fall from 2010 to 2013, while the stock market boomed. In contrast, the percentage of households with higher incomes and greater wealth who owned stocks rose from 2010 to 2013. In other words, the rich got richer, in part because the slump in stocks in 2008 did not deter them from continuing to invest in the market. Less wealthy households bought stocks when market values were high, sold them when the market crashed, and failed to benefit from the subsequent stock market recovery.

(Source: Josh Zumbrun, "Bad Stock-Market Timing Fueled Wealth Disparity," http://www.wsj.com/articles/bad-stock-market-timing-fueled-wealth-disparity-1414355341, accessed 6/26/2015.)

---

attracted new entrants in the first place. Yet there is ample evidence that managers do pay a larger premium when they acquire firms that experienced rapid growth prior to the acquisition, even though the prospect of sustaining the growth is low.

Underreaction In certain instances, representativeness can cause investors to underreact to new information. Consider this problem from statistics. On a table are 100 sacks, each of which contains 1,000 poker chips. Forty-five of these sacks contain 70% black chips and 30% red chips. The other 55 bags hold 70% red chips and 30% black chips. If you pick one bag at random, what is the likelihood that it will contain mostly black chips?

Most people get this answer right. If 45 out of 100 bags contain mostly black chips, then the probability of picking a bag at random that has mostly black chips is 45%. Here is a much harder problem. Suppose you choose one bag at random and then take out 12 chips, without looking at the others. Of the 12 chips that you pull out, 8 are black and 4 are red. What is the probability that the bag you picked contains mostly black chips?

Intuitively, people know that if the sample of 12 chips taken from the bag has a majority of black chips, then that means the probability that the bag has mostly black chips is higher than in the first problem where we select a bag at random and learn nothing more about it. But how much higher? Few people come close to guessing that the probability is over 95%! In other words, people tend to underreact to the new information they obtain in the second version of the question.

Let's make an analogy between drawing poker chips out of a bag and reading firms' earnings announcements. Earnings announcements contain a mix of good and bad news that varies over time. When a company announces particularly good (or bad) news, representativeness may cause investors to underreact to the new information. That is, investors may not appreciate that very good earnings news this quarter probably means the likelihood of good news next quarter has gone up (and vice versa for bad news this quarter). When the firm announces the next quarter's earnings, investors are surprised by how positive the news is, and the firm's stock price goes up again. That could explain the post earnings announcement drift (or momentum) phenomenon discussed earlier.

WATCH YOUR BEHAVIOR

Who Underreacts to News? A recent study found that it is primarily individual investors who underreact to information such as earnings announcements. For example, after firms release good earnings news, individuals tend to sell their shares too quickly before prices have risen high enough to incorporate the new information. Who's buying these shares from individuals? Professional investors like mutual fund managers.

A careful reader may object that we have asserted that representativeness can lead to both overreaction (in the case of value stocks) and underreaction (in the case of momentum). Keep in mind that there are important differences in the nature of the information that investors are reacting to in each case. In the value phenomenon, investors see a common string of information—several good years or several bad years in a row. This causes them to discount the role of chance in the outcome and *overreact to the series of events*. In the case of earnings announcement drift, investors are responding to a single new piece of information that is extreme—particularly good or particularly bad. In that case, representativeness may lead investors to *underreact to the new information* they've received.

Narrow Framing Many people tend to analyze a situation in isolation, while ignoring the larger context. This behavior is called **narrow framing**. A common example in investments relates to the asset allocation decisions that investors make in their retirement plans. The table below summarizes the retirement savings plans offered to employees of two firms. Firm A offers its employees two options for investing retirement savings—a stock fund and a bond fund. Firm B also offer two options—a stock fund and a blended fund that holds 50% stocks and 50% bonds.

Fund Offered	Company A	Company B
Stock fund (100% stocks)	Yes	Yes
Bond fund (100% bonds)	Yes	Not available
Blended fund (50% stocks, 50% bonds)	Not available	Yes

Research shows that many investors view this decision through the narrow frame of two choices, and they follow a simple guideline—put 50% into one fund and 50% into the other. It is as if investors know that they should diversify, so they divide their investments equally between the available options. However, investors seemingly fail to recognize how the asset allocation of the individual funds influences the resulting composition of their overall portfolios. The narrow frame (splitting money evenly between two funds) combined with the options offered by each company produces an odd outcome. Employees of Company A who divide their money between the stock fund and the bond fund will wind up with portfolios containing 50% stocks and 50% bonds. Employees of Company B also divide their money equally between the two funds, but in this case the two funds are the stock fund and the blended fund. Splitting money equally between those options results in an overall portfolio allocation of 75% stocks and 25% bonds. The retirement portfolios held by employees of Company B are much riskier than those held by workers at Company A, but not necessarily because Company B's employees prefer to take more risk. Instead, framing influences the risk of their portfolios.

Belief Perseverance People typically ignore information that conflicts with their existing beliefs, a phenomenon called **belief perseverance**. If they believe a stock is good and purchase it, for example, they later tend to discount any signs of trouble. In many cases, they even avoid gathering new information for fear it will contradict their initial opinion. It would be better to view each stock owned as a "new" stock when periodically reviewing a portfolio and to ask whether the information available at that time would cause you to buy or sell the stock.

Anchoring **Anchoring** refers to a phenomenon in which individuals attempting to predict or estimate some unknown quantity place too much weight on information that they have at hand, even when that information is not particularly relevant. For example, it is reasonably well known that a firm's past rate of growth in revenues is a very poor predictor of its future growth rate. Even so, when individuals are ask to predict the sales growth rate for a firm, if they are given information about the firm's past growth rate, that information appears to influence their projections. Specifically, individuals tend to predict faster (slower) sales growth when they know that a firm's past growth rate has been high (low).

A key component of the capital asset pricing model is the expected return on the market. To use the CAPM, an investor must form an expectation for the market's future return. How do investors estimate future returns? It appears in part that they anchor on the market's recent past returns. More specifically, surveys of investors reveal that when the previous year's stock market return was high, investor's expect a higher return in the subsequent year compared to cases in which the previous market return was low. In fact, high past returns are generally not a reliable signal for high future returns, so when investors based their forecast on recent past returns (i.e., when they anchor on last year's market return), they were overestimating the market's return, and that in turn would lead them to overestimate returns on specific stocks via the CAPM.

Familiarity Bias In this text we have discussed a number of analytical methods that investors can use to decide whether they want to purchase a particular investment. It turns out that in many cases people simply invest in things that are familiar to them, a behavior called **familiarity bias**. Research has shown that investors tend to invest in stocks located close to their homes. Even professional investors are not immune to this bias. A recent study found that mutual fund managers tend to invest more heavily in stocks located in their home states.

Investing something familiar is not necessarily a bad thing. Perhaps being more familiar with a company helps investors determine whether that company's stock is a good buy. However, if familiarity helps give investors an information edge, then investors should earn higher returns on the investments that they make based on familiarity (e.g., investments in companies located nearby). Even among professional investors, the evidence on this question is mixed. One study found that mutual fund managers earned unusually high returns on their investments in nearby firms, but other studies found that investing in companies based on familiarity influenced fund managers to form portfolios that were not fully diversified. As a result, those funds did not earn higher returns, but they did experience higher risk.

Investing heavily in familiar stocks does have one serious potential drawback. Industries are often concentrated in specific geographic areas. Think of the concentration of high-tech firms in Silicon Valley, for example. If investors in northern California invest mostly in companies from that region, they will form portfolios that are heavily weighted in tech firms, neglecting other sectors of the economy. Thus, familiarity bias may lead investors to hold underdiversified portfolios. Investors who do not take full advantage of diversification opportunities bear more risk than they need to without necessarily earning higher returns.

Implications of Behavioral Finance for Security Analysis

Our discussion of the psychological factors that affect financial decisions suggests that behavioral finance can play an important role in investing. Naturally, the debate on the efficiency of markets rages on and will continue to do so for many years. The

TABLE 7.1   USING BEHAVIORAL FINANCE TO IMPROVE INVESTMENT RESULTS

Studies have documented a number of behavioral factors that appear to influence investors' decisions and adversely affect their returns. By following some simple guidelines, you can avoid making mistakes and improve your portfolio's performance. A little common sense goes a long way in the financial markets!

- **Don't hesitate to sell a losing stock.** If you buy a stock at $20 and its price drops to $10, ask yourself whether you would buy that same stock if you came into the market today with $10 in cash. If the answer is yes, then hang onto it. If not, sell the stock and buy something else.
- **Don't chase performance.** The evidence suggests that past performance is at best a very noisy guide to future performance. For example, the best performing mutual funds in the last year or even the last five years are not especially likely to perform best in subsequent years. Don't buy last year's hottest mutual fund based solely on its performance. Always keep your personal investment objectives and constraints in mind.
- **Be humble and open-minded.** Many investment professionals, some of whom are extremely well paid, are frequently wrong in their predictions. Admit your mistakes and don't be afraid to take corrective action. The fact is, reviewing your mistakes can be a very rewarding exercise—all investors make mistakes, but the smart ones learn from them. Winning in the market is often about not losing, and one way to avoid loss is to learn from your mistakes.
- **Review the performance of your investments on a periodic basis.** Remember the old saying, "Out of sight, out of mind." Don't be afraid to face the music and to make changes as your situation changes. Nothing runs on "autopilot" forever—including investment portfolios.
- **Don't trade too much.** Investment returns are uncertain, but transaction costs are guaranteed. Considerable evidence indicates that investors who trade frequently perform poorly.

contribution of behavioral finance is to identify psychological factors that can lead investors to make systematic mistakes and to determine whether those mistakes may contribute to predictable patterns in stock prices. If that's the case, the mistakes of some investors may be the profit opportunities for others. See Table 7.1 for our advice on how to keep your own mistakes to a minimum.

CONCEPTS IN REVIEW

Answers available at
http://www.pearsonhighered.com/smart

7.4   How can behavioral finance have any bearing on investor returns? Do supporters of behavioral finance believe in efficient markets? Explain.

7.5   Briefly explain how behavioral finance can affect each of the following:

    a. The trading activity of investors

    b. The tendency of value stocks to outperform growth stocks

    a. The tendency of stock prices to drift up (down) after unusually good (bad) earnings news

Technical Analysis

  In the first section of this chapter we introduced the idea of market efficiency and suggested that there are many good reasons to believe that stock prices (and prices in other financial markets) are inherently unpredictable. The second section presented the behavioral finance challenge to market efficiency and discussed the evidence that there is at least some predictability in stock returns. In this section we introduce **technical analysis**, which is the practice of searching the historical record of stock prices and returns for patterns. If these patterns repeat, investors who know about them and can spot them early may have an opportunity to earn better-than-average returns.

Because it focuses on using past price movements to predict future returns, technical analysis is fundamentally at odds with even the weak form of market efficiency. For this reason, the practice of technical analysis remains controversial. For some investors, it's another piece of information to use when deciding whether to buy, hold, or sell a stock. For others, it's the only input they use in their investment decisions. Still others regard technical analysis as a waste of time.

Analyzing market behavior dates back to the 1800s, when there was no such thing as industry or company analysis. Detailed financial information about individual companies simply was not made available to stockholders, let alone the general public. About the only thing investors could study was the market itself. Some investors used detailed charts to monitor what large market operators were doing. These charts were intended to show when major buyers were moving into or out of particular stocks and to provide information useful for profitable buy-and-sell decisions. The charts centered on stock price movements. These movements were said to produce certain "formations," indicating when the time was right to buy or sell a particular stock. The same principle is still applied today. Technical analysts argue that internal market factors, such as trading volume and price movements, often reveal the market's future direction long before it is evident in financial statistics.

Measuring the Market

If using technical analysis to assess the overall market is a worthwhile endeavor, then we need some sort of tool or measure to do it. Charts are popular with many investors because they provide a visual summary of the behavior of the market and the price movements of individual stocks. As an alternative or supplement to charting, some investors prefer to study various market statistics. They might look at trends in market indexes or track other aspects of market behavior such as trading volume, short selling, or trading behavior of small investors (e.g., odd-lot transactions).

Technical analysis addresses those factors in the marketplace that can (or may) have an effect on the price movements of stocks in general. The idea is to understand the general condition (or "tone") of the market and to gain some insights into where the market may be headed over the next few months. Several approaches try to do just that, and we summarize some of the more common approaches below.

The Confidence Index   One measure that attempts to capture the tone of the market is the **confidence index**, which deals not with the stock market but with bond returns. Computed and published by *Barron's*, the confidence index is a ratio that reflects the spread between the average yield on high-grade corporate bonds relative to the yield on average- or intermediate-grade corporate bonds. Technically, the index is computed by relating the average yield on 10 high-grade corporate bonds to the yield on 10 intermediate-grade bonds. The formula is as follows:

Equation 7.3

$$\text{Confidence index} = \frac{\text{Average yield on 10 high-grade corporate bonds}}{\text{Average yield on 10 intermediate-grade bonds}}$$

Thus, the index measures the yield spread between high-grade bonds and intermediate-grade bonds. Because the yield on high-grade bonds should always be lower than the average yield on a sample of intermediate-grade bonds, the confidence index should never exceed 1.0. Indeed, as the measure approaches 1.0 (or 100%), the spread between the two sets of bonds will get smaller and smaller, which, according to the theory, is a positive sign. The idea is that as investors become more confident about the economy, they will be willing to invest in riskier bonds, driving down their yields and pushing up the confidence index. Those who follow the confidence index interpret a rise in the index as a positive sign for future stock returns.

Consider, for example, a point in time where high-grade bonds are yielding 4.50%, while intermediate-grade bonds, on average, are yielding 5.15%. This would amount to a yield spread of 65 "basis points," or 65/100 of 1% (i.e., 5.15% − 4.50% = 0.65%), and a confidence index of 4.50 ÷ 5.15 = 87.38%. Now, look what happens when yields (and yield spreads) fall or rise:

	Yields (Yield Spreads)	
	Fall	Rise
Yields on high-grade bonds	4.25%	5.25%
Yields on average bonds	4.50%	6.35%
Yield spread	0.25%	1.10%
Confidence index	94.44%	82.68%

Lower-yield spreads, in effect, lead to higher confidence indexes. These, in turn, indicate that investors are demanding a lower premium in yield for the lower-rated (riskier) bonds and in so doing are showing more confidence in the economy. This theory implies that the trend of "smart money" is usually revealed in the bond market before it shows up in the stock market, meaning that a rise in the confidence index today foreshadows a rise in the stock market.

Market Volume   Market volume is an obvious reflection of the amount of investor interest in stocks. As a rule, technical analysts who follow market volume say that increasing volume during a rising market is a positive sign that the upward movement in stocks will continue. On the other hand, when stocks are falling, a decline in volume may suggest that the decline in stock prices is approaching an end. In a similar vein, when stocks have been moving up and volume begins to drop off, that may signal the end of the bull market. Numerous financial periodicals and websites report total market volume daily, so it is an easy statistic to track.

Breadth of the Market   Each trading day, some stocks go up in price and others go down. In market terminology, some stocks advance and others decline. Breadth of the market deals with these advances and declines. The principle behind this indicator is that the number of advances and declines reflects the underlying sentiment of investors.

Analysts who use market breadth to help guide their investment decisions interpret the numbers as follows. As long as the number of stocks that advance in price on a given day exceeds the number that decline, the market is strong. The extent of that strength depends on the spread between the number of advances and declines. For example, if the spread narrows (the number of declines starts to approach the number of advances), market strength deteriorates. Similarly, the market is weak when the number of declines repeatedly exceeds the number of advances. When the mood is optimistic, advances outnumber declines. Again, data on advances and declines

WATCH YOUR BEHAVIOR

Plane Crashes and Sentiment
Investor sentiment is a tricky thing to define, and it's even harder to quantify. One study looked at how major airline disasters affected investor sentiment and stock returns. The author of the study found that the average one-day return on the U.S. stock market is about 4 basis points (0.04%), but the average return on a day with a major airline disaster was negative 32 basis points (−0.32%). That one-day dip represented an aggregate market value loss of $60 billion per airline disaster, but over the next two weeks as sentiment returned to normal, the market recovered most of its losses.

(Source: Guy Kaplanski, "Sentiment and Stock Prices: The Case of Aviation Disasters," *Journal of Financial Economics*, 2010, Vol. 95, pp. 174–201.)

FIGURE 7.5

Basic Market Statistics

Here is an example of the kind of information on market volume, advances, and declines that is easily accessible on the web. (Source: http://finance.yahoo.com/advances, accessed August 12, 2015.)

Advances & Declines

	NYSE	AMEX	NASDAQ	BB
Advancing Issues	922 (28%)	448 (30%)	781 (27%)	100 (37%)
Declining Issues	2,216 (68%)	976 (66%)	1,997 (70%)	112 (42%)
Unchanged Issues	121 (4%)	65 (4%)	91 (3%)	57 (21%)
Total Issues	**3,259**	**1,489**	**2,869**	**269**
New Highs	**76**	**17**	**132**	**11**
New Lows	**39**	**25**	**41**	**25**
Up Volume	645,655,898 (21%)	204,871,316 (40%)	435,985,588 (27%)	322,898,146 (66%)
Down Volume	2,342,076,687 (77%)	290,403,641 (57%)	1,162,111,459 (72%)	130,996,046 (27%)
Unchanged Volume	68,657,120 (2%)	11,132,061 (2%)	19,031,533 (1%)	38,445,283 (8%)
Total Volume	**3,056,389,705**[1]	**506,407,018**[1]	**1,617,128,580**[1]	**492,339,475**[1]

[1]Volume totals include pre-market and regional exchanges. Advancers & Decliners calculations are delayed 15 minutes.

are widely available. Figure 7.5 illustrates data on market volume, advances, and declines taken from Yahoo! Finance.

Short Interest When investors anticipate a market decline, they sometimes sell a stock short. That is, they sell borrowed stock. The number of shares of stocks sold short in the market at any point in time is known as the **short interest**. The more stocks that are sold short, the higher the short interest. Because all short sales must eventually be "covered" (the borrowed shares must be returned), a short sale in effect ensures future demand for the stock. Thus, the market is viewed optimistically when the level of short interest becomes relatively high by historical standards. The logic is that as shares are bought back to cover outstanding short sales, the additional demand will push stock prices up. The amount of short interest on the NYSE, the Amex, and Nasdaq's National Market is published in the *Wall Street Journal*, *Barron's*, and other sources.

Keeping track of the level of short interest can indicate future market demand, but it can also reveal present market optimism or pessimism. Knowledgeable investors usually do short selling, and a significant buildup or decline in the level of short interest hints at the sentiment of sophisticated investors about the current state of the market or a company. For example, a significant shift upward in short interest might indicate pessimism concerning the current state of the market, even though it may signal optimism with regard to future levels of demand.

Odd-Lot Trading A rather cynical saying on Wall Street suggests that the best thing to do is just the opposite of whatever the small investor is doing. The reasoning behind this is that as a group, small investors exhibit notoriously bad timing. The investing public usually does not come into the market in force until after a bull market has pretty much run its course, and it does not get out until late in a bear market. Although its validity is debatable, this is the premise behind a widely followed technical indicator and is the basis for the **theory of contrary opinion**. This theory uses the amount and type of odd-lot trading as an indicator of the current state of the market and pending changes.

Because many individual investors deal in transactions of fewer than 100 shares, their combined sentiments are supposedly captured in odd-lot figures. The idea is to see what odd-lot investors "on balance" are doing. So long as there is little or no difference in the spread between the volume of odd-lot purchases and sales, the theory of contrary opinion holds that the market will probably continue along its current line (either up or down). A dramatic change in the balance of odd-lot purchases and sales may be a signal that a bull or bear market is about to end. For example, if the amount of odd-lot purchases starts to exceed odd-lot sales by an ever-widening margin, speculation on the part of small investors may be starting to get out of control—an ominous signal that the final stages of a bull market may be at hand.

Two trends have diminished the usefulness of odd-lot trading as a market indicator. First, transactions costs have fallen dramatically in recent decades, so the cost advantage of trading in round lots rather than odd lots has diminished. Second, it has become more common for larger traders to break their orders into smaller parts to disguise their activities. For both of these reasons, it is less clear today than it used to be that an individual investor is behind an odd-lot trade. If the purpose of watching odd-lot trades is to assess the trading behavior of individuals rather than professionals, that purpose is harder to achieve today than it once was.

Trading Rules and Measures

Market technicians—analysts who believe it is chiefly (or solely) supply and demand that drive stock prices—use a variety of mathematical equations and measures to assess the underlying condition of the market. These analysts often use computers to produce the measures, plotting them on a daily basis. They then use those measures as indicators of when to get into or out of the market or a particular stock. In essence, they develop trading rules based on these market measures. Technical analysts almost always use several of these market measures, rather than just one (or two), because one measure rarely works the same way for all stocks. Moreover, they generally look for confirmation of one measure by another. In other words, market analysts like to see three or four of these ratios and measures all pointing in the same direction.

Although dozens of these market measures and trading rules exist, we'll confine our discussion here to some of the more widely used technical indicators: (1) advance-decline lines, (2) new highs and lows, (3) the Arms index, (4) the mutual fund cash ratio, (5) on-balance volume, and (6) the relative strength index (RSI).

Advance-Decline Line   Each trading day, the NYSE, Amex, and Nasdaq publish statistics on how many of their stocks closed higher on the day (i.e., advanced in price) and how many closed lower (declined in price). The *advance-decline (A/D) line* is simply the difference between these two numbers. To calculate it, you take the number of stocks that have risen in price and subtract the number that have declined, usually for the previous day. For example, if 1,000 issues advanced on a day when 450 issues declined, the day's net number would be 550 (i.e., $1,000 - 450$). If 450 advanced and 1,000 declined, the net number would be -550. Each day's net number is then added to (or subtracted from) the running total, and the results are plotted on a graph.

If the graph is rising, the advancing issues are dominating the declining issues, and the technical analysts conclude that the market is strong. When declining issues start to dominate, the graph will turn down as the market begins to soften. Technicians use the A/D line as a signal for when to buy or sell stocks.

New Highs–New Lows This measure is similar to the advance-decline line but looks at price movements over a longer period of time. A stock is defined as reaching a "new high" if its current price is at the highest level it has been over the past year (sometimes referred to as the "52-week high"). Conversely, a stock reaches a "new low" if its current price is at the lowest level it has been over the past year.

The *new highs–new lows (NH-NL) indicator* equals the number of stocks reaching new 52-week highs minus the number reaching new lows. Thus, you end up with a net number, which can be either positive (when new highs dominate) or negative (when new lows exceed new highs), just like with the advance-decline line. To smooth out the daily fluctuations, the net number is often added to (or subtracted from) a 10-day moving average and then plotted on a graph.

As you might have guessed, a graph that's increasing over time indicates a strong market, where new highs are dominating. A declining graph indicates a weak market, where new lows are more common than new highs. Technicians following a momentum-based strategy will buy stocks when new highs dominate and sell them when there are more new lows than new highs. Alternatively, they might use the indicator to rotate money into stocks when the market looks strong and to rotate money out of stocks and into cash or bonds when the market looks weak.

The Arms Index This indicator, also known as the TRIN, for *trading index*, builds on the advance-decline line by considering the volume in advancing and declining stocks in addition to the number of stocks rising or falling in price. The formula is

Equation 7.4

$$\text{TRIN} = \frac{\text{Number of up stocks}}{\text{Number of down stocks}} \div \frac{\text{Volume in up stocks}}{\text{Volume in down stocks}}$$

For example, suppose we are analyzing the S&P 500. Assume on a given day 300 of these stocks rose in price and 200 fell in price. Also assume that the total trading volume in the rising ("up") stocks was 400 million shares, and the total trading volume in the falling ("down") stocks was 800 million shares. The value of the TRIN for the day would be

$$\text{TRIN} = \frac{300}{200} \div \frac{400 \text{ million}}{800 \text{ million}} = 3.0$$

Alternatively, suppose the volume in up stocks was 700 million shares, and the volume in down stocks was 300 million. The value of the TRIN then would be

$$\text{TRIN} = \frac{300}{200} \div \frac{700 \text{ million}}{300 \text{ million}} = 0.64$$

Higher TRIN values are interpreted as being bad for the market because even though more stocks rose than fell, the trading volume in the falling stocks was much greater. The underlying idea is that a strong market is characterized by more stocks rising in price than falling, along with greater volume in the rising stocks than in the falling ones, as in the second example.

Mutual Fund Cash Ratio This indicator looks at the cash position of mutual funds as an indicator of future market performance. The *mutual fund cash ratio (MFCR)* measures the percentage of mutual fund assets that are held in cash. It is computed as follows:

Equation 7.5 $\text{MFCR} = \text{Mutual fund cash position} \div \text{Total assets under management}$

The assumption is that the higher the MFCR, the stronger the market. Indeed, the ratio is considered very bullish when it moves to abnormally high levels (i.e., when mutual fund cash exceeds 10% to 12% of assets). It is seen as bearish when the ratio drops to very low levels (e.g., less than 5% of assets). The logic goes as follows: When fund managers hold a lot of cash (when the MFCR is high), that's good news for the market because they will eventually have to invest that cash, buying stocks and causing prices to rise. If fund managers hold very little cash, investors might be concerned for two reasons. First, there is less demand for stocks if most of the cash is already invested. Second, if the market takes a downturn, investors might want to withdraw their money. Fund managers will then have to sell some of their stocks to accommodate these redemptions (because they don't have much accumulated cash), putting additional downward pressure on prices.

On-Balance Volume Technical analysts usually consider stock prices to be the key measure of market activity. However, they also consider trading volume as a secondary indicator. *On-balance volume (OBV)* is a momentum indicator that relates volume to price change. It uses trading volume in addition to price and tracks trading volume as a running total. In this way, OBV indicates whether volume is flowing into or out of a security. When the security closes higher than its previous close, all the day's volume is considered "up-volume," all of which is added to the running total. In contrast, when a stock closes lower, all the day's volume is considered "down-volume," which is then subtracted from the running total.

The OBV indicator is used to confirm price trends. According to this measure, you want to see a lot of volume when a stock's price is rising because that would suggest that the stock will go even higher. On the other hand, if prices are rising but OBV is falling, technical analysts would describe the situation as a divergence and interpret it as a sign of possible weakness.

When analyzing OBV, it is the direction or trend that is important, not the actual value. To begin the computation of OBV, you can start with an arbitrary number, such as 50,000. Suppose you are calculating the OBV for a stock that closed yesterday at a price of $50 per share, and you start with an OBV value of 50,000. Assume that the stock trades 80,000 shares today and closes at $49. Because the stock declined in price, we would subtract the full 80,000 shares from the previous balance (our starting point of 50,000); now the OBV is 50,000 − 80,000 = −30,000 (Note that the OBV is simply the trading volume running total.) If the stock trades 120,000 shares on the following day and closes up at $52 per share, we would then add all of those 120,000 shares to the previous day's OBV: −30,000 + 120,000 = +90,000. This process would continue day after day. The normal procedure is to plot these daily OBVs on a graph. As long as the graph is moving up, it's bullish; when the graph starts moving down, it's bearish.

Relative Strength One of the most widely used technical indicators is the *relative strength index (RSI)*, an index measuring a security's strength of advances and declines over time. The RSI indicates a security's momentum and gives the best results when used for short trading periods. It also helps identify market extremes, signaling that a security is approaching its price top or bottom and may soon reverse trend. The RSI is the ratio of average price change on "up days" to the average price change on "down days" during the same period. The index formula is

Equation 7.6

$$RSI = 100 - \left[100 \div \left(1 + \frac{\text{Average price change on up days}}{\text{Average price change on down days}} \right) \right]$$

The average price change in this formula is usually calculated over a 9-, 14-, or 25-day period. In the RSI calculation, both price increases and price decreases are treated as positive values. In other words, if a stock fell by $0.05 for 14 days in a row, then the average price change on down days would be 0.05, and the same would hold if a stock rose by $0.05 for 14 days in a row.

The RSI ranges between 0 and 100, with most RSIs falling between 30 and 70. Generally, values above 70 or 80 indicate an *overbought* condition (more and stronger buying than fundamentals would justify). RSI values below 30 indicate a possible *oversold* condition (more selling than fundamentals may indicate). When the RSI crosses these points, it signals a possible trend reversal. The wider 80–20 range is often used with the 9-day RSI, which tends to be more volatile than longer-period RSIs. In bull markets, 80 may be a better upper indicator than 70; in bear markets, 20 is a more accurate lower level. Different sectors and industries may have varying RSI threshold levels.

To use the RSI in their own trading, investors set buy and sell ranges—such as sell when the RSI crosses above 70 and buy when it moves below 30. Another strategy is to compare RSIs with stock charts. Most of the time both move in the same direction, but a divergence between RSI and a price chart can be a strong predictor of a changing trend.

Charting

Charting is perhaps the best-known activity of the technical analyst. Indeed, technical analysts use various types of charts to plot the behavior of everything from the Dow Jones Industrial Average and share price movements of individual stocks to moving averages (see below) and advance-decline lines. In fact, as noted above, just about every type of technical indicator is charted in one form or another.

Practice Your Charting
Skills

Charts are popular because they provide a visual summary of activity over time. Perhaps more important (in the eyes of technicians, at least), they contain valuable information about developing trends and the future behavior of the market or individual stocks. Chartists believe price patterns evolve into chart formations that provide signals about the future course of the market or a stock.

Chart Formations A chart by itself tells you little more than where the market or a stock has been. But to chartists, those price patterns yield formations that tell them what to expect in the future. Chartists believe that history repeats itself, so they study the historical reactions of stocks (or the market) to various formations, and they devise trading rules based on these observations. It makes no difference to chartists whether they are following the market or an individual stock. It is the formation that matters, not the issue being plotted. Chartists believe that they can see formations building and recognize buy and sell signals. These chart formations are often given exotic names, such as *head and shoulders*, *falling wedge*, *scallop and saucer*, *ascending triangle*, and *island reversal*, to name just a few.

Figure 7.6 shows six of these formations. The patterns form "support levels" and "resistance lines" that when combined with the basic formations, yield buy and sell signals. Panel A is an example of a buy signal that occurs when prices break out above a resistance line in a particular pattern. In contrast, when prices break out below a support level, as they do at the end of the formation in panel B, a sell signal is said to occur. Supposedly, a sell signal means everything is in place for a major drop in the market (or in the price of a share of stock). A buy signal indicates that the opposite is about to occur.

FIGURE 7.6

Some Popular Chart Formations

To chartists, each of these formations has meaning about the future course of events.

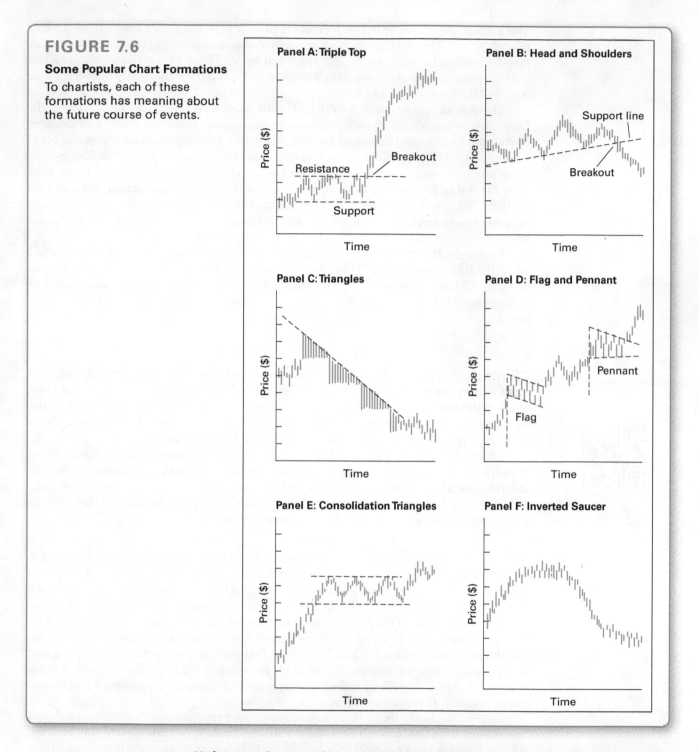

Panel A: Triple Top

Panel B: Head and Shoulders

Panel C: Triangles

Panel D: Flag and Pennant

Panel E: Consolidation Triangles

Panel F: Inverted Saucer

Unfortunately, one of the major problems with charting is that the formations rarely appear as neatly and cleanly as those in Figure 7.6. Rather, identifying and interpreting them often demands considerable imagination.

Moving Averages?   One problem with daily price charts is that they may contain a lot of short-term price swings that mask the overall trend in prices. As a result, technical analysts often use moving averages not only to eliminate those minor blips but also to highlight underlying trends. A **moving average** is a mathematical procedure that records the average value of a series of prices, or other data, over time. Because they incorporate a stream of these average values, moving averages will smooth out a data series and make it easier to spot trends. The moving average is one of the oldest and most popular technical indicators. It can, in fact, be used not only with share prices but also with market indexes and even other technical measures.

Moving averages are computed over time periods ranging from 10 to 200 days—meaning that from 10 to 200 data points are used in each calculation. For example, a series of 15 data points is used in a 15-day moving average. The length of the time period has a bearing on how the MA will behave. Shorter periods (10 to 30 days) are more sensitive and tend to more closely track actual daily behavior. Longer periods (say, 100 to 200 days) are smoother and only pick up the major trends. Several types of moving averages exist, with the most common (and the one we'll use here) being the *simple average*, which gives equal weight to each observation. In contrast, there are other procedures that give more weight to the most recent data points (e.g., the "exponential" and "weighted" averages) or apply more weight to the middle of the time period (e.g., "triangular" averages).

Using closing share prices as the basis of discussion, we can calculate the simple moving average by adding up the closing prices over a given time period (e.g., 10 days) and then dividing this total by the length of the time period. Thus, the simple moving average is nothing more than the arithmetic mean. To illustrate, consider the following stream of closing share prices:

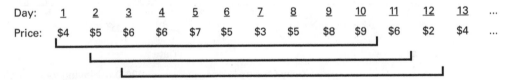

Day:	1	2	3	4	5	6	7	8	9	10	11	12	13	...
Price:	$4	$5	$6	$6	$7	$5	$3	$5	$8	$9	$6	$2	$4	...

Using a 10-day moving average, we add up the closing prices for days 1 through 10 ($4 + $5 + ⋯ + $8 + $9 = $58) and then divide this total by 10($58 ÷ 10 = $5.8). Thus, the average closing price for this 10-day period was $5.80. The next day, the process is repeated once again for days 2 through 11; that turns out to be $60 ÷ 10 = $6.00. This procedure is repeated each day, so that over time we have a series of these individual averages that, when linked together, form a moving-average line. This line is then plotted on a chart, either by itself or along with other market information.

Figure 7.7 shows a 100-day moving average (i.e., the red line) plotted against the daily closing prices for Facebook (i.e., the blue line) starting with its May 2012 IPO and continuing through June 2015. In contrast to the actual closing prices, the moving average provides a much smoother line, without all the short-term fluctuations; it clearly reveals the general trend in prices for this stock.

Technicians often use charts like the one in Figure 7.7 to help them make buy and sell decisions about a stock. Specifically, if the security's price starts moving above the moving average, they read that situation as a good time to buy because prices should be drifting up (e.g., see the buy signal). In contrast, a sell signal occurs when the security's price moves below the moving-average line (e.g., see the sell signal). A problem arises when volatility in the stock price leads to repeated buy and sell signals. For example, for Facebook, the red and blue lines cross 11 times between April 4, 2014 and May 6, 2014, resulting in six sell signals and five buy signals all within a single month. Trading based on the moving-average indicator during that period would result in a lot of transactions costs, but not much profit.

FIGURE 7.7

Daily Closing Prices and 100-Day Moving-Average Line for Facebook

Moving-average lines are often plotted along with the actual daily closing prices for a stock. They're also widely used with market indexes, such as the S&P 500, and with a variety of technical indicators, including the advance-decline line.

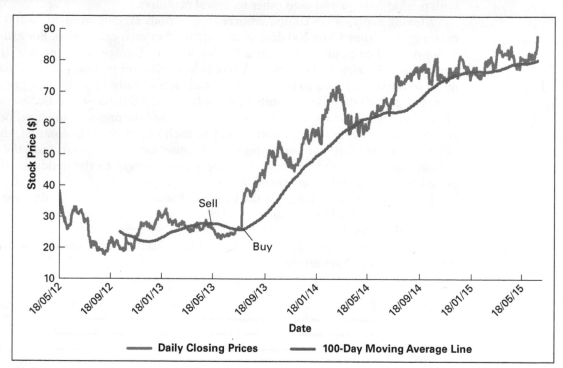

CONCEPTS IN REVIEW

Answers available at
http://www.pearsonhighered.com/
smart

7.6   What is the purpose of technical analysis? Explain how and why it is used by technicians; note how it can be helpful in timing investment decisions.

7.7   Can the market really have a measurable effect on the price behavior of individual securities? Explain.

7.8   Describe the confidence index, and note the feature that makes it unique.

7.9   Briefly describe each of the following and explain how it is used in technical analysis:

    a. Breadth of the market
    b. Short interest
    c. Odd-lot trading

7.10 Briefly describe each of the following and note how it is computed and how it is used by technicians:

    a. Advance-decline lines
    b. Arms index
    c. On-balance volume
    d. Relative strength index
    e. Moving averages

7.11 What is a stock chart? What kind of information can be put on charts, and what is the purpose of charting?

MyFinanceLab

Here is what you should know after reading this chapter. MyFinanceLab will help you identify what you know and where to go when you need to practice.

What You Should Know	Key Terms	Where to Practice
LG1 Describe the characteristics of an efficient market, explain what market anomalies are, and note some of the challenges that investors face when markets are efficient. An efficient market is one in which prices fully reflect all available information; in an efficient market, price movements are nearly random. If markets are efficient, then investors should not expect to earn above-average returns consistently by using either technical or fundamental analysis.	abnormal return, *p. 221* alpha, *p. 221* arbitrage, *p. 224* behavioral finance, *p. 229* efficient market, *p. 220* efficient markets hypothesis (EMH), *p. 220* market anomalies, *p. 226* random walk hypothesis, *p. 220* semi-strong form (EMH), *p. 222* strong form (EMH), *p. 223* weak form (EMH), *p. 221*	MyFinanceLab Study Plan 7.1
LG2 Summarize the evidence which suggests that the stock market is efficient. Early research on the market efficiency question found that stock prices were essentially unpredictable and moved at random. Other studies found that even professional investors did not consistently earn returns that beat market averages.		MyFinanceLab Study Plan 7.2
LG3 List four "decision traps" that may lead investors to make systematic errors in their investment decisions. Behavioral finance asserts that investors are subject to a variety of decision traps, which include overconfidence, loss aversion, representativeness, narrow framing, and belief perseverance. If investors do indeed make systematic errors in their investment decisions, then those errors may influence prices in financial markets.	anchoring, *p. 237* belief perseverance, *p. 236* familiarity bias, *p. 239* loss aversion, *p. 231* narrow framing, *p. 236* overconfidence, *p. 230* representativeness, *p. 233* self-attribution bias, *p. 230*	MyFinanceLab Study Plan 7.3
LG4 Explain how behavioral finance links market anomalies to investors' cognitive biases. A market anomaly represents a pattern in stock prices that would appear to present investors with an opportunity to earn above-average returns without taking above-average risk. Behavioral finance suggests that some market anomalies exist because investors make systematic errors, such as undervaluing stocks that have performed poorly in recent years.		MyFinanceLab Study Plan 7.4
LG5 Describe some of the approaches to technical analysis, including, among others, moving averages, charting, and various indicators of the technical condition of the market. Market analysts look at those factors in the marketplace that can affect the price behavior of stocks in general. This analysis can be done by assessing the overall condition of the market, by informally or formally studying various internal market statistics (e.g., short interest or advance-decline lines), or by charting various aspects of the market (including the use of moving averages).	confidence index, *p. 239* market technician, *p. 242* short interest, *p. 243* technical analysis, *p. 238* theory of contrary opinion, *p. 242*	MyFinanceLab Study Plan 7.5 Video Learning Aid for Problems P7.2, P7.6

What You Should Know	Key Terms	Where to Practice
LG6 **Compute and use technical trading rules for individual stocks and the market as a whole.** Technical analysts use a number of mathematical equations and measures to gauge the direction of the market, including advance-decline lines, new highs and lows, the trading index, the mutual fund cash ratio, on-balance volume, and the relative strength index. They test different indicators using historical price data to find those that generate profitable trading strategies, which then are developed into trading rules used to guide buy and sell decisions.	charting, *p. 245* moving average (MA), *p. 247*	MyFinanceLab Study Plan 7.6

Log into MyFinanceLab, take a chapter test, and get a personalized Study Plan that tells you which concepts you understand and which ones you need to review. From there, MyFinanceLab will give you further practice, tutorials, animations, videos, and guided solutions.
Log into http://www.myfinancelab.com

Discussion Questions

LG1   **Q7..1**   Much has been written about the concept of an efficient market. It's probably safe to say that some of your classmates believe the markets are efficient and others believe they are not. Have a debate to see whether you can resolve this issue (at least among you and your classmates). Pick a side, either for or against efficient markets, and then develop your "ammunition." Be prepared to discuss these three aspects:
a. What is an efficient market? Do such markets really exist?
b. Are stock prices always (or nearly always) correctly set in the market? If so, does that mean little opportunity exists to find undervalued stocks?
c. Can you cite any reasons to use fundamental or technical analysis in your stock selection process? If not, how would you go about selecting stocks?

LG1 LG2   **Q7..2**   Each year financial periodicals like the *Wall Street Journal* and *Money Magazine* publish a list of the top performing mutual fund managers. And every year there are some fund managers who earn much higher returns than the market average, and in some cases they do so without taking above-average risk. Is this inconsistent with the efficient markets hypothesis?

LG3 LG4   **Q7..3**   Briefly define each of the following terms and describe how it can affect investors' decisions.
a. Loss aversion
b. Representativeness
c. Narrow framing
d. Overconfidence
e. Biased self-attribution

LG3 LG4   **Q7..4**   Describe how representativeness may lead to biases in stock valuation.

LG5   **Q7..5**   Briefly describe how technical analysis is used as part of the stock valuation process. What role does it play in an investor's decision to buy or sell a stock?

LG5 **Q7..6** Describe each of the following approaches to technical analysis and note how it would be used by investors.

    a. Confidence index

    b. Arms index

    c. Trading action

    d. Odd-lot trading

    e. Charting

    f. Moving averages

    g. On-balance volume

Which of these approaches is likely to involve some type of mathematical equation or ratio?

LG5 **Q7..7** Briefly define each of the following and note the conditions that would suggest the market is technically strong.

    a. Breadth of the market

    b. Short interest

    c. Relative strength index

    d. Theory of contrary opinion

    e. Head and shoulders

Problems

All problems are available on http://www.myfinancelab.com

LG5 **LG6** **P7.1** Compute the Arms index for the S&P 500 over the following three days:

Day	Number of Stocks **Rising** in Price	Number of Stocks **Falling** in Price	Volume for Stocks **Rising** in Price	Volume for Stocks **Falling** in Price
1	350	150	850 million shares	420 million shares
2	275	225	450 million shares	725 million shares
3	260	240	850 million shares	420 million shares

Which of the three days would be considered the most bullish? Explain why.

LG5 **LG6** **P7.2** Listed below are data that pertain to the corporate bond market. (*Note:* Each "period" below covers a span of six months.)

	Period 1	Period 2	Period 3	Period 4
Average yield on 10 high-grade corporate bonds	5.30%	5.70%	5.10%	?
Yield on the Dow Jones average of 40 corporate bonds	6.50%	?	6.00%	4.90%
Yield spread (in basis points)	?	155	?	25
Confidence index				

    a. Compute the confidence index for each of the four periods listed above.

    b. Assume that the latest confidence index (for period 0, in effect) amounts to 86.83%, while the yield spread between high- and average-grade corporate bonds is 85 basis points. Based on your calculations, what's happening to bond yield spreads and the confidence index over the period of time covered in the problem (i.e., from period 0 through period 4)?

c. Based on the confidence index measures you computed, what would be your overall assessment of the stock market? In which one or more of the periods (1 through 4) is the confidence index bullish? In which one(s) is it bearish?

LG5 LG6 **P7.3** Compute the level of on-balance volume (OBV) for the following three-day period for a stock, if the beginning level of OBV is 50,000 and the stock closed yesterday at $25.

Day	Closing Price	Trading Volume (shares)
1	$27	70,000
2	$26	45,000
3	$29	120,000

Does the movement in OBV appear to confirm the rising trend in prices? Explain.

LG5 LG6 **P7.4** Below are figures representing the number of stocks making new highs and new lows for each month over a six-month period:

Month	New Highs	New Lows
July	117	22
August	95	34
September	84	41
October	64	79
November	53	98
December	19	101

Would a technical analyst consider the trend to be bullish or bearish over this period? Explain.

LG5 LG6 **P7.5** You hear a market analyst on television say that the advance/decline ratio for the session was 1.2. What does that mean?

LG5 LG6 **P7.6** At the end of a trading day you find that on the NYSE 2,200 stocks advanced and 1,000 stocks declined. What is the value of the advance-decline line for that day?

LG5 LG6 **P7.7** You are given the following information for the number of stocks making new highs and new lows for each day:

Day	New Highs	New Lows
1 (yesterday)	117	22
2	95	34
3	84	41
4	64	79
5	53	98
6	19	101
7	19	105
8	18	110
9	19	90
10	22	88

a. Calculate the 10-day moving-average NH-NL indicator.

b. If there are 120 new highs and 20 new lows today, what is the new 10-day moving-average NH-NL indicator?

LG5 LG6 **P7.8** You have collected the following NH-NL indicator data:

Day	NH-NL Indicator
1 (yesterday)	100
2	95
3	61
4	43
5	−15
6	−45
7	−82
8	−86
9	−92
10	−71

If you are a technician following a momentum-based strategy, are you buying or selling today?

LG5 LG6 **P7.9** You are presented with the following data:

Week	Mutual Fund Cash Position	Mutual Fund Total Assets
Most recent	$281,478,000	$2,345,650,000
2	$258,500,000	$2,350,000,000
3	$234,800,000	$2,348,000,000
4	$211,950,000	$2,355,000,000
5	$188,480,000	$2,356,000,000

Calculate the MFCR for each week. Based on the result, are you bullish or bearish?

LG5 LG6 **P7.10** You find the closing prices for a stock you own. You want to use a 10-day moving average to monitor the stock. Calculate the 10-day moving average for days 11 through 20. Based on the data in the table below, are there any signals you should act on? Explain.

Day	Closing Price	Day	Closing Price
1	$25.25	11	$30.00
2	$26.00	12	$30.00
3	$27.00	13	$31.00
4	$28.00	14	$31.50
5	$27.00	15	$31.00
6	$28.00	16	$32.00
7	$27.50	17	$29.00
8	$29.00	18	$29.00
9	$27.00	19	$28.00
10	$28.00	20	$27.00

LG5 LG6   **P7.11**   Data on a stock's closing price and its price change for the last 14 trading days appears below.

Day	Closing Price	Price Change	Price Increase	Price Decrease
1	$22.50	+$0.14	$0.14	
2	$22.28	−$0.22		$0.22
3	$22.32	+$0.04	$0.04	
4	$23.01	+$0.69	$0.69	
5	$22.82	−$0.19		$0.19
6	$23.41	+$0.59	$0.59	
7	$23.83	+$0.42	$0.42	
8	$23.67	−$0.16		$0.16
9	$24.02	+$0.35	$0.35	
10	$24.14	+$0.12	$0.12	
11	$23.99	−$0.15		$0.15
12	$24.54	+$0.55	$0.55	
13	$25.17	+$0.63	$0.63	
14	$25.01	−$0.16		$0.16

a. Over this 14-day period what is the average gain on up days? (*Note:* to calculate the average, divide the sum of all gains by 14, not by the number of days on which the stock went up.)

b. Over this 14-day period, what is the average loss on down days?

c. What is the RSI?

d. Is the RSI sending a strong buy or sell signal?

Visit **http://www.myfinancelab.com** for web exercises, spreadsheets, and other online resources.

Case problem 7.1   Brett Runs Some Technical Measures on a Stock

LG5   Brett Daly is an active stock trader and an avid market technician. He got into technical analysis about 10 years ago, and although he now uses the Internet for much of his analytical work, he still enjoys running some of the numbers and doing some of the charting himself. Brett likes to describe himself as a serious stock trader who relies on technical analysis for some—but certainly not all—of the information he uses to make an investment decision; unlike some market technicians, he does not totally ignore a stock's fundamentals. Right now he's got his eye on a stock that he's been tracking for the past three or four months.

The stock is Nautilus Navigation, a mid-sized high-tech company that's been around for a number of years and has a demonstrated ability to generate profits year-in and year-out. The problem is that the earnings are a bit erratic, tending to bounce up and down from year to year, which causes the price of the stock to be a bit erratic as well. And that's exactly why Brett likes the stock—the volatile prices enable him, as a trader, to move in and out of the stock over relatively short (three- to six-month) periods of time.

Brett has already determined that the stock has "decent" fundamentals, so he does not worry about its basic soundness. Hence, he can concentrate on the technical side of the stock. In particular, he wants to run some technical measures on the market price behavior of the security. He's obtained recent closing prices on the stock, which are shown in the table below.

Recent Price Behavior: Nautilus Navigation

$14 (8/15/16)	$18.55	$20	$17.50
$14.25	$17.50	$20.21	$18.55
$14.79	$17.50	$20.25	$19.80
$15.50	$17.25	$20.16	$19.50
$16	$17	$20	$19.25
$16	$16.75	$20.25	$20
$16.50	$16.50	$20.50	$20.90
$17	$16.55	$20.80	$21
$17.25	$16.15	$20	$21.75
$17.20	$16.80	$20	$22.50
$18	$17.15	$20.25	$23.25
$18 (9/30/16)	$17.22	$20	$24
$18.55	$17.31 (10/31/16)	$19.45	$24.25
$18.65	$17.77	$19.20	$24.15
$18.80	$18.23	$18.25 (11/30/16)	$24.75
$19	$19.22	$17.50	$25
$19.10	$20.51	$16.75	$25.50
$18.92	$20.15	$17	$25.55 (12/31/16)

Nautilus shares are actively traded on the Nasdaq Global Market and enjoy considerable market interest.

Questions

a. Use the closing share prices in the table above to compute the stock's relative strength index for (1) the 20-day period from 9/30/16 to 10/31/16; and (2) the 22-day period from 11/30/16 to 12/31/16. [*Hint:* Use a simple (unweighted) average to compute the numerator (average price change on up days) and denominator (average price change on down days) of the RSI formula.]

    1. Contrast the two RSI measures you computed. Is the index getting bigger or smaller, and is that good or bad?

    2. Is the latest RSI measure giving a buy or a sell signal? Explain.

b. Based on the above closing share prices, prepare a moving-average line covering the period shown in the table; use a 10-day time frame to calculate the individual average values.

    1. Plot the daily closing prices for Nautilus from 8/15/16 through 12/31/16 on a graph/chart.

    2. On the same graph/chart, plot a moving-average line using the individual average values computed earlier. Identify any buy or sell signals.

    3. As of 12/31/16, was the moving-average line giving a buy, hold, or sell signal? Explain. How does that result compare to what you found with the RSI in part a? Explain.

c. Based on the technical measures and charts you've prepared, what course of action would you recommend that Brett take with regard to Nautilus Navigation? Explain.

Case problem 7.2   Deb Takes Measure of the Market

LG5   Several months ago, Deb Forrester received a substantial sum of money from the estate of her late aunt. Deb initially placed the money in a savings account because she was not sure what to do with it. Since then, however, she has taken a course in investments at the local university. The textbook for the course was, in fact, this one, and the class just completed this chapter. Excited about what she has learned in class, Deb has decided that she definitely wants to invest in stocks. But before she does, she wants to use her newfound knowledge in technical analysis to determine whether now would be a good time to enter the market.

Deb has decided to use all of the following measures to help her determine if now is, indeed, a good time to start putting money into the stock market:

- Advance-decline line
- New highs-new lows indicator (Assume the current 10-day moving average is 0 and the last 10 periods were each 0.)
- Arms index
- Mutual fund cash ratio

Deb goes to the Internet and, after considerable effort, is able to put together the accompanying table of data.

Questions

a. Based on the data presented in the table, calculate a value (where appropriate) for periods 1 through 5, for each of the four measures listed above. Chart your results, where applicable.

b. Discuss each measure individually and note what it indicates for the market, as it now stands. Taken collectively, what do these four measures indicate about the current state of the market? According to these measures, is this a good time for Deb to consider getting into the market, or should she wait a while? Explain.

c. Comment on the time periods used in the table, which are not defined here. What if they were relatively long intervals of time? What if they were relatively short? Explain how the length of the time periods can affect the measures.

	Period 1	Period 2	Period 3	Period 4	Period 5
Dow Jones Industrial Average	8,300	7,250	8,000	9,000	9,400
Dow Transportation Average	2,375	2,000	2,000	2,850	3,250
New highs	$ 68	$ 85	$ 85	$ 120	$ 200
New lows	$ 75	$ 60	$ 80	$ 75	$ 20
Volume up	600,000,000	836,254,123	275,637,497	875,365,980	1,159,534,297
Volume down	600,000,000	263,745,877	824,362,503	424,634,020	313,365,599
Mutual fund cash (trillions of dollars)	$0.31	$0.32	$0.47	$0.61	$0.74
Total assets managed (trillions of dollars)	$6.94	$6.40	$6.78	$6.73	$7.42
Advancing issues (NYSE)	1,120	1,278	1,270	1,916	1,929
Declining issues (NYSE)	2,130	1,972	1,980	1,334	1,321

Excel@Investing

| Excel@Investing |

Technical analysis looks at the demand and supply for securities based on trading volumes and price studies. Charting is a common method used to identify and project price trends in a security. A well-known technical indicator is the Bollinger Band. It creates two bands, one above and one below the price performance of a stock. The upper band is a resistance level and represents the level above which the stock is unlikely to rise. The bottom forms a support level and shows the price that a stock is unlikely to fall below.

According to technicians, if you see a significant "break" in the upper band, the expectation is that the stock price will fall in the immediate future. A "break" in the lower band signals that the security is about to rise in value. Either of these occurrences will dictate a unique investment strategy.

Replicate the following technical analysis for Amazon.com (AMZN)

- Go to http://www.finance.yahoo.com
- Symbol(s): **AMZN**
- In the left-hand column, click on Interactive Chart.
- Select a 5-year chart.
- Click on Indicator.
- Choose Bollinger Bands.
- The price performance graph for Amazon stock with an upper and lower Bollinger Band should appear.
- Make sure that the graph covers, at a minimum, the first six months of 2015.

Questions

a. On approximately April 20, 2015, what happened to the upper band (resistance level) of Amazon stock?

b. During the following nine days, how did the price of the stock behave?

c. Is this in line with what a technician would predict?

d. What strategy would a technician have undertaken on April 20?

e. At around the same time, what happened to the lower band (support level) of Amazon stock?

f. How did the stock behave through the month of May 2015?

8

Bond Valuation

LEARNING GOALS

After studying this chapter, you should be able to:

LG1 Explain the behavior of market interest rates and identify the forces that cause interest rates to change.

LG2 Describe the term structure of interest rates and note how investors can use yield curves.

LG3 Understand how investors value bonds in the marketplace.

LG4 Describe the various measures of yield or return and explain how investors use these standards of performance to value bonds.

LG5 Understand the basic concept of duration, how it can be measured, and its use in the management of bond portfolios.

LG6 Discuss various bond investment strategies and the different ways investors can use these securities.

oney market investors made very little money during the Great Recession due to historically low interest rates on the short-term debt securities that comprise the U.S. money market. At the start of 2007, U.S. Treasury bills with 6-month maturities were earning yields slightly better than 5%. Over the next few years, Treasury bill yields tumbled to record lows. By the end of 2009, investors who purchased a 6-month bill at the Treasury auction earned only one-fifth of 1 percent (0.20%) on their money. Even worse, by September of 2014, investors in 6-month bills received a yield of just 3 basis points (0.03%).

Investors in other parts of the world faced even lower, unprecedented rates. In April 2015 Switzerland issued 10-year government bonds that offered investors a yield of −5 basis points (−0.05%). In other words, investors who purchased these bonds were actually paying the Swiss government for that privilege. That marked the first time in history that any 10-year bond was successfully sold with a negative yield. Presumably hoping to take advantage of historically low interest rates in Europe, Mexico issued its own bonds, denominated in euros. What made Mexico's bonds unique was their maturity—100 years. Prior to Mexico's bond issue, no one had ever issued 100-year bonds in euros.

The low interest rates were a result of actions by the U.S. Federal Reserve, the European Central Bank, and other authorities around the world who were trying to stimulate their economies to help pull out of (or prevent) a recession. The resulting low rates around the world sparked a borrowing binge.

In this chapter we'll learn about the forces that move market interest rates up and down and how those movements affect bonds and the investors who buy them.

(Source: Emese Bartha, Chiara Albanese, and Anthony Harp, "New Era in Bonds: Zero Yield, or Less," *The Wall Street Journal*, April 9, 2015, p. 1.)

The Behavior of Market Interest Rates

LG1 LG2   Recall from earlier discussions that rational investors try to earn a return that fully compensates them for risk. In the case of bondholders, that required return (r_i) has three components: the real rate of return (r^*), an expected inflation premium (IP), and a risk premium (RP). Thus, the required return on a bond can be expressed by the following equation:

Equation 8.1 $$r_i = r^* + IP + RP$$

The real rate of return and inflation premium are external economic factors, which together equal the risk-free rate (r_f). To find the required return, we need to consider the unique features and properties of the bond issue itself that influence its risk. After we do this, we add a risk premium to the risk-free rate to obtain the required rate of return. A bond's risk premium (RP) will take into account key issue and issuer characteristics, including such variables as the type of bond, the issue's term to maturity, its call features, and its bond rating.

Together, the three components in Equation 8.1 (r^*, IP, and RP) drive the required return on a bond. Recall in the previous chapter that we identified five types of risks to which bonds are exposed. All of these risks are embedded in a bond's required rate of return. That is, the bond's risk premium addresses, among other things, the business and financial (credit) risk characteristics of an issue, along with its liquidity and call risks, whereas the risk-free rate (r_f) takes into account interest rate and purchasing power risks.

Because these interest rates have a significant bearing on bond prices and yields, investors watch them closely. For example, more conservative investors watch interest rates because one of their major objectives is to lock in high yields. Aggressive traders also have a stake in interest rates because their investment programs are often built on the capital gains opportunities that accompany major swings in rates.

Keeping Tabs on Market Interest Rates

The bond market is not a single market. Rather, it consists of many different sectors. Similarly, there is no single interest rate that applies to all segments of the bond market. Instead, different interest rates apply to different segments. Granted, the various rates do tend to drift in the same direction over time, but it is also common for **yield spreads** (interest rate differentials) to exist among the various market sectors. Some important factors to keep in mind when you think about interest rates on bonds are as follows:

- Municipal bonds usually offer the lowest market rates because of their tax-exempt feature. As a rule, their market yields are about 20% to 30% lower than corporate bond yields.

- In the municipal sector, revenue bonds pay higher rates than general obligation bonds.

- In the taxable sector, Treasury securities have the lowest yields (because they have the least risk), followed by agency bonds and then corporate bonds, which provide the highest returns.

FAMOUS FAILURES IN FINANCE

Signs of a Recession

When short-term interest rates on treasury bills exceed the rates on long-term treasury bonds, watch out. That is often the precursor to a recession. This "inversion" in the relationship between short-term and long-term rates has occurred prior to each of the last five U.S. recessions. Just as important, this indicator has rarely issued a false recession warning signal.

- Issues that normally carry bond ratings (e.g., municipals or corporates) generally display the same behavior: the lower the rating, the higher the yield.

- Most of the time, bonds with long maturities provide higher yields than short-term issues. However, this rule does not always hold. When short-term bond yields exceed yields on longer-term bonds, as they did in February 2006, that may be an early signal that a recession is coming.

- Bonds that are freely callable generally pay the highest interest rates, at least at date of issue. These are followed by deferred call obligations and then by noncallable bonds, which offer lower yields.

As an investor, you should pay close attention to interest rates and yield spreads. Try to stay abreast of both the current state of the market and the future direction of market rates. Thus, if you are a conservative (income-oriented) investor and think that rates have just about peaked, that should be a signal to try to lock in the prevailing high yields with some form of call protection. (For example, buy bonds, such as Treasuries or AA-rated utilities that are noncallable or still have lengthy call deferments.) In contrast, if you're an aggressive bond trader who thinks rates have peaked (and are about to drop), that should be a clue to buy bonds that offer maximum price appreciation potential (low-coupon bonds that still have a long time before they mature).

But how do you formulate such expectations? Unless you have considerable training in economics, you will probably need to rely on various published sources. Fortunately, a wealth of such information is available. Your broker is an excellent source for such reports, as are investor services like Moody's and Standard & Poor's. Also, of course, there are numerous online sources. Finally, there are widely circulated business and financial publications (like the *Wall Street Journal*, *Forbes*, *Business Week*, and *Fortune*) that regularly address the current state and future direction of market interest rates. Predicting the direction of interest rates is not easy. However, by taking the time to read some of these publications and reports regularly and carefully, you can at least get a sense of what experts predict is likely to occur in the near future.

What Causes Rates to Move?

Although the determination of interest rates is a complex economic issue, we do know that certain forces are especially important in influencing rate movements. Serious bond investors should make it a point to become familiar with the major determinants of interest rates and try to monitor those variables, at least informally.

WATCH YOUR BEHAVIOR

Anchoring on Credit Spreads The credit spread is the difference in yield between a risky bond and a safe bond. In theory, credit spreads are determined by forward-looking economic fundamentals that measure a borrower's capacity to repay its debts. A recent study found that borrowers and lenders appear to focus excessively (i.e., to anchor) on past deal terms when setting spreads for a new bond issue. The study found that when a firm's most recent past debt issue had a credit spread that was higher than an upcoming issue, the interest rate on the upcoming deal was higher than fundamentals could justify. In other words, both the firm and its lenders were anchored to the older, higher interest rate.

(Source: Casey Dougal, Joseph Engelberg, Christopher A. Parsons, & Edward D. Van Wesep, "Anchoring on Credit Spreads," *Journal of Finance*, June 2015.)

In that regard, perhaps no variable is more important than inflation. Changes in the inflation rate, or to be more precise, changes in the expected inflation rate, have a direct and profound effect on market interest rates. When investors expect inflation to slow down, market interest rates generally fall as well. To gain an appreciation of the extent to which interest rates are linked to inflation, look at Figure 8.1. The figure plots the behavior of the interest rate on a 10-year U.S. Treasury bond and the inflation rate from 1963 to 2014. The blue line in the figure tracks the actual inflation rate over time, although as we have already noted, the expected inflation rate has a more direct effect on interest rates. Even so, there is a clear link between actual inflation and interest rates. Note that, in general, as inflation drifts up, so do interest rates. On the other hand, a decline in inflation is matched by a similar decline in interest rates. Most of the time, the rate on the 10-year bond exceeded the inflation rate, which is exactly what you should expect. When that was not the case, such as in the 1970s and more recently in 2012, investors in the 10-year Treasury bond did not earn enough interest to keep up with inflation. Notice that in 2009 as the U.S. struggled to recover from the Great Recession, the inflation rate was negative and the Treasury yields dropped sharply. On average, the 10-year Treasury yield exceeded the inflation rate by about 2.4 percentage points per year.

FIGURE 8.1   The Impact of Inflation on the Behavior of Interest Rates

The behavior of interest rates has always been closely tied to the movements in the rate of inflation. Since 1963 the average spread between the U.S. 10-year Treasury rate and inflation is 2.4 percentage points. This spread fluctuates quite a bit over time. Some extreme examples occurred in 1974 when the rate of inflation exceeded the 10-year Treasury rate by 4.1 percentage points and in 1985 when 10-year Treasury rates outpaced inflation by 8 percentage points.

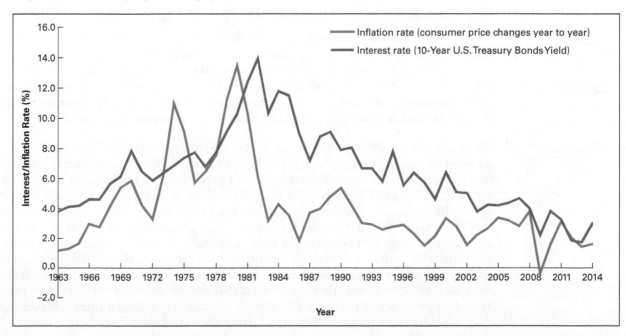

In addition to inflation, five other important economic variables can significantly affect the level of interest rates:

- *Changes in the money supply.* An increase in the money supply pushes rates down (as it makes more funds available for loans), and vice versa. This is true only up to a point, however. If the growth in the money supply becomes excessive, it can lead to inflation, which, of course, means higher interest rates.

- *The size of the federal budget deficit.* When the U.S. Treasury has to borrow large amounts to cover the budget deficit, the increased demand for funds exerts an upward pressure on interest rates. That's why bond market participants become so concerned when the budget deficit gets bigger and bigger—other things being equal, that means more upward pressure on market interest rates.

- *The level of economic activity.* Businesses need more capital when the economy expands. This need increases the demand for funds, and rates tend to rise. During a recession, economic activity contracts, and rates typically fall.

- *Policies of the Federal Reserve.* Actions of the Federal Reserve to control inflation also have a major effect on market interest rates. When the Fed wants to slow actual (or anticipated) inflation, it usually does so by driving up interest rates, as it did repeatedly in the mid- and late 1970s. Unfortunately, such actions sometimes have the side effect of slowing down business activity as well. Likewise, when the Federal Reserve wants to stimulate the economy, it takes action to push interest rates down, as it did repeatedly during and after the 2008-2009 recession.

- *The level of interest rates in major foreign markets.* Today investors look beyond national borders for investment opportunities. Rising rates in major foreign markets put pressure on rates in the United States to rise as well; if U.S. rates don't keep pace, foreign investors may be tempted to dump their dollars to buy higher-yielding foreign securities.

The Term Structure of Interest Rates and Yield Curves

Living Yield Curve

Bonds having different maturities typically have different interest rates. The relationship between interest rates (yield) and time to maturity for any class of similar-risk securities is called the **term structure of interest rates**. This relationship can be depicted graphically by a **yield curve**, which shows the relation between time to maturity and yield to maturity for a group of bonds having similar risk. The yield curve constantly changes as market forces push bond yields at different maturities up and down.

Types of Yield Curves   Two types of yield curves are illustrated in Figure 8.2. By far, the most common type is curve 1, the red upward-sloping curve. It indicates that yields tend to increase with longer maturities. That's partly because the longer a bond has to maturity, the greater the potential for price volatility. Investors, therefore, require higher-risk premiums to induce them to buy the longer, riskier bonds. Long-term rates may also exceed short-term rates if investors believe short-term rates will rise. In that case, rates on long-term bonds might have to be higher than short-term rates to attract investors. That is, if investors think short-term rates are rising, they will not want to tie up their money for long at today's lower rates. Instead, they would prefer to invest in a short-term security so that they can reinvest that money quickly after rates have risen. To induce investors to purchase a long-term bond, the bond must offer a higher rate than investors think they could earn by buying a series of short-term bonds, with each new bond in that series offering a higher rate than the one before.

FIGURE 8.2

Two Types of Yield Curves

A yield curve plots the relation between term to maturity and yield to maturity for a series of bonds that are similar in terms of risk. Although yield curves come in many shapes and forms, the most common is the upward-sloping curve. It shows that yields increase with longer maturities.

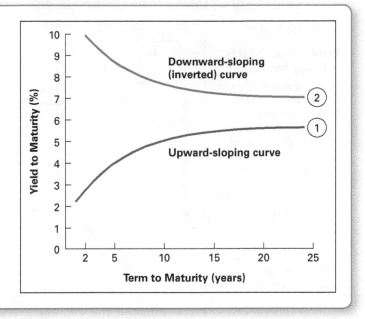

Occasionally, the yield curve becomes inverted, or downward sloping, as shown in curve 2, which occurs when short-term rates are higher than long-term rates. This curve sometimes results from actions by the Federal Reserve to curtail inflation by driving short-term interest rates up. An inverted yield curve may also occur when firms are very hesitant to borrow long-term (such as when they expect a recession). With very low demand for long-term loans, long-term interest rates fall. In addition to these two common yield curves, two other types appear from time to time: the *flat* yield curve, when rates for short- and long-term debt are essentially the same, and the *humped* yield curve, when intermediate-term rates are the highest.

Historical Yield Curves

Plotting Your Own Curves   Yield curves are constructed by plotting the yields for a group of bonds that are similar in all respects but maturity. Treasury securities (bills, notes, and bonds) are typically used to construct yield curves. There are several reasons for this. Treasury securities have no risk of default. They are actively traded, so their prices and yields are easy to observe, and they are relatively homogeneous with regard to quality and other issue characteristics. Investors can also construct yield curves for other classes of debt securities, such as A-rated municipal bonds, Aa-rated corporate bonds, and even certificates of deposit.

Figure 8.3 shows the yield curves for Treasury securities on March 7, 2007, and March 16, 2015. To draw these curves, you need Treasury quotes from the U.S. Department of the Treasury or some other similar source. (Note that actual quoted yields for curve 1 are highlighted in yellow in the table below the graph.) Given the required quotes, select the yields for the Treasury bills, notes, and bonds maturing in approximately 1 month, 3 months, 6 months, and 1, 2, 3, 5, 7, 10, 20, and 30 years. That covers the full range of Treasury issues' maturities. Next, plot the points on a graph whose horizontal (x) axis represents time to maturity in years and whose vertical (y) axis represents yield to maturity. Now, just connect the points to create the curves shown in Figure 8.3. You'll notice that curve 1 is upward sloping, while curve 2 is downward sloping. Downward-sloping yield curves are less common,

FIGURE 8.3

Yield Curves on U.S. Treasury Issues

Here we see two yield curves constructed from actual market data obtained from the U.S. Department of the Treasury. Curve 2 shows a less common downward-sloping yield curve. The yields that make up the more common upward-sloping curve 1 are near U.S. record low levels.

(Source: U.S. Department of the Treasury, June 4, 2015.)

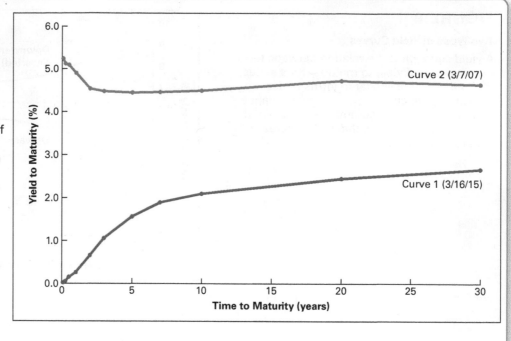

Date	1 mo	3 mo	6 mo	1 yr	2 yr	3 yr	5 yr	7 yr	10 yr	20 yr	30 yr
03/02/15	0.02	0.02	0.08	0.22	0.66	1.06	1.57	1.89	2.08	2.46	2.68
03/03/15	0.01	0.02	0.08	0.26	0.68	1.09	1.61	1.94	2.12	2.49	2.71
03/04/15	0.01	0.01	0.08	0.26	0.66	1.07	1.6	1.93	2.12	2.49	2.72
03/05/15	0.02	0.02	0.08	0.25	0.65	1.05	1.57	1.9	2.11	2.49	2.71
03/06/15	0.02	0.01	0.08	0.27	0.73	1.16	1.7	2.04	2.24	2.63	2.83
03/09/15	0.01	0.02	0.1	0.27	0.7	1.13	1.66	1.99	2.2	2.58	2.8
03/10/15	0.03	0.02	0.1	0.25	0.7	1.1	1.62	1.94	2.14	2.51	2.73
03/11/15	0.03	0.03	0.1	0.25	0.7	1.09	1.6	1.92	2.11	2.47	2.69
03/12/15	0.03	0.03	0.1	0.24	0.67	1.06	1.59	1.91	2.1	2.47	2.69
03/13/15	0.03	0.03	0.11	0.24	0.68	1.07	1.6	1.93	2.13	2.48	2.7
03/16/15	0.02	0.05	0.15	0.26	0.66	1.06	1.57	1.9	2.1	2.45	2.67

thankfully so because they often signal an upcoming recession. For example, the downward-sloping yield curve shown in Figure 8.3 signaled the Great Recession that officially ran from December 2007 to June of 2009. While curve 1 is the more typical upward-sloping yield curve, it nonetheless reflects the historically low interest rates that prevailed as the U.S. economy recovered from a deep recession.

Explanations of the Term Structure of Interest Rates As we noted earlier, the shape of the yield curve can change over time. Three commonly cited theories—the expectations hypothesis, the liquidity preference theory, and the market segmentation theory—explain more fully the reasons for the general shape of the yield curve.

Expectations Hypothesis   The **expectations hypothesis** suggests that the yield curve reflects investor expectations about the future behavior of interest rates. This theory argues that the relationship between short-term and long-term interest rates today reflects investors' expectations about how interest rates will change in the future. When the yield curve slopes upward, and long-term rates are higher than short-term rates, the expectations hypothesis interprets this as a sign that investors expect short-term rates to rise. That's why long-term bonds pay a premium compared to short-term bonds. People will not lock their money away in a long-term investment when they think interest rates are going to rise unless the rate on the long-term investment is higher than the current rate on short-term investments.

For example, suppose the current interest rate on a 1-year Treasury bill is 5%, and the current rate on a 2-year Treasury note is 6%. The expectations hypothesis says that this pattern of interest rates reveals that investors believe that the rate on a 1-year Treasury bill will go up to 7% next year. Why? That's the rate that makes investors today indifferent between locking their money away for 2 years and earning 6% on the 2-year note versus investing in the 1-year T-bill today at 5% and then next year reinvesting the money from that instrument into another 1-year T-bill paying 7%.

Investment Strategy	(1) Rate Earned This Year	(2) Rate Earned Next Year	(3) Return over 2 Years [(1) + (2)]
Buy 2-year note today	6%	6%	12%
Buy 1-year T-bill, then reinvest in another T-bill next year	5%	7%	12%

Only if the rate on a 1-year T-bill rises from 5% this year to 7% next year will investors be indifferent between these 2 strategies. Thus, according to the expectations hypothesis, an upward-sloping yield curve means that investors expect interest rates to rise, and a downward-sloping yield curve means that investors expect interest rates to fall.

Example

> Suppose the yield curve is inverted, and 1-year bonds offer a 5% yield while 2-year bonds pay a 4.5% yield. According to the expectations hypothesis, what do investors expect the 1-year bond yield to be 1 year from now? Remember that the expectations hypothesis says today's short-term and long-term interest rates are set at a level which makes investors indifferent between short-term and long-term bonds, given their beliefs about where interest rates are headed. Therefore, to determine the expected 1-year bond yield next year, you must determine what return in the second year would make investors just as happy to buy two 1-year bonds as they are to buy one 2-year bond.
>
> $$\text{Return on a 2-year bond} = 4.5\% + 4.5\%$$
> $$\text{Return on two 1-year bonds} = 5.0\% + x$$
>
> The x in the second equation represents the expected rate on the 1-year bond next year. The top equation shows that an investor earns 9% over 2 years by purchasing a 2-year bond, so to achieve the same return on a series of two 1-year bonds, the return in the second year must be 4%.

Liquidity Preference Theory   More often than not, yield curves have an upward slope. The expectations hypothesis would interpret this as a sign that investors *usually* expect rates to rise. That seems somewhat illogical. Why would investors expect interest rates to rise more often than they expect rates to fall? Put differently, why would investors expect interest rates to trend up over time? There is certainly no historical pattern to lead one to hold that view. One explanation for the frequency of upward-sloping yield curves is the **liquidity preference theory**. This theory states that long-term bond rates should be higher than short-term rates because of the added risks involved with the longer maturities. In other words, because of the risk differential between long- and short-term debt securities, rational investors will prefer the less risky, short-term obligations unless they can be motivated, via higher interest rates, to invest in longer-term bonds. Even if investors do not expect short-term rates to rise, long-term bonds will still have to offer higher yields to attract investors.

Actually, there are a number of reasons why rational investors should prefer short-term securities. To begin with, they are more liquid (more easily converted to cash) and less sensitive to changing market rates, which means there is less price volatility. For a given change in market rates, the prices of longer-term bonds will show considerably more movement than the prices of short-term bonds. In addition, just as investors tend to require a premium for tying up funds for longer periods, borrowers will also pay a premium in order to obtain long-term funds. Borrowers thus assure themselves that funds will be available, and they avoid having to roll over short-term debt at unknown and possibly unfavorable rates. All of these preferences explain why higher rates of interest should be associated with longer maturities and why it's perfectly rational to expect upward-sloping yield curves.

Market Segmentation Theory   Another often-cited theory, the **market segmentation theory**, suggests that the market for debt is segmented on the basis of the maturity preferences of different financial institutions and investors. According to this theory, the yield curve changes as the supply and demand for funds within each maturity segment determines its prevailing interest rate. The equilibrium between the financial institutions that supply the funds for short-term maturities (e.g., banks) and the borrowers of those short-term funds (e.g., businesses with seasonal loan requirements) establishes interest rates in the short-term markets. Similarly, the equilibrium between suppliers and demanders in such long-term markets as life insurance and real estate determines the prevailing long-term interest rates.

AN ADVISOR'S PERSPECTIVE

Ryan McKeown
Senior VP–Financial Advisor, **Wealth Enhancement Group**

"I pay very close attention to the yield curve."

MyFinanceLab

The shape of the yield curve can slope either upward or downward, as determined by the general relationship between rates in each market segment. When supply outstrips demand for short-term loans, short-term rates are relatively low. If, at the same time, the demand for long-term loans is higher than the available supply of funds, then long-term rates will move up, and the yield curve will have an upward slope. If supply and demand conditions are reversed—with excess demand for borrowing in the short-term market and an excess supply of funds in the long-term market—the yield curve could slope down.

Which Theory Is Right?   All three theories of the term structure have at least some merit in explaining the shape of the yield curve. These theories tell us that, at any time, the slope of the yield curve is affected by the interaction of (1) expectations regarding future interest rates, (2) liquidity preferences, and (3) the supply and demand conditions in the short- and long-term market segments. Upward-sloping yield curves result from expectations of rising interest rates, lender preferences for shorter-maturity loans, and a greater supply of short- than of long-term loans relative to the respective demand in each market segment. The opposite conditions lead to a downward-sloping yield curve.

More about the Yield Curve

Using the Yield Curve in Investment Decisions   Bond investors often use yield curves in making investment decisions. Analyzing the changes in yield curves provides investors with information about future interest rate movements, which in turn affect the prices and returns on different types of bonds. For example, if the entire yield curve begins to move upward, it usually means that inflation is starting to heat up or is expected to do so in the near future. In that case, investors can expect that interest rates, too, will rise. Under these conditions, most seasoned bond investors will turn to short or intermediate (three to five years) maturities, which provide reasonable returns and at the same time minimize exposure to capital loss when interest rates go up. A downward-sloping yield curve signals that rates have peaked and are about to fall and that the economy is slowing down.

Another factor to consider is the difference in yields on different maturities—the "steepness" of the curve. For example, a steep yield curve is one where long-term rates are much higher than short-term rates. This shape is often seen as an indication that the spread between long-term and short-term rates is about to fall, either because long-term rates will fall or short-term rates will rise. Steep yield curves are generally viewed as a bullish sign. For aggressive bond investors, they could be the signal to start moving into long-term securities. Flatter yield curves, on the other hand, sharply reduce the incentive for going long-term since the difference in yield between the 5- and 30-year maturities can be quite small. Under these conditions, investors would be well advised to just stick with the 5- to 10-year maturities, which will generate about the same yield as long bonds but without the risks.

CONCEPTS IN REVIEW

Answers available at
http://www.pearsonhighered.com/smart

8.1 Is there a single market rate of interest applicable to all segments of the bond market, or is there a series of market yields? Explain and note the investment implications of such a market environment.

8.2 Explain why interest rates are important to both conservative and aggressive bond investors. What causes interest rates to move, and how can you monitor such movements?

8.3 What is the term structure of interest rates and how is it related to the yield curve? What information is required to plot a yield curve? Describe an upward-sloping yield curve and explain what it has to say about the behavior of interest rates. Do the same for a flat yield curve.

8.4 How might you, as a bond investor, use information about the term structure of interest rates and yield curves when making investment decisions?

The Pricing of Bonds

LG3 No matter who the issuer is, what kind of bond it is, or whether it's fully taxable or tax-free, all bonds are priced using similar principles. That is, all bonds (including notes with maturities of more than one year) are priced according to the present value of their future cash flow streams. Indeed, once the prevailing or expected market yield is known, the whole process becomes rather mechanical.

Market yields largely determine bond prices. That's because in the marketplace, investors first decide what yield is appropriate for a particular bond, given its risk, and then they use that yield to find the bond's price (or market value). As we saw earlier, the appropriate yield on a bond is a function of certain market and economic forces (e.g., the risk-free rate of return and inflation), as well as key issue and issuer characteristics (like years to maturity and the issue's bond rating). Together these forces combine to form the required rate of return, which is the rate of return the investor would like to earn in order to justify an investment in a given fixed-income security. The required return defines the yield at which the bond should be trading and serves as the discount rate in the bond valuation process.

The Basic Bond Valuation Model

Generally speaking, when you buy a bond you receive two distinct types of cash flow: (1) periodic interest income (i.e., coupon payments) and (2) the principal (or par value) at the end of the bond's life. Thus, in valuing a bond, you're dealing with an annuity of coupon payments for a specified number of periods plus a large single cash flow at maturity. You can use these cash flows, along with the required rate of return on the investment, in a present value-based bond valuation model to find the dollar value, or price, of a bond. Using annual compounding, you can calculate the price of a particular bond (BPi) using the following equation:

Equation 8.2

$$BP_i = \sum_{t=1}^{N} \frac{C}{(1 + r_i)^t} + \frac{PV_N}{(1 + r_i)^N}$$

$$= \frac{\text{Present value of}}{\text{coupon payments}} + \frac{\text{Present value of}}{\text{bond's par value}}$$

where

$BP_i =$ current price (or value) of a particular bond i
$C =$ annual coupon (interest) payment
$PV_N =$ par value of the bond, at maturity
$N =$ number of years to maturity
$r_i =$ prevailing market yield, or required annual return on bonds similar to bond i

In this form, you can compute the bond's current value, or what you would be willing to pay for it, given that you want to generate a certain rate of return, as defined by r_i. Alternatively, if you already know the bond's price, you can solve for r_i in the equation, in which case you'd be looking for the yield to maturity embedded in the current market price of the bond.

In the discussion that follows, we will demonstrate the bond valuation process in two ways. First, we'll use annual compounding—that is, because of its computational simplicity, we'll assume we are dealing with coupons that are paid once a year. Second, we'll examine bond valuation under conditions of semiannual compounding, which is the way most bonds actually pay their interest.

Annual Compounding

You need the following information to value a bond: (1) the annual coupon payment, (2) the par value (usually $1,000), and (3) the number of years (i.e., time periods) remaining to maturity. You then use the prevailing market yield, r_i, as the discount rate to compute the bond's price, as follows:

Equation 8.3

$$\text{Bond price} = \frac{\text{Present value of}}{\text{coupon payments}} + \frac{\text{Present value of}}{\text{bond's par value}}$$

Equation 8.3a

$$BP_i = \frac{C}{(1+r_i)^1} + \frac{C}{(1+r_i)^2} + \cdots + \frac{C}{(1+r_i)^N} + \frac{\$1,000}{(1+r_i)^N}$$

where again

C = annual coupon payment
N = number of years to maturity

Example

A 20-year, 4.5% bond is priced to yield 5%. That is, the bond pays an annual coupon of 4.5% (or $45), has 20 years left to maturity, and has a yield to maturity of 5%, which is the current market rate on bonds of this type. We can use Equation 8.3 to find the bond's price.

$$BP_i = \frac{\$45}{(1+0.05)^1} + \frac{\$45}{(1+0.05)^2} + \cdots + \frac{\$45}{(1+0.05)^{20}} + \frac{\$1,000}{(1+0.05)^{20}} = \$937.69$$

Note that because this is a coupon-bearing bond, we have an annuity of coupon payments of $45 a year for 20 years, plus a single cash flow of $1,000 that occurs at the end of year 20. Thus, we find the present value of the coupon annuity and then add that amount to the present value of the recovery of principal at maturity. In this particular case, you should be willing to pay almost $938 for this bond, as long as you're satisfied with earning 5% on your money.

Notice that this bond trades at a discount of $62.31 ($1,000 − $937.69). It trades at a discount because its coupon rate (4.5%) is below the market's required return (5%). You can directly link the size of the discount on this bond to the present value of the difference between the coupons that it pays ($45) and the coupons that would be required if the bond matched the market's 5% required return ($50). In other words, this bond's coupon payment is $5 less than what the market requires, so if you take the present value of that difference over the bond's life, you will calculate the size of the bond's discount:

$$\frac{\$5}{(1+0.05)^1} + \frac{\$5}{(1+0.05)^2} + \cdots + \frac{\$5}{(1+0.05)^{20}} = \$62.31$$

In a similar vein, for a bond that trades at a premium, the size of that premium equals the present value of the difference between the coupon that the bond pays and the (lower) coupon that the market requires.

Bonds initially sell for a price close to par value because bond issuers generally set the bond's coupon rate equal or close to the market's required return at the time the bonds are issued. If market interest rates change during the life of the bond, then the bond's price will adjust up or down to reflect any differences between the bond's coupon rate and the market interest rate. Although bonds can sell at premiums or discounts over their lives, as the maturity date arrives, bond prices will converge to par value. This happens because as time passes and a bond's maturity date approaches, there are fewer interest payments remaining (so any premium or discount is diminishing) and the principal to be repaid at maturity is becoming an ever bigger portion of the bond's price since the periods over which it is being discounted are disappearing.

CALCULATOR USE For annual compounding, to price a 20-year, 4.5% bond to yield 5%, use the keystrokes shown in the margin, where:

$$N = \text{number of years to maturity}$$
$$I = \text{required annual return on the bond (what the bond is being priced to yield)}$$
$$PMT = \text{annual coupon payment}$$
$$FV = \text{par value of the bond}$$
$$PV = \text{computed price of the bond}$$

Input	Function
20	N
5.0	I
45	PMT
1000	FV
	CPT
	PV

Solution
-937.69

Financial Calculator
Tutorials

Recall that the calculator result shows the bond's price as a negative value, which indicates that the price is a cash outflow for an investor when buying the bond's cash flows.

SPREADSHEET USE The bond's price can also be calculated as shown on the following Excel spreadsheet.

	A	B
1	**Bond's Price**	
2	Par value	$1,000
3	Annual coupon rate	4.5%
4	Annual coupon payment	$45
5	Number of years to maturity	20
6	Required annual return	5.0%
7	Bond's price	-$937.69
8	Entry in Cell B7 is =PV(B6,B5,B4,B2,0). The minus sign appears before the $937.69 in B7 because the price of the bond is treated as a cash outflow.	

Semiannual Compounding

Although using annual compounding simplifies the valuation process a bit, it's not the way most bonds are actually valued in the marketplace. In practice, most bonds pay interest every six months, so it is appropriate to use semiannual compounding to value bonds. Fortunately, it's relatively easy to go from annual to semiannual compounding: All you need to do is cut the annual interest income and the required rate of return in half and double the number of periods until maturity. In other words, rather than one compounding and payment interval per year, there are two (i.e., two 6-month periods per year). Given these changes, finding the price of a bond under conditions of semiannual compounding is much like pricing a bond using annual compounding. That is:

Equation 8.4

$$\begin{array}{ccc} \text{Bond price (with semi-} & = & \text{Present value of the annuity of} & + & \text{Present value of the} \\ \text{annual compounding)} & & \text{semiannual coupon payments} & & \text{bond's par value} \end{array}$$

Equation 8.4a

$$BP_i = \frac{C/2}{\left(1 + \frac{r_i}{2}\right)^1} + \frac{C/2}{\left(1 + \frac{r_i}{2}\right)^2} + \cdots + \frac{C/2}{\left(1 + \frac{r_i}{2}\right)^{2N}} + \frac{\$1{,}000}{\left(1 + \frac{r_i}{2}\right)^{2N}}$$

where, in this case,

$$C/2 = \text{semiannual coupon payment, or the amount of interest paid every 6 months}$$
$$r_i/2 = \text{the required rate of return per 6-month period}$$

Example

In the previous bond-pricing example, you priced a 20-year bond to yield 5%, assuming annual interest payments of $45. Suppose the bond makes semiannual interest payments instead. With semiannual payments of $22.50, you adjust the semiannual return to 2.5% and the number of periods to 40. Using Equation 8.4, you'd have:

$$BP_i = \frac{\$45/2}{\left(1 + \dfrac{0.05}{2}\right)^1} + \frac{\$45/2}{\left(1 + \dfrac{0.05}{2}\right)^2} + \cdots + \frac{\$45/2}{\left(1 + \dfrac{0.05}{2}\right)^{40}} + \frac{1,000}{\left(1 + \dfrac{0.05}{2}\right)^{40}} = \$937.24$$

The price of the bond in this case ($937.24) is slightly less than the price we obtained with annual compounding ($937.69).

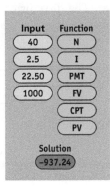

Input	Function
40	N
2.5	I
22.50	PMT
1000	FV
	CPT
	PV

Solution
-937.24

CALCULATOR USE For *semiannual compounding,* to price a 20-year, 4.5% semiannual-pay bond to yield 5%, use the keystrokes shown in the margin, where:

N = number of 6-month periods to maturity ($20 \times 2 = 40$)
I = yield on the bond, adjusted for semiannual compounding ($5\% \div 2 = 2.5\%$)
PMT = semiannual coupon payment ($\$45.00 \div 2 = \$22.50$)
FV = par value of the bond
PV = computed price of the bond

SPREADSHEET USE You can calculate the bond's price with semiannual coupon payments as shown on the following Excel spreadsheet. Notice that in cell B8 the required annual return is divided by coupon payment frequency to find the required rate of return per 6-month period, and the number of years to maturity is multiplied times the coupon payment frequency to find the total number of 6-month periods remaining until maturity.

	A	B
1	**Bond's Price**	
2	Par value	$1,000
3	Coupon rate	4.5%
4	Coupon payment frequency	2
5	Coupon payment	$22.50
6	Number of years to maturity	20
7	Required annual return	5.0%
8	Bond's price	-$937.24
9	Entry in Cell B8 is =PV(B7/B4,B6*B4,B5,B2,0). The minus sign appears before the $937.24 in B8 because the price of the bond is treated as a cash outflow.	

Accrued Interest

Most bonds pay interest every six months, but you can trade them any time that the market is open. Suppose you own a bond that makes interest payments on January 15 and July 15 each year. What happens if you sell this bond at some time between the scheduled coupon payment dates? For example, suppose you sell the bond on October 15, a date that is roughly halfway between two payment dates. Fortunately, interest accrues on bonds between coupon payments, so selling the bond prior to a coupon payment does not mean that you sacrifice any interest that you earned. **Accrued interest** is the amount of interest earned on a bond since the last coupon payment. When you sell a bond in between coupon dates, the bond buyer adds accrued interest to the bond's price (the price calculated using Equation 8.3 or 8.4 depending on whether coupons arrive annually or semiannually).

> **Example**
>
> Suppose you purchase a $1,000 par value bond that pays a 6% coupon in semi-annual installments of $30. You received a coupon payment two months ago, and now you are ready to sell the bond. Contacting a broker, you learn that the bond's current market price is $1,010. If you sell the bond, you will receive not only the market price, but also accrued interest. Because you are about one-third of the way between the last coupon payment and the next one, you receive accrued interest of $10 (i.e., 1/3 × $30), so the total cash that you receive in exchange for your bond is $1,020.

Traders in the bond market sometimes refer to the price of a bond as being either clean or dirty. The **clean price** of a bond equals the present value of its cash flows, as in Equations 8.3 and 8.4. As a matter of practice, bond price quotations that you may find in financial periodicals or online are nearly always clean prices. The **dirty price** of a bond is the clean price plus accrued interest. In the example above, the clean price is $1,010, and the dirty price is $1,020.

CONCEPTS IN REVIEW

Answers available at
http://www.pearsonhighered.com/smart

8.5 Explain how market yield affects the price of a bond. Could you price a bond without knowing its market yield? Explain.

8.6 Why are bonds generally priced using semiannual compounding? Does it make much difference if you use annual compounding?

Measures of Yield and Return

 In the bond market, investors focus as much on a bond's yield to maturity as on its price. As you have seen, the yield to maturity helps determine the price at which a bond trades, but it also measures the rate of return on the bond. When you can observe the price of a bond that is trading in the market, you can simply reverse the bond valuation process described above to solve for the bond's yield to maturity rather than its price. That gives you a pretty good idea of the return that you might earn if you purchased the bond at its current market price. Actually, there are three widely used metrics to assess the return on a bond: the current yield, the yield to maturity, and the yield to call (for bonds that are callable). We'll look at all three measures here, along with a concept known as the *expected return*, which measures the expected (or actual) rate of return earned over a specific holding period.

Current Yield

The **current yield** is the simplest of all bond return measures, but it also has the most limited application. This measure looks at just one source of return: a bond's annual interest income. In particular, it indicates the amount of current income a bond provides relative to its prevailing market price. The current yield equals:

Equation 8.5

$$\text{Current yield} = \frac{\text{Annual interest income}}{\text{Current market price of the bond}}$$

Example

> An 8% bond would pay $80 per year in interest for every $1,000 of principal. However, if the bond was currently priced at $800, it would have a current yield of $80 ÷ $800 = 0.10 = 10%. The current yield measures a bond's annual interest income, so it is of interest primarily to investors seeking high levels of current income, such as endowments or retirees.

Yield to Maturity

The **yield to maturity (YTM)** is the most important and most widely used measure of the return provided by a bond. It evaluates the bond's interest income and any gain or loss that results from differences between the price that an investor pays for a bond and the par value that the investor receives at maturity. The YTM takes into account all of the cash flow received over a bond's life. Also known as the **promised yield**, the YTM shows the rate of return earned by an investor, given that the bond is held to maturity and all principal and interest payments are made in a prompt and timely fashion. In addition, the YTM calculation implicitly assumes that the investor can reinvest all the coupon payments at an interest rate equal to the bond's yield to maturity. This "reinvestment assumption" plays a vital role in the YTM, which we will discuss in more detail later in this chapter (see the section entitled Yield Properties).

The yield to maturity is used not only to gauge the return on a single issue but also to track the behavior of the market in general. In other words, market interest rates are basically a reflection of the average promised yields that exist in a given segment of the market. The yield to maturity provides valuable insights into an issue's investment merits that investors can use to assess the attractiveness of different bonds. Other things being equal, the higher the promised yield of an issue, the more attractive it is.

Although there are a couple of ways to compute the YTM, the best and most accurate procedure is derived directly from the bond valuation model described above. That is, you can use Equations 8.3 and 8.4 to determine the YTM for a bond. The difference is that now instead of trying to determine the price of the bond, you know its price and are trying to find the discount rate that will equate the present value of the bond's cash flow (coupon and principal payments) to its current market price. This procedure may sound familiar. It's just like the internal rate of return measure described earlier in the text. Indeed, the YTM is basically the internal rate of return on a bond. When you find that, you have the bond's yield to maturity.

Using Annual Compounding Finding yield to maturity is a matter of trial and error. In other words, you try different values for YTM until you find the one that solves the equation. Let's say you want to find the YTM for a 7.5% ($1,000 par value) annual-coupon-paying bond that has 15 years remaining to maturity and is currently trading in the market at $809.50. From Equation 8.3, we know that

$$BP_i = \$809.50 = \frac{\$75}{(1 + r_i)^1} + \frac{\$75}{(1 + r_i)^2} + \cdots + \frac{\$75}{(1 + r_i)^{15}} + \frac{\$1,000}{(1 + r_i)^{15}}$$

Notice that this bond sells below par (i.e., it sells at a discount). What do we know about the relationship between the required return on a bond and its coupon rate when the bond sells at a discount? Bonds sell at a discount when the required return (or yield to maturity) is higher than the coupon rate, so the yield to maturity on this bond must be higher than 7.5%.

Through trial and error, we might initially try a discount rate of 8% or 9% (or, since it sells at a discount, any value above the bond's coupon). Sooner or later, we'll try a discount rate of 10%, and at that discount rate, the present value of the bond's cash flows is $809.85 (use Equation 8.3 to verify this), which is very close to the bond's market price.

Because the computed price of $809.85 is reasonably close to the bond's current market price of $809.50, we can say that 10% represents the approximate yield to maturity on this bond. That is, 10% is the discount rate that leads to a computed bond price that's equal (or very close) to the bond's current market price. In this case, if you were to pay $809.50 for the bond and hold it to maturity, you would expect to earn a YTM very close to 10.0%. Doing trial and error by hand can be time consuming, so you can use a handheld calculator or computer software to calculate the YTM.

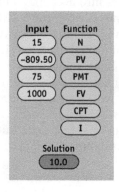

CALCULATOR USE For annual compounding, to find the YTM of a 15-year, 7.5% bond that is currently priced in the market at $809.50, use the keystrokes shown in the margin. The present value (PV) key represents the current market price of the bond, and all other keystrokes are as defined earlier.

SPREADSHEET USE The bond's YTM can also be calculated as shown on the following Excel spreadsheet.

	A	B
1	**Bond's YTM**	
2	Par value	$1,000
3	Annual coupon rate	7.5%
4	Annual coupon payment	$75
5	Number of years to maturity	15
6	Bond's price	-$809.50
7	Bond's YTM	10.0%
8	Entry in Cell B7 is =RATE(B5,B4,B6,B2,0). The minus sign appears before the $809.50 in B6 because the price of the bond is treated as a cash outflow.	

Using Semiannual Compounding Given some fairly simple modifications, it's also possible to find the YTM using semiannual compounding. To do so, we cut the annual coupon and discount rate in half and double the number of periods to maturity. Returning to the 7.5%, 15-year bond, let's see what happens when you use Equation 8.4 and try an initial discount rate of 10%.

$$BP_i = \frac{\$75.00/2}{\left(1 + \frac{0.10}{2}\right)^1} \frac{\$75.00/2}{\left(1 + \frac{0.10}{2}\right)^2} + \cdots + \frac{\$75.00/2}{\left(1 + \frac{0.10}{2}\right)^{30}} + \frac{\$1,000}{\left(1 + \frac{0.10}{2}\right)^{30}} = \$807.85$$

As you can see, a semiannual discount rate of 5% results in a computed bond value that's well short of the market price of $809.50. Given the inverse relationship between price and yield, it follows that if you need a higher price, you have to try a lower YTM (discount rate). Therefore, you know the semiannual yield on this bond has to be something less than 5%. By trial and error, you would determine that the yield to maturity on this bond is just a shade under 5% per half year—approximately 4.99%. Remember that this is the yield expressed over a 6-month period. The market convention is to simply state the annual yield as twice the semiannual yield. This practice produces what the market refers to as the **bond equivalent yield**. Returning to the YTM problem started above, you know that the issue has a semiannual yield of about 4.99%.

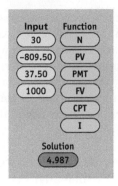

Input	Function
30	N
−809.50	PV
37.50	PMT
1000	FV
	CPT
	I

Solution
4.987

According to the bond equivalent yield convention, you double the semiannual rate to obtain the annual rate of return on this bond. Doing this results in an annualized yield to maturity (or promised yield) of approximately 4.99% × 2 = 9.98%. This is the annual rate of return you will earn on the bond if you hold it to maturity.

CALCULATOR USE For semiannual compounding, to find the YTM of a 15-year, 7.5% bond that is currently priced in the market at $809.50, use the keystrokes shown here. As before, the *PV* key is the current market price of the bond, and all other keystrokes are as defined earlier. Remember that to find the bond equivalent yield, you must double the computed value of *I*, 4.987%. That is 4.987% × 2 = 9.97%. The difference between our answer here, 9.97%, and the 9.98% figure in the previous paragraph is simply due to the calculator's more precise rounding.

SPREADSHEET USE A semiannual bond's YTM and bond equivalent yield can also be calculated as shown on the following Excel spreadsheet.

	A	B
1	**Bond's YTM**	
2	Par value	$1,000
3	Coupon rate	7.5%
4	Coupon payment frequency	2
5	Coupon payment	$37.50
6	Number of years to maturity	15
7	Bond's price	−$809.50
8	Bond's YTM	4.99%
9	Bond-equivalent yield	9.97%
10	Entry in Cell B8 is =RATE(B6*B4,B5,B7,B2,0). The minus sign appears before the $809.50 in B7 because the price of the bond is treated as a cash outflow.	

Yield Properties Actually, in addition to holding the bond to maturity, there are several other critical assumptions embedded in any yield to maturity figure. The promised yield measure—whether computed with annual or semiannual compounding—is based on present value concepts and therefore contains important reinvestment assumptions. To be specific, the YTM calculation assumes that when each coupon payment arrives, you can reinvest it for the remainder of the bond's life at a rate that is equal to the YTM. When this assumption holds, the return that you earn over a bond's life is in fact equal to the YTM. In essence, the calculated yield to maturity figure is the return "promised" only as long as the issuer meets all interest and principal obligations on a timely basis and the investor reinvests all interest income at a rate equal to the computed promised yield. In our example above, you would need to reinvest each of the coupon payments and earn a 10% return on those reinvested funds. Failure to do so would result in a realized yield of less than the 10% YTM. If you made no attempt to reinvest the coupons, you would earn a realized yield over the 15-year investment horizon of just over 6.5%—far short of the 10% promised return. On the other hand, if you could reinvest coupons at a rate that exceeded 10%, the actual yield on your bond over the 15 years would be higher than its 10% YTM. The bottom line is that unless you are dealing with a zero-coupon bond, a significant portion of the bond's total return over time comes from reinvested coupons.

When we use present value-based measures of return, such as the YTM, there are actually three components of return: (1) coupon/interest income, (2) capital gains (or losses), and (3) interest on interest. Whereas current income and capital gains make up the profits from an investment, interest on interest is a measure of what you do with those profits. In the context of a bond's yield to maturity, the computed YTM defines the required, or minimum, reinvestment rate. Put your investment profits (i.e., interest income) to work at this rate and you'll earn a rate of return equal to YTM. This rule applies to any coupon-bearing bond—as long as there's an annual or semiannual flow of interest income, the reinvestment of that income and interest on interest are matters that you must deal with. Also, keep in mind that the bigger the coupon and/or the longer the maturity, the more important the reinvestment assumption. Indeed, for many long-term, high-coupon bond investments, interest on interest alone can account for well over half the cash flow.

Finding the Yield on a Zero   You can also use the procedures described above (Equation 8.3 with annual compounding or Equation 8.4 with semiannual compounding) to find the yield to maturity on a zero-coupon bond. The only difference is that you can ignore the coupon portion of the equation because it will, of course, equal zero. All you need to do to find the promised yield on a zero-coupon bond is to solve the following expression:

$$\text{Yield} = \left(\frac{\$1,000}{\text{Price}}\right)^{\frac{1}{N}} - 1$$

Example

> Suppose that today you could buy a 15-year zero-coupon bond for $315. If you purchase the bond at that price and hold it to maturity, what is your YTM?
>
> $$\text{Yield} = \left(\frac{\$1,000}{\$315}\right)^{\frac{1}{15}} - 1 = 0.08 = 8\%$$
>
> The zero-coupon bond pays an annual compound return of 8%. Had we been using semiannual compounding, we'd use the same equation except we'd substitute 30 for 15 (because there are 30 semiannual periods in 15 years). The yield would change to 3.93% per half year, or 7.86% per year.

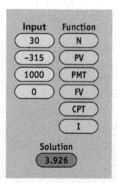

Input	Function
30	N
−315	PV
1000	PMT
0	FV
	CPT
	I

Solution
3.926

CALCULATOR USE   For semiannual compounding, to find the YTM of a 15-year zero-coupon bond that is currently priced in the market at $315, use the keystrokes shown in the margin. *PV* is the current market price of the bond, and all other keystrokes are as defined earlier. To find the bond equivalent yield, double the computed value of *I*, 3.926%. That is, 3.926% × 2 = 7.85%.

SPREADSHEET USE   A semiannual bond's YTM and bond equivalent yield can also be calculated as shown on the following Excel spreadsheet. Notice that the spreadsheet also shows 7.85% for the bond equivalent yield.

	A	B
1	**Bond's YTM**	
2	Par value	$1,000
3	Coupon rate	0.0%
4	Coupon payment frequency	2
5	Coupon payment	$0.00
6	Number of years to maturity	15
7	Bond's price	−$315.00
8	Bond's YTM	3.93%
9	Bond-equivalent yield	7.85%
10	Entry in Cell B8 is =RATE(B6*B4,B5,B7,B2,0). The minus sign appears before the $315.00 in B7 because the price of the bond is treated as a cash outflow.	

Yield to Call

Bonds can be either noncallable or callable. Recall that a noncallable bond prohibits the issuer from calling the bond prior to maturity. Because such issues will remain outstanding to maturity, you can value them by using the standard yield to maturity measure. In contrast, a callable bond gives the issuer the right to retire the bond before its maturity date, so the issue may not remain outstanding to maturity. As a result, the YTM may not always provide a good measure of the return that you can expect if you purchase a callable bond. Instead, you should consider the impact of the bond being called away prior to maturity. A common way to do that is to use a measure known as the **yield to call (YTC)**, which shows the yield on a bond if the issue remains outstanding not to maturity but rather until its first (or some other specified) call date.

The YTC is commonly used with bonds that carry deferred-call provisions. Remember that such issues start out as noncallable bonds and then, after a call deferment period (of 5 to 10 years), become freely callable. Under these conditions, the YTC would measure the expected yield on a deferred-call bond assuming that the issue is retired at the end of the call deferment period (that is, when the bond first becomes freely callable). You can find the YTC by making two simple modifications to the standard YTM equation (Equation 8.3 or 8.4). First, define the length of the investment horizon (N) as the number of years to the first call date, not the number of years to maturity. Second, instead of using the bond's par value ($1,000), use the bond's call price (which is stated in the indenture and is frequently greater than the bond's par value).

For example, assume you want to find the YTC on a 20-year, 10.5% deferred-call bond that is currently trading in the market at $1,204 but has five years to go to first call (that is, before it becomes freely callable), at which time it can be called in at a price of $1,085. Rather than using the bond's maturity of 20 years in the valuation equation (Equation 8.3 or 8.4), you use the number of years to first call (five years), and rather than the bond's par value, $1,000, you use the issue's call price, $1,085. Note, however, you still use the bond's coupon (10.5%) and its current market price ($1,204). Thus, for annual compounding, you would have:

Equation 8.6

$$BP_i = \$1,204 = \frac{\$105}{(1+r_i)^1} + \frac{\$105}{(1+r_i)^2} + \frac{\$105}{(1+r_i)^3} + \frac{\$105}{(1+r_i)^4} + \frac{\$105}{(1+r_i)^5} + \frac{\$1,085}{(1+r_i)^5}$$

Through trial and error, you could determine that at a discount rate of 7%, the present value of the future cash flows (coupons over the next five years, plus call price) will exactly (or very nearly) equal the bond's current market price of $1,204.

Thus, the YTC on this bond is 7%. In contrast, the bond's YTM is 8.37%. In practice, bond investors normally compute both YTM and YTC for deferred-call bonds that are trading at a premium. They do this to find which yield is lower; the market convention is *to use the lower, more conservative measure of yield (YTM or YTC) as the appropriate indicator of the bond's return.* As a result, the premium bond in our example would be valued relative to its yield to call. The assumption is that because interest rates have dropped so much (the YTM is two percentage points below the coupon rate), it will be called in the first chance the issuer gets. However, the situation is totally different when this or any bond trades at a discount. Why? Because the YTM on any discount bond, whether callable or not, will always be less than the YTC. Thus, the YTC is a totally irrelevant measure for discount bonds—it's used only with premium bonds.

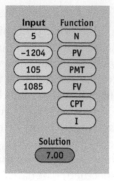

Input	Function
5	N
−1204	PV
105	PMT
1085	FV
	CPT
	I

Solution
7.00

CALCULATOR USE For annual compounding, to find the YTC of a 20-year, 10.5% bond that is currently trading at $1,204 but can be called in five years at a call price of $1,085, use the keystrokes shown in the margin. In this computation, N is the number of years to first call date, and FV represents the bond's call price. All other keystrokes are as defined earlier.

SPREADSHEET USE A callable bond's YTC can also be calculated as shown on the following Excel spreadsheet.

	A	B
1	**Bond's YTC**	
2	Par value	$1,000
3	Annual coupon rate	10.5%
4	Annual coupon payment	$105
5	Number of years to maturity	5
6	Call price	$1,085.00
7	Bond's price	-$1,204.00
8	Bond's YTM	7.0%
9	Entry in Cell B8 is =RATE(B5,B4,B7,B6,0). The minus sign appears before the $1,204.00 in B7 because the price of the bond is treated as a cash outflow.	

Expected Return

Rather than just buying and holding bonds, some investors prefer to actively trade in and out of these securities over fairly short investment horizons. As a result, measures such as yield to maturity and yield to call have relatively little meaning, other than as indicators of the rate of return used to price the bond. These investors obviously need an alternative measure of return that they can use to assess the investment appeal of those bonds they intend to trade. Such an alternative measure is the **expected return**. It indicates the rate of return an investor can expect to earn by holding a bond over a period of time that's less than the life of the issue. (Expected return is also known as **realized yield** because it shows the return an investor would realize by trading in and out of bonds over short holding periods.)

The expected return lacks the precision of the yield to maturity (and YTC) because the major cash flow variables are largely the product of investor estimates. In particular, going into the investment, both the length of the holding period and the future selling price of the bond are pure estimates and therefore subject to uncertainty. Even so, you can use essentially the same procedure to find a bond's realized yield as you did to find the promised yield. That is, with some simple modifications to the standard bond-pricing formula, you can use the following equation to find the expected return on a bond.

Equation 8.7

$$\text{Bond price} = \begin{matrix}\text{Present value of the bond's} \\ \text{annual coupon payments} \\ \text{over the holding period}\end{matrix} + \begin{matrix}\text{Present value of the bond's} \\ \text{future price at the end} \\ \text{of the holding period}\end{matrix}$$

Equation 8.7a

$$BP_i = \frac{C}{(1 + r_i)^1} + \frac{C}{(1 + r_i)^2} + \cdots + \frac{C}{(1 + r_i)^N} + \frac{FV}{(1 + r_i)^N}$$

where this time N represents the length of the holding period (not years to maturity), and FV is the expected future price of the bond.

As indicated above, you must determine the future price of the bond when computing its expected return. This is done by using the standard bond price formula, as described earlier. The most difficult part of deriving a reliable future price is, of course, coming up with future market interest rates that you feel will exist when the bond is sold. By evaluating current and expected market interest rate conditions, you can estimate the YTM that you expect the issue to provide at the date of sale and then use that yield to calculate the bond's future price.

To illustrate, take one more look at our 7.5%, 15-year bond. This time, let's assume that you feel the price of the bond, which is now trading at a discount, will rise sharply as interest rates fall over the next few years. In particular, assume the bond is currently priced at $809.50 (to yield 10%) and you anticipate holding the bond for three years. Over that time, you expect market rates to drop to 8%. With that assumption in place, and recognizing that three years from now the bond will have 12 remaining coupon payments, you can use Equation 8.3 to estimate that the bond's price will be approximately $960 in three years. Thus, you are assuming that you will buy the bond today at a market price of $809.50 and sell it three years later—after interest rates have declined to 8%—at a price of $960. Given these assumptions, the expected return (realized yield) on this bond is 14.6%, which is the discount rate in the following equation that will produce a current market price of $809.50.

$$BP_i = \$809.50 = \frac{\$75}{(1 + r_i)^1} + \frac{\$75}{(1 + r_i)^2} + \frac{\$75}{(1 + r_i)^3} + \frac{\$960}{(1 + r_i)^3}$$

where $r_i = 0.146 = 14.6\%$.

The return on this investment is fairly substantial, but keep in mind that this is only an estimate. It is, of course, subject to variation if things do not turn out as anticipated, particularly with regard to the market yield expected at the end of the holding period. This example uses annual compounding, but you could just as easily have used semiannual compounding, which, everything else being the same, would have resulted in an expected yield of 14.4% rather than the 14.6% found with annual compounding.

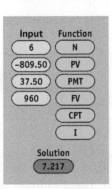

CALCULATOR USE For semiannual compounding, to find the expected return on a 7.5% bond that is currently priced in the market at $809.50 but is expected to rise to $960 within a three-year holding period, use the keystrokes shown in the margin. In this computation, PV is the current price of the bond, and FV is the expected price of the bond at the end of the (three-year) holding period. All other keystrokes are as defined earlier. To find the bond equivalent yield, double the computed value of I, 7.217%. That is 7.217% × 2 = 14.43%.

SPREADSHEET USE The expected return for semiannual compounding can also be calculated as shown on the following Excel spreadsheet. Notice that the spreadsheet shows 14.43% for the bond equivalent yield.

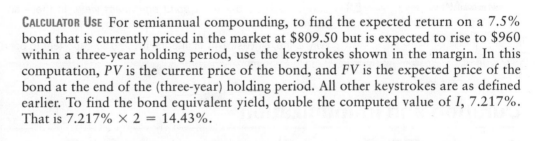

	A	B
1	**Bond's YTM**	
2	Par value	$1,000
3	Coupon rate	7.5%
4	Coupon payment frequency	2
5	Coupon payment	$37.50
6	Holding period in years	3
7	Bond's current price	-$809.50
8	Bond's future price	$960.00
9	Bond's YTM	7.22%
10	Bond-equivalent yield	14.43%
11	Entry in Cell B9 is =RATE(B6*B4,B5,B7,B8,0). The minus sign appears before the $809.50 in B7 because the price of the bond is treated as a cash outflow.	

Valuing a Bond

Depending on their objectives, investors can estimate the return that they will earn on a bond by calculating either its yield to maturity or its expected return. Conservative, income-oriented investors focus on the YTM. Earning interest income over extended periods of time is their primary objective, above earning a quick capital gain if interest rates fall. Because these investors intend to hold most of the bonds that they buy to maturity, the YTM (or the YTC) is a reliable measure of the returns that they can expect over time—assuming, of course, the reinvestment assumptions embedded in the yield measure are reasonable. More aggressive bond traders, who hope to profit from swings in market interest rates, calculate the expected return to estimate the return that they will earn on a bond. Earning capital gains by purchasing and selling bonds over relatively short holding periods is their chief concern, so the expected return is more important to them than the YTM.

In either case, the promised or expected yield provides a measure of return that investors can use to determine the relative attractiveness of fixed-income securities. But to evaluate the merits of different bonds, we must evaluate their returns and their risks. Bonds are no different from stocks in that the return (promised or expected) that they provide should be sufficient to compensate investors for the risks that they take. Thus, the greater the risk, the greater the return the bond should generate.

CONCEPTS IN REVIEW

Answers available at http://www.pearsonhighered .com/smart

8.7 What's the difference between current yield and yield to maturity? Between promised yield and realized yield? How does YTC differ from YTM?

8.8 Briefly describe the term *bond equivalent yield*. Is there any difference between promised yield and bond equivalent yield? Explain.

8.9 Why is the reinvestment of interest income so important to bond investors?

Duration and Immunization

 One of the problems with the yield to maturity is that it assumes you can reinvest the bond's periodic coupon payments at the same rate over time. If you reinvest this interest income at a lower rate (or if you spend it), your actual return will be lower than the YTM. Another flaw is that YTM assumes the investor will hold the bond to maturity. If you sell a bond prior to its maturity, the price that you receive will reflect prevailing interest rates, which means that the return that you will earn will probably differ from the YTM. If rates have moved up since you purchased the bond, the bond will sell at a discount, and your return will be less than the YTM. If interest rates have dropped, the opposite will happen.

The problem with yield to maturity, then, is that it fails to take into account the effects of reinvestment risk and price (or market) risk. To see how reinvestment and price risks behave relative to one another, consider a situation in which market interest rates have undergone a sharp decline. Under such conditions, bond prices will rise. You might be tempted to cash out your holdings and take some gains (i.e., do a little "profit taking"). Indeed, selling before maturity is the only way to take advantage of falling interest rates because a bond will pay its par value at maturity, regardless of prevailing interest rates. That's the good news about falling rates, but there is a downside. When interest rates fall, so do the opportunities to reinvest at high rates. Therefore, although you gain on the price side, you lose on the reinvestment side. Even if you don't sell out, you are faced with decreased reinvestment opportunities. To earn the YTM promised on your bonds, you must reinvest each coupon payment at the same YTM rate. Obviously, as rates fall, you'll find it increasingly difficult to reinvest the stream of coupon payments at that rate. When market rates rise, just the opposite happens. The price of the bond falls, but your reinvestment opportunities improve.

Bond investors need a measure that helps them judge just how significant these risks are for a particular bond. Such a yardstick is provided by something called **duration**. It captures in a single measure the extent to which the price of a bond will react to different interest rate environments. Because duration gauges the price volatility of a bond, it gives you a better idea of how likely you are to earn the return (YTM) you expect. That, in turn, will help you tailor your holdings to your expectations of interest rate movements.

The Concept of Duration

The concept of duration was first developed in 1938 by actuary Frederick Macaulay to help insurance companies match their cash inflows with payments. When applied to bonds, duration recognizes that the amount and frequency of interest payments, the yield to maturity, and the term to maturity all affect the interest rate risk of a particular bond. Term to maturity is important because it influences how much a bond's price will rise or fall as interest rates change. In general, when rates move, bonds with longer maturities fluctuate more than shorter issues. On the other hand, while the amount of price risk embedded in a bond is related to the issue's term to maturity, the amount of reinvestment risk is directly related to the size of a bond's coupon. Bonds that pay high coupons have greater reinvestment risk simply because there's more to reinvest.

As it turns out, both price and reinvestment risk are related in one way or another to interest rates, and therein lies the conflict. Any change in interest rates (whether up or down) will cause price risk and reinvestment risk to push and pull bonds in opposite directions. An increase in rates will produce a drop in price but will increase reinvestment opportunities. Declining rates, in contrast, will boost prices but decrease reinvestment opportunities. At some point in time, these two forces should exactly offset each other. That point in time is a bond's duration.

In general, bond duration possesses the following properties:

- Higher *coupons* result in shorter durations.

- Longer *maturities* mean longer durations.

- Higher *yields* (YTMs) lead to shorter durations.

Together these variables—coupon, maturity, and yield—interact to determine an issue's duration. Knowing a bond's duration is helpful because it captures the bond's underlying price volatility. That is, since a bond's duration and volatility are directly related, it follows that the shorter the duration, the less volatility in bond prices—and vice versa, of course.

Measuring Duration

Duration is a measure of the average maturity of a fixed-income security. The term *average maturity* may be confusing because bonds have only one final maturity date. An alternative definition of average maturity might be that it captures the average timing of the bond's cash payments. For a zero-coupon bond that makes only one cash payment on the final maturity date, the bond's duration equals its maturity. But because coupon-paying bonds make periodic interest payments, the average timing of these payments (i.e., the average maturity) is different from the actual maturity date. For instance, a 10-year bond that pays a 5% coupon each year distributes a small cash flow in year 1, in year 2, and so on up until the last and largest cash flow in year 10. Duration is a measure that puts some weight on these intermediate payments, so that the "average maturity" is a little less than 10 years.

You can think of duration as the *weighted-average life of a bond*, where the weights are the fractions of the bond's total value accounted for by each cash payment that the bond makes over its life. Mathematically, we can find the duration of a bond as follows:

Equation 8.8
$$\text{Duration} = \sum_{t=1}^{N}\left[\frac{PV(C_t)}{BP} \times t\right]$$

where

$$PV(C_t) = \text{present value of a future coupon or principal payment}$$
$$BP = \text{current market price of the bond}$$
$$t = \text{year in which the cash flow (coupon or principal) payment is received}$$
$$N = \text{number of years to maturity}$$

The duration measure obtained from Equation 8.8 is commonly referred to as *Macaulay duration*—named after the actuary who developed the concept.

Although duration is often computed using semiannual compounding, Equation 8.8 uses annual coupons and annual compounding to keep the ensuing discussion and calculations as simple as possible. Even so, the formula looks more formidable than it really is. If you follow the basic steps noted below, you'll find that duration is not tough to calculate.

Step 1. Find the present value of each annual coupon or principal payment [$PV(C_t)$]. Use the prevailing YTM on the bond as the discount rate.

Step 2. Divide this present value by the current market price of the bond (BP). This is the weight, or the fraction of the bond's total value accounted for by each individual payment. Because a bond's value is just the sum of the present values of its cash payments, these weights must sum to 1.0.

Step 3. Multiply this weight by the year in which the cash flow is to be received (t).

Step 4. Repeat steps 1 through 3 for each year in the life of the bond, and then add up the values computed in step 3.

TABLE 8.1 DURATION CALCULATION FOR A 7.5%, 15-YEAR BOND PRICED TO YIELD 8%

(1) Year t	(2) Annual Cash Flow C_t	(3) Present Value at 8% of Annual Cash Flow $(2) \div (1.08)^t$	(4) Present Value of Annual Cash Flow Divided by Price of the Bond $(3) \div \$957.20$	(5) Time-Weighted Relative Cash Flow $(1) \times (4)$
1	$ 75	$ 69.44	0.0725	0.0725
2	$ 75	$ 64.30	0.0672	0.1344
3	$ 75	$ 59.54	0.0622	0.1866
4	$ 75	$ .55.13	0.0576	0.2304
5	$ 75	$ 51.04	0.0533	0.2666
6	$ 75	$ 47.26	0.0494	0.2963
7	$ 75	$ 43.76	0.0457	0.3200
8	$ 75	$ 40.52	0.0423	0.3387
9	$ 75	$ 37.52	0.0392	0.3528
10	$ 75	$ 34.74	0.0363	0.3629
11	$ 75	$ 32.17	0.0336	0.3696
12	$ 75	$ 29.78	0.0311	0.3734
13	$ 75	$ 27.58	0.0288	0.3745
14	$ 75	$ 25.53	0.0267	0.3735
15	$1,075	$338.88	0.3540	5.3106
	Price of Bond: $957.20		1.00	Duration: 9.36 yr

Duration for a Single Bond   Table 8.1 illustrates the four-step procedure for calculating the duration of a 7.5%, 15-year bond priced at $957.20 to yield 8%. Table 8.1 provides the basic input data: Column (1) shows the year t in which each cash flow arrives. Column (2) provides the dollar amount of each annual cash flow (C_t) (coupons and principal) made by the bond. Column (3) lists the present value of each annual cash flow in year t at an 8% discount rate (which is equal to the prevailing YTM on the bond). For example, in row 1 of Table 8.1, we see that in year 1 the bond makes a $75 coupon payment, and discounting that to the present at 8% reveals that the first coupon payment has a present value of $69.44. If we sum the present value of the annual cash flows in column (3), we find that the current market price of the bond is $957.20.

Next, in column 4 we divide the present value in column 3 by the current market price of the bond. If the present value of this bond's first coupon payment is $69.45 and the total price of the bond is $957.20, then that first payment accounts for 7.25% of the bond's total value (i.e., $69.45 ÷ $957.20 = 0.0725) Therefore, 7.25% is the "weight" given to the cash payment made in year 1. If you sum the weights in column 4, you will see that they add to 1.0. Multiplying the weights from column 4 by the year t in which the cash flow arrives results in a time-weighted value for each of the annual cash flow streams shown in column 5. Adding up all the values in column 5 yields the duration of the bond. As you can see, the duration of this bond is a lot less than its maturity. In addition, keep in mind that the duration on any bond will change over time as YTM and term to maturity change. For example, the duration on this 7.5%, 15-year bond will fall as the bond nears maturity and/or as the market yield (YTM) on the bond increases.

INVESTOR FACTS

Different Bonds, Same Durations Sometimes, you really can't judge a book—or a bond, for that matter—by its cover. Here are three bonds that, on the surface, appear to be totally different:

- An 8-year, zero-coupon bond priced to yield 6%
- A 12-year, 8.5% bond that trades at a yield of 8%
- An 18-year, 10.5% bond priced to yield 13%

Although these bonds have different coupons and different maturities, they have one thing in common: they all have identical durations of eight years. Thus, if interest rates went up or down by 50 to 100 basis points, the market prices of these bonds would all behave pretty much the same!

Duration for a Portfolio of Bonds   The concept of duration is not confined to individual bonds only. It can also be applied to whole portfolios of fixed-income securities. The duration of an entire portfolio is fairly easy to calculate. All we need are the durations of the individual securities in the portfolio and their weights (i.e., the proportion that each security contributes to the overall value of the portfolio). Given this, the duration of a portfolio is the weighted average of the durations of the individual securities in the portfolio. Actually, this weighted-average approach provides only an approximate measure of duration. But it is a reasonably close approximation and, as such, is widely used in practice—so we'll use it, too.

To see how to measure duration using this approach, consider the following five-bond portfolio:

Bond	Amount Invested*	Weight	×	Bond Duration	=	Portfolio Duration
Government bonds	$ 270,000	0.15		6.25		0.9375
Aaa corporates	$ 180,000	0.10		8.90		0.8900
Aa utilities	$ 450,000	0.25		10.61		2.6525
Agency issues	$ 360,000	0.20		11.03		2.2060
Baa industrials	$ 540,000	0.30		12.55		3.7650
	$1,800.000	1.00				10.4510

*Amount invested = Current market price × Par value of the bonds. That is, if the government bonds are quoted at 90 and the investor holds $300,000 in these bonds, then 0.90 × $300,000 = $270,000.

In this case, the $1.8 million bond portfolio has an average duration of approximately 10.5 years.

If you want to change the duration of the portfolio, you can do so by (1) changing the asset mix of the portfolio (shift the weight of the portfolio to longer- or shorter-duration bonds, as desired) and/or (2) adding new bonds to the portfolio with the desired duration characteristics. As we will see below, this approach is often used in a bond portfolio strategy known as *bond immunization*.

Bond Duration and Price Volatility

A bond's price volatility is, in part, a function of its term to maturity and, in part, a function of its coupon. Unfortunately, there is no exact relationship between bond maturities and bond price volatilities with respect to interest rate changes. There is, however, a fairly close relationship between bond duration and price volatility—as long as the market doesn't experience wide swings in interest rates. A bond's duration can be used as a viable predictor of its price volatility only as long as the yield swings are relatively small (no more than 50 to 100 basis points or so). That's because as interest rates change, bond prices change in a nonlinear (convex) fashion. For example, when interest rates fall, bond prices rise at an increasing rate. When interest rates rise, bond prices fall at a decreasing rate. The duration measure essentially predicts that as interest rates change, bond prices will move in the opposite direction in a linear fashion. This means that when interest rates fall, bond prices will rise a bit faster than the duration measure would predict, and when interest rates rise, bond prices will fall at a slightly slower rate than the duration measure would predict. The bottom line is that the duration measure helps investors understand how bond prices will respond to changes in market rates, as long as those changes are not too large.

The mathematical link between changes in interest rates and changes in bond prices involves the concept of *modified duration*. To find modified duration, we simply take the (Macaulay) duration for a bond (as found from Equation 8.8) and divide it by the bond's yield to maturity.

Equation 8.9
$$\text{Modified duration} = \frac{(\text{Macaulay}) \text{ Duration in years}}{1 + \text{Yield to maturity}}$$

Thus, the modified duration for the 15-year bond discussed above is

$$\text{Modified duration} = \frac{9.36}{1 + 0.08} = \underline{8.67}$$

Note that here we use the bond's computed (Macaulay) duration of 9.36 years and the same YTM we used to compute duration in Equation 8.8; in this case, the bond was priced to yield 8%, so we use a yield to maturity of 8%.

To determine, in percentage terms, how much the price of this bond would change as market interest rates increased by 50 basis points from 8% to 8.5%, we multiply the modified duration value calculated above first by −1 (because of the inverse relationship between bond prices and interest rates) and then by the change in market interest rates. That is,

Equation 8.10
$$\begin{aligned}
\frac{\text{Percent change}}{\text{in bond price}} &= -1 \times \text{Modified duration} \times \text{Change in interest rates} \\
&= -1 \times 8.67 \times 0.5\% = \underline{-4.33}
\end{aligned}$$

Thus, a 50-basis-point (or ½ of 1%) increase in market interest rates will lead to an approximate 4.33% drop in the price of this 15-year bond. Such information is useful to bond investors seeking—or trying to avoid—price volatility.

Effective Duration

One problem with the duration measures that we've studied so far is that they do not always work well for bonds that may be called or converted before they mature. That is, the duration measures we've been using assume that the bond's future cash flows are paid as originally scheduled through maturity, but that may not be the case with callable or convertible bonds. An alternative duration measure that is used for these types of bonds is the effective duration. To calculate effective duration (ED), you use Equation 8.11:

Equation 8.11
$$\text{ED} = \frac{BP(r_i\downarrow) - BP(r_i\uparrow)}{2 \times BP \times \Delta r_i}$$

where

$BP(r_i\uparrow)$ = the new price of the bond if market interest rates go up
$BP(r_i\downarrow)$ = the new price of the bond if market interest rates go down
BP = the original price of the bond
Δr_i = the change in market interest rates

Example

Suppose you want to know the effective duration of a 25-year bond that pays a 6% coupon semiannually. The bond is currently priced at $882.72 for a yield of 7%. Now suppose the bond's yield goes up by 0.5% to 7.5%. At that yield the new price would be $831.74 (using a calculator, N = 50, I = 3.75, PMT = 30, and PV = 1,000). What if the yield drops by 0.5% to 6.5%? In that case, the price rises to $938.62 (N = 50, I = 3.25, PMT = 30, PV = 1,000). Now we can use Equation 8.11 to calculate the bond's effective duration.

Effective duration = ($938.62 − $831.74) ÷ (2 × $882.72 × 0.005) = 12.11

This means that if interest rates rise or fall by a full percentage point, the price of the bond would fall or rise by approximately 12.11%. Note that you can use effective duration in place of modified duration in Equation 8.10 to find the percent change in the price of a bond when interest rates move by more or less than 1.0%. When calculating the effective duration of a callable bond, one modification may be necessary. If the calculated price of the bond when interest rates fall is greater than the bond's call price, then use the call price in the equation rather than $BP(r_i\downarrow)$ and proceed as before.

Uses of Bond Duration Measures

You can use duration analysis in many ways to guide your decisions about investing in bonds. For example, as we saw earlier, you can use modified duration or effective duration to measure the potential price volatility of a particular issue. Another equally important use of duration is in the structuring of bond portfolios. That is, if you thought that interest rates were about to increase, you could reduce the overall duration of the portfolio by selling higher-duration bonds and buying shorter-duration bonds. Such a strategy could prove useful because shorter-duration bonds do not decline in value to the same degree as longer-duration bonds. On the other hand, if you felt that interest rates were about to decline, the opposite strategy would be appropriate.

Active, short-term investors frequently use duration analysis in their day-to-day operations. Longer-term investors also employ it in planning their investment decisions. Indeed, a strategy known as *bond portfolio immunization* represents one of the most important uses of duration.

Bond Immunization Some investors hold portfolios of bonds not for the purpose of "beating the market," but rather to accumulate a specified level of wealth by the end of a given investment horizon. For these investors, bond portfolio **immunization** often proves to be of great value. Immunization allows you to derive a specified rate of return from bond investments over a given investment interval regardless of what happens to market interest rates over the course of the holding period. In essence, you are able to "immunize" your portfolio from the effects of changes in market interest rates over a given investment horizon.

To understand how and why bond portfolio immunization is possible, you will recall from our earlier discussion that changes in market interest rates will lead to two distinct and opposite changes in bond valuation. The first effect is known as the *price effect*, and the second is known as the *reinvestment effect*. Whereas an increase in rates has a negative effect on a bond's price, it has a positive effect on the reinvestment of coupons. Therefore, when interest rate changes do occur, the price and reinvestment effects work against each other from the standpoint of the investor's wealth.

Excel@Investing

TABLE 8.2 BOND IMMUNIZATION

Year t	Cash Flow from Bond						Terminal Value of Reinvested Cash Flow
1	$ 80	×	$(1.08)^4$	×	$(1.06)^3$	=	$ 129.63
2	$ 80	×	$(1.08)^3$	×	$(1.06)^3$	=	$ 120.03
3	$ 80	×	$(1.08)^2$	×	$(1.06)^3$	=	$ 111.14
4	$ 80	×	(1.08)	×	$(1.06)^3$	=	$ 102.90
5	$ 80	×	$(1.06)^3$			=	$ 95.28
6	$ 80	×	$(1.06)^2$			=	$ 89.89
7	$ 80	×	(1.06)			=	$ 84.80
8	$ 80					=	$ 80.00
8	$1,036.67						$1,036.67
					Total		$1,850.33
					Investor's required wealth at 8%		$1,850.93
					Difference		$ 0.60

When the average duration of the portfolio just equals the investment horizon, these counteracting effects offset each other and leave your position unchanged. This should not come as much of a surprise because such a property is already embedded in the duration measure. If that relationship applies to a single bond, it should also apply to the weighted-average duration of a whole bond portfolio. When such a condition (of offsetting price and reinvestment effects) exists, a bond portfolio is immunized. More specifically, your wealth is immunized from the effects of interest rate changes when the weighted-average duration of the bond portfolio exactly equals your desired investment horizon. Table 8.2 provides an example of bond immunization using a 10-year, 8% coupon bond with a duration of 8 years. Here, we assume that your desired investment horizon is also 8 years.

The example in Table 8.2 assumes that you originally purchased the 8% coupon bond at par. It further assumes that market interest rates for bonds of this quality drop from 8% to 6% at the end of the fifth year. Because you had an investment horizon of exactly 8 years and desire to lock in an interest rate return of exactly 8%, it follows that you expect to accumulate cash totaling $1,850.93 [i.e., $1,000 invested at 8% for 8 years = $1,000 × $(1.08)^8$ = $1,850.93], regardless of interest rate changes in the interim. As you can see from the results in Table 8.2, the immunization strategy netted you a total of $1,850.33—just 60 cents short of your desired goal. Note that in this case, although reinvestment opportunities declined in years 5, 6, and 7 (when market interest rates dropped to 6%), that same lower rate led to a higher market price for the bond. That higher price, in turn, provided enough capital gains to offset the loss in reinvested income. This remarkable result clearly demonstrates the power of bond immunization and the versatility of bond duration. And note that even though the table uses a single bond for purposes of illustration, the same results can be obtained from a bond portfolio that is maintained at the proper weighted-average duration.

Maintaining a fully immunized portfolio (of more than one bond) requires continual portfolio rebalancing. Indeed, every time interest rates change, the duration of a portfolio changes. Because effective immunization requires that the portfolio have a duration value equal in length to the remaining investment horizon, the composition of the portfolio must be rebalanced each time interest rates change. Further, even in the absence of interest rate changes, a bond's duration declines more slowly than its term to maturity. This, of course, means that the mere passage of time will dictate changes in portfolio composition. Such changes will ensure that the duration of the portfolio continues to match the remaining time in the investment horizon. In summary, portfolio immunization strategies can be extremely effective, but immunization is not a passive strategy and is not without potential problems, the most notable of which are associated with portfolio rebalancing.

8.10 What does the term *duration* mean to bond investors and how does the duration of a bond differ from its maturity? What is modified duration, and how is it used? What is effective duration, and how does it differ from modified duration?

8.11 Describe the process of bond portfolio immunization, and explain why an investor would want to immunize a portfolio. Would you consider portfolio immunization a passive investment strategy comparable to, say, a buy-and-hold approach? Explain.

Bond Investment Strategies

Generally speaking, bond investors tend to follow one of three kinds of investment programs. First, there are those who live off the income. They are conservative, quality-conscious, income-oriented investors who seek to maximize current income. Second, there are the speculators (bond traders). Their investment objective is to maximize capital gains, often within a short time span. Finally, there are the long-term investors. Their objective is to maximize total return—from both current income and capital gains—over fairly long holding periods.

In order to achieve the objectives of any of these programs, you need to adopt a strategy that is compatible with your goals. Professional money managers use a variety of techniques to manage the multimillion- (or multibillion-) dollar bond portfolios under their direction. These range from passive approaches, to semiactive strategies, to active, fully managed strategies using interest rate forecasting and yield spread analysis. Most of these strategies are fairly complex and require substantial computer support. Even so, we can look briefly at some of the more basic strategies to gain an appreciation of the different ways in which you can use fixed-income securities to reach different investment objectives.

Passive Strategies

The bond immunization strategies we discussed earlier are considered to be primarily passive in nature. Investors using these tools typically are not attempting to beat the market but to lock in specified rates of return that they deem acceptable, given the risks involved. As a rule, passive investment strategies are characterized by a lack of input regarding investor expectations of changes in interest rates and/or bond prices. Further, these strategies typically do not generate significant transaction costs. A buy-and-hold strategy is perhaps the most passive of all investment strategies. All that is required is that the investor replace bonds that have deteriorating credit ratings, have matured, or have been called. Although buy-and-hold investors restrict their ability to earn above-average returns, they also minimize the losses that transaction costs represent.

One popular approach that is a bit more active than buy-and-hold is the use of **bond ladders**. In this strategy, equal amounts are invested in a series of bonds with staggered maturities. Here's how a bond ladder works. Suppose you want to confine your investing to fixed-income securities with maturities of 10 years or less. Given that maturity constraint, you could set up a ladder by investing (roughly) equal amounts in, say, 3-, 5-, 7-, and 10-year issues. When the 3-year issue matures, you would put the money from it (along with any new capital) into a new 10-year note. You would continue this rolling-over process so that eventually you would hold a full ladder of staggered 10-year notes. By rolling into new 10-year issues every 2 or 3 years, the interest income on your portfolio will be an average of the rates available over time. The laddered approach is a safe, simple, and almost automatic way of investing for the long haul. A key ingredient of this or any other passive strategy is, of course, the use of high-quality investments that possess attractive features, maturities, and yields.

Trading on Forecasted Interest Rate Behavior

In contrast to passive strategies, a more risky approach to bond investing is the *forecasted interest rate* approach. Here, investors seek attractive capital gains when they expect interest rates to decline and preservation of capital when they anticipate an increase in interest rates. This strategy is risky because it relies on the imperfect forecast of future interest rates. The idea is to increase the return on a bond portfolio by making strategic moves in anticipation of interest rate changes. Such a strategy is essentially *market timing*. An unusual feature of this tactic is that most of the trading is done with investment-grade securities because these securities are the most sensitive to interest rate movements, and that sensitivity is what active traders hope to profit from.

This strategy brings together interest rate forecasts and the concept of duration. For example, when a decline in rates is anticipated, aggressive bond investors often seek to lengthen the duration of their bonds (or bond portfolios) because bonds with longer durations (e.g., long-term bonds) rise more in price than do bonds with shorter durations. At the same time, investors look for low-coupon and/or moderately discounted bonds because these bonds have higher durations, and their prices will rise more when interest rates fall. Interest rate swings may be short-lived, so bond traders try to earn as much as possible in as short a time as possible. When rates start to level off and move up, these investors begin to shift their money out of long, discounted bonds and into high-yielding issues with short maturities. In other words, they do a complete reversal and look for bonds with shorter durations. During those periods when bond prices are dropping, investors are more concerned about preservation of capital, so they take steps to protect their money from capital losses. Thus, they tend to use such short-term obligations as Treasury bills, money funds, short-term (two- to five-year) notes, or even variable-rate notes.

Bond Swaps

In a **bond swap**, an investor simultaneously liquidates one position and buys a different issue to take its place. Swaps can be executed to increase current yield or yield to maturity, to take advantage of shifts in interest rates, to improve the quality of a portfolio, or for tax purposes. Although some swaps are highly sophisticated, most are fairly simple transactions. They go by a variety of colorful names, such as "profit takeout," "substitution swap," and "tax swap," but they are all used for one basic reason: portfolio improvement. We will briefly review two types of bond swaps that are fairly simple and hold considerable appeal: the yield pickup swap and the tax swap.

In a **yield pickup swap**, an investor switches out of a low-coupon bond into a comparable higher-coupon issue in order to realize an instantaneous pickup of current yield and yield to maturity. For example, you would be executing a yield pickup swap if you sold 20-year, A-rated, 6.5% bonds (which were yielding 8% at the time) and replaced them with an equal amount of 20-year, A-rated, 7% bonds that were priced to yield 8.5%. By executing the swap, you would improve your current yield (your interest income would increase from $65 a year to $70 a year) as well as your yield to maturity (from 8% to 8.5%). Such swap opportunities arise because of the yield spreads that normally exist between different types of bonds. You can execute such swaps simply by watching for swap candidates and asking your broker to do so. In fact, the only thing you must be careful of is that transaction costs do not eat up all the profits.

Another popular type of swap is the **tax swap**, which is also relatively simple and involves few risks. You can use this technique whenever you have a substantial tax liability as a result of selling some security holdings at a profit. The objective is to execute a swap to eliminate or substantially reduce the tax liability accompanying the capital gains. This is done by selling an issue that has undergone a capital loss and replacing it with a comparable obligation.

For example, assume that you had $10,000 worth of corporate bonds that you sold (in the current year) for $15,000, resulting in a capital gain of $5,000. You can eliminate the tax liability accompanying the capital gain by selling securities that have capital losses of $5,000. Let's assume you find you hold a 20-year, 4.75% municipal bond that has undergone a $5,000 drop in value. Thus, you have the required tax shield in your portfolio. Now you need to find a viable swap candidate. Suppose you find a comparable 20-year, 5% municipal issue currently trading at about the same price as the issue being sold. By selling the 4.75s and simultaneously buying a comparable amount of the 5s, you will not only increase your tax-free yields (from 4.75% to 5%) but will also eliminate the capital gains tax liability.

The only precaution in doing tax swaps is that you cannot use identical issues in the swap transactions. The IRS would consider that a "wash sale" and disallow the loss. Moreover, the capital loss must occur in the same taxable year as the capital gain. Typically, at year-end, tax loss sales and tax swaps multiply as knowledgeable investors hurry to establish capital losses.

CONCEPTS IN REVIEW

Answers available at
http://www.pearsonhighered.com/smart

8.12 Briefly describe a bond ladder and note how and why an investor would use this investment strategy. What is a tax swap and why would it be used?

8.13 What strategy would you expect an aggressive bond investor (someone who's looking for capital gains) to employ?

8.14 Why is interest sensitivity important to bond speculators? Does the need for interest sensitivity explain why active bond traders tend to use high-grade issues? Explain.

MyFinanceLab

Here is what you should know after reading this chapter. MyFinanceLab will help you identify what you know and where to go when you need to practice.

What You Should Know	Key Terms	Where to Practice
LG1 **Explain the behavior of market interest rates and identify the forces that cause interest rates to change.** The behavior of interest rates is the most important force in the bond market. It determines not only the amount of current income an investor will receive but also the investor's capital gains (or losses). Changes in market interest rates can have a dramatic impact on the total returns obtained from bonds over time.	yield spreads, *p. 259*	MyFinanceLab Study Plan 8.1
LG2 **Describe the term structure of interest rates and note how investors can use yield curves.** Many forces drive the behavior of interest rates over time, including inflation, the cost and availability of funds, and the level of interest rates in major foreign markets. One particularly important force is the term structure of interest rates, which relates yield to maturity to term to maturity. Yield curves essentially plot the term structure and are often used by investors as a way to get a handle on the future behavior of interest rates.	expectations hypothesis, *p. 265* liquidity preference theory, *p. 266* market segmentation theory, *p. 266* term structure of interest rates, *p. 262* yield curve, *p. 262*	MyFinanceLab Study Plan 8.2
LG3 **Understand how investors value bonds in the marketplace.** Bonds are valued (priced) in the marketplace on the basis of their required rates of return (or market yields). The process of pricing a bond begins with the yield it should provide. Once that piece of information is known (or estimated), a standard, present value-based model is used to find the dollar price of a bond.	accrued interest, *p. 271* clean price, *p. 272* dirty price, *p. 272*	MyFinanceLab Study Plan 8.3 Video Learning Aid for Problems P8.1, P8.2
LG4 **Describe the various measures of yield and return and explain how investors use these standards of performance to value bonds.** Four types of yields are important to investors: current yield, promised yield, yield to call, and expected yield (or return). Promised yield (yield to maturity) is the most widely used bond valuation measure. It captures both the current income and the price appreciation of an issue. Yield to call, which assumes the bond will be outstanding only until its first (or some other) call date, also captures both current income and price appreciation. The expected return, in contrast, is a valuation measure used by aggressive bond traders to show the total return that can be earned from trading in and out of a bond long before it matures.	bond equivalent yield, *p. 274* current yield, *p. 272* expected return, *p. 278* promised yield, *p. 273* realized yield, *p. 278* yield to call (YTC), *p. 277* yield to maturity (YTM), *p. 277*	MyFinanceLab Study Plan 8.4

What You Should Know	Key Terms	Where to Practice
LG5 Understand the basic concept of duration, how it can be measured, and its use in the management of bond portfolios. Bond duration takes into account the effects of both reinvestment and price (or market) risks. It captures in a single measure the extent to which the price of a bond will react to different interest rate environments. Equally important, duration can be used to immunize whole bond portfolios from the often-devastating forces of changing market interest rates.	duration, *p. 281* immunization, *p. 286*	MyFinanceLab Study Plan 8.5 Excel Tables 8.1, 8.2
LG6 Discuss various bond investment strategies and the different ways investors can use these securities. Bonds can be used as a source of income, as a way to seek capital gains by speculating on interest rate movement, or as a way to earn long-term returns. Investors often employ one or more of the following strategies: passive strategies such as buy-and-hold, bond ladders, and portfolio immunization; bond trading based on forecasted interest rate behavior; and bond swaps.	bond ladders, *p. 289* bond swap, *p. 289* tax swap, *p. 290* yield pickup swap, *p. 290*	MyFinanceLab Study Plan 8.6

Log into MyFinanceLab, take a chapter test, and get a personalized Study Plan
that tells you which concepts you understand and which ones you need to
review. From there, MyFinanceLab will give you further practice, tutorials,
animations, videos, and guided solutions.
Log into http://www.myfinancelab.com

Discussion Questions

LG1   **Q8.1**   Briefly describe each of the following theories of the term structure of interest rates.
a. Expectations hypothesis
b. Liquidity preference theory
c. Market segmentation theory

According to these theories, what conditions would result in a downward-sloping yield curve? What conditions would result in an upward-sloping yield curve? Which theory do you think is most valid, and why?

LG2   **Q8.2**   Using the *Wall Street Journal*, *Barron's*, or an online source, find the bond yields for Treasury securities with the following maturities: 3 months, 6 months, 1 year, 3 years, 5 years, 10 years, 15 years, and 20 years. Construct a yield curve based on these reported yields, putting term to maturity on the horizontal (x) axis and yield to maturity on the vertical (y) axis. Briefly discuss the general shape of your yield curve. What conclusions might you draw about future interest rate movements from this yield curve?

LG5   **Q8.3**   Briefly explain what will happen to a bond's duration measure if each of the following events occur.
a. The yield to maturity on the bond falls from 8.5% to 8%.
b. The bond gets 1 year closer to its maturity.

c. Market interest rates go from 8% to 9%.

d. The bond's modified duration falls by half a year.

LG6 **Q8.4** Assume that an investor comes to you looking for advice. She has $200,000 to invest and wants to put it all into bonds.

a. If she considers herself a fairly aggressive investor who is willing to take the risks necessary to generate the big returns, what kind of investment strategy (or strategies) would you suggest? Be specific.

b. What kind of investment strategies would you recommend if your client were a very conservative investor who could not tolerate market losses?

c. What kind of investor do you think is most likely to use

1. an immunized bond portfolio?

2. a yield pickup swap?

3. a bond ladder?

4. a long-term, zero-coupon bond when interest rates fall?

LG4 LG5 **Q8.5** Using the resources at your campus or public library (or on the Internet), select any six bonds you like, consisting of two Treasury bonds, two corporate bonds, and two agency issues. Determine the latest current yield and promised yield for each. (For promised yield, use annual compounding.) In addition, find the duration and modified duration for each bond.

a. Assuming that you put an equal amount of money into each of the six bonds you selected, find the duration for this six-bond portfolio.

b. What would happen to your bond portfolio if market interest rates fell by 100 basis points?

c. Assuming that you have $100,000 to invest, use at least four of these bonds to develop a bond portfolio that emphasizes either the potential for capital gains or the preservation of capital. Briefly explain your logic.

Problems

All problems are available on http://www.myfinancelab.com

LG3 **P8.1** You are considering the purchase of a $1,000 par value bond with an 6.5% coupon rate (with interest paid semiannually) that matures in 12 years. If the bond is priced to provide a required return of 8%, what is the bond's current price?

LG3 **P8.2** Two bonds have par values of $1,000. One is a 5%, 15-year bond priced to yield 8%. The other is a 7.5%, 20-year bond priced to yield 6%. Which of these has the lower price? (Assume annual compounding in both cases.)

LG3 **P8.3** Using semiannual compounding, find the prices of the following bonds.

a. A 10.5%, 15-year bond priced to yield 8%

b. A 7%, 10-year bond priced to yield 8%

c. A 12%, 20-year bond priced at 10%

Repeat the problem using annual compounding. Then comment on the differences you found in the prices of the bonds.

LG3 **P8.4** You have the opportunity to purchase a 25-year, $1,000 par value bond that has an annual coupon rate of 9%. If you require a YTM of 7.6%, how much is the bond worth to you?

LG3 **P8.5** A $1,000 par value bond has a current price of $800 and a maturity value of $1,000 and matures in five years. If interest is paid semiannually and the bond is priced to yield 8%, what is the bond's annual coupon rate?

LG3 **P8.6** A 20-year bond has a coupon of 10% and is priced to yield 8%. Calculate the price per $1,000 par value using semiannual compounding. If an investor purchases this bond two months before a scheduled coupon payment, how much accrued interest must be paid to the seller?

LG4   **P8.7**   Three years ago you purchased a 10% coupon bond that pays semiannual coupon payments for $975. What would be your bond equivalent yield if you sold the bond for current market price of $1,050?

LG4   **P8.8**   A bond is priced in the market at $1,150 and has a coupon of 8%. Calculate the bond's current yield.

LG4   **P8.9**   A $1,000 par value bond with a 7.25% coupon rate (semiannual interest) matures in seven years and currently sells for $987. What is the bond's yield to maturity and bond equivalent yield?

LG4   **P8.10**   What is the current yield for a $1,000 par value bond that pays interest semiannually, has nine years to maturity, and is currently selling for $937 with a bond equivalent yield of 12%?

LG3   **P8.11**   An investor is considering the purchase of an 8%, 18-year corporate bond that's being priced to yield 10%. She thinks that in a year, this bond will be priced in the market to yield 9%. Using annual compounding, find the price of the bond today and in one year. Next, find the holding period return on this investment, assuming that the investor's expectations are borne out.

LG4   **P8.12**   You notice in the WSJ a bond that is currently selling in the market for $1,070 with a coupon of 11% and a 20-year maturity. Using annual compounding, calculate the promised yield on this bond.

LG4   **P8.13**   A bond is currently selling in the market for $1,098.62. It has a coupon of 9% and a 20-year maturity. Using annual compounding, calculate the yield to maturity on this bond.

LG4   **P8.14**   Compute the current yield of a 10%, 25-year bond that is currently priced in the market at $1,200. Use annual compounding to find the promised yield on this bond. Repeat the promised yield calculation, but this time use semiannual compounding to find yield to maturity.

LG4   **P8.15**   You are evaluating an outstanding issue of $1,000 par value bonds with an 8.75% coupon rate that mature in 25 years and make quarterly interest payments. If the current market price for the bonds is $865, what is the quoted annual yield to maturity for the bonds?

LG4   **P8.16**   A 10%, 25-year bond has a par value of $1,000 and a call price of $1,075. (The bond's first call date is in five years.) Coupon payments are made semiannually (so use semiannual compounding where appropriate).
a. Find the current yield, YTM, and YTC on this issue, given that it is currently being priced in the market at $1,200. Which of these three yields is the highest? Which is the lowest? Which yield would you use to value this bond? Explain.
b. Repeat the three calculations above, given that the bond is being priced at $850. Now which yield is the highest? Which is the lowest? Which yield would you use to value this bond? Explain.

LG4   **P8.17**   Assume that an investor is looking at two bonds: Bond A is a 20-year, 9% (semiannual pay) bond that is priced to yield 10.5%. Bond B is a 20-year, 8% (annual pay) bond that is priced to yield 7.5%. Both bonds carry 5-year call deferments and call prices (in 5 years) of $1,050.
a. Which bond has the higher current yield?
b. Which bond has the higher YTM?
c. Which bond has the higher YTC?

LG4   **P8.18**   A zero-coupon bond that matures in 15 years is currently selling for $209 per $1,000 par value. What is the promised yield on this bond?

LG4   **P8.19**   What is the price of a zero-coupon ($1,000 par value) bond that matures in 20 years and has a promised yield of 9.5%?

LG4   **P8.20**   A 25-year, zero-coupon bond was recently being quoted at 11.625% of par. Find the current yield and the promised yield of this issue, given that the bond has a par value of $1,000. Using semiannual compounding, determine how much an investor would have to pay for this bond if it were priced to yield 12%.

LG4 **P8.21** Assume that an investor pays $800 for a long-term bond that carries an 8% coupon. In three years, he hopes to sell the issue for $950. If his expectations come true, what yield will this investor realize? (Use annual compounding.) What would the holding period return be if he were able to sell the bond (at $950) after only nine months?

LG4 **P8.22** Using annual compounding, find the yield to maturity for each of the following bonds.
a. A 9.5%, 20-year bond priced at $957.43
b. A 16%, 15-year bond priced at $1,684.76
c. A 5.5%, 18-year bond priced at $510.65

Now assume that each of the above bonds is callable as follows: Bond **a** is callable in seven years at a call price of $1,095; bond **b** is callable in five years at $1,250; and bond **c** is callable in three years at $1,050. Use annual compounding to find the yield to call for each bond.

LG5 **P8.23** A bond has a Macaulay duration equal to 9.5 and a yield to maturity of 7.5%. What is the modified duration of this bond?

LG5 **P8.24** A bond has a Macaulay duration of 8.62 and is priced to yield 8%. If interest rates go up so that the yield goes to 8.5%, what will be the percentage change in the price of the bond? Now, if the yield on this bond goes down to 7.5%, what will be the bond's percentage change in price? Comment on your findings.

LG5 **P8.25** An investor wants to find the duration of a 25-year, 6% semiannual-pay, noncallable bond that's currently priced in the market at $882.72, to yield 7%. Using a 50 basis point change in yield, find the effective duration of this bond. (Hint: Use Equation 8.11.)

LG5 **P8.26** Find the Macaulay duration and the modified duration of a 20-year, 10% corporate bond priced to yield 8%. According to the modified duration of this bond, how much of a price change would this bond incur if market yields rose to 9%? Using annual compounding, calculate the price of this bond in one year if rates do rise to 9%. How does this price change compare to that predicted by the modified duration? Explain the difference.

LG5 **P8.27** Which one of the following bonds would you select if you thought market interest rates were going to fall by 50 basis points over the next six months?
a. A bond with a Macaulay duration of 8.46 years that's currently being priced to yield 7.5%
b. A bond with a Macaulay duration of 9.30 years that's priced to yield 10%
c. A bond with a Macaulay duration of 8.75 years that's priced to yield 5.75%

LG5 **LG6** **P8.28** Stacy Picone is an aggressive bond trader who likes to speculate on interest rate swings. Market interest rates are currently at 9%, but she expects them to fall to 7% within a year. As a result, Stacy is thinking about buying either a 25-year, zero-coupon bond or a 20-year, 7.5% bond. (Both bonds have $1,000 par values and carry the same agency rating.) Assuming that Stacy wants to maximize capital gains, which of the two issues should she select? What if she wants to maximize the total return (interest income and capital gains) from her investment? Why did one issue provide better capital gains than the other? Based on the duration of each bond, which one should be more price volatile?

LG5 **LG6** **P8.29** Elliot Karlin is a 35-year-old bank executive who has just inherited a large sum of money. Having spent several years in the bank's investments department, he's well aware of the concept of duration and decides to apply it to his bond portfolio. In particular, Elliot intends to use $1 million of his inheritance to purchase four U.S. Treasury bonds:
a. An 8.5%, 13-year bond that's priced at $1,045 to yield 7.47%
b. A 7.875%, 15-year bond that's priced at $1,020 to yield 7.60%
c. A 20-year stripped Treasury that's priced at $202 to yield 8.22%
d. A 24-year, 7.5% bond that's priced at $955 to yield 7.90%
1. Find the duration and the modified duration of each bond.
2. Find the duration of the whole bond portfolio if Elliot puts $250,000 into each of the four U.S. Treasury bonds.
3. Find the duration of the portfolio if Elliot puts $360,000 each into bonds **a** and **c** and $140,000 each into bonds **b** and **d**.

4. Which portfolio—b or c—should Elliot select if he thinks rates are about to head up and he wants to avoid as much price volatility as possible? Explain. From which portfolio does he stand to make more in annual interest income? Which portfolio would you recommend, and why?

Visit **http://www.myfinancelab.com** for web exercises, spreadsheets, and other online resources.

Case problem 8.1   The Bond Investment Decisions of Dave and Marlene Carter

LG3 LG4 LG6   Dave and Marlene Carter live in the Boston area, where Dave has a successful orthodontics practice. Dave and Marlene have built up a sizable investment portfolio and have always had a major portion of their investments in fixed-income securities. They adhere to a fairly aggressive investment posture and actively go after both attractive current income and substantial capital gains. Assume that it is now 2016 and Marlene is currently evaluating two investment decisions: one involves an addition to their portfolio, the other a revision to it.

The Carters' first investment decision involves a short-term trading opportunity. In particular, Marlene has a chance to buy a 7.5%, 25-year bond that is currently priced at $852 to yield 9%; she feels that in two years the promised yield of the issue should drop to 8%.

The second is a bond swap. The Carters hold some Beta Corporation 7%, 2029 bonds that are currently priced at $785. They want to improve both current income and yield to maturity and are considering one of three issues as a possible swap candidate: (a) Dental Floss, Inc., 7.5%, 2041, currently priced at $780; (b) Root Canal Products of America, 6.5%, 2029, selling at $885; and (c) Kansas City Dental Insurance, 8%, 2030, priced at $950. All of the swap candidates are of comparable quality and have comparable issue characteristics.

Questions

a. Regarding the short-term trading opportunity:

1. What basic trading principle is involved in this situation?

2. If Marlene's expectations are correct, what will the price of this bond be in two years?

3. What is the expected return on this investment?

4. Should this investment be made? Why?

b. Regarding the bond swap opportunity:

1. Compute the current yield and the promised yield (use semiannual compounding) for the bond the Carters currently hold and for each of the three swap candidates.

2. Do any of the swap candidates provide better current income and/or current yield than the Beta Corporation bonds the Carters now hold? If so, which one(s)?

3. Do you see any reason why Marlene should switch from her present bond holding into one of the other issues? If so, which swap candidate would be the best choice? Why?

Case problem 8.2   Grace Decides to Immunize Her Portfolio

LG4 LG5 LG6   Grace Hesketh is the owner of an extremely successful dress boutique in downtown Chicago. Although high fashion is Grace's first love, she's also interested in investments, particularly bonds and other fixed-income securities. She actively manages her own investments and over time has built up a substantial portfolio of securities. She's well versed on the latest investment techniques and is not afraid to apply those procedures to her own investments.

Grace has been playing with the idea of trying to immunize a big chunk of her bond portfolio. She'd like to cash out this part of her portfolio in seven years and use the proceeds to buy a vacation home in her home state of Oregon. To do this, she intends to use the $200,000 she now has invested in the following four corporate bonds (she currently has $50,000 invested in each one).

1. A 12-year, 7.5% bond that's currently priced at $895
2. A 10-year, zero-coupon bond priced at $405
3. A 10-year, 10% bond priced at $1,080
4. A 15-year, 9.25% bond priced at $980

(*Note:* These are all noncallable, investment-grade, nonconvertible/straight bonds.)

Questions

a. Given the information provided, find the current yield and the promised yield for each bond in the portfolio. (Use annual compounding.)

b. Calculate the Macaulay and modified durations of each bond in the portfolio and indicate how the price of each bond would change if interest rates were to rise by 75 basis points. How would the price change if interest rates were to fall by 75 basis points?

c. Find the duration of the current four-bond portfolio. Given the seven-year target that Grace has set, would you consider this an immunized portfolio? Explain.

d. How could you lengthen or shorten the duration of this portfolio? What's the shortest portfolio duration you can achieve? What's the longest?

e. Using one or more of the four bonds described above, is it possible to come up with a $200,000 bond portfolio that will exhibit the duration characteristics Grace is looking for? Explain.

f. Using one or more of the four bonds, put together a $200,000 immunized portfolio for Grace. Because this portfolio will now be immunized, will Grace be able to treat it as a buy-and-hold portfolio-one she can put away and forget about? Explain.

Excel@Investing

 Excel@Investing

All bonds are priced according to the present value of their future cash flow streams. The key components of bond valuation are par value, coupon interest rate, term to maturity, and market yield. It is market yield that drives bond prices. In the market for bonds, the appropriate yield at which the bond should sell is determined first, and then that yield is used to find the market value of the bond. The market yield can also be referred to as the required rate of return. It implies that this is the rate of return that a rational investor requires before he or she will invest in a given fixed-income security.

Create a spreadsheet to model and answer the following bond valuation questions.

Questions

a. One of the bond issues outstanding by H&W Corporation has an annual-pay coupon of 5.625% plus a par value of $1,000 at maturity. This bond has a remaining maturity of 23 years. The required rate of return on securities of similar-risk grade is 6.76%. What is the value of this corporate bond today?

b. What is the current yield for the H&W bond?

c. In the case of the H&W bond issue from question a, if the coupon interest payment is compounded on a semiannual basis, what would be the value of this security today?

d. How would the price of the H&W bond react to changing market interest rates? To find out, determine how the price of the issue reacts to changes in the bond's yield to maturity. Find the value of the security when the YTM is (1) 5.625%, (2) 8.0%, and (3) 4.5%. Label your findings as being a premium, par, or discount bond. Comment on your findings.

e. The Jay & Austin Company has a bond issue outstanding with the following characteristics: par of $1,000, a semiannual-pay coupon of 6.5%, remaining maturity of 22 years, and a current price of $878.74. What is the bond's YTM?

9

Stock Valuation

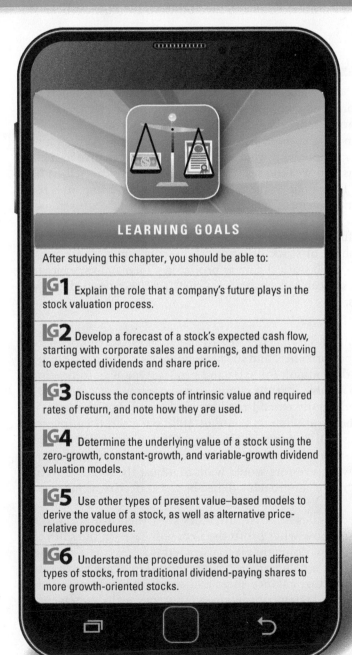

LEARNING GOALS

After studying this chapter, you should be able to:

LG1 Explain the role that a company's future plays in the stock valuation process.

LG2 Develop a forecast of a stock's expected cash flow, starting with corporate sales and earnings, and then moving to expected dividends and share price.

LG3 Discuss the concepts of intrinsic value and required rates of return, and note how they are used.

LG4 Determine the underlying value of a stock using the zero-growth, constant-growth, and variable-growth dividend valuation models.

LG5 Use other types of present value–based models to derive the value of a stock, as well as alternative price-relative procedures.

LG6 Understand the procedures used to value different types of stocks, from traditional dividend-paying shares to more growth-oriented stocks.

What drives a stock's value? Many factors come into play, including how much profit the company earns, how its new products fare in the marketplace, and the overall state of the economy. But what matters most is what investors believe about the company's future.

Nothing illustrates this principle better than the stock of the oil driller, Helmerich & Payne (ticker symbol HP). The company announced its financial results for the first quarter of its fiscal year on January 29, 2015, reporting earnings per share of $1.85 with total revenue of $1.06 billion. Wall Street stock analysts had been expecting the company to earn just $1.55 per share with $977 million in total revenue, so the company's performance was much better than expected. Even so, HP's stock price slid nearly 5% in response to the earnings news. Why would investors drive down the stock price of a company that was outperforming expectations? The answer had to do with the company's future rather than its past earnings. In its earnings report, HP warned investors that its earnings for the rest of 2015 would likely be hit by falling oil prices. Indeed, in early 2015 oil prices were lower than they had been in six years, and many analysts believed that the market had not yet hit bottom. Stock analysts who followed HP acknowledged that the company had experienced solid revenue growth and used a reasonable amount of debt. Nevertheless, these analysts advised investors who did not already own HP to stay away from the stock because of the company's poor return on equity and lackluster growth in earnings per share.

How do investors determine a stock's true value? This chapter explains how to determine a stock's intrinsic value by using dividends, free cash flow, price/earnings, and other valuation models.

(Source: Richard Saintvilus, "Helmerich & Payne Stock Falls on Outlook Despite Earnings Beat," http://www.thestreet.com/story/13027986/1/helmerich-payne-stock-falls-on-outlook-despite-earnings-beat.html, accessed on May 27, 2015.)

Valuation: Obtaining a Standard of Performance

LG1 LG2 LG3 Obtaining an estimate of a stock's intrinsic value that investors can use to judge the merits of a share of stock is the underlying purpose of **stock valuation**. Investors attempt to resolve the question of whether and to what extent a stock is under- or over-valued by comparing its current market price to its intrinsic value. At any given time, the price of a share of stock depends on investors' expectations about the future performance of the company. When the outlook for the company improves, its stock price will probably go up. If investors' expectations become less rosy, the price of the stock will probably go down.

Valuing a Company Based on Its Future Performance

Thus far we have examined several aspects of security analysis including macroeconomic factors, industry factors, and company-specific factors. But as we've said, for stock valuation the future matters more than the past. The primary reason for looking at past performance is to gain insight about the firm's future direction. Although past performance provides no guarantees about what the future holds, it can give us a good idea of a company's strengths and weaknesses. For example, history can tell us how well the company's products have done in the marketplace, how the company's fiscal health shapes up, and how management tends to respond to difficult situations. In short, the past can reveal how well the company is positioned to take advantage of the things that may occur in the future.

Because the value of a share of stock depends on the company's future performance, an investor's task is to use historical data to project key financial variables into the future. In this way, he or she can judge whether a stock's market price aligns well with the company's prospects.

Forecasted Sales and Profits The key to the forecast is, of course, the company's future performance, and the most important aspects to consider in this regard are the outlook for sales and profits. One way to develop a sales forecast is to assume that the company will continue to perform as it has in the past and simply extend the historical trend. For example, if a firm's sales have been growing at a rate of 10% per year, then investors might assume sales will continue at that rate. Of course, if there is some evidence about the economy, industry, or company that hints at a faster or slower rate of growth, investors would want to adjust the forecast accordingly. Often, this "naive" approach will be about as effective as more complex techniques.

Once they have produced a sales forecast, investors shift their attention to the net profit margin. We want to know what profit the firm will earn on the sales that it achieves. One of the best ways of doing that is to use what is known as a **common-size income statement**. Basically, a common-size statement takes every entry found on an ordinary income statement or balance sheet and converts it to a percentage. To create a common-size income statement, divide every item on the statement by *sales*—which, in effect, is the common denominator. An example of this appears in Table 9.1, which shows the 2016 dollar-based and common-size income statements for Universal Office Furnishings.

Excel@Investing

TABLE 9.1   COMPARATIVE DOLLAR-BASED AND COMMON-SIZE INCOME STATEMENT UNIVERSAL OFFICE FURNISHINGS, INC. 2016 INCOME STATEMENT

	($ millions)	(Common-Size)*
Net Sales	$1,938.0	100.0%
Cost of goods sold	$1,128.5	58.2%
Gross operating Profit	**$ 809.5**	**41.8%**
Selling, general, & administrative expenses	$ 496.7	25.6%
Depreciation & amortization	$ 77.1	4.0%
Other expenses	$ 0.5	0.0%
Total operating expenses	**$ 574.3**	**29.6%**
Earnings before interest & taxes (EBIT)	**$ 235.2**	**12.1%**
Interest Expense	$ 13.4	0.7%
Income taxes	$ 82.1	4.2%
Net profit after taxes	**$ 139.7**	**7.2%**

*Common-size figures are found by using 'Net Sales" as the common denominator, and then dividing all entries by net sales. For example, cost of goods sold = $1,128.5 ÷ $1,938.0 = 58.2%; EBIT = $235.2 ÷ $1,938.0 = 12.1%.

Example

To understand how to construct these statements, let's use the gross profit margin (41.8%) as an illustration. In this case, divide the gross operating profit of $809.5 million by sales of $1,938.0 million:

$$\$809.5 \div \$1,938.0 = 0.4177 = 41.8\%$$

Use the same procedure for every other entry on the income statement. Note that a common-size statement adds up, just like its dollar-based counterpart. For example, sales of 100.0% minus costs of goods sold of 58.2% equals a gross profit margin of 41.8%. (You can also work up common-size balance sheets, using total assets as the common denominator.)

Securities analysts and investors use common-size income statements to compare operating results from one year to the next. The common-size format helps investors identify changes in profit margins and highlights possible causes of those changes. For example, a common-size income statement can quickly reveal whether a decline in a firm's net profit margin is caused by a reduction in the gross profit margin or a rise in other expenses. That information also helps analysts make projections of future profits. For example, analysts might use the most recent common-size statement (or perhaps an average of the statements that have prevailed for the past few years) combined with a sales forecast to create a forecasted income statement a year or two ahead. Analysts can make adjustments to specific line items to sharpen their projections. For example, if analysts know that a firm has accumulated an unusually large amount of inventory this year, it is likely that the firm will cut prices next year to reduce its inventory holdings, and that will put downward pressure on profit margins. Adjustments like these (hopefully) improve the accuracy of forecasts of profits.

Given a satisfactory sales forecast and estimate of the future net profit margin, we can combine these two pieces of information to arrive at future earnings (i.e., profits).

Equation 9.1

$$\text{Future after-tax earnings in year } t = \text{Estimated sales in year } t \times \text{Net profit margin expected in year } t$$

The *year t* notation in this equation simply denotes a future calendar or fiscal year. Suppose that in the year just completed, a company reported sales of $100 million. Based on the company's past growth rate and on industry trends, you estimate that revenues will grow at an 8% annual rate, and you think that the net profit margin will be about 6%. Thus, the forecast for next year's sales is $108 million (i.e., $100 million ×1.08), and next year's profits will be $6.5 million:

$$\text{Future after-tax earnings next year} = \$108 \text{ million} \times 0.06 = \underline{\underline{\$6.5 \text{ million}}}$$

Using this same process, investors could estimate sales and earnings for other years in the forecast period.

Forecasted Dividends and Prices At this point the forecast provides some insights into the company's future earnings. The next step is to evaluate how these results will influence the company's stock price. Given a corporate earnings forecast, investors need three additional pieces of information:

- An estimate of future dividend payout ratios
- The number of common shares that will be outstanding over the forecast period
- A future price-to-earnings (P/E) ratio

For the first two pieces of information, lacking evidence to the contrary, investors can simply project the firm's recent experience into the future. Except during economic downturns, payout ratios are usually fairly stable, so recent experience is a fairly good indicator of what the future will bring. Similarly, the number of shares outstanding does not usually change a great deal from one year to the next, so using the current number in a forecast will usually not lead to significant errors. Even when shares outstanding do change, companies usually announce their intentions to issue new shares or repurchase outstanding shares, so investors can incorporate this information into their forecasts.

Getting a Handle on the P/E Ratio The most difficult issue in this process is coming up with an estimate of the future P/E ratio—a figure that has considerable bearing on the stock's future price behavior. Generally speaking, the P/E ratio (also called the P/E multiple) is a function of several variables, including the following:

- The growth rate in earnings
- The general state of the market
- The amount of debt in a company's capital structure
- The current and projected rate of inflation
- The level of dividends

As a rule, higher P/E ratios are associated with higher rates of growth in earnings, an optimistic market outlook, and lower debt levels (less debt means less financial risk).

The link between the inflation rate and P/E multiples, however, is a bit more complex. Generally speaking, as inflation rates rise, so do the interest rates offered by bonds. As returns on bonds increase, investors demand higher returns on stocks because they are riskier than bonds. Future returns on stocks can increase if companies earn higher profits and pay higher dividends, but if earnings and profits remain fixed, investors will only earn higher future returns if stock prices are lower today. Thus, inflation often puts downward pressure on stock prices and P/E multiples. On the other hand, declining inflation (and interest) rates normally have a positive effect on the economy, and that translates into higher P/E ratios and stock prices. Holding all other factors constant, a higher dividend payout ratio leads to a higher P/E ratio. In practice, however, most companies with high P/E ratios have *low* dividend payouts because firms that have the opportunity to grow rapidly tend to reinvest most of their earnings. In that case, the prospect of earnings growth drives up the P/E, more than offsetting the low dividend payout ratio.

A Relative Price-to-Earnings Multiple A useful starting point for evaluating the P/E ratio is the *average market multiple*. This is simply the average P/E ratio of all the stocks in a given market index, like the S&P 500 or the DJIA. The average market multiple indicates the general state of the market. It gives us an idea of how aggressively the market, in general, is pricing stocks. Other things being equal, the higher the P/E ratio, the more optimistic the market, though there are exceptions to that general rule. Figure 9.1 plots the S&P 500 price-to-earnings multiple from 1901 to 2015. This figure calculates the market P/E ratio by dividing prices at the beginning of the year by earnings over the previous 12 months. The figure shows that market multiples move over a fairly wide range. For example, in 2009, the market P/E ratio was at an all-time high of more than 70, but just one year later the ratio had fallen to just under 21. It is worth noting that the extremely high P/E ratio in 2009 was not primarily the result of stock prices hitting all-time highs. Instead, the P/E ratio at the time was high because earnings over the preceding 12 months had been extraordinarily low due to a severe recession. This illustrates that you must be cautious when interpreting P/E ratios as a sign of the health of individual stocks or of the overall market.

FIGURE 9.1   Average P/E Ratio of S&P 500 Stocks

The average price-to-earnings ratio for stocks in the S&P 500 Index fluctuated around a mean of 13 from 1940 to 1990 before starting an upward climb. Increases in the P/E ratio do not necessarily indicate a bull market. The P/E ratio spiked in 2009 not because prices were high, but because earnings were very low due to the recession. (Source: Data from http://www.multpl.com.)

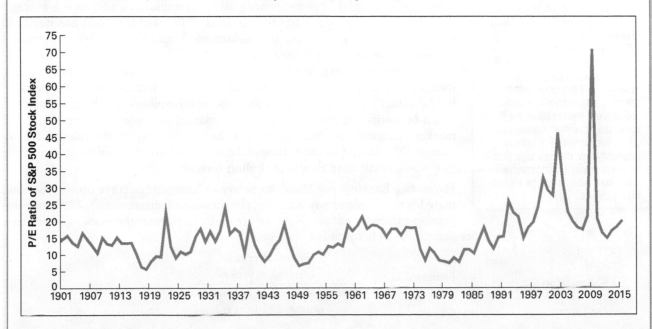

P/E Ratios Can Be Misleading

The most recent spike in the S&P 500 P/E ratio cannot be explained by a booming economy or a rising stock market. Recall that in 2008 stock prices fell dramatically, with the overall market declining by more than 30%. Yet, as 2009 began the average P/E ratio stood at an extraordinarily high level. The reason is that with the deep recession of 2008, corporate earnings declined even more sharply than stock prices did. So, in the market P/E ratio, the denominator (last year's earnings) declined more rapidly than the numerator (prices), and the overall P/E ratio jumped. In fact, in mid-2009 the average S&P 500 P/E ratio reached an all-time high of 144!

Looking at Figure 9.1, you can see that the market's P/E ratio has increased in recent years. From 1900 to 1990, the market P/E averaged about 13, but since then its average value has been above 24 (or more than 22 if you exclude the peak in 2009). At least during the 1990s, that upward trend could easily be explained by the very favorable state of the economy. Business was booming and new technologies were emerging at a rapid pace. There were no recessions from 1991 to 2000. If investors believed that the good times would continue indefinitely, then it's easy to understand why they might be willing to pay higher and higher P/E ratios over time.

With the market multiple as a benchmark, investors can evaluate a stock's P/E performance relative to the market. That is, investors can calculate a **relative P/E multiple** by dividing a stock's P/E by a market multiple. For example, if a stock currently has a P/E of 35 and the market multiple for the S&P 500 is, say, 25, the stock's relative P/E is $35 \div 25 = 1.4$. Looking at the relative P/E, investors can quickly get a feel for how aggressively the stock has been priced in the market and what kind of relative P/E is normal for the stock.

Other things being equal, a high relative P/E is desirable—up to a point, at least. For just as abnormally high P/Es can spell trouble (i.e., the stock may be overpriced and headed for a fall), so too can abnormally high relative P/Es. Given that caveat, it follows that the higher the relative P/E measure, the higher the stock will be priced in the market. But watch out for the downside: High relative P/E multiples can also mean lots of price volatility, which means that both large gains and large losses are possible. (Similarly, investors use average industry multiples to get a feel for the kind of P/E multiples that are standard for a given industry. They use that information, along with market multiples, to assess or project the P/E for a particular stock.)

The next step is to generate a forecast of the stock's future P/E over the anticipated *investment horizon* (the period of time over which an investor expects to hold the stock). For example, with the existing P/E multiple as a base, an increase might be justified if investors believe the market multiple will increase (as the market becomes more bullish) even if they do not expect the relative P/E to change. Of course, if investors believe the stock's relative P/E will increase as well, that would result in an even more bullish forecast.

Estimating Earnings per Share So far we've been able to come up with an estimate for the dividend payout ratio, the number of shares outstanding, and the price-to-earnings multiple. Now we are ready to forecast the stock's future earnings per share (EPS) as follows:

INVESTOR FACTS

How to Spot an Undervalued (or Overvalued) Market Just as shares of common stock can become over- or undervalued, so can the market as a whole. How can you tell if the market is overvalued? One of the best ways is to examine the overall market P/E ratio relative to its long-term average. When the market's P/E ratio is above its long-term average, that is a good sign that the market is overvalued and subsequent market returns will be lower than average. Conversely, when the market's P/E ratio is unusually low, that is a sign that the market may be undervalued and future returns will be higher than average.

Equation 9.2

$$\text{Estimated EPS in year } t = \frac{\text{Future after-tax earnings in year } t}{\text{Number of shares of common stock outstanding in year } t}$$

Earnings per share is a critical part of the valuation process. Investors can combine an EPS forecast with (1) the dividend payout ratio to obtain (future) dividends per share and (2) the price-to-earnings multiple to project the (future) price of the stock.

Equation 9.2 simply converts total corporate earnings to a per-share basis by dividing forecasted company profits by the expected number of shares outstanding. Although this approach works quite effectively, some investors may want to analyze earnings per share from a slightly different perspective. One way to do this begins by measuring a firm's ROE. For example, rather than using Equation 9.2 to calculate EPS, investors could use Equation 9.3 as follows:

Equation 9.3

$$\text{EPS} = \frac{\text{After-tax earnings}}{\text{Book value of equity}} \times \frac{\text{Book value of equity}}{\text{Shares outstanding}} = \text{ROE} \times \text{Book value per share}$$

This formula will produce the same results as Equation 9.2. The major advantage of this form of the equation is that it highlights how much a firm earns relative to the book value of its equity. As we've already seen, earnings divided by book equity is the firm's ROE. Return on equity is a key financial measure because it captures the amount of success the firm is having in managing its assets, operations, and capital structure. And as we see here, ROE is not only important in defining overall corporate profitability, but it also plays a crucial role in defining a stock's EPS.

To produce an estimated EPS using Equation 9.3, investors would go directly to the two basic components of the formula and try to estimate how those components might change in the future. In particular, what kind of growth in the firm's book value per share is reasonable to expect, and what's likely to happen to the company's ROE? In the vast majority of cases, ROE is really the driving force, so it's important to produce a good estimate of that variable. Investors often do that by breaking ROE into its component parts— net profit margin, total asset turnover, and the equity multiplier.

With a forecast of ROE and book value per share in place, investors can plug these figures into Equation 9.3 to produce estimated EPS. The bottom line is that, one way or another (using the approach reflected in Equation 9.2 or that in Equation 9.3), investors have to arrive at a forecasted EPS number that they are comfortable with. After that, it's a simple matter to use the forecasted payout ratio to estimate dividends per share:

Equation 9.4

$$\frac{\text{Estimated dividends}}{\text{per share in year } t} = \frac{\text{Estimated EPS}}{\text{for year } t} \times \frac{\text{Estimated}}{\text{payout ratio}}$$

Finally, estimate the future value of the stock by multiplying expected earnings times the expected P/E ratio:

Equation 9.5

$$\frac{\text{Estimated share price}}{\text{at end of year } t} = \frac{\text{Estimated EPS}}{\text{in year } t} \times \frac{\text{Estimated P/E}}{\text{ratio}}$$

Pulling It All Together Now, to see how all of these components fit together, let's continue with the example we started above. Using the aggregate sales and earnings approach, if the company had two million shares of common stock outstanding and investors expected that to remain constant, then given the estimated earnings of $6.5 million obtained from Equation 9.1, the firm should generate earnings per share next year of

$$\frac{\text{Estimated EPS}}{\text{next year}} = \frac{\$6.5 \text{ million}}{2 \text{ million}} = \underline{\$3.25}$$

An investor could obtain the same figure using forecasts of the firm's ROE and its book value per share. For instance, suppose we estimate that the firm will have an ROE of 15% and a book value per share of $21.67. According to Equation 9.3, those conditions would also produce an estimated EPS of $3.25 (i.e., $0.15 \times \$21.67$). Using this EPS figure, along with an estimated payout ratio of 40%, dividends per share next year should equal

$$\frac{\text{Estimated dividends}}{\text{per share next year}} = \$3.25 \times .40 = \underline{\$1.30}$$

Keep in mind that firms don't always adjust dividends in lockstep with earnings. A firm might pay the same dividend for many years if managers are not confident that an increase in earnings can be sustained over time. In a case like this, when a firm has a history of adjusting dividends slowly if at all, it may be that past dividends are a better guide to future dividends than projected earnings are. Finally, if it has been estimated that the stock should sell at 17.5 times earnings, then a share of stock in this company should be trading at $56.88 by the end of next year.

$$\frac{\text{Estimated share price}}{\text{at the end of next year}} = \$3.25 \times 17.5 = \underline{\$56.88}$$

Actually, an investor would be most interested in the price of the stock at the end of the anticipated investment horizon. Thus, the $56.88 figure would be appropriate for an investor who had a one-year horizon. However, for an investor with a three-year holding period, extending the EPS figure for two more years and repeating these calculations with the new data would be a better approach. The bottom line is that the estimated share price is important because it has embedded in it the capital gains portion of the stock's total return.

Developing a Forecast of Universal's Financial Performance

Using information obtained from Universal Office Furnishings (UVRS), we can illustrate the forecasting procedures we discussed above. Recall that our earlier assessment of the economy and the office equipment industry was positive and that the company's operating results and financial condition looked strong, both historically and relative to industry standards. Because everything looks favorable for Universal, we decide to take a look at the future prospects of the company and its stock.

Let's assume that an investor considering Universal common stock has a three-year investment horizon. Perhaps the investor believes (based on earlier studies of economic and industry factors) that the economy and the market for office equipment stocks will start running out of steam near the end of 2019 or early 2020. Or perhaps the investor plans to sell any Universal common stock purchased today to finance a major expenditure in three years. Regardless of the reason behind the investor's three-year horizon, we will focus on estimating Universal's performance for 2017, 2018, and 2019.

TABLE 9.2   SELECTED HISTORICAL FINANCIAL DATA, UNIVERSAL OFFICE FURNISHINGS

	2012	2013	2014	2015	2016
Total assets (millions)	$554.20	$ 694.90	$ 755.60	$ 761.50	$ 941.20
Total asset turnover	1.72	1.85	1.98	2.32	2.06
Sales revenue (millions)	$953.20	$1,283.90	$1,495.90	$1,766.20	$1,938.00
Annual rate of growth in sales*	−1.07%	34.69%	16.51%	18.07%	9.73%
Net profit margin	4.20%	6.60%	7.50%	8.00%	7.20%
Payout ratio	6.80%	5.20%	5.50%	6.00%	6.60%
Price/earnings ratio	13.5	16.2	13.9	15.8	18.4
Number of common shares outstanding (millions)	77.7	78.0	72.8	65.3	61.8

*To find the annual rate of growth in sales divide sales in one year by sales in the previous year and then subtract one. For example, the annual rate of growth in sales for 2016 = ($1,938.00 − $1,766.20) ÷ $1,766.20 − 1 = 9.73%.

Table 9.2 provides selected historical financial data for the company, covering a five-year period (ending with the latest fiscal year) and provides the basis for much of our forecast. The data reveal that, with one or two exceptions, the company has performed at a fairly steady pace and has been able to maintain a very attractive rate of growth. Our previous economic analysis suggested that the economy is about to pick up, and our research indicated that the industry and company are well situated to take advantage of the upswing. Therefore, we conclude that the rate of growth in sales should pick up from the 9.7% rate in 2016, attaining a growth rate of over 20% in 2017—a little higher than the firm's five-year average. After a modest amount of pent-up demand is worked off, the rate of growth in sales should drop to about 19% in 2018 and to 15% in 2019.

The essential elements of the financial forecast for 2017 through 2019 appear in Table 9.3. Highlights of the key assumptions and the reasoning behind them are as follows:

- *Net profit margin.* Various published industry and company reports suggest a comfortable improvement in earnings, so we decide to use a profit margin of 8.0% in 2017 (up a bit from the latest margin of 7.2% recorded in 2016). We're projecting even better profit margins (8.5%) in 2018 and 2019, as Universal implements some cost improvements.

- *Common shares outstanding.* We believe the company will continue to pursue its share buyback program, but at a substantially slower pace than in the 2013–2016 period. From a current level of 61.8 million shares, we project that the number of shares outstanding will drop to 61.5 million in 2017, to 60.5 million in 2018, and to 59.0 million in 2019.

- *Payout ratio.* We assume that the dividend payout ratio will hold at a steady 6% of earnings.

- *P/E ratio.* Primarily on the basis of expectations for improved growth in revenues and earnings, we are projecting a P/E multiple that will rise from its present level of 18.4 times earnings to roughly 20 times earnings in 2017. Although this is a fairly conservative increase in the P/E, when it is coupled with the hefty growth in EPS, the net effect will be a big jump in the projected price of Universal stock.

TABLE 9.3   SUMMARY FORECAST STATISTICS, UNIVERSAL OFFICE FURNISHINGS

	Latest Actual Figure (Fiscal 2016)	Weighted Average in Recent Years (2012–2016)	Forecasted Figures**		
			2017	2018	2019
Annual rate of growth in sales	9.7%	15.0%	22.0%	19.0%	15.0%
Net sales (millions)	$1,938.0	N/A*	$2,364.4	$2,813.6	$3,235.6
× Net profit margin	7.2%	5.6%	8.0%	8.5%	8.5%
= Net after-tax earnings (millions)	$ 139.7	N/A	$ 189.1	$ 239.2	$ 275.0
÷ Common shares outstanding (millions)	61.8	71.1	61.5	60.5	59.0
= Earnings per share	$ 2.26	N/A	$ 3.08	$ 3.95	$ 4.66
× Payout ratio	6.6%	6.2%	6.0%	6.0%	6.0%
= Dividends per share	$ 0.15	$0.08	$ 0.18	$ 0.24	$ 0.28
Earnings per share	$ 2.26	N/A	$ 3.08	$ 3.95	$ 4.66
× P/E ratio	18.4	16.8	20.0	20.0	20.0
= Share price at year end	$ 41.58	N/A	$ 61.51	$ 79.06	$ 93.23

*N/A: Not applicable.

**Forecasted sales figures: Sales from preceding year × (1 + growth rate in sales) = forecasted sales.

For example, for 2017: $1,938.0 × (1 + 0.22) = $2,364.4.

Excel@Investing

Table 9.3 also shows the sequence involved in arriving at forecasted dividends and share price behavior; that is:

1. The company dimensions of the forecast are handled first. These include sales and revenue estimates, net profit margins, net earnings, and the number of shares of common stock outstanding.

2. Next we estimate earnings per share by dividing expected earnings by shares outstanding.

3. The bottom line of the forecast is, of course, the returns in the form of dividends and capital gains expected from a share of Universal stock, given that the assumptions about sales, profit margins, earnings per share, and so forth hold up. We see in Table 9.3 that dividends should go up to 28 cents per share, which is a big jump from where they are now (15 cents per share). Even with a big dividend increase, it's clear that dividends still won't account for much of the stock's return. In fact, our projections indicate that the dividend yield in 2019 will fall to just 0.3% (divide the expected $0.28 dividend by the anticipated $93.23 price to get a yield of just 0.3%). Clearly, our forecast implies that the returns from this stock are going to come from capital gains, not dividends. That's obvious when we look at year-end share prices, which we expect to more than double over the next three years. That is, if our projections are valid, the price of a share of stock should rise from around $41.50 to more than $93.00 by year-end 2019.

We now have an idea of what the future cash flows of the investment are likely to be. We can now use that information to establish an intrinsic value for Universal Office Furnishings stock.

The Valuation Process

Valuation is a process by which an investor determines the worth of a security keeping in mind the tradeoff between risk and return. This process can be applied to any asset that produces a stream of cash—a share of stock, a bond, a piece of real estate, or an oil well. To establish the value of an asset, the investor must determine certain key inputs, including the amount of future cash flows, the timing of these cash flows, and the rate of return required on the investment.

In terms of common stock, the essence of valuation is to determine what the stock ought to be worth, given estimated cash flows to stockholders (future dividends and capital gains) and the amount of risk. Toward that end we employ various types of stock valuation models, the end product of which represents the elusive intrinsic value we have been seeking. That is, the stock valuation models determine either an expected rate of return or the intrinsic worth of a share of stock, which in effect represents the stock's "justified price." In this way, we obtain a standard of performance, based on forecasted stock behavior, which we can use to judge the investment merits of a particular security.

Either of two conditions would make us consider a stock a worthwhile investment candidate: (1) the expected rate of return equals or exceeds the return we feel is warranted given the stock's risk, or (2) the justified price (intrinsic worth) is equal to or greater than the current market price. In other words, a security is a good investment if its expected return is at least as high as the return that an investor demands based on the security's risk or if its intrinsic value equals or exceeds the current market price of the security. There is nothing irrational about purchasing a security in those circumstances. In either case, the security meets our minimum standards to the extent that it is giving investors the rate of return they wanted.

Remember this, however, about the valuation process: Even though valuation plays an important part in the investment process, there is absolutely no assurance that the actual outcome will be even remotely similar to the projections. The stock is still subject to economic, industry, company, and market risks, any one of which could negate *all* of the assumptions about the future. Security analysis and stock valuation models are used not to guarantee success but to help investors better understand the return and risk dimensions of a potential transaction.

Required Rate of Return One of the key ingredients in the stock valuation process is the **required rate of return**. Generally speaking, the return that an investor requires should be related to the investment's risk. In essence, the required return establishes a level of compensation compatible with the amount of risk involved. Such a standard helps determine whether the expected return on a stock (or any other security) is satisfactory. Because investors don't know for sure what the cash flow of an investment will be, they should expect to earn a rate of return that reflects this uncertainty. Thus, the greater the perceived risk, the more investors should expect to earn. This is basically the notion behind the capital asset pricing model (CAPM).

Recall that using the CAPM, we can define a stock's required return as

Equation 9.6
$$\text{Required rate of return} = \text{Risk-free rate} + \left[\text{Stock's beta} \times \left(\text{Market return} - \text{Risk-free rate} \right) \right]$$

Two of the required inputs for this equation are readily available. You can obtain a stock's beta from many online sites or print sources. The risk-free rate is the current return provided by a risk-free investment such as a Treasury bill or a Treasury bond.

Estimating the expected return on the overall stock market is not as straightforward. A simple way to calculate the market's expected return is to use a long-run average return on the stock market. This average return may, of course, have to be adjusted up or down a bit based on what investors expect the market to do over the next year or so.

In the CAPM, the risk of a stock is captured by its beta. For that reason, the required return on a stock increases (or decreases) with increases (or decreases) in its beta. As an illustration of the CAPM at work, consider Universal's stock, which we'll assume has a beta of 1.30. If the risk-free rate is 3.5% and the expected market return is 10%, according to the CAPM model, this stock would have a required return of

$$\text{Required return} = 3.5\% + [1.30 \times (10.0\% - 3.5\%)] = \underline{11.95\%}$$

This return—let's round it to 12%—can now be used in a stock valuation model to assess the investment merits of a share of stock. To accept a lower return means you'll fail to be fully compensated for the risk you must assume.

AN ADVISOR'S PERSPECTIVE

Rod Holloway
Equity Portfolio Manager,
CFCI

"The higher the beta, the more that stock will move up if the market is going up."

MyFinanceLab

CONCEPTS IN REVIEW

Answers available at
http://www.pearsonhighered.com/smart

9.1 What is the purpose of stock valuation? What role does intrinsic value play in the stock valuation process?

9.2 Are the expected future earnings of the firm important in determining a stock's investment suitability? Discuss how these and other future estimates fit into the stock valuation framework.

9.3 Can the growth prospects of a company affect its price-to-earnings multiple? Explain. How about the amount of debt a firm uses? Are there any other variables that affect the level of a firm's P/E ratio?

9.4 What is the market multiple and how can it help in evaluating a stock's P/E ratio? Is a stock's relative P/E the same thing as the market multiple? Explain.

9.5 In the stock valuation framework, how can you tell whether a particular security is a worthwhile investment candidate? What roles does the required rate of return play in this process? Would you invest in a stock if all you could earn was a rate of return that just equaled your required return? Explain.

Stock Valuation Models

LG4 LG5 LG6 Investors employ several stock valuation models. Although they are usually aimed at a security's future cash flows, their approaches to valuation are nonetheless considerably different. Some models, for example, focus heavily on the dividends that a stock will pay over time. Other models emphasize the cash flow that a firm generates, focusing less attention on whether the company pays that cash out as dividends, uses it to repurchase shares, or simply holds it in reserve.

There are still other stock valuation models in use—models that employ such variables as dividend yield, abnormally low P/E multiples, relative price performance over time, and even company size or market cap as key elements in the decision-making process. For purposes of our discussion, we'll focus on several stock valuation models that derive value from the fundamental performance of the company. We'll look first at stocks that pay dividends and at a procedure known as the dividend valuation model. From there, we'll look at several valuation procedures that can be used with companies that pay little or nothing in dividends. Finally, we'll move on to procedures that set the price of a stock based on how it behaves relative to earnings, cash flow, sales, or book value. The stock valuation procedures that we'll examine in this chapter are the same as those used by many professional security analysts and are, in fact, found throughout the "Equity Investments" portion of the CFA exam, especially at Level-I. And, of course, an understanding of these valuation models will enable you to better evaluate analysts' recommendations.

The Dividend Valuation Model

In the valuation process, the intrinsic value of any investment equals the present value of its expected cash benefits. For common stock, this amounts to the cash dividends received each year plus the future sale price of the stock. One way to view the cash flow benefits from common stock is to assume that the dividends will be received over an infinite time horizon—an assumption that is appropriate as long as the firm is considered a "going concern." Seen from this perspective, the value of a share of stock is equal to the present value of all the future dividends it is expected to provide over an infinite time horizon.

When an investor sells a stock, from a strictly theoretical point of view, what he or she is really selling is the right to all future dividends. Thus, just as the current value of a share of stock is a function of future dividends, the future price of the stock is also a function of future dividends. In this framework, the future price of the stock will rise or fall as the outlook for dividends (and the required rate of return) changes. This approach, which holds that the value of a share of stock is a function of its future dividends, is known as **dividend valuation model (DVM)**.

There are three versions of the dividend valuation model, each based on different assumptions about the future rate of growth in dividends:

1. *The zero-growth model* assumes that dividends will not grow over time.

2. *The constant-growth model* assumes that dividends will grow by a constant rate over time.

3. *The variable-growth model* assumes that the rate of growth in dividends will vary over time.

In one form or another, the DVM is widely used in practice to solve many kinds of valuation problems.

Zero Growth The simplest way to picture the dividend valuation model is to assume the stock has a fixed stream of dividends. In other words, dividends stay the same year in and year out, and they're expected to do so in the future. Under such conditions, the value of a zero-growth stock is simply the present value of its annual dividends. To find the present value, just divide annual dividends by the required rate of return:

Equation 9.7
$$\text{Value of a share of stock} = \frac{\text{Annual dividends}}{\text{Required rate of return}}$$

FAMOUS FAILURES IN FINANCE

Ethical Conflicts Faced by Stock Analysts: Don't Always Believe the Hype

Buy, sell, or hold? Unfortunately, many investors have learned the hard way not to trust analysts' recommendations.

Consider the late 1990s stock market bubble. As the market began to fall in 2000, 95% of publicly traded stocks were free of sell recommendations, according to investment research firm Zacks, and 5% of stocks that did have a sell rating had exactly that: one sell rating from a single analyst. When the market began its climb back up, analysts missed the boat again. From 2000 to 2004, stocks that analysts told investors to sell rose 19% per annum on average, while their "buys" and "holds" rose just 7%.

Why were the all-star analysts wrong so often? Conflict of interest is one explanation. Analysts often work for investment banks who have business relationships with the companies that analysts follow. Analysts may feel pressure to make positive comments to please current or prospective investment banking clients. Also, analysts' buy recommendations may induce investors to trade, and those trades generate commissions for the analysts' employers.

Analyst hype is a real problem for both Wall Street and Main Street, and the securities industry has taken steps to correct it. The SEC's Regulation Fair Disclosure requires that all company information be released to the public rather than quietly disseminated to analysts. Some brokerages ban analysts from owning stocks they cover. In 2003 the SEC ruled that compensation for analyst research must be separated from investment banking fees, so that the analyst's job is to research stock rather than solicit clients.

Most important, investors must learn how to read between the lines of analysts' reports. In early 2014 there were nearly eight times as many "buy" recommendations for stocks in the S&P 500 as there were "sell" recommendations. If analysts were really unbiased, it seems very unlikely that their recommendations would be so heavily tilted toward the buy side. What should investors do? To start, they should probably lower analysts' ratings by one notch. A strong buy could be interpreted as a buy or a buy as a hold, and a hold or neutral as a sell. Also, investors should give more weight to negative ratings than to positive ones. A recent study found that sell recommendations were followed by an immediate drop of 3% in the price of downgraded stocks, whereas buy recommendations had either a more muted effect or no effect at all. Downgrades and those rare sell recommendations may signal future problems. Investors should also pay attention to forecasts in which a ratings change is accompanied by an earnings forecast revision in the same direction. That is, if an analyst moves a stock from sell to buy and simultaneously raises the earnings forecast for the stock, that is more credible than a report that simply changes the rating to "buy." Finally, when in doubt, investors should do their own homework, using the techniques taught in this text.

Critical Thinking Question Why do you think sell ratings tend to cause stock prices to fall, while buy ratings do not lead to stock price increases?

(Sources: Jack Hough, "How to Make Money off Analysts' Stock Recommendations," *Smart Money*, January 19, 2012, http://www.smartmoney.com/invest/stocks/how-to-make-money-off-analysts-stock-recommendations-1326759491635/; Rich Smith, "Analysts Running Scared," *The Motley Fool*, April 5, 2006, http://www.fool.com.)

Example

Suppose a stock pays a dividend of $3 per share each year, and you don't expect that dividend to change. If you want a 10% return on your investment, how much should you be willing to pay for the stock?

$$\text{Value of stock} = \$3 \div 0.10 = \$30$$

If you paid a higher price, you would earn a rate of return less than 10%, and likewise if you could acquire the stock for less, your rate of return would exceed 10%.

As you can see, the only cash flow variable that's used in this model is the fixed annual dividend. Given that the annual dividend on this stock never changes, does that mean the price of the stock never changes? Absolutely not! For as the required rate of return (capitalization rate) changes, so will the price of the stock. Thus, if the required rate of return goes up to 15%, the price of the stock will fall to $20 ($3 ÷ 0.15). Although this may be a very simplified view of the valuation model, it's actually not as far-fetched as it may appear, for this is basically the procedure used to price preferred stocks in the marketplace.

Constant Growth The zero-growth model is a good beginning, but it does not take into account a growing stream of dividends. The standard and more widely recognized version of the dividend valuation model assumes that dividends will grow over time at a specified rate. In this version, the value of a share of stock is still considered to be a function of its future dividends, but such dividends are expected to grow forever at a constant rate of growth, g. Accordingly, we can find the value of a share of stock as follows:

Equation 9.8

$$\frac{\text{Value of a}}{\text{share of stock}} = \frac{\text{Next year's dividends}}{\text{Required rate} - \text{Dividend growth}}$$
$$\text{of return} \qquad \text{rate}$$

Equation 9.8a

$$V = \frac{D_1}{r - g}$$

where

D_1 = annual dividend expected next year (the first year in the forecast period)
r = the required rate of return on the stock
g = the annual rate of growth in dividends, which must be less than r

Even though this version of the model assumes that dividends will grow at a constant rate forever, it is important to understand that doesn't mean we assume the investor will hold the stock forever. Indeed, the dividend valuation model makes no assumptions about how long the investor will hold the stock, for the simple reason that the investment horizon has no bearing on the computed value of a stock. Thus, with the constant-growth DVM, it is irrelevant whether the investor has a one-year, five-year, or ten-year expected holding period. The computed value of the stock will be the same under all circumstances. So long as the input assumptions (r, g, and D_1) are the same, the value of the stock will be the same regardless of the intended holding period.

Note that this model succinctly captures the essence of stock valuation. Increase the cash flow (through D or g) or decrease the required rate of return (r), and the stock value will increase. We know that, in practice, there are potentially two components that make up the total return to a stockholder: dividends and capital gains. This model captures both components. If you solve Equation 9.8a for r, you will find that $r = D_1/V + g$. The first term in this sum, D_1/V, represents the dividend expected next year relative to the stock's current price. In other words, D_1/V is the stock's expected dividend yield. The second term, g, is the expected dividend growth rate. But if dividends grow at rate g, the stock price will grow at that rate too, so g also represents the capital gain component of the stock's total return. Therefore, the stock's total return is the sum of its dividend yield and its capital gain.

The constant-growth model should not be used with just any stock. Rather, it is best suited to the valuation of mature, dividend-paying companies that have a long track record of increasing dividends. These are probably large-cap (or perhaps even some mature mid-cap) companies that have demonstrated an ability to generate steady—although perhaps not spectacular—rates of growth year in and year out. The growth rates may not be identical from year to year, but they tend to move within a relatively narrow range. These are companies that have established dividend policies and fairly predictable growth rates in earnings and dividends.

INVESTOR FACTS

Steady Stream of Dividends The Canadian company Power Financial Corp. paid a $0.35 dividend for 27 consecutive quarters from December 2008 to December 2014. After receiving the same dividend for so long, did investors value Power Financial based on the assumption that it would pay $1.40 per year ($0.35 per quarter 4 times per year) forever? If we assume that investors required an 8% return on the stock, then under the assumption of constant dividends, the stock would sell for $17.50 per share (i.e., 1.40 ÷ 0.08). In fact, the stock traded in the $30 range in December 2014. Therefore, we can surmise that investors either required a return that was lower than 8% or they expected dividends to rise. In fact, the company did announce a dividend increase a few months later in March 2015.

Example

> In the 25 years between 1990 and 2015, the food company General Mills increased its dividend payments by about 7% per year. The food industry is not one where we would expect explosive growth. Food consumption is closely tied to population growth, so profits in this business should grow relatively slowly over time. In April 2015 General Mills was paying an annual dividend of $1.76 per share, so for 2016 investors were expecting a modest increase in General Mills dividends over the coming year to $1.88 per share (7% more than the 2015 dividend). If the required return on General Mills stock is 10%, then investors should have been willing to pay $62.67 for the stock ($1.88 ÷ (0.10 − 0.07)) in 2015. In fact, General Mills stock was trading in a range between $55 and $57 at the time, so our application of the constant growth model suggests that General Mills was slightly undervalued. That is, its intrinsic value ($62.67) was a little higher than the stock's market price. Of course, our estimate of intrinsic value might be too high if the required return on General Mills shares is higher than 10% or if the long-run growth rate in dividends in less than 7%. Indeed, one drawback to the constant growth model is that the estimate of value that it produces is very sensitive to the assumptions one makes about the required return and the dividend growth rate. For example, if we assumed that the required return on General Mills stock was 11% rather than 10%, our estimate of intrinsic value would fall from $62.67 to $47!

Analysts sometimes use the constant-growth DVM to estimate the required return on a stock based on the assumption that the stock's market price is equal to its intrinsic value. In other words, analysts plug the stock's market price and an estimate of the dividend growth rate into Equation 9.8a and solve for r rather than solving for V. For General Mills, if the stock's market price is $56, the next dividend is $1.88, and the dividend growth rate is 7%, we can estimate the required return on General Mills' stock as follows:

$$\$56 = \$1.88 \div (r - 0.07)$$

Solving this equation for r, we find that the required return on General Mills' stock is about 10.36%.

Estimating the Dividend Growth Rate   Use of the constant-growth DVM requires some basic information about the stock's required rate of return, its current level of dividends, and the expected rate of growth in dividends. A fairly simple, albeit naïve, way to find the dividend growth rate, g, is to look at the historical behavior of dividends. If they are growing at a relatively constant rate, you can assume they will continue to grow at (or near) that average rate in the future. You can get historical dividend data in a company's annual report or from various online sources

With the help of a calculator or spreadsheet, we can use basic present value arithmetic to find the growth rate embedded in a stream of dividends. For example, compare the dividend that a company is paying today to the dividend it paid several years ago. If dividends have been growing steadily, dividends today will be higher than they were in the past. Next, use your calculator to find the discount rate that equates the present value of today's dividend to the dividend paid several years earlier. When you find that rate, you've found the dividend growth rate. In this case, the discount rate is the average rate of growth in dividends. (See Chapter 10 for a detailed discussion of how to calculate growth rates.)

Example

> In 2015 General Mills paid an annual dividend of $1.76 per share. The company had been increasing dividends steadily since 1990, when the annual dividend was just $0.32 per share. The table below shows the present value of the 2015 dividend, discounted back 25 years at various interest rates. You can see that when the discount rate is 7%, the present value of the 2015 dividend is approximately equal to the dividend paid in 1990, so 7% is the growth rate in dividends from 1990 to 2015.
>
> | Discount rate | PV of 2015 dividend ($1.76) |
> | --- | --- |
> | 5% | $0.52 |
> | 6% | $0.41 |
> | 7% | $0.32 (matches actual 1990 dividend) |
> | 8% | $0.26 |

Growth Rate Calculator

Once you've determined the dividend growth rate, you can find next year's dividend, D_1, as $D_0 \times (1 + g)$, where D_0 equals the current dividend. In 2015 General Mills was paying dividends at an annual rate of $1.76 per share. If you expect those dividends to grow at the rate of 7% a year, you can find the expected 2016 dividend as follows: $D_1 = D_0(1 + g) = \$1.76 (1 + 0.07) = \$1.88$. The only other information you need is the required rate of return (capitalization rate), r. (Note that r must be greater than g for the constant-growth model to be mathematically operative.) As we have already seen, if we assume that the required return on General Mills stock is 10%, that assumption, combined with an expected dividend next year of $1.88 and a projected dividend growth rate of 7%, produces an estimate of General Mills' stock value of $62.67.

Stock-Price Behavior over Time The constant-growth model implies that a stock's price will grow over time at the same rate that dividends grow, g, and that the growth rate plus the dividend yield equals the required return. To see how this works, consider the following example.

Suppose that today's date is January 2, 2016, and a stock just paid (on January 1) its annual dividend of $2.00 per share. Suppose too that investors expect this dividend to grow at 5% per year, so they believe that next year's dividend (which will be paid on January 1, 2017) will be $2.10, which is 5% more than the previous year's dividend. Finally, assume that investors require a 9% return on the stock. Based on those assumptions, we can estimate the price of the stock on January 2, 2016, as follows:

$$\text{Price on January 2, 2016} = \text{Dividend on January 1, 2017} \div (r - g)$$
$$\text{Price} = \$2.10 \div (0.09 - 0.05) = \$52.50.$$

Imagine that an investor purchases this stock for $52.50 on January 2 and holds it for one year. The investor receives the next dividend on January 1, 2017, and then sells the stock a day later on January 2, 2017. To estimate the expected return on this purchase, we must calculate the expected stock price that the investor will receive when she sells the stock on January 2, 2017.

$$\text{Price on January 2, 2017} = \text{Dividend on January 1, 2018} \div (r - g)$$
$$\text{Price} = \$2.10(1 + 0.05) \div (0.09 - 0.05)$$
$$\text{Price} = \$2.205 \div (0.09 - 0.05) = \$55.125$$

Now let's look at the investor's expected return during the calendar year 2016. She purchases the stock for $52.50 at the beginning of the year. One year later on January 1, 2017, she receives a dividend of $2.10 per share, and then she sells the stock for $55.125. Her total return equals the dividend plus the capital gain, divided by the original purchase price.

$$\text{Total return} = (\text{dividend} + \text{capital gain}) \div \text{purchase price}$$
$$\text{Total return} = (\$2.10 + \$55.125 - \$52.50) \div \$52.50 = 0.09 = 9.0\%$$

The investor expects to earn 9% over the year, which is exactly the required return on the stock. Notice that during the year the stock price increased by 5% from $52.50 to $55.125. So the stock price increased at the same rate that the dividend payment did. Furthermore, the dividend yield that the investor earned was 4% ($2.10 /$52.50). Therefore the 9% total return consists of a 5% capital gain and a 4% dividend yield.

Repeating this process allows you to estimate the stock price on January 2 of any succeeding year. As the table below shows, each and every year the stock price increases by 5%, and the stock's dividend yield is 4%. Therefore, an investor in this stock earns exactly the 9% required return year after year.

Year	Dividend paid on January 1	Stock price on January 2*
2016	$2.000	$52.50
2017	$2.100	$55.125
2018	$2.205	$57.881
2019	$2.315	$60.775

*As determined by the dividend valuation mode, given $g = 0.05$ and $r = 0.09$.

Variable Growth Although the constant-growth dividend valuation model is an improvement over the zero-growth model, it still has some shortcomings. The most obvious deficiency is that the model does not allow for changes in expected growth rates. To overcome this problem, we can use a form of the DVM that allows for variable rates of growth over time. Essentially, the variable-growth dividend valuation model calculates a stock price in two stages. In the first stage, dividends grow rapidly but not necessarily at a single rate. The dividend growth rate can rise or fall during this initial stage. In the second stage, the company matures and dividend growth settles down to some long-run, sustainable rate. At that point, it is possible to value the stock using the constant-growth version of the DVM. The variable-growth version of the model finds the value of a share of stock as follows:

Equation 9.9

$$\begin{array}{c} \text{Value of a share} \\ \text{of stock} \end{array} = \begin{array}{c} \text{Present value of} \\ \text{future dividends} \\ \text{during the initial} \\ \text{variable-growth period} \end{array} + \begin{array}{c} \text{Present value of the price} \\ \text{of the stock at the end of} \\ \text{the variable-growth period} \end{array}$$

Equation 9.9a

$$V = \frac{D_1}{(1+r)^1} + \frac{D_2}{(1+r)^2} + \cdots \frac{D_v}{(1+r)^v} + \frac{\dfrac{D_v(1+g)}{(r-g)}}{(1+r)^v}$$

where

D_1, D_2, etc. = future annual dividends

v = number of years in the initial variable-growth period

Note that the last element in this equation is the standard constant-growth dividend valuation model, which is used to find the price of the stock at the end of the initial variable-growth period, discounted back v periods.

This form of the DVM is appropriate for companies that are expected to experience rapid or variable rates of growth for a period of time—perhaps for the first three to five years—and then settle down to a more stable growth rate thereafter. This, in fact, is the growth pattern of many companies, so the model has considerable application in practice. It also overcomes one of the operational shortcomings of the constant-growth DVM in that r does not have to be greater than g during the initial stage. That is, during the variable-growth period, the rate of growth, g, can be greater than the required rate of return, r, and the model will still be fully operational.

Finding the value of a stock using Equation 9.9 is actually a lot easier than it looks. To do so, follow these steps:

1. Estimate annual dividends during the initial variable-growth period and then specify the constant rate, g, at which dividends will grow after the initial period.

2. Find the present value of the dividends expected during the initial variable-growth period.

3. Using the constant-growth DVM, find the price of the stock at the end of the initial growth period.

4. Find the present value of the price of the stock (as determined in step 3). Note that the price of the stock is discounted for the same length of time as the last dividend payment in the initial growth period because the stock is being priced (per step 3) at the end of this initial period.

5. Add the two present value components (from steps 2 and 4) to find the value of a stock.

Applying the Variable-Growth DVM To see how this works, let's apply the variable-growth model to Sweatmore Industries (SI). Let's assume that dividends will grow at a variable rate for the first three years (2016, 2017, and 2018). After that, the annual dividend growth rate will settle down to 3% and stay there indefinitely. Starting with the latest (2015) annual dividend of $2.21 a share, we estimate that Sweatmore's dividends should grow by 20% next year (in 2016), by 16% in 2017, and then by 13% in 2018 before dropping to a 3% rate. Finally, suppose that SI's investors require an 11% rate of return.

Using these growth rates, we project that dividends in 2016 will be $2.65 a share ($2.21 × 1.20) and will rise to $3.08($2.65 × 1.16) in 2017 and to $3.48($3.08 × 1.13) in 2018. Dividing 2019's $3.58 dividend by 8% ($r - g$) gives us the present value in 2018 of all dividends paid in 2019 and beyond. We now have all the inputs we need to put a value on Sweatmore Industries. Table 9.4 shows the variable-growth DVM in action. The value of Sweatmore stock, according to the variable-growth DVM, is $40.19 a share. In essence, that's the maximum price an investor should be willing to pay for the stock to earn an 11% rate of return.

Defining the Expected Growth Rate Mechanically, application of the DVM is really quite simple. It relies on just three key pieces of information: future dividends, future

TABLE 9.4   USING THE VARIABLE-GROWTH DVM TO VALUE SWEATMORE STOCK

Step

1. Projected annual dividends:

Most recent dividend	2015	$2.21
Future dividends	2016	$2.65
	2017	$3.08
	2018	$3.48

Estimated annual rate of growth in dividends, g, for 2019 and beyond: 3%

2. Present value of dividends, using a required rate of return, r, of 11%, during the initial variable-growth period:

Year	Dividends	Present Value
2016	$2.65	$2.39
2017	$3.08	$2.50
2018	$3.48	$2.54
	Total	$7.43 (to step 5)

3. Price of the stock at the end of the initial growth period:

$$P_{2018} = \frac{D_{2019}}{r - g} = \frac{D_{2018} \times (1 - g)}{r - g} = \frac{\$3.48 \times (1.03)}{0.11 - 0.03} = \frac{\$3.58}{0.08} = \underline{\$44.81}$$

4. Discount the price of the stock (as computed above) back to its present value, at r, of 11%:

$$\$44.81 \div (1.11)^3 = \$32.76 \text{ (to step 5)}$$

5. Add the present value of the initial dividend stream (step 2) to the present value of the price of the stock at the end of the initial growth period (step 4):

Value of Sweatmore stock: $7.43 + \$32.76 = \underline{\$40.19}$

growth in dividends, and a required rate of return. But this model is not without its difficulties. One of the most difficult (and most important) aspects of the DVM is specifying the appropriate growth rate, g, over an extended period of time. Whether you are using the constant-growth or the variable-growth version of the dividend valuation model, the growth rate, g, has an enormous impact on the value derived from the model. As a result, in practice analysts spend a good deal of time trying to come up with a good way to estimate a company's dividend growth rate.

As we saw earlier, we can estimate the growth rate by looking at a company's historical dividend growth. While that approach might work in some cases, it does have some serious shortcomings. What's needed is a procedure that looks at the key forces that actually drive the growth rate. Fortunately, there is such an approach that is widely used in practice. This approach assumes that future dividend growth depends on the rate of return that a firm earns and the fraction of earnings that managers reinvest in the company. Equation 9.10 illustrates this idea:

Equation 9.10 $g = \text{ROE} \times \text{The firm's retention rate, } rr$

where

Equation 9.10a $rr = 1 - \text{Dividend payout ratio}$

Both variables in Equation 9.10 (ROE and *rr*) are directly related to the firm's future growth rate. The retention rate represents the percentage of its profits that the firm plows back into the company. Thus, if the firm pays out 35% of its earnings in dividends (i.e., it has a dividend payout ratio of 35%), then it has a retention rate of 65%: *rr* = 1 − 0.35 = 0.65. The retention rate indicates the amount of capital that is flowing back into the company to finance growth. Other things being equal, the more money managers reinvest in the company, the higher the growth rate.

The other component of Equation 9.10 is the familiar return on equity (ROE). Clearly, the more the company can earn on its retained capital, the higher the growth rate. Remember that ROE is the product of three things: the net profit margin, total asset turnover, and the equity multiplier.

Example

> Consider a situation where a company retains, on average, about 80% of its earnings and generates an ROE of around 18%. (Driving the firm's ROE is a net profit margin of 7.5%, a total asset turnover of 1.20, and an equity multiplier of 2.0.) Under these circumstances, we would expect the firm to have a growth rate of 14.4%:
>
> $$g = \text{ROE} \times rr = 0.18 \times 0.80 = 14.4\%$$

This firm might even achieve faster growth if it raises more capital through a stock offering or borrows more money and thereby increases its equity multiplier. If the firm chooses not to do any of those things, Equation 9.10 gives you a good idea of what growth the company might be able to achieve. To further refine your estimate of a company's growth rate, consider the two key components of the formula (ROE and *rr*) to see whether they're likely to undergo major changes in the future. If so, then what impact is the change in ROE or *rr* likely to have on the growth rate? The idea is to take the time to study the forces (ROE and *rr*) that drive the growth rate because the DVM itself is so sensitive to the rate of growth being used. Employ a growth rate that's too high and you'll end up with an intrinsic value that's way too high also. The downside, of course, is that you may end up buying a stock that you really shouldn't.

Other Approaches to Stock Valuation

In addition to the DVM, the market has developed other ways of valuing stock. One motivation for using these approaches is to find techniques that allow investors to estimate the values of non-dividend-paying stocks. In addition, for a variety of reasons, some investors prefer to use procedures that don't rely on corporate earnings as the basis of valuation. For these investors, it's not earnings that matter, but instead things like cash flow, sales, or book value.

One approach that many investors use is the *free cash flow to equity method* (or simply *the flow to equity method*), which estimates the cash flow that a firm generates for common stockholders, whether it pays those out as dividends or not. Another is the *P/E approach*, which builds the stock valuation process around the stock's price-to-earnings ratio. One of the major advantages of these procedures is that they don't rely on dividends as the primary input. Accordingly, investors can use these methods to value stocks that are more growth-oriented and that pay little or nothing in dividends. Let's take a closer look at both of these approaches, as well as a technique that arrives at the expected return on the stock (in percentage terms) rather than a (dollar-based) "justified price."

Free Cash Flow to Equity As we saw earlier, the value of a share of stock is a function of the amount and timing of future cash flows that stockholders receive and the risk associated with those cash flows. The **free cash flow to equity method** estimates the cash flow that a company generates over time for its shareholders and discounts that to the present to determine the company's total equity value. The model does not consider whether a firm distributes free cash flow by paying dividends or repurchasing shares or whether it merely retains free cash flow. Instead, the model simply accounts for the cash that "flows to equity," meaning that it is the residual cash flow produced by the firm that is not needed to pay bills or fund new investments. The model begins by estimating the free cash flow that a company is expected to generate over time.

Free cash flow to equity is the cash flow that remains after a firm pays all of its expenses and makes necessary investments in working capital and fixed assets. It includes a company's after-tax earnings, plus any noncash expenses like depreciation, minus new investments in working capital and fixed assets. Using the flow-to-equity method requires forecasts of the cash flow going to equity far out into the future, just as the dividend valuation model requires long-term dividend forecasts. With cash flow forecasts in hand, analysts calculate the stock's intrinsic value by taking the present value of free cash flow going to equity and dividing by the number of shares outstanding. We can summarize the flow-to-equity model with the following equations:

Equation 9.11

$$\text{Value of a share of stock} = \frac{\text{present value of future free cash flows going to equity}}{\text{shares outstanding}}$$

$$\text{Free cash flow} = \text{after-tax earnings} + \text{depreciation}$$
$$- \text{investments in working capital} - \text{investments in fixed assets}$$

Equation 9.11a

$$V = \frac{\dfrac{FCF_1}{(1+r)^1} + \dfrac{FCF_2}{(1+r)^2} + \cdots}{N}$$

where

FCF_t = free cash flow in year t
N = number of common shares outstanding

Note that there are similarities here to the dividend-growth model. Equation 9.11a is a present-value calculation, except that we are discounting future free cash flows rather than future dividends. As in the dividend-growth model, we may assume that free cash flows remain constant over time, grow at a constant rate, or grow at a rate that varies over time.

Zero Growth in Free Cash Flow Victor's Secret Sauce is a specialty retail company that sells a variety of bottled sauces for home cooks. Last year (2015) the company generated $2.2 million in after-tax earnings. Victor's took depreciation charges against its fixed assets equal to $250,000, and it invested $50,000 in new working capital and $40,000 in new fixed assets. Thus, the company's free cash flow last year was:

Victor's Secret Sauce free cash flow (2015) = $2,200,000 + $250,000 −
$50,000 − $40,000 = $2,360,000

Victor's had four million common shares outstanding, and the firm's shareholders expected a 9% rate of return on their investment. Suppose you believe that Victor's would continue to generate $2.36 million in free cash flow indefinitely, without additional growth. In other words, you would treat Victor's free cash flow like a perpetuity, so the present value of all of the company's future cash flows would equal:

$$\text{PV of future cash flows} = \$2,360,000 \div 0.09 = \$26,222,222$$

Given that the company has four million outstanding shares, the intrinsic value of the company's stock would be:

Value of Victor's common shares $= \$26,222,222 \div 4,000,000$ shares $= \$6.56$ per share

Our calculation here is analogous to the approach we took in dividend valuation model when dividends were not expected to grow. In this case, however, we are discounting free cash flow rather than dividends, and we take no stand on whether the firm will actually pay this cash out as a dividend in the current year or not.

Constant Growth in Free Cash Flow Now suppose that you expect Victor's free cash flow to grow over time at a constant rate of 2%. This implies that the company will generate cash flow next year (in 2016) that is 2% higher than last year's cash flow. Clearly, with a growing cash flow, Victor's shares should be more valuable than in the no-growth case, and indeed, that is what we find.

$$\text{PV (in 2015) of future cash flows} = \text{Cash flow (in 2016)} \div (r - g)$$
$$\text{PV of future cash flows} = \$2,360,000(1 + 0.02) \div (0.09 - 0.02)$$
$$= \$34,388,571$$
$$\text{Value of common shares} = \$34,388,571 \div 4,000,000 = \$8.60 \text{ per share}$$

Notice that we obtained the present value of Victor's future cash flows in the same way that we did in the constant-growth version of the dividend valuation model. We divided the cash flow expected next year, which is 2% greater than the previous year's free cash flow, by the difference between the required return on the stock and the expected growth rate in cash flow.

Variable Growth in Free Cash Flow Finally, suppose that you expected Victor's Secret Sauce to experience rapid growth in free cash flow for the next couple of years. To be specific, suppose that Victor's cash flow grows 20% next year, 10% the year after that, and then 2% per year for all subsequent years. To value the company's stock, we follow the same method that we used when valuing a company whose dividends grew at a variable rate.

First, calculate the expected free cash flow for 2016 and 2017. If last year's cash flow was $2.36 million, then next year's cash flow will be 20% higher, or $2,832,000 (i.e., $2,360,000 × 1.20). The year after, Victor's cash flow rises another 10% to $3,115,200 (i.e., $2,832,000 × 1.10). Using the required return of 9%, we can calculate the present value of the cash flow generated in the next two years.

Year	Cash Flow	Present Value
2016	$2,832,000	$2,832,000 \div 1.09 = \$2,598,165$
2017	$3,115,200	$3,115,200 \div 1.09^2 = \$2,622,002$

Next, calculate the present value as of 2017 of all the cash flows that Victor's will generate in years 2018 in beyond. In 2018, the company will generate 2% more in cash flow than it did the prior year, and from that point forward, cash flows grow at the constant 2% rate. We can calculate the present value (as of 2017) of all cash flows generated in years 2018 and beyond as follows:

$$PV_{2017} = FCF_{2018} \div (r - g) = FCF_{2017}(1 + g) \div (r - g)$$
$$PV_{2017} = \$3,115,200(1 + 0.02) \div (0.09 - 0.02) = \$45,392,914$$

As of 2017, the present value of all free cash flow that Victor's generates in 2018 and beyond is almost $45.4 million. As an additional step, we need to discount this figure two more years, so we have the present value as of 2015.

$$PV_{2015} = \$45,392,914 \div 1.09^2 = \$38,206,308$$

Now we are ready to calculate the present value of all future free cash flows generated by the company, including the cash flows produced during the rapid growth stage (2016 and 2017) and the cash flows earned during the constant-growth phase (2018 and beyond). Dividing that total by 4,000,000 shares outstanding gives us an estimate of Victor's intrinsic value.

PV of all future cash flows = $2,598,165 + $2,622,002 + $38,206,308
                            = $43,426,474

Value of common shares = $43,426,474 ÷ 4,000,000 = $10.86 per share

To summarize, our estimate of the value of Victor's is $6.56 when we expect no growth in cash flow, $8.60 when we expect steady 2% growth, and $10.86 when we expect rapid growth for two years followed by constant 2% growth. Because the free cash flow to equity method does not focus on the timing and amount of dividends that a company pays, but instead emphasizes the cash flow that the firm generates for its stockholders, it is well suited for valuing younger companies that have not yet established a dividend-paying history.

Using IRR to Solve for the Expected Return Sometimes investors find it more convenient to think about what a stock's expected return will be, given its current market price, rather than try to estimate the stock's intrinsic value. This is no problem, nor is it necessary to sacrifice the present value dimension of the stock valuation model to achieve such an end. You can find the expected return by using a trial-and-error approach to find the discount rate that equates the present value of a company's future free cash flows going to equity (or its future dividends if the firm pays dividends) to the current market value of the firm's common stock. Having estimated the stock's expected return, an investor would then decide whether that return is sufficient to justify buying the stock given its risk.

To see how to estimate a stock's expected return, look once again at the variable growth scenario for Victor's Secret Sauce. Recall that as of the end of 2015, we had the following projections for Victor's free cash flow going to equity:

2016	$2,832,000
2017	$3,115,200

Remember that cash flow in 2018 is 2% higher than in 2017 and that cash flow will continue to grow at 2% indefinitely starting in 2018. This means that as of 2017, the present value of all cash flow that Victor's will generate for stockholders from 2018 and beyond can be calculated as:

$$PV_{2017} = \frac{3,115,200\,(1.02)}{(r - 0.02)} = \frac{3,177,504}{(r - 0.02)}$$

Therefore, if we wanted to calculate the present value in 2015 of Victor's cash flow going to equity, we could use this equation:

$$PV = \frac{2,832,000}{(1 + r)} + \frac{3,115,200}{(1 + r)^2} + \frac{3,177,504 \div (r - 0.02)}{(1 + r)^2}$$

Suppose we know that in 2015 the price of Victor's common stock is $12 per share. With four million common shares outstanding, the total value of Victor's common equity is $48 million. What does that value imply about the expected return on Victor's shares? Just plug $48 million into the equation above as the present value of Victor's free cash flow going to equity, and then use a trial and error method to solve for *r*. If you do this, you will find that the value of *r* that solves the equation is roughly 8.34%. Again, this means that given the cash flow forecast for Victor's and given the company's current stock price, its expected return is 8.34%. An investor who believed that Victor's stock ought to pay a 9% return based on its risk would not see Victor's as an attractive stock at its current $12 per share market price.

The Price-to-Earnings (P/E) Approach One of the problems with the stock valuation procedures we've looked at so far is that they require long-term forecasts of either dividends or free cash flows. They involve a good deal of "number crunching," and naturally the valuations that these models produce are only as good as the forecasts that go into them. Fortunately, there is a simpler approach. That alternative is the **price-to-earnings (P/E) approach** to stock valuation.

The P/E approach is a favorite of professional security analysts and is widely used in practice. It's relatively simple to use. It's based on the standard P/E formula first introduced previously. We showed that a stock's P/E ratio is equal to its market price divided by the stock's EPS. Using this equation and solving for the market price of the stock, we have

Equation 9.12 $$\text{Stock price} = \text{EPS} \times \text{P/E ratio}$$

Equation 9.12 basically captures the P/E approach to stock valuation. That is, given an estimated EPS figure, you decide on a P/E ratio that you feel is appropriate for the stock. Then you use it in Equation 9.12 to see what kind of price you come up with and how that compares to the stock's current price.

Actually, this approach is no different from what's used in the market every day. Look at the stock quotes in the *Wall Street Journal* or online at Yahoo! Finance. They include the stock's P/E ratio and show what investors are willing to pay for each dollar of earnings. Essentially, this ratio relates the company's earnings per share for the last 12 months (known as *trailing earnings*) to the latest price of the stock. In practice, however, investors buy stocks not for their past earnings but for their expected future earnings. Thus, in Equation 9.12, it's customary to use forecasted EPS for next year—that is, to use projected earnings one year out.

The first thing you have to do to implement the P/E approach is to come up with an expected EPS figure for next year. In the early part of this chapter, we saw how this might be done (see, for instance, Equations 9.2 and 9.3 on pages 302 and 303). Given the forecasted EPS, the next step is to evaluate the variables that drive the P/E ratio. Most of that assessment is intuitive. For example, you might look at the stock's expected rate of growth in earnings, any potential major changes in the firm's capital structure or dividends, and any other factors such as relative market or industry P/E multiples that might affect the stock's multiple. You could use such inputs to come up with a base P/E ratio. Then adjust that base, as necessary, to account for the perceived state of the market and/or anticipated changes in the rate of inflation.

Along with estimated EPS, we now have the P/E ratio we need to compute (via Equation 9.12) the price at which the stock should be trading. Take, for example, a stock that's currently trading at $37.80. One year from now, it's estimated that this stock should have an EPS of $2.25 a share. If you feel that the stock should be trading at a P/E ratio of 20 times projected earnings, then it should be valued at $45 a share (i.e., $2.25 × 20). By comparing this targeted price to the current market price of the stock, you can decide whether the stock is a good buy. In this case, you would consider the stock undervalued and therefore a good buy, since the computed price of the stock of $45 is more than its market price of $37.80.

Other Price-Relative Procedures

As we saw with the P/E approach, price-relative procedures base their valuations on the assumptions that the value of a share of stock should be directly linked to a given performance characteristic of the firm, such as earnings per share. These procedures involve a good deal of judgment and intuition, and they rely heavily on the market expertise of the analysts. Besides the P/E approach, there are several other price-relative procedures that are used by investors who, for one reason or another, want to use some measure other than earnings to value stocks. They include:

- The price-to-cash-flow (P/CF) ratio
- The price-to-sales (P/S) ratio
- The price-to-book-value (P/BV) ratio

Like the P/E multiple, these procedures determine the value of a stock by relating share price to cash flow, sales, or book value. Let's look at each of these in turn to see how they're used in stock valuation.

A Price-to-Cash-Flow (P/CF) Procedure This measure has long been popular with investors who believe that cash flow provides a more accurate picture of a company's true value than do net earnings. When used in stock valuation, the procedure is almost identical to the P/E approach. That is, analysts use a P/CF ratio along with projected cash flow per share to estimate the stock's value.

Although it is quite straightforward, this procedure nonetheless has one problem—defining the appropriate cash flow measure. While some investors use cash flow from operating activities, as obtained from the statement of cash flows, others use free cash flow. The one measure that seems to be the most popular with professional analysts is EBITDA (earnings before interest, taxes, depreciation, and amortization), which we'll use here. EBITDA represents "pretax cash earnings" to the extent that the major noncash expenditures (depreciation and amortization) are added back to operating earnings (EBIT).

The price-to-cash-flow ratio is computed as follows:

Equation 9.13
$$\text{P/CF ratio} = \frac{\text{Market price of common stock}}{\text{Cash flow per share}}$$

where cash flow per share = EBITDA ÷ number of common shares outstanding.

Before you can use the P/CF procedure to assess the current market price of a stock, you first have to come up with a forecasted cash flow per share one year out and then define an appropriate P/CF multiple to use. For most firms, it is very likely that the cash flow (EBITDA) figure will be larger than net earnings available to stockholders. As a result, the cash flow multiple will probably be lower than the P/E multiple. In any event, once you determine an appropriate P/CF multiple (subjectively and with the help of any historical market information), simply multiply it by the expected cash flow per share one year from now to find the price at which the stock should be trading. That is, the computed price of a share of stock = cash flow per share × P/CF ratio.

Example

> Assume a company currently is generating an EBITDA of $325 million, which is expected to increase by some 12% to around $364 million (i.e., $325 million × 1.12) over the course of the next 12 months. Suppose the company has 56 million shares of stock outstanding. The company's projected cash flow per share is $6.50. If we feel this stock should be trading at about eight times its projected cash flow per share, then it should be valued at around $52 a share. Thus, if it is currently trading in the market at $45.50 (or at seven times its projected cash flow per share), we can conclude, once again, that the stock is undervalued and, therefore, should be considered a viable investment candidate.

Price-to-Sales (P/S) and Price-to-Book-Value (P/BV) Ratios Some companies, like high-tech startups, have little, if any, earnings. Or if they do have earnings, they tend to be quite volatile and therefore highly unpredictable. In these cases, valuation procedures based on earnings (and even cash flows) aren't much help. So investors turn to other procedures—those based on sales or book value, for example. While companies may not have much in the way of profits, they almost always have sales and, ideally, some book value.

Investors use the P/S and P/BV ratios exactly like the P/E and P/CF procedures:

$$\text{P/BV ratio} = \frac{\text{Market price of common stock}}{\text{Book value per share}}$$

We can define the P/S ratio in a similar fashion:

Equation 9.14

$$\text{P/S ratio} = \frac{\text{Market price of common stock}}{\text{Sales per share}}$$

INVESTOR FACTS

Crafty Investors Spot Problem with Etsy's IPO In April 2015, Etsy, Inc., the online marketplace for hand-crafted goods, became a public company by issuing shares to the public in an IPO. Initially priced at $16 per share, Etsy's common stock doubled on its first trading day. That runup put Etsy's price-to-sales ratio into double digits, several times higher than the P/S of the S&P 500, and even higher than some of the most rapidly growing tech stocks. Etsy's inflated P/S ratio was a sign of trouble to come, as the stock lost more than 40% of its value in its first two months of trading.

where sales per share equals net annual sales (or revenues) divided by the number of common shares outstanding.

Many bargain-hunting investors look for stocks with P/S ratios of 2.0 or less. They believe that these securities offer the most potential for future price appreciation. Especially attractive to these investors are very low P/S multiples of 1.0 or less. Think about it: With a P/S ratio of, say, 0.9, you can buy $1 in sales for only 90 cents! As long as the company can convert some of the sales into cash flow and earnings for shareholders, such low P/S multiples may well be worth pursuing.

Keep in mind that while the emphasis may be on low multiples, high P/S ratios aren't necessarily bad. To determine if a high multiple—more than 3.0 or 4.0, for example—is justified, look at the company's net profit margin. Companies that can consistently generate high net profit margins often have high P/S ratios. Here's a valuation rule to remember: High profit margins should go hand-in-hand with high P/S multiples. That makes sense because a company with a high profit margin brings more of its sales down to the bottom line in the form of profits.

You would also expect the price-to-book-value measure to be low, but probably not as low as the P/S ratio. Indeed, unless the market becomes grossly overvalued (think about what happened in 1999 and 2000), most stocks are likely to trade at multiples of less than three to five times their book values. And in this case, unlike with the P/S multiple, there's usually little justification for abnormally high price-to-book-value ratios—except perhaps for firms that have abnormally low levels of equity in their capital structures. Other than that, high P/BV multiples are almost always caused by "excess exuberance." As a rule, when stocks start trading at seven or eight times their book values, or more, they are becoming overvalued.

CONCEPTS IN REVIEW

Answers available at http://www.pearsonhighered.com/smart

9.6 Briefly describe the dividend valuation model and the three versions of this model. Explain how CAPM fits into the DVM.

9.7 What is the difference between the variable-growth dividend valuation model and the free cash flow to equity approach to stock valuation? Which procedure would work better if you were trying to value a growth stock that pays little or no dividends? Explain.

9.8 How would you go about finding the expected return on a stock? Note how such information would be used in the stock selection process.

9.9 Briefly describe the P/E approach to stock valuation and note how this approach differs from the variable-growth DVM. Describe the P/CF approach and note how it is used in the stock valuation process. Compare the P/CF approach to the P/E approach, noting the relative strengths and weaknesses of each.

9.10 Briefly describe the price-to-sales ratio and explain how it is used to value stocks. Why not just use the P/E multiple? How does the P/S ratio differ from the P/BV measure?

MyFinanceLab

Here is what you should know after reading this chapter. MyFinanceLab will help you identify what you know and where to go when you need to practice.

What You Should Know	Key Terms	Where to Practice
LG 1 Explain the role that a company's future plays in the stock valuation process. The final phase of security analysis involves an assessment of the investment merits of a specific company and its stock. The focus here is on formulating expectations about the company's prospects and the risk and return behavior of the stock. In particular, we would want some idea of the stock's future earnings, dividends, and share prices, which are ultimately the basis of return.	common-size income statement, *p. 300* relative P/E multiple, *p. 304* stock valuation, *p. 300* target price, *p. 306*	MyFinanceLab Study Plan 9.1 Excel Table 9.1

What You Should Know	Key Terms	Where to Practice
LG2 Develop a forecast of a stock's expected cash flow, starting with corporate sales and earnings, and then moving to expected dividends and share price. Because the value of a share of stock is a function of its future returns, investors must formulate expectations about what the future holds for the company. Look first at the company's projected sales and earnings, and then translate those data into forecasted dividends and share prices. These variables define an investment's future cash flow and, therefore, investor returns.	valuation, *p.* 309	MyFinanceLab Study Plan 9.2 Excel Table 9.3
LG3 Discuss the concepts of intrinsic value and required rates of return, and note how they are used. Information such as projected sales, forecasted earnings, and estimated dividends are important in establishing intrinsic value. This is a measure, based on expected return and risk exposure, of what the stock ought to be worth. A key element is the investor's required rate of return, which is used to define the amount of return that should be earned given the stock's perceived exposure to risk.	required rate of return, *p. 309*	MyFinanceLab Study Plan 9.3 Video Learning Aid for Problem P9.18
LG4 Determine the underlying value of a stock using the zero-growth, constant-growth, and variable-growth dividend valuation models. The dividend valuation model derives the value of a share of stock from the stock's future growth in dividends. There are three versions of the DVM. Zero-growth valuation assumes that dividends are fixed and won't change. Constant-growth valuation assumes that dividends will grow at a constant rate into the future. Variable-growth valuation assumes that dividends will initially grow at varying (or abnormally high) rates before eventually settling down to a constant rate of growth.	dividend valuation model (DVM), *p.* 311	MyFinanceLab Study Plan 9.4 Excel Table 9.4 Video Learning Aid for Problem P9.9
LG5 Use other types of present value-based models to derive the value of a stock, as well as alternative price-relative procedures. The DVM works well with some types of stocks but not so well with others. Investors may turn to other stock-valuation approaches, including the free cash flow to equity approach, as well as certain price-relative procedures, like the P/E, P/CF, P/S, and P/BV methods. The free cash flow to equity model projects the free cash flows that a firm will generate over time, discounts them to the present, and divides by the number of shares outstanding to estimate a common stock's intrinsic value. Several price-relative procedures exist as well, such as the price-to-earnings approach, which uses projected EPS and the stock's P/E ratio to determine whether a stock is fairly valued.	free cash flow to equity method, *p. 320* free cash flow, *p. 320* price-to-earnings (P/E) approach, *p. 323*	MyFinanceLab Study Plan 9.5 Video Learning Aid for Problem P9.18

What You Should Know	Key Terms	Where to Practice
LG6 Understand the procedures used to value different types of stocks, from traditional dividend-paying shares to more growth-oriented stocks. All sorts of stock valuation models are used in the market; this chapter examined several widely used procedures. One thing that becomes apparent in stock evaluation is that one approach definitely does not fit all situations. Some approaches (e.g., the DVM) work well with mature, dividend-paying companies. Others (e.g., the P/E and P/CF approaches) are more suited to growth-oriented firms, which may not pay dividends. Other price-relative procedures (e.g., P/S and P/BV) are often used to value companies that have little or nothing in earnings or whose earnings records are sporadic.		MyFinanceLab Study Plan 9.6

Log into MyFinanceLab, take a chapter test, and get a personalized Study Plan that tells you which concepts you understand and which ones you need to review. From there, MyFinanceLab will give you further practice, tutorials, animations, videos, and guided solutions.
Log into http://www.myfinancelab.com

Discussion Questions

LG1   **Q9.1**   Select a company from *Yahoo! Finance* or another online source that would be of interest to you. (*Hint*: Pick a company that's been publicly traded for at least 10 years and avoid public utilities, banks, and other financial institutions.) Using the historical and forecasted data reported in the source you select, along with one of the valuation techniques described in this chapter, calculate the maximum (i.e., justified) price you'd be willing to pay for this stock. Use the CAPM to find the required rate of return on your stock. (For this problem, use a market rate of return of 10%, and for the risk-free rate, use the latest three-month Treasury bill rate.)
   a.   How does the justified price you computed compare to the latest market price of the stock?
   b.   Would you consider this stock to be a worthwhile investment candidate? Explain.

LG5   **LG6**   **Q9.2**   In this chapter, we examined nine stock valuation procedures:
   • Zero-growth DVM
   • Constant-growth DVM
   • Variable-growth DVM
   • Free cash flow to equity approach
   • Expected return (IRR) approach
   • P/E approach
   • Price-to-cash-flow ratio
   • Price-to-sales ratio
   • Price-to-book-value ratio

    a. Which one (or more) of these procedures would be appropriate when trying to put a value on:

       1. A growth stock that pays little or nothing in dividends?

       2. The S&P 500?

       3. A relatively new company that has only a brief history of earnings?

       4. A large, mature, dividend-paying company?

       5. A preferred stock that pays a fixed dividend?

       6. A company that has a large amount of depreciation and amortization?

    b. Of the nine procedures listed above, which three do you think are the best? Explain.

    c. If you had to choose just one procedure to use in practice, which would it be? Explain. (*Note:* Confine your selection to the list above.)

LG1 LG3 Q9.3 Explain the role that the future plays in the stock valuation process. Why not just base the valuation on historical information? Explain how the intrinsic value of a stock is related to its required rate of return. Illustrate what happens to the value of a stock when the required rate of return increases.

LG4 Q9.4 Assume an investor uses the constant-growth DVM to value a stock. Listed below are various situations that could affect the computed value of a stock. Look at each one of these individually and indicate whether it would cause the computed value of a stock to go up, go down, or stay the same. Briefly explain your answers.

    a. Dividend payout ratio goes up.

    b. Stock's beta rises.

    c. Equity multiplier goes down.

    d. T-bill rates fall.

    e. Net profit margin goes up.

    f. Total asset turnover falls.

    g. Market return increases.

Assume throughout that the current dividend (D_0) remains the same and that all other variables in the model are unchanged.

Problems

All problems are available on http://www.myfinancelab.com

LG1 P9.1 An investor estimates that next year's sales for Dursley's Hotels, Inc., should amount to about $100 million. The company has five million shares outstanding, generates a net profit margin of about 10%, and has a payout ratio of 50%. All figures are expected to hold for next year. Given this information, compute the following.

    a. Estimated net earnings for next year

    b. Next year's dividends per share

    c. The expected price of the stock (assuming the P/E ratio is 24.5 times earnings)

    d. The expected holding period return (latest stock price: $40 per share)

LG2 P9.2 GrowthCo had sales of $55 million in 2016 and is expected to have sales of $83,650,000 for 2017. The company's net profit margin was 5% in 2016 and is expected to increase to 8% by 2017. Estimate the company's net profit for 2017.

LG2 P9.3 Granger Toothpaste Corp. has total equity of $600 million and 125 million shares outstanding. Its ROE is 18%. Calculate the company's EPS.

LG2 P9.4 Goodstuff Corporation has total equity of $500 million and 100 million shares outstanding. Its ROE is 15%. The dividend payout ratio is 33.3%. Calculate the company's dividends per share (round to the nearest penny).

LG2   **P9.5**   HighTeck has an ROE of 15%. Its earnings per share are $2.00, and its dividends per share are $0.20. Estimate HighTeck's growth rate.

LG2   **P9.6**   Last year, InDebt Company paid $75 million of interest expense, and its average rate of interest for the year was 10%. The company's ROE is 15%, and it pays no dividends. Estimate next year's interest expense assuming that interest rates will fall by 25% and the company keeps a constant equity multiplier of 20%.

LG2   **P9.7**   From 2010 to 2015 Steller Strollers, Inc., has paid dividends of $1.06, $1.13, $1.21, $1.25, $1.31, and $1.38. Use an Excel spreadsheet like the template below to find Steller's historical dividend growth rate.

	A	B
1	**GROWTH RATE FOR A DIVIDEND STREAM**	
2	Year	Dividend
3		
4		
5		
6		
7		
8		
9	Annual Growth Rate	=RATE((A8-A3),0,-B3,B8,0)
10	Entry in Cell B9 is =RATE((A8-A3),0,-B3,B8,0). The expression (A8-A3) in the entry calculates the number of years of growth. The minus sign appears before B3 because the dividend in 2002 is treated as a cash outflow.	

LG2   **P9.8**   Melissa Popp is thinking about buying some shares of R. H. Lawncare Equipment, at $48 per share. She expects the price of the stock to rise to $60 over the next three years. During that time she also expects to receive annual dividends of $4 per share.
   a.   What is the intrinsic worth of this stock, given a 12% required rate of return?
   b.   What is its expected return?

LG4   **P9.9**   Investors expect that Amalgamated Aircraft Parts, Inc., will pay a dividend of $2.50 in the coming year. Investors require a 12% rate of return on the company's shares, and they expect dividends to grow at 7% per year. Using the dividend valuation model, find the intrinsic value of the company's common shares.

LG4   **P9.10**   Danny is considering a stock purchase. The stock pays a constant annual dividend of $2.00 per share and is currently trading at $20. Danny's required rate of return for this stock is 12%. Should he buy this stock?

LG4   **LG5**   **P9.11**   Larry and Curley are brothers. They're both serious investors, but they have different approaches to valuing stocks. Larry, the older brother, likes to use the dividend valuation model. Curley prefers the free cash flow to equity valuation model.
   As it turns out, right now, both of them are looking at the same stock—American Home Care Products, Inc. (AHCP). The company has been listed on the NYSE for over 50 years and is widely regarded as a mature, rock-solid, dividend-paying stock. The brothers have gathered the following information about AHCP's stock:

Current dividend (D_0) = $2.50/share

Current free cash flow (FCF_0) = $1 million

Expected growth rate of dividends and cash flows (g) = 5.0%

Required rate of return (r) = 12.0%

Shares outstanding = 400,000

How would Larry and Curley each value this stock?

LG5 **P9.12** Assume you've generated the following information about the stock of Bufford's Burger Barns: The company's latest dividends of $4 a share are expected to grow to $4.32 next year, to $4.67 the year after that, and to $5.04 in three years. After that, you think dividends will grow at a constant 6% rate.

    a. Use the variable growth version of the dividend valuation model and a required return of 15% to find the value of the stock.

    b. Suppose you plan to hold the stock for three years, selling it immediately after receiving the $5.04 dividend. What is the stock's expected selling price at that time? As in part (a), assume a required return of 15%.

    c. Imagine that you buy the stock today paying a price equal to the value that you calculated in part (a). You hold the stock for three years, receiving the dividends as described above. Immediately after receiving the third dividend, you sell the stock at the price calculated in part **b**. Use the IRR approach to calculate the expected return on the stock over three years. Could you have guessed what the answer would be before doing the calculation?

    d. Suppose the stock's current market price is actually $44.65. Based on your analysis from part **a**, is the stock overvalued or undervalued?

    e. A friend of yours agrees with your projections of Bufford's future dividends, but he believes that in three years, just after the company pays the $5.04 dividend, the stock will be selling in the market for $53.42. Given that belief, along with the stock's current market price from part **d**, calculate the return that your friend expects to earn on this stock over the next three years.

LG6 **P9.13** Let's assume that you're thinking about buying stock in West Coast Electronics. So far in your analysis, you've uncovered the following information: The stock pays annual dividends of $5.00 a share indefinitely. It trades at a P/E of 10 times earnings and has a beta of 1.2. In addition, you plan on using a risk-free rate of 3% in the CAPM, along with a market return of 10%. You would like to hold the stock for three years, at the end of which time you think EPS will be $7 a share. Given that the stock currently trades at $62, use the IRR approach to find this security's expected return. Now use the dividend valuation model (with constant dividends) to put a price on this stock. Does this look like a good investment to you? Explain.

LG6 **P9.14** The price of Myrtle's Plumbing Supply Co. is now $80. The company pays no dividends. Ms. Bossard expects the price three years from now to be $110 per share. Should she buy Myrtle's Plumbing stock if she desires a 10% rate of return? Explain.

LG5 **P9.15** This year, Shoreline Light and Gas (SL&G) paid its stockholders an annual dividend of $3 a share. A major brokerage firm recently put out a report on SL&G predicting that the company's annual dividends would grow at the rate of 10% per year for each of the next five years and then level off and grow at 6% thereafter.

    a. Use the variable-growth DVM and a required rate of return of 12% to find the maximum price you should be willing to pay for this stock.

    b. Redo the SL&G problem in part **a**, this time assuming that after year 5, dividends stop growing altogether (for year 6 and beyond, $g = 0$). Use all the other information given to find the stock's intrinsic value.

    c. Contrast your two answers and comment on your findings. How important is growth to this valuation model?

LG5 **P9.16** Assume there are three companies that in the past year paid exactly the same annual dividend of $2.25 a share. In addition, the future annual rate of growth in dividends for each of the three companies has been estimated as follows:

Buggies-Are-Us	Steady Freddie, Inc.	Gang Buster Group	
$g = 0$	$g = 6\%$	Year 1	$2.53
(i.e., dividends	(for the	2	$2.85
are expected to	foreseeable	3	$3.20
remain at	future)	4	$3.60
$2.25/share)		Year 5 and beyond: $g = 6\%$	

Assume also that as the result of a strange set of circumstances, these three companies all have the same required rate of return ($r = 10\%$).

a. Use the appropriate DVM to value each of these companies.

b. Comment briefly on the comparative values of these three companies. What is the major cause of the differences among these valuations?

LG5 **P9.17** New Millennium Company earned $2.5 million in net income last year. It took depreciation deductions of $300,000 and made new investments in working capital and fixed assets of $100,000 and $350,000, respectively.

a. What was New Millennium's free cash flow last year?

b. Suppose that the company's free cash flow is expected to grow at 5% per year forever. If investor's require an 8% return on Millennium stock, what is the present value of Millennium's future free cash flows?

c. New Millennium has 3.5 million shares of common stock outstanding. What is the per-share value of the company's common stock?

d. What is the company's P/E ratio based on last year's earnings (i.e., trailing earnings)?

e. What is the company's P/E ratio based on next year's earnings (assume that earnings grow at the same rate as free cash flow).

LG6 **P9.18** A particular company currently has sales of $250 million; sales are expected to grow by 20% next year (year 1). For the year after next (year 2), the growth rate in sales is expected to equal 10%. Over each of the next two years, the company is expected to have a net profit margin of 8% and a payout ratio of 50% and to maintain the common stock outstanding at 15 million shares. The stock always trades at a P/E of 15 times earnings, and the investor has a required rate of return of 20%. Given this information,

a. Find the stock's intrinsic value (its justified price).

b. Use the IRR approach to determine the stock's expected return, given that it is currently trading at $15 per share.

c. Find the holding period returns for this stock for year 1 and for year 2.

LG3 **LG5** **P9.19** Assume a major investment service has just given Oasis Electronics its highest investment rating, along with a strong buy recommendation. As a result, you decide to take a look for yourself and to place a value on the company's stock. Here's what you find: This year Oasis paid its stockholders an annual dividend of $3 a share, but because of its high rate of growth in earnings, its dividends are expected to grow at the rate of 12% a year for the next four years and then to level out at 9% a year. So far, you've learned that the stock has a beta of 1.80, the risk-free rate of return is 5%, and the expected return on the market is 11%. Using the CAPM to find the required rate of return, put a value on this stock.

LG5 **P9.20** Consolidated Software doesn't currently pay any dividends but is expected to start doing so in four years. That is, Consolidated will go three more years without paying dividends and then is expected to pay its first dividend (of $3 per share) in the fourth year. Once the company starts paying dividends, it's expected to continue to do so. The company is expected to have a dividend payout ratio of 40% and to maintain a return on equity of

20%. Based on the DVM, and given a required rate of return of 15%, what is the maximum price you should be willing to pay for this stock today?

LG5 P9.21 Assume you obtain the following information about a certain company:

Total assets	$50,000,000
Total equity	$25,000,000
Net income	$3,750,000
EPS	$5.00 per share
Dividend payout ratio	40%
Required return	12%

Use the constant-growth DVM to place a value on this company's stock.

LG6 P9.22 You're thinking about buying some stock in Affiliated Computer Corporation and want to use the P/E approach to value the shares. You've estimated that next year's earnings should come in at about $4.00 a share. In addition, although the stock normally trades at a relative P/E of 1.15 times the market, you believe that the relative P/E will rise to 1.25, whereas the market P/E should be around 18.5 times earnings. Given this information, what is the maximum price you should be willing to pay for this stock? If you buy this stock today at $87.50, what rate of return will you earn over the next 12 months if the price of the stock rises to $110.00 by the end of the year? (Assume that the stock doesn't pay dividends.)

LG5 P9.23 AviBank Plastics generated an EPS of $2.75 over the last 12 months. The company's earnings are expected to grow by 25% next year, and because there will be no significant change in the number of shares outstanding, EPS should grow at about the same rate. You feel the stock should trade at a P/E of around 30 times earnings. Use the P/E approach to set a value on this stock.

LG6 P9.24 Newco is a young company that has yet to make a profit. You are trying to place a value on the stock, but it pays no dividends and you obviously cannot calculate a P/E ratio. As a result, you decide to look at other stocks in the same industry as Newco to see if you can find a way to value this company. You find the following information:

	Per-Share Data ($)			
	Newco	Adolescentco	Middle-Ageco	Oldco
Sales	$10	$200	$800	$800
Profit	–$10	$ 10	$ 60	$ 80
Book value	–$ 2	$ 2	$ 5	$ 8
Market value	?	$ 20	$ 80	$ 75

Estimate a market value for Newco. Discuss how your estimate could change if Newco was expected to grow much faster than the other companies.

LG4 P9.25 World Wide Web Wares (4W, for short) is an online retailer of small kitchen appliances and utensils. The firm has been around for a few years and has created a nice market niche for itself. In fact, it actually turned a profit last year, albeit a fairly small one. After doing some basic research on the company, you've decided to take a closer look. You plan to use the price-to-sales ratio to value the stock, and you have collected P/S multiples on the following Internet retailer stocks:

Company	P/S Multiples
Amazing.com	4.5
ReallyCooking.com	4.1
Fixtures & Appliances Online	3.8

Find the average P/S ratio for these three firms. Given that 4W is expected to generate $40 million in sales next year and will have 10 million shares of stock outstanding, use the average P/S ratio you computed above to put a value on 4W's stock.

Visit **http://www.myfinancelab.com** for web exercises, spreadsheets, and other online resources

Case Problem 9.1   Chris Looks for a Way to Invest His Wealth

LG1 LG2 LG4   Chris Norton is a young Hollywood writer who is well on his way to television superstardom. After writing several successful television specials, he was recently named the head writer for one of TV's top-rated sitcoms. Chris fully realizes that his business is a fickle one, and on the advice of his dad and manager, he has decided to set up an investment program. Chris will earn about a half-million dollars this year. Because of his age, income level, and desire to get as big a bang as possible from his investment dollars, he has decided to invest in speculative, high-growth stocks.

Chris is currently working with a respected Beverly Hills broker and is in the process of building up a diversified portfolio of speculative stocks. The broker recently sent him information on a hot new issue. She advised Chris to study the numbers and, if he likes them, to buy as many as 1,000 shares of the stock. Among other things, corporate sales for the next three years have been forecasted as follows:

Year	Sales ($ millions)
1	$22.5
2	$35.0
3	$50.0

The firm has 2.5 million shares of common stock outstanding. They are currently being traded at $70 a share and pay no dividends. The company has a net profit rate of 20%, and its stock has been trading at a P/E of around 40 times earnings. All these operating characteristics are expected to hold in the future.

Questions

a. Looking first at the stock:
1. Compute the company's net profits and EPS for each of the next 3 years.
2. Compute the price of the stock three years from now.
3. Assuming that all expectations hold up and that Chris buys the stock at $70, determine his expected return on this investment.
4. What risks is he facing by buying this stock? Be specific.
5. Should he consider the stock a worthwhile investment candidate? Explain.

b. Looking at Chris's investment program in general:
1. What do you think of his investment program? What do you see as its strengths and weaknesses?
2. Are there any suggestions you would make?
3. Do you think Chris should consider adding foreign stocks to his portfolio? Explain.

Case Problem 9.2   An Analysis of a High-Flying Stock

LG2 LG6   Marc Dodier is a recent university graduate and a security analyst with the Kansas City brokerage firm of Lippman, Brickbats, and Shaft. Marc has been following one of the hottest issues on Wall Street, C&I Medical Supplies, a company that has turned in an outstanding performance lately and, even more important, has exhibited excellent growth potential. It has five million shares outstanding and pays a nominal annual dividend of $0.05 per share. Marc has decided to take a closer look at C&I to assess its investment potential. Assume the company's sales for the past five years have been as follows:

Year	Sales ($ millions)
2012	$10.0
2013	$12.5
2014	$16.2
2015	$22.0
2016	$28.5

Marc is concerned with the future prospects of the company, not its past. As a result, he pores over the numbers and generates the following estimates of future performance:

Expected net profit margin	12%
Estimated annual dividends per share	5¢
Number of common shares outstanding	No change
P/E ratio at the end of 2017	35
P/E ratio at the end of 2018	50

Questions

a. Determine the average annual rate of growth in sales over the past five years. (Assume sales in 2011 amounted to $7.5 million.)

   1. Use this average growth rate to forecast revenues for next year (2017) and the year after that (2018).

   2. Now determine the company's net earnings and EPS for each of the next two years (2017 and 2018).

   3. Finally, determine the expected future price of the stock at the end of this two-year period.

b. Because of several intrinsic and market factors, Marc feels that 25% is a viable figure to use for a desired rate of return.

   1. Using the 25% rate of return and the forecasted figures you came up with in question a, compute the stock's justified price.

   2. If C&I is currently trading at $32.50 per share, should Marc consider the stock a worthwhile investment candidate? Explain.

Excel@Investing

Excel@Investing   Fundamental to the valuation process is the determination of the intrinsic value of a security, where an investor calculates the present value of the expected future cash benefits of the investment. Specifically, in the case of common stock, these future cash flows are defined by expected future dividend payments and future potential price appreciation. A simple but useful way to view stock value is that it is equal to the present value of all expected future dividends it may provide over an infinite time horizon.

Based on this latter concept, the dividend valuation model (DVM) has evolved. It can take on any one of three versions—the zero-growth model, the constant-growth model, and the variable-growth model.

Create a spreadsheet that applies the variable-growth model to predict the intrinsic value of the Rhyhorn Company common stock. Assume that dividends will grow at a variable rate for the next three years (2016, 2017, and 2018). After that, the annual rate of growth in dividends is expected to be 7% and stay there for the foreseeable future. Starting with the latest (2015) annual dividend of $2.00 per share, Rhyhorn's earnings and dividends are estimated to grow by 18% in 2016, by 14% in 2017, and by 9% in 2018 before dropping to a 7% rate. Given the risk profile of the firm, assume a minimum required rate of return of at least 12%. The spreadsheet for Table 9.4, which you can view on http://www.myfinance.lab.com, is a good reference for solving this problem.

Questions

a. Calculate the projected annual dividends over the years 2016, 2017, and 2018.

b. Determine the present value of dividends during the initial variable-growth period.

c. What do you believe the price of Rhyhorn stock will be at the end of the initial growth period (2018)?

d. Having determined the expected future price of Rhyhorn stock in part c, discount the price of the stock back to its present value.

e. Determine the total intrinsic value of Rhyhorn stock based on your calculations above.

Chapter-Opening Problem

At the beginning of this chapter you read about a 2015 earnings announcement from HP in which earnings per share were reported as $1.85 for the quarter. Let's make a simple assumption and say that earnings for the year were four times as much, or $7.40 per share. At the time of that announcement, the average P/E for stocks in the U.S. was close to 15.

a. If you use the market's P/E and HP's current earnings to estimate the stock's intrinsic value, what value do you obtain?

b. The actual price of HP after the earnings announcement was about $73. What does this tell you about your answer to part a?

c. Suppose HP paid out all of its earnings as a dividend. Suppose also that investors expected the firm to continue doing that forever, and because the company was not reinvesting any earnings, investors expected no growth in dividends. If the required return on HP stock is 9%, what is the stock price?

d. Comment on your answer to part c in light of HP's market price at the time.

10

Return and Risk

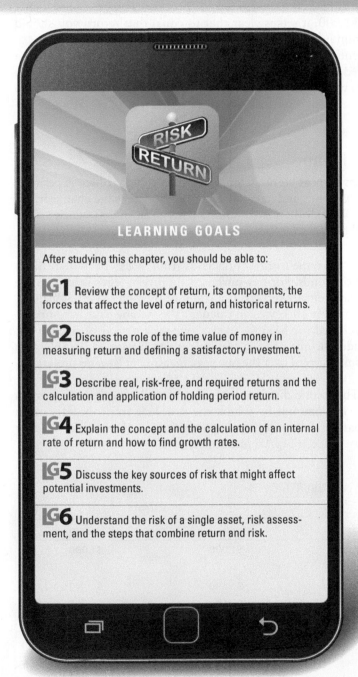

LEARNING GOALS

After studying this chapter, you should be able to:

LG1 Review the concept of return, its components, the forces that affect the level of return, and historical returns.

LG2 Discuss the role of the time value of money in measuring return and defining a satisfactory investment.

LG3 Describe real, risk-free, and required returns and the calculation and application of holding period return.

LG4 Explain the concept and the calculation of an internal rate of return and how to find growth rates.

LG5 Discuss the key sources of risk that might affect potential investments.

LG6 Understand the risk of a single asset, risk assessment, and the steps that combine return and risk.

An old saying often attributed to Mark Twain advises, "Buy land—they're not making it anymore." That bit of folk wisdom gained enormous popularity during the U.S. real estate boom. According to the S&P/Case-Shiller Index, which tracks home prices in 20 large cities, U.S. homeowners saw their property values increase more than 100% from 2000 to 2005. Over the same six years, the U.S. stock market (as measured by the S&P 500 Index) lost more than 7% of its value.

Moreover, the tantalizing returns on real estate seemed to come without much risk. The average home price rose every single month from July 1996 to May 2006. No wonder, then, that investing in real estate became fashionable, as evidenced by the introduction of television shows such as A&E's *Flip This House*. It seemed that no one could lose money by investing in residential real estate.

Unfortunately, home prices began to decline in late summer 2006, and their fall continued through March 2012. Over that period, average home prices dropped 34% and millions of properties were lost to foreclosure, reminding homeowners that investing in real estate has both rewards and risks. After hitting bottom in March 2012 the S&P/Case-Shiller Index rose 29% by the end of 2014; however, this rebound lagged behind the S&P 500 Index return of 46% over the same period.

The boom and bust cycles in both the housing and stock markets over the last decade provide great examples of the almost inextricable link between risk and return. Some investments may deliver high returns for several consecutive years, just as housing did in the mid 2000s, but high returns tend to be associated with high risks, as investors in housing learned after 2006. This chapter and the next discuss tools that will help you quantify the tradeoff between risk and return.

(Source: S&P/Case-Shiller price indexes downloaded from http://www.standardandpoors.com and http://www.realtytrac.com/, "Year-End 2014 U.S. Foreclosure Market Report.")

The Concept of Return

LG1 LG2 People are motivated to invest in a given asset by its expected return. The **return** is the level of profit from an investment—that is, the reward for investing. Suppose you have $1,000 in an insured savings account paying 2% annual interest, and a business associate asks you to lend her that much money. If you lend her the money for one year, at the end of which she pays you back, your return will depend on the amount of interest you charge. If you make an interest-free loan, your return will be 0. If you charge 2% interest, your return will be $20 (i.e., 0.02 × $1,000). Because you are already earning a safe 2% on the $1,000, it seems clear that to equal that return you should charge your associate a minimum of 2% interest.

Some investments guarantee a return, but most do not. The return on a bank deposit insured by the federal government is virtually certain. The return earned on a loan to your business associate might be less certain. The size and the certainty of the expected return are important factors in choosing a suitable investment.

Components of Return

The return on an investment comes from two sources. One source is periodic payments, such as dividends and interest. The other source is the change in the investment's price. We call these two components of an investment's return *current income* and *capital gains* (or *capital losses*), respectively.

Income Income may take the form of dividends from stocks or mutual funds or interest received on bonds. For our purposes, an investment's **income** is the cash that investors periodically receive as a result of owning the investment.

Using the data in Table 10.1, we can calculate the income from investments A and B, both purchased for $1,000, over a one-year period of ownership. Investment A provides income of $80, and investment B pays $120. Solely on the basis of the income received over the one year, investment B seems preferable.

Capital Gains (or Losses) The second dimension of return focuses on the change in an investment's market value. The amount by which the proceeds from the sale of an investment exceed its original purchase price is a *capital gain*. If an investment sells for less than its original purchase price, a *capital loss* results.

> ### INVESTOR FACTS
>
> **Burrito Bonds are Easy to Swallow** In the summer of 2014, the London-based restaurant chain, Chilango, sold bonds to investors that promised cash interest payments of 8% per year, plus vouchers for free burritos. Though those burritos undoubtedly have some value to Chilango's investors, when we calculate an investment's return, we'll focus on the cash payments that the investment makes, ignoring any in-kind payments like free burritos.
>
> (Source: Based on "Will Chilango's £2m Success Herald an Affordable Mini Bond Revolution?" http://www.forbes.com/sites/trevorclawson/2014/08/28/will-chilangos-2m-success-herald-an-affordable-mini-bond-revolution/, accessed April 23, 2015.)

TABLE 10.1   PROFILES OF TWO INVESTMENTS

	Investment	
	A	B
Purchase price (beginning of year)	$1,000	$1,000
Cash received		
1st quarter	$ 10	$ 0
2nd quarter	$ 20	$ 0
3rd quarter	$ 20	$ 0
4th quarter	$ 30	$ 120
Total income (for year)	$ 80	$ 120
Sale price (end of year)	$1,100	$ 960

TABLE 10.2 TOTAL RETURNS OF TWO INVESTMENTS

	Investment	
Return	A	B
Income	$ 80	$120
Capital gain (loss)	$100	$(40)
Total return	$180	$ 80

We can calculate the capital gain or loss of the investments shown in Table 10.1. Investment A experiences a capital gain of $100 (i.e., $1,100 sale price −$1,000 purchase price) over the one-year period. Investment B, on the other hand, earned a $40 capital loss because the sale price of $960 is $40 less than the $1,000 purchase price.

Combining the capital gain (or loss) with the income (calculated in the preceding section) gives the **total return**. Table 10.2 shows the total return for investments A and B over the year. Investment A earns a $180 total return, compared to just $80 earned by investment B.

It is generally preferable to use *percentage returns* rather than dollar returns. Percentages allow direct comparison of different sizes and types of investments. Investment A earned an 18% return, which equals $180 divided by $1,000; B produced only an 8% return (i.e., $80 ÷ $1,000). At this point investment A appears preferable, but as we'll see, differences in risk might cause some investors to prefer B.

Why Return Is Important

An asset's return is a key variable in the investment decision because it indicates how rapidly an investor can build wealth. Naturally, because most people prefer to have more wealth rather than less, they prefer investments that offer high returns rather than low returns if all else is equal. However, we've already said that the returns on most investments are uncertain, so how do investors distinguish assets that offer high returns from those likely to produce low returns? One way to make this kind of assessment is to examine the returns that different types of investments have produced in the past.

Historical Performance Most people recognize that future performance is not guaranteed by past performance, but past data often provide a meaningful basis for future expectations. A common practice in the investment world is to look closely at the historical record when formulating expectations about the future.

Consider the data for ExxonMobil Corporation presented in Table 10.3. ExxonMobil paid dividends every year from 2005 through 2014. ExxonMobil's stock price generally rose during this decade, starting at $51.26 and ending at $92.45. Despite the overall upward trend, the company's stock price fell in 2008 and 2009 (largely due to the Great Recession and the corresponding drop in oil prices), and it declined again in 2014 (largely due to a rapid increase in the supply of oil and shrinking worldwide demand for oil).

Two aspects of these data are important. First, we can determine the *annual total return* generated by this investment over the past 10 years. The average annual total return earned by ExxonMobil's shareholders (column 6) over this period was 9.6%, performance that put ExxonMobil ahead of

TABLE 10.3 HISTORICAL INVESTMENT DATA FOR EXXONMOBIL CORP. (XOM)

Year	Market Value (Price)				Yearly Total Return	
	(1) Dividend Income	(2) Beginning of Year	(3) End of Year	(4) (3) – (2) Capital Gain	(5) (1) + (4)	(6) (5) ÷ (2)
2005	$1.14	$51.26	$56.17	$ 4.91	$ 6.05	11.8%
2006	$1.28	$56.17	$76.63	$20.46	$21.74	38.7%
2007	$1.37	$76.63	$93.69	$17.06	$18.43	24.1%
2008	$1.55	$93.69	$79.83	–$13.86	–$12.31	–13.1%
2009	$1.66	$79.83	$68.19	–$11.64	–$ 9.98	–12.5%
2010	$1.74	$68.19	$73.12	$ 4.93	$ 6.67	9.8%
2011	$1.85	$73.12	$84.76	$11.64	$13.49	18.4%
2012	$2.18	$84.76	$86.55	$ 1.79	$ 3.97	4.7%
2013	$2.46	$86.55	$101.20	$14.65	$17.11	19.8%
2014	$2.70	$101.20	$92.45	–$ 8.75	–$ 6.05	–6.0%
Average	$1.79			$ 4.12	$ 5.91	9.6%

(Source: Dividends and end-of-year closing prices were obtained from Yahoo! Finance.)

Excel@Investing

many other stocks for the same period. Second, observe that there was considerable variation in ExxonMobil's return from one year to the next. The firm's best year was 2006, during which its investors earned a total return of 38.7%. But in 2008, ExxonMobil's worst year, shareholders lost 13.1%.

Expected Return In the final analysis, of course, it's the future that matters when we make investment decisions. Therefore an investment's **expected return** is a vital measure of its performance. It's what you think the investment will earn in the future that determines what you should be willing to pay for it.

To demonstrate, let's return to the data in Table 10.3. A naive investor might estimate ExxonMobil's expected return to be the same as its average return from the prior decade, 9.6%. That's not necessarily a bad starting point, but it would be wise to ask, "What contributed to ExxonMobil's past returns, and is it likely that the same factors will occur in the future?" Central to ExxonMobil's success in the recent past was a generally upward trend in oil prices. In early 2005, crude oil traded for around $58 per barrel, but prices rose steadily until they peaked around $140 per barrel in June 2008. Even though prices fell sharply for a brief period during the recession, the price of oil did not fall below $70 at any point from June 2009 to October 2014, so this was a very favorable period for ExxonMobil. This suggests that the historical returns shown in Table 10.3 might represent a better-than-average period for the company. An investor who believed that oil prices would not continue to move up indefinitely, but rather would stabilize, might estimate ExxonMobil's expected return by looking at its historical performance during a period of relatively stable oil prices.

Level of Return

The level of return achieved or expected from an investment will depend on a variety of factors. The key factors are internal characteristics and external forces.

Fears of Deflation Worry Investors

For most of your lifetime, prices of most goods and services have been rising. There are important exceptions, such as the prices of consumer electronics and computers, but from one year to the next, the overall price level rose continuously in the United States from 1955 through 2007. However, as the recession deepened in 2008, consumer prices in the United States began to decline, falling in each of the last five months that year. Countries in the European Union experienced a brief deflationary period around the same time. The news raised fears among some investors that the recession might turn into a depression like the one that had brought about a price decline of −27% from November 1929 to March 1933. Although prices began to rise again, fears of deflation resurfaced again in late 2014 and early 2015. Prices in the United States were flat or down in the first three months of 2015, while countries in the European Union experienced falling prices for four consecutive months starting in December 2015.

Critical Thinking Question Suppose you own an investment that pays a fixed return in dollars year after year. How do you think inflation (rising prices) or deflation (falling prices) would influence the value of this type of investment?

Internal Characteristics Certain characteristics of an investment affect its return. For investments issued by companies, the important characteristics include things such as the type of investment (e.g., stocks or bonds), the quality of the firm's management, and whether the firm finances its operations with debt or equity. For example, investors might expect a different return on the common stock of a large, well-managed, completely equity-financed plastics manufacturer than they would anticipate from the common stock of a small, poorly managed, largely debt-financed clothing manufacturer. As we will see in later chapters, assessing internal factors and their impact on return is one important step in analyzing possible investments.

What Is Inflation?

External Forces External forces such as Federal Reserve actions, recessions, wars, and political events may also affect an investment's return. None of these are under the control of the issuer of the investment, and investments react differently to these forces. For example, if investors expect oil prices to rise, they may raise their expected return for ExxonMobil stock and lower it for the stock of an automobile manufacturer that produces gas guzzlers. Likewise, the economies of various countries respond to external forces in different ways.

Another external force is the *general level of price changes*, either up—**inflation**—or down—**deflation**. How inflation (or deflation) affects investment returns is complex, but it depends in part on whether investors correctly anticipate the rate of inflation. Generally speaking, when investors expect inflation to occur, they will demand higher returns. For example, when we look back through history, we see that interest rates on bonds were usually higher in periods when inflation was higher. However, when investors are caught off guard and the rate of inflation is higher or lower than they expected, returns on investments may rise or fall in response. The way that investment returns respond to unexpected changes in inflation will vary from one type of investment to another, and that response can be influenced by investors' beliefs about how policymakers will react to changing inflation. For example, if inflation unexpectedly rises, investors might anticipate that the Federal Reserve will take action to slow economic growth to bring inflation back down. In that case, returns on some investments might fall even as inflation is accelerating.

TABLE 10.4   HISTORICAL RETURNS FOR MAJOR ASSET CLASSES (1900–2014)

	Average Annual Return			
	Stocks	Long-Term Government Bonds	Short-Term Government Bills	Inflation
Australia	11.4%	5.6%	4.5%	3.8%
Belgium	7.9%	5.5%	4.8%	5.1%
Canada	8.9%	5.3%	4.5%	3.0%
Denmark	9.3%	7.2%	6.0%	3.8%
Finland	12.9%	7.3%	6.6%	7.1%
France	10.4%	7.2%	4.0%	7.0%
Germany	8.4%	3.2%	2.2%	4.7%
Ireland	8.5%	5.8%	4.8%	4.1%
Italy	10.3%	7.0%	4.4%	8.2%
Japan	11.2%	5.8%	4.8%	6.8%
Netherlands	8.0%	4.7%	3.5%	2.9%
New Zealand	10.0%	5.8%	5.4%	3.7%
Norway	8.0%	5.6%	4.8%	3.7%
South Africa	12.7%	6.9%	6.0%	4.9%
Spain	9.5%	7.6%	6.0%	5.7%
Sweden	9.4%	6.3%	5.3%	3.4%
Switzerland	6.8%	4.6%	3.0%	2.2%
United Kingdom	9.4%	5.5%	4.8%	3.9%
United States	9.6%	5.0%	3.8%	2.9%

(Source: Data from *Credit Suisse Global Investment Returns Yearbook 2015.*)

Historical Returns

Returns vary both over time and among types of investments. By averaging historical yearly returns over a long period of time, it is possible to observe the differences in annual returns earned by various types of investments. Table 10.4 shows the average annual rates of return for three major asset classes (stocks, treasury bonds, and treasury bills) in 19 countries over the 115-year period from 1900 to 2014. With more than 100 years of data to draw on, some clear patterns emerge. You can see that significant differences exist among the average annual rates of return realized on stocks, long-term government bonds, and short-term government bills. In all 19 countries, stocks earn higher returns than government bonds, which in turn earn higher average returns than short-term government bills. Later in this chapter, we will see how we can link these differences in return to differences in the risk of each of these investments.

We now turn our attention to the role that time value of money principles play in determining investment returns.

The Time Value of Money and Returns

The phrase *the time value of money* refers to the fact that it is generally better to receive cash sooner rather than later. For example, consider two investments, A and B. Investment A will pay you $100 next year and $100 the year after that. Investment B pays you $200 in two years. Assume that neither investment has any risk, meaning that you are certain that you will receive these cash payments. Clearly both investments pay $200 over two years, but investment A is preferable because you can reinvest the $100 you receive in the first year to earn more interest the second year. You should always consider time value of money principles when making investment decisions.

We now review the key computational aids for streamlining time value of money calculations, and then we demonstrate the application of time value of money techniques to determine an acceptable investment.

Computational Aids for Use in Time Value of Money Calculations The once time-consuming calculations involved in applying time value of money techniques can be simplified with a number of computational aids. Throughout this text we will demonstrate the use of hand-held financial calculators and electronic spreadsheets. Financial calculators include numerous preprogrammed financial routines. To demonstrate the calculator keystrokes for various financial computations, we show a keypad, with the keys defined below.

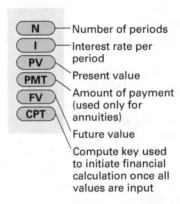

Electronic spreadsheet use has become a prime skill for today's investors. Like financial calculators, spreadsheets have built-in routines that simplify time value of money calculations. For most time value of money calculations in the text, we show spreadsheet solutions with clearly identified cell entries.

Determining a Satisfactory Investment You can use time value of money techniques to determine whether an investment's return is satisfactory given the investment's cost. Ignoring risk at this point, a **satisfactory investment** would be one for which the present value of benefits (discounted at the appropriate discount rate) equals or exceeds its cost. The three possible cost–benefit relationships and their interpretations follow:

1. If the present value of the benefits equals the cost, you would earn a rate of return equal to the discount rate.

2. If the present value of benefits exceeds the cost, you would earn a rate of return greater than the discount rate.

3. If the present value of benefits is less than the cost, you would earn a rate of return less than the discount rate.

You would prefer only those investments for which the present value of benefits equals or exceeds its cost—situations 1 and 2. In these cases, the rate of return would be equal to or greater than the discount rate.

Excel@Investing

TABLE 10.5   PRESENT VALUE APPLIED TO AN INVESTMENT

End of Year	(1) Income	(2) Present Value Calculation at 8%	(3) Present Value at 8%
1	$ 90	$ 90/(1.08)^1	$ 83.33
2	$ 100	$ 100/(1.08)^2	$ 85.73
3	$ 110	$ 110/(1.08)^3	$ 87.32
4	$ 120	$ 120/(1.08)^4	$ 88.20
5	$ 100	$ 100/(1.08)^5	$ 68.06
6	$ 100	$ 100/(1.08)^6	$ 63.02
7	$1,200	$1,200/(1.08)^7	$ 700.19
		Total Present Value	$1,175.85

Time Is Money

The information in Table 10.5 demonstrates the application of present value to investment decision making. (*Note:* You can use a financial calculator or an Excel spreadsheet to convert the algebraic expression in column 2 to the numeric value in column 3.) This investment makes a series of payments over the next seven years. Because the payments arrive at different times, we calculate the present value of each payment to determine how much each payment is worth in today's dollars. The present value of the benefits (i.e., the income) provided by this investment over its seven-year life is $1,175.85. If the cost of the investment today is $1,175.85 or less, then the investment is acceptable, and an investor would earn a rate of return equal to at least 8%. At a cost above the $1,175.85 present value, the investment would not be acceptable because the rate of return would be less than 8%. In that case it would be preferable to find an alternative investment with a present value of benefits that equals or exceeds its cost.

For your convenience, Appendix 10A provides a complete review of the key time value of money techniques. Be sure to review it before reading ahead, to make sure you have adequate understanding of this important financial concept.

CONCEPTS IN REVIEW

Answers available at
http://www.pearsonhighered
.com/smart

10.1   Explain what is meant by the return on an investment. Differentiate between the two components of return—income and capital gains (or losses).

10.2   What role do historical performance data play in estimating an investment's expected return? Discuss the key factors affecting investment returns—internal characteristics and external forces.

10.3   What is a satisfactory investment? When the present value of benefits exceeds the cost of an investment, what can you conclude about the rate of return earned by the investor relative to the discount rate?

Measuring Return

LG3 LG4   Thus far, we have discussed the concept of return in terms of its two components (income and capital gains) and the key factors that affect the level of return (internal characteristics and external forces). These discussions intentionally oversimplified the computations involved in determining the historical or expected return. To compare returns from different investments, we need to incorporate time value of money concepts that explicitly consider differences in the timing of investment income and capital gains. We must also be able to calculate the present value of future benefits. Here we will look at several measures that enable us to compare alternative investments. First, we must define and consider the relationships among various rates of return.

Real, Risk-Free, and Required Returns

Inflation and Returns Glance back at Table 10.4, which reports that in the United States the average annual return on a short-term government Treasury bill was 3.8% between 1900 and 2014. The table also shows that the average annual inflation rate was 2.9%. It's no coincidence that the T-bill rate of return exceeds the inflation rate because investors want to earn returns that exceed the inflation rate. Inflation erodes the purchasing power of money. For example, if prices of most goods and services rise by 3% in a year, $1 buys about 3% fewer goods and services at the end of the year than at the beginning. Thus, if investors seek to increase their purchasing power over time, they must earn returns that exceed the inflation rate.

The **nominal rate of return** on an investment is the return that the investment earns expressed in current dollars. For example, if you put $50 into an investment that promises to pay 3% interest, at the end of the year you will have $51.50 (the initial $50 plus a $1.50 return). Your nominal return is 3%, but this does not necessarily mean that you are better off financially at the end of the year because the nominal return does not take into account the effects of inflation.

To continue the example, assume that at the beginning of the year, one bag of groceries costs $50. During the year, suppose grocery prices rise by 3%. This means that by the end of the year one bag of groceries costs $51.50. In other words, at the beginning of the year you could have used your $50 either to buy one bag of groceries or to make the investment that promised a 3% return. If you invested your money rather than spending it on groceries, by the end of the year you would have had $51.50, still just enough to buy one bag of groceries. In other words, your purchasing power did not increase at all during the year. The **real rate of return** on an investment measures the increase in purchasing power that the investment provides. In our continuing example, the real rate of return is 0% even though the nominal rate of return is 3%. In dollar terms, by investing $50 you increased your wealth by 3% to $51.50, but in terms of purchasing power you are no better off because you can only buy the same amount of goods that you could have bought before you made the investment. In mathematical terms, the real rate of return is approximately equal to the nominal rate of return minus the inflation rate.

Example

Suppose you have $50 today and are trying to decide whether to invest that money or spend it. If you invest it, you believe that you can earn a nominal return of 10%, so after one year your money will grow to $55. If you spend the money today, you plan to feed your caffeine habit by purchasing 20 lattes at your favorite coffee shop at $2.50 each. You decide to save and invest your money, so a year later you have $55. How many more lattes can you buy because you chose to invest your money rather than spend it right away? Unfortunately, during the year inflation caused the price of a latte to increase by 4.8% from $2.50 to $2.62. At the new price, you can just about afford to buy 21 lattes (i.e., 21 × $2.62 = $55.02). That extra latte represents an increase in your purchasing power of 5% (21 is 5% more than 20), so your real return on the investment is 5% because it enabled you to buy 5% more than you could before you invested. Notice that the real return is approximately equal to the difference between the investment's nominal return (10%) and the inflation rate (4.8%):

Real return ≈ Nominal return − Inflation rate
5% ≈ 10% − 4.8%

Risk and Returns Investors are generally *risk averse*, meaning that they do not like risk and will only take risk when they expect compensation for doing so. The greater the risk associated with any particular investment, the greater the return that investors will require to make that investment. The rate of return that fully compensates for an investment's risk is called the **required return**. Note that the required return is a kind of forecast. If an investor expects an investment to earn a return equal to or greater than the required return, the investor will want to buy the investment. However, the return that an investment actually earns can be quite different from the investor's required return.

The required return on any investment j consists of three components: the real rate of return, an expected inflation premium, and a risk premium, as noted in Equation 10.1.

Equation 10.1	$\dfrac{\text{Required return}}{\text{on investment } j} = \dfrac{\text{Real rate}}{\text{of return}} + \dfrac{\text{Expected inflation}}{\text{premium}} + \dfrac{\text{Risk premium}}{\text{for investment } j}$
Equation 10.1a	$r_j = r^* + IP + RP_j$

The **expected inflation premium** represents the rate of inflation expected over an investment's life. Although the historical average inflation rate in the United States has been close to 3.0%, investors' expectations may deviate from the historical norm for many reasons. For instance, most inflation forecasts for 2016 projected very low inflation due to the lingering effects of the global recession. By adding the first two terms in Equation 10.1, we obtain the **risk-free rate**. This is the rate of return that can be earned on a risk-free investment, such as a short-term U.S. Treasury bill. The formula for this rate appears in Equation 10.2.

Equation 10.2	$\text{Risk-free rate} = \dfrac{\text{Real rate}}{\text{of return}} + \dfrac{\text{Expected inflation}}{\text{premium}}$
Equation 10.2a	$r_f = r^* + IP$

The required return can be found by adding to the risk-free rate a **risk premium**, which varies depending on specific issue and issuer characteristics. *Issue characteristics* are the type of investment (stock, bond, etc.), its maturity (two years, five years, infinity, etc.), and its features (voting/nonvoting, callable/noncallable, etc.). *Issuer characteristics* are industry and company factors such as the line of business and financial condition of the issuer. Together, the issue and issuer factors contribute to the overall risk of an investment and cause investors to require a risk premium above the risk-free rate.

Substituting the risk-free rate, r_f, from Equation 10.2a into Equation 10.1a for the first two terms to the right of the equal signs $(r^* + IP)$, we get Equation 10.3.

Equation 10.3	$\dfrac{\text{Required return}}{\text{on investment } j} = \dfrac{\text{Risk-free}}{\text{rate}} + \dfrac{\text{Risk premium}}{\text{for investment } j}$
Equation 10.3a	$r_j = r_f + RP_j$

For example, if the required return on Nike common stock is 7% when the risk-free rate is 2%, investors require a 5% risk premium as compensation for the risk associated with common stock (the issue) and Nike (the issuer). Notice also that if investors expect 1% inflation, then the real required rate on Nike is approximately 6%. Later, we will explore further the relationship between the risk premium and required returns.

Next, we consider the specifics of return measurement. We look at two return measures—one used primarily for short-term investments and the other for longer-term investments.

Holding Period Return

The return to a *saver* is the amount of interest earned on a given deposit. Of course, the amount "invested" in a savings account does not change in value, as does the amount invested in stocks, bonds, and mutual funds. Because we are concerned with a broad range of investments, we need a measure of return that captures both periodic income and changes in value. One such measure is the *holding period return*.

The **holding period** is the period of time over which one wishes to measure the return on an investment. When comparing returns, be sure to use holding periods of the same length. For example, comparing the return on a stock over a six-month period with the return on a bond over a one-year period could result in a poor investment decision. To avoid this problem, be sure you define the holding period. It is common practice to annualize the holding period and use that as a standard.

Understanding Return Components Earlier in this chapter we identified the two components of investment return: income and capital gains (or losses). The income received by the investor during the investment period is a **realized return**. Capital gains and losses, on the other hand, are realized only when the investor sells an asset at the end of the investment period. Until the sale occurs, the capital gain or loss is called a **paper return** or an unrealized return.

For example, the capital gain return on an investment that increases in market value from $50 to $70 during a year is $20. For that capital gain to be realized, you would sell the investment for $70 at the end of that year. An investor who purchased the same investment but plans to hold it for another three years would also experience the $20 capital gain return during the first year, but he or she would not have realized the gain by collecting the $20 profit in cash. However, even if the capital gain is not realized, it must be included in the total return calculation.

A second point to recognize about returns is that both the income and the capital gains components can have a negative value. Occasionally, an investment may have negative income. That is, you may be required to pay out cash to meet certain obligations. (This situation is most likely to occur in various types of property investments that require periodic maintenance.) A capital loss can occur on any investment. Stocks, bonds, mutual funds, options, futures, real estate, and gold can all decline in value.

Computing the Holding Period Return The **holding period return (HPR)** is the total return earned from holding an investment for a specified time (the holding period). Analysts typically use the HPR with holding periods of one year or less. (We'll explain why later.) It represents the sum of income and capital gains (or losses) achieved over the holding period, divided by the beginning investment value (market price). The annual total returns in Table 10.3 are calculated in this fashion. The equation for HPR is

Equation 10.4

$$\text{Holding period return} = \frac{\text{Income during period} + \text{Capital gain (or loss) during period}}{\text{Beginning investment value}}$$

Equation 10.4a

$$\text{HPR} = \frac{\text{Inc} + \text{CG}}{V_0}$$

where

Equation 10.5

$$\text{Capital gain (or loss) during period} = \text{Ending investment value} - \text{Beginning investment value}$$

Equation 10.5a

$$CG = V_n - V_0$$

The HPR equation provides a convenient method for either measuring the total return earned or estimating the total return expected. For example, Table 10.6 summarizes the key financial variables for four investments over the past year. The total income and capital gain or loss during the investment period appear in the lines labeled (1) and (3), respectively. The total return over the year is calculated, as shown in line (4), by adding these two sources of return. Dividing the total return value [line (4)] by the beginning-of-year investment value [line (2)], we find the holding period return, given in line (5). Over the one-year holding period the common stock had the highest HPR (12.25%). The savings account had the lowest (6%).

As these calculations show, to find the HPR we need the beginning-of-period and end-of-period investment values, along with income received during the period. Note that if the current income and capital gain (or loss) values in lines (1) and (3) of Table 10.6 had been drawn from a 6-month rather than a one-year period, the HPR values calculated in line (5) would have been the same.

Excel@Investing

TABLE 10.6   KEY FINANCIAL VARIABLES FOR FOUR INVESTMENTS

	Investment			
	Savings Account	Common Stock	Bond	Real Estate
Cash Received				
1st quarter	$ 15	$ 10	$ 0	$ 0
2nd quarter	$ 15	$ 10	$ 70	$ 0
3rd quarter	$ 15	$ 10	$ 0	$ 0
4th quarter	$ 15	$ 15	$ 70	$ 0
(1) Total current income	$ 60	$ 45	$ 140	$ 0
Investment Value				
End-of-year	$ 1,000	$2,200	$ 970	$3,300
(2) Beginning-of-year	–$ 1,000	–$2,000	–$ 1,000	–$3,000
(3) Capital gain (loss)	$ 0	$ 200	–$ 30	$ 300
(4) Total return [(1) + (3)]	$ 60	$ 245	$ 110	$ 300
(5) Holding period return [(4) ÷ (2)]	6.00%	12.25%	11.00%	10.00%

An investment's holding period return can be negative or positive. You can use Equation 10.4 to calculate HPRs using either historical data (as in the preceding example) or forecast data.

Using the HPR in Investment Decisions The holding period return is easy to use in making investment decisions. It measures an investment's return (including both the income and capital gains components) relative to the investment's initial cost, and in so doing makes it easier to compare the performance of investments that may differ greatly in terms of the amount of money required from an investor.

If we look only at the total returns in dollars calculated for each of the investments in Table 10.6 [line (4)], the real estate investment appears best because it has the highest total return. However, the real estate investment would require the largest dollar outlay ($3,000). The holding period return (or total return expressed as a percentage of the investment's cost) offers a *relative comparison*, by dividing the total return by the amount of the investment. Comparing HPRs [line (5)], we find that common stock is the investment alternative with the highest return per invested dollar at 12.25%. Because the return per invested dollar reflects the efficiency of the investment, the HPR provides a logical method for evaluating and comparing investment returns, particularly for holding periods of one year or less.

The Internal Rate of Return

For investments with holding periods greater than one year, an alternative way to define a satisfactory investment is in terms of the annual rate of return it earns. Why do we need an alternative to the HPR? Because the HPR calculation fails to fully account for the time value of money, and the HPRs for competing investments are not always comparable. Instead, sophisticated investors prefer to use a present value–based measure, called the **internal rate of return (IRR)**, to determine the annual rate of return earned on investments held for longer than one year. An investment's IRR is the discount rate that equates the investment's cost to the present value of the benefits that it provides for the investor.

Once you know the IRR, you can decide whether an investment is acceptable. If the IRR on an investment is equal to or greater than the required return, then the investment is acceptable. An investment with an IRR below the required return is unacceptable.

The IRR on an investment providing a single future cash flow is relatively easy to calculate. The IRR on an investment providing a stream of future cash flows generally involves more complex calculations. Hand-held financial calculators or Excel spreadsheets simplify these calculations.

IRR for a Single Cash Flow Some investments, such as U.S. savings bonds, stocks paying no dividends, and zero-coupon bonds, provide no periodic income. Instead, investors pay a lump sum up front to purchase these investments, and in return investors expect to receive a single, future cash flow when they sell the investment or when the investment matures. The IRR on such an investment is easy to calculate using a financial calculator or an Excel spreadsheet.

CALCULATOR USE Assume you wish to find the IRR on an investment that costs $1,000 today and will pay you $1,400 in five years. To compute the IRR for this investment on a financial calculator, you treat the investment's cost as a present value, PV, and the investment's payoff as a future value, FV. (*Note:* Most calculators require you to enter either the PV or FV as a negative number to calculate an unknown IRR. Generally, the PV is entered as a negative value since it represents the initial cost of an investment.) Using the inputs shown at the left, you can verify that the IRR is 6.96%.

SPREADSHEET USE You can calculate the IRR for the single cash flow as shown on the following Excel spreadsheet.

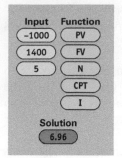

Excel@Investing

	A	B
1	**IRR FOR A SINGLE CASH FLOW**	
2	Investment	Cash Flow
3	Cost (PV)	-$1,000
4	Payoff (FV)	$1,400
5	Number of Years	5
6	IRR	6.96%
7	Entry in Cell B6 is =Rate(B5,0,B3,B4,0). The minus sign appears before the $1,000 in B3 because the cost of the investment is treated as a cash outflow.	

IRR for a Stream of Income Investments such as income-oriented stocks and bonds typically provide the investor with an income stream. The IRR on an investment that pays income periodically is the discount rate that equates the present value of the investment's cash flows to its current price.

Example

Consider once more the investment presented in Table 10.5. The table illustrates that the present value of the investment's cash flows given a discount rate of 8% is $1,175.85. If the market price of the investment is also $1,175.85 (equal to the present value), then 8% is its internal rate of return, because at that discount rate the present value and the market price are the same. Suppose that the price of this investment falls to $1,100. At that price, what IRR does the investment offer? Table 10.7 uses a trial-and-error approach in an attempt to find the answer. If we discount the investment's cash flows at 9%, the present value of those cash flows is $1,117.75. That's above the investment's market price, so the IRR must be above 9%. Table 10.7 shows that at a 10% discount rate, the present value of the cash flows is $1,063.40, so the investment's IRR must be below 10%. Therefore, you need to keep searching for the exact discount rate at which the investment's cash flows equal $1,100. You can do that using a financial calculator or an Excel spreadsheet.

Excel@Investing

TABLE 10.7   PRESENT VALUE APPLIED TO AN INVESTMENT

End of Year	(1) Income	(2) Present Value Calculation at 9%	(3) Present Value at 9%	(4) Present Value Calculation at 10%	(5) Present Value at 10%
1	$ 90	$ 90/(1 + 0.09)^1	$ 82.57	$ 90/(1 + 0.1)^1	$ 81.82
2	$ 100	$ 100/(1 + 0.09)^2	$ 84.17	$ 100/(1 + 0.1)^2	$ 82.64
3	$ 110	$ 110/(1 + 0.09)^3	$ 84.94	$ 110/(1 + 0.1)^3	$ 82.64
4	$ 120	$ 120/(1 + 0.09)^4	$ 85.01	$ 120/(1 + 0.1)^4	$ 81.96
5	$ 100	$ 100/(1 + 0.09)^5	$ 64.99	$ 100/(1 + 0.1)^5	$ 62.09
6	$ 100	$ 100/(1 + 0.09)^6	$ 59.63	$ 100/(1 + 0.1)^6	$ 56.45
7	$1,200	$1,200/(1 + 0.09)^7	$ 656.44	$1,200/(1 + 0.1)^7	$ 615.79
Total Present Value			$1,117.75		$1,063.40

CALCULATOR USE Using a financial calculator to find an investment's IRR typically involves three steps: (1) Enter the cost of the investment (typically referred to as the *cash outflow* at time 0). (2) Enter all of the income expected each period (typically referred to as the *cash inflow* in year *x*). (3) Calculate the IRR.

SPREADSHEET USE We can also calculate the IRR for a stream of income as shown on the following Excel spreadsheet.

Excel@Investing

	A	B
1	IRR FOR A STREAM OF INCOME	
2	Year	Cash Flow
3	0	-$1,100
4	1	$90
5	2	$100
6	3	$110
7	4	$120
8	5	$100
9	6	$100
10	7	$1,200
11	IRR	9.32%
12	Entry in Cell B11 is =IRR(B3:B10). The minus sign appears before the $1,100 in B3 because the cost of the investment is treated as a cash outflow.	

Interest on Interest: The Critical Assumption The IRR is a measure of the return that an investment provides, but the IRR calculation contains a subtle assumption. That assumption is that the investor can reinvest all of the income that the investment provides, and that the return earned on reinvested income equals the return on the original investment. This concept can best be illustrated with a simple example. Suppose you buy a $1,000 U.S. Treasury bond that pays 8% annual interest ($80) over its 20-year life. Each year you receive $80, and at maturity you get the $1,000 principal back. To earn an 8% IRR on this investment, you must be able to reinvest the $80 annual interest income for the remaining 20-year life at the same annual rate of return of 8%.

Figure 10.1 shows the elements of return on this investment to demonstrate the point. If you don't *reinvest* the interest income of $80 per year, you'll end up earning an IRR of about 4.9%. You'll have $2,600—the $1,000 principal plus $1,600 in interest ($80 per year for 20 years)—at the end of 20 years. (The IRR on a single cash flow of $1,000 today that will be worth $2,600 in 20 years is about 4.9%.) Alternatively, if you reinvest each $80 annual interest payment, and if those reinvestment payments earn an 8% return from the time that they are received until the end of the bond's 20-year life, then at the end of 20 years you'll have $4,661—the $1,000 principal plus the $3,661 future value of the $80 interest payments reinvested at 8%. (The IRR on a single cash flow of $1,000 today that will be worth $4,661 in 20 years is 8%.) Figure 10.1 shows that this investment's future value is $2,061 greater ($4,661 −$2,600) with interest payments reinvested compared to the case when interest payments are not reinvested.

It should be clear to you that if you buy an investment that makes periodic cash payments, and if you want an 8% return on that investment, you must earn that same 8% rate of return when reinvesting your income to earn the full IRR. The rate of

FIGURE 10.1

Earning Interest on Interest

If you invested in a $1,000, 20-year bond with an annual interest rate of 8%, you would have only $2,600 at the end of 20 years if you did not reinvest the $80 annual interest payments. That is roughly equivalent to investing $1,000 today and letting it grow at 5% for 20 years.

If you reinvested the interest payments at 8%, you would have $4,661 at the end of 20 years. That's the same amount that you would have by investing $1,000 today and letting that grow at 8% per year for 20 years. To achieve the calculated IRR of 8%, you must therefore be able to earn interest on interest at that same 8% rate.

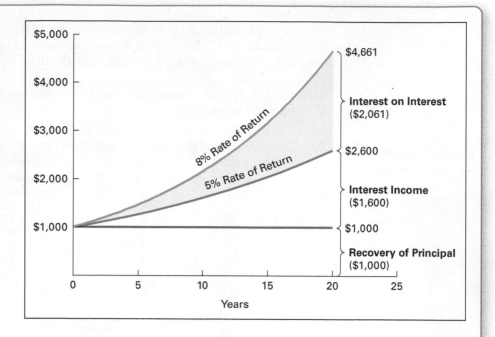

return you start with is the required, or minimum, **reinvestment rate**. This is the rate of return earned on interest or other income received over the relevant investment horizon. By putting your income to work at this rate, you'll earn the rate of return you set out to earn. If you must reinvest income at a lower rate, your return will decline accordingly.

Because the IRR calculation assumes that you can earn interest on the periodic income that you receive, financial experts say that the IRR is a **fully compounded rate of return**. That simply means that the IRR calculation accounts for the fact that you earn a higher return on an investment when you can reinvest its cash flows.

Interest on interest is a particularly important element of return for investment programs that involve a lot of income. You must actively reinvest income. (With capital gains, the money is automatically reinvested unless you sell the asset to realize the gain.) It follows, therefore, that for investment programs that lean toward income-oriented securities, the continued reinvestment of income plays an important role in investment success.

Finding Growth Rates

In addition to finding compound annual rates of return, we frequently need to find the **rate of growth**. This is the compound annual *rate of change* in some financial quantity, such as the price of a stock or the size of its dividend. Here we use an example to demonstrate a simple technique for estimating growth rates using a financial calculator and an Excel spreadsheet.

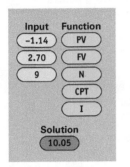

Excel@Investing

CALCULATOR USE Imagine that you wish to determine the rate at which ExxonMobil Corp. dividends grew from 2005 to 2014. Exxon's dividends appear in Table 10.3. The table presents 10 years of dividend payments, which means that the dividend had 9 years to grow from its 2005 value through 2014.

To use a financial calculator to find the growth rate for ExxonMobil dividends shown in Table 10.3, you treat the earliest (2005) value as a present value, PV, and the latest (2014) value as a future value, FV. (*Note:* Most calculators require you to key in either the PV or the FV as a negative number to calculate an unknown growth rate.) As noted above, although 10 years of dividends appear in Table 10.3, there are only nine years of growth ($N = 9$) because the earliest year (2005) must be defined as the base year (year 0). Using the inputs shown at the left, we calculate the growth rate to be 10.05%.

SPREADSHEET USE You can also calculate the growth rate using an Excel spreadsheet as shown below. Like the calculator, the spreadsheet equation simply calculates the annualized rate of change from the first dividend paid in 2005 to the last dividend paid in 2014. (Notice that only the first and last dividends and the nine years between them were necessary to find the annual growth rate.)

	A	B
1	GROWTH RATE FOR A DIVIDEND STREAM	
2	Year	Dividend
3	2005	$1.14
4	2006	$1.28
5	2007	$1.37
6	2008	$1.55
7	2009	$1.66
8	2010	$1.74
9	2011	$1.85
10	2012	$2.18
11	2013	$2.46
12	2014	$2.70
13	Annual Growth Rate	10.05%
14	Entry in Cell B13 is =RATE((A12-A3),0,-B3,B12,0). The expression (A12-A3) in the entry calculates the number of years of growth. The minus sign appears before B3 because the dividend in 2002 is treated as a cash outflow.	

10.4 Define the following terms and explain how they are used to find the risk-free rate of return and the required rate of return for a given investment.

    a. *Real rate of return*
    b. *Expected inflation premium*
    c. *Risk premium* for a given investment

10.5 What is meant by the holding period, and why is it advisable to use holding periods of equal length when comparing alternative investments? Define the *holding period return*, and explain for what length holding periods it is typically used.

10.6 Define *internal rate of return*. When is it appropriate to use IRR rather than the HPR to measure the return on an investment?

10.7 Explain why you must earn 10% on all income received from an investment during its holding period in order for its IRR actually to equal the 10% value you've calculated.

10.8 Explain how either the present value (of benefits versus cost) or the IRR measure can be used to find a satisfactory investment. Given the following data, indicate which, if any, of these investments is acceptable. Explain your findings.

	Investment		
	A	B	C
Cost	$200	$160	$500
Required return	7%	10%	9%
Present value of income	—	$150	—
IRR	8%	—	8%

Risk: The Other Side of the Coin

LG5 LG6 Thus far, our primary concern in this chapter has been the return on an investment. However, we cannot consider return without also looking at risk. *Risk* is the uncertainty surrounding the actual return that an investment will generate.

    The risk associated with a given investment is directly related to its expected return. In general, the greater the investment's risk, the higher the expected return it must offer to attract investors. Riskier investments should provide higher returns. Otherwise, what incentive is there for an investor to risk his or her money?

    This relationship between risk and return is called the **risk-return tradeoff**. In general, investors want to obtain the highest possible return for the level of risk that they are willing to take. To introduce this concept, we begin by examining the key sources of risk. We then consider the measurement and assessment of risk: the risk of a single asset, the assessment of risk associated with a potential investment, and the steps by which return and risk can be combined in the decision process.

How Are Risk and Return Related?

Sources of Risk

The risk associated with an investment may come from many different sources. A prudent investor considers how the major sources of risk might affect potential investments. The combined effect of different risks will be reflected in the investment's *risk premium*. As discussed earlier and shown in Equation 10.3, you can find the required return on an investment by adding its risk premium to the risk-free rate. This premium in a broad sense results from the sources of risk, which derive from characteristics of both the investment and the entity issuing the investment.

Business Risk In general, **business risk** is the degree of uncertainty associated with an investment's earnings and the investment's ability to pay the returns (interest, principal, dividends) that investors expect. For example, business owners may receive no return if the firm's earnings are not adequate to meet obligations. Debt holders, on the other hand, are likely to receive some (but not necessarily all) of the amount owed them because of the preferential treatment legally accorded to debt.

The business risk associated with an investment is tied to the firm's industry. For example, the business risk in a public utility common stock differs from the risk in the stock of a high-fashion clothing manufacturer or an Internet start-up. Generally, investments in similar kinds of firms have similar business risk, although differences in management, costs, and location can cause varying risk levels.

Financial Risk Many firms raise money both by issuing common stock to investors and by borrowing money. When firms borrow money, they commit themselves to make future interest and principal payments, and those payments are generally not linked to a firm's profits but are instead fixed according to a contract between the firm and its lender. Therefore, when business conditions are good and profits are high, shareholders benefit from the use of debt because payments to lenders do not rise with profits, leaving more for shareholders. All other things being equal, a firm that uses debt will generate higher profits for its shareholders compared to a firm that uses no debt, but only when business conditions are good. When business conditions are poor, firms must repay their debts even if they are not making a profit. In that case, debt magnifies the losses that shareholders must endure, so in bad times a firm that uses debt will experience greater losses compared to a firm that has no debt. If a firm using debt has higher profits in good times and steeper losses in bad times (compared to a firm that borrows no money), we can say that debt magnifies a firm's business risk. Firms in all industries are subject to the ups and downs that we refer to as business risk, but firms that use debt take even more risk. That is why debt is also referred to as *leverage*. The increased uncertainty that results when a firm borrows money is called **financial risk**. The more debt used to finance a firm, the greater its financial risk.

Purchasing Power Risk The chance that unanticipated changes in price levels (inflation or deflation) will adversely affect investment returns is **purchasing power risk**. Specifically, this risk is the chance that an unexpected increase in prices (inflation) will reduce purchasing power (the goods and services that can be purchased with a dollar).

In general, investments whose values move with general price levels have low purchasing power risk and are most profitable during periods of rising prices. Those that provide fixed returns have high purchasing power risk, and they are most profitable during periods of low inflation or declining price levels. The returns on stocks of durable-goods manufacturers, for example, tend to move with the general price level, whereas returns from deposit accounts and bonds do not, at least in the short run.

Interest Rate Risk Securities are especially affected by interest rate risk. This is particularly true for those securities that offer purchasers a fixed periodic return. **Interest rate risk** is the chance that changes in interest rates will adversely affect a security's value. The interest rate changes themselves result from changes in the general relationship between the supply of and the demand for money.

As interest rates change, the prices of many securities fluctuate. The prices of fixed-income securities (bonds and preferred stock) typically drop when interest rates rise. As interest rates rise, new securities become available in the market, and those new securities pay the new, higher rates. Securities that are already outstanding make cash payments that reflect lower market rates from the past, so they are not competitive in the higher rate environment. Investors sell them, and their prices fall. The opposite occurs when interest rates fall. Prices of outstanding securities that make cash payments above the current market rate become more attractive, and their prices rise.

A second, more subtle aspect of interest rate risk is associated with reinvestment of income. When interest rates rise, bond prices fall, but bondholders have the opportunity to reinvest interest payments that they receive at a new, higher rate. This opportunity boosts the compound rate of return that investors earn on their bonds. In other words, a rise in interest rates causes bond returns to drop because bond prices fall, but income reinvested at the new higher interest rate partially offsets that effect. This offsetting effect is larger for bonds that make higher interest payments, and it is entirely absent for zero-coupon bonds.

A final aspect of interest rate risk is related to investing in short-term securities such as U.S. Treasury bills and certificates of deposit. Investors face the risk that when short-term securities mature, they may have to invest those proceeds in lower-yielding, new short-term securities. By initially making a long-term investment, you can lock in a return for a period of years rather than face the risk of declines in short-term interest rates. Clearly, when interest rates are declining, the returns from investing in short-term securities are adversely affected. (On the other hand, interest rate increases have a positive impact on such a strategy.) The chance that interest rates will decline is therefore the interest rate risk of a strategy of investing in short-term securities.

Most investments are subject to interest rate risk. Although interest rate movements most directly affect fixed-income securities, they also affect other long-term investments such as common stock and mutual funds. Holding other factors constant, the higher the interest rate, the lower the value of an investment, and vice versa.

Liquidity Risk The risk of not being able to sell (or liquidate) an investment quickly without reducing its price is called **liquidity risk**. One can generally sell an investment by significantly cutting its price. However, a liquid investment is one that investors can sell quickly without having an adverse impact on its price. For example, a security recently purchased for $1,000 would not be viewed as highly liquid if it could be quickly sold only at a greatly reduced price, such as $500.

An investment's liquidity is an important consideration. In general, investments traded in thin markets, where transaction volume is low, tend to be less liquid than those traded in broad markets. Assets such as stocks issued by large companies and bonds issued by the U.S. Treasury are generally highly liquid; others, such as artwork and antique furniture, are relatively illiquid.

Tax Risk The chance that Congress will make unfavorable changes in tax laws is known as **tax risk**. The greater the chance that such changes will drive down the after-tax returns and market values of certain investments, the greater the tax risk. Unfavorable changes in tax laws include elimination of tax exemptions, limitation of deductions, and increases in tax rates. For example, a new tax on investment income went into effect on January 1, 2013, as part of the Affordable Care Act. That tax requires certain high-income taxpayers to pay an additional 3.8% tax on their net investment income.

Event Risk **Event risk** occurs when something happens to a company that has a sudden and substantial impact on its financial condition. Event risk goes beyond business and financial risk. It does not necessarily mean the company or market is doing poorly. Instead, it involves an unexpected event that has a significant and usually immediate effect on the underlying value of an investment. An example of event risk is the May 2015 death of the president of American Express. On the day he died returning on a plane from a business trip to New York, the market value of American Express stock fell by about $400 million.

Event risk can take many forms and can affect all types of investments. Fortunately, its impact tends to be isolated in most cases.

Market Risk **Market risk** is the risk that investment returns will decline because of factors that affect the broader market, not just one company or one investment. Examples include political, economic, and social events, as well as changes in investor tastes and preferences. Market risk actually embodies a number of different risks including purchasing power risk, interest rate risk, and tax risk.

The impact of market factors on investment returns is not uniform. Both the degree and the direction of change in return differ among investments. For example, a rapid economic boom would likely increase the value of companies that produce luxury goods, while it might have a more muted positive effect (or even a slight negative effect) on companies like Walmart and Dollar General that focus on selling goods at bargain prices. Essentially, market risk is reflected in a stock's sensitivity to these broad market forces. In other words, if a stock tends to move up or down sharply when the overall market moves, that stock has a high degree of market risk.

Risk of a Single Asset

Most people have at some time in their lives asked themselves how risky some anticipated course of action is. In such cases, the answer is usually a subjective judgment. In finance, we seek to quantify risk because doing so improves comparisons between investments and enhances decision making.

We can use statistical concepts to measure the risk of both single assets and portfolios of assets. First, we focus solely on the risk of single assets, and we show how the concept of standard deviation provides insights regarding an investment's risk. We will consider the risk and return of portfolios of assets later.

Standard Deviation: An Absolute Measure of Risk One indicator of an asset's risk is the **standard deviation, s.** It measures the dispersion (variation) of returns around an asset's average or expected return. The formula is

Equation 10.6

$$\text{Standard deviation} = \sqrt{\frac{\sum_{t=1}^{n}\left(\begin{array}{cc}\text{Return for} & \text{Average or} \\ \text{outcome } t & \text{expected return}\end{array}\right)^2}{\begin{array}{c}\text{Total number} \\ \text{of outcomes}\end{array} - 1}}$$

Equation 10.6a

$$s = \sqrt{\frac{\sum_{t=1}^{n}(r_t - \bar{r})^2}{n-1}}$$

Consider two competing investments—shares of stock in Target Corporation (TGT) and American Eagle Outfitters, Inc. (AEO)—described in Table 10.8. From 2005 to 2014, Target earned an average return of 7.7%, but American Eagle Outfitters achieved a superior average return of 12.4%. Looking at the returns each year, you can see that American Eagle Outfitters returns fluctuated over a much wider range (from –53.5% to 105.8%) than did Target returns (from –30.0% to 42.5%).

The standard deviation provides a quantitative tool for comparing investment risk. Table 10.9 demonstrates the standard deviation calculations for Target and American Eagle Outfitters. (Note: Values in column 4 may not appear to equal the square of values in column 3, but that is simply due to rounding. See the available Excel file for the exact calculations.) We can see that the standard deviation of 21.5% for the returns on Target is, not surprisingly, considerably below the standard deviation of 51.9% for American Eagle Outfitters. The fact that American Eagle Outfitters stock returns fluctuate over a very wide range is reflected in its larger standard deviation and indicates that American Eagle Outfitters is a more volatile investment than Target. Of course, these figures are based on historical data. There is no assurance that the risks of these two investments will remain the same in the future.

Historical Returns and Risk We can now use the standard deviation as a measure of risk to assess the historical (1900–2014) investment return data in Table 10.4. Table 10.10 reports the average return and the standard deviation associated with stocks, bonds, and bills in many countries. Within each country, a close relationship exists between the average return and the standard deviation of different types of investments. Stocks earn higher returns than bonds, and bonds earn higher returns than bills. Similarly, stock returns are more volatile than bond returns, with bill returns displaying the least volatility (i.e., the lowest standard deviation). Regardless of the country, the general pattern is clear: Investments with higher average

Excel@Investing

TABLE 10.8 HISTORICAL ANNUAL RETURNS FOR TARGET AND AMERICAN EAGLE OUTFITTERS

	Annual Rate of Return* (r_t)%	
Year (*t*)	Target	American Eagle Outfitters
2005	6.6%	–1.4%
2006	4.7%	105.8%
2007	–11.6%	–32.4%
2008	–30.0%	–53.6%
2009	42.5%	86.5%
2010	26.3%	–8.4%
2011	–13.0%	8.0%
2012	18.2%	47.5%
2013	9.5%	–28.1%
2014	23.8%	0.3%
Average ($\bar{r}$)	**7.7%**	**12.4%**

*Annual rate of return is calculated based on end-of-year closing prices.

(Source: End-of-year closing prices are obtained from Yahoo! Finance and are adjusted for dividends and stock splits.)

TABLE 10.9 CALCULATION OF STANDARD DEVIATIONS OF RETURNS FOR TARGET AND AMERICAN EAGLE OUTFITTERS

			Target	
Year (t)	(1) Return r_t	(2) Average Return $\bar{r}$	(3) (1) − (2) $r_t - \bar{r}$	(4) $(3)^2$ $(r_t - \bar{r})^2$
2005	6.6%	7.7%	−1.1%	1.2%^{2}
2006	4.7%	7.7%	−3.0%	9.2%^{2}
2007	−11.6%	7.7%	−19.3%	371.4%^{2}
2008	−30.0%	7.7%	−37.7%	1421.3%^{2}
2009	42.5%	7.7%	34.8%	1208.6%^{2}
2010	26.3%	7.7%	18.6%	347.0%^{2}
2011	−13.0%	7.7%	−20.7%	427.6%^{2}
2012	18.2%	7.7%	10.5%	109.6%^{2}
2013	9.5%	7.7%	1.8%	3.2%^{2}
2014	23.8%	7.7%	16.1%	260.3%^{2}
			Sum	4159.5%^{2}
		Variance %^{2}	$S^2_{TGT} =$	462.2%^{2}
		Standard deviation %	$S_{TGT} =$	21.5%

$$S_{TGT} = \sqrt{\frac{\sum_{t=1}^{10}(r_t - \bar{r})^2}{n-1}} = \sqrt{\frac{4,159.5}{10-1}} = \sqrt{462.2} = 21.5\%$$

			American Eagle Outfitters	
Year (t)	(1) Return r_t	(2) Average Return $\bar{r}$	(3) (1) − (2) $r_t - \bar{r}$	(4) $(3)2$ $(r_t - \bar{r})^2$
2005	−1.4%	12.4%	−13.8%	190.0%^{2}
2006	105.8%	12.4%	93.4%	8,718.2%^{2}
2007	−32.4%	12.4%	−44.8%	2,010.1%^{2}
2008	−53.6%	12.4%	−66.0%	4,355.4%^{2}
2009	86.5%	12.4%	74.0%	5,482.4%^{2}
2010	−8.4%	12.4%	−20.8%	433.8%^{2}
2011	8.0%	12.4%	−4.4%	19.5%^{2}
2012	47.5%	12.4%	35.1%	1,229.6%^{2}
2013	−28.1%	12.4%	−40.5%	1,639.2%^{2}
2014	0.3%	12.4%	−12.1%	147.2%^{2}
			Sum	24,225.5%^{2}
		Variance %^{2}	$s^2_{AOE} =$	2,691.7%^{2}
		Standard deviation %	$s_{AEO} =$	51.9%

$$S_{AEO} = \sqrt{\frac{\sum_{t=1}^{10}(r_t - \bar{r})^2}{n-1}} = \sqrt{\frac{24,225.5}{10-1}} = \sqrt{2,691.7} = 51.9\%$$

Excel@Investing

returns have higher standard deviations. Because higher standard deviations are associated with greater risk, the historical data confirm the existence of a positive relationship between risk and return. That relationship reflects the fact that market participants require higher returns as compensation for greater risk.

TABLE 10.10 HISTORICAL RETURNS AND STANDARD DEVIATIONS FOR SELECT ASSET CLASSES (1900–2014)

	Stocks		Long-Term Government Bonds		Short-Term Government Bills	
	Average Annual Return	Standard Deviation of Returns	Average Annual Return	Standard Deviation of Returns	Average Annual Return	Standard Deviation of Returns
Australia	11.4%	18.3%	5.6%	11.5%	4.5%	3.9%
Belgium	7.9%	24.5%	5.5%	10.1%	4.8%	3.0%
Canada	8.9%	17.0%	5.3%	8.9%	4.5%	3.6%
Denmark	9.3%	22.0%	7.2%	10.5%	6.0%	3.5%
Finland	12.9%	31.2%	7.3%	6.1%	6.6%	3.4%
France	10.4%	25.1%	7.2%	8.8%	4.0%	2.4%
Germany	8.4%	33.6%	3.2%	13.7%	2.2%	9.5%
Ireland	8.5%	23.1%	5.8%	13.0%	4.8%	4.0%
Italy	10.3%	33.3%	7.0%	10.1%	4.4%	3.3%
Japan	11.2%	29.2%	5.8%	14.1%	4.8%	2.5%
Netherlands	8.0%	22.9%	4.7%	8.3%	3.5%	2.4%
New Zealand	10.0%	20.4%	5.8%	8.2%	5.4%	4.2%
Norway	8.0%	28.0%	5.6%	8.9%	4.8%	3.5%
South Africa	12.7%	22.9%	6.9%	9.6%	6.0%	5.5%
Spain	9.5%	22.8%	7.6%	11.2%	6.0%	4.1%
Sweden	9.4%	21.8%	6.3%	9.7%	5.3%	3.2%
Switzerland	6.8%	18.9%	4.6%	6.0%	3.0%	1.8%
United Kingdom	9.4%	21.4%	5.5%	12.0%	4.8%	3.8%
United States	9.6%	19.8%	5.0%	9.1%	3.8%	2.8%

(Source: Data from Elroy Dimson, Paul Marsh, and Mike Staunton, *Credit Suisse Global Investment Returns Sourcebook 2015*.)

Assessing Risk

Techniques for quantifying the risk of an investment are quite useful. However, they will be of little value if you are unaware of your feelings toward risk. Individual investors typically seek answers to these questions: "Is the amount of perceived risk worth taking to get the expected return?" "Can I get a higher return for the same level of risk, or can I earn the same return while taking less risk?" A look at the general risk-return characteristics of alternative investments and at the question of an acceptable level of risk will shed light on how to evaluate risk.

Risk-Return Characteristics of Alternative Investments A very rough generalization of the risk-return characteristics of the major types of investments appears in Figure 10.2. Of course, within each category, specific investments can vary dramatically in terms of their risk and return characteristics. For instance, some common stocks offer low returns and low risk, while others offer high returns and high risk. In other words, once you have selected the appropriate type of investment, you must decide which specific security to acquire.

An Acceptable Level of Risk Individuals differ in the amount of risk that they are willing to bear and the return that they require as compensation for bearing that risk. Broadly speaking, we can talk about investors' attitudes toward risk by defining three distinct categories of investors whose preferences regarding risk vary in fundamental

FIGURE 10.2

Risk-Return Tradeoffs for Various Investments

A risk-return tradeoff exists such that for a higher risk one expects a higher return, and vice versa. In general, low-risk/low-return investments include U.S. government securities and deposit accounts. High-risk/high-return investments include real estate and other tangible investments, common stocks, options, and futures.

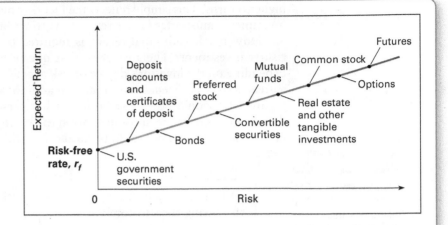

ways, as depicted in Figure 10.3. The figure shows how the required return on an investment is related to risk for investors with different preferences. The three categories are risk-indifferent, risk-averse, and risk-seeking investors.

- For **risk-indifferent** (or risk-neutral) investors, the required return does not change as risk changes. For example, in Figure 10.3, the horizontal blue line indicates that the risk-indifferent investor will accept the same return even if an investment's risk increases from x_1 to x_2.

- For **risk-averse** investors, the required return increases with risk. Because they do not like risk, these investors require higher expected returns to compensate them for taking greater risk. In Figure 10.3, the preferences of risk-averse investors are depicted by the upward sloping green line.

- For the **risk-seeking** investor, the required return decreases as risk increases. These investors simply enjoy the thrill of taking a risk, so they willingly give up some return to take more risk, as indicated by the downward sloping red line in Figure 10.3.

We have already seen historical data on the risk and return of different investments from all over the world, and that data indicate that riskier investments tend to pay

FIGURE 10.3

Risk Preferences

The risk-indifferent investor requires no change in return for a given increase in risk. The risk-averse investor requires an increase in return for a given risk increase. The risk-seeking investor gives up some return for more risk. The majority of investors are risk averse.

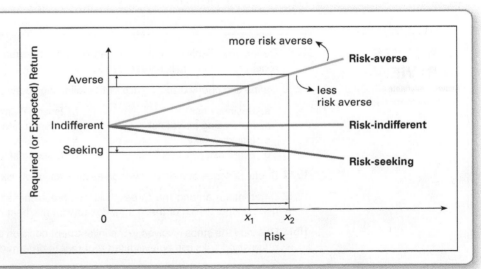

higher returns. This simply reflects the fact that most investors are risk averse, so riskier investments must offer higher returns to attract buyers.

How much additional return is required to convince an investor to purchase a riskier investment? The answer to that question varies from one person to another depending on the investor's degree of risk aversion. A very risk-averse investor requires a great deal of compensation to take on additional risk, meaning that the green line in Figure 10.3 would be very steep for such a person. Someone who is less risk averse does not require as much compensation to be persuaded to accept risk, so for that sort of person the green line would be flatter (but still upward sloping).

Steps in the Decision Process: Combining Return and Risk

When you are deciding among alternative investments, you should take the following steps to combine return and risk.

- Using historical or projected return data, estimate the expected return over a given holding period. Be sure that your estimate of an investment's expected return takes into account the time value of money.

- Using historical or projected return data, assess the risk associated with the investment. You can assess an investment's risk by making a subjective judgment, by calculating the standard deviation of an investment's returns, or by using one of the more sophisticated methods that we discuss elsewhere.

- Evaluate the risk-return characteristics of each investment option to make sure that the return that you expect is reasonable given the risk that you are taking. If other investments with lower levels of risk provide equal or greater expected returns, or if other investments with the same level of risk provide higher returns, the investment is not acceptable.

- Select the investments that offer the highest returns associated with the level of risk you are willing to take. As long as you get the highest expected return for your acceptable level of risk, you have made a "good investment."

Probably the most difficult step in this process is assessing risk. Aside from return and risk considerations, other factors such as taxes and liquidity affect the investment decision. You will learn more about assessing these other factors in subsequent chapters.

CONCEPTS IN REVIEW

Answers available at
http://www.pearsonhighered
.com/smart

10.9 Define *risk*. Explain what we mean by the *risk-return tradeoff*. What happens to the required return as risk increases? Explain.

10.10 Define and briefly discuss each of the following sources of risk.

    a. Business risk   b. Financial risk
    c. Purchasing power risk   d. Interest rate risk
    e. Liquidity risky   f. Tax risk
    g. Event risk   h. Market risk

10.11 Briefly describe standard deviation as a measure of risk or variability.

10.12 Differentiate among the three basic risk preferences: risk-indifferent, risk-averse, and risk-seeking. Which of these attitudes toward risk best describes most investors?

10.13 Describe the steps involved in the investment decision process. Be sure to mention how returns and risks can be evaluated together to determine acceptable investments.

MyFinanceLab

Here is what you should know after reading this chapter. MyFinanceLab will help you identify what you know and where to go when you need to practice.

What You Should Know	Key Terms	Where to Practice
LG1 Review the concept of return, its components, the forces that affect the level of return, and historical returns. Return is the reward for investing. The total return provided by an investment includes income and capital gains (or losses). Return is commonly calculated on a historical basis and then used to project expected returns. The level of return depends on internal characteristics and external forces, which include the general level of price changes. Significant differences exist among the average annual rates of return realized over time on various types of security investments.	deflation, *p. 341* expected return, *p. 340* income, *p. 338* inflation, *p. 341* return, *p. 338* total return, *p. 339*	MyFinanceLab Study Plan 10.1 Excel Table 10.3
LG2 Discuss the role of time value of money in measuring return and defining a satisfactory investment. Because investors have opportunities to earn interest on their funds, money has a time value. Time value of money concepts should be considered when making investment decisions. Financial calculators and electronic spreadsheets can be used to streamline time value of money calculations. A satisfactory investment is one for which the present value of its benefits equals or exceeds the present value of its costs.	satisfactory investment, *p. 343*	MyFinanceLab Study Plan 10.2 Excel Table 10.5
LG3 Describe real, risk-free, and required returns and the calculation and application of holding period return. The required return is the rate of return an investor must earn to be fully compensated for an investment's risk. It represents the sum of the real rate of return and the expected inflation premium (which together represent the risk-free rate), plus the risk premium. The risk premium varies depending on issue and issuer characteristics. The holding period return (HPR) is the return earned over a specified period of time. It is frequently used to compare returns earned in periods of 1 year or less.	expected inflation premium, *p. 346* holding period, *p. 347* holding period return (HPR), *p. 347* nominal rate of return, *p. 345* paper return, *p. 347* real rate of return, *p. 345* realized return, *p. 347* required return, *p. 346* risk-free rate, *p. 346* risk premium, *p. 346*	MyFinanceLab Study Plan 10.3 Excel Table 10.6 Video Learning Aid for Problem P10.10

What You Should Know	Key Terms	Where to Practice
LG4 **Explain the concept and the calculation of IRR and how to find growth rates.** Internal rate of return is the compound annual rate of return earned on investments held for more than 1 year. If the IRR is greater than or equal to the required return, the investment is acceptable. The concept of IRR assumes that the investor will be able to earn interest at the calculated IRR on all income from the investment. Present value techniques can be used to find a rate of growth, which is the compound annual rate of change in the value of a stream of income, particularly dividends or earnings.	fully compounded rate of return, *p. 352* rate of growth, *p. 353* reinvestment rate, *p. 352* internal rate of return, *p. 349*	MyFinanceLab Study Plan 10.4 Excel Table 10.7
LG5 **Discuss the key sources of risk that might affect potential investments.** Risk is uncertainty surrounding the actual return that an investment will generate. Risk results from a combination of sources: business, financial, purchasing power, interest rate, liquidity, tax, market, and event risk. These risks have varying effects on different types of investments. The combined impact of any of the sources of risk in a given investment would be reflected in its risk premium.	business risk, *p. 355* event risk, *p. 357* financial risk, *p. 355* interest rate risk, *p. 355* liquidity risk, *p. 356* market risk, *p. 357* purchasing power risk, *p. 355* risk-return tradeoff, *p. 354* tax risk, *p. 356*	MyFinanceLab Study Plan 10.5
LG6 **Understand the risk of a single asset, risk assessment, and the steps that combine return and risk.** The standard deviation measures the volatility of both single assets and portfolios of assets. Investors require higher returns as compensation for greater risk. Generally, each type of investment displays certain risk-return characteristics. Most investors are risk averse: For a given increase in risk, they require an increase in expected return. Investors estimate the return and risk of each alternative and then select investments that offer the highest returns for the level of acceptable risk.	risk-averse, *p. 361* risk-indifferent, *p. 361* risk-seeking, *p. 361* standard deviation, *s, p. 357*	MyFinanceLab Study Plan 10.6 Excel Table 10.9

Log into MyFinanceLab, take a chapter test, and get a personalized Study Plan that tells you which concepts you understand and which ones you need to review. From there, MyFinanceLab will give you further practice, tutorials, animations, videos, and guided solutions.

Log into http://www.myfinancelab.com

Discussion Questions

LG1 **Q10.1** Choose a publicly traded company that has been listed on a major exchange or in the over-the-counter market for at least five years. Use any data source of your choice to find the annual cash dividend, if any, paid by the company in each of the past five calendar years. Also find the closing price of the stock at the end of each of the preceding six years.
  a. Calculate the return for each of the five one-year periods.
  b. Create a graph that shows the return that the investment earned on the y-axis and the year in which the return was earn on the x-axis.
  c. On the basis of the graph in part **b**, estimate the return for the coming year, and explain your answer.

LG2 **Q10.2** Two investments offer a series of cash payments over the next four years, as shown in the following table.

Investment	Year 1	Year 2	Year 3	Year 4
1	$100	$200	$300	$400
2	$250	$250	$250	$250

  a. What is the total amount of money paid by each investment over the four years?
  b. From a time value of money perspective, which of these investments is more attractive?
  c. Can you think of a reason why investors might prefer Investment 1?

LG4 **Q10.3** Access appropriate estimates of the expected inflation rate over the next year, and the current yield on one-year, risk-free securities (the yield on these securities is referred to as the *nominal* rate of interest). Use the data to estimate the current risk-free *real* rate of interest.

LG3 LG6 **Q10.4** Choose three NYSE-listed stocks and maintain a record of their dividend payments, if any, and closing prices each week over the next six weeks.
  a. At the end of the six-week period, calculate the one-week HPRs for each stock for each of the six weeks.
  b. For each stock, average the six weekly HPRs calculated in part **a** and compare them.
  c. Use the averages you computed in part **b** and compute the standard deviation of the six HPRs for each stock. Discuss the stocks' relative risk and return behavior. Did the stocks with the highest risk earn the greatest return?

Problems

All problems are available on http://www.myfinancelab.com

LG1 **P10.1** How much would an investor earn on a stock purchased one year ago for $45 if it paid an annual cash dividend of $2.25 and had just been sold for $52.50? Would the investor have experienced a capital gain? Explain.

LG1 **P10.2** An investor buys a bond for $10,000. The bond pays $200 interest every 6 months. After 18 months, the investor sells the bond for $9,500. Describe the types of income and/or loss the investor had.

LG1 **P10.3** Assuming you purchased a share of stock for $50 one year ago, sold it today for $60, and during the year received three dividend payments totaling $2.70, calculate the following.
  a. Income
  b. Capital gain (or loss)
  c. Total return
    (1) In dollars
    (2) As a percentage of the initial investment

LG1 **P10.4** Assume you purchased a bond for $9,500. The bond pays $300 interest every 6 months. You sell the bond after 18 months for $10,000. Calculate the following.
  a. Income
  b. Capital gain or loss
  c. Total return in dollars and as a percentage of the original investment

LG1 **P10.5** Consider the historical data for an investment given in the accompanying table.
  a. Calculate the total return (in dollars) for each year.
  b. Indicate the level of return you would expect in 2018 and in 2019.
  c. Comment on your forecast.

		Market Value	
Year	Income	Beginning	Ending
2013	$1.00	$30.00	$32.50
2014	$1.20	$32.50	$35.00
2015	$1.30	$35.00	$33.00
2016	$1.60	$33.00	$40.00
2017	$1.75	$40.00	$45.00

LG1 **P10.6** Refer to the table in Problem 10.5. What is the total return in dollars and as a percentage of your original investment if you purchased 100 shares of the investment at the beginning of 2013 and sold it at the end of 2015?

LG3 **P10.7** Given a real rate of interest of 2%, an expected inflation premium of 3%, and risk premiums for investments A and B of 4% and 6%, respectively, find the following.
  a. The risk-free rate of return, r_f
  b. The required returns for investments A and B

LG3 **P10.8** The risk-free rate is 3%, and expected inflation is 1.5%. If inflation expectations change such that future expected inflation rises to 2.5%, what will the new risk-free rate be?

LG3 **P10.9** Calculate a one-year holding period return for the following two investment alternatives. Which investment would you prefer, assuming they are of equal risk? Explain.

	Investment	
	X	Y
Cash received		
1st quarter	$ 1.00	$ 0.00
2nd quarter	$ 1.20	$ 0.00
3rd quarter	$ 0.00	$ 0.00
4th quarter	$ 2.30	$ 2.00
Investment value		
Beginning of year	$30.00	$50.00
End of year	$29.00	$56.00

LG3 **P10.10** You are considering two investment alternatives. The first is a stock that pays quarterly dividends of $0.25 per share and is trading at $20 per share; you expect to sell the stock in six months for $24. The second is a stock that pays quarterly dividends of $0.50 per share and is trading at $27 per share; you expect to sell the stock in one year for $30. Which stock will provide the better annualized holding period return?

LG3 **P10.11** You are considering purchasing a bond that pays annual interest of $50 per $1,000 of par value. The bond matures in one year, and at that time you will collect the par value and the interest payment. If you can purchase this bond for $950, what is the holding period return?

LG4 **P10.12** Assume you invest $4,000 today in an investment that promises to return $9,000 in exactly 10 years.

a. Use the present value technique to estimate the IRR on this investment.

b. If a minimum annual return of 9% is required, would you recommend this investment?

LG4 **P10.13** You invest $7,000 in stock and receive dividends of $65, $70, $70, and $65 over the following four years. At the end of the four years, you sell the stock for $7,900. What was the IRR on this investment?

LG4 **P10.14** Your friend asks you to invest $10,000 in a business venture. Based on your estimates, you would receive nothing for three years, at the end of year four you would receive $4,900, and at the end of year five you would receive $14,500. If your estimates are correct, what would be the IRR on this investment?

LG4 **P10.15** Use a financial calculator or an Excel spreadsheet to estimate the IRR each of the following investments.

Investment	Initial Investment	Future Value	End of Year
A	$ 1,000	$ 1,200	5
B	$10,000	$20,000	7
C	$ 400	$ 2,000	20
D	$ 3,000	$ 4,000	6
E	$ 5,500	$25,000	30

LG4 **P10.16** Sara Holliday must earn a return of 10% on an investment that requires an initial outlay of $2,500 and promises to return $6,000 in eight years.

a. Use present value techniques to estimate the IRR on this investment.

b. On the basis of your finding in part **a**, should Sara make the proposed investment? Explain.

LG4 **P10.17** Use a financial calculator or an Excel spreadsheet to estimate the IRR for each of the following investments.

	Investment	
	A	B
Initial Investment	$8,500	$9,500
End of Year	Income	
1	$2,500	$2,000
2	$2,500	$2,500
3	$2,500	$3,000
4	$2,500	$3,500
5	$2,500	$4,000

LG4 **P10.18** Elliott Dumack must earn a minimum rate of return of 11% to be adequately compensated for the risk of the following investment.

Initial Investment	$14,000
End of Year	Income
1	$6,000
2	$3,000
3	$5,000
4	$2,000
5	$2,100

    a. Use present value techniques to estimate the IRR on this investment.

    b. On the basis of your finding in part a, should Elliott make the proposed investment? Explain.

P10.19 Assume that an investment generates the following income stream and can be purchased at the beginning of 2017 for $1,000 and sold at the end of 2020 for $1,200. Estimate the IRR for this investment. If a minimum return of 9% is required, would you recommend this investment? Explain.

End of Year	Income Stream
2017	$140
2018	$120
2019	$100
2020	$ 80
2021	$ 60
2022	$ 40
2023	$ 20

P10.20 For each of the following streams of dividends, estimate the compound annual rate of growth between the earliest year for which a value is given and 2017.

	Dividend Stream		
Year	A	B	C
2008		$1.50	
2009		$1.55	
2010		$1.61	
2011		$1.68	$2.50
2012		$1.76	$2.60
2013	$5.10	$1.85	$2.65
2014	$5.60	$1.95	$2.65
2015	$6.40	$2.06	$2.80
2016	$7.20	$2.17	$2.85
2017	$7.90	$2.28	$2.90

P10.21 A company paid dividends of $1.00 per share in 2009 and just announced that it will pay $2.21 in 2016. Estimate the compound annual growth rate of the dividends.

P10.22 A company reported net income in 2012 of $350 million. In 2016 the company expects net income to be $446.9 million. Estimate the annual compound growth rate of net income.

P10.23 The historical returns for two investments—A and B—are summarized in the following table for the period 2013 to 2017. Use the data to answer the questions that follow.

	A	B
Year	Rate of Return	
2013	19%	8%
2014	1%	10%
2015	10%	12%
2016	26%	14%
2017	4%	16%
Average	12%	12%

a. On the basis of a review of the return data, which investment appears to be more risky? Why?

b. Calculate the standard deviation for each investment's returns.

c. On the basis of your calculations in part **b**, which investment is more risky? Compare this conclusion to your observation in part **a**.

Visit http://www.myfinancelab.com for web exercises, spreadsheets, and other online resources.

Case Problem 10.1   Coates's Decision

LG2 LG4   On January 1, 2017, Dave Coates, a 23-year-old mathematics teacher at Xavier High School, received a tax refund of $1,100. Because Dave didn't need this money for his current living expenses, he decided to make a long-term investment. After surveying a number of alternative investments costing no more than $1,100, Dave isolated two that seemed most suitable to his needs.

Each of the investments cost $1,050 and was expected to provide income over a 10-year period. Investment A provided a relatively certain stream of income. Dave was a little less certain of the income provided by investment B. From his search for suitable alternatives, Dave found that the appropriate discount rate for a relatively certain investment was 4%. Because he felt a bit uncomfortable with an investment like B, he estimated that such an investment would have to provide a return at least 4% higher than investment A. Although Dave planned to reinvest funds returned from the investments in other vehicles providing similar returns, he wished to keep the extra $50 ($1,100 − $1,050) invested for the full 10 years in a savings account paying 3% interest compounded annually.

As he makes his investment decision, Dave has asked for your help in answering the questions that follow the expected return data for these investments.

End of Year	Expected Returns	
	A	B
2017	$ 50	$ 0
2018	$ 50	$150
2019	$ 50	$150
2020	$ 50	$150
2021	$ 50	$200
2022	$ 50	$250
2023	$ 50	$200
2024	$ 50	$150
2025	$ 50	$100
2026	$1,050	$ 50

Questions

a. Assuming that investments A and B are equally risky and using the 4% discount rate, apply the present value technique to assess the acceptability of each investment and to determine the preferred investment. Explain your findings.

b. Recognizing that investment B is more risky than investment A, reassess the two alternatives, adding the 4% risk premium to the 4% discount rate for investment A and therefore applying a 8% discount rate to investment B. Compare your findings relative to acceptability and preference to those found for question a.

c. From your findings in questions **a** and **b**, indicate whether the IRR for investment A is above or below 4% and whether that for investment B is above or below 8%. Explain.

d. Use the present value technique to estimate the IRR on each investment. Compare your findings and contrast them with your response to question **c**.

e. From the information given, which, if either, of the two investments would you recommend that Dave make? Explain your answer.

f. Indicate to Dave how much money the extra $50 will have grown to by the end of 2026, assuming he makes no withdrawals from the savings account.

Case Problem 10.2   The Risk-Return Tradeoff: Molly O'Rourke's Stock Purchase Decision

LG3 LG6   Over the past 10 years, Molly O'Rourke has slowly built a diversified portfolio of common stock. Currently her portfolio includes 20 different common stock issues and has a total market value of $82,500.

Molly is at present considering the addition of 50 shares of either of two common stock issues—X or Y. To assess the return and risk of each of these issues, she has gathered dividend income and share price data for both over the last 10 years (2007–2016). Molly's investigation of the outlook for these issues suggests that each will, on average, tend to behave in the future just as it has in the past. She therefore believes that the expected return can be estimated by finding the average HPR over the past 10 years for each of the stocks. The historical dividend income and stock price data collected by Molly are given in the accompanying table.

| | Stock X | | | Stock Y | | |
| | | Share Price | | | Share Price | |
Year	Dividend Income	Beginning	Ending	Dividend Income	Beginning	Ending
2007	$1.00	$20.00	$22.00	$1.50	$20.00	$20.00
2008	$1.50	$22.00	$21.00	$1.60	$20.00	$20.00
2009	$1.40	$21.00	$24.00	$1.70	$20.00	$21.00
2010	$1.70	$24.00	$22.00	$1.80	$21.00	$21.00
2011	$1.90	$22.00	$23.00	$1.90	$21.00	$22.00
2012	$1.60	$23.00	$26.00	$2.00	$22.00	$23.00
2013	$1.70	$26.00	$25.00	$2.10	$23.00	$23.00
2014	$2.00	$25.00	$24.00	$2.20	$23.00	$24.00
2015	$2.10	$24.00	$27.00	$2.30	$24.00	$25.00
2016	$2.20	$27.00	$30.00	$2.40	$25.00	$25.00

Questions

a. Determine the HPR for each stock in each of the preceding 10 years. Find the expected return for each stock, using the approach specified by Molly.

b. Use the HPRs and expected return calculated in question **a** to find the standard deviation of the HPRs for each stock over the 10-year period.

c. Use your findings to evaluate and discuss the return and risk associated with stocks X and Y. Which stock seems preferable? Explain.

d. Ignoring her existing portfolio, what recommendations would you give Molly with regard to stocks X and Y?

Excel@Investing

Excel@Investing

From her Investment Analysis class, Laura has been given an assignment to evaluate several securities on a risk-return tradeoff basis. The specific securities to be researched are International Business Machines, Helmerich & Payne, Inc., and the S&P 500 Index. The respective ticker symbols for the stocks are IBM and HP. She finds the following data on the securities in question.

Year	2009	2010	2011	2012	2013	2014
Price$_{IBM}$	$130.90	$146.76	$183.88	$191.55	$187.57	$160.44
Dividend$_{IBM}$	$ 2.15	$ 2.50	$ 2.90	$ 3.30	$ 3.70	$ 4.25
Price$_{HP}$	$ 39.88	$ 48.48	$ 58.36	$ 56.01	$ 84.08	$ 67.42
Dividend$_{HP}$	$ 0.20	$ 0.22	$ 0.26	$ 0.28	$ 1.30	$ 2.63
Value$_{S&P}$	1115.10	1257.64	1257.60	1426.19	1848.36	2058.90

Note: The value of the S&P 500 Index includes dividends.

Questions

Part One

a. Use the data that Laura has found on the three securities and create a spreadsheet to calculate the holding period return for each year and the average return over a five-year period. Specifically, the HPR will be based upon five unique one-year periods (i.e., 2009 to 2010, 2010 to 2011, 2011 to 2012, 2012 to 2013, 2013 to 2014). Use the following formula:

$$HPR = [Inc + (V_n - V_0)]/V_0$$

where

Inc = income during period

V_n = ending investment value

V_0 = beginning investment value

Part Two

Create a spreadsheet similar to the spreadsheet for Table 10.9, which can be viewed at http://www.myfinancelab.com, in order to evaluate the risk-return tradeoff.

b. Calculate the standard deviations of the returns for IBM, HP, and the S&P 500 Index.

c. What industries are associated with IBM and HP?

d. Based on your answer in part c and your results for the average return and the standard deviation, what conclusions can Laura make about investing in either IBM or HP?

Chapter-Opening Problem

The table below shows the annual change in the average U.S. home price from 2005 to 2014 according to the S&P/Case-Shiller Index. Calculate the average annual return and its standard deviation. Compare this to the average return and standard deviation for Target Corporation and American Eagle Outfitters, Inc., shown in Table 10.9. In terms of average return and standard deviation, how does residential real estate compare as an investment relative to those two common stocks?

Year	% Change
2005	15.5%
2006	0.7%
2007	− 9.0%
2008	− 18.6%
2009	− 3.1%
2010	− 2.4%
2011	− 4.1%
2012	6.9%
2013	13.4%
2014	4.5%

11

Modern Portfolio Concepts

LEARNING GOALS

After studying this chapter, you should be able to:

LG1 Understand portfolio objectives and the procedures used to calculate portfolio return and standard deviation.

LG2 Discuss the concepts of correlation and diversification and the key aspects of international diversification.

LG3 Describe the components of risk and the use of beta to measure risk.

LG4 Explain the capital asset pricing model (CAPM) conceptually, mathematically, and graphically.

LG5 Review the traditional and modern approaches to portfolio management.

LG6 Describe portfolio betas, the risk-return tradeoff, and reconciliation of the two approaches to portfolio management.

United Rentals Inc. (URI) rents construction and industrial equipment to contractors, businesses, governments, and individuals. The company specializes in heavy equipment such as earth-moving machines and forklifts. During the recession that began in 2007, many companies found that they did not have enough work to do to keep the machines they already owned running, so naturally the demand for rental equipment suffered. URI stock reached a 2007 peak of over $35 per share in May, but after that began a long slide, hitting bottom at $2.52 in March 2009.

That spring, the economy began to show signs of life, and URI stock surged, rising nearly 200% from its low point by August 2009. Heiko Ihle, a stock analyst for the Gabelli & Co. money management firm, issued a "buy" rating on URI despite the fact that the company had high leverage (meaning that it borrowed a lot of money to finance its operations). Ihle noted that URI stock had a high beta, meaning that it moved sharply when the broader market shifted.

Mr. Ihle's recommendation proved to be a good one. From the end of August 2009 to the end of August 2014, the value of URI stock climbed almost 1,200% and was trading above $119 per share. Over that same period of time, the S&P 500 Index, a widely used indicator of the overall stock market, rose by a less dramatic 95%.

In this chapter we continue to explore the tradeoff between risk and return, and we'll see that a stock's beta—its sensitivity to movements in the overall stock market—has a big effect on both the stock's risk and the return that it offers investors.

(Sources: Yahoo! Finance; "U.S. Hot Stocks: Legg Mason, JDA Software Active in Late Trading," July 20, 2009; The Wall Street Journal Digital Network, http://online.wsj.com/article/BT-CO-20090720-713541.html.)

Principles of Portfolio Planning

LG1 LG2 Investors benefit from holding portfolios of investments rather than single investments. Without necessarily sacrificing returns, investors who hold portfolios can reduce risk. Surprisingly, the volatility of a portfolio may be less than the volatilities of the individual assets that make up the portfolio. In other words, when it comes to portfolios and risk, the whole is less than the sum of its parts!

A *portfolio* is a collection of investments assembled to meet one or more investment goals. Of course, different investors have different objectives for their portfolios. The primary goal of a **growth-oriented portfolio** is long-term price appreciation. An **income-oriented portfolio** is designed to produce regular dividends and interest payments.

Portfolio Objectives

Setting portfolio objectives involves definite tradeoffs, such as the tradeoff between risk and return or between potential price appreciation and income. How investors evaluate these tradeoffs will depend on their tax bracket, current income needs, and ability to bear risk. The key point is that portfolio objectives must be established *before* one begins to invest.

The ultimate goal of an investor is an **efficient portfolio,** one that provides the highest return for a given risk level. Efficient portfolios aren't necessarily easy to identify. Investors usually must search out investment alternatives to get the best combinations of risk and return.

Portfolio Return and Standard Deviation

The first step in forming a portfolio is to analyze the characteristics of the securities that an investor might include in the portfolio. Two of the most important characteristics to examine are the returns that each asset might be expected to earn and the uncertainty surrounding that expected return. As a starting point, we will examine historical data to see what returns stocks have earned in the past and how much those returns have fluctuated to get a feel for what the future might hold.

The portfolio return is calculated as a weighted average of returns on the assets (i.e., the investments) that make up the portfolio. You can calculate the portfolio return, r_p, by using Equation 11.1. The portfolio return depends on the returns of each asset in the portfolio and on the fraction invested in each asset, w_j.

Equation 11.1

$$\text{Portfolio Return} = \begin{pmatrix} \text{Proportion of} \\ \text{portfolio's total} \\ \text{dollar value} \\ \text{invested in} \\ \text{asset 1} \end{pmatrix} \times \begin{matrix} \text{Return} \\ \text{on asset} \\ 1 \end{matrix} + \begin{pmatrix} \text{Proportion of} \\ \text{portfolio's total} \\ \text{dollar value} \\ \text{invested in} \\ \text{asset 2} \end{pmatrix} \times \begin{matrix} \text{Return} \\ \text{on asset} \\ 2 \end{matrix} + \cdots +$$

$$\begin{pmatrix} \text{Proportion of} \\ \text{portfolio's total} \\ \text{dollar value} \\ \text{invested in} \\ \text{asset } n \end{pmatrix} \times \begin{matrix} \text{Return} \\ \text{on asset} \\ n \end{matrix} = \sum_{j=1}^{n} \begin{pmatrix} \text{Proportion of} \\ \text{portfolio's total} \\ \text{dollar value} \\ \text{invested in} \\ \text{asset } j \end{pmatrix} \times \begin{matrix} \text{Return} \\ \text{on asset} \\ j \end{matrix}$$

Equation 11.1a

$$r_p = (w_1 \times r_1) + (w_2 \times r_2) + \cdots + (w_n \times r_n) = \sum_{j=1}^{n} (w_j \times r_j)$$

The fraction invested in each asset, w_j, is also known as a portfolio weight because it indicates the weight that each asset receives in the portfolio. Of course, $\sum_{j=1}^{n} w_j = 1$, which means that the sum of the portfolio weights must equal 100%. In other words, when you add up the fractions invested in all of the assets, that sum must equal 1.0.

Panel A of Table 11.1 shows the historical annual returns on two stocks, International Business Machines Corp. (IBM) and Celgene Corp. (CELG), from 2005 through 2014. Over that period, IBM earned an average annual return of 9.0%, which is close to the average annual return on the U.S. stock market during the past century. In contrast, Celgene Corp. earned a spectacular 40.7% average annual return. Although Celgene may not repeat that kind of performance over the next decade, it is still instructive to examine the historical figures.

Excel@Investing

TABLE 11.1   INDIVIDUAL AND PORTFOLIO RETURNS AND STANDARD DEVIATION OF RETURNS FOR INTERNATIONAL BUSINESS MACHINES (IBM) AND CELGENE (CELG)

A. Individual and Portfolio Returns

	(1)	(2)	(3)		(4)
	Historical Returns*		Portfolio Weights		Portfolio Return
Year (t)	r_{IBM}	r_{CELG}	$W_{IBM} = 0.86$	$W_{CELG} = 0.14$	r_p
2005	−15.8%	144.3%	(0.86 × −15.8%) + (0.14 × 144.3%) =		6.6%
2006	19.8%	77.5%	(0.86 × 19.8%) + (0.14 × 77.5%) =		27.9%
2007	12.8%	−19.7%	(0.86 × 12.8%) + (0.14 × −19.7%) =		8.3%
2008	−20.8%	19.7%	(0.86 × −20.8%) + (0.14 × 19.7%) =		−15.1%
2009	58.6%	0.7%	(0.86 × 58.6%) + (0.14 × 0.7%) =		50.5%
2010	14.3%	6.2%	(0.86 × 14.3%) + (0.14 × 6.2%) =		13.1%
2011	27.4%	14.3%	(0.86 × 27.4%) + (0.14 × 14.3%) =		25.6%
2012	5.9%	16.1%	(0.86 × 5.9%) + (0.14 × 16.1%) =		7.3%
2013	−0.2%	115.3%	(0.86 × −0.2%) + (0.14 × 115.3%) =		16.0%
2014	−12.4%	32.4%	(0.86 × −12.4%) + (0.14 × 32.4%) =		−6.1%
Average Return	9.0%	40.7%			13.4%

B. Individual and Portfolio Standard Deviations

Standard Deviation Calculation for IBM:

$$s_{IBM} = \sqrt{\frac{\sum_{t=1}^{10}(r_t - \bar{r})^2}{n-1}} = \sqrt{\frac{(-15.8\% - 9.0\%)^2 + \ldots + (-12.4\% - 9.0\%)^2}{10-1}} = \sqrt{\frac{5015.4\%^2}{10-1}} = 23.6\%$$

Standard Deviation Calculation for CELG:

$$s_{CELG} = \sqrt{\frac{\sum_{t=1}^{10}(r_t - \bar{r})^2}{n-1}} = \sqrt{\frac{(144.3\% - 40.7\%)^2 + \ldots + (32.4\% - 40.7\%)^2}{10-1}} = \sqrt{\frac{2,5913.3\%^2}{10-1}} = 53.7\%$$

Standard Deviation Calculation for Portfolio:

$$s_p = \sqrt{\frac{\sum_{t=1}^{10}(r_t - \bar{r})^2}{n-1}} = \sqrt{\frac{(6.6\% - 13.4\%)^2 + \ldots + (-6.1\% - 13.4\%)^2}{10-1}} = \sqrt{\frac{3045.8\%^2}{10-1}} = 18.4\%$$

*Annual rate of return is calculated based on end-of-year closing prices.

Source: End-of-year closing prices are obtained from Yahoo Finance and are adjusted for dividends and stock splits.

Suppose we want to calculate the return on a portfolio containing investments in both IBM and Celgene. The first step in that calculation is to determine how much of each stock to hold. In other words, we must to decide what weight each stock should receive in the portfolio. Let's assume that we want to invest 86% of our money in IBM and 14% in CELG. What kind of return would such a portfolio earn?

We know that over this period, Celgene earned much higher returns than IBM, so intuitively we might expect that a portfolio containing both stocks would earn a return higher than IBM's but lower than Celgene's. Furthermore, because most (i.e., 86%) of the portfolio is invested in IBM, you might guess that the portfolio's return would be closer to IBM's than to Celgene's.

Columns 3 and 4 in Panel A show the portfolio's return each year. The average annual return on this portfolio was 13.4% and as expected it is higher than the return on IBM and lower than the return on Celgene. By investing a little in Celgene, an investor could earn a higher return than would be possible by holding IBM stock in isolation.

What about the portfolio's risk? To examine the risk of this portfolio, start by measuring the risk of the stocks in the portfolio. Recall that one measure of an investment's risk is the standard deviation of its returns. Panel B of Table 11.1 applies the formula for standard deviation that we introduced earlier to calculate the standard deviation of returns on IBM and Celgene stock. Or, if you prefer, rather than using the formulas in Table 11.1 to find the standard deviation of returns for IBM and CELG, you can construct an Excel spreadsheet to do the calculations, as shown below. The standard deviation of IBM's returns is 23.6%, and for Celgene's stock returns the standard deviation is 53.7%. Here again we see evidence of the tradeoff between risk and return. Celgene's stock earned much higher returns than IBM's stock, but Celgene returns fluctuate a great deal more as well.

	A	B	C	D
1	STANDARD DEVIATION OF RETURNS FOR IBM, CELG, AND PORTFOLIO			
2	Year (t)	r_{IBM}	r_{CELG}	r_p
3	2005	-15.8%	144.3%	6.6%
4	2006	19.8%	77.5%	27.9%
5	2007	12.8%	-19.7%	8.3%
6	2008	-20.8%	19.7%	-15.1%
7	2009	58.6%	0.7%	50.5%
8	2010	14.3%	6.2%	13.1%
9	2011	27.4%	14.3%	25.6%
10	2012	5.9%	16.1%	7.3%
11	2013	-0.2%	115.3%	16.0%
12	2014	-12.4%	32.4%	-6.1%
13	Standard deviation	23.6%	53.7%	18.4%
14	Entries in Cells B13, C13, and D13 are =STDEV(B3:B12), =STDEV(C3:C12), and			
15	=STDEV(D3:D12), respectively.			

Because Celgene's returns are more volatile than IBM's, you might expect that a portfolio containing both stocks would have a standard deviation that is higher than IBM's but lower than Celgene's. In fact, that's not what happens. The final calculation in Panel B inserts the IBM-Celgene portfolio return data from column 4 in Panel A into the standard deviation formula to calculate the portfolio's standard deviation. Panel B shows the surprising result that the portfolio's returns are less volatile than are the returns of either stock in the portfolio! The portfolio's standard deviation is just 18.4%. This is great news for investors. An investor who held only IBM shares would have earned an average return of only 9.0%, but to achieve that return the investor would have had to endure IBM's 23.6% standard deviation. By selling a few IBM shares and using the proceeds to buy a few Celgene shares (resulting in the 0.86 and 0.14 portfolio weights shown in Table 11.1), an investor could have simultaneously increased his or her return to 13.4% and reduced the standard deviation to 18.4%. In other words, the investor could have had more return and less risk at the same time. This means that an investor who owns nothing but IBM shares holds an inefficient portfolio—an alternative portfolio exists that has a better return-to-risk tradeoff. That's the power of diversification. Next, we will see that the key factor in making this possible is a low correlation between IBM and Celgene returns.

Correlation and Diversification

Diversification involves the inclusion of a number of different investments in a portfolio, and it is an important aspect of creating an efficient portfolio. Underlying the intuitive appeal of diversification is the statistical concept of correlation. Effective portfolio planning requires an understanding of how correlation and diversification influence a portfolio's risk.

Correlation Correlation is a statistical measure of the relationship between two series of numbers. If two series tend to move in the same direction, they are **positively correlated**. For instance, if each day we record the number of hours of sunshine and the average daily temperature, we would expect those two series to display positive correlation. Days with more sunshine tend to be days with higher temperatures. If the series tend to move in opposite directions, they are **negatively correlated**. For example, if each day we record the number of hours of sunshine and the amount of rainfall, we would expect those two series to display negative correlation because, on average, rainfall is lower on days with lots of sunshine. Finally, if two series bear no relationship to each other, then they are **uncorrelated**. For example, we would probably expect no correlation between the number of hours of sunshine on a particular day and the change in the value of the U.S. dollar against other world currencies on the same day. There is no obvious connection between sunshine and world currency markets.

The degree of correlation—whether positive or negative—is measured by the **correlation coefficient**, which is usually represented by the Greek symbol rho (ρ). It's easy to use Excel to calculate the correlation coefficient between IBM and Celgene stock returns, as shown in the following spreadsheet.

	A	B	C
1	**CORRELATION COEFFICIENT OF RETURNS FOR IBM AND CELG**		
2	Year (t)	r_{IBM}	r_{CELG}
3	2005	-15.8%	144.3%
4	2006	19.8%	77.5%
5	2007	12.8%	-19.7%
6	2008	-20.8%	19.7%
7	2009	58.6%	0.7%
8	2010	14.3%	6.2%
9	2011	27.4%	14.3%
10	2012	5.9%	16.1%
11	2013	-0.2%	115.3%
12	2014	-12.4%	32.4%
13		Correlation coefficient	-0.43
14	Entry in Cell B13 is		
15	=CORREL(B3:B12,C3:C12).		

Excel will quickly tell you that the correlation coefficient between IBM and Celgene during the 2005–2014 period was −0.43. The negative figure means that there was a tendency over this period for the two stocks to move in opposite directions. In other words, years in which IBM's return was better than average tended to be years in which Celgene's return was worse than average, and vice versa. A negative correlation between two stocks is somewhat unusual because most stocks are affected in the same way by large, macroeconomic forces. In other words, most stocks tend to move in the same direction as the overall economy, which means that most stocks will display at least some positive correlation with each other.

Because IBM is a major provider of information technology services and Celgene is a biopharmaceutical manufacturer, it is not too surprising that the correlation between these two stocks is not strongly positive. The companies compete in entirely different industries, have different customers and suppliers, and operate within very different regulatory constraints; however, the relatively large (i.e., −0.43) magnitude of their negative correlation raises concerns and should cause us to question the validity of basing investment decisions on this correlation measure. Perhaps the sample period we are using to estimate this correlation is too short or is not truly representative of the investment performance of these two stocks. The 2005 to 2014 period that we are focusing on consists of just 10 yearly return observations, and during this particular period there were no fewer than three strong systematic market-wide events (i.e., a financial crisis, a Great Recession, and an economic recovery). Those sharp macroeconomic fluctuations tended to drive most securities' returns up and down at the same time, which in turn leads to a positive correlation between most pairs of stocks, even when those stocks are drawn from different industries. Ten yearly observations is without question a small sample size, and it may be too small, at least in this case, to accurately capture a meaningful measure of correlation between IBM and Celgene. One way to address this concern is to increase the period of time over which the correlation is being measured and in this way increase the number of yearly observations. Alternatively, one could use monthly returns over the same 10-year period, thereby increasing the number of observations by a factor of 12.

For any pair of investments that we might want to study, the correlation coefficient ranges from +1.0 for **perfectly positively correlated** series to −1.0 for **perfectly negatively correlated** series. Figure 11.1 illustrates these two extremes for two pairs of

What's the Correlation?

FIGURE 11.1

The Correlations of Returns between Investments M and P and Investments M and N.

Investments M and P produce returns that are perfectly positively correlated and move exactly together. On the other hand, returns on investments M and N move in exactly opposite directions and are perfectly negatively correlated. In most cases, the correlation between any two investments will fall between these two extremes.

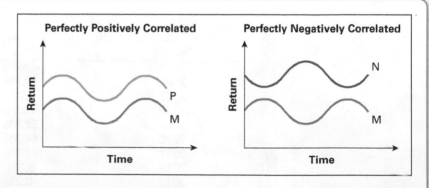

investments: M and P, and M and N. M and P represent the returns on two investments that move perfectly in sync, so they are perfectly positively correlated. In the real world it is extremely rare to find two investments that are perfectly correlated like this, but you could think of M and P as representing two companies that operate in the same industry, or even two mutual funds that invest in the same types of stocks. In contrast, returns on investments M and N move in exactly opposite directions and are perfectly negatively correlated. While these two extreme cases can be illustrative, the correlations between most asset returns exhibit some degree (ranging from high to low) of positive correlation. Negative correlation is the exception.

Diversification As a general rule, the lower the correlation between any two assets, the greater the risk reduction that investors can achieve by combining those assets in a portfolio. Figure 11.2 shows negatively correlated assets F and G, both having the same average return, $\bar{r}$. The portfolio that contains both F and G has the same return, $\bar{r}$, but has less risk (variability) than either of the individual assets because some of the fluctuations in asset F cancel out fluctuations in G. As a result, the combination of F and G is less volatile than either F or G alone. Even if assets are not negatively correlated, the lower the positive correlation between them, the lower the resulting risk.

Table 11.2 shows the average return and the standard deviation of returns for many combinations of IBM and Celgene stock. Columns 1 and 2 show the percentage of the portfolio invested in IBM and Celgene, respectively, and columns 3 and 4 show the portfolio average return and standard deviation. Notice that as you move from the top of the table to the bottom (i.e., from investing the entire portfolio in IBM to investing all of it in Celgene), the portfolio return goes up. That makes sense because as you move from top to bottom, the percentage invested in Celgene increases, and Celgene's average return is higher than IBM's. The general conclusion from column 3 is that when a portfolio contains two stocks, with one having a higher average return than the other, the portfolio's return rises the more you invest in the stock with the higher return.

FIGURE 11.2

Combining Negatively Correlated Assets to Diversify Risk

Investments F and G earn the same return on average, $\bar{r}$, but they are negatively correlated, so movements in F sometimes partially offset movements in G. As a result, a portfolio containing F and G (shown in the rightmost graph) exhibits less variability than the individual assets display on their own while earning the same return.

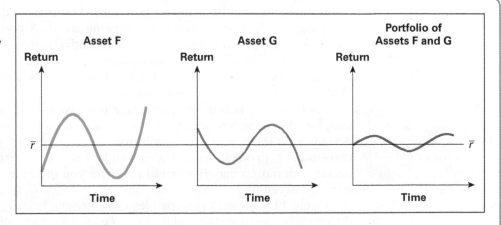

Excel@Investing

TABLE 11.2   PORTFOLIO RETURNS AND STANDARD DEVIATIONS FOR INTERNATIONAL BUSINESS MACHINES (IBM) AND CELGENE (CELG)

(1)	(2)	(3)		(4)
Portfolio Weights		Portfolio Return		Portfolio Standard Deviation
W_{IBM}	W_{CELG}	$\bar{r}_{IBM} = 9.0\%$	$\bar{r}_{CELG} = 40.7\%$	
1.0	0.0	$(1.0 \times 9.0\%) + (0.0 \times 40.7\%) = 9.0\%$		23.6%
0.9	0.1	$(0.9 \times 9.0\%) + (0.1 \times 40.7\%) = 12.1\%$		19.6%
0.8	0.2	$(0.8 \times 9.0\%) + (0.2 \times 40.7\%) = 15.3\%$		17.3%
0.7	0.3	$(0.7 \times 9.0\%) + (0.3 \times 40.7\%) = 18.5\%$		17.5%
0.6	0.4	$(0.6 \times 9.0\%) + (0.4 \times 40.7\%) = 21.7\%$		20.0%
0.5	0.5	$(0.5 \times 9.0\%) + (0.5 \times 40.7\%) = 24.8\%$		24.3%
0.4	0.6	$(0.4 \times 9.0\%) + (0.6 \times 40.7\%) = 28.0\%$		29.4%
0.3	0.7	$(0.3 \times 9.0\%) + (0.7 \times 40.7\%) = 31.2\%$		35.1%
0.2	0.8	$(0.2 \times 9.0\%) + (0.8 \times 40.7\%) = 34.3\%$		41.1%
0.1	0.9	$(0.1 \times 9.0\%) + (0.9 \times 40.7\%) = 37.5\%$		47.3%
0.0	1.0	$(0.0 \times 9.0\%) + (1.0 \times 40.7\%) = 40.7\%$		53.7%

Example: Calculation of the Standard Deviation for the Equally Weighted Portfolio

$s_{IBM} = 23.6\%$

$s_{CELG} = 53.7\%$

$\rho_{IBM, CELG} = -0.43$

$s_p = \sqrt{w_i^2 s_i^2 + w_j^2 s_j^2 + 2 w_i w_j \rho_{i,j} s_i s_j}$

$s_p = \sqrt{0.5^2 \times 23.6\%^2 + 0.5^2 \times 53.7\%^2 + 2(0.5 \times 0.5 \times -0.43 \times 23.6\% \times 53.7\%)} = 24.3\%$

Column 4 shows the standard deviation of returns for different portfolios of IBM and Celgene. Here again we see a surprising result. A portfolio invested entirely in IBM has a standard deviation of 23.6%. Intuitively, it might seem that reducing the investment in IBM slightly and increasing the investment in Celgene would increase the portfolio's standard deviation because Celgene stock is so much more volatile than IBM stock. However, the opposite is true, at least up to a point. The portfolio standard deviation initially falls as the percentage invested in Celgene rises. Eventually, however, increasing the amount invested in Celgene does increase the portfolio's standard deviation. So the general conclusion from column 4 is that when a portfolio contains two stocks, with one having a higher standard deviation than the other, the portfolio's standard deviation may rise or fall the more you invest in the stock with the higher standard deviation.

Figure 11.3 illustrates the two lessons emerging from Table 11.2. The curve plots the return (*y*-axis) and standard deviation (*x*-axis) for each portfolio listed in Table 11.2. As the portfolio composition moves from 100% IBM to a mix of IBM and Celgene, the portfolio return rises, but the standard deviation initially falls. Therefore, portfolios of IBM and Celgene trace out a backward-bending arc. Clearly no investor should place all of his or her money in IBM because the investor could earn a higher return with a lower standard deviation by holding at least some stock in Celgene. However, investors who want to earn the highest possible returns, and who therefore will invest heavily in Celgene, have to accept a higher standard deviation.

FIGURE 11.3

Portfolios of IBM and Celgene

Because the returns of IBM and Celgene are not highly correlated, investors who hold only IBM shares can simultaneously increase the portfolio return and reduce its standard deviation by holding at least some Celgene shares. At some point, however, investing more in Celgene does increase the portfolio volatility while also increasing its expected return.

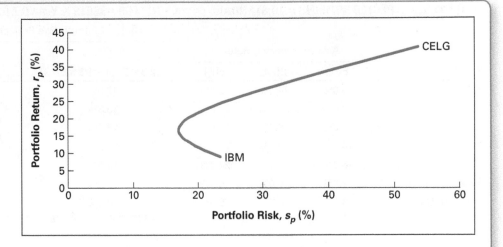

INVESTOR FACTS

Not an Ideal [Cor]relationship
During periods of economic uncertainty and high stock market volatility, the correlation between different assets tends to rise. In the summer of 2011, with concerns about European economies rocking markets, the correlation between the different sectors of the S&P 500 stock index reached 97.2%, the highest correlation since the 2008 financial crisis. During these periods, macroeconomic news announcements have a larger impact on stock returns than individual events at specific companies, so the correlation between stocks rises and the benefits of diversification fall.

(Source: Charles Rotblut, "AAII Investor Update: Highly Correlated Stock Returns Are Temporary," September 16, 2011, http://seekingalpha.com/article/294067-aaii-investor-update-highly-correlated-stock-returns-are-temporary.)

The relationship between IBM and Celgene is obviously a special case, so let's look at the more general patterns that investors encounter in the markets. Table 11.3 presents the projected returns from three assets—X, Y, and Z—in each of the next five years (2018–2022). Table 11.3 also shows the average return that we expect each asset to earn over the five-year period and the standard deviation of each asset's returns. Asset X has an average return of 12% and a standard deviation of 3.2%. Assets Y and Z each have an average return of 16% and a standard deviation of 6.3%. Thus, we can view asset X as having a low-return, low-risk profile while assets Y and Z are high-return, high-risk stocks. The returns of assets X and Y are perfectly negatively correlated—they move in exactly opposite directions over time. The returns of assets X and Z are perfectly positively correlated—they move in precisely the same direction.

Portfolio XY (shown in Table 11.3) is constructed by investing $\frac{2}{3}$ in asset X and $\frac{1}{3}$ in asset Y. The average return on this portfolio, 13.3%, is a weighted average of the average returns of assets X and Y $\left(\frac{2}{3} \times 12\% + \frac{1}{3} \times 16\%\right)$. To calculate the portfolio's standard deviation, use the equation shown in Table 11.2 with a value of −1.0 for the correlation between X and Y. Notice that portfolio XY generates a predictable 13.3% return every year. In other words, the portfolio is risk-free and has a standard deviation of 0.

Now consider portfolio XZ, which is created by investing $\frac{2}{3}$ in asset X and $\frac{1}{3}$ in asset Z. Like portfolio XY, portfolio XZ has an expected return of 13.3%. Notice, however, that portfolio XZ does not provide a risk-free return. Its return fluctuates from year to year, and its standard deviation is 4.2%.

To summarize, the two portfolios, XY and XZ, have identical average returns, but they differ in terms of risk. The reason for that difference is correlation. Movements in X are offset by movements in Y, so by combining the two assets in a portfolio, the investor can reduce or eliminate risk. Assets X

TABLE 11.3   EXPECTED RETURNS AND STANDARD DEVIATIONS FOR ASSETS X, Y, AND Z AND PORTFOLIOS XY AND XZ

Year (t)	Asset's Projected Returns			Portfolio's Projected Returns	
				$E(r_{xy})$	$E(r_{xz})$
	$E(r_X)$	$E(r_Y)$	$E(r_Z)$	$[2/3 \times E(r_X) + 1/3 \times E(r_Y)]$	$[2/3 \times E(r_X) + 1/3 \times E(r_Z)]$
2018	8.0%	24.0%	8.0%	13.3%	8.0%
2019	10.0%	20.0%	12.0%	13.3%	10.7%
2020	12.0%	16.0%	16.0%	13.3%	13.3%
2021	14.0%	12.0%	20.0%	13.3%	16.0%
2022	16.0%	8.0%	24.0%	13.3%	18.7%
Average Return	12.0%	16.0%	16.0%	13.3%	13.3%
Standard Deviation	3.2%	6.3%	6.3%	0.0%	4.2%

Excel@Investing

and Z move together, so movements in one cannot offset movements in the other, and the standard deviation of portfolio XZ cannot be reduced below the standard deviation of asset X.

Figure 11.4 illustrates how the relation between a portfolio's expected return and standard deviation depends on the correlation between the assets in the portfolio. The black line illustrates a case like portfolio XY where the correlation coefficient is −1.0. In that case, it is possible to combine two risky assets in just the right proportions so that the portfolio return is completely predictable (i.e., has no risk). Notice that in this situation, it would be very unwise for an investor to hold an undiversified position in the least risky asset. By holding a portfolio of assets rather than just one, the investor moves up and to the left along the black line to earn a higher return while taking less risk. Beyond some point, however, increasing the investment in the more risky asset pushes both the portfolio return and risk higher, so the investor's portfolio moves up and to the right along the second segment of the black line.

The red line in Figure 11.4 illustrates a situation like portfolio XZ in which the correlation coefficient is +1.0. In that instance, when an investor decreases his or her investment in the low-risk asset to hold more of the high-risk asset, the portfolio's expected return rises, but so does its standard deviation. The investor moves up and to

FIGURE 11.4

Risk and Return for Combinations of Two Assets with Various Correlation Coefficients

This graph illustrates how a low-return, low-risk asset can be combined with a high-return, high-risk asset in a portfolio, and how the performance of that portfolio depends on the correlation between the two assets. In general, as an investor shifts the portfolio weight from the low-return to the high-return investment, the portfolio return will rise. But the portfolio's standard deviation may rise or fall depending on the correlation. In general, the lower the correlation, the greater the risk reduction that can be achieved through diversification.

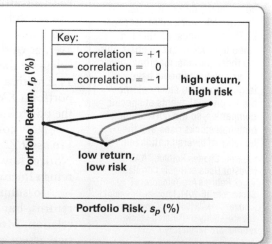

the right along the red line. An investor might choose to invest in both assets, but making that decision is a matter of one's risk tolerance, and not all investors will make that choice. In other words, when the correlation between two assets is −1.0, diversifying is definitely the right move, but when the correlation is +1.0, whether to diversify or not is less obvious.

The blue line in Figure 11.4 illustrates an intermediate case in which the correlation coefficient is between −1.0 and +1.0. This is what investors encounter in real markets most of the time—assets are neither perfectly negatively correlated nor perfectly positively correlated. When the correlation coefficient is between the extremes, portfolios of two assets lie along an arc (i.e., the blue line). When two assets have very low correlation, that arc may bend back upon itself, as was the case with IBM and Celgene. When the correlation is higher, but still below 1.0, the arc merely curves up and to the right. Even then, the benefits of diversification are better than when the correlation is 1.0, meaning that portfolios along the blue arc earn higher returns for the same risk compared to portfolios along the red line.

International Diversification

Diversification is clearly a primary consideration when constructing an investment portfolio. As noted earlier, many opportunities for international diversification are now available. Here we consider three aspects of international diversification: effectiveness, methods, and costs.

Effectiveness of International Diversification Investing internationally offers greater diversification than investing only domestically. That is true for U.S. investors as well as for investors in countries with capital markets that offer much more limited diversification opportunities than are available in the United States. Broadly speaking, the diversification benefits from investing internationally come from two sources. The first source is that returns in different markets around the world do not move exactly in sync. In other words, the correlation between markets is less than +1.0. As you have already seen, the lower the correlation is between investments, the larger are the benefits from diversification. Unfortunately, as globalization has brought about greater integration of markets (both financial markets and markets for goods and services) around the world, the correlation in returns across national markets has risen. This trend reduces the benefit of international diversification.

However, the second source of the benefits of international diversification has been on the rise for many years. Over time, the number of stock markets around the world has been increasing. For example, at the beginning of the 20th century fewer than 40 countries in the world had active stock markets, but by the end of the century the number of stock markets had more than doubled. Just as someone who invests only in domestic stocks will generally have a more diversified portfolio if there are more stocks in the portfolio, so it is for investors who can diversify across many stock markets around the world rather than just a few.

On net, there is little question that it benefits investors to diversify internationally, even if the rising correlation across markets (especially the larger, more developed markets) limits these benefits to an extent. Next, we discuss how investors can access international markets to diversify their portfolios.

Methods of International Diversification Later in this text we will examine a wide range of alternatives for international portfolio diversification. We will see that investors can make investments in bonds and other debt instruments in U.S. dollars or in foreign currencies—either directly or via foreign mutual funds. Foreign currency investment, however, brings currency exchange risk. Investors can hedge this risk with contracts such as currency forwards, futures, and options. Even if there is little or no currency exchange risk, investing abroad is generally less convenient, more expensive, and riskier than investing domestically. When making direct investments abroad, you must know what you're doing. You should have a clear idea of the benefits being sought and enough time to monitor foreign markets.

U.S. investors can capture at least some of the benefits of international diversification without having to send money abroad. Investors can buy stock of foreign companies listed on U.S. exchanges. Many foreign issuers, both corporate and government, sell their bonds (called *Yankee bonds*) in the United States. The stocks of more than 2,000 foreign companies, from more than 60 countries, trade in the United States in the form of American depositary shares (ADSs). Finally, international mutual funds provide foreign investment opportunities.

You might wonder whether it is possible to achieve the benefits of international diversification by investing in a portfolio of U.S.-based multinational corporations. The answer is yes and no. Yes, a portfolio of U.S. multinationals is more diversified than a portfolio of wholly domestic firms. Multinationals generate revenues, costs, and profits in many markets and currencies, so when one part of the world is doing poorly, another part may be doing well.

Investors who invest only in U.S.-based multinationals will still not enjoy the full benefits of international diversification. That's because a disproportionate share of the revenues and costs generated by these firms *is* still in the United States. Thus, to fully realize the benefits of international diversification, it is necessary to invest in firms located outside the United States.

Costs of International Diversification You can find greater returns overseas than in the United States, and you can reduce a portfolio's risk by including foreign investments. Still, you should not jump to the conclusion that it is wise to invest all of your money in overseas assets. A successful global investment strategy depends on many things, just as a purely domestic strategy does. The percentage of your portfolio that you should allocate to foreign investments depends on your overall investment goals and risk preferences. Many investment advisers suggest allocations to foreign investments of about 20% to 30%, with two-thirds of this allocation in established foreign markets and the other one-third in emerging markets.

In general, investing directly in foreign-currency-denominated instruments is very costly. Unless you have hundreds of thousands of dollars to invest, the transaction costs of buying securities directly on foreign markets will tend to be high. A less costly approach to international diversification is to invest in international mutual funds, which offer diversified foreign investments and the professional expertise of fund managers. You could also purchase ADSs to make foreign investments in individual stocks. With either mutual funds or ADSs, you can obtain international diversification along with low cost, convenience, transactions in U.S. dollars, and protection under U.S. security laws.

11.1   What is an efficient portfolio, and what role should such a portfolio play in investing?

11.2   How do you calculate the return and standard deviation of a portfolio? Compare the calculation of a portfolio's standard deviation to that for a single asset.

11.3   What is correlation, and why is it important with respect to portfolio returns? Describe the characteristics of returns that are (a) positively correlated, (b) negatively correlated, and (c) uncorrelated. Differentiate between perfect positive correlation and perfect negative correlation.

11.4   What is diversification? How does the diversification of risk affect the risk of the portfolio compared to the risk of the individual assets it contains?

11.5   Discuss how the correlation between asset returns affects the risk and return behavior of the resulting portfolio. Describe the potential range of risk and return when the correlation between two assets is (a) perfectly positive, (b) uncorrelated, and (c) perfectly negative.

11.6   What benefit, if any, does international diversification offer the individual investor? Compare and contrast the methods of achieving international diversification by investing abroad versus investing domestically.

The Capital Asset Pricing Model

LG3 LG4   Intuitively we would expect that any risky investment should offer a return that exceeds what investors can earn on a risk-free investment. In other words, the return that investors expect to earn on a risky asset equals the risk-free rate plus a risk premium. But what determines the magnitude of the risk premium? In the previous section we learned that investors can reduce or eliminate many types of risk simply by diversifying their portfolios, a process that is neither particularly time consuming nor expensive. However, diversification can't eliminate risk entirely. Therefore, from an investor's perspective, the most worrisome risk is *undiversifiable risk*—the risk that can't be eliminated through diversification. The more undiversifiable risk that a particular investment entails, the higher the risk premium it must offer to attract investors.

That logic provides the underpinning for a theory that links return and risk for all assets. The theory is called the *capital asset pricing model*, or the *CAPM*. The CAPM says that the expected return on a risky asset equals the risk-free rate plus a risk premium, and the risk premium depends on how much of the asset's risk is undiversifiable. In this section, we introduce the concept of undiversifiable risk, and we explain how the CAPM quantifies that risk and links it to investment returns.

Components of Risk

The risk of an investment consists of two components: diversifiable and undiversifiable risk. **Diversifiable risk,** sometimes called **unsystematic risk,** results from factors that are firm-specific, such as whether a new product succeeds or fails, the performance of senior managers, or a firm's relationships with its customers and suppliers. Unsystematic risk is the portion of an investment's risk that can be eliminated through diversification. **Undiversifiable risk,** also called **systematic risk** or **market risk,** is the inescapable portion of an investment's risk. In other words, it's the risk that remains even if a portfolio is well diversified. Systematic risk is associated with broad forces such as economic growth, inflation, interest rates, and political events that affect all investments and therefore are not unique to any single investment. The sum of undiversifiable risk and diversifiable risk is called **total risk.**

Equation 11.2   Total risk = Diversifiable risk + Undiversifiable risk

Any careful investor can reduce or virtually eliminate diversifiable risk by holding a diversified portfolio of securities. Studies have shown that investors can eliminate most diversifiable risk by carefully selecting a portfolio of as few as two or three dozen securities, and most investors hold many more securities than that through investments such as mutual funds and pension funds. Because it is relatively easy to eliminate unsystematic risk through diversification, there is no reason for investors to expect a reward (i.e., higher returns) for bearing this kind of risk. Investors who fail to diversify are simply bearing more risk than they have to without getting a reward for doing so.

But no matter how many securities are in a portfolio, some systematic risk will remain. Remember, undiversifiable risk refers to the broad forces that tend to affect most stocks simultaneously, such as whether the economy is booming or in recession. Some stocks are more sensitive to these forces than others. For example, companies that produce luxury goods tend to do very well when the economy is surging, but when a recession hits, these companies struggle to find customers. On the other hand, some stocks are relatively insulated from swings in the business cycle. Companies that produce food and other basic necessities do not see their revenues and profits rise and fall sharply with the ups and downs of the economy.

This discussion implies that systematic risk varies from one stock to another, and stocks with greater systematic risk must offer higher returns to attract investors. To identify these stocks, we need a way to measure the undiversifiable risk associated with any particular stock. The CAPM provides just such a measure called the stock's *beta*.

Beta: A Measure of Undiversifiable Risk

During the past 50 years, the finance discipline has developed much theory on the measurement of risk and its use in assessing returns. The two key components of this theory are beta, which is a measure of systematic risk, and the capital asset pricing model, which links an investment's beta to its return.

First we will look at **beta**, a number that quantifies undiversifiable risk. A security's beta indicates how the security's return responds to fluctuations in market returns, which is why market risk is synonymous with undiversifiable risk. The more sensitive the return of a security is to changes in market returns, the higher that security's beta. When we speak of returns on the overall market, what we have in mind is something like the return on a broad portfolio of stocks or on a stock index. Analysts commonly use changes in the value of the Standard & Poor's 500 Index or some other broad stock index to measure market returns. To calculate a security's beta, you gather historical returns on the security and on the overall market to see how they relate to each other. You don't have to calculate betas yourself; you can easily obtain them for actively traded securities from a variety of published and online sources. But you should understand how betas are derived, how to interpret them, and how to apply them to portfolios.

Deriving Beta We can demonstrate graphically the relationship between a security's return and the market return. Figure 11.5 plots the relationship between the returns of two securities, United Parcel Service, Inc. (UPS) and FedEx Corporation (FDX), and the market return measured as the return on the S&P 500 (GSPC). The return data necessary to plot the relationships shown in Figure 11.5 are easily obtained from numerous online financial websites. In this case, we obtained historical closing prices from Yahoo! Finance by entering the security ticker symbols and downloading the end-of-year historical prices to a spreadsheet. In a spreadsheet, we used the end-of-year

FIGURE 11.5

Graphical Derivation of Beta for Securities C and D

Betas can be derived graphically by plotting the coordinates for the market return and security return at various points in time and using statistical techniques to fit the "characteristic line" to the data points. The slope of the characteristic line is beta. For FedEx the beta is about 1.12, and for UPS the beta is about 0.76.

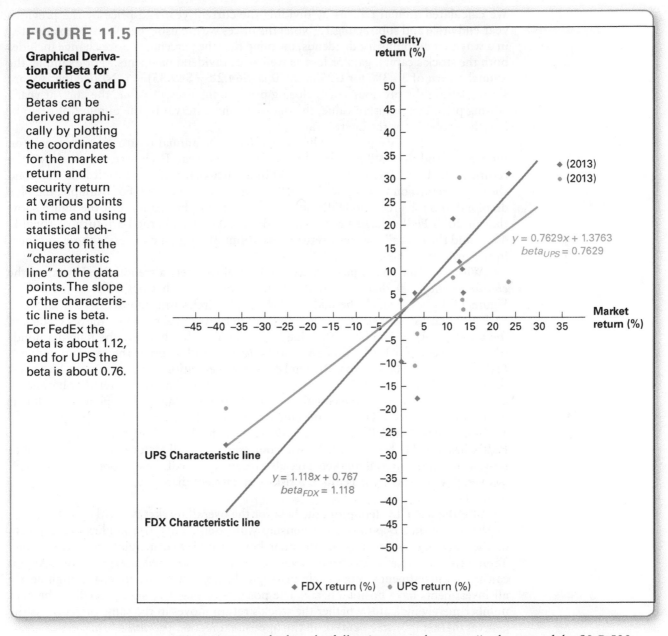

security prices to calculate the following annual returns (in the case of the S&P 500, we calculated annual returns based on the index level):

	A	B	C	D	E	F	G
1	Year	December month-ending index level	S&P 500 return	December month-ending price	UPS return	December month-ending price	FDX return
2	2004	1211.9		$64.93		$93.50	
3	2005	1248.3	3.0%	$58.10	-10.5%	$98.49	5.3%
4	2006	1418.3	13.6%	$59.12	1.8%	$103.80	5.4%
5	2007	1468.4	3.5%	$57.05	-3.5%	$85.53	-17.6%
6	2008	903.3	-38.5%	$45.79	-19.7%	$61.86	-27.7%
7	2009	1115.1	23.5%	$49.35	7.8%	$81.12	31.1%
8	2010	1257.6	12.8%	$64.28	30.3%	$90.92	12.1%
9	2011	1257.6	0.0%	$66.75	3.8%	$82.14	-9.7%
10	2012	1426.2	13.4%	$69.32	3.9%	$90.79	10.5%
11	2013	1848.4	29.6%	$101.57	46.5%	$143.06	57.6%
12	2014	2058.9	11.4%	$110.38	8.7%	$173.66	21.4%

We calculated annual returns by dividing the current year-end price by the previous year-end price and subtracting 1. (Note: the prices we are using here have been adjusted in a way that accounts for dividends, meaning that the percentage price change includes both the stock's capital gain or loss as well as its dividend payments.) For example, the annual return of 30.3% for UPS in 2010 is ($64.28 ÷ $49.35) − 1. Notice that we are simply letting the previous year's closing price be the present value, the current year's closing price be the future value, the one-year time interval be the number of periods, and then solving for the interest rate.

In Figure 11.5 we plot coordinates showing the annual return on each stock (on the *y*-axis) and the S&P 500 (on the *x*-axis) in each year. Each green circle shows the return earned by UPS and the S&P 500 in a particular year, and each blue diamond shows the return on FedEx and the S&P 500 in a particular year. For example, the blue diamond and the green circle diamond in the upper right quadrant of the figure show that in 2013 FedEx earned a return of about 60%, UPS earned a return of roughly 45%, and the overall market's return was about 30% (you can verify these numbers in the previous table).

With the data points plotted, we used Excel to insert a trendline (also called the *characteristic line*) that best fit the coordinates for each stock. The green line in Figure 11.5 goes through the middle of the green circles (the coordinates for UPS and S&P 500 returns), so it shows the general relation between the return on the S&P 500 and the return on UPS. Similarly, the blue line is the line that best fits the blue diamonds (the coordinates for FedEx and S&P 500 returns), and it shows the relation between FedEx and S&P 500 returns. Remember that the equation for any straight line takes the form $y = mx + b$, where m represents the slope of the line, or the relation between x and y. Figure 11.5 shows the equation for each trendline, and the slope for each line is the beta for that stock. For UPS, the equation for the characteristic line is $y = 0.7629x + 1.3763$, so the beta of UPS stock is 0.7639. The beta for FedEx is higher at 1.118. Because FedEx has a higher beta than UPS, we would say that FedEx stock is more sensitive to movements in the overall market. This also means that FedEx has more systematic risk, so overall we conclude the FedEx is a riskier investment than UPS.

Interpreting Beta By definition, the beta for the overall market is equal to 1.0 (i.e., the market moves in a one-to-one relationship with itself). That also implies that the beta of the "average" stock is 1.0. All other betas are viewed in relation to this value. Table 11.4 shows some selected beta values and their associated interpretations. As you can see, an investment's beta can, in principle, be positive or negative, although nearly all investments have positive betas. The positive or negative sign preceding the beta number merely indicates whether the stock's return moves in the same direction as the general market (*positive beta*) or in the opposite direction (*negative beta*).

TABLE 11.4   SELECTED BETAS AND ASSOCIATED INTERPRETATIONS

Beta	Comment	Interpretation
2.0	Move in same direction as the market	Twice as responsive as the market
1.0		Same response as the market
0.5		One half as responsive as the market
0.0		Unaffected by market movement
−0.5	Move in opposite direction of the market	One-half as responsive as the market
−1.0		Same response as the market
−2.0		Twice as responsive as the market

Most stocks have betas that fall between 0.50 and 1.75. The return of a stock that is half as responsive as the market ($b = 0.5$) will, on average, change by ½ of 1% for each 1% change in the return of the market portfolio. A stock that is twice as responsive as the market ($b = 2$) will, on average, experience a 2% change in its return for each 1% change in the return of the market portfolio. Listed here, for illustration purposes, are the actual betas for some popular stocks, as reported on Yahoo! Finance on February 27, 2015:

Stock	Beta	Stock	Beta
Amazon.com Inc.	1.27	Int'l Business Machines Corp.	0.88
Molson Coors Brewing Co.	1.45	Goldman Sachs Inc.	1.64
Bank of America Corp.	1.33	Microsoft Corp.	0.79
Procter & Gamble Co.	0.93	Nike Inc.	0.51
Walt Disney Co.	1.02	Celgene Corp.	1.84
eBay Inc.	0.82	Qualcomm Inc.	1.2
ExxonMobil Corp.	1.16	Sempra Energy	0.39
The Gap Inc.	1.63	Walmart Stores Inc.	0.29
Ford Motor Co.	0.76	Xerox Corp.	1.34
INTEL Corp.	0.95	YAHOO! Inc.	1.27

How to Estimate a Beta

Applying Beta Individual investors will find beta useful. It can help in assessing the risk of a particular investment and in understanding the impact the market can have on the return expected from a share of stock. In short, beta reveals how a security responds to market forces. For example, if the market is expected to experience a 10% increase in its rate of return over the next period, we would expect a stock with a beta of 1.5 to experience an increase in return of about 15% ($1.5 \times 10\%$).

For stocks with positive betas, increases in market returns result in increases in security returns. Unfortunately, decreases in market returns are translated into decreasing security returns. In the preceding example, if the market is expected to experience a 10% decrease in its rate of return, then a stock with a beta of 1.5 should experience a 15% decrease in its return. Because the stock has a beta greater than 1.0, it is riskier than an average stock and will tend to experience dramatic swings when the overall market moves.

Stocks that have betas less than 1.0 are, of course, less responsive to changing returns in the market and are therefore less risky. For example, a stock with a beta of 0.50 will increase or decrease its return by about half that of the market as a whole. Thus, if the market return went down by 8%, such a stock's return would probably experience only about a 4% ($0.50 \times 8\%$) decline.

Here are some important points to remember about beta:

- Beta measures the undiversifiable (or market) risk of a security.

- The beta for the market as a whole, and for the average stock, is 1.0.

- In theory, stocks may have positive or negative betas, but most stocks have positive betas.

- Stocks with betas greater than 1.0 are more responsive than average to market fluctuations and therefore are more risky than average. Stocks with betas less than 1.0 are less risky than the average stock.

INVESTOR FACTS

Which Beta? Working with betas is not an exact science. A researcher recently found that by browsing through 16 financial websites, one could find estimates of beta for the same company (Walt Disney) ranging from 0.72 to 1.39. If you try to estimate betas on your own, you will find that your estimates will vary depending on how much historical data you use in your analysis and the frequency with which returns are measured.

(Source: Data from Pablo Fernández. (2009, May). "Betas Used by Professors: A Survey with 2,500 Answers." Working paper, IESE Business School, University of Navarra.)

FAMOUS FAILURES IN FINANCE

Bulging Betas

Ford Motor Company has always been considered a cyclical stock whose fortunes rise and fall with the state of the economy. Ford's beta was as high as 2.80 during the financial crisis, which hit auto manufacturers particularly hard and resulted in the bankruptcy of Ford's major competitor,

General Motors. Bank of America, another firm in an industry hit hard by the recession, had a beta of 1.96 during the crisis, indicating that it too was extremely sensitive to movements in the overall economy. Notice that both Ford and Bank of America have lower betas now than they did during the last recession.

The CAPM: Using Beta to Estimate Return

Intuitively, we expect riskier investments to provide higher returns than less risky investments. If beta measures the risk of a stock, then stocks with higher betas should earn higher returns, on average, than stocks with lower betas. About 50 years ago, finance professors William F. Sharpe and John Lintner developed a model that uses beta to formally link the notions of risk and return. Called the **capital asset pricing model (CAPM)**, it attempts to quantify the relation between risk and return for different investments. It also provides a mechanism whereby investors can assess the impact of a proposed security investment on their portfolio's risk and return. The CAPM predicts that a stock's expected return depends on three things: the risk-free rate, the expected return on the overall market, and the stock's beta.

The Equation With beta, b, as the measure of undiversifiable risk, the capital asset pricing model defines the expected return on an investment as follows.

Equation 11.3

$$\text{Expected return on investment } j = \text{Risk-free rate} + \left[\text{Beta for investment } j \times \left(\text{Expected market return} - \text{Risk-free rate} \right) \right]$$

Equation 11.3a

$$r_j = r_{rf} + \left[b_j \times (r_m - r_{rf}) \right]$$

where

r_j = the expected return on investment j, given its risk as measured by beta

r_{rf} = the risk-free rate of return; the return that can be earned on a risk-free investment

b_j = beta coefficient, or index of undiversifiable risk for investment j

r_m = the expected market return; the average return on all securities (typically measured by the average return on all securities in the Standard & Poor's 500 Composite Index or some other broad stock market index)

The CAPM can be divided into two parts: (1) the risk-free rate of return, r_{rf}, and (2) the *risk premium*, $b_j \times (r_m - r_{rf})$. The risk premium is the return investors require beyond the risk-free rate to compensate for the investment's undiversifiable risk as measured by beta. The equation shows that as beta increases, the stock's risk premium increases, thereby causing the expected return to increase.[1]

---

[1] Note that we are using the terms *expected return* and *required return* interchangeably here. Investors require investments to earn a return that is sufficient compensation based on the investment's risk, and in equilibrium, the return that they require and the return that they expect to earn are the same.

Example

We can demonstrate use of the CAPM with the following example. Assume you are thinking about investing in Bank of America stock, which has a beta of 1.33. At the time you are making your investment decision, the risk-free rate (r_{rf}) is 2% and the expected market return (r_m) is 8%. Substituting these data into the CAPM equation, Equation 11.3a, we get:

$$r = 2\% + 1.33(8\% - 2\%) = 10\%$$

You should therefore expect—indeed, require—a 10% return on this investment as compensation for the risk you have to assume, given the security's beta of 1.33.

If the beta were lower, say, 1.0, the required return would be lower. In fact, in this case the required return on the stock is the same as the expected (or required) return on the market.

$$r = 2\% + 1.0(8\% - 2\%) = 8\%$$

If the beta were higher, say 2.0, the required return would be higher:

$$r = 2\% + 2.0(8\% - 2\%) = 14\%$$

Clearly, the CAPM reflects the positive tradeoff between risk and return: The higher the risk (beta), the higher the risk premium, and therefore the higher the required return.

The Graph: The Security Market Line Figure 11.6 depicts the CAPM graphically. The line in the figure is called the **security market line (SML)**, and it shows the expected return (y-axis) for any security given its beta (x-axis). For each level of undiversifiable risk (beta), the SML shows the return that the investor should expect to earn in the marketplace.

We can plot the CAPM by simply calculating the required return for a variety of betas. For example, as we saw earlier, using a 2% risk-free rate and an 8% market return, the required return is 10% when the beta is 1.33. Increase the beta to 2.0, and the required return equals 14% [2% + 2.0(8% − 2%)]. Similarly, we can find the required return for a number of betas and end up with the following combinations of risk (beta) and required return.

Risk (beta)	Required Return
0.0	2%
0.5	5%
1.0	8%
1.5	11%
2.0	14%
2.5	17%

Plotting these values on a graph (with beta on the horizontal axis and required return on the vertical axis) would yield a straight line like the one in Figure 11.6. It is clear from the SML that as risk (beta) increases, so do the risk premium and required return, and vice versa.

Some Closing Comments The capital asset pricing model generally relies on historical data in the sense that the value of beta used in the model is typically based on calculations using historical returns. A company's risk profile may change at any time as the company moves in and out of different lines of business, issues or retires debt, or takes

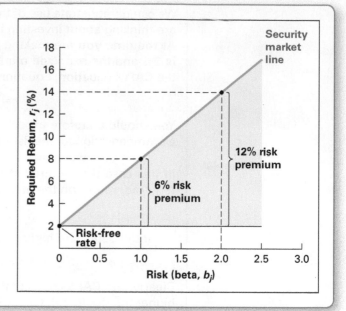

FIGURE 11.6

The Security Market Line (SML)

The security market line clearly depicts the tradeoff between risk and return. At a beta of 0, the required return is the risk-free rate of 2%. At a beta of 1.0, the required return is the market return of 8%. Given these data, the required return on an investment with a beta of 2.0 is 14% and its risk premium is 12% (14% – 2%).

other actions that affect the risk of its common stock. Therefore, betas estimated from historical data may or may not accurately reflect how the company's stock will perform relative to the overall market in the future. Therefore, the required returns specified by the model can be viewed only as rough approximations. Analysts who use betas commonly make subjective adjustments to the historically determined betas based on other information that they possess.

Despite its limitations, the CAPM provides a useful conceptual framework for evaluating and linking risk and return. Its simplicity and practical appeal cause beta and CAPM to remain important tools for investors who seek to measure risk and link it to required returns in security markets. The CAPM also sees widespread use in corporate finance. Before they spend large sums of money on big investment projects, companies need to know what returns their shareholders require. Many surveys show that the primary method that companies use to determine the required rate of return on their stock is the CAPM.

CONCEPTS IN REVIEW

Answers available at http://www.pearsonhighered.com/smart

11.7 Briefly define and give examples of each of the following components of total risk. Which type of risk matters, and why?

   a. Diversifiable risk
   b. Undiversifiable risk

11.8 Explain what is meant by beta. What type of risk does beta measure? What is the market return? How is the interpretation of beta related to the market return?

11.9 What range of values does beta typically exhibit? Are positive or negative betas more common? Explain.

11.10 What is the capital asset pricing model (CAPM)? What role does beta play in the model? What is the risk premium? How is the security market line (SML) related to the CAPM?

11.11 Is the CAPM a predictive model? Why do beta and the CAPM remain important to investors?

Traditional Versus Modern Portfolio Management

LG5 LG6 Individual and institutional investors currently use two approaches to plan and construct their portfolios. The traditional approach refers to the less quantitative methods that investors have been using since the evolution of the public securities markets. Modern portfolio theory (MPT) is a more mathematical approach that relies on quantitative analysis to guide investment decisions.

The Traditional Approach

Traditional portfolio management emphasizes balancing the portfolio by assembling a wide variety of stocks and/or bonds. The typical emphasis is *interindustry diversification*. This produces a portfolio with securities of companies from a broad range of industries. Investors construct traditional portfolios using security analysis techniques that we will discuss later.

Table 11.5 presents some of the industry groupings and the percentages invested in them by a typical mutual fund that is managed by professionals using the traditional approach. This fund, American Funds' Growth Fund of America (AGTHX), is an open-end mutual fund with a net asset value of $145.2 billion as of December 31, 2014. Its objective is to invest in a wide range of companies that appear to offer superior opportunities for growth of capital. The Growth Fund of America holds shares of more than 280 different companies and short-term securities issued from a wide range of industries. The AGTHX fund is most heavily invested in information technology, representing 21.7% of the portfolio. The consumer discretionary and health care industries represent 17.9% and 17.8% of the fund's investment, respectively.

TABLE 11.5 THE GROWTH FUND OF AMERICA (AGTHX) INVESTMENTS IN SELECT INDUSTRY GROUPS AS OF DECEMBER 31, 2014

The Growth Fund of America appears to adhere to the traditional approach to portfolio management. Its total portfolio value is $145.2 billion, of which 80.8% ($117.3 billion) is U.S. equities, 10.2% ($14.8 billion) is non-U.S. equities, 0.2% ($290.4 million) is U.S. bonds, and 8.8% ($12.8 billion) is cash & equivalents.

Sector Breakdown	Percentage
Information technology	21.7%
Consumer discretionary	17.9%
Health care	17.8%
Industrials	9.6%
Financials	8.2%
Energy	7.7%
Consumer staples	4.6%
Materials	2.8%
Telecommunication services	0.6%
Utilities	0.1%

(Source: Data from The Growth Fund of America, Class A Shares, Quarterly Fund Fact Sheet, December 31, 2014.)

Analyzing the stock position of the Growth Fund of America, which accounts for 91% of the fund's assets, we observe the traditional approach to portfolio management at work. This fund holds numerous stocks from a broad cross-section of the universe of available stocks. The stocks are a mix of large and small companies. The fund's largest individual holding is Amazon.com Inc., which accounts for 3.7% of the portfolio. Google Inc., the world's do-everything search engine, ranks second, at 3.3%. The third largest holding, 2.3%, is Gilead Sciences. Although many of the fund's stocks are those of large, recognizable companies, its portfolio does include stocks of smaller, less recognizable firms.

Those who manage traditional portfolios tend to invest in well-known companies for three reasons. First, fund managers and investors may believe that investing in well-known companies is less risky than investing in lesser-known firms. Second, the securities of large firms are more liquid and are available in large quantities. Third, institutional investors prefer successful, well-known companies because it is easier to convince clients to invest in them. Called *window dressing*, this practice of loading up a portfolio with successful, well-known stocks makes it easier for institutional investors to sell their services.

One tendency often attributed to institutional investors during recent years is that of "herding"—investing in securities similar to those held by their competitors. These institutional investors effectively mimic the actions of their competitors. In the case of The Growth Fund of America, for example, its managers would buy stocks in companies that are held by other large, growth-oriented mutual funds. While we don't know for certain why The Growth Fund of America's managers bought specific stocks, it is clear that most funds with similar objectives hold many of the same well-known stocks.

Modern Portfolio Theory

During the 1950s, Harry Markowitz, a trained mathematician, first developed the theories that form the basis of modern portfolio theory. In the years since Markowitz's pioneering work, many other scholars and investment experts have contributed to the theory. **Modern portfolio theory** (**MPT**) uses several basic statistical measures to develop a portfolio plan. Portfolios formed using MPT principles estimate the average returns, standard deviations, and correlations among many combinations of investments to find an optimal portfolio. According to MPT, the maximum benefits of diversification occur when investors find securities that are relatively uncorrelated and put those securities together in a portfolio. Two important aspects of MPT are the efficient frontier and portfolio betas.

The Efficient Frontier At any point in time, you are faced with hundreds of investments from which to choose. You can form any number of possible portfolios. In fact, using only a few different assets, you could create an unlimited number of portfolios by changing the proportion of each asset in the portfolio.

If we were to create all possible portfolios, calculate the return and risk of each, and plot each risk-return combination on a graph, we would have the *feasible*, or *attainable*, *set* of possible portfolios. This set is represented by the shaded area in Figure 11.7. It is the area bounded by ABYOZCDEF. As defined earlier, an *efficient portfolio* is a portfolio that provides the highest return for

FIGURE 11.7

The Feasible, or Attainable, Set and the Efficient Frontier

The feasible, or attainable, set (shaded area) represents the risk-return combinations attainable with all possible portfolios; the efficient frontier is the locus of all efficient portfolios. The point O, where the investor's highest possible indifference curve is tangent to the efficient frontier, is the optimal portfolio. It represents the highest level of satisfaction the investor can achieve given the available set of portfolios.

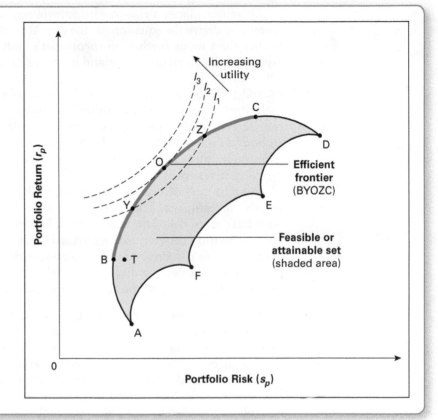

a given level of risk. For example, let's compare portfolio T to portfolios B and Y shown in Figure 11.7. Portfolio Y appears preferable to portfolio T because it has a higher return for the same level of risk. Portfolio B also "dominates" portfolio T because it has lower risk for the same level of return.

The boundary BYOZC of the feasible set of portfolios represents all efficient portfolios—those portfolios that provide the best tradeoff between risk and return. This boundary is the **efficient frontier**. All portfolios on the efficient frontier are preferable to all other portfolios in the feasible set. Any portfolios that would fall to the left of the efficient frontier are not available for investment because they fall outside of the attainable set. For example, anyone would love to buy an investment with an extremely high return and no risk at all, but no such investment exists. Portfolios that fall to the right of the efficient frontier are not desirable because their risk-return tradeoffs are inferior to those of portfolios on the efficient frontier.

We can, in theory, use the efficient frontier to find the highest level of satisfaction the investor can achieve given the available set of portfolios. To do this, we would plot on the graph an *investor's indifference curves*. These curves indicate, for a given level of utility (satisfaction), the set of risk-return combinations about which an investor would be indifferent. These curves, labeled I_1, I_2, and I_3 in Figure 11.7, reflect increasing satisfaction as we move from I_1 to I_2 to I_3. The optimal portfolio, O, is the point at which indifference curve I_2 meets the efficient frontier. The investor cannot achieve the higher utility provided by I_3 because there is no investment available that offers a combination of risk and return falling on the curve I_3.

If we introduced a risk-free investment-paying return r_f into Figure 11.7, we could eventually derive the equation for the capital asset pricing model introduced previously. Rather than focus further on theory, let's shift our attention to the more practical aspects of the efficient frontier and its extensions.

Portfolio Betas As we have noted, investors strive to diversify their portfolios by including a variety of noncomplementary investments that allow investors to reduce risk while meeting their return objectives. Remember that investments embody two basic types of risk: (1) diversifiable risk, the risk unique to a particular investment, and (2) undiversifiable risk, the risk possessed, at least to some degree, by every investment.

A great deal of research has been conducted on the topic of risk as it relates to security investments. The results show that, in general, to earn a higher return, you must bear more risk. Just as important, however, are research results showing that the positive relation between risk and return holds only for undiversifiable risk. High levels of diversifiable risk do not result in correspondingly high levels of return. Because there is no reward for bearing diversifiable risk, investors should minimize this form of risk by diversifying the portfolio so that only undiversifiable risk remains.

Risk Diversification As we've seen, diversification minimizes diversifiable risk by off-setting the below-average return on one investment with the above-average return on another. Minimizing diversifiable risk through careful selection of investments requires that the investments chosen for the portfolio come from a wide range of industries.

To better understand how diversification benefits investors, let's examine what happens when we begin with a single asset (security) in a portfolio and then expand the portfolio by randomly selecting additional securities. Using the standard deviation, s_p, to measure the portfolio's total risk, we can depict the behavior of the total portfolio risk as more securities are added in Figure 11.8. As we add securities to the portfolio (*x*-axis), the total portfolio risk (*y*-axis) declines because of the effects of diversification, but there is a limit to how much risk reduction investors can achieve.

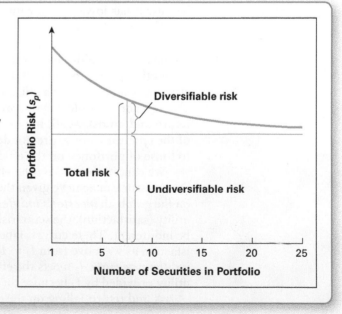

FIGURE 11.8

Portfolio Risk and Diversification

As more securities are combined to create a portfolio, the total risk of the portfolio (measured by its standard deviation, s_p) declines. The portion of the risk eliminated is the diversifiable risk; the remaining portion is the undiversifiable, or relevant, risk.

On average, most of the risk-reduction benefits of diversification can be gained by forming portfolios containing two or three dozen carefully selected securities, but our recommendation is to hold 40 or more securities to achieve efficient diversification. This suggestion tends to support the popularity of investment in mutual funds.

Because any investor can create a portfolio of assets that will eliminate virtually all diversifiable risk, the only **relevant risk** is that which is undiversifiable. You must therefore be concerned solely with undiversifiable risk. The measurement of undiversifiable risk is thus of primary importance.

Calculating Portfolio Betas As we saw earlier, beta measures the undiversifiable, or relevant, risk of a security. The beta for the market is equal to 1.0. Securities with betas greater than 1.0 are more risky than the market, and those with betas less than 1.0 are less risky than the market. The beta for the risk-free asset is 0.

The **portfolio beta**, b_p, is merely the weighted average of the betas of the individual assets in the portfolio. You can easily calculate a portfolio's beta by using the betas of the component assets. To find the portfolio beta, b_p, calculate a weighted average of the betas of the individual stocks in the portfolio, where the weights represent the percentage of the portfolio's value invested in each security, as shown in Equation 11.4.

Equation 11.4

$$\text{Portfolio beta} = \begin{pmatrix} \text{Proportion of} \\ \text{portfolio's total} \\ \text{dollar value} \\ \text{in asset 1} \end{pmatrix} \times \begin{matrix} \text{Beta} \\ \text{for} \\ \text{asset 1} \end{matrix} + \begin{pmatrix} \text{Proportion of} \\ \text{portfolio's total} \\ \text{dollar value} \\ \text{in asset 2} \end{pmatrix} \times \begin{matrix} \text{Beta} \\ \text{for} \\ \text{asset 2} \end{matrix} + \cdots +$$

$$\begin{pmatrix} \text{Proportion of} \\ \text{portfolio's total} \\ \text{dollar value} \\ \text{in asset } n \end{pmatrix} \times \begin{matrix} \text{Beta} \\ \text{for} \\ \text{asset } n \end{matrix} = \sum_{j=1}^{n} \begin{pmatrix} \text{Proportion of} \\ \text{portfolio's total} \\ \text{dollar value} \\ \text{in asset } j \end{pmatrix} \times \begin{matrix} \text{Beta} \\ \text{for} \\ \text{asset } j \end{matrix}$$

Equation 11.4a

$$b_p = (w_1 \times b_1) + (w_2 \times b_2) + \cdots + (w_n \times b_n) = \sum_{j=1}^{n} (w_j \times b_j)$$

Of course, $\sum_{j=1}^{n} w_j = 1$, which means that 100% of the portfolio's assets must be included in this computation.

Portfolio betas are interpreted in exactly the same way as individual asset betas. They indicate the degree of responsiveness of the portfolio's return to changes in the market return. For example, when the market return increases by 10%, a portfolio with a beta of 0.75 will experience a 7.5% increase in its return ($0.75 \times 10\%$). A portfolio with a beta of 1.25 will experience a 12.5% increase in its return ($1.25 \times 10\%$). Low-beta portfolios are less responsive, and therefore less risky, than high-beta portfolios.

To demonstrate, consider the Austin Fund, a large investment company that wishes to assess the risk of two portfolios, V and W. Both portfolios contain five assets, with the proportions and betas shown in Table 11.6. We can calculate the betas for portfolios V and W, b_v and b_w, by substituting the appropriate data from the table into Equation 11.4, as follows.

TABLE 11.6 AUSTIN FUND'S PORTFOLIOS V AND W

Asset	Portfolio V		Portfolio W	
	Proportion	Beta	Proportion	Beta
1	0.10	1.65	0.10	0.80
2	0.30	1.00	0.10	1.00
3	0.20	1.30	0.20	0.65
4	0.20	1.10	0.10	0.75
5	0.20	1.25	0.50	1.05
Total	1.00		1.00	

$$b_v = (0.10 \times 1.65) + (0.30 \times 1.00) + (0.20 \times 1.30) + (0.20 \times 1.10) + (0.20 \times 1.25)$$
$$= 0.165 + 0.300 + 0.260 + 0.220 + 0.250 = 1.195 \approx \underline{1.20}$$
$$b_w = (0.10 \times 0.80) + (0.10 \times 1.00) + (0.20 \times 0.65) + (0.10 \times 0.75) + (0.50 \times 1.05)$$
$$= 0.080 + 0.100 + 0.130 + 0.075 + 0.525 = \underline{0.91}$$

Portfolio V's beta is 1.20, and portfolio W's is 0.91. These values make sense because portfolio V contains relatively high-beta assets and portfolio W contains relatively low-beta assets. Clearly, portfolio V's returns are more responsive to changes in market returns—and therefore more risky—than portfolio W's.

Interpreting Portfolio Betas If a portfolio has a beta of 1.0, the portfolio experiences changes in its rate of return equal to changes in the market's rate of return. The 1.0 beta portfolio would tend to experience a 10% increase in return if the stock market as a whole experienced a 10% increase in return. Conversely, if the market return fell by 6%, the return on the 1.0 beta portfolio would also fall by 6%.

Table 11.7 lists the expected returns for three portfolio betas in two situations: an increase in market return of 10% and a decrease in market return of 10%. The portfolio with a beta of 2.0 moves twice as much (on average) as the market does. When the market return increases by 10%, the portfolio return increases by 20%. When the market return declines by 10%, the portfolio's return will fall by 20%. This portfolio would be considered a high-risk, high-return portfolio.

The middle, 0.5 beta portfolio is considered a low-risk, low-return portfolio. This would be a conservative portfolio for investors who wish to maintain a low-risk investment posture. The 0.5 beta portfolio is half as volatile as the market.

A portfolio with a beta of −1.0 moves in the opposite direction from the market. A bearish investor would probably want to own a negative-beta portfolio because this

TABLE 11.7 PORTFOLIO BETAS AND ASSOCIATED CHANGES IN RETURNS

Portfolio Beta	Changes in Market Return (%)	Change in Expected Portfolio Return (%)
+ 2.0	+ 10.0%	+ 20.0%
	− 10.0%	− 20.0%
+ 0.5	+ 10.0%	+ 5.0%
	− 10.0%	− 5.0%
− 1.0	+ 10.0%	− 10.0%
	− 10.0%	+ 10.0%

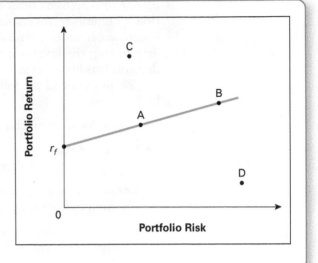

FIGURE 11.9

The Portfolio Risk-Return Tradeoff

As the risk of an investment portfolio increases from 0, the return provided should increase above the risk-free rate, r$_f$. Portfolios A and B offer returns commensurate with their risk, portfolio C provides a high return at a low-risk level, and portfolio D provides a low return for high risk. Portfolio C is highly desirable; portfolio D should be avoided.

type of investment tends to rise in value when the stock market declines, and vice versa. Finding securities with negative betas is difficult, however. Most securities have positive betas because they tend to experience return movements in the same direction as changes in the stock market.

The Risk-Return Tradeoff: Some Closing Comments Another valuable outgrowth of modern portfolio theory is the specific link between undiversifiable risk and investment returns. The basic premise is that an investor must have a portfolio of relatively risky investments to earn a relatively high rate of return. That relationship is illustrated in Figure 11.9. The upward-sloping line shows the **risk-return tradeoff**. The point where the risk-return line crosses the return axis is called the **risk-free rate**, *r$_f$*. This is the return an investor can earn on a risk-free investment such as a U.S. Treasury bill or an insured money market deposit account.

As we proceed upward along the risk-return tradeoff line, portfolios of risky investments appear, as depicted by four investment portfolios, A through D. Portfolios A and B are investment opportunities that provide a level of return commensurate with their respective risk levels. Portfolio C provides a high return at a relatively low risk level—and therefore would be an excellent investment. Portfolio D, in contrast, offers high risk but low return—an investment to avoid.

Reconciling the Traditional Approach and MPT

We have reviewed two fairly different approaches to portfolio management: the traditional approach and MPT. The question that naturally arises is which technique should you use? There is no definite answer; the question must be resolved by the judgment of each investor. However, we can offer a few useful ideas.

The average individual investor does not have the resources and the mathematical acumen to implement a total MPT portfolio strategy. But most individual investors can extract and use ideas from both the traditional and MPT approaches. The traditional approach stresses security selection, which we will discuss later in this text. It also emphasizes diversification of the portfolio across industry lines. MPT stresses reducing correlations between securities within the portfolio. This approach calls for diversification to minimize diversifiable risk. Thus, diversification must be accomplished to ensure satisfactory performance with either strategy. Also, beta is a useful tool for determining the level of a portfolio's undiversifiable risk and should be part of the decision-making process.

We recommend the following portfolio management policy, which uses aspects of both approaches:

- Determine how much risk you are willing to bear.

- Seek diversification among types of securities and across industry lines, and pay attention to how the return from one security is related to that from another.

- Consider how a security responds to the market, and use beta in diversifying your portfolio to keep the portfolio in line with your acceptable risk level.

- Evaluate alternative portfolios to make sure that the portfolio selected provides the highest return for the acceptable level of risk.

CONCEPTS IN REVIEW

Answers available at
http://www.pearsonhighered
.com/smart

11.12 Describe traditional portfolio management. Give three reasons why traditional portfolio managers like to invest in well-established companies.

11.13 What is modern portfolio theory (MPT)? What is the feasible or attainable set of all possible portfolios? How is it derived for a given group of investments?

11.14 What is the efficient frontier? How is it related to the attainable set of all possible portfolios? How can it be used with an investor's utility function to find the optimal portfolio?

11.15 Define and differentiate among the diversifiable, undiversifiable, and total risk of a portfolio. Which is considered the relevant risk? How is it measured?

11.16 Define beta. How can you find the beta of a portfolio when you know the beta for each of the assets included within it?

11.17 Explain how you can reconcile the traditional and modern portfolio approaches.

MyFinanceLab

Here is what you should know after reading this chapter. MyFinanceLab will help you identify what you know and where to go when you need to practice.

What You Should Know	Key Terms	Where to Practice
LG1 **Understand portfolio objectives and the procedures used to calculate portfolio return and standard deviation.** A portfolio is a collection of investments assembled to achieve one or more investment goals. It produces potential price appreciation and current income, subject to a tradeoff between risk and return. The return on a portfolio is calculated as a weighted average of the returns of the assets from which it is formed. The standard deviation of a portfolio's returns is found by applying the same formula that is used to find the standard deviation of a single asset.	efficient portfolio, *p. 374* growth-oriented portfolio, *p. 374* income-oriented portfolio, *p. 374*	Study Plan 11.1 Excel Table 11.1 Video Learning Aid for Problem P11.5

What You Should Know	Key Terms	Where to Practice
Discuss the concepts of correlation and diversification and the key aspects of international diversification. Correlation is a statistic used to measure the relationship between the returns on assets. To diversify, it is best to add assets with negatively correlated returns. In general, the less positive and more negative the correlation between asset returns, the more effectively a portfolio can be diversified to reduce its risk. Diversification can reduce the risk (standard deviation) of a portfolio below the risk of the least risky asset (sometimes to 0). The return of the resulting portfolio will be no lower than the smallest return of its component assets. For any two-asset portfolio, the ability to reduce risk depends on both the degree of correlation and the proportion of each asset in the portfolio. International diversification may allow an investor to reduce portfolio risk without necessarily imposing a corresponding reduction in return. It can be achieved by investing abroad or through domestic investment in foreign companies or funds, but it typically cannot be achieved by investing in U.S. multinationals. The preferred method of international diversification for individual investors is the use of ADSs or international mutual funds available in the United States. Although opportunities to earn "excess" returns in international investments are diminishing over time, international investments continue to provide an effective way to diversify.	correlation, p. 377 correlation coefficient, p. 377 negatively correlated, p. 377 perfectly negatively correlated, p. 378 perfectly positively correlated, p. 378 positively correlated, p. 377 uncorrelated, p. 377	Study Plan 11.2 Excel Tables 11.2, 11.3
LG3 Describe the components of risk and the use of beta to measure risk. The two basic components of total risk are diversifiable (unsystematic) and undiversifiable (systematic) risk. Undiversifiable risk is the relevant risk. Beta measures the undiversifiable, or market, risk associated with a security investment. It is derived from the historical relationship between a security's return and the market return.	beta, p. 386 diversifiable (unsystematic) risk, p. 385 market risk, p. 385 undiversifiable (systematic) risk, p. 385 total risk, p. 386	MyFinanceLab Study Plan 11.3 Video Learning Aid for Problem P11.22
LG4 Explain the capital asset pricing model conceptually, mathematically, and graphically. The CAPM relates risk (as measured by beta) to return. It can be divided into (1) the risk-free rate of return, r_{rf}, and (2) the risk premium, $b \times (r_m - r_{rf})$. The graphic depiction of the CAPM is the security market line (SML). The CAPM reflects increasing required returns for increasing risk.	capital asset pricing model (CAPM), p. 390 security market line (SML), p. 391	MyFinanceLab Study Plan 11.4
LG5 Review the traditional and modern approaches to portfolio management. The traditional approach constructs portfolios by combining a large number of securities issued by companies from a broad cross-section of industries. Modern portfolio theory (MPT) uses statistical diversification to develop efficient portfolios. To determine the optimal portfolio, MPT finds the efficient frontier and couples it with an investor's risk-indifference curves.	efficient frontier, p. 395 modern portfolio theory (MPT), p. 394 portfolio beta, b_p, p. 397 relevant risk, p. 402 risk-return tradeoff, p. 309 risk-free rate, r_{rf}, p. 309 traditional portfolio management, p. 393	MyFinanceLab Study Plan 11.5

What You Should Know	Key Terms	Where to Practice
LG6 Describe portfolio betas, the risk-return tradeoff, and reconciliation of the two approaches to portfolio management. Portfolio betas can be used to develop efficient portfolios consistent with the investor's risk-return preferences. Portfolio betas are merely a weighted average of the betas of the individual assets in the portfolio. Generally, investors use elements of both the traditional approach and MPT to create portfolios. This approach involves determining how much risk you are willing to bear, seeking diversification, using beta to diversify your portfolio, and evaluating alternative portfolios to select the one that offers the highest return for an acceptable level of risk.		MyFinanceLab Study Plan 11.6 Video Learning Aid for Problem P11.22

Log into MyFinanceLab, take a chapter test, and get a personalized Study Plan that tells you which concepts you understand and which ones you need to review. From there, MyFinanceLab will give you further practice, tutorials, animations, videos, and guided solutions.
Log into http://www.myfinancelab.com

Discussion Questions

LG1 **Q11.1** State your portfolio objectives. Then construct a 10-stock portfolio that you feel is consistent with your objectives. (Use companies that have been public for at least five years.) Obtain annual dividend and price data for each of the past five years.
a. Calculate the historical return for each stock for each year.
b. Using your findings in part **a**, calculate the historical portfolio return for each of the five years.
c. Use your findings in part **b** to calculate the average portfolio return over the five years.
d. Use your findings in parts **b** and **c** to find the standard deviation of the portfolio's returns over the five-year period.
e. Use the historical average return from part **c** and the standard deviation from part **d** to evaluate the portfolio's return and risk in light of your stated portfolio objectives.

LG2 **Q11.2** Using the following guidelines, choose the stocks—A, B, and C—of three firms that have been public for at least 10 years. Stock A should be one you are interested in buying. Stock B should be a stock, possibly in the same line of business or industry, that you feel will have the highest possible return correlation with stock A. Stock C should be one you feel will have the lowest possible return correlation with stock A.
a. Calculate the annual rates of return for each of the past 10 years for each stock.
b. Plot the 10 annual return values for each stock on the same set of axes, where the x-axis is the year and the y-axis is the annual return in percentage terms.
c. Join the points for the returns for each stock on the graph. Evaluate and describe the returns of stocks A and B in the graph. Do they exhibit the expected positive correlation? Why or why not?
d. Evaluate and describe the relationship between the returns of stocks A and C in the graph. Do they exhibit negative correlation? Why or why not?
e. Compare and contrast your findings in parts **c** and **d** to the expected relationships among stocks A, B, and C. Discuss your findings.

LG2   **Q11.3** From the *Wall Street Journal*, a website such as Yahoo! Finance, or some other source, obtain a current estimate of the risk-free rate (use a 10-year Treasury bond). Use the *Value Line Investment Survey* or Yahoo! Finance to obtain the beta for each of the following stocks:

Ford (autos)
Dell (computers)
Sempra Energy (utilities)
Kroger (groceries)
Bank of America (financial services)

Use the information you gathered along with the market risk premium on large stocks given in the chapter to find the required return for each stock with the capital asset pricing model.

LG3 LG4   **Q11.4** From the *Wall Street Journal*, a website such as Yahoo! Finance, or some other source, obtain a current estimate of the risk-free rate (use a 10-year Treasury bond). Use the *Value Line Investment Survey* or Yahoo! Finance to obtain the beta for each of the companies listed on page 186.
a. Compare the current betas to the February 27, 2015 betas given in the chapter for each of the companies.
b. What might cause betas to change over time, even in a stable economic environment?
c. Use the current betas, along with a market risk premium on stocks of 8.5%, to find the required return for each stock with the CAPM.
d. Compare and discuss your findings in part **c** with regard to the specific business of each company.

LG2 LG5 LG6   **Q11.5** Obtain a prospectus and an annual report for a major mutual fund that includes some international securities. Carefully read the prospectus and annual report and study the portfolio's composition in light of the fund's stated objectives.
a. Evaluate the amount of diversification and the types of industries and companies held. Is the portfolio well diversified?
b. Discuss the additional risks faced by an investor in this fund compared to an investor in a domestic stock portfolio such as the S&P 500.

LG6   **Q11.6** Use Yahoo! Finance or some other source to select four stocks with betas ranging from about 0.50 to 1.50. Record the current market prices of each of these stocks. Assume you wish to create a portfolio that combines all four stocks in such a way that the resulting portfolio beta is about 1.10.
a. Through trial and error, use all four stocks to create a portfolio with the target beta of 1.10.
b. If you have $100,000 to invest in this portfolio, on the basis of the weightings determined in part a, what dollar amounts would you invest in each stock?
c. Approximately how many shares of each of the four stocks would you buy given the dollar amounts calculated in part **b**?
d. Repeat parts **a**, **b**, and **c** with a different set of weightings that still result in a portfolio beta of 1.10. Can only one unique portfolio with a given beta be created from a given set of stocks?

Problems

All problems are available on http://www.myfinancelab.com

LG1   **P11.1** Your portfolio had the values in the following table for the four years listed. There were no withdrawals or contributions of new funds to the portfolio. Calculate your average return over the four-year period.

Year	Beginning Value	Ending Value
2013	$50,000	$55,000
2014	$55,000	$58,000
2015	$58,000	$65,000
2016	$65,000	$70,000

LG1　**P11.2** Using your data from Problem 11.1, calculate the portfolio standard deviation.

LG1 LG2　**P11.3** Assume you are considering a portfolio containing two assets, L and M. Asset L will represent 40% of the dollar value of the portfolio, and asset M will account for the other 60%. The projected returns over the next six years, 2018–2023, for each of these assets are summarized in the following table.

	Projected Return	
Year	Asset L	Asset M
2018	14%	20%
2019	14%	18%
2020	16%	16%
2021	17%	14%
2022	17%	12%
2023	19%	10%

a. Use an Excel spreadsheet to calculate the projected portfolio return, $\bar{r}_p$, for each of the six years.
b. Use an Excel spreadsheet to calculate the average portfolio return, $\bar{r}_p$, over the six-year period.
c. Use an Excel spreadsheet to calculate the standard deviation of expected portfolio returns, s_p, over the six-year period.
d. How would you characterize the correlation of returns of the assets L and M?
e. Discuss any benefits of diversification achieved through creation of the portfolio.

LG1 LG2　**P11.4** Refer to Problem 11.3. Assume that asset L represents 60% of the portfolio and asset M is 40%. Calculate the average return and standard deviation of this portfolio's returns over the six-year period. Compare your answers to the answers from Problem 11.3.

LG1 LG2　**P11.5** You have been given the following return data on three assets—F, G, and H—over the period 2018–2021.

	Expected Return		
Year	Asset F	Asset G	Asset H
2018	16%	17%	14%
2019	17%	16%	15%
2020	18%	15%	16%
2021	19%	14%	17%

Using these assets, you have isolated three investment alternatives:

Alternative	Investment
1	100% of asset F
2	50% of asset F and 50% of asset G
3	50% of asset F and 50% of asset H

a. Calculate the portfolio return over the four-year period for each of the three alternatives.

b. Calculate the standard deviation of returns over the four-year period for each of the three alternatives.

c. On the basis of your findings in parts **a** and **b**, which of the three investment alternatives would you recommend? Why?

LG1 LG2 **P11.6** You have been asked for your advice in selecting a portfolio of assets and have been supplied with the following data.

	Projected Return		
Year	Asset A	Asset B	Asset C
2018	12%	16%	12%
2019	14%	14%	14%
2020	16%	12%	16%

You have been told that you can create two portfolios—one consisting of assets A and B and the other consisting of assets A and C—by investing equal proportions (50%) in each of the two component assets.

a. What is the average return, $\bar{r}$, for each asset over the three-year period?

b. What is the standard deviation, s, for each asset's return?

c. What is the average return, $\bar{r}_p$, for each of the portfolios?

d. How would you characterize the correlations of returns of the two assets in each of the portfolios identified in part **c**?

e. What is the standard deviation of expected returns, s_p, for each portfolio?

f. Which portfolio do you recommend? Why?

LG1 LG2 **P11.7** Referring to Problem 11.6, what would happen if you constructed a portfolio consisting of assets A, B, and C, equally weighted? Would this reduce risk or enhance return?

LG1 LG2 **P11.8** Assume you wish to evaluate the risk and return behaviors associated with various combinations of assets V and W under three assumed degrees of correlation: perfect positive, uncorrelated, and perfect negative. The following average return and risk values were calculated for these assets.

Asset	Average Return, $\bar{r}$	Risk (Standard Asset Deviation), s
V	8%	5%
W	13%	10%

a. If the returns of assets V and W are perfectly positively correlated (correlation coefficient = +1), describe the range of (1) return and (2) risk associated with all possible portfolio combinations.

b. If the returns of assets V and W are uncorrelated (correlation coefficient = 0), describe the approximate range of (1) return and (2) risk associated with all possible portfolio combinations.

c. If the returns of assets V and W are perfectly negatively correlated (correlation coefficient = −1), describe the range of (1) return and (2) risk associated with all possible portfolio combinations.

LG1 **P11.9** The following table contains annual returns for the stocks of Home Depot (HD) and Lowe's (LOW). The returns are calculated using end-of-year prices (adjusted for dividends and stock splits) retrieved from **http://www.finance.yahoo.com/**. Use Excel to create a spreadsheet that calculates annual portfolio returns for an equally weighted portfolio of HD and LOW. Also, calculate the average annual return for both stocks and the portfolio.

Year	HD Returns	LOW Returns
2005	−4.3%	16.1%
2006	1.0%	−6.1%
2007	−31.1%	−26.8%
2008	−11.4%	−3.3%
2009	30.5%	10.6%
2010	25.0%	9.2%
2011	23.5%	3.4%
2012	50.3%	42.9%
2013	35.9%	41.8%
2014	30.2%	41.2%

LG1 LG2 **P11.10** Use the table of annual returns in Problem 11.9 for Home Depot (HD) and Lowe's (LOW) to create an Excel spreadsheet that calculates the standard deviation of annual returns for HD, LOW, and the equally weighted portfolio of HD and LOW.

LG1 LG2 **P11.11** Use the table of annual returns in Problem 11.9 for Home Depot (HD) and Lowe's (LOW) to create an Excel spreadsheet that calculates the correlation coefficient for HD and LOW annual returns.

LG1 LG2 **P11.12** Use the table of annual returns in Problem 11.9 for Home Depot (HD) and Lowe's (LOW) to create an Excel spreadsheet that calculates returns for portfolios that comprise HD and LOW using the following, respective, weightings: (1.0, 0.0), (0.9, 0.1), (0.8, 0.2), (0.7, 0.3), (0.6, 0.4), (0.5, 0.5), (0.4, 0.6), (0.3, 0.7), (0.2, 0.8), (0.1, 0.9), and (0.0, 1.0). Also, calculate the portfolio standard deviation associated with each portfolio composition. You will need to use the standard deviations found previously for HD and LOW and their correlation coefficient.

LG1 LG2 **P11.13** Create an Excel spreadsheet that graphs the portfolio return and standard deviation combinations found in Problem 11.12 for Home Depot and Lowe's.

LG1 LG2 **P11.14** The following table contains annual returns for the stocks of M and N. Use Excel to create a spreadsheet that calculates the average, standard deviation, and correlation coefficient for the two annual return series. Next, use the averages, standard deviations, and correlation coefficient along with the portfolios shown in the lower table to calculate a range of portfolio return and risk combinations. Finally, graph the range of return and risk combinations. (Hint: Review Figure 11.3)

Year	M Returns	N Returns
2015	40.6%	7.6%
2016	−37.9%	−30.0%
2017	18.1%	63.2%
2018	4.8%	20.9%
2019	−18.2%	50.0%
2020	17.4%	80.3%
2021	10.4%	−17.0%
2022	−23.2%	22.3%
2023	56.2%	13.6%
2024	11.9%	8.9%

Portfolio Weights	
w_M	w_N
1.0	0.0
0.9	0.1
0.8	0.2
0.7	0.3
0.6	0.4
0.5	0.5
0.4	0.6
0.3	0.7
0.2	0.8
0.1	0.9
0.0	1.0

LG3 **P11.15** Imagine you wish to estimate the betas for two investments, A and B. You have gathered the following return data for the market and for each of the investments over the past 10 years, 2008–2017.

		Historical Returns	
		Investment	
Year	Market	A	B
2008	6%	11%	16%
2009	2%	8%	11%
2010	−13%	−4%	10%
2011	−4%	3%	3%
2012	−8%	0%	3%
2013	16%	19%	30%
2014	10%	14%	22%
2015	15%	18%	29%
2016	8%	12%	19%
2017	13%	17%	26%

    a. On a set of market return (x-axis)–investment return (y-axis) axes, use the data to draw the characteristic lines for investments A and B on the same graph.
    b. Use the characteristic lines from part **a** to estimate the betas for investments A and B.
    c. Use the betas found in part **b** to comment on the relative risks of investments A and B.

LG3 **P11.16** You are evaluating two possible stock investments, Buyme Co. and Getit Corp. Buyme Co. has an expected return of 14% and a beta of 1.0. Getit Corp. has an expected return of 14% and a beta of 1.2. Based only on this data, which stock should you buy and why?

LG3 **P11.17** Referring to Problem 11.16, if you expected a significant market rally, would your decision be altered? Explain.

LG3 **P11.18** A security has a beta of 1.2. Is this security more or less risky than the market? Explain. Assess the impact on the required return of this security in each of the following cases.
    a. The market return increases by 15%.
    b. The market return decreases by 8%.
    c. The market return remains unchanged.

LG3 **P11.19** Assume the betas for securities A, B, and C are as shown here.

Security	Beta
A	1.4
B	0.8
C	−0.9

a. Calculate the change in return for each security if the market experiences an increase in its rate of return of 13.2% over the next period.
b. Calculate the change in return for each security if the market experiences a decrease in its rate of return of 10.8% over the next period.
c. Rank and discuss the relative risk of each security on the basis of your findings. Which security might perform best during an economic downturn? Explain.

LG3 **LG6** **P11.20** Referring to Problem 11.19, assume you have a portfolio with $20,000 invested in each of investments A, B, and C. What is your portfolio beta?

LG3 **LG6** **P11.21** Referring to Problem 11.20, using the portfolio beta, what would you expect the value of your portfolio to be if the market rallied 20%? Declined 20%?

LG2 **P11.22** Use the capital asset pricing model to find the required return for each of the following securities in light of the data given.

Security	Risk-Free Rate	Market Return	Beta
A	5%	8%	1.3
B	8%	13%	0.9
C	9%	12%	0.2
D	10%	15%	1.0
E	6%	10%	0.6

LG4 **P11.23** Jay is reviewing his portfolio of investments, which include certain stocks and bonds. He has a large amount tied up in U.S. Treasury bills paying 3%. He is considering moving some of his funds from the T-bills into a stock. The stock has a beta of 1.25. If Jay expects a return of 14% from the stock (a little better than the current market return of 13%), should he buy the stock or leave his funds in the T-bill?

LG4 **P11.24** The risk-free rate is currently 3%, and the market return is 10%. Assume you are considering the following investments.

Investment	Beta
A	1.5
B	1.0
C	0.75
D	0.0
E	2.0

a. Which investment is most risky? Least risky?
b. Use the capital asset pricing model to find the required return on each of the investments.
c. Using your findings in part b, draw the security market line.
d. On the basis of your findings in part c, what relationship exists between risk and return? Explain.

LG5 LG6 **P11.25** Portfolios A through J, which are listed in the following table along with their returns (r_p) and risk (measured by the standard deviation, s_p), represent all currently available portfolios in the feasible or attainable set.

Portfolio	Return, r_p	Risk, s_p
A	9%	8%
B	3%	3%
C	14%	10%
D	12%	14%
E	7%	11%
F	11%	6%
G	10%	12%
H	16%	16%
I	5%	7%
J	8%	4%

a. Plot the feasible, or attainable, set represented by these data on a graph showing portfolio risk, s_p (x-axis), and portfolio return, r_p (y-axis).

b. Draw the efficient frontier on the graph in part a.

c. Which portfolios lie on the efficient frontier? Why do these portfolios dominate all others in the feasible set?

d. How would an investor's utility function or risk-indifference curves be used with the efficient frontier to find the optimal portfolio?

LG5 LG6 **P11.26** For his portfolio, Jack Cashman randomly selected securities from all those listed on the New York Stock Exchange. He began with one security and added securities one by one until a total of 20 securities were held in the portfolio. After each security was added, Jack calculated the portfolio standard deviation, s_p. The calculated values follow.

Number of Securities	Portfolio Risk, s_p	Number of Securities	Portfolio Risk, s_p
1	14.5%	11	7.00%
2	13.3%	12	6.80%
3	12.2%	13	6.70%
4	11.2%	14	6.65%
5	10.3%	15	6.60%
6	9.5%	16	6.56%
7	8.8%	17	6.52%
8	8.2%	18	6.5%
9	7.7%	19	6.48%
10	7.3%	20	6.47%

a. On a graph showing the number of securities in the portfolio (x-axis) and portfolio risk, s_p (y-axis), plot the portfolio risk given the data in the preceding table.

b. Divide the portfolio risk in the graph into its undiversifiable and diversifiable risk components, and label each of these on the graph.

c. Describe which of the two risk components is the relevant risk, and explain why it is relevant. How much of this risk exists in Jack Cashman's portfolio?

LG3 LG6 **P11.27** If portfolio A has a beta of 1.5 and portfolio Z has a beta of −1.5, what do the two values indicate? If the return on the market rises by 20%, what impact, if any, would this have on the returns from portfolios A and Z? Explain.

LG3 LG6 **P11.28** Stock A has a beta of 0.8, stock B has a beta of 1.4, and stock C has a beta of −0.3.
   a. Rank these stocks from the most risky to the least risky.
   b. If the return on the market portfolio increases by 12%, what change in the return for each of the stocks would you expect?
   c. If the return on the market portfolio declines by 5%, what change in the return for each of the stocks would you expect?
   d. If you felt the stock market was about to experience a significant decline, which stock would you be most likely to add to your portfolio? Why?
   e. If you anticipated a major stock market rally, which stock would you be most likely to add to your portfolio? Why?

LG6 **P11.29** Jeanne Lewis is attempting to evaluate two possible portfolios consisting of the same five assets but held in different proportions. She is particularly interested in using beta to compare the risk of the portfolios and, in this regard, has gathered the following data.

		Portfolio Weights	
Asset	Asset Beta	Portfolio A	Portfolio B
1	1.3	10%	30%
2	0.7	30%	10%
3	1.25	10%	20%
4	1.1	10%	20%
5	0.9	40%	20%
Total		100%	100%

   a. Calculate the betas for portfolios A and B.
   b. Compare the risk of each portfolio to the market as well as to each other. Which portfolio is more risky?

LG4 **P11.30** Referring to Problem 11.29, if the risk-free rate is 2% and the market return is 7%, calculate the required return for each portfolio using the CAPM.

LG5 LG6 **P11.31** Referring to Problem 11.30, assume that you believe that each of the five assets will earn the return shown in the table below. Based on these figures and the weights in Problem 11.29, what returns do you believe that Portfolios A and B will earn. Which portfolio would you invest in and why?

Asset	Returns
1	16.5%
2	12.0%
3	15.0%
4	13.0%
5	7.0%

Visit **http://www.myfinancelab.com** for web exercises, spreadsheets, and other online resources.

Case Problem 11.1   Traditional Versus Modern Portfolio Theory: Who's Right?

LG5 LG6 Walt Davies and Shane O'Brien are district managers for Lee, Inc. Over the years, as they moved through the firm's sales organization, they became (and still remain) close friends. Walt, who is 33 years old, currently lives in Princeton, New Jersey. Shane, who is 35, lives in Houston, Texas.

Recently, at the national sales meeting, they were discussing various company matters, as well as bringing each other up to date on their families, when the subject of investments came up. Each had always been fascinated by the stock market, and now that they had achieved some degree of financial success, they had begun actively investing.

As they discussed their investments, Walt said he thought the only way an individual who does not have hundreds of thousands of dollars can invest safely is to buy mutual fund shares. He emphasized that to be safe, a person needs to hold a broadly diversified portfolio and that only those with a lot of money and time can achieve independently the diversification that can be readily obtained by purchasing mutual fund shares.

Shane totally disagreed. He said, "Diversification! Who needs it?" He thought that what one must do is look carefully at stocks possessing desired risk-return characteristics and then invest all one's money in the single best stock. Walt told him he was crazy. He said, "There is no way to measure risk conveniently—you're just gambling." Shane disagreed. He explained how his stockbroker had acquainted him with beta, which is a measure of risk. Shane said that the higher the beta, the more risky the stock, and therefore the higher its return. By looking up the betas for potential stock investments on the Internet, he can pick stocks that have an acceptable risk level for him. Shane explained that with beta, one does not need to diversify; one merely needs to be willing to accept the risk reflected by beta and then hope for the best.

The conversation continued, with Walt indicating that although he knew nothing about beta, he didn't believe one could safely invest in a single stock. Shane continued to argue that his broker had explained to him that betas can be calculated not just for a single stock but also for a portfolio of stocks, such as a mutual fund. He said, "What's the difference between a stock with a beta of, say, 1.2 and a mutual fund with a beta of 1.2? They have the same risk and should therefore provide similar returns."

As Walt and Shane continued to discuss their differing opinions relative to investment strategy, they began to get angry with each other. Neither was able to convince the other that he was right. The level of their voices now raised, they attracted the attention of the company's vice president of finance, Elinor Green, who was standing nearby. She came over and indicated she had overheard their argument about investments and thought that, given her expertise on financial matters, she might be able to resolve their disagreement. She asked them to explain the crux of their disagreement, and each reviewed his own viewpoint. After hearing their views, Elinor responded, "I have some good news and some bad news for each of you. There is some validity to what each of you says, but there also are some errors in each of your explanations. Walt tends to support the traditional approach to portfolio management. Shane's views are more supportive of modern portfolio theory." Just then, the company president interrupted them, needing to talk to Elinor immediately. Elinor apologized for having to leave and offered to continue their discussion later that evening.

Questions

a. Analyze Walt's argument and explain why a mutual fund investment may be overdiversified. Also explain why one does not necessarily have to have hundreds of thousands of dollars to diversify adequately.

b. Analyze Shane's argument and explain the major error in his logic relative to the use of beta as a substitute for diversification. Explain the key assumption underlying the use of beta as a risk measure.

c. Briefly describe the traditional approach to portfolio management and relate it to the approaches supported by Walt and Shane.

d. Briefly describe modern portfolio theory and relate it to the approaches supported by Walt and Shane. Be sure to mention diversifiable risk, undiversifiable risk, and total risk, along with the role of beta.

e. Explain how the traditional approach and modern portfolio theory can be blended into an approach to portfolio management that might prove useful to the individual investor. Relate this to reconciling Walt's and Shane's differing points of view.

Case Problem 11.2   Susan Lussier's Inherited Portfolio: Does It Meet Her Needs?

LG3 LG4   Susan Lussier is 35 years old and employed as a tax accountant for a major oil and gas explora-
LG5 LG6   tion company. She earns nearly $135,000 a year from her salary and from participation in the
company's drilling activities. An expert on oil and gas taxation, she is not worried about job
security—she is content with her income and finds it adequate to allow her to buy and do whatever she wishes. Her current philosophy is to live each day to its fullest, not concerning herself
with retirement, which is too far in the future to require her current attention.

A month ago, Susan's only surviving parent, her father, was killed in a sailing accident. He
had retired in La Jolla, California, two years earlier and had spent most of his time sailing. Prior
to retirement, he managed a children's clothing manufacturing firm in South Carolina. Upon
retirement he sold his stock in the firm and invested the proceeds in a security portfolio that
provided him with supplemental retirement income of over $30,000 per year. In his will, he left
his entire estate to Susan. The estate was structured in such a way that in addition to a few family
heirlooms, Susan received a security portfolio having a market value of nearly $350,000 and
about $10,000 in cash.

Susan's father's portfolio contained 10 securities: 5 bonds, 2 common stocks, and 3 mutual
funds. The following table lists the securities and their key characteristics. The common stocks
were issued by large, mature, well-known firms that had exhibited continuing patterns of dividend payment over the past five years. The stocks offered only moderate growth potential—
probably no more than 2% to 3% appreciation per year. The mutual funds in the portfolio were
income funds invested in diversified portfolios of income-oriented stocks and bonds. They provided stable streams of dividend income but offered little opportunity for capital appreciation.

The Securities Portfolio That Susan Lussier Inherited

Bonds						
Par Value	Issue	S&P Rating	Interest Income	Quoted Price	Total Cost	Current Yield
$40,000	Delta Power and Light 10.125% due 2029	AA	$4,050	$ 98	$39,200	10.33%
$30,000	Mountain Water 9.750% due 2021	A	$2,925	$102	$30,600	9.56%
$50,000	California Gas 9.500% due 2016	AAA	$4,750	$ 97	$48,500	9.79%
$20,000	Trans-Pacific Gas 10.000% due 2027	AAA	$2,000	$ 99	$19,800	10.10%
$20,000	Public Service 9.875% due 2017	AA	$1,975	$100	$20,000	9.88%

Common Stocks						
Number of Shares	Company	Dividend per Share	Dividend Income	Price per Share	Total Cost	Beta	Dividend Yield
2,000	International Supply	$2.40	$4,800	$22	$44,900	0.97	10.91%
3,000	Black Motor	$1.50	$4,500	$17	$52,000	0.85	8.82%

Mutual Funds

Number of Shares	Fund	Dividend per Share Income	Dividend Income	Price per Share	Total Cost	Beta	Dividend Yield
2,000	International Capital Income A Fund	$0.80	$1,600	$10	$20,000	1.02	8.00%
1,000	Grimner Special Income Fund	$2.00	$2,000	$15	$15,000	1.10	7.50%
4,000	Ellis Diversified Income Fund	$1.20	$4,800	$12	$48,000	0.90	10.00%
		Total annual income: $33,400		Portfolio value: $338,000		Portfolio current yield: 9.88%	

Now that Susan owns the portfolio, she wishes to determine whether it is suitable for her situation. She realizes that the high level of income provided by the portfolio will be taxed at a rate (federal plus state) of about 40%. Because she does not currently need it, Susan plans to invest the after-tax income primarily in common stocks offering high capital gain potential. During the coming years she clearly needs to avoid generating taxable income. (Susan is already paying out a sizable portion of her income in taxes.) She feels fortunate to have received the portfolio and wants to make certain it provides her with the maximum benefits, given her financial situation. The $10,000 cash left to her will be especially useful in paying brokers' commissions associated with making portfolio adjustments.

Questions

a. Briefly assess Susan's financial situation and develop a portfolio objective for her that is consistent with her needs.

b. Evaluate the portfolio left to Susan by her father. Assess its apparent objective and evaluate how well it may be doing in fulfilling this objective. Use the total cost values to describe the asset allocation scheme reflected in the portfolio. Comment on the risk, return, and tax implications of this portfolio.

c. If Susan decided to invest in a security portfolio consistent with her needs—indicated in response to question **a**—describe the nature and mix, if any, of securities you would recommend she purchase. Discuss the risk, return, and tax implications of such a portfolio.

d. From the response to question **b**, compare the nature of the security portfolio inherited by Susan with what you believe would be an appropriate security portfolio for her, based on the response to question **c**.

e. What recommendations would you give Susan about the inherited portfolio? Explain the steps she should take to adjust the portfolio to her needs.

Excel@Investing

Excel@Investing

Katie plans to form a portfolio consisting of two securities, Intel (INTC) and Procter & Gamble (PG), and she wonders how the portfolio's return will depend on the amount that she invests in each stock. Katie's professor suggests that she use the capital asset pricing model to define the required returns for the two companies. (Refer to Equations 11.3 and 11.3a.)

$$r_j = r_{rf} + [b_j \times (r_m - r_{rf})]$$

Katie measures r_{rf} using the current long-term Treasury bond return of 5%. Katie determines that the average return on the S&P 500 Index over the last several years is 6.1%, so she uses that figure to measure r_m. She researches a source for the beta information and follows these steps:

- Go to http://money.msn.com

- In the Get Quote box, type INTC and press Get Quote.

- On the next page, look for the stock's beta.
- Repeat the steps for the PG stock.

Questions

a. What are the beta values for INTC and PG? Using the CAPM, create a spreadsheet to determine the required rates of return for both INTC and PG.

b. Katie has decided that the portfolio will be distributed between INTC and PG in a 60% and 40% split, respectively. Hence, a weighted average can be calculated for both the returns and betas of the portfolio. This concept is shown in the spreadsheet for Table 11.2, which can be viewed at **http://www.myfinancelab.com**. Create a spreadsheet using the following models for the calculations:

$$\text{war} = (w_i \times r_i) + (w_j \times r_j)$$

where

 war = weighted average required rate of return for the portfolio

 w_i = weight of security i in the portfolio

 r_i = required return of security i in the portfolio

 w_j = weight of security j in the portfolio

 r_j = required return of security j in the portfolio

$$\text{wab} = (w_i \times b_i) + (w_j \times b_j)$$

where

 wab = weighted average beta for the portfolio

 w_i = weight of security i in the portfolio

 b_i = beta for security i

 w_j = weight of security j in the portfolio

 b_j = beta for security j

Chapter-Opening Problem

In this problem we will visit United Rentals Inc. (URI), which was introduced at the beginning of the chapter. The following table shows the monthly return on URI stock and on the S&P 500 stock index from January 2009 to December 2014.

Month/Year	S&P 500 Return	United Rentals Return	Month/Year	S&P 500 Return	United Rentals Return
1/2/2009	−8.6%	−38.8%	10/1/2009	−2.0%	−7.9%
2/2/2009	−11.0%	−27.4%	11/2/2009	5.7%	−2.8%
3/2/2009	8.5%	4.0%	12/1/2009	1.8%	6.4%
4/1/2009	9.4%	43.9%	1/4/2010	−3.7%	−18.3%
5/1/2009	5.3%	−21.6%	2/1/2010	2.9%	−5.7%
6/1/2009	0.0%	36.6%	3/1/2010	5.9%	24.2%
7/1/2009	7.4%	15.1%	4/1/2010	1.5%	53.1%
8/3/2009	3.4%	23.0%	5/3/2010	−8.2%	−15.4%
9/1/2009	3.6%	12.1%	6/1/2010	−5.4%	−23.3%

Month/Year	S&P 500 Return	United Rentals Return	Month/Year	S&P 500 Return	United Rentals Return
7/1/2010	6.9%	41.4%	10/1/2012	−2.0%	24.3%
8/2/2010	−4.7%	−14.6%	11/1/2012	0.3%	2.1%
9/1/2010	8.8%	31.9%	12/3/2012	0.7%	9.6%
10/1/2010	3.7%	26.6%	1/2/2013	5.0%	11.2%
11/1/2010	−0.2%	4.4%	2/1/2013	1.1%	5.5%
12/1/2010	6.5%	16.0%	3/1/2013	3.6%	2.9%
1/3/2011	2.3%	17.1%	4/1/2013	1.8%	−4.3%
2/1/2011	3.2%	16.2%	5/1/2013	2.1%	8.0%
3/1/2011	−0.1%	7.4%	6/3/2013	−1.5%	−12.2%
4/1/2011	2.8%	−11.6%	7/1/2013	4.9%	14.8%
5/2/2011	−1.4%	−7.1%	8/1/2013	−3.1%	−4.4%
6/1/2011	−1.8%	−7.1%	9/3/2013	3.0%	6.4%
7/1/2011	−2.1%	−9.4%	10/1/2013	4.5%	10.8%
8/1/2011	−5.7%	−27.5%	11/1/2013	2.8%	6.4%
9/1/2011	−7.2%	1.0%	12/2/2013	2.4%	13.4%
10/3/2011	10.8%	39.0%	1/2/2014	−3.6%	3.8%
11/1/2011	−0.5%	20.2%	2/3/2014	4.3%	9.1%
12/1/2011	0.9%	5.0%	3/3/2014	0.7%	7.5%
1/3/2012	4.4%	29.4%	4/1/2014	0.6%	−1.2%
2/1/2012	4.1%	9.0%	5/1/2014	2.1%	7.7%
3/1/2012	3.1%	2.9%	6/2/2014	1.9%	3.6%
4/2/2012	−0.7%	8.8%	7/1/2014	−1.5%	1.1%
5/1/2012	−6.3%	−26.0%	8/1/2014	3.8%	11.1%
6/1/2012	4.0%	−1.5%	9/2/2014	−1.6%	−5.6%
7/2/2012	1.3%	−15.1%	10/1/2014	2.3%	−0.9%
8/1/2012	2.0%	11.8%	11/3/2014	2.5%	3.0%
9/4/2012	2.4%	1.2%	12/1/2014	−0.4%	−10.0%

Questions

a. Using an Excel spreadsheet calculate the average monthly return on URI stock and on the S&P 500.

b. Using an Excel spreadsheet calculate the standard deviation of monthly returns for URI and the S&P 500. What do your answers tell you about diversifiable risk, undiversifiable risk, and total risk?

c. Using an Excel spreadsheet plot the returns of URI on the vertical axis and the returns of the S&P 500 on the horizontal axis of a graph. Does it appear that URI and the S&P 500 are correlated? If so, are they correlated positively or negatively?

d. Using an Excel spreadsheet add a trend line that best fits the scatterplot of points that you created in part c. What is the slope of this line? How can you interpret the slope? What does it say about the risk of URI compared to the risk of the S&P 500?

12

Risk and Return
Capital Market Theory

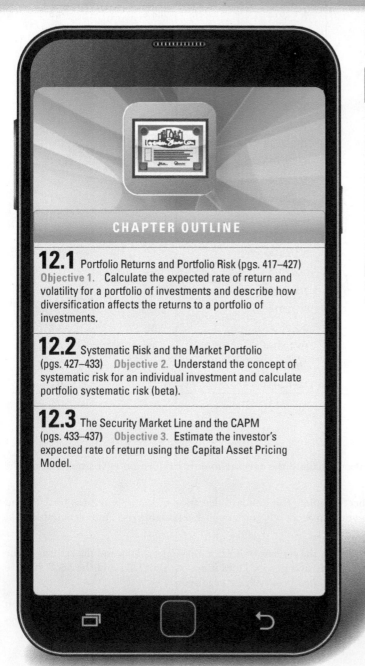

CHAPTER OUTLINE

12.1 Portfolio Returns and Portfolio Risk (pgs. 417–427)
Objective 1. Calculate the expected rate of return and
volatility for a portfolio of investments and describe how
diversification affects the returns to a portfolio of
investments.

12.2 Systematic Risk and the Market Portfolio
(pgs. 427–433) Objective 2. Understand the concept of
systematic risk for an individual investment and calculate
portfolio systematic risk (beta).

12.3 The Security Market Line and the CAPM
(pgs. 433–437) Objective 3. Estimate the investor's
expected rate of return using the Capital Asset Pricing
Model.

Principles P2 and P4 Applied

In this chapter we will continue our discussion of
P Principle 2: **There Is a Risk–Return Tradeoff.** In particular,
we will extend our analysis of risk and return to consider
portfolios of risky investments and the beneficial effects of
portfolio diversification on risk. In addition, we will learn more
about what types of risk are associated with both higher and
lower expected rates of return. To do this we first develop the
tools needed to calculate both the expected rate of return and
the variance of the return of a portfolio consisting of many
investments. Having developed these tools, we then
investigate the concept of diversification and define what is
meant by an investment's diversifiable and non-diversifiable
risks. Finally, we describe the Capital Asset Pricing Model
(CAPM), which helps us understand how the risk of an
individual investment should be measured. In addition, as
P Principle 4: **Market Prices Reflect Information** states, as new
information arrives and changes investors' risk and return
expectations, prices will change.

Good News Plus Bad News Equals No News

On Monday, April 28, 2008, Veeco Instruments Inc. (VECO) reported quarterly earnings that exceeded analysts' expectations for the quarter by 200 percent. The surprise earnings performance was greeted by a 6 percent rise in the company's share price for the day. On the same day, Travelzoo Inc. (TZOO) reported quarterly earnings that were dramatically below the level that was expected, and the company's stock price declined by more than 7 percent. Taken individually, Veeco's shareholders would be very happy at the end of the day, but Travelzoo's stockholders would not. Yet if you held a portfolio that included both company's shares, its value may not have changed much at all.

  This example illustrates how diversification can reduce risk. **Diversification** is simply "not putting all your eggs in one basket." For example, if your portfolio consists only of stocks of oil companies such as ExxonMobil (XOM) and ConocoPhillips (COP), you would lose a substantial amount of money if the price of oil fell. Similarly, if your portfolio consists entirely of banking stocks such as that of Bank of America (BAC) and JPMorgan Chase (JPM), you are likely to lose a lot of money when the default rate on loans increases. On the other hand, if you were to invest half your money in oil stocks and the other half in banking stocks, the ups and downs of these investments would tend to offset one another, which would reduce the extreme returns on the downside as well as the upside. This is diversification.

REGARDLESS OF YOUR MAJOR...

"Risk and Your Personal Investment Plan"

Vanguard, one of the leading mutual fund families, identifies four key guidelines you should consider when making personal investment decisions:

1. Select investment products suited to your objective.
2. Find a comfortable balance between risk and return.
3. Diversify wisely to help manage risks.
4. Evaluate your portfolio periodically.

Notice that two of these four common-sense suggestions deal with risk. When you set up your own personal investment plan, which you might create for a variety of reasons—a rainy day fund, a down payment on a home, an education fund for your children, or simply retirement—you will need to determine your comfort level with risk and adjust your investments accordingly.

  Some people can live with the substantial ups and downs of very risky investments. Others reach for the antacid when the value of their investments takes a plunge.

Your Turn: See Study Question 12–1.

12.1 Portfolio Returns and Portfolio Risk

The most important thing that we learn in this chapter is that with appropriate diversification, you can lower the risk of your portfolio without lowering the portfolio's expected rate of return. How does this concept of diversification relate to ▣ Principle 2: **There Is a Risk–Return Tradeoff?** What we learn in this chapter is that some risk can be eliminated by diversification, and that those risks that can be eliminated are not necessarily rewarded in the financial marketplace. To understand this, we must delve into the computation of portfolio expected return and portfolio risk.

Calculating the Expected Return of a Portfolio

The expected rate of return for a portfolio of investments is simply a weighted average of the expected rates of return of the individual investments in that portfolio. To calculate a portfolio's expected rate of return we *weight* each individual investment's expected rate of return using the fraction of the portfolio invested in that particular investment. For instance, if you put half your money in the stock of ExxonMobil, with an expected rate of return of 12 percent, and the other half in General Electric (GE) stock, with an expected rate of return of 8 percent, then we can calculate the expected rate of return of the portfolio as follows: $(1/2 \times 12\%) + (1/2 \times 8\%) = 10\%$.

In general, we calculate the expected rate of return of a portfolio that includes n different assets as follows:

$$
\begin{aligned}
\text{Expected Portfolio Return} = &\left(\begin{array}{c} \text{Fraction of Portfolio} \\ \text{Invested in Asset 1} \end{array} \times \begin{array}{c} \text{Expected Rate of} \\ \text{Return on Asset 1} \end{array} \right) \\
+ &\left(\begin{array}{c} \text{Fraction of Portfolio} \\ \text{Invested in Asset 2} \end{array} \times \begin{array}{c} \text{Expected Rate of} \\ \text{Return on Asset 2} \end{array} \right) \\
+ &\left(\begin{array}{c} \text{Fraction of Portfolio} \\ \text{Invested in Asset 3} \end{array} \times \begin{array}{c} \text{Expected Rate of} \\ \text{Return on Asset 3} \end{array} \right) \\
+ \cdots + &\left(\begin{array}{c} \text{Fraction of Portfolio} \\ \text{Invested in Asset } n \end{array} \times \begin{array}{c} \text{Expected Rate of} \\ \text{Return on Asset } n \end{array} \right)
\end{aligned}
$$

Because the number of elements used to calculate the portfolio expected return is somewhat lengthy, we generally abbreviate the formula using symbols as follows:

Portfolio Expected Rate of Return

Equation 12.1 $E(r_{portfolio}) = [W_1 \times E(r_1)] + [W_2 \times E(r_2)] + [W_3 \times E(r_3)] + \cdots + [W_n \times E(r_n)]$

Important Definitions and Concepts:

- $E(r_{portfolio})$ = the expected rate of return on a portfolio of n assets.
- W_i = the portfolio weight for asset i.
- $E(r_i)$ = the expected rate of return earned by asset i. In this chapter we will assume that this calculation has already been made and that the expected rate of return for risky assets is known.
- $[W_1 \times E(r_1)]$ = the contribution of asset 1 to the portfolio expected return.
- Note that the expected rate of return on a portfolio of n assets is simply a weighted average of the expected rates of return on each of the n assets.

Evaluating Portfolio Risk

In the last section we showed that the expected rate of return of a portfolio is simply the weighted average of the expected rates of returns of the individual investments that make up the portfolio. Next we calculate the risk of a portfolio using the standard deviation of portfolio returns. However, as we will illustrate in this section, the standard deviation of a portfolio's return is generally *not* equal to the weighted average of the standard deviations of the returns of the individual investments held in the portfolio. To understand why this is the case, we must look deeper into the concept of diversification.

Portfolio Diversification In most cases, combining investments in a portfolio leads to risk reduction. This effect of reducing risks by including a large number of investments in a portfolio is called diversification. As a consequence of diversification, the standard deviation of a portfolio's return is typically less than the average of the standard deviations of the returns of each of the portfolio's individual investments.

To illustrate this, suppose you open a shop to cater to the tourist trade on a beautiful Caribbean island. The two products that you consider selling are sunglasses and umbrellas. Sunglasses generate a 20 percent rate of return during the sunny season and a 0 percent return during the rainy season. In contrast, umbrellas generate a 0 percent rate of return during the sunny season, but during the rainy season the umbrella business will generate a 20 percent return. So if the probability of a rainy year is 50 percent and the probability of a mostly sunny year is 50 percent, then the expected rate of return from each of these items is 10 percent. The problem comes into play when rainy and sunny seasons vary in length. For example, if you only sold sunglasses and the sunny season only lasted for 2 months, you wouldn't do very well at all; likewise, if you only invested in umbrellas and the sunny season lasted for 10 months, you would likewise do poorly.

In this example the revenues from both products, when viewed in isolation, are quite risky. However, if you invest half of your money in sunglasses and the other half in umbrellas, you will earn 10 percent on your total investment regardless of how long the sunny season lasts because at all times one of your products will be returning 20 percent while the other will be returning 0 percent. In effect, when you combine sunglasses and umbrellas, you completely eliminate risk.

Do you always get this diversification benefit when two investments are combined? Not necessarily. For example, if you were currently selling sunglasses and added sunscreen, which also returns 20 percent in the sunny season and 0 percent in the rainy season, there would be no benefit to diversification because the returns of the sunscreen and sunglasses investments are perfectly *correlated*. As a result, if the rainy season lasted for three-quarters of the year, you would only earn 5 percent that year. Moreover, your return would be the same whether you only invested in sunglasses or you invested half your money in sunglasses and half in sunscreen. In effect, you will achieve no diversification gains when investments are perfectly correlated.

The concept of correlation is critical to our understanding of portfolio diversification. We measure the degree to which the returns on two investments are correlated using the **correlation coefficient**, a measure of the relationship of the return earned by one investment to another. The correlation coefficient can range from -1.0 (perfect negative correlation), meaning that two variables move in perfectly opposite directions (e.g., the sales of umbrellas and sunglasses), to $+1.0$ (perfect positive correlation), meaning that two assets move exactly together (e.g., the sales of sunglasses and sunscreen increase and decrease simultaneously). A correlation coefficient of 0.0 means that there is no relationship between the returns earned by the two assets.

In the previous example, sunglasses and sunscreen sales are perfectly *positively* correlated with one another. This means that their returns move up and down exactly in unison. The sale of umbrellas, on the other hand, goes up when sunscreen and sunglass sales fall, and vice versa. So umbrella sales are perfectly *negatively* correlated with sunscreen and sunglass sales. In most cases, the returns of two different investments will neither be perfectly correlated positively nor perfectly correlated negatively. However, there will be a tendency for most investment returns to move together, that is, in positive correlation. As long as the investment returns are not perfectly positively correlated, there will be diversification benefits. However, the diversification benefits will be greater when the correlations are low or negative.

Checkpoint 12.1

Calculating a Portfolio's Expected Rate of Return

Penny Simpson has her first full-time job and is considering how to invest her savings. Her dad suggested she invest no more than 25 percent of her savings in the stock of her employer, Emerson Electric (EMR), so she is considering investing the remaining 75 percent in a combination of a risk-free investment in U.S. Treasury bills, currently paying 4 percent, and Starbucks (SBUX) common stock. Penny's father has invested in the stock market for many years and suggested that Penny might expect to earn 8 percent on the Emerson shares and 12 percent from the Starbucks shares. Penny decides to put 25 percent in Emerson, 25 percent in Starbucks, and the remaining 50 percent in Treasury bills. Given Penny's portfolio allocation, what rate of return should she expect to receive on her investment?

STEP 1: Picture the problem

The following figure shows the expected rates of return for each investment in Penny's portfolio.

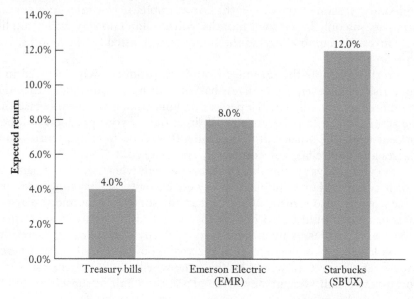

The expected rate of return for Penny's portfolio can be calculated as a weighted average of these expected rates of return, where the weights are the proportions of each investment.

STEP 2: Decide on a solution strategy

The portfolio expected rate of return is simply a weighted average of the expected rates of return of the investments in the portfolio. So we use Equation (12–1) to calculate the expected rate of return for Penny's portfolio. Fill in the *shaded cells* under the "Product" column in the following table to calculate a weighted average.

	E(Return) ×	Weight =	Product
U.S. Treasury bills	4.0%	0.50	
Emerson Electric (EMR)	8.0%	0.25	
Starbucks (SBUX)	12.0%	0.25	
Portfolio E(Return) = Sum of product column			

STEP 3: Solve

We can use Equation (12–1) to calculate the expected rate of return for the portfolio as follows:

$$E(r_{portfolio}) = W_{Treasury\ Bills}E(r_{Treasury\ Bills}) + W_{EMR}E(r_{EMR}) + W_{SBUX}E(r_{SBUX})$$

$$= (1/2 \times .04) + (1/4 \times .08) + (1/4 \times .12) = .07\ or\ 7\%$$

Alternatively, by filling out the table described above we get the same result.

	E(Return)	Weight	Product
Treasury bills	4.0%	0.50	2.0%
Emerson Electric (EMR)	8.0%	0.25	2.0%
Starbucks (SBUX)	12.0%	0.25	3.0%
	Portfolio E(Return) =		7.0%

STEP 4: Analyze

The expected rate of return for the portfolio composed of 50 percent invested in Treasury bills, 25 percent in Emerson Electric stock, and the remaining 25 percent in Starbucks stock is 7 percent. Note that we have referred to the Treasury bill rate as its expected rate of return. This is technically accurate because this return is assumed to be risk-free. That is, if you purchase a Treasury bill that promises to pay you 4 percent, because this security is risk-free, this is the only possible outcome. This is not the case for either of the other investment alternatives. We can calculate the expected rate of return for the portfolio in exactly the same way regardless of the risk of the investments contained in the portfolio. However, as we learn next, the risk of the portfolio is affected by the riskiness of the returns of the individual investments contained in the portfolio.

STEP 5: Check yourself

Evaluate the expected return for Penny's portfolio in which she places a quarter of her money in Treasury bills, half in Starbucks stock, and the remainder in Emerson Electric stock.

ANSWER: 9 percent.

Your Turn: For more practice, do related **Study Problems** 12–1 and 12–5 at the end of this chapter.   **>> END Checkpoint 12.1**

Diversification Lessons We can take away two key lessons from this initial look at portfolio risk and diversification:

- First, a portfolio can be less risky than the average risk of its individual investments in the portfolio.

- Second, the key to reducing risk through diversification is to combine investments whose returns do not move together and thus are not perfectly positively correlated (such as the sales of sunglasses and umbrellas).

Calculating the Standard Deviation of a Portfolio's Returns

Consider the problem faced by Patty. Patty just received $20,000 from her Aunt Gladys, who suggests she invest the money in the stock market. Patty told her aunt that she is considering the possibility of investing the money in the common stock of either Apple (AAPL) or Coca-Cola (KO). When she hears this, Aunt Gladys advises Patty to put half the money in Apple stock and half in Coca-Cola stock.

To analyze Aunt Gladys's suggested investment strategy, let's calculate the expected return and standard deviation of a portfolio that includes both Apple and Coca-Cola stocks. We saw from Equation (12–1) that the expected return is simply the weighted average of the expected returns of the individual securities in the portfolio. So if we assume that individually, Apple and Coca-Cola stocks have the same expected rate of return of 14 percent, and Patty invests in each equally, then the portfolio consisting of both stocks will have the same expected rate of return as the individual stocks, or 14 percent:

$$E(r_{portfolio}) = W_{Apple}E(r_{Apple}) + W_{CocaCola}E(r_{CocaCola}) = (1/2 \times .14) + (1/2 \times .14) = .14 \text{ or } 14\%$$

Now let's consider the riskiness of Patty's portfolio. To measure the portfolio's risk, we use the standard deviation of the portfolio. As we noted earlier, the standard deviation of the portfolio is *not* simply a weighted average of the respective standard deviations of the two stock investments. Indeed, if the returns on investing in Apple stock are less than perfectly correlated with the returns on Coca-Cola stock, the standard deviation of the portfolio that combines the two firms' shares will be less than this simple weighted average of the two firms' standard deviations. This reduction in portfolio standard deviation is due to the effects of diversification. The magnitude of the reduction in the portfolio's standard deviation resulting from diversification will depend on the extent to which the returns are correlated. This can be understood by looking at the mathematics for calculating the standard deviation of a portfolio with two stocks. The mathematics may look forbidding at first, but it offers a useful key to understanding how diversification works.

Standard deviation is the square root of the variance, so we first calculate the variance and then take the square root of the result. In the following formula, we will substitute Apple stock for asset 1 and Coca-Cola stock for asset 2. To illustrate, consider the following formula for the variance of a two-asset portfolio comprised of asset 1 and asset 2:

Equation 12.2

$$\sigma_{portfolio} = \sqrt{W_1^2\sigma_1^2 + W_2^2\sigma_2^2 + 2W_1W_2\rho_{1,2}\sigma_1\sigma_2}$$

Important Definitions and Concepts:

- $\sigma_{portfolio}$ = the standard deviation in portfolio returns,
- W_i = the proportion of the portfolio that is invested in asset i,
- σ_i = the standard deviation in the rate of return earned by asset i, and
- $\rho_{i,j}$ = correlation between the rates of return earned by assets i and j. The symbol $\rho_{i,j}$ (pronounced "rho") represents correlation between the rates of return for asset 1 and asset 2.

Once again, correlation tells us the strength of the linear relationship between two assets. It can take on a value that ranges from 1.0, meaning these two assets move in a perfectly opposite linear manner as in the sunglasses and umbrellas example, to +1.0, which means that these two assets move in a perfectly linear manner together as in the sunglasses and sunscreen example. A value of 0.0 would mean that there is no linear relationship between the movements of the two assets. The amount of risk reduction that takes place as a result of diversification is a function of correlation. The higher correlation between two assets, the less benefit, or risk reduction, there is from diversification.[1]

Now, let's look at the calculation of the standard deviation of this two-asset portfolio and let the correlation coefficient vary between −1.0 and +1.0. Let's also assume the following:

- Patty invests half of her money in each of the two company's shares.

---

[1]The correlation coefficient is actually a standardized covariance. The covariance provides an absolute measure of how two securities move over time; however, because it depends upon the volatility of the two series of returns, it can be hard to interpret. For this reason we generally standardize the covariance by the variability of the two series of returns, and that way it varies between 1.0 and +1.0.

- The standard deviation for both Apple and Coca-Cola's individual stock returns is .20.

- Correlation between the stock returns of Apple and Coca-Cola is .75.

Substituting into Equation (12–2) we get the following result:

$$\sigma_{portfolio} = \sqrt{W_{Apple}^2\sigma_{Apple}^2 + W_{Coke}^2\sigma_{Coke}^2 + 2W_{Apple}W_{Coke}\rho_{Apple,Coke}\sigma_{Apple}\sigma_{Coke}}$$

$$= \sqrt{(.5^2 \times .20^2) + (.5^2 \times .20^2) + (2 \times .5 \times .5 \times .75 \times .20 \times .20)}$$

$$= \sqrt{.035} = .187$$

> Correlation coefficient of $+0.75$ indicates the stock returns of the two firms move together but not in perfect unison.

Because the standard deviation of each of the stocks is equal to .20, a simple weighted average of the standard deviations of the Apple and Coca-Cola stock returns would produce a portfolio standard deviation of .20. However, a correlation coefficient of .75 indicates that the stocks are not perfectly correlated and produces a portfolio standard deviation of 0.187. To see how the correlation between the investments influences the portfolio standard deviation, let's look at what happens when we substitute a correlation coefficient of 1.0 into Equation (12–2):

$$\sigma_{portfolio} = \sqrt{W_{Apple}^2\sigma_{Apple}^2 + W_{Coke}^2\sigma_{Coke}^2 + 2W_{Apple}W_{Coke}\rho_{Apple,Coke}\sigma_{Apple}\sigma_{Coke}}$$

$$= \sqrt{(.5^2 \times .20^2) + (.5^2 \times .20^2) + (2 \times .5 \times .5 \times 1.00 \times .20 \times .20)}$$

$$= \sqrt{.040} = .20$$

> Correlation coefficient of $+1.0$ indicates the stock returns of the two firms move in exact unison.

When the two stocks' rates of return are perfectly positively correlated (move in unison), the standard deviation of the portfolio is simply the weighted average of their individual standard deviations. When this is the case, there is no benefit to diversification. However, when the correlation coefficient is less than $+1.0$, the standard deviation of the portfolio is less than the weighted average of the individual stock standard deviations, indicating a benefit from diversification.

Figure 12.1 illustrates the importance of the correlation coefficient as a determinant of the portfolio standard deviation. Note that the lower the correlation between the returns of the investments in the portfolio, the greater the benefit of diversification. For example, consider the diversification benefits derived from combining two investments whose returns are perfectly positively correlated $(+1)$, uncorrelated (0), and perfectly negatively correlated (-1):

Correlation between Investment Returns	Diversification Benefits
$+1$	None. No risk has been eliminated because there is no diversification realized by combining the investments because they move together perfectly. This is exactly the case we saw earlier in this chapter when we combined the sunglasses product line with the sunscreen lotion—no elimination of risk.
0.0	There is substantial value to diversification.
-1	Diversification is extremely effective in reducing portfolio risk. In fact, it is possible to select the portfolio weights for two investments whose returns are perfectly negatively correlated, such that all variability is eliminated from the portfolio return and the portfolio standard deviation is zero. Earlier, we encountered a correlation of -1.0 when we considered the sunglasses and umbrellas example.

FIGURE 12.1

Diversification and the Correlation Coefficient—Apple and Coca-Cola

The effects of diversification on the risk of the portfolio are contingent on the degree of correlation between the assets included in the portfolio. If the correlation is +1 (meaning the two assets are perfectly correlated and move together in lockstep, as was the case with sunglasses and sunscreen), then there is no benefit to diversification. However, if the correlation is −1 (meaning the two assets move in lockstep in opposite directions, as was the case with sunglasses and umbrellas), it will be possible to construct a portfolio that completely eliminates risk.

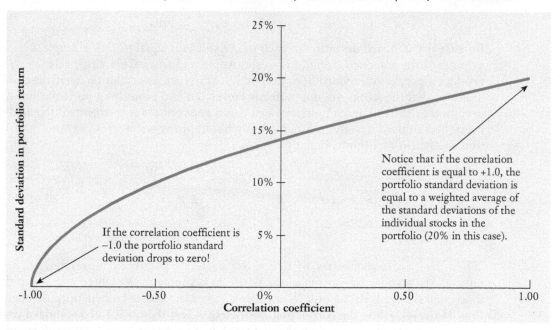

LEGEND:

Correlation	E(Return)	Standard Deviation
−1.00	0.14	0%
−0.80	0.14	6%
−0.60	0.14	9%
−0.40	0.14	11%
−0.20	0.14	13%
0.0	0.14	14%
0.20	0.14	15%
0.40	0.14	17%
0.60	0.14	18%
0.80	0.14	19%
1.00	0.14	20%

All portfolios are comprised of equal investments in Apple and Coca-Cola shares.

Finance in a Flat World
International Diversification

One of the great things about diversification is that it reduces risk without reducing expected return. That is, whereas returns are simply the weighted average of the returns on the investments that make up your portfolio, the portfolio's risk, as measured by its standard deviation, is less than the weighted average of the standard deviations of these investments. In effect, the less closely the returns of the investments move together over time, the greater the benefit of diversification. The key, then, is to include stocks in your portfolio that are not too highly correlated with each other.

One way to do this is to include more international stocks in your portfolio. International and domestic securities tend to react differently to the same economic or market information. For example, historically, when the price of oil rises, the prices of U.S. auto companies react differently than those of their Japanese counterparts because Japanese consumers prefer fuel-efficient economy cars to gas-guzzling SUVs that are a mainstay of the U.S. automakers. Thus, the price increase for oil may be bad for the economy in general, but it is worse news for domestic automakers than for Toyota and Nissan. Because of this, a portfolio that includes Japanese as well as U.S. auto stocks will be less risky than a portfolio that includes only U.S. auto stocks.

Unfortunately, international diversification appears to be less effective than it used to be. Over the past 20 years, the returns of U.S. stocks and foreign stocks have become more highly correlated. This is one of the side effects of economic globalization. Only time will tell the full extent of this trend, but it still makes sense to invest beyond the U.S. borders as part of an effort to effectively diversify.

Checkpoint 12.2

Evaluating a Portfolio's Risk and Return

Sarah Marshall Tipton is considering her 401(k) retirement portfolio and wonders if she should move some of her money into international investments. To this point in her short working life (she graduated just four years ago), she has simply put her retirement savings into a mutual fund with an investment strategy that mimicked the returns of the S&P 500 stock index (large company stocks). This fund has historically earned a return averaging 12 percent over the last 80 or so years, but recently the returns were depressed somewhat, as the economy was languishing in a mild recession. Sarah is considering an international mutual fund that diversifies its holdings around the industrialized economies of the world and has averaged a 14 percent annual rate of return. The international fund's higher average return is offset by the fact that the standard deviation in its returns is 30 percent compared to only 20 percent for the domestic index fund. Upon closer investigation, Sarah learned that the domestic and international funds tend to earn high returns and low returns at about the same times in the business cycle, such that correlation is .75. Suppose Sarah moves half her money into the international fund and leaves the remainder in the domestic fund. What is the expected return and standard deviation of the combined portfolio?

STEP 1: Picture the problem

We can visualize the expected rates of return and corresponding standard deviations as follows:

Investment Fund	Expected Return	Standard Deviation	Investment Proportion
S&P 500 Fund	12%	20%	50%
International Fund	14%	30%	50%
Portfolio			100%

The challenge Sarah faces is estimating the portfolio's expected return and standard deviation when she places half her money in each of the two mutual funds. She needs answers to place in the shaded squares in the grid.

STEP 2: Decide on a solution strategy

The portfolio expected rate of return is simply a weighted average of the expected rates of return of the investments in the portfolio. However, the standard deviation is a bit more complicated, as diversification can lead to a reduction in the standard deviation below the weighted average of the standard deviations of the investments in the portfolio. We use Equations (12–1) and (12–2) to calculate the expected rate of return and standard deviation for the portfolio.

STEP 3: Solve

Calculating the Expected Return for the Portfolio.

We use Equation (12–1) to calculate the expected rate of return for the portfolio as follows:

$$E(r_{portfolio}) = W_{S\&P\ 500}E(r_{S\&P\ 500}) + W_{International}E(r_{International})$$

$$= (1/2 \times .12) + (1/2 \times .14) = .13\ or\ 13\%$$

Calculating the Standard Deviation for the Portfolio.

The standard deviation can be calculated using Equation (12–2) as follows:

$$\sigma_{portfolio} = \sqrt{W_1^2\sigma_1^2 + W_2^2\sigma_2^2 + 2W_1W_2\rho_{1,2}\sigma_1\sigma_2}$$

$$= \sqrt{(.5^2 \times .20^2) + (.5^2 \times .30^2) + (2 \times .5 \times .5 \times .75 \times .20 \times .30)}$$

$$= .235\ or\ 23.5\%$$

STEP 4: Analyze

The expected rate of return for the portfolio comprised of 50 percent in the S&P 500 fund and 50 percent in the international fund is 13 percent, which plots exactly halfway between the two investments' expected returns on the following graph:

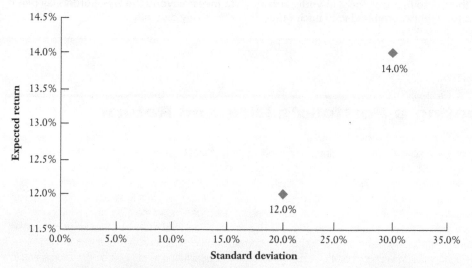

However, the standard deviation of the portfolio is not equal to 25 percent, the midpoint between the standard deviations of 20 percent and 30 percent (i.e., the weighted average of the two investments' standard deviations). It is, instead, equal to only 23.5 percent, which shows that we gain something from diversifying between the international and domestic markets. The returns in these two markets are not perfectly positively correlated, so there is some reduction in the standard deviation of the portfolio that is gained by putting the two investment alternatives together.

STEP 5: Check yourself

Evaluate the expected return and standard deviation of the portfolio of the S&P 500 and international fund where correlation is estimated to be .20 and Sarah still places half of her money in each of the funds.

ANSWER: Expected return = 13 percent and standard deviation = 19.6 percent.

Your Turn: For more practice, do related **Study Problem** 12–2 at the end of this chapter.

>> END Checkpoint 12.2

Tools of Financial Analysis—Portfolio Mean and Variance

Name of Tool	Formula	What It Tells You
Expected Portfolio Return, $E(r_{portfolio})$	$[W_1 \times E(r_1)] + [W_2 \times E(r_2)] + \ldots + [W_n \times E(r_n)]$ • $E(r_{portfolio})$ = the expected rate of return for a portfolio of n assets. • W_i = the proportion of the portfolio that is invested in asset i. • $E(r_i)$ = the expected rate of return earned by asset i.	• Measures the expected rate of return from investing in a portfolio of n different assets or securities • The portfolio return is simply an average of the rates of return expected from each security in the portfolio, where the weights reflect the relative amount of funds invested in each security.
Portfolio Variance, $\sigma_{Portfolio}$	$\sqrt{W_1\sigma_2^2 + W_2\sigma_2^2 + 2W_1\sigma_2^2 + 2W_1W_2\rho_{1,2}\sigma_1\sigma_1}$ • $\sigma_{portfolio}$ = the standard deviation in portfolio returns, • W_i = the proportion of the portfolio that is invested in asset i, • σ_i = the standard deviation in the rate of return earned by asset i, and • $\rho_{i,j}$ = correlation between the rate of return earned by assets i and j. The symbol $\rho_{i,j}$ (pronounced "rho") represents correlation between the rates of return for asset 1 and asset 2.	• Measures the return from investing in a security as a percent of the dollars invested • A higher rate of return means a greater return earned by the investment (measured as a percent of the initial investment).

Before you move on to 12.2

CONCEPT CHECK: 12.1

1. How is the expected rate of return on a portfolio related to the expected rates of return of the individual assets contained in the portfolio?

2. When the returns of two risky investments are perfectly negatively correlated, how does combining them in a portfolio affect the overall riskiness of the portfolio?

3. When the returns of two risky investments are perfectly positively correlated, how does combining them in a portfolio affect the overall riskiness of the portfolio?

12.2 Systematic Risk and the Market Portfolio

In the last section, we showed that the correlation between the returns of two stocks in a portfolio plays a key role in determining the overall risk of the portfolio. The intuition that combining imperfectly correlated investments into a portfolio reduces risk also applies to portfolios that include many different investments. In particular, those investments whose returns have low correlations with other investments in the portfolio contribute less to the overall riskiness of a diversified portfolio than those investments whose returns are highly correlated with the other investments in the portfolio.

This logic implies that we cannot simply say that the standard deviation of an individual investment is the relevant measure of the investment's risk. The standard deviation ignores how the investment's returns are correlated with the returns of other investments, and thus cannot tell us how the investment would contribute to the overall risk of an investor's portfolio. However, because there are thousands of possible investments, it is impractical to calculate all of the correlations of each investment's returns with all other investments, so coming up with a simple measure of the riskiness of an investment is clearly a challenge.

Fortunately, we have a theory, known as the **Capital Asset Pricing Model (CAPM)**, that provides a relatively simple measure of risk. This theory, which was recognized in

1990 in the Nobel Memorial Prize in Economics for Harry Markowitz and William Sharpe, assumes that investors choose to hold the optimally diversified portfolio that includes *all* risky investments. This optimally diversified portfolio that includes all of the economy's assets is generally referred to as the **market portfolio**. According to the CAPM, the relevant risk of an investment relates to how the investment contributes to the risk of this market portfolio.

To understand how an investment contributes to the risk of the market portfolio, it is useful to categorize the risks of the individual investments into two categories—*systematic* and *unsystematic*. The **systematic risk** component measures the contribution of the investment to the risk of the market portfolio. In contrast, the **unsystematic risk** component is the element of risk that does not contribute to the risk of the market portfolio. This component is effectively diversified away when the investment is combined with other investments. In summary, we can think of the total risk of an investment as follows:

Equation 12.3

$$\text{Total risk} = \text{Systematic risk} + \text{Unsystematic risk}$$

Intuitively, systematic risk refers to those risks that affect the returns of almost all investments. This is the common element of investment returns that causes the returns to be correlated. For example, if the economy were to slip into a recession, virtually all investments would experience negative returns. Alternatively, if all wars in the world were suddenly ended, it is likely that all stocks (with the exception of the firms that supply armaments and weapons of war) would experience positive returns.

The returns of some investments are more sensitive to systematic (or market-wide) risk than those of other investments. The returns of these investments will tend to be more highly correlated with the returns of most of the other stocks in a portfolio, and will thus make a substantial contribution to the portfolio's overall risk. Unsystematic risk is simply the variability in the returns of an investment that is due to events that are specific to the investment. For example, variation in the stock returns of a particular company can result from the death of the firm's CEO, a product recall, a major fire at a manufacturing plant, or perhaps an event that helps one industry at the expense of other industries. If the risk of an investment comes mainly from unsystematic risk, the investment will tend to have a low correlation with the returns of most of the other stocks in the portfolio, and will thus make only a minor contribution to the portfolio's overall risk. Thus, an investment's systematic risk is far more important than its unsystematic risk.

Diversification and Unsystematic Risk

A more descriptive term for systematic risk is **non-diversifiable risk**. Likewise, unsystematic risk is **diversifiable risk**. The idea here is that large diversified portfolios are still subject to systematic risk—in other words, systematic risk is non-diversifiable. However, unsystematic risk contributes almost nothing to the standard deviation of large diversified portfolios—in other words, unsystematic risk can be diversified away. We illustrate in Figure 12.2 that as the number of securities in a portfolio increases, the contribution of unsystematic risk to the standard deviation of the portfolio declines. This happens because the unsystematic risk of the individual stocks is uncorrelated, so the unsystematic components of the individual stock returns tend to offset one another. If a portfolio consists of stocks in different industries with very different characteristics, then as the number of stocks gets large, virtually all of the variation of the portfolio will come from systematic risk, and virtually none will come from unsystematic risk. The unsystematic component of risk has been diversified away and portfolio risk is comprised almost entirely of the systematic risk of the portfolio stocks.

Diversification and Systematic Risk

Diversification leads to the reduction and eventual elimination of unsystematic risk (the dark green area in Figure 12.2), but this does not hold true for systematic risk. Because systematic risk is common to most investments, it is a source of correlation between the returns. Indeed, by definition, the systematic sources of risk are perfectly correlated. As we learned earlier, when the returns of two investments are perfectly positively correlated, there is no risk reduction benefit to be gained by diversifying. This means that very large and diversified portfolios are likely to be influenced by the risks associated with interest rates, inflation, wars, and all other factors that affect all companies' stock returns.

Systematic Risk and Beta

Up to this point, we have examined the basic intuition behind systematic risk and why it is important to any investor. In this section, we will describe how systematic risk is measured. Recall that we have defined systematic risk as that portion of an asset's return variation that is shared with many other investments. Because investments with a high level of systematic risk tend to be highly correlated with the returns of many other investments, they are also highly correlated with the returns of a broad market portfolio that includes all investments. This suggests that we can measure the

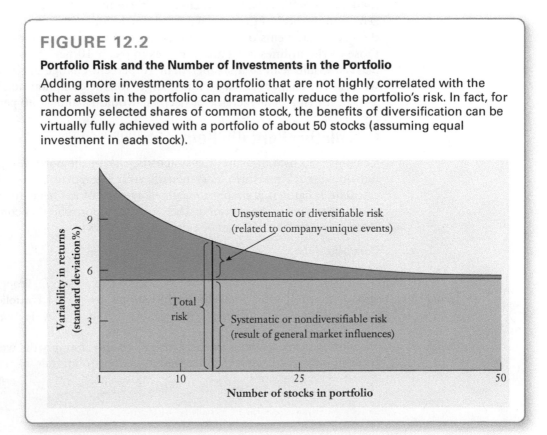

FIGURE 12.2

Portfolio Risk and the Number of Investments in the Portfolio

Adding more investments to a portfolio that are not highly correlated with the other assets in the portfolio can dramatically reduce the portfolio's risk. In fact, for randomly selected shares of common stock, the benefits of diversification can be virtually fully achieved with a portfolio of about 50 stocks (assuming equal investment in each stock).

systematic risk of an investment using the extent to which the returns of the investment correlate with the returns on the overall market portfolio.

To measure the systematic risk of an investment, we estimate what is referred to as the investment's **beta coefficient**, often simply called beta. The beta of an investment, which is referenced using the Greek letter β, measures the extent to which a particular investment's returns vary with the returns of the market portfolio. Specifically, our measure of systematic risk is referred to as the investment's beta because in practice it is estimated as the slope of a straight line such as the one found in Figure 12.3. Note that the figure contains historical monthly rates of return earned by Home Depot (HD) and a market index (the S&P 500) for the period November 2010 through October 2012. The beta for Home Depot is simply the slope of the straight line that best fits the market and Home Depot stock return pattern. In this case the slope is .67, which means that if the market increases by 10 percent over the year, Home Depot would only increase by 6.7 percent. In other words, the systematic risk of Home Depot's shares is less than the average for all stocks (the index, which has a beta of 1.00). This may seem a bit odd, but remember that we are talking about only that portion of Home Depot's return volatility that is shared with the market portfolio, or its systematic risk. The rest of the volatility in Home Depot's stock returns is unsystematic and can be diversified away by simply investing in a diversified portfolio.

Although we could estimate betas ourselves, this is generally not necessary because these estimates are readily available from a wide variety of sources. Table 12.1 contains beta estimates for several well-known companies. Note that the beta estimates vary between Yahoo Finance and MoneyCentral.com. The difference reflects differences in the time intervals of data used in the estimate. To get some perspective on the size of these beta coefficients, we can compare them to the beta of a risk-free bond, which is zero, and the beta of the overall market portfolio, which is 1. Moreover, it appears that the beta coefficients of the computer and software companies are much higher than those of the utilities companies. For example, a 10 percent rise or fall in the overall market would lead to a smaller than 10 percent change in the utility stock returns, whereas the change would be much larger for the computer and software companies. In fact, for Apple the increase or decrease would be almost 30 percent.

Calculating Portfolio Beta

The **portfolio beta** measures the systematic risk of the portfolio, just like a beta for an individual stock measures its systematic risk. The portfolio beta is straightforward to calculate because it is simply a weighted average of the betas for the individual investments contained in the portfolio. Therefore, for a portfolio that contains n different risky assets, the portfolio beta can be calculated as follows:

Portfolio Beta

$$
\begin{array}{l}
\text{Portfolio} \\
\text{Beta}
\end{array}
=
\left(
\begin{array}{l}
\text{Proportion of} \\
\text{Portfolio Invested} \times
\begin{array}{l}
\text{Beta for} \\
\text{Asset 1}
\end{array} \\
\text{in Asset 1 } (W_1) \quad\quad (\beta_1)
\end{array}
\right)
+
\left(
\begin{array}{l}
\text{Proportion of} \\
\text{Portfolio Invested} \times
\begin{array}{l}
\text{Beta for} \\
\text{Asset 2}
\end{array} \\
\text{in Asset 2 } (W_2) \quad\quad (\beta_2)
\end{array}
\right)
+ \cdots +
\left(
\begin{array}{l}
\text{Proportion of} \\
\text{Portfolio Invested} \times
\begin{array}{l}
\text{Beta for} \\
\text{Asset } n
\end{array} \\
\text{in Asset } n \ (W_n) \quad\quad (\beta_n)
\end{array}
\right)
$$

Equation 12.4 Or, written using symbols, the beta for a portfolio is simply the weighted average of the betas of individual assets that are held in the portfolio, that is,

$$\beta_{portfolio} = W_1\beta_1 + W_2\beta_2 + \cdots + W_n\beta_n$$

FIGURE 12.3

Estimating Home Depot's (HD) Beta Coefficient

A firm's beta coefficient is the slope of a straight line that fits the relationship between the firm's stock returns and those of a broad market index. In the following graph, the market index used is the Standard and Poor's (S&P) 500 index.

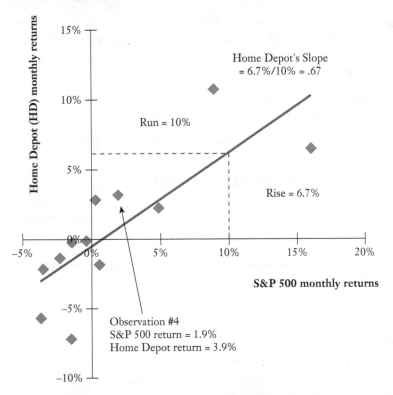

Calculating beta:

1. Visual—the slope of a straight line can be estimated visually by drawing a straight line that best "fits" the scatter of Home Depot's stock returns and those of the market index. The beta coefficient then is the "rise over the run." The blue dots on the graph correspond to values indicated on the chart.

2. Financial calculator—financial calculators have built-in functions for computing the beta coefficient. However, because the procedure varies from one calculator to another we do not present it here.

3. Excel—Excel's Slope function can be used to calculate the slope as follows: =slope(C2:C12,B2:B12)

4. Internet—there are a number of resources that can be used to obtain beta estimates on the Internet, including Yahoo! Finance and Google finance. The estimates can differ depending on the time period used to make the estimate.

Observation	Date	S&P 500 Returns	Home Depot Stock Returns
1	Nov-10	–0.23%	–1.47%
2	Dec-10	6.53%	16.05%
3	Jan-11	2.26%	4.88%
4	Feb-11	3.90%	1.90%
5	Mar-11	–0.10%	–0.43%
6	Apr-11	2.85%	0.24%
7	May-12	–1.35%	–2.34%
8	Jun-12	–1.83%	0.52%
9	Jul-12	–2.15%	–3.56%
10	Aug-12	–5.68%	–3.72%
11	Sep-12	–7.18%	–1.53%
12	Oct-12	10.77%	8.91%

Important Definitions and Concepts:

- W_i = the proportion of the portfolio that is invested in asset i,
- β_i = the beta coefficient for asset i, and
- $\beta_{portfolio}$ = the portfolio beta, which is a weighted average of the betas for the individual assets contained in the portfolio.

For example, consider the following portfolio that is comprised of three investments with betas equal to 1.20, .70, and .25. If half of the portfolio is invested in the first investment and one-fourth in each of the remaining investments, we can calculate the portfolio beta using Equation (12–4) as follows:

$$\beta_{portfolio} = W_1\beta_1 + W_2\beta_2 + W_3\beta_3$$
$$= (.50 \times 1.20) + (.25 \times .70) + (.25 \times .25) = .8375$$

The beta for the three-investment portfolio is therefore .8375.

TABLE 12.1   BETA COEFFICIENTS FOR SELECTED COMPANIES

This table contains two sources of beta estimates (Yahoo.com and MSN.com). These estimates were accessed on the same day and can vary over time because historical stock and market returns are used to calculate the beta estimates.

Company	Yahoo Finance (Yahoo.com)	Microsoft Money Central (MSN.com)
Computers and Software		
Apple Inc. (AAPL)	2.90	2.58
Dell Inc. (DELL)	1.81	1.37
Hewlett Packard (HPQ)	1.27	1.47
Utilities		
American Electric Power Co. (AEP)	0.74	0.73
Duke Energy Corp. (DUK)	0.40	0.56
Centerpoint Energy (CNP)	0.82	0.91

What if the first asset in the preceding example is a risk-free Treasury bond, which by definition has a zero beta? In this case, the portfolio beta calculation would be as follows:

$$\beta_{portfolio} = W_1\beta_1 + W_2\beta_2 + W_3\beta_3$$
$$= (.50 \times 0.00) + (.25 \times .70) + (.25 \times .25) = .2375$$

Tools of Financial Analysis—Portfolio Beta

Name of Tool	Formula	What It Tells You
Portfolio Beta, $\beta_{Portfolio}$	$(W_1 \times \beta_1) + (W_2 \times \beta_2) + \cdots + (W_n \times \beta_n)$ • $\beta_{portfolio}$ = the weighted average beta for the portfolio. • W_i = the weight of the ith security's beta, which reflects the proportion of the portfolio invested in that security.	• Measures the systematic risk of a portfolio of securities • The average is weighted by the fraction of the portfolio invested in each security.

Before you move on to 12.3
CONCEPT
CHECK: 12.2

1. What are some factors that influence the returns of a company such as Home Depot that would constitute a source of systematic risk? Unsystematic risk?

2. How many different stocks are required to essentially diversify away unsystematic risk?

12.3 The Security Market Line and the CAPM

In addition to suggesting that an investment's beta is the appropriate measure of its risk, the Capital Asset Pricing Model (or the CAPM) describes how these betas relate to the expected rates of return that investors require on their investments. *The key insights of the CAPM are that investments with the same beta have the same expected rate of return and that investors will require a higher rate of return on investments with higher betas.*

To understand the CAPM expected return equation that comes from this theory, recall that the beta of a portfolio equals the average beta of the investments in the portfolio, and the expected return of a portfolio equals the average expected return of the investments in the portfolio. For example, let's consider the relation between the beta and expected return of a portfolio invested 80 percent in the market portfolio, W_M equals 80 percent, and 20 percent in a risk-free security. The market portfolio has a beta of 1.0 and, for purposes of this example, we will assume that the expected return for the market portfolio, $E(r_M)$ is 11 percent. The risk-free security has a beta of 0, and we will assume it offers a 6 percent risk-free return, r_f equals 6 percent. The expected rate of return using Equation (12–1) for this two-investment portfolio is then:

$$E(r_{portfolio}) = \begin{pmatrix} \text{Percent of} \\ \text{Funds Invested} \\ \text{in the Market} \\ \text{Portfolio } (W_M) \end{pmatrix} \begin{pmatrix} \text{Expected Return} \\ \text{on the Market} \\ \text{Portfolio } [E(r_m)] \end{pmatrix} + \left[1 - \begin{pmatrix} \text{Percent of} \\ \text{Funds Invested} \\ \text{in the Market} \\ \text{Portfolio } (W_M) \end{pmatrix} \right] \begin{pmatrix} \text{Risk-free} \\ \text{Rate } (r_f) \end{pmatrix}$$

Because all money is invested in either the market portfolio or the risk-free security, the proportion invested in the risk-free security is equal to $(1 - W_M.)$.

$$E(r_{portfolio}) = W_M[E(r_M)] + (1 - W_M)r_f = 0.8 \times 11\% + (1 - 0.8) \times 6\% = 9.3\%$$

If we rearrange the terms in this equation slightly we have,

Equation 12.5 $E(r_{portfolio}) = r_f + W_M[E(r_M) - r_f]$

Similarly, we can calculate the portfolio beta using Equation (12–4), which says that a portfolio beta should be equal to the weighted average of the individual assets' betas that make up the portfolio. For this two-investment portfolio:

The beta coefficient for the risk-free security, β_{rf}, is equal to 0.0 because it has zero systematic risk.

$$\beta_{portfolio} = W_M \times \beta_M + (1 - W_M)\beta_f = 0.8 \times 1.0 + (1 - 0.8) \times 0.0 = 0.80$$

Figure 12.4 provides the expected returns and betas for a variety of portfolios comprised of the market portfolio and the risk-free asset. However, because the CAPM specifies that all investments with the same betas have the same expected returns, the expected return and beta combinations illustrated in this figure apply to all investments, not just to portfolios consisting of the market and the risk-free rate.

The straight-line relationship between the betas and expected returns in Figure 12.4 is called the **security market line**, and its slope is often referred to as the reward-to-risk ratio. Note that the security market line is simply a graphical representation of the Capital Asset Pricing Model. We can measure the slope of the security market line by computing the ratio of the change in expected rate of return measured along the vertical axis divided by the corresponding change in the beta for the portfolios with these two expected returns. To illustrate how this is done we compare the expected rates of return for a portfolio with zero beta (the risk-free security, which earns 6 percent) and a portfolio that has an expected rate of return of 9 percent and has a beta of 0.60. The slope then is calculated as follows:

$$\text{Slope} = \frac{\text{Rise}}{\text{Run}} = \frac{.09 - .06}{0.60 - 0.0} = \frac{.03}{.60} = 0.05 \text{ or } 5\%$$

The security market line can be expressed as the following equation, which is often referred to as the CAPM pricing equation:

Equation 12.6

$$\begin{array}{ccccc} \text{Expected Return on} \\ \text{Risky Asset } j \end{array} = \begin{array}{c} \text{Risk-free} \\ \text{Rate of Return} \end{array} + \begin{array}{c} \text{Beta for} \\ \text{Asset } j \end{array} \times \left(\begin{array}{c} \text{Expected Return} \\ \text{on the Market Portfolio} \end{array} - \begin{array}{c} \text{Risk-free} \\ \text{Rate of Return} \end{array} \right)$$

$$E(r_{Asset\,j}) = r_f + \beta_{Asset\,j}[E(r_{Market}) - r_f]$$

Note that Equation (12–6) looks very much like Equation (12–5). The weight associated with the market portfolio, W_M, in Equation (12–5) is equal to the portfolio beta in Equation (12–6). In other words, if we substitute beta for W_M in Equation (12–5), we get Equation (12–6). Hence, according to the CAPM, low-beta investments are equivalent to portfolios that are mostly invested in the risk-free investment and just slightly invested in the market portfolio. These portfolios are less risky and thus require lower rates of return. In contrast, higher-beta investments are equivalent to portfolios that are more heavily invested in the market portfolio, and hence require a higher expected rate of return. Of course, most investments cannot be viewed as simply a combination of the market and the risk-free investment. They also contain unsystematic risk. However, because unsystematic risk can be eliminated in a diversified portfolio, it is does not affect the investment's expected rate of return.

A critically important learning point here is that because systematic risk cannot be eliminated through diversification and must be borne by the investor, this is the source of risk that is reflected in expected returns. The higher the systematic risk of an investment, other things remaining the same, the higher will be the expected rate of return an investor would require to invest in the asset. This is a simple restatement of **P** Principle 2: **There Is a Risk–Return Tradeoff.**

Using the CAPM to Estimate Expected Rates of Return

The CAPM provides a theory of how risk and expected return are connected or traded off in the capital markets. For example, earlier we estimated the beta for Home Depot to be .92. If the risk-free rate of interest in the economy is currently about 3 percent, and if the **market risk premium**, which is the difference between the expected return on the market portfolio and the risk-free rate of return, is estimated to be 5 percent, we can estimate the expected rate of return on Home Depot's common stock using the CAPM from Equation (12–6) as follows:

$$E(r_{Home\,Depot}) = r_{risk\text{-}free} + \beta_{Home\,Depot}[E(r_{market}) - r_{risk\text{-}free}]$$
$$E(r_{Home\,Depot}) = .03 + .92[.05] = .076 \text{ or } 7.6\%$$

FIGURE 12.4

Risk and Return for Portfolios Containing the Market and the Risk-Free Security

The following graph depicts the systematic risk and expected rate of return for portfolios comprised of the risk-free security (with beta of zero) plus the market portfolio of all risky assets (with a beta of 1). In the most extreme case, we invest 120 percent in the market portfolio by borrowing 20 percent of the funds and paying the risk-free rate. The risk-free rate is assumed to be 6 percent, and the market risk premium (difference in the expected rate of return on the market portfolio and the risk-free rate) is 5 percent.

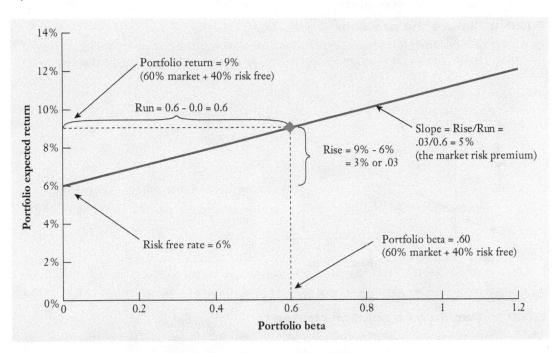

% Market Portfolio, W_{Market}	% Risk-Free Asset, $W_{Risk-free}$	Portfolio Beta, $\beta_{Portfolio}$	Expected Portfolio Return, $E(r_{Portfolio})$
0%	100%	0.0	6.0%
20%	80%	0.2	7.0%
40%	60%	0.4	8.0%
60%	**40%**	**0.6**	**9.0%**
80%	20%	0.8	10.0%
100%	0%	1.0	11.0%
120%	−20%	1.2	12.0%

The systematic risk of Home Depot's shares is reflected in the beta, which was only .92, suggesting that the shares have very nearly the same systematic risk as the market portfolio which has a beta of 1.0.

Estimating the Expected Rate of Return Using the CAPM

Jerry Allen graduated from the University of Texas with a finance degree in the spring of 2013 and took a job with a Houston-based investment banking firm as a financial analyst. One of his first assignments is to investigate the investor-expected rates of return for three technology firms: Apple (APPL), Dell (DELL), and Hewlett Packard (HPQ). Jerry's supervisor suggests that he make his estimates using the CAPM, where the risk-free rate is 4.5 percent, the expected return on the market is 10.5 percent, and the risk premium for the market as a whole (the difference between the expected return on the market and the risk-free rate) is 6 percent. Use the two estimates of beta provided for these firms in Table 12.1 to calculate two estimates of the investor-expected rates of return for the sample firms.

STEP 1: Picture the problem

Calculating the expected rates of return using the CAPM can be viewed graphically using the security market line, where the intercept of the line equals the risk-free rate (4.5 percent in this case) and the slope is equal to the market risk premium (6 percent in this case):

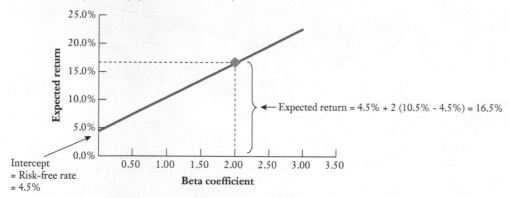

Thus, using Equation (12–6) and a beta coefficient of 2.00, the investor's expected rate of return is 16.5 percent.

STEP 2: Decide on a solution strategy

Although the expected rates of return plot along the security market line, we can solve for them directly by substituting into the CAPM formula found in Equation (12–6):

$$E(r_j) = r_f + \beta[E(r_{Market}) - r_f]$$

STEP 3: Solve

Solving for the expected return for Apple using the beta from Yahoo, the beta from MSN, a risk-free rate of 4.5 percent, and a market risk premium of 6 percent yields the following:

- Apple expected return assuming a beta of 2.90 (the Yahoo estimate of beta): 4.5% + 2.90(6.0%) = 4.5% + 17.4% = 21.9%
- Apple expected return assuming a beta of 2.58 (the MSN estimate of beta): 4.5% + 2.58(6.0%) = 4.5% + 15.48% = 19.98%

Calculating the expected return with the CAPM equation using each of the beta estimates found in Table 12.1 for the three technology firms yields the following results:

	Beta		E(return)	
	Yahoo	MSN	Yahoo	MSN
Apple Inc. (APPL)	2.90	2.58	21.90%	19.98%
Dell Inc. (DELL)	1.81	1.37	15.36%	12.72%
Hewlett Packard (HPQ)	1.27	1.47	12.12%	13.32%

(12.3 CONTINUED >> ON NEXT PAGE)

STEP 4: Analyze

The expected rate of return for the individual stocks varies somewhat depending upon the source of the beta estimate. This raises a question as to whether it makes sense to carry our estimates out to multiple decimal places.

STEP 5: Check yourself

Estimate the expected rates of return for the three utility companies found in Table 12.1, using the 4.5 percent risk-free rate and market risk premium of 6 percent.

ANSWER: American Electric Power (AEP) estimates are 8.94 percent and 8.88 percent for the Yahoo! and MSN beta estimates, respectively.

Your Turn: For more practice, do related **Study Problems** 8–8 and 8–10 at the end of this chapter.   >> **END Checkpoint 12.3**

Tools of Financial Analysis—Portfolio Beta

Name of Tool	Formula	What It Tells You
Capital Asset Pricing Model	$\dfrac{Risk\text{-}free}{Rate\ of\ Return} + \dfrac{Beta\ for}{Asset\ j} \times \left(\dfrac{Expected\ Return}{on\ the\ Market\ Portfolio} - \dfrac{Risk\text{-}free}{Rate\ of\ Return} \right)$	• Measures the expected rate of return for a risky security, where risk is measured by its systematic (or non-diversifiable) risk.

Before you begin end-of-chapter material

CONCEPT CHECK: 12.3

1. Who are Harry Markowitz and William Sharpe, and what did they do that was so important in finance?

2. How is the portfolio beta related to the betas of the individual investments in the portfolio?

3. Explain the concept of the security market line.

4. What is the market risk premium, and how is it related to the Capital Asset Pricing Model?

Applying the Principles of Finance to Chapter 12

P Principle 2: **The Risk–Return Tradeoff** The Capital Asset Pricing Model provides a model that links the risk of an investment as measured by its beta coefficient to its expected rate of return.

P Principle 4: **Market Prices Reflect Information** Market prices reflect the risk and return expectations of investors.

Chapter Summaries

Summary	Key Terms

12.1 Calculate the expected rate of return and volatility for a portfolio of investments and describe how diversification affects the returns to a portfolio of investments. (pgs. 418–427)

A portfolio is a combination of several individual investments. The expected rate of return for a portfolio is calculated as a weighted average of the expected rates of return of the individual investments. However, the calculation of the risk of a portfolio (which is reflected in the volatility of the portfolio returns) is more complicated because diversification can influence the overall volatility of the portfolio returns. Consequently, when we compute the portfolio variance or its square root, the standard deviation, we must consider the correlation of the returns of the various individual investments in the portfolio.

Correlation coefficient, page 224 A measure of the degree to which the variation in one variable is related to the variation in another. The coefficient ranges from −1 for a perfectly negative relationship to +1 for perfectly positive dependence.

Diversification, page 221 The reduction in risk that comes about by combining two or more risky assets into a portfolio where the individual assets are less than perfectly positively correlated.

Key Equations

Equation 12.1
$$E(r_{portfolio}) = [W_1 \times E(r_1)] + [W_2 \times E(r_2)] + [W_3 \times E(r_3)] + \cdots + [W_n \times E(r_n)]$$

Equation 12.2
$$\sigma_{portfolio} = \sqrt{W_1^2\sigma_1^2 + W_2^2\sigma_2^2 + 2W_1 W_2 \rho_{1,2}\sigma_1\sigma_2}$$

where

$\sigma_{portfolio} =$ the standard deviation in portfolio returns,

$W_i =$ the proportion of the portfolio that is invested in asset i,

$\sigma_i =$ the standard deviation in the rate of return earned by asset i, and

ρ_{ij} (pronounced "rho") = correlation between the rates of return earned by assets i and j.

$E(r_{portfolio}) =$ the expected rate of return on a portfolio of n assets.

$E(r_i) =$ the expected rate of return earned by asset i.

Concept Check: 12.1

1. How is the expected rate of return on a portfolio related to the expected rates of return of the individual assets contained in the portfolio?

2. When the returns of two risky investments are perfectly negatively correlated, how does combining them in a portfolio affect the overall riskiness of the portfolio?

3. When the returns of two risky investments are perfectly positively correlated, how does combining them in a portfolio affect the overall riskiness of the portfolio?

Summary	Key Terms

12.2 Understand the concept of systematic risk for an individual investment and calculate portfolio systematic risk (beta). (pgs. 427–437)

We have made an important distinction between systematic and non-systematic risk. The distinction is important because non-systematic risk can be eliminated in large diversified portfolios. Because this risk can be diversified away in large portfolios, investors do not require a premium for holding diversifiable risk. Beta measures the average sensitivity of a security's returns to the movement of the general market, such as the S&P 500. If beta is 1, the security's returns move on average 1 percent for each 1 percent change in the market returns; if beta is 1.5, the security's returns will on average move up and down 1.5 percent for every 1 percent change in the market's returns, and so forth.

Beta coefficient, page 429 A measure of the relationship between the returns of a security such as a share of common stock and the returns of the portfolio of all risky assets.

Capital Asset Pricing Model (CAPM), page 427 A model that describes the theoretical link between the expected rate of return on a risky security such as a share of stock and the security's risk as measured by its beta coefficient.

Diversifiable risk, page 428 Risk that can be eliminated through diversification.

Market portfolio, page 427 The portfolio of all risky and risk-free assets.

Non-diversifiable risk, page 428 Risk that cannot be eliminated through diversification.

Portfolio beta, page 432 The beta coefficient of a portfolio of different investments.

Systematic risk, page 428 See Non-diversifiable risk.

Unsystematic risk, page 428 See Diversifiable risk.

Key Equations

Equation 12.3
$$\text{Total risk} = \text{Systematic risk} + \text{Unsystematic risk}$$

$$\begin{array}{c} \text{Portfolio} \\ \text{Beta} \end{array} = \left(\begin{array}{c} \text{Proportion of} \\ \text{Portfolio Invested} \times \begin{array}{c}\text{Beta for} \\ \text{Asset 1} \end{array} \\ \text{in Asset 1 } (W_1) \quad\quad (\beta_1) \end{array} \right) + \left(\begin{array}{c} \text{Proportion of} \\ \text{Portfolio Invested} \times \begin{array}{c}\text{Beta for} \\ \text{Asset 2} \end{array} \\ \text{in Asset 2 } (W_2) \quad\quad (\beta_2) \end{array} \right)$$

Equation 12.4
$$+ \quad + \cdots + \left(\begin{array}{c} \text{Proportion of} \\ \text{Portfolio Invested} \times \begin{array}{c}\text{Beta for} \\ \text{Asset } n \end{array} \\ \text{in Asset } n \ (W_n) \quad\quad (\beta_n) \end{array} \right)$$

Concept Check: 12.2

1. What are some factors that influence the returns of a company such as Home Depot that would constitute a source of systematic risk? Unsystematic risk?

2. How many different stocks are required to essentially diversify away unsystematic risk?

Summary	Key Terms

12.3 Estimate an investor's expected rate of return using the Capital Asset Pricing Model. (pgs. 437–441)

The Capital Asset Pricing Model (CAPM) provides an intuitive framework for understanding the risk–return relationship. The CAPM suggests that the expected rate of return on an investment is determined by the investment's systematic risk. The model can be stated as follows:

$$\text{Expected Return on Risky Asset } j = \text{Risk-free Rate of Return} + \text{Beta for Asset } j \times \left(\text{Expected Return on the Market Portfolio} - \text{Risk-free Rate of Return} \right)$$

Note that the expected rate of return on risky asset j is equal to the risk-free rate of interest plus a risk premium that is specifically tailored to asset j by the systematic risk of the asset as measured by its beta coefficient. If the beta is equal to 1, then the expected return for the risky asset is simply the expected rate of return for the market portfolio of all risky assets.

Market risk premium, page 237 The difference in the expected rate of return on the market portfolio and the risk-free rate of return.

Security market line, page 237 A graphical representation of the Capital Asset Pricing Model.

Key Equations

Equation 12.6

$$\text{Expected Return on Risky Asset } j = \text{Risk-free Rate of Return} + \text{Beta for Asset } j \times \left(\text{Expected Return on the Market Portfolio} - \text{Risk-free Rate of Return} \right)$$

Concept Check: 12.3

1. Who are Harry Markowitz and William Sharpe, and what did they do that was so important in finance?
2. How is the portfolio beta related to the betas of the individual investments in the portfolio?
3. Explain the concept of the security market line.
4. What is the market risk premium, and how is it related to the Capital Asset Pricing Model?

Study Questions

Q12.1. Related to Regardless of Your Major: Risk and Your Personal Investment Plan on page 222) In the *Regardless of Your Major* feature box, what are the four guidelines suggested for analyzing your personal investment decisions?

Q12.2. What did Depression-era humorist Will Rogers mean when he said "People tell me about the great return I'm going to get *on* my investment, but I'm more concerned about the return *of* my investment"?

Q12.3. Describe the relationship between the expected rate of return for an individual investment and the expected rate of return for a portfolio of several investments.

Q12.4. On a recent trip home for fall break, your grandfather tells you that he has purchased the stock of two firms in the automobile industry: Toyota and Ford. He goes on to discuss the merits of his decision and one of the points he makes is that he has avoided the risk of purchasing only one company's stock by diversifying his holdings across two stocks. What do you think of his argument? Be specific and describe to your grandfather what you have learned about portfolio diversification.

Q12.5. True or false: Portfolio diversification is affected by the volatility of the returns of the individual investments in the portfolio as well as the correlation among the returns. Explain this statement.

Q12.6. Describe what is meant by systematic and unsystematic risk. How is this distinction related to an investment's beta?

Q12.7. How is the beta of a portfolio related to the betas of the individual investments in the portfolio?

Q12.8. What is the security market line? What do the slope and intercept of this line represent?

Q12.9. Describe what the Capital Asset Pricing Model tells you to your father, who has never had a course in finance. What is the key insight we gain from this model?

Q12.10. Why would we expect the reward-to-risk ratio (slope of the security market line) to be the same across all risky investments? Assume that you are able to earn 5 percent per unit of risk for investing in the stock of Company A and 7 percent for investing in Company B. How would you expect investors to act in light of this difference in reward-to-risk ratio? (Hint: Which stock do you think investors would want to buy?)

Q12.11. Presently you own shares of stock in Company A and are considering adding some shares in either Company B or Company C. The standard deviations of all three firms are exactly the same but the correlation between the common stock returns for Company A and Company B is .5, whereas it is −.5 between the common stock of Company A and Company C. How will the risk or standard deviation of your investment returns change if you decide to invest in A and B's common stock? How will the risk or standard deviation of your portfolio returns change if you decide to invest in A and C's common stock? If the expected return on the stock of all three companies is the same, how will your portfolio's expected return be impacted by your decision to invest in either B or C along with A?

Q12.12. True or false: If the standard deviation of Company A's stock returns is greater than the standard deviation of Company B's stock returns, then the beta of Stock A *must* be greater than the beta of Stock B. Explain your answer.

Q12.13. If a company's beta jumped from 1.5 to 4.5, would its expected rate of return triple? Explain why or why not. (Hint: Assume the risk-free rate is 4 percent and the market risk premium is 5 percent.)

Study Problems Portfolio Returns and Portfolio Risk

Go to
www.myfinancelab.com
to complete these
exercises online and get
instant feedback.

P12.1 (Related to Checkpoint 12.1 on page 420) (**Expected rate of return**) James Fromholtz is considering whether to invest in a newly formed investment fund. The fund's investment objective is to acquire home mortgage securities at what it hopes will be bargain prices. The fund sponsor has suggested to James that the fund's performance will hinge on how the national economy performs in the coming year. Specifically, he suggested the following possible outcomes:

State of the Economy	Probability	Fund Return
Rapid expansion and recovery	5%	100%
Modest growth	45%	35%
Continued recession	45%	5%
Falls into depression	5%	−100%

a. Based on these potential outcomes, what is your estimate of the expected rate of return from this investment opportunity?
b. Would you be interested in making such an investment? Note that you lose all your money in one year if the economy collapses into the worst state or you double your money if the economy enters into a rapid expansion.

P12.2 (Related to Checkpoint 12.2 on page 425) (**Computing the standard deviation for an individual investment**) Calculate the standard deviation in the anticipated returns found in Problem 12–1.

P12.3 (**Computing the standard deviation for a portfolio of two risky investments**) Mary Guilott recently graduated from college and is evaluating an investment in two companies' common stock. She has collected the following information about the common stock of Firm A and Firm B:

	Expected Return	Standard Deviation
Firm A's common stock	0.15	0.12
Firm B's common stock	0.1	0.06
Correlation coefficient	0.4	

a. If Mary invests half her money in each of the two common shares, what is the expected rate of return and standard deviation in portfolio return?
b. Answer question a, where correlation between the two common stock investments is equal to zero.
c. Answer question a, where correlation between the two common stock investments is equal to +1.
d. Answer question a, where correlation between the two common stock investments is equal to −1.
e. Using your responses to questions a–d, describe the relationship between correlation and the risk and return of the portfolio.

P12.4 (**Computing the standard deviation for a portfolio of two risky investments**) Answer the following questions using the information provided in Problem 12–3:
a. Answer question a of Problem 12–3, where Mary decides to invest 10 percent of her money in Firm A's common stock and 90 percent in Firm B's common stock.
b. Answer question a of Problem 12–3, where Mary decides to invest 90 percent of her money in Firm A's common stock and 10 percent in Firm B's common stock.
c. Recompute your responses to both questions a and b, where the correlation between the two firms' stock returns is –4.
d. Summarize what your analysis tells you about portfolio risk when combining risky assets in a portfolio.

P12.5 (Related to Checkpoint 12.1 on page 420) (**Portfolio expected rate of return**) Penny Francis inherited a $100,000 portfolio of investments from her grandparents when she turned 21 years of age. The portfolio is comprised of the following three investments:

	Expected Return	$ Value
Treasury bills	4.5%	40,000
Ford (F)	8.0%	30,000
Harley Davidson (HOG)	12.0%	30,000

a. Based on the current portfolio composition and the expected rates of return, what is the expected rate of return for Penny's portfolio?
b. If Penny wants to increase her expected portfolio rate of return, she could increase the allocated weight of the portfolio she has invested in stock (Ford and Harley Davidson) and decrease her holdings of Treasury bills. If Penny moves all her money out of Treasury bills and splits it evenly between the two stocks, what will be her expected rate of return?
c. If Penny does move money out of Treasury bills and into the two stocks she will reap a higher expected portfolio return, so why would anyone want to hold Treasury bills in their portfolio?

P12.6 (**Portfolio expected rate of return**) Barry Swifter is 60 years of age and considering retirement. Barry's retirement portfolio currently is valued at $750,000 and is allocated in Treasury bills, an S&P 500 index fund, and an emerging-market fund as follows:

	Expected Return	$ Value
Treasury bills	4.5%	75,000
S&P 500 Index Fund	8.0%	450,000
Emerging Market Fund	12.0%	225,000

a. Based on the current portfolio composition and the expected rates of return, what is the expected rate of return for Barry's portfolio?

b. Barry is considering a reallocation of his investments to include more Treasury bills and less exposure to emerging markets. If Barry moves all of his money from the emerging market fund and puts it in Treasury bills, what will be the expected rate of return on the resulting portfolio?

P12.7 (**Expected rate of return and risk**) Kelly B. Stites, Inc., is considering an investment in one of two portfolios. Given the information that follows, which investment is better, based on risk (as measured by the standard deviation) and the expected rate of return?

	Portfolio A		Portfolio B
Probability	Return	Probability	Return
.20	−2%	.10	5%
.50	19%	.30	7%
.30	25%	.40	12%
		.20	14%

Systematic Risk and the Market Portfolio

P12.8 (Related to Checkpoint 12.3 on page 436) (**Systematic risk and expected rates of return**) Table 12.1 contains beta coefficient estimates for six firms and from two different sources. Calculate the expected increase in the value of each firm's shares if the market portfolio were to increase by 10 percent (use either the Yahoo Finance or Microsoft Money Central beta estimates). Perform the same calculation where the market drops by 10 percent. Which set of firms has the most variable or volatile stock returns?

P12.9 (**Estimating betas**) Consider the following stock returns for B&A Trucking, Inc. and the market index:

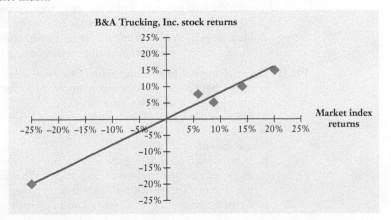

Use the visual method described in Figure 12.3 to estimate the beta for B&A. Is the firm more or less risky than the market portfolio? Explain.

The Security Market Line and the CAPM

P12.10 (Related to Checkpoint 12.3 on page 436) (**CAPM and expected returns**)
a. Given the following holding-period returns, compute the average returns and the standard deviations for the Sugita Corporation and for the market.

Month	Sugita Corp.	Market
1	1.8%	1.5%
2	−0.5	1.0
3	2.0	0.0
4	−2.0	−2.0
5	5.0	4.0
6	5.0	3.0

b. If Sugita's beta is 1.18 and the risk-free rate is 4 percent, what would be an expected return for an investor owning Sugita? (Note: Because the preceding returns are based on monthly data, you will need to annualize the returns to make them comparable with the risk-free rate. For simplicity, you can convert from monthly to yearly returns by multiplying the average monthly returns by 12.)
c. How does Sugita's historical average return compare with the return you should expect based on the Capital Asset Pricing Model and the firm's systematic risk?

P12.11 (**CAPM and expected returns**)
a. Given the following holding-period returns, compute the average returns and the standard deviations for the Zemin Corporation and for the market.

Month	Zemin Corp.	Market
1	6%	4%
2	3	2
3	1	−1
4	−3	−2
5	5	2
6	0	2

b. If Zemin's beta is 1.54 and the risk-free rate is 4 percent, what would be an expected return for an investor owning Zemin? (Note: Because the preceding returns are based on monthly data, you will need to annualize the returns to make them comparable with the risk-free rate. For simplicity, you can convert from monthly to yearly returns by multiplying the average monthly returns by 12.)
c. How does Zemin's historical average return compare with the return you believe you should expect based on the capital asset pricing model and the firm's systematic risk?

P12.12 (**Security market line**) James Fromholtz from Problem 12–1 is evaluating the investment posed in that problem and wants to apply his recently acquired understanding of the security market line concept to his analysis.
a. If the risk-free rate of interest is currently 2.5 percent, and the beta for the investment is 2, what is the slope of the security market line for the real estate mortgage security investment?
b. James is also considering the investment of his money in a market index fund that has an expected rate of return of 10 percent. What is the slope of the security market line (i.e., the reward-to-risk ratio) for this investment opportunity?
c. Based on your analysis of parts a and b, which investment should James take? Why?

P12.13 (Expected rate of return using CAPM)
a. Compute the expected rate of return for Intel common stock, which has a 1.2 beta. The risk-free rate is 3.5 percent and the market portfolio (composed of New York Stock Exchange stocks) has an expected return of 16 percent.
b. Why is the rate you computed the expected rate?

P12.14 (Expected rate of return using CAPM)
a. Compute the expected rate of return for Acer common stock, which has a 1.5 beta. The risk-free rate is 4.5 percent and the market portfolio (composed of New York Stock Exchange stocks) has an expected return of 10 percent.
b. Why is the rate you computed the expected rate?

P12.15 (Capital Asset Pricing Model) Johnson Manufacturing, Inc., is considering several investments. The rate on Treasury bills is currently 4 percent, and the expected return for the market is 10 percent. What should be the the expected rates of return for each investment (using the CAPM)?

Security	Beta
A	1.50
B	.82
C	.60
D	1.15

P12.16 (Capital Asset Pricing Model) Bobbi Manufacturing, Inc., is considering several investments. The rate on Treasury bills is currently 3.75 percent, and the expected return for the market is 10 percent. What should be the expected rates of return for each investment (using the CAPM)?

Security	Beta
A	1.40
B	.75
C	.80
D	1.20

P12.17 (Capital Asset Pricing Model) Breckenridge, Inc., has a beta of .85. If the expected market return is 10.5 percent and the risk-free rate is 3.5 percent, what is the appropriate expected return of Breckenridge (using the CAPM)?

P12.18 (Capital Asset Pricing Model) CSB, Inc. has a beta of .765. If the expected market return is 10.5 percent and the risk-free rate is 3.5 percent, what is the appropriate expected rate of return of CSB (using the CAPM)?

P12.19 (Capital Asset Pricing Model) The expected return for the general market is 10.3 percent, and the risk premium in the market is 5.3 percent. Tasaco, LBM, and Exxos have betas of .864, .693, and .575, respectively. What are the appropriate expected rates of return for the three securities?

P12.20 (Portfolio beta and security market line) You own a portfolio consisting of the following stocks:

Stock	Percentage of Portfolio	Beta	Expected Return
1	20%	1.00	16%
2	30%	0.85	14%
3	15%	1.20	20%
4	25%	0.60	12%
5	10%	1.60	24%

The risk-free rate is 3 percent. Also, the expected return on the market portfolio is 10.5 percent.

a. Calculate the expected return of your portfolio. (Hint: The expected return of a portfolio equals the weighted average of the individual stock's expected return, where the weights are the percentage invested in each stock.)

b. Calculate the portfolio beta.

c. Given the preceding information, plot the security market line on paper. Plot the stocks from your portfolio on your graph.

d. From your plot in part c, which stocks appear to be your winners and which ones appear to be losers?

e. Why should you consider your conclusion in part d to be less than certain?

P12.21 (Security market line) Your father just learned from his financial advisor that his retirement portfolio has a beta of 1.80. He has turned to you to explain to him what this means. Specifically, describe what you would expect to happen to the value of his retirement fund if the following were to occur:

a. The value of the market portfolio rises by 7 percent.

b. The value of the market portfolio drops by 7 percent.

c. Is your father's retirement portfolio more or less risky than the market portfolio? Explain.

P12.22 (Security market line) You are considering the construction of a portfolio comprised of equal investments in each of four different stocks. The betas for each stock on next page:

Security	Beta
A	2.5
B	1.0
C	0.5
D	−1.5

a. What is the portfolio beta for your proposed investment portfolio?

b. How would a 25 percent increase in the expected return on the market impact the expected return of your portfolio?

c. How would a 25 percent decrease in the expected return on the market impact the expected return on each asset?

d. If you are interested in decreasing the beta of your portfolio by changing your portfolio allocation to two stocks, which stock would you decrease and which would you increase? Why?

P12.23 (Portfolio beta and CAPM) You are putting together a portfolio made up of four different stocks. However, you are considering two possible weightings:

		Portfolio Weightings	
Asset	Beta	First Portfolio	Second Portfolio
A	2.5	10%	40%
B	1.0	10%	40%
C	0.5	40%	10%
D	−1.5	40%	10%

a. What is the beta on each portfolio?

b. Which portfolio is riskier?

c. If the risk-free rate of interest were 4 percent and the market risk premium were 5 percent, what rate of return would you expect to earn from each of the portfolios?

P12.24 (**Security market line**) If the risk-free rate of return is 4 percent and the expected rate of return on the market portfolio is 10 percent.
   a. Graph the security market line (SML). Also, calculate and label the market risk premium on the graph.
   b. Using your graph from question a, identify the expected rates of return on a portfolio with beta of .4 and a beta of 1.8, respectively.
   c. Now assume that because of a financial crisis the economy slows down and anticipated inflation drops. As a result, the risk-free rate of return drops to 2 percent and the expected rate of return on the market portfolio drops to 8 percent. Draw the resulting security market line.
   d. Now assume that because of economic fears, investors have become more risk averse, demanding a higher return on all assets that have any risk. This results in an increase in the expected rate of return on the market portfolio to 12 percent (with the risk-free rate equal to 4 percent). Draw the resulting SML. What can you conclude about the effect of a financial crisis on expected rates of return?

P12.25 (**Portfolio beta and security market line**) You own a portfolio consisting of the following stocks:

Stock	Percentage of Portfolio	Beta	Return Expected
1	10%	1.00	12%
2	25	0.75	11
3	15	1.30	15
4	30	0.60	9
5	20	1.20	14

The risk-free rate is 4 percent. Also, the expected return on the market portfolio is 10 percent.
   a. Calculate the expected return of your portfolio. (Hint: The expected return of a portfolio equals the weighted average of the individual stock's expected return, where the weights are the percentage invested in each stock.)
   b. Calculate the portfolio beta.
   c. Given the preceding information, plot the security market line on paper. Plot the stocks from your portfolio on your graph.
   d. From your plot in part c, which stocks appear to be your winners and which ones appear to be losers?
   e. Why should you consider your conclusion in part d to be less than certain?

P12.26 (**Capital Asset Pricing Model**) Anita, Inc. is considering the following investments. The current rate on Treasury bills is 4.5 percent, and the expected return for the market is 11 percent. Using the CAPM, what rates of return should Anita require for each individual security?

Stock	Beta
H	0.75
T	1.4
P	0.95
W	1.25

P12.27 (Capital Asset Pricing Model) Grace Corporation is considering the following investments. The current rate on Treasury bills is 2.5 percent and the expected return for the market is 9 percent.

Stock	Beta
K	1.12
G	1.3
B	0.75
U	1.02

a. Using the CAPM, what rates of return should Grace require for each individual security?

b. How would your evaluation of the expected rates of return for Grace change if the risk-free rate were to rise to 4.5 percent and the market risk premium were to be only 5 percent?

c. Which market risk premium scenario (from part a or b) best fits a recessionary environment? A period of economic expansion? Explain your response.

Mini-Case

Larry Lynch has been working for a year as an analyst for an investment company that specializes in serving very wealthy clients. These clients often purchase shares in closely held investment funds with very limited numbers of stockholders. In the fall of 2008, the market for certain types of securities based on real estate loans simply collapsed as the subprime mortgage scandal unfolded. Larry's firm, however, sees this market collapse as an opportunity to put together a fund that purchases some of these mortgage-backed securities that investors have shunned by acquiring them at bargain prices and holding them until the underlying mortgages are repaid or the market for these securities recovers.

The investment company began putting together sales information concerning the possible performance of the new fund and has made the following predictions regarding the possible performance of the new fund over the coming year as a function of how well the economy does:

State of the Economy	Probability	Fund Return
Rapid expansion	10%	50%
Modest growth	50%	35%
No growth	40%	5%
Recession	5%	−100%

Larry's boss has asked him to perform a preliminary analysis of the new fund's performance potential for the coming year. Specifically, he has asked that Larry address each of the following issues:

1. What are the expected rate of return and standard deviation?

2. What is the reward-to-risk ratio for the fund based on the fund's standard deviation as a measure of risk?

3. What is the expected rate of return for the fund based on the Capital Asset Pricing Model?

In addition to the information provided above, Larry has observed that the risk-free rate of interest for the coming year is 4.5 percent, the market risk premium is 5.5 percent, and the beta for the new investment is 3.55.

Based on your analysis, do you think that the proposed fund offers a fair return given its risk? Explain.

13

Options: Puts and Calls

LEARNING GOALS

After studying this chapter, you should be able to:

LG1 Discuss the basic nature of options in general and puts and calls in particular and understand how these investments work.

LG2 Describe the options market and note key options provisions, including strike prices and expiration dates.

LG3 Explain how put and call options are valued and the forces that drive option prices in the marketplace.

LG4 Describe the profit potential of puts and calls and note some popular put and call investment strategies.

LG5 Explain the profit potential and loss exposure from writing covered call options and discuss how writing options can be used as a strategy for enhancing investment returns.

LG6 Describe market index options, puts and calls on foreign currencies, and LEAPS and discuss how these securities can be used by investors.

Would you spend $229 million to keep a promise to your college roommate? That's what GoPro Inc. founder Nick Woodman did in May of 2015. Ten years earlier, Woodman made a promise to Neil Dana, his then-roommate at the University of California at San Diego, that he would pay Dana 10% of any proceeds that he received from the sale of GoPro shares. Later, Woodman and Dana struck a new agreement in which Dana would receive six million GoPro stock options rather than cash in the event that the company was sold. If Dana ever exercised those options, Woodman would have to repay GoPro by turning in some of his own shares to the company. When Dana exercised his stock options, he spent $3.6 million to acquire stock valued at $229 million. True to his word, Woodman turned in millions of his own shares to repay GoPro for their payout to his former roommate.

(Source: "GoPro's CEO Just Dropped $229 Million to Fulfill a Promise to His College Roommate," http://www.bloomberg.com/news/articles/2015-05-13/gopro-billionaire-returns-229-million-to-satisfy-10-year-vow, accessed July 6, 2015.)

Call and Put Options

LG1 LG2   When investors buy shares of common or preferred stock, they are entitled to all the rights and privileges of ownership such as receiving dividends or, in the case of common stock, having the right to vote at shareholder meetings. Investors who acquire bonds or convertible issues are also entitled to certain benefits of ownership such as receiving periodic interest payments. Stocks, bonds, and convertibles are all examples of *financial assets*. They represent financial claims on the issuing organization. In contrast, investors who buy options acquire nothing more than the right to subsequently buy or sell other, related securities. An **option** gives the holder the right to buy or sell an underlying asset (such as common stock) at a fixed price over a limited period of time.

Options are contractual instruments, whereby two parties enter into an agreement to exchange something of value. The option buyer has the right to buy or sell an underlying asset, and in exchange for this right the option buyer makes an up-front payment to the seller. The option seller receives the payment and then stands ready to buy or sell the underlying asset to the option holder according to the terms of the contract. In this chapter we'll look at two basic kinds of options: *calls and puts*.

Before we get into the details of call and put options, note that there are two other types of options: *rights* and *warrants*. Rights are issued by corporations to their existing shareholders, and they entitle shareholders to buy new shares that the company plans to issue in the near future, usually at a price that is slightly below the stock's market value. By using their rights to buy new shares, existing stockholders can avoid having their ownership stake diluted when the company issues new shares. If they do not wish to purchase new shares, existing stockholders can sell their rights on the open market. These rights typically expire within 30 to 60 days, so they hold very little investment appeal for the average individual investor.

In contrast, warrants are long-term options that grant the right to buy shares in a certain company for a given period of time (often fairly long—5 to 10 years or more). Warrants are usually created as "sweeteners" to bond issues and are used to make the issues more attractive to investors. That is, some bonds come with warrants attached, which gives bondholders the opportunity to earn higher returns if the underlying stock performs well. In essence, the buyer of one of these bonds also receives one or more warrants, and the additional upside potential that these bonds provide is called an *equity kicker*.

Basic Features of Calls and Puts

Stock options began trading on the Chicago Board Options Exchange in the early 1970s. Soon the interest in options spilled over to other kinds of financial assets. Today investors can trade puts and calls on common stock, stock indexes, exchange-traded funds, foreign currencies, debt instruments, and commodities and financial futures. For the most part, we will focus on options on common stock, though many of the principles that apply to stock options also apply to options on other kinds of financial assets.

As we will see, although the underlying financial assets may vary, the basic features of different types of options are very similar. Perhaps the most important feature to understand is that options allow investors to benefit from price changes in the underlying asset without investing much capital.

The Option Contract   Call and put options allow the holder to buy or sell an underlying security at a fixed price known as the *strike price* or *exercise price*. We'll focus our attention on calls and puts that grant the right to buy or sell shares of common stock.

A **call** enables the holder to buy the underlying stock at the strike price over a set period of time. A **put,** in contrast, gives the holder the right to sell the stock at the strike price within a set period of time. In most cases, calls and puts allow investors to buy or sell 100 shares of the underlying stock. Calls and puts are entitled to no voting rights, no privileges of ownership, and no interest or dividend income. Instead, calls and puts possess value to the extent that they allow the holder to benefit from price movements of the underlying asset.

Because call and put options derive their value from the price of some other underlying asset, they are known as **derivative securities**. In other words, call and put options derive their value from the price of the underlying asset. Rights and warrants, as well as futures contracts (which we'll study later), are also derivative securities. Although certain segments of the derivative market are for big institutional investors only, there's still ample room for the individual investor. Many of these securities—especially those listed on exchanges—are readily available for individuals to trade.

The price that an investor pays to buy an option is called the **option premium**. As we will see, an option's premium depends on the option's characteristics such as its strike price and expiration date and on the price and volatility of the underlying asset. However, don't let the word *premium* confuse you. It's just the market price of the option.

One of the key features of puts and calls is the attractive **leverage** opportunities they offer. Option buyers can invest a relatively small amount of capital, yet the potential return on that capital can be very large. To illustrate, consider a call on a common stock that gives an investor the right to buy a share of stock at a strike price of $45 a share. If that stock currently sells for $45, the call option would cost just a few dollars—for the sake of illustration, let's say $3 per option or $300 total since the option contract covers 100 shares. Next, suppose that a month or two later the underlying stock's price has increased by $10 to $55. At that point, the investor might exercise his right to buy 100 shares for $45 each. He pays $4,500 to acquire the shares and then immediately resells them at the market price for $5,500, pocketing a gain of $1,000. Thus, in a short period of time his $300 up-front investment grew to $1,000, a gain of 233%. The percentage increase in the stock over this period was just 22.2% ($10 ÷ $45), so the percentage gain on the option is much greater than the percentage gain on the stock. That's the benefit of the leverage the options provide.

Seller versus Buyer Puts and calls are a unique type of security because they are not issued by the organizations that issue the underlying stock. Instead, they are created by investors. It works like this. Suppose Abby wants to sell Carli the right to buy 100 shares of Fitbit common stock (i.e., Abby wants to sell a Fitbit call option to Carli). Abby does this by "writing a call." More generally, the individual (or institution) writing the option is known as the **option seller** or **option writer**. As the option writer, Abby sells the option in the market, so she is entitled to receive the price paid by Carli for the call option. However, Abby does have an obligation. If Carli later decides that she wants to exercise her right to buy Fitbit stock, Abby must sell those shares to her. If Abby does not already own Fitbit shares, she must go into the open market to buy them. Her obligation is legally binding, so she cannot walk away from the deal if it turns out to be a money loser for her. In contrast, Carli has no obligation. She has an option. She can buy Fitbit shares if she wants to, but she is under no obligation to do so. Puts work in much the same way. If Abby sold Carli a put option, then Carli would have the right to sell Fitbit shares to Abby, but she would not be obligated to do so. Abby, on the other hand, must stand behind her promise to buy Fitbit shares from Carli if Carli chooses to sell them. It is important to note that no matter what happens

American or European? Put and call options can be issued in either American or European form. Actually, this has absolutely nothing to do with where the options are traded but rather with when they can be exercised. An American option can be exercised on any business day that the option is traded. A European option can be exercised only on the day of expiration. Because the right to exercise is more flexible with American options than with European options, the American variety is often more desirable, and hence more valuable in the market. But that's not always true. Having the right to exercise an option prior to its expiration date does not mean that it is optimal to do so. In many cases, an investor is better off selling the option in the open market than exercising it, and in those instances, the prices of American and European options are similar.

in these transactions between Abby and Carli, Fitbit Inc. is not affected. They do not receive any money, nor do they issue or retire any common shares.

Investors trade calls and puts with the help of securities brokers and dealers. In fact, options are as easy to buy and sell as common stocks. A simple phone call, or a few mouse clicks, is all it takes. Investors trade options for a variety of reasons, many of which we will explore in this chapter. At this point, suffice it to say that trading options can be a viable investment strategy.

How Calls and Puts Work Taking the buyer's point of view, we will briefly examine how calls and puts work and how they derive their value. To start, it is best to look at their profit-making potential. For example, consider the call described earlier that has a $45 strike price and sells for $3. A buyer of the call option hopes for a rise in the price of the underlying common stock. What is the profit potential from this transaction if the price of the stock does indeed move up to, say, $75 by the expiration date on the call?

The answer is that the buyer will earn $30 ($75 − $45) on each of the 100 shares of stock in the call, minus the original $300 cost of the option. In other words, the buyer earns a gross profit of $3,000 from the $300 investment. This is so because the buyer has the right to buy 100 shares of the stock, from the option seller, at a price of $45 each, and then immediately turn around and sell them in the market for $75 a share.

Could an investor have made the same gross profit ($3,000) by investing directly in the common stock? Yes, if the investor had purchased 100 shares of stock. Buying 100 shares of a $45 stock requires an initial investment of $4,500 compared to the $300 investment needed to buy the options. As a consequence, the rate of return from buying the shares is much less than the rate of return from buying the options. The return potential of common stocks and calls differs considerably. This difference attracts investors and speculators to calls whenever the price outlook for the underlying financial asset is positive. Such differential returns are, of course, the direct result of leverage, which is similar to buying a stock on margin. We learned earlier that buying stock on margin raises the potential return that an investor might earn, but it also increases the risk of the investment.

To see the downside of buying a call option, suppose that the stock price in the previous example did not increase to $75, but instead fell to $40.50. That represents just a 10% decline from the initial $45 stock price, but when the stock is worth $40.50, the call option will not be exercised. No investor would choose to pay the $45 strike price to buy the stock when they can simply purchase shares in the open market at a cheaper price. Therefore, if the option contract expires when the stock price is at $40.50, the option will be worthless, and the option buyer's $300 initial investment will be worth nothing. Another way to say this is that the option buyer earns a return of −100% even though the stock price fell just 10%. Clearly call options have a lot of upside potential, but the risk of a total loss is also very real.

A similar situation can be worked out for puts. Assume that for the same stock (which has a current price of $45) an investor could pay $250 to buy a put option, which gives the investor the right to sell 100 shares of the stock at a strike price of $45 each. As the buyer of a put, the investor wants the price of the stock to drop. Assume that the investor's expectations are correct and the price of the stock does indeed drop to $25 a share. The investor goes into the market and purchases 100 shares for $25 each, and then she immediately exercises her put option by selling those shares for $45 each (note: the person who sold the put option is obligated to buy these shares at $45 each). The investor makes a gross profit of $20 per share, or $2,000 total on her initial investment of $250. That represents a rate of return of 700%! Of course, put options are risky just as call options are. If the stock price had risen to $50 rather than falling to $25, the put option buyer's $250 investment would be totally lost.

In some cases, investors who buy calls and puts do not actually have to trade the underlying asset to realize their profits. Instead, investors can "cash settle" their options, meaning that they receive the profits from their option in cash. This arrangement is most common when the underlying asset is difficult to trade, as would be the case when the underlying asset is a stock index rather than stock of a single company. Though most options that have a single common stock as the underlying asset are settled by exchanging the stock, to keep things simple we will illustrate the cash settlement process for a basic stock option. For example, consider once more the call option that had a strike price of $45. Suppose the underlying stock price rises to $75, so on paper at least, the call option buyer has made a gross profit of $30 per share. Rather than pay the $45 exercise price, take delivery of the shares from the call writer, and then resell the shares in the open market for $75, the call buyer may simply receive a $30 per share or $3,000 total cash payment from the call seller in exchange for the option. Settling options in cash eliminates the need for the option buyer and seller to exchange the underlying shares and the need for the option buyer to sell shares in the open market to monetize his or her profit.

Investors can trade options in the secondary market, just as they can trade other securities such as stocks and bonds. The value of both calls and puts is directly linked to the market price of the underlying common stock. For example, the secondary market price of a call increases as the market price of the underlying stock rises. Likewise, the price of a put increases as the underlying common stock price declines. Thus, another way that investors can realize their profits on options is simply to sell them in the secondary market after they have increased in value.

Advantages and Disadvantages The major advantage of investing in puts and calls is the leverage they offer. This feature allows investors to earn large profits from relatively small movements in the underlying asset without investing a large amount of money up front. Another advantage is that options allow investors to profit whether the underlying stock price goes up or down. Investors who believe that the underlying stock price will go up can buy calls, and those who believe that the stock price will fall can buy puts.

A major disadvantage of calls and puts is that the holder enjoys neither interest or dividend income nor any other ownership benefits. Moreover, because options have limited lives, there is a limited time during which the underlying asset can move in the direction that makes the option profitable. Finally, while it is possible to buy calls and puts without investing a lot of money up front, the likelihood that an investor will lose 100% of the money that he or she does invest is much higher with options than with stocks. That's because if the underlying stock moves just a little in the wrong direction, a call or put option on that stock may be totally worthless when it expires.

Options Markets

Although the concept of options can be traced back to the writings of Aristotle, options trading in the United States did not begin until the late 1700s. Even then, up to the early 1970s, this market remained fairly small, largely unorganized, and the almost-private domain of a handful of specialists and traders. All of this changed, however, on April 26, 1973, when the Chicago Board Options Exchange (CBOE) opened.

Conventional Options Prior to the creation of the CBOE, options trading occurred in the over-the-counter market through a handful of specialized dealers. Investors who wished to purchase options contacted their own brokers, who contacted the options dealers. The dealers would find investors willing to write the options. If the buyer wished to exercise an option, he or she did so with the writer and no one else—a system that largely prohibited any secondary trading. Options were written on New York and American exchange stocks, as well as on regional and over-the-counter securities, for as short a time as 30 days and for as long as a year. Over-the-counter options, known today as **conventional options**, are not as widespread as they once were. Accordingly, our attention in this chapter will focus on listed markets, like the CBOE, where individual investors do most of their options trading.

Listed Options The creation of the CBOE signaled the birth of **listed options**, a term that describes options traded on organized exchanges. The CBOE launched trading in calls on just 16 firms. From these rather humble beginnings, there evolved in a relatively short time a large and active market for listed options. Today trading in listed options in the United States is done in both calls and puts and takes place on several exchanges, the most active of which are the CBOE, the International Securities Exchange (ISE), the BATS Exchange, and the Nasdaq PHLX. Collectively those four exchanges accounted for more than half of all options trading in 2015. In total, put and call options are now traded on thousands of different stocks, with many of those options listed on multiple exchanges. In addition to stocks, the options exchanges also offer listed options on stock indexes, exchange-traded funds, debt securities, foreign currencies, and even commodities and financial futures.

Listed options provide not only a convenient market for calls and puts but also standardized expiration dates and exercise prices. The listed options exchanges created a clearinghouse that eliminated direct ties between buyers and sellers of options and reduced the cost of executing put and call transactions. They also developed an active secondary market, with wide distribution of price information. As a result, it is now as easy to trade a listed option as a listed stock.

Stock Options

The advent of the CBOE and the other listed option exchanges had a dramatic impact on the trading volume of puts and calls. Today 4.3 billion listed options contracts are traded each year, most of which are stock options. In 2015 about 89% of listed options contracts were stock options.

Listed options exchanges have unquestionably added a new dimension to investing. In order to avoid serious (and possibly expensive) mistakes with these securities, however, investors must fully understand their basic features. In the sections that follow, we will look closely at the investment attributes of stock options and the trading strategies for using them. Later, we'll explore stock-index (and ETF) options and then briefly look at other types of calls and puts, including interest rate and currency options, and long-term options.

Stock Option Provisions Because of their low unit cost, stock options (or *equity options*, as they're also called) are very popular with individual investors. Except for the underlying financial asset, they are like any other type of call or put, subject to the same kinds of contract provisions and market forces. Two provisions are especially important for stock options: (1) the price—known as the *strike price*—at which the stock can be bought or sold, and (2) the amount of time remaining until expiration. As we'll see, both the strike price and the time remaining to expiration have a significant bearing on the market value of an option.

Strike Price The **strike price** is the fixed, contract price at which an option holder has the right to buy (in the case of a call option) or sell (in the case of a put option) the underlying stock. With conventional (OTC) options, there are no constraints on the strike price, meaning that two parties can agree to whatever strike price they desire. With listed options, strike prices are standardized by the exchanges on which options trade. Generally speaking, options strike prices are set as follows:

- Stocks selling for less than $25 per share carry strike prices that are set in $2.50 increments ($7.50, $10.00, $12.50, $15, and so on).

- In general, the increments jump to $5 for stocks selling between $25 and $200 per share, although a number of securities in the $25 to $50 range are now allowed to use $2.50 increments.

- For stocks that trade at more than $200 a share, the strike price is set in $10 increments.

- Unlike most equity options, options on exchange-traded funds (discussed more fully later in this chapter) usually have strike prices set in $1 increments.

In all cases, the strike price is adjusted for stock splits. Strike prices are not adjusted for cash dividends (except for large "special" dividends), but they are adjusted when firms pay significant stock dividends (e.g., dividends paid in additional shares).

Expiration Date The **expiration date** is also an important provision. It specifies the life of the option, just as the maturity date indicates the life of a bond. The expiration date, in effect, specifies the length of the contract between the holder and the writer of the option. Thus, if you hold a six-month call on Sears with a strike price of, say, $70, that option gives you the right to buy 100 shares of Sears common stock at $70 per share at any time over the next six months. No matter what happens to the market price of the stock, you can use your call option to buy 100 shares of Sears at $70 a share. If the price of the stock moves up, you stand to make money. If it goes down, you'll be out the cost of the option.

Technically, some options can be exercised at any time up until the expiration date, while others can be exercised only on the expiration date. *American options* allow investors to exercise their right to buy or sell the underlying asset at any time up to the expiration date, while *European options* only permit investors to exercise on the expiration date. All exchange-listed options in the United States are American options, so unless otherwise noted, we will focus on those.

Expiration dates are standardized in the listed options market. The exchanges initially created three expiration cycles for all listed options:

- January, April, July, and October

- February, May, August, and November

- March, June, September, and December

Each issue is assigned to one of these cycles. The exchanges still use the same three expiration cycles, but they've been altered so that investors are always able to trade in the two nearest (current and following) months, plus the next two closest months in the option's regular expiration cycle. For reasons that are pretty obvious, this is sometimes referred to as a *two-plus-two* schedule.

For example, if the current month (also called the *front month*) is January, then available options in the *January cycle* would be January, February, April, and July. These represent the two current months (January and February) and the next two months in the cycle (April and July). Likewise, maintaining the assumption that the current month is January, available contracts for the *February cycle* would be January, February, May, and August; available contracts for the *March cycle* would be January, February, March, and June. The expiration dates, based on the front months, continue rolling over in this way during the course of the year. The following table demonstrates the available contracts under the two-plus-two system for the months of February and June:

Front Month	Cycle	Available Contracts
February	January	February, March, April, July
February	February	February, March, May, August
February	March	February, March, June, September
June	January	June, July, October, January
June	February	June, July, August, November
June	March	June, July, September, December

Given the month of expiration, the actual day of expiration is always the same: the third Friday of each expiration month. Thus, for all practical purposes, *listed options always expire on the third Friday of the month of expiration.*

Look Up an Option Chain

Put and Call Transactions Option traders are subject to commission and transaction costs when they buy or sell an option. These costs effectively represent compensation to the broker or dealer for selling the option.

Listed options have their own marketplace and quotation system. Finding the price (or *premium*) of a listed stock option is fairly easy since there are lots of online sources for option quotations. Figure 13.1 illustrates a quotation from **Nasdaq.com** for an *option chain* in which Facebook stock serves as the underlying asset. An **option chain** is a listing of all options (calls and puts) on an underlying asset for a given expiration period. The quotation in Figure 13.1 shows only a small subset of the entire option chain for Facebook, seven call option contracts on the left and seven put option contracts on the right along with their strike prices and premiums for contracts that expire on August 21, 2015. Generating a quotation for all current option contracts on Facebook produces an option chain with several hundred call and put option quotes.

Each row of Figure 13.1 provides important details about a particular option contract. Notice that in the upper left portion of the figure is a column heading that says "Calls," indicating that the first several columns in the figure contain information about various call options on Facebook stock. Moving to the right, notice the column header, "Puts," which indicates that the right side of the figure provides information about put options on Facebook shares. All of the options shown in Figure 13.1 expire on August 21, 2015. The columns headed "Last" provide the most recent market price (or premium) for each option, and the columns headed "Chg" show the change in the price of each option from the previous day's closing price. Other columns show the bid and ask prices for the options, the day's trading volume, and the open interest, which is a measure of the number of outstanding option contracts. Notice that the column headed "Root" shows the ticker symbol for Facebook, which is the underlying asset for all of these options.

Perhaps the most salient information in Figure 13.1 is the market price of each option. For example, on July 6, 2015, an August Facebook call with a strike price of $85 was quoted at $4.90 (which translates into a price of $490 because stock options trade in 100 share lots), and an August put option with the same strike price sold for $2.68.

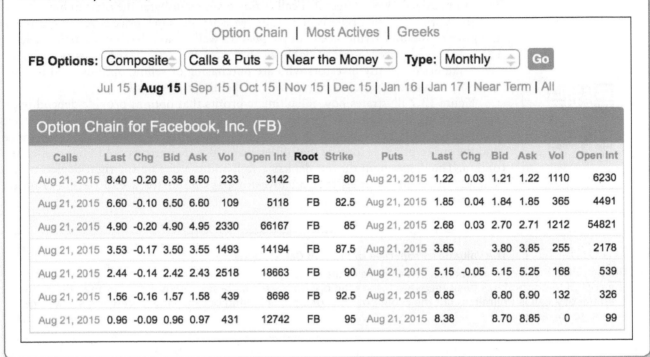

FIGURE 13.1 **Quotations for Facebook Stock Options**
The quotes for calls and puts of a specified expiration period are listed down either side of the strike price. In addition to the last price the option traded at for the day and its end-of-day bid and ask price, the change from the previous day's last transaction price is shown. (Source: Data from http://www.nasdaq.com, accessed July 6, 2015.)

Option Chain | Most Actives | Greeks

FB Options: Composite ⇕ Calls & Puts ⇕ Near the Money ⇕ **Type:** Monthly ⇕ Go

Jul 15 | **Aug 15** | Sep 15 | Oct 15 | Nov 15 | Dec 15 | Jan 16 | Jan 17 | Near Term | All

Option Chain for Facebook, Inc. (FB)

Calls	Last	Chg	Bid	Ask	Vol	Open Int	**Root**	Strike	Puts	Last	Chg	Bid	Ask	Vol	Open Int
Aug 21, 2015	8.40	-0.20	8.35	8.50	233	3142	FB	80	Aug 21, 2015	1.22	0.03	1.21	1.22	1110	6230
Aug 21, 2015	6.60	-0.10	6.50	6.60	109	5118	FB	82.5	Aug 21, 2015	1.85	0.04	1.84	1.85	365	4491
Aug 21, 2015	4.90	-0.20	4.90	4.95	2330	66167	FB	85	Aug 21, 2015	2.68	0.03	2.70	2.71	1212	54821
Aug 21, 2015	3.53	-0.17	3.50	3.55	1493	14194	FB	87.5	Aug 21, 2015	3.85		3.80	3.85	255	2178
Aug 21, 2015	2.44	-0.14	2.42	2.43	2518	18663	FB	90	Aug 21, 2015	5.15	-0.05	5.15	5.25	168	539
Aug 21, 2015	1.56	-0.16	1.57	1.58	439	8698	FB	92.5	Aug 21, 2015	6.85		6.80	6.90	132	326
Aug 21, 2015	0.96	-0.09	0.96	0.97	431	12742	FB	95	Aug 21, 2015	8.38		8.70	8.85	0	99

CONCEPTS IN REVIEW
Answers available at
http://www.pearsonhighered.com/smart

13.1 Describe call and put options. Are they issued like other corporate securities?

13.2 What are listed options, and how do they differ from conventional options?

13.3 What are the main investment attractions of call and put options? What are the risks?

13.4 What is a stock option? What is the difference between a stock option and a derivative security? Describe a derivative security and give several examples.

13.5 What is a strike price? How does it differ from the market price of the stock?

13.6 Why do call and put options have expiration dates? Is there a market for options that have passed their expiration dates?

Options Pricing and Trading

LG3 LG4 LG5 The value of an option depends to a large extent on the price of the underlying asset, but several other factors also influence option prices. Being a good options trader requires an understanding of these factors and how they influence option values. Let's look now at the basic principles of options pricing. We'll start with a brief review of how profits are derived from puts and calls. Then we'll take a look at several ways in which investors can use these options.

The Profit Potential from Puts and Calls

Although the quoted market price of a call or put is affected by such factors as time to expiration, stock volatility, and market interest rates, by far the most important variable is the price of the underlying common stock. This is the variable that drives the most significant moves in an option's price. When the price of the underlying stock moves up, calls do well. After all, a call option gives an investor the right to buy a stock at a fixed price, and that right is most valuable when the stock price is very high. When the price of the underlying stock drops, puts do well. Again, having the right to sell a stock at a fixed price is most valuable when the market price of the stock is far below the strike price. Clearly investors who are purchasing or selling options need to have some awareness of the potential behavior of the underlying stock.

Figure 13.2 illustrates how the ultimate profits that options provide depend upon the underlying stock price. By "profit" we mean the gain that an investor would receive from exercising the option just before it expires—the difference between the stock price and the strike price (as long as that difference is positive) minus the initial cost of the option. The diagram on the left depicts a call, and the one on the right depicts a put. The call diagram assumes that an investor pays $500 for a call option contract

Call Option Payoff Diagrams

FIGURE 13.2   The Valuation Properties of Put and Call Options

The payoff of a call or put depends on the price of the underlying common stock (or other financial asset). The cost of the option has been recovered when the option passes its breakeven point. After that, the profit potential of a call is unlimited, but the profit potential of a put is limited because the underlying stock price cannot go lower than $0.

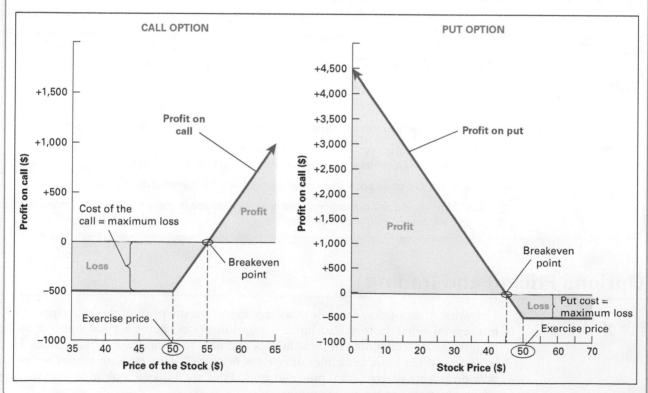

(i.e., 100 calls at $5 per call) and that the call has a strike price of $50. The graph shows how the option profit increases as the stock price rises. Observe that a call provides no cash inflow unless the price of the stock advances past the stated exercise price ($50). In other words, when the underlying stock price is below $50, the call generates a net loss of $500, which is just what the investor spent on the call. If the market price of the stock is below $50, no rational investor would exercise the option and pay $50 to buy the stock—it would be cheaper to simply buy the stock in the open market, and therefore the call expires worthless in that case.

The call option does not begin to move toward profitability until the stock price starts to move above $50. Because it costs $500 to buy the call, the stock has to move up to $55 ($5 above the strike price) for the investor to recover the $500 premium and thereby reach a breakeven point. Note, however, that even if the stock price is between $50 and $55, it's still best to exercise the option because doing so reduces the option holder's net loss. For example, if the stock price is $52, exercising the option generates a cash inflow of $200, which partially offsets the $500 option premium. For each dollar by which the stock price exceeds the breakeven point ($55), the call option's profit goes up by $100. The potential profit from the call position is unlimited because there is no upper limit on the underlying stock's price.

The value of a put is also derived from the price of the underlying stock, except that the put value goes up when the stock price goes down and vice versa. The put diagram in Figure 13.2 assumes you buy a put for $500 and obtain the right to sell the underlying stock at $50 a share. It shows that the profit of the put is −$500 unless the market price of the corresponding stock drops below the exercise price ($50) on the put. The further the stock price is below $50, the more the profit of the put option increases. Again, note that because the put cost $500, the put doesn't reach a breakeven point until the stock price reaches $45. At stock prices lower than that, the put is profitable, and it becomes more profitable the further the stock price drops. However, notice an important difference between puts and calls. The put option has a maximum profit of $4,500 because the stock price cannot fall below zero. As noted, a call's profit potential is unlimited because there is no upper limit on the stock price.

Intrinsic Value

As we have seen, the payoff of a put or call depends ultimately on the exercise price stated on the option, as well as on the prevailing market price of the underlying common stock. The relationship between an option's strike price and the underlying stock's market price determines the options intrinsic value. **Intrinsic value** represents the gross amount of money that an investor would receive if he chose to exercise a call option. For example, suppose a call option has a strike price of $50 and the underlying stock price is $60. By exercising this option an investor could receive $10 (or $1,000 for a call contract on 100 shares of stock), and that is the option's intrinsic value. If the stock price were just $45, the investor would not choose to exercise the option (because the stock is cheaper in the open market) and the call's intrinsic value would be zero. More specifically, the intrinsic value of a call is determined according to the following simple formula.

Equation 13.1

$$\text{Intrinsic value of a call} = (\text{Stock price} - \text{Strike price}) \times 100$$
$$\text{or 0, whichever is greater}$$

In other words, the intrinsic value of a call is merely the difference between the stock's market price and the option's strike price times 100. When the stock price is below the strike price, the intrinsic value is zero. As implied in Equation 13.1, a call has an intrinsic value whenever the market price of the underlying financial asset exceeds the strike price stipulated on the call. If a call option has a strike price of $50 and the underlying stock sells for $60, then the option's intrinsic value is $1,000.

A put, on the other hand, cannot be valued in the same way because puts and calls allow the holder to do different things. To find the intrinsic value of a put, we must change the order of the equation a bit:

Equation 13.2

$$\text{Intrinsic value of a put} = (\text{Strike price} - \text{Stock price}) \times 100$$
$$\text{or } 0, \text{ whichever is greater}$$

In this case, a put has intrinsic value as long as the market price of the underlying stock (or financial asset) is less than the strike price stipulated on the put.

In-the-Money/Out-of-the-Money When a call has a strike price that is less than the market price of the underlying common stock, it has a positive intrinsic value and is known as an **in-the-money** option. Look back at Figure 13.1 and notice that the first three call options listed in the figure are highlighted in yellow. Those call options have strike prices of $80, $82.50, and $85, and they are highlighted in yellow because on the day that these option quotes were retrieved, Facebook stock was selling just above $87. This means that the highlighted call options in Figure 13.1 are in the money (i.e., their strike prices are below Facebook's stock price).

When the strike price of the call exceeds the market price of the stock, the call has no intrinsic value, in which case it is known as an **out-of-the-money** option. In Figure 13.1, the calls with strike prices of $87.50, $90, $92.50, and $95 are not highlighted because they were out of the money at the time (i.e., Facebook's stock price was below the strike prices). However, an out-of-the-money call option is not worthless as long as there is still time before it expires because there is a chance that the stock price will rise above the strike price. In other words, when a call is out-of-the-money, its intrinsic value is zero but its market value is greater than zero. In such a case, we say that the option has no intrinsic value but it still has time value. An option's **time value** is the difference between its market price and its intrinsic value. In Figure 13.1, notice that the Facebook call option with a strike price of $87.50 has a quoted price of $3.53. Because the option had more than a month left before it expired, it still had plenty of time value even though its intrinsic value was zero. In the special case when the strike price of the option and the market price of the stock are the same, we say that the call option is **at-the-money**.

As you might expect, the situation is reversed for put options. A put is in-the-money when its strike price is greater than the market price of the stock. Remember, a put option grants the holder the right to sell a stock at the strike price, so that right is most valuable when the strike price is higher than the stock's current market price. In Figure 13.1, the in-the-money put options (highlighted in yellow) have strike prices of $87.50, $90, $92.50, and $95. For all four of those put options, the strike price is above the stock's then-current market price, so the options have a positive intrinsic value. A put option is out-of-the-money when the market price of the stock exceeds the strike price, which is the case in Figure 13.1 for the put options with strike prices of $80, $82.50, and $85. As with calls, an out-of-the-money put still has a positive market value as long as there is some time before the expiration date. For example, the put option with a strike price of $85 in Figure 13.1 has a market price of $2.68. This put's

FAMOUS FAILURES IN FINANCE

Ethical Lapse or Extraordinarily Good Timing?

A finance professor conducting research on executive stock option grants discovered that firms awarding these grants seemed to display extraordinarily good timing, setting the exercise prices just before a large run-up in the stock price. Perhaps firms were withholding good news until after they awarded stock option grants, knowing that when they released the news, their stock prices would rise. A few years later, Erik Lie and Randall Heron solved the puzzle of executives' remarkable timing abilities. Some firms apparently backdated their option grants, using hindsight to set the exercise price on the one date in the prior several weeks when their stock price was at its lowest point. Backdating works like this. A firm announces on June 1 that it had granted its executives stock options on April 15, using the market price of the stock that day as the option's exercise price. In fact, the firm did not actually award the options on April 15 but rather chose that date several weeks later. That gave the firm the benefit of hindsight, meaning that the firm knew that the stock's lowest point in the preceding month or two had in fact been April 15. By the time the firm announced the option grant on June 1, the options were already in-the-money because the stock price was much higher than it had been on the retroactively set grant date. In backdating options, firms failed to disclose the true value of the option grants they awarded, which in turn affected their reported earnings and taxes.

That research and the press coverage it generated prompted investigations of at least 257 firms' options grants. Some firms launched their own internal investigations, but many other companies became the target of SEC investigations. Firms involved in options backdating scandals endured serious consequences. Some executives paid fines or went to prison. Other firms settled lawsuits without admitting wrongdoing, such as Broadcom, which paid $118 million to settle a shareholder lawsuit. Most of the firms investigated saw their stock prices decline by as much as 10%.

The opportunity for senior management to engage in meaningful options backdating was largely eliminated by the Sarbanes-Oxley Act, which requires companies to publicly disclose option grants within two days. Indeed, researchers verified that the unusual market timing associated with stock option grants seemed to vanish soon after the passage of Sarbanes-Oxley.

(Source: Kenneth Carow, Randall Heron, Erik Lie, and Robert Neal, "Option Grant Backdating Investigations and Capital Market Discipline," *Journal of Corporate Finance,* Volume 15, Issue 5, December 2009, pages 562–572.)

intrinsic value is zero, but its time value is $2.68. Finally, a put is at-the-money when the strike price equals the stock price.

When firms grant stock options to their employees, they typically grant at-the-money options, meaning that the strike prices of the options are set equal to the price of the underlying stock on the date of the option grant. However, as the accompanying Famous Failures in Finance box explains, many companies got into trouble for using a bit of hindsight (and failing to disclose that) when selecting their option grant dates. This practice came to be known as options backdating.

Put-Call Parity Newcomers to options are often surprised to learn that as different as put and call options are from each other, their prices are linked under certain conditions. As long as a put and call option have the same underlying asset, the same strike price, and the same expiration date, their prices do not, and in fact cannot move independently of each other without creating an arbitrage opportunity. To explain why, consider the following example.

Suppose Nick forms a portfolio containing one share of Dow Chemical common stock and one put option with an exercise price of $50 (which we will denote $X = 50). The Dow put option expires in one year. Nick's wife Nora forms a different portfolio. She purchases a Dow call option, also having an exercise price of $50 and a one-year expiration, but Nora also buys a risk-free, zero-coupon bond with a face value of $50 (which matches the option's strike price) and a maturity of one year. Unlike Nora's call

TABLE 13.1   ILLUSTRATION OF PUT-CALL PARITY

	Price of Dow Chemical Stock in One Year						
	$35	$40	$45	$50	$55	$60	$65
Nick's portfolio							
Put with X = 50	$15	$10	$ 5	$ 0	$ 0	$ 0	$ 0
Share of stock	$35	$40	$45	$50	$55	$60	$65
Total value	**$50**	**$50**	**$50**	**$50**	**$55**	**$60**	**$65**
Nora's portfolio							
Call with X = $50	$ 0	$ 0	$ 0	$ 0	$ 5	$ 10	$15
Bond with FV = $50	$50	$50	$50	$50	$50	$50	$50
Total value	**$50**	**$50**	**$50**	**$50**	**$55**	**$60**	**$65**

option, the bond is an absolutely safe investment that will pay her $50 in one year with certainty. Let's assume that the put and call options that Nick and Nora have purchased are European options, meaning that they can only be exercised when they expire in one year.

Because Nick and Nora have invested in options on Dow common stock, the value of their portfolios will clearly depend on how Dow's stock performs. Table 13.1 shows what each portfolio will be worth next year, just as the options are about to expire, for a range of possible Dow stock values. Let's look at Nick's portfolio first. Suppose Dow stock does not perform well at all, trading at $35 next year. In that case, Nick will be fortunate to have purchased a put option. If Dow stock is trading at $35, the put option will be in the money by $15, and its market value will be $15 too since it is about to expire. Combined with the share of stock that Nick owns (which is worth $35), the total portfolio value is $50. Notice that Nick's portfolio value is fixed at $50 as long as Dow's stock price is $50 or lower. That should make sense because the put option guarantees that Nick can sell his Dow share for $50. If Dow stock finishes the year above $50 per share, the put option expires out of the money and will be worthless, but the share of Dow that Nick owns gives his portfolio upside potential. To summarize, one year from now, Nick's portfolio will be worth at least $50, and it could be worth more if Dow's stock price ends the year above $50.

Now let's turn to Nora's portfolio, and again let's start by asking what happens to her portfolio when Dow's performance is poor and the stock ends the year at $35. In that case, Nora's call option expires out of the money and has no value. However, Nora at least receives the $50 payment from her risk-free bond, so her total portfolio value is $50. The same will be true at any Dow price of $50 or lower, because when Dow's price is in that range, the call option will be worthless, and Nora will only receive the $50 bond payment. What happens if Dow stock ends the year higher, say at $55? In that scenario, Nora's call option will be worth $5, and her total portfolio will be worth $55. If Dow stock ends the year even higher, then Nora's portfolio will be worth more too because the call value will increase in step with the underlying stock. To summarize Nora's position, her portfolio will be worth at least $50, and it could be worth more if Dow's stock price ends the year above $50.

By now it should be clear that the portfolios that Nick and Nora created have identical future values, no matter what happens to the price of Dow stock. Both investors have guaranteed that their portfolio will be worth at least $50, and both will benefit from an even higher payoff if Dow stock ends the year above $50. In technical terms, we would say that Nick and Nora have *replicating portfolios*, meaning that their portfolios provide identical payoffs (i.e., Nora's portfolio replicates Nick's and vice versa) even though the portfolios contain different securities. This leads to an important concept in option pricing called put-call parity. **Put-call parity** says that the future payoffs of a portfolio containing a put option and a share of the underlying stock are the same as the payoffs of a portfolio containing a call option and a risk-free bond. Again, remember that the put and call options have to have the same underlying asset, the same exercise price, and the same expiration date. But if those conditions hold, as they do for Nick and Nora's portfolios, then put-call parity holds.

Put-call parity is important because it tells us something about the market prices of puts and calls. To be specific, if the future payoff of a put option and a stock equals the future payoff of a call option and a risk-free bond, then the prices of those two portfolios must be the same at any moment in time. If that were not true there would be an arbitrage opportunity. Remember that arbitrage means buying and selling identical assets at different prices to earn an instant, risk-free profit. Hypothetically, if the value of the portfolio containing a put and a share of stock exceeded the value of the portfolio containing a call and a risk-free bond, the traders could sell short the first portfolio and buy the second one to earn a profit. Such transactions would put upward pressure on the prices of the call and the bond, and they would put downward pressure on the prices of the stock and the put, until the values of the two portfolios were equal again. Put-call parity says that because the portfolio containing the put and the stock is essentially the same as the portfolio containing the call and the risk-free bond, the prices of those portfolios must also be the same. We can express this mathematically as follows:

Equation 13.3

$$\text{Price of a put option} + \text{Price of a stock} = \text{Price of a call option} + \text{Price of a risk-free bond}$$

Example

Suppose a certain stock sells for $71.75. You want to know the value of a put option on this stock if the strike price is $70 and the expiration date is three months from now. A call option on the same underlying stock has a strike price of $70, and it expires in three months. That call option currently sells for $6.74. There is also a risk-free, zero-coupon bond available in the market with a maturity in three months and a face value of $70 (notice the bond's face value is the same as the option's strike price). The current risk-free rate is 2% per year, or about 0.5% for a quarter (three months). This means that the bond's market price is just the present value of $70 discounted for three months, or $69.65 ($70/0.005). You can use put-call parity (Equation 13.3) to find the put option's market price:

Price of a put + Price of a stock = Price of a call + Price of a risk-free bond
Price of a put + $71.75 = $6.74 + 69.65
Price of a put = $6.74 + $69.65 − $71.75 = $4.64

Now we know one way to find the value of an option. If we know the price of the underlying stock, the risk-free interest rate, and the price of a call option, we can use put-call parity to find the value of a put. Or, if we know the value of the put, we can use it to find the value of a call. But what if we don't know the value of either option? To explore that question, let's turn our attention to the underlying forces that influence option prices.

TABLE 13.2   OPTION PRICE COMPONENTS FOR CALL OPTIONS

Stock Price	Strike Price	Options Expiring in One Month			Options Expiring in Three Months		
		Market Price	Intrinsic Value	Time Value	Market Price	Intrinsic Value	Time Value
$71.75	$65.00	$7.69	$6.75	$0.94	$9.68	$6.75	$2.93
$71.75	$70.00	$4.28	$1.75	$2.53	$6.74	$1.75	$4.99
$71.75	$75.00	$2.04	$0.00	$2.04	$4.50	$0.00	$4.50

Excel@Investing

What Drives Option Prices

Option prices can be reduced to two separate components. The first is the intrinsic value of the option, which is driven by the gap between the current market price of the underlying financial asset and the option's strike price. As we saw in Equations 13.1 and 13.2, the greater the difference between the market price of the underlying asset and the strike price on the option, the greater the intrinsic value of the call or put. We can summarize these relationships by saying that a call value is greater when (1) the strike price is lower or (2) the stock price is higher. Conversely, a put value is greater when (2) the strike price is higher or (3) the stock price is lower.

Time Value and Time to Expiration   The second component of an option price is the time value. It represents the amount by which an option's price exceeds its intrinsic value. Table 13.2 illustrates this concept by listing market prices, intrinsic values, and time values for six different call options. Three of the options expire in one month, and the other three options expire in three months. In addition, there are two call options with a strike price of $65, two with a strike of $70, and two with a $75 strike price. The current market price of the underlying stock is $71.75, so the call options with $65 and $70 strike prices are in the money, but the options with a $75 strike price are out of the money.

Look first at the call option with a strike price of $65 expiring in one month. Table 13.2 lists its market price as $7.69. This option is in-the-money and has an intrinsic value of $6.75 because it allows the option holder to buy a stock for $65 when that stock is actually worth $71.75. The option's market price is $0.94 higher than its intrinsic value, so $0.94 is the option's time value. Why would investors be willing to pay $7.69 for this option when they will only earn $6.75 if they exercise it today?

Because the option does not expire for another month, there is some chance that the underlying stock price will rise, and that possibility gives the option its time value. Moving to the right in Table 13.2, observe that the call with a $65 strike price expiring in three months has an even higher market value, $9.68. The intrinsic value of this option is also $6.75, but its time value is higher because there is more time for the stock price to move in a favorable direction.

Now look at the options with a $75 strike price. These options are out of the money, so their intrinsic values are zero. Yet both have time value. The option expiring in one month is worth $2.04, and the option expiring in three months sells for $4.50. Investors are willing to pay for out-of-the-money options because with time left before they expire, there is still a chance that the underlying stock price will rise, and it will become profitable to exercise the options. Clearly the option expiring in three months is more valuable than the one expiring next month.

There are two important general lessons from Table 13.2. The first is that the market price of an option will almost always be higher than its intrinsic value. The main exception to that general rule is that an option's price will equal its intrinsic value just before it expires. As long as an option has some time left before it expires, it will generally be worth more than its intrinsic value. The second important lesson is that an option's price will usually be higher if the option has more time remaining before it expires.

Volatility and Option Prices For most financial assets, higher volatility means higher risk, and higher risk means that investors demand a higher rate of return. Because an asset's value is linked to the present value of its cash flows, if investors discount those cash flows at a higher rate of interest, the asset's value will be lower. Think of a bond, for example. A bond's cash flows are contractually fixed, so if investors perceive that the bond's risk has increased, they will discount those cash flows at a higher rate, which in turn leads to a lower bond price. So in most cases, we can say that if an asset's volatility is higher, its value will be lower, holding everything else constant.

That's not really true with options. The reason is that options have asymmetric pay-offs. Consider a call option that is near its expiration date. As the underlying stock price rises above the call's strike price, the option's payoff rises too. So on the upside, the call's payoff moves in step with the stock. But when the stock falls below the call's strike price, the option is out-of-the-money and will not be worth exercising. That is true whether the stock price is $1 below the call's strike price or $10 below it or even $100 below the strike price. On the downside, the call's payoff is fixed at zero no matter how the stock price goes, so there is an asymmetry between a call's upside and its downside.

This asymmetry makes options more valuable if the underlying stock price is more volatile. To see this clearly, consider two stocks, A and B, which are both currently selling for $50 per share. Suppose we want to evaluate the investment potential of call options on these two stocks. Suppose these call options are at-the-money, so their strike prices are $50, and they expire in one year. Suppose A is not a particularly volatile stock, and you think that a year from now, the value of stock A will be in a range between $40 and $60. The following table shows how the payoff on a call option will vary depending on the price of stock A next year.

Price of Stock A	$40	$44	$48	$52	$56	$60
Payoff of Call	$ 0	$ 0	$ 0	$ 2	$ 6	$10

Now stock B is more volatile than stock A, so you believe that in one year its price will be in a range from $32 to $68. The following table below how payoffs on a call option will vary depending on the price of stock B.

Price of Stock B	$32	$36	$40	$44	$48	$52	$56	$60	$64	$68
Payoff of a Call	$ 0	$ 0	$ 0	$ 0	$ 0	$ 2	$ 6	$10	$14	$18

Notice that the payoffs of this option are the same as the call option on stock A when the stock price ends the year below $50, but call options on stock B offer more upside. This means that the market price of a call option on stock B must be higher than the price of a call option on stock A. To say this more generally, *the value of an option (call or put) is greater if the volatility of the underlying stock is greater.*

Interest Rates and Option Prices Previously we said that one way to value options is by using put-call parity, and part of that valuation process involves pricing a risk-free

FAMOUS FAILURES IN FINANCE

The Volatility Index

Because the volatility of the underlying asset plays a major role in option valuation, options traders track the volatility of individual stocks and of the market as a whole very closely. In fact, there is an index, called the VIX (which stands for volatility index), which provides an estimate of the volatility of the overall market. From about 1990 to 2007, the average volatility of the U.S. stock market as measured by VIX was close to 20% per year. But in the fall of 2008, after the failure of Lehman Brothers, the VIX index peaked at nearly 90%, more than four times its long-run average! Throughout the Great Recession (December 2007 through June 2009) the VIX index spiked several times to levels above its historical average, but it has been mainly below average in recent years.

bond. In general, options prices do depend on interest rates, just as the prices of other financial assets do. The general relationship is that the value of a call rises when the risk-free rate rises, and the value of a put falls with rising interest rates. Intuitively, a call option grants the holder the right to buy something at some future date. In a sense then, part of what a call option provides is the right to defer payment for a stock. When is the right to defer paying for something most valuable? It's when interest rates are high. With high rates, investors prefer to keep their money invested as long as possible, so having the right to defer payment for something is particularly valuable.

Puts work in just the opposite way. A put option gives the holder the right to sell something, that is, to receive cash in exchange for stock at some future date. Therefore, part of what a put option provides is a deferred receipt. Having to wait to receive money is never a good thing, but it is worse when interest rates are high. Thus, put values fall when the risk-free interest rate rises.

To summarize what we've learned so far, there are five major forces that influence the price of an option. They are (1) the price of the underlying financial asset, (2) the option's strike price, (3) the amount of time remaining to expiration, (4) the underlying asset's volatility, and (5) the risk-free interest rate. For stocks that pay dividends, the dividend yield can also influence the price of an option, with higher dividends leading to lower call values and higher put values.

Option-Pricing Models Some fairly sophisticated option-pricing models have been developed, notably by Myron Scholes and the late Fisher Black, to value options. Options traders use these models to try to identify and trade over- and undervalued options. Not surprisingly, these models are based on the same five variables we identified above. The Black and Scholes option-pricing model prices a European call option using this equation:

Equation 13.4

$$\text{Call price} = SN(d_1) - PV(X)N(d_2)$$

In Equation 13.4, S represents the market price of the underling stock, $PV(X)$ represents the present value of the option's strike price, and $N(d_1)$ and $N(d_2)$ are probabilities ranging from 0 to 1. Loosely speaking, these probabilities are related to the odds that the call option will expire in-the-money. In other words, as these probabilities get closer and closer to 1.0, the option is more and more likely to be exercised, and hence it is more and more valuable. The probabilities $N(d_1)$ and $N(d_2)$ depend on the numerical values of d_1 and d_2, which come from these equations:

Equation 13.4a

$$d_1 = \frac{\ln\left(\dfrac{S}{X}\right) + \left(r + \dfrac{\sigma^2}{2}\right)T}{\sigma\sqrt{T}}$$

Equation 13.4b

$$d_2 = d_1 - \sigma\sqrt{T}$$

In these two equations, S and X again represent the stock price and the strike price, respectively, T represents the time remaining before the option expires (expressed in years), σ represents the annual standard deviation of the stock's return (so σ^2 represents the variance of the stock's return), and r represents the annual risk-free interest rate. Once values for d_1 and d_2 are calculated, they must then be converted into probabilities using the standard normal distribution function. The normal distribution is simply the familiar bell curve, and the standard normal distribution is a bell curve with a mean of zero and a standard deviation of 1. The probabilities we need in Equation 13.4 represent the likelihood of drawing a number less than or equal to d_1 (and d_2) from this distribution. Figure 13.3 provides a graphical illustration of the probability that we seek. Suppose we use Equation 13.4a and find that d_1 equals 0.9. To obtain $N(d_1)$ for Equation 13.4, we need to know the area under the curve in Figure 13.3 to the left of the value 0.9.

Fortunately, Excel provides a useful function that makes it easy to calculate these standard normal probabilities. That function is denoted with = normsdist(0.9), and Excel reveals that the appropriate probability is 0.8159.

FIGURE 13.3

The Standard Normal Distribution

The standard normal distribution has a 0 mean and a standard deviation of 1. The shaded area to the left of d_1 represents the probability of drawing a value at random from this distribution that is less than or equal to d_1.

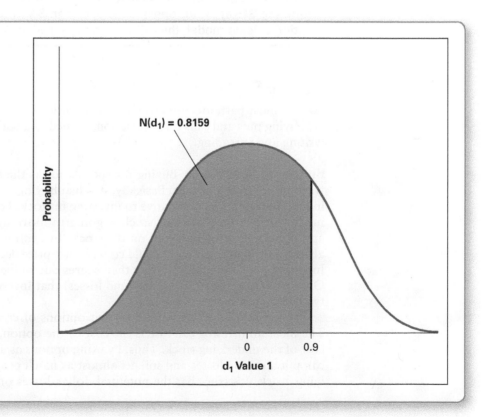

$N(d_1) = 0.8159$

Now we are ready to price a call option using Black and Scholes.

Suppose we want to price a call option that expires in three months (one-quarter of a year). The option has a strike price of $45, and the market price of the underlying stock is currently $44. The standard deviation of this stock's returns is about 50% per year, and the risk-free rate is 2%.

To price this option, start by solving for the quantities d_1 and d_2:

$$d_1 = \frac{\ln\left(\left(\frac{44}{45}\right) + \left(0.02 + \frac{0.50^2}{2}\right)0.25\right)}{0.50\sqrt{0.25}} = \frac{-0.0225 + (0.145)0.25}{0.25} = 0.0551$$

$$d_2 = 0.0551 - 0.50\sqrt{0.25} = -0.1949$$

Next, use Excel to find the standard normal probabilities attached to these values:

$$N(d_1) = \text{normsdist}\ (0.0551) = 0.5220$$

$$N(d_2) = \text{normsdist}\ (-0.1949) = 0.4227$$

Finally, plug the values for $N(d_1)$ and $N(d_2)$ into Equation 13.4 to obtain the call price:

Call price $= \$44(0.5220) - [\$45 \div (1.02)^{0.25}](0.4227) = \$22.97 - \$18.93 = \$4.04$

In this last equation, we calculate the present value of the strike price by discounting $45 at 2% for one quarter of a year. So, according to the Black-Scholes option-pricing model, the call should be priced at $4.04.

Example

Trading Strategies

For the most part, investors can use stock options in three kinds of trading strategies: (1) buying puts and calls for speculation, (2) hedging with puts and calls, and (3) option writing and spreading.

Buying for Speculation Buying for speculation is the simplest and most straightforward use of puts and calls. Basically, it is like buying stock ("buy low, sell high") and, in fact, represents an alternative to investing in stock. For example, if investors feel the market price of a particular stock is going to move up, they can capture that price appreciation by buying a call on the stock. In contrast, if investors feel the stock is about to drop in price, a put could convert that price decline into a profitable situation. Investors may buy options rather than shares due to the leverage that options provide. On a percentage basis, the gains (and losses) that investors can realize on options are typically much higher than on stocks.

Sometimes investors will argue that options offer valuable downside protection. The most an investor can lose is the cost of the option, which is always less than the cost of the underlying stock. Thus, by using options as a tool for speculation, investors can put a cap on losses and still get almost as much profit potential as with the underlying stock. It's true that the potential dollar losses on one option are less than the potential losses on one share of stock, but don't be fooled into thinking that options are less risky than stock. The likelihood of buying an option and earning a return of −100% (i.e., losing the entire investment) is quite high, whereas buying a share of stock and seeing its value drop to nothing is very unusual.

Speculating with Calls To illustrate the essentials of speculating with options, imagine that you own a stock that you feel will move up in price over the next six months. What would happen if you were to buy a call on this stock rather than investing directly in the stock? To find out, let's see what the numbers show. The price of the stock is now $49, and you anticipate that within six months it will rise to about $65. You need to determine the expected return associated with each of your investment alternatives. Because (most) options have relatively short lives, and because we're dealing with an investment horizon of only six months, we can use holding period return to measure the investment's performance. Thus, if your expectations about the stock are correct, it should go up by $16 a share and will provide you with a 33% holding period return: ($65 − $49) ÷ $49 = $16 ÷ $49 = 0.33.

But there are also some listed options available on this stock. Let's see how they would do. For illustrative purposes, we will use two six-month calls that carry a $40 and a $50 strike price, respectively. Table 13.3 compares the behavior of these two calls with the behavior of the underlying common stock. Clearly, from a holding period return perspective, either call option represents a superior investment to buying the stock itself. The dollar amount of profit may be a bit more with the stock, but note that the size of the required investment, $4,900, is a lot more too, so that alternative has the lowest HPR.

Observe that one of the calls is an in-the-money option (the one with the $40 strike price). The other is out-of-the-money. The difference in returns generated by these calls is rather typical. That is, investors are usually able to generate much better rates of return with lower-priced (out-of-the-money) options, but of course there is a greater

Excel@Investing

TABLE 13.3 SPECULATING WITH CALL OPTIONS

	100 Shares of Underlying Common Stock	Six-Month Call Options on the Stock	
		$40 Strike Price	$50 Strike Price
Today			
Market value of stock (at $49/share)	$4,900		
Market price of calls*		$1,100	$ 530
Six Months Later			
Expected value of stock (at $65/share)	$6,500		
Expected price of calls		$2,500	$1,500
Profit	$1,600	$1,400	$ 970
Holding Period Return**	**33%**	**127%**	**183%**

*The price of the calls was computed using the Black and Scholes option-pricing model, assuming a six-month expiration, 2% risk-free rate, and 40% standard deviation.
**Holding period return (HPR) = (Ending price of the stock or option − Beginning price of the stock or option) ÷ Beginning price of the stock or option.

risk that these options will expire worthless. A major drawback of out-of-the-money options is that their price is made up solely of investment premium—a sunk cost that will be lost if the stock does not move in price.

Speculating with Puts To see how you can speculate in puts, consider the following situation. You're looking at a stock that's now priced at $51, but you anticipate a drop in price to about $35 per share within the next six months. If that occurs, you could sell the stock short and make a profit of $16 per share.

Alternatively, you can purchase an out-of-the-money put (with a strike price of $50) for, say, $500. Again, if the price of the underlying stock drops, you will make money with the put. The profit and rate of return on the put are summarized below, along with the comparative returns from short selling the stock. Once again, in terms of holding period return, the stock option is the superior investment vehicle by a wide margin.

Comparative Performance Given Price of Stock Moves from $51 to $35/Share over a 6-Month Period	Buy 1 Put ($50 strike price)	Short Sell 100 Shares of Stock
Purchase price (today)*	−$ 500	
Selling price (six months later)	$1,500	
Short sell (today)		$5,100
Cover (six months later)	———	−$3,500
Profit	$1,000	$1,600
Holding period return	200%	63%**

*The purchase price of the put was computed using the Black and Scholes option-pricing model to value an identical call, then using put-call parity to value the put. Assumed 2% risk-free rate and 40% standard deviation.
**Assumes the short sale was made with a required margin deposit of 50% ($2,550).

Of course, not all option investments perform as well as the ones in our examples. Success with this strategy rests on picking the right underlying common stock. Thus, security analysis and proper stock selection are critical dimensions of this technique. It is a highly risky investment strategy, but it may be well suited for the more speculatively inclined investor.

Hedging: Modifying Risks A **hedge** is simply a combination of two or more securities into a single investment position for the purpose of reducing risk. Let's say you hold a stock and want to reduce the amount of downside risk in this investment. You can do that by setting up a hedge. In essence, you are using the hedge as a way to modify your exposure to risk. To be more specific, you are trying to change not only the chance of loss but also the amount lost if the worst does occur. A simple hedge might involve nothing more than buying stock and simultaneously buying a put on that stock with a strike price equal to the current stock price. This strategy guarantees that you can sell the stock for at least the strike price of the option, but you might be able to sell the stock for more than the strike price if the stock performs well. Another hedge strategy might consist of selling some stock short and then buying a call. There are many types of hedges, some of which are very simple and others very sophisticated. Investors use them for one basic reason: to earn or protect a profit without exposing the investor to excessive loss.

An options hedge may be appropriate if you have generated a profit from an earlier common stock investment and wish to protect that profit. Or it may be appropriate if you are about to make a common stock investment and wish to protect your money by limiting potential capital loss. If you hold a stock that has gone up in price, the purchase of a put would provide the type of downside protection you need; the purchase of a call, in contrast, would provide protection to a short seller of common stock. Thus, option hedging always involves two transactions: (1) the initial common stock position (long or short) and (2) the simultaneous or subsequent purchase of the option.

Protective Puts: Limiting Capital Loss Let's examine a simple option hedge in which you use a put to limit your exposure to capital loss. Assume that you want to buy 100 shares of stock. Being a bit apprehensive about the stock's outlook, you decide to use an option hedge to protect your capital against loss. Therefore, you simultaneously (1) buy the stock and (2) buy a put on the stock (which fully covers the 100 shares owned) with strike price equal to the stock's current market price. This type of hedge is known as a *protective put*. Suppose you purchase 100 shares of the common stock at $25 a share and pay $150 for a put with a $25 strike price. Now, no matter what happens to the price of the stock over the life of the put, you can always sell the stock for at least $25. Your maximum loss is $150, which occurs if the stock price stays at $25. In that case, there is no gain on the stock and the put expires worthless too, so your loss equals your investment in the put. At the same time, there's no limit on the gains. If the price of the stock goes up (as hoped), the put becomes worthless, and you will earn the capital gains on the stock (less the cost of the put, of course).

Table 13.4 shows the essentials of this option hedge. The $150 paid for the put is sunk cost. That's lost no matter what happens to the price of the stock. In effect, it is the price paid for the insurance this hedge offers. Moreover, this hedge is good only for the life of the put. When this put expires, you will have to replace it with another put or forget about hedging your capital.

Excel@Investing

TABLE 13.4 LIMITING CAPITAL LOSS WITH A PUT HEDGE

		Stock	Put*
Today			
Purchase price of the stock		$25	
Purchase price of the put			$1.50
Sometime Later			
A. Price of stock goes up to:		$50	
Value of put			$ 0
Profit:			
100 shares of stock ($50 – $25)	$2,500		
Less: Cost of Put	–$ 150		
Profit:	**$2,350**		
B. Price of stock goes down to:		$10	
Value of put			$ 15
Profit:			
100 shares of stock (loss $10 – $25)	–$1,500		
Value of put (profit)	$1,500		
Less: Cost of put	–$ 150		
Loss:	**$ 150**		

*The put is purchased simultaneously and carries a strike price of $25.

TABLE 13.5   PROTECTING PROFITS WITH A PUT HEDGE

		Stock	3-month Put with $75 Strike Price
Purchase price of the stock		$ 35	
Today			
Marketprice of the stock		$ 75	
Market price of the put			$2.50
Three Months Later			
A. Price of stock goes down to:		$ 50	
Value of put			$ 25
Profit:			
100 shares of stock ($50 – $35)	$1,500		
Value of put (profit)	$2,500		
Less: Cost of put	–$ 250		
Profit	**$3,750**		
B. Price of stock goes up to:		$100	
Value of put			$ 0
Profit:			
100 shares of stock ($100 – $35)	$6,500		
Less: Cost of Put	–$ 250		
Profit:	**$6,250**		

Protective Puts: Protecting Profits   The other basic use of an option hedge involves entering into the options position after a profit has been made on the underlying stock. This could be done because of investment uncertainty or for tax purposes (to carry over a profit to the next taxable year). For example, if you bought 100 shares of a stock at $35 and it moved to $75, there would be a profit of $40 per share to protect. You could protect the profit with an option hedge by buying a put. Assume you buy a three-month put with a $75 strike price at a cost of $250. Now, regardless of what happens to the price of the stock over the life of the put, you are guaranteed a minimum profit of $3,750 (the $4,000 profit in the stock made so far, less the $250 cost of the put).

You can see this in Table 13.5. Note that if the price of the stock should fall to $50, you still earn a profit of $3,750. Plus, there is still no limit on how much profit can be made. For example, if the stock goes up to $100, you earn a profit of $6,250.

Unfortunately, the cost of this kind of insurance can become very expensive just when it's needed the most—that is, when market prices are falling. Under such circumstances, it's not uncommon to find put options trading at price premiums of 20% to 30%, or more, above their prevailing intrinsic values. Essentially, that means the price of the stock position you're trying to protect has to fall 20% to 30% before the protection even starts to kick in. Clearly, as long as high option price premiums prevail, the hedging strategies described above are a lot less attractive. They still may prove to be helpful, but only for very wide swings in value—and for those that occur over fairly short periods of time, as defined by the life of the put option.

Although the preceding discussion pertained to put hedges, call hedges can also be set up to limit the loss or protect a profit on a short sale. For example, when selling a stock short, you can purchase a call to protect yourself against a rise in the price of the stock—with the same basic results as outlined above.

Enhancing Returns: Options Writing and Spreading The advent of listed options has led to many intriguing options-trading strategies. Yet, despite the appeal of these techniques, the experts agree on one important point: Such specialized trading strategies should be left to experienced investors who fully understand their subtleties. Our goal at this point is not to master these specialized strategies but to explain in general terms what they are and how they operate. We will look at two types of specialized options strategies here: (1) writing options and (2) spreading options.

Writing Options Generally, investors write options because they believe the price of the underlying stock is going to move in their favor. That is, it is not going to rise as much as the buyer of a call expects, nor will it fall as much as the buyer of a put hopes. Option writing represents an investment transaction to the writers. They receive the full option premium (less normal transaction costs) in exchange for agreeing to live up to the terms of the option.

Naked Options Investors can write options in two ways. One is to write **naked options**, which involves writing options on stock not owned by the writer. An investor simply writes the put or call, collects the option premium, and hopes the price of the underlying stock does not move against him or her. If successful, naked writing can be highly profitable because it requires essentially no capital up front. Remember, though, the amount of return to the writer is always limited to the amount of option premium received. The catch is that there is really no limit to loss exposure. The price of the underlying stock can rise or fall by just about any amount over the life of the option and, thus, can deal a real blow to the writer of a naked put or call.

Covered Options The amount of risk exposure is a lot less for those who write **covered options**. That's because these options are written against stocks the investor (writer) already owns or has a position in. For example, an investor could write a call against stock he owns or write a put against stock he has short sold. The investor can use the long or short position to meet the terms of the option. Such a strategy is a fairly conservative way to generate attractive rates of return. The object is to write a slightly out-of-the-money option, pocket the option premium, and hope the price of the underlying stock will move up or down to (but not exceed) the option's strike price. In effect, you are adding an option premium to the other usual sources of return (dividends and/or capital gains). But there's more. While the option premium adds to the return, it also reduces risk. It can cushion a loss if the price of the stock moves against the investor.

There is a hitch to all this, of course. The amount of return the covered option investor can realize is limited. Once the price of the underlying common stock exceeds the strike price on the option, the option becomes valuable. When that happens, the investor starts to lose money on the options. From this point on, for every dollar the investor makes on the stock position, he loses an equal amount on the option position. That's a major risk of writing covered call options—if the price of the underlying stock takes off, the call writer misses out on the added profits.

To illustrate the ins and outs of covered call writing, let's assume you own 100 shares of PFP, Inc., an actively traded, high-yielding common stock. The stock is currently trading at $73.50 and pays quarterly dividends of $1 a share. You decide to write a three-month call on PFP, giving the buyer the right to take the stock off your hands at $80 a share. Such options are trading in the market at $2.50, so you receive $250 for writing the call. You fully intend to hold on to the stock, so you'd like to see the price of

TABLE 13.6   COVERED CALL WRITING

	Stock	3-Month Call with $80 Strike Price
Current market price of the stock	$73.50	
Current market price of the call		$2.50
Three Months Later		
A. Price of the stock is *unchanged*:	$73.50	
Value of the call		$0
Profit:		
Quarterly dividends received	$ 100	
Proceeds from sale of call	$ 250	
Total Profit:	**$ 350**	
B. Price of the stock goes up to:	$80	**Price Where Maximum Profit Occurs**
Value of the call		$0
Profit:		
Quarterly dividends received	$ 100	
Proceeds from sale of call	$ 250	
Capital gains on stock ($80 – $73.5)	$ 650	
Total Profit:	**$1,000**	
C. Price of the stock goes up to:	$90	
Value of the call		$10.00
Profit:		
Quarterly dividends received	$ 100	
Proceeds from sale of call	$ 250	
Capital gains on stock ($90 – $73.5)	$1,650	
Less: Loss on call	–$1,000	
Net Profit:	**$1,000**	
D. Price of the stock drops to:	$71	**Breakeven Price**
Value of the call		$0
Profit:		
Quarterly dividends received	$ 100	
Proceeds from sale of call	$ 250	
Capital loss on stock ($71 – $73.50)	–$ 250	
Net Profit:	**$ 100**	

Excel@Investing

PFP stock rise to no more than $80 by the expiration date on the call. If that happens, the call option will expire worthless. As a result, not only will you earn the dividends and capital gains on the stock, but you also get to pocket the $250 you received when you wrote the call. Basically, you've just added $250 to the quarterly return on your stock.

Table 13.6 summarizes the profit and loss characteristics of this covered call position. Note that the maximum profit on this transaction occurs when the market price of the stock equals the strike price on the call. If the price of the stock keeps going up, you miss out on the added profits. Even so, the $1,000 profit you earn at a stock price of $80 or above translates into a (three-month) holding period return of 13.6% ($1,000 ÷ $7,350). That represents an annualized return of nearly 55%! With this kind of return potential, it's not difficult to see why covered call writing is so popular. Moreover, as situation D in the table illustrates, covered call writing adds a little cushion to losses. The price of the stock has to drop more than $2.50 (which is what you received when you wrote/sold the call) before you start losing money.

Besides covered calls and protective puts, there are many ways to combine options with other types of securities to achieve a given investment objective. Probably none is more unusual than the creation of so-called synthetic securities. Here's an example. Say you want to buy a convertible bond on a certain company but that company doesn't have any convertibles outstanding. You can create your own customized convertible by combining a straight (nonconvertible) bond with a listed call option on your targeted company.

Spreading Options **Option spreading** is nothing more than the combination of two or more options into a single transaction. You could create an option spread, for example, by simultaneously buying and writing options on the same underlying stock. These would not be identical options; they would differ with respect to strike price and/or expiration date. Spreads are a very popular use of listed options, and they account for a substantial amount of the trading activity on the listed options exchanges. These spreads go by a variety of exotic names, such as *bull spreads, bear spreads, money spreads, vertical spreads,* and *butterfly spreads.* Each spread is different and each is constructed to meet a certain type of investment goal.

Consider, for example, a *vertical spread.* It would be set up by buying a call at one strike price and then writing a call (on the same stock and for the same expiration date) at a higher strike price. For instance, you could buy an August call on Facebook at a strike price of, say, $80 and simultaneously sell (write) an August call on Facebook at a strike price of $85. If you refer back to Figure 13.1, you will see that the first option would cost you $8.40, while the option that you sell would bring in $4.90. Therefore, the net cost of this position is $3.50. Strange as it may sound, such a position would generate a hefty return if the price of the underlying stock went up by just a few points. Suppose, for example, that when these options expire, the price of Facebook stock is $88. The call option that you purchased would pay you $8, but you'd have to pay $3 to the buyer of the option you wrote, so your net cash payoff at expiration would be $5. A $5 return on an investment of $3.50 represents a rate of return of almost 43%! Other spreads are used to profit from a falling market. Still others try to make money when the price of the underlying stock moves either up or down.

Whatever the objective, most spreads are created to take advantage of differences in prevailing option prices. The payoff from spreading is usually substantial, but so is the risk. In fact, some spreads that seem to involve almost no risk may end up with devastating results if the market and the difference between option premiums move against the investor.

How Do Straddles Work?

Option Straddles A variation on this theme involves an **option straddle.** This is the simultaneous purchase (or sale) of both a put and a call on the same underlying common stock. Unlike spreads, straddles normally involve the same strike price and expiration date. Here the object is to earn a profit from either a big or a small swing in the price of the underlying common stock.

For example, in a *long straddle* you buy an equal number of puts and calls. You make money in a long straddle when the underlying stock undergoes a big change in price—either up or down. If the price of the stock shoots way up, you make money on the call side of the straddle but are out the cost of the puts. If the price of the stock plummets, you make money on the puts, but the calls are useless. In either case, so long as you make more money on one side than the cost of the options for the other side, you're ahead of the game.

As an example, refer again to Figure 13.1. Imagine that you buy a Facebook call and a put, both having a strike of $87.50 and an August expiration date. The call costs

$3.53, and the put costs $3.85, so the total cost of this position is $7.38. To make money on this transaction, Facebook stock would have to fall more than $7.38 below the $87.50 strike price or rise more than $7.38 above it. If Facebook stock stays within that range, your position loses money.

In a similar fashion, in a *short straddle,* you sell/write an equal number of puts and calls with the same underlying stock, the same strike price, and the same expiration date. You make money in this position when the price of the underlying stock goes nowhere. In effect, you get to keep all or most of the option premiums you collected when you wrote the options.

Except for obvious structural differences, the principles that underlie the creation of straddles are much like those for spreads. The object is to combine options that will enable you to capture the benefits of certain types of stock price behavior. But keep in mind that if the prices of the underlying stock and/or the option premiums do not behave in the anticipated manner, you lose. Spreads and straddles are extremely tricky and should be used only by knowledgeable investors.

CONCEPTS IN REVIEW

Answers available at
http://www.pearsonhighered
.com/smart

13.7   Briefly explain how you would make money on (a) a call option and (b) a put option. Do you have to exercise the option to capture the profit?

13.8   How do you find the intrinsic value of a call? Of a put? Does an out-of-the-money option have intrinsic value?

13.9   Name five variables that can affect the price of options, and briefly explain how each affects prices. How important are intrinsic value and time value to in-the-money options? To out-of-the-money options?

13.10   Describe three ways in which investors can use stock options.

13.11   What's the most that can be made from writing calls? Why would an investor want to write covered calls? Explain how you can reduce the risk on an underlying common stock by writing covered calls.

Stock-Index and Other Types of Options

 Imagine being able to buy or sell a major stock market index like the S&P 500—and at a reasonable cost. Think of what you could do. If you felt the market was heading up, you could invest in a security that tracks the price of the S&P 500 Index and make money when the market goes up. No longer would you have to go through the process of selecting specific stocks that you hope will capture the market's performance. Rather, you could play the market as a whole. Of course, you can do this by purchasing a mutual fund or an ETF that is indexed to the S&P 500, but you can also accomplish that goal with stock-index options—puts and calls that are written on major stock market indexes. Index options have been around since 1983 and have become immensely popular with both individual and institutional investors. Here we will take a closer look at these popular and often highly profitable investments.

Contract Provisions of Stock-Index Options

Basically, a **stock-index option** is a put or call written on a specific stock market index. The underlying security in this case is the specific market index. Thus, when the market index moves in one direction or another, the value of the index option moves accordingly. Because there are no stocks or other financial assets backing these options, settlement is defined in terms of cash. Specifically, the cash value of an index option is equal to 100 times the published market index that underlies the option. For example, if the S&P 500 is at 2,100, then the value of an S&P 500 Index option will be $100 \times 2,100 = $210,000$. If the underlying index moves up or down in the market, so will the cash value of the option. In addition, whereas most options on individual stocks are American options and can be exercised at any time, stock index options may be American or European options, so they may be exercisable only on the expiration date.

Today put and call options are available on more than 100 stock indexes. These include options on just about every major U.S. stock market index or average (such as the Dow Jones Industrial Average, the S&P 500, the Russell 2000, and the Nasdaq 100), options on a handful of foreign markets (e.g., China, Mexico, Japan, Hong Kong, and the Europe sector), and options on different segments of the market (pharmaceuticals, oil services, semiconductors, bank, and utility indexes). In 2015 about 10% of traded option contracts were index options, and a large percentage of these contracts were on five of the leading stock indexes:

- S&P 500 Index (SPX)

- Russell 2000 Index (RUT)

- Nasdaq 100 Index (NDX)

- S&P 100 Index (OEX)

- Dow Jones Industrial Average (DJX)

The S&P 500 Index captures the market behavior of large-cap stocks. The Russell 2000 Index measures the performance of the small-cap stocks in the United States. The Nasdaq 100 Index tracks the behavior of the 100 largest nonfinancial stocks listed on Nasdaq and is composed of mostly large, high-tech companies (such as Intel and Cisco). The S&P 100 Index is another large-cap index composed of 100 stocks, drawn from the S&P 500, that have actively traded stock options. Another popular index is the DJIA Index, which measures the blue-chip segment of the market and is one of the most actively traded index options. Options on the S&P 500 are, by far, the most popular instruments. Indeed, there's more trading in SPX options contracts than in all the other index options combined. Among the options exchanges that currently deal in index options, the CBOE dominates the market, accounting for more than 98% of the trades in 2015.

Both puts and calls are available on index options. They are valued and have issue characteristics like any other put or call. That is, a put lets a holder profit from a drop in the market. (When the underlying market index goes down, the value of a put goes up.) A call enables the holder to profit from a market that's going up. Also, as Figure 13.4 shows, index options have a quotation system that is the same as for stock options, except for the fact that the strike price is an index level.

Putting a Value on Stock-Index Options As is true of equity options, the market price of index options is a function of the difference between the strike price on the option (stated in terms of the underlying index) and the latest published stock market index. To illustrate, consider the highly popular S&P 500 Index traded on the CBOE.

Let's say the S&P 500 Index recently closed at 2058 and the August call has a strike price of 2055. A stock-index call will have a positive value so long as the underlying index exceeds the index strike price (just the opposite for puts). The intrinsic value of this call is 2058 − 2053 = 3.

Suppose that the call actually trades at 49.92, which is 46.92 points above the call's intrinsic value. This difference is the option's time value.

Example

If the S&P 500 Index in our example were to go up to, say, 2200 by late August (the expiration date of the call), this option would be quoted at 2200 − 2055 = 145. Because index options (like stock options) are valued in multiples of $100, this contract would be worth $14,500. Thus, if you had purchased this option when it was trading at $49.92, it would have cost you $49.92 × $100 = $4,992 and, in less than a month, would have generated a profit of $14,500 −$4,992 = $9,508. That translates into a holding period return of a whopping 90%.

FIGURE 13.4   Quotations on Index Options

The quotation system used with index options is just like that used with stock options: strikes and expiration dates are shown along with option prices and volumes. The biggest differences are that the option strikes and closing values for the underlying asset are shown as index levels. The closing S&P 500 Index level on the day of this quotation was 2051. (Source: Data from http://www.nasdaq.com, accessed July 9, 2015.)

Option Chain | Most Actives | Greeks

SPX Options: Composite | Calls & Puts | Near the Money | **Type:** Monthly | Go

Jul 15 | **Aug 15** | Sep 15 | Oct 15 | Dec 15 | Jan 16 | Mar 16 | Jun 16 | Dec 16 | Jun 17 | Dec 17 | Near Term | All

Option Chain for S&P 500 (SPX)

Calls	Last	Chg	Bid	Ask	Vol	Open Int	Root	Strike	Puts	Last	Chg	Bid	Ask	Vol	Open Int
Aug 21, 2015	47.50		50.40	52.00	0	473	SPX	2045	Aug 21, 2015	42.10	-6.00	42.60	44.40	216	517
Aug 21, 2015	48.25	3.05	47.30	48.80	1671	10615	SPX	2050	Aug 21, 2015	45.78	-6.22	44.40	46.20	3445	38172
Aug 21, 2015	49.92	7.67	44.10	45.60	12	557	SPX	2055	Aug 21, 2015	44.45	-6.55	46.30	48.10	32	506
Aug 21, 2015	42.20	2.90	41.40	43.20	40	969	SPX	2060	Aug 21, 2015	49.64	-5.91	48.40	50.50	99	3221
Aug 21, 2015	39.05	3.30	38.40	39.60	400	369	SPX	2065	Aug 21, 2015	47.00	-10.75	49.70	52.50	121	765
Aug 21, 2015	36.35	3.35	35.50	37.40	8	1420	SPX	2070	Aug 21, 2015	49.90	-10.84	51.80	54.60	7	7177

Full Value versus Fractional Value Most broad-based index options use the full market value of the underlying index for purposes of options trading and valuation. That's not the case, however, with two of the Dow Jones measures: The option on the Dow Jones Industrial Average is based on 1% of the actual Industrial Average, and the Dow Transportation Average option is based on 10% of the actual average. For example, if the DJIA is at 11,260, the index option would be valued at 1% of that amount, or 112.60. Thus, the cash value of this option is not $100 times the underlying DJIA but $100 times 1% of the DJIA, which equals the Dow Jones Industrial Average itself: $100 \times 112.60 = \$11,260$.

Fortunately, the option strike prices are also based on the same 1% of the Dow, so there is no effect on option valuation. What matters is the difference between the strike price on the option and 1% of the DJIA. For instance, suppose that the DJIA closes at 11,260, which means that the DJIA option index would close at 112.60. A call option on this index might have a strike price of 110, which would mean that the call is slightly in-the-money with an intrinsic value of 2.60. If the option were not set to expire immediately, its market price would be higher, with the difference between the market price and 2.60 being the option's time value.

Another type of option that is traded at 10% $(1 \div 10)$ of the value of the underlying index is the "mini" index option. For example, the Mini-NDX Index (MNX) is set at 10% of the value of the Nasdaq 100. "Minis" also exist for the Nasdaq composite, the S&P 500, the Russell 2000, and the FTSE 250 (an index of mid-cap stocks in the United Kingdom), among others.

Investment Uses

Although index options, like equity options, can be used in spreads, straddles, or even covered calls, they are perhaps used most often for speculating or for hedging. When used as a speculative investment, index options give investors an opportunity to play the market as a whole, with a relatively small amount of capital. Like any other put or call, index options provide attractive leverage opportunities and at the same time limit exposure to loss to the price paid for the option.

Index Options as Hedging Vehicles Index options are equally effective as hedging vehicles. In fact, hedging is a major use of index options and accounts for a good deal of the trading in these securities. To see how these options can be used for hedging, assume that you hold a diversified portfolio of, say, a dozen different stocks and you think the market is heading down. One way to protect your capital would be to sell all of your stocks. However, that could be expensive, especially if you plan to get back into the market after it drops, and it could lead to a good deal of unnecessary taxes. Fortunately, there is a way to "have your cake and eat it, too" and that is to hedge your stock portfolio with a stock index put. In this way, if the market does go down, you'll make money on your puts, which you then can use to buy more stocks at the lower prices. On the other hand, if the market continues to go up, you'll be out only the cost of the puts. That amount could well be recovered from the increased value of your stock holdings. The principles of hedging with stock-index options are exactly the same as those for hedging with equity options. The only difference is that with stock-index options, you're trying to protect a whole portfolio of stocks rather than individual stocks.

Like hedging with individual equity options, the cost of protecting your portfolio with index options can become very expensive (with price premiums of 20% to 30% or more) when markets are falling and the need for this type of portfolio insurance is the greatest. That, of course, will have an impact on the effectiveness of this strategy.

Also, the amount of profit you make or the protection you obtain depends in large part on how closely the behavior of your stock portfolio is matched by the behavior of the stock-index option you employ. There is no guarantee that the two will behave in the same way. You should therefore select an index option that closely reflects the nature of the stocks in your portfolio. If, for example, you hold a number of small-cap stocks, you might select something like the Russell 2000 index option as the hedging vehicle. If you hold mostly blue chips, you might choose the DJIA index option. You probably can't get dollar-for-dollar portfolio protection, but you should try to get as close a match as possible.

A Word of Caution   Given their effectiveness for either speculating or hedging, it's little wonder that index options have become popular with investors. But a word of caution is in order. Although trading index options appears simple and seems to provide high rates of return, these investments involve high risk and are subject to considerable price volatility. Amateurs should not use them. True, there's only so much you can lose with these options. The trouble is that it's very easy to lose all of that investment, however small it may be. These securities are not investments you can buy and then forget about until just before they expire. With the wide market swings that are so common today, you must monitor these securities daily.

Other Types of Options

Options on stocks and stock indexes account for most of the market activity in listed options. But you also can obtain put and call options on various other securities. Let's now take a brief look at these other kinds of options, starting with options on ETFs.

Options on Exchange-Traded Funds   In addition to various market indexes, put and call options are also available on several hundred exchange-traded funds (ETFs). As you've already learned, ETFs are like mutual funds that have been structured to track the performance of a wide range of market indexes—in other words, ETFs are a type of index fund. They trade like shares of common stock on listed exchanges and cover everything from broad market measures, such as the DJIA, the S&P 500, and the Nasdaq 100, to market sectors like energy, financials, health care, and semiconductors.

There's a good deal of overlap in the markets and market segments covered by index options and ETF options. In addition to their similar market coverage, they perform very much the same in the market, are valued the same, and are used for many of the same reasons (particularly for speculation and hedging). After all, an ETF option is written on an underlying index fund (for example, one that tracks the S&P 500) just like an index option is written on the same underlying market index (the S&P 500). Both do pretty much the same thing—either directly or indirectly track the performance of a market measure—so of course they should behave in the same way. The only real difference is a structural detail. Options on ETFs are operationally like stock options in that each option covers 100 shares of the underlying exchange-traded fund rather than $100 of the underlying market index, as is the case with index options. In the end, though, both trade at 100 times the underlying index (or ETF). Thus, while operationally ETF options may be closer to stock options, they function more like index options. As such, the market views them as viable alternatives to index options. These contracts have definitely caught the fancy of investors, especially those who track the major market indexes.

Interest Rate Options Puts and calls on fixed-income (debt) securities are known as **interest rate options**. At the present time, interest rate options are written only on U.S. Treasury securities with 30-year, 10-year, 5-year, or 13-week maturities. These options are yield-based rather than price-based. This means they track the yield (rather than the price) of the underlying Treasury security. Other types of options (equity and index options) are set up so that they react to movements in the price (or value) of the underlying asset. Interest rate options, in contrast, are set up to react to the yield of the underlying Treasury security (i.e., the exercise price is an interest rate). Thus, when yields rise, the value of a call goes up, and the value of a put goes down. In effect, because bond prices and yields move in opposite directions, the value of an interest rate call option goes up at the very time that the price (or value) of the underlying debt security is going down. The opposite is true for puts.

Currency Options Foreign exchange options, or **currency options** as they're more commonly called, provide a way for investors to speculate on foreign exchange rates or to hedge foreign currency or foreign security holdings. Currency options are available on the currencies of most of the countries with which the United States has strong trading ties. These options are traded on several exchanges and over the counter and include the following currencies:

- British pound
- Swiss franc
- Australian dollar
- Canadian dollar
- Japanese yen
- Euro

Puts and calls on foreign currencies give the holders the right to sell or buy large amounts of the specified currency. However, in contrast to the standardized contracts used with stock and stock-index options, the specific unit of trading in this market varies with the particular underlying currency. Table 13.7 spells out the details. Currency options are traded in full or fractional cents per unit of the underlying currency, relative to the amount of foreign currency involved. Thus, if a put or call on the British pound were quoted at, say, 6.40 (which is read as "6.4 cents"), it would be valued at $640 because 10,000 British pounds underlie this option (that is, $10,000 \times 0.064 = 640).

The value of a currency option is linked to the exchange rate between the U.S. dollar and the underlying foreign currency. For example, if the Canadian dollar

TABLE 13.7 FOREIGN CURRENCY OPTION CONTRACTS ON THE PHILADELPHIA EXCHANGE

Underlying Currency*	Size of Contracts	Underlying Currency*	Size of Contracts
British pound	10,000 pounds	Canadian dollar	10,000 dollars
Swiss franc	10,000 francs	Japanese yen	1,000,000 yen
Euro	10,000 euros	Australian dollar	10,000 dollars

*The British pound, Swiss franc, euro, Canadian dollar, and Australian dollar are all quoted in full cents. The Japanese yen is quoted in hundredths of a cent.

becomes stronger relative to the U.S. dollar, causing the exchange rate to go up, the price of a call option on the Canadian dollar will increase, and the price of a put will decline. (*Note:* Some cross-currency options are available in the market, but such options/trading techniques are beyond the scope of this text. Here, we will focus solely on foreign currency options (or futures) linked to U.S. dollars.)

The strike price on a currency option is stated in terms of exchange rates. Thus, a strike price of 150 implies that each unit of the foreign currency (such as one British pound) is worth 150 cents, or $1.50, in U.S. money. If you held a 150 call on this foreign currency, you would make money if the foreign currency strengthened relative to the U.S. dollar so that the exchange rate rose—say, to 155. In contrast, if you held a 150 put, you would profit from a decline in the exchange rate—say, to 145. Success in forecasting movements in foreign exchange rates is obviously essential to a profitable foreign currency options program.

LEAPS They look like regular puts and calls, and they behave pretty much like regular puts and calls, but they're not regular puts and calls. We're talking about **LEAPS**, which are puts and calls with lengthy expiration dates. Basically, LEAPS are long-term options. Whereas standard options have maturities of eight months or less, LEAPS have expiration dates as long as three years. Known formally as *Long-term Equity AnticiPation Securities,* they are listed on all of the major options exchanges. LEAPS are available on hundreds of stocks, stock indexes, and ETFs.

Aside from their time frame, LEAPS work like any other equity or index option. For example, a single (equity) LEAPS contract gives the holder the right to buy or sell 100 shares of stock at a predetermined price on or before the specified expiration date. LEAPS give you more time to be right about your bets on the direction of a stock or stock index, and they give hedgers more time to protect their positions. But there's a price for this extra time. You can expect to pay a lot more for a LEAPS than you would for a regular (short-term) option. That should come as no surprise. LEAPS, being nothing more than long-term options, are loaded with time value. And as we saw earlier in this chapter, other things being equal, *the more time an option has to expiration, the higher the quoted price.*

CONCEPTS IN REVIEW

Answers available at
http://www.pearsonhighered.com/smart

13.12 Briefly describe the differences and similarities between stock-index options and stock options. Do the same for foreign currency options and stock options.

13.13 Identify and briefly discuss two ways to use stock-index options. Do the same for foreign currency options.

13.14 Why would an investor want to use index options to hedge a portfolio of common stock? Could the same objective be obtained using options on ETFs? If the investor thinks the market is in for a fall, why not just sell the stock?

13.15 What are LEAPS? Why would an investor want to use a LEAPS option rather than a regular listed option?

MyFinanceLab	Here is what you should know after reading this chapter. MyFinanceLab will help you identify what you know and where to go when you need to practice.	
What You Should Know	**Key Terms**	**Where to Practice**
LG1 Discuss the basic nature of options in general and puts and calls in particular and understand how these investments work. An option gives the holder the right to buy or sell a certain amount of some real or financial asset at a set price for a set period of time. Puts and calls are the most widely used types of options. These derivative securities offer considerable leverage potential. A put enables the holder to sell a certain amount of a specified security at a specified price over a specified time period. A call gives the holder the right to buy the security at a specified price over a specified period of time.	call, *p. 451* derivative securities, *p. 451* leverage, *p. 451* option, *p. 451* option premium, *p. 451* option writer (or seller), *p. 451* put, *p. 451*	MyFinanceLab Study Plan 13.1
LG2 Describe the options market and note key options provisions, including strike prices and expiration dates. The options market is made up of conventional (OTC) options and listed options. OTC options are used predominantly by institutional investors. Listed options are traded on organized exchanges such as the CBOE. The creation of listed options exchanges led to standardized options features and to widespread use of options by individual investors. Among the option provisions are the strike price (the stipulated price at which the underlying asset can be bought or sold) and the expiration date (the date when the contract expires).	conventional options, *p. 454* expiration date, *p. 455* listed options, *p. 454* option chain, *p. 456* strike price, *p. 455*	MyFinanceLab Study Plan 13.2
LG3 Explain how put and call options are valued and the forces that drive option prices in the marketplace. The intrinsic value of a call is the market price of the underlying security less the strike price on the call. The intrinsic value of a put is its strike price less the market price of the security. The market value of an option is its intrinsic value plus its time value. The value of an option is driven by the current market price of the underlying asset, as well as by the option's strike price, its time to expiration, the risk-free interest rate, and the volatility of the underlying asset.	at-the-money out-of-the money, *p. 460* intrinsic value in-the-money, *p. 460* put-call parity time value, *p. 461*	MyFinanceLab Study Plan 13.3 Excel Table 4.2 Video Learning Aid for Problems P13.5, P13.11
LG4 Describe the profit potential of puts and calls and note some popular put and call investment strategies. Investors who hold puts make money when the value of the underlying asset goes down over time. Call investors make money when the underlying asset moves up in price. Aggressive investors use puts and calls either for speculation or in highly specialized writing and spreading programs. Conservative investors like the low unit costs and the limited risk that puts and calls offer in absolute dollar terms. Conservative investors often use options to hedge positions in other securities.	hedge, *p. 470*	MyFinanceLab Study Plan 13.4 Excel Tables 4.3, 4.4

What You Should Know	Key Terms	Where to Practice
LG5 Explain the profit potential and loss exposure from writing covered call options and discuss how writing options can be used as a strategy for enhancing investment returns. Covered call writers have limited loss exposure because they write options against securities they already own. The maximum profit occurs when the price of the stock equals the strike price of the call. If the stock price goes above the strike price, then any loss on the option is offset by a gain on the stock position. If the stock price goes down, part of the loss on the stock is offset by the proceeds from the call option. Option writing can be combined with other securities to create investment strategies for specific market conditions.	covered options, *p. 473* naked options, *p. 473* option spreading, *p. 475* option straddle, *p. 473*	MyFinanceLab Study Plan 13.5 Excel Table 13.5 Video Learning Aid for Problem P13.11
LG6 Describe market index options, puts and calls on foreign currencies, and LEAPS and discuss how these securities can be used by investors. Standardized put and call options are available on stock-market indexes, like the S&P 500 (in the form of index options or ETF options), and on a number of foreign currencies (currency options). Also available are LEAPS, which are listed options that carry lengthy expiration dates. Although these securities can be used just like stock options, the index and currency options tend to be used primarily for speculation or to develop hedge positions.	currency options, *p. 481* interest rate options, *p. 481* LEAPS, *p. 482* stock-index option, *p. 476*	MyFinanceLab Study Plan 13.6

Log into MyFinanceLab, take a chapter test, and get a personalized Study Plan
that tells you which concepts you understand and which ones you need to
review. From there, MyFinanceLab will give you further practice, tutorials,
animations, videos, and guided solutions.
Log into http://www.myfinancelab.com

Discussion Questions

LG2 **Q13.1** Using the Facebook stock option quotations in Figure 13.1, find the option premium, the time value, and the stock index breakeven point for the following puts and calls.
   a. The August put with a strike price of $82.50
   b. The August call with a strike price of $85

LG3 **Q13.2** In Table 13.2, notice that among the options expiring in one month, the option with the highest time value is the one with a strike price of $70. Likewise, among the options expiring in three months, the option with a $70 strike has more time value than the options with $65 and $75 strike prices. Why do you think this is so?

LG5 **Q13.3** Alcan stock recently closed at $52.51. Assume that you write a covered call on Alcan by writing one September call with a strike price of $55 and buying 100 shares of stock at the market price. The option premium that you obtain from writing the call is $370. Assume the stock will pay no dividends between now and the expiration date of the option.

a. What is the total profit if the stock price remains unchanged?

b. What is the total profit if the stock price goes up to $55?

c. What is the total loss if the stock price goes down to $49?

LG6 **Q13.4** Assume you hold a well-balanced portfolio of common stocks. Under what conditions might you want to use a stock-index (or ETF) option to hedge the portfolio?

a. Briefly explain how such options could be used to hedge a portfolio against a drop in the market.

b. Discuss what happens if the market does, in fact, go down.

c. What happens if the market goes up instead?

LG3 **LG4** **Q13.5** Using the resources at your campus or public library (or on the Internet), complete each of the following tasks. (*Note:* Show your work for all calculations.)

a. Find an in-the-money call that has two or three months to expiration. (Select an equity option that is at least $2 or $3 in-the-money.) What's the intrinsic value of this option and what is its time value? Using the current market price of the underlying stock (the one listed with the option), determine what kind of dollar and percentage return the option would generate if the underlying stock goes up 10%. How about if the stock goes down 10%?

b. Repeat part a, but this time use an in-the-money put. (Choose an equity option that's at least $2 or $3 in-the-money and has two or three months to expiration.) Answer the same questions as above.

c. Repeat once more the exercise in part a, but this time use an out-of-the-money call. (Select an equity option, at least $2 or $3 out-of-the-money with two or three months to expiration.) Answer the same questions.

d. Compare the valuation properties and performance characteristics of in-the-money calls and out-of-the-money calls (from parts a and c). Note some of the advantages and disadvantages of each.

Problems

All problems are available on http://www.myfinancelab.com

LG3 **P13.1** Apple stock is selling for $120 per share. Call options with a $117 exercise price are priced at $12. What is the intrinsic value of the option, and what is the time value?

LG3 **P13.2** Twitter is trading at $34.50. Call options with a strike price of $35 are priced at $2.30. What is the intrinsic value of the option, and what is the time value?

LG3 **P13.3** Verizon is trading at $36. Put options with a strike price of $45 are priced at $10.50. What is the intrinsic value of the option, and what is the time value?

LG3 **P13.4** Abercrombie & Fitch is trading at $21.50. Put options with a strike price of $20.50 are priced at $0.85. What is the intrinsic value of the option, and what is the time value?

LG3 **P13.5** A six-month call option contract on 100 shares of Home Depot common stock with a strike price of $60 can be purchased for $600. Assuming that the market price of Home Depot stock rises to $75 per share by the expiration date of the option, what is the call holder's profit? What is the holding period return?

LG4 **P13.6** Suppose that a call option with a strike price of $45 expires in one year and has a current market price of $5.16. The market price of the underlying stock is $46.21, and the risk-free rate is 1%. Use put-call parity to calculate the price of a put option on the same underlying stock with a strike of $45 and an expiration of one year.

LG4 P13.7 Look at the Facebook option quotes in Figure 13.1, and focus on the call and put options with a strike price of $80. Can you use put-call parity to infer what the market price of Facebook stock must have been when these option prices were quoted? To keep things simple, assume the options expire in one month, and that the risk-free rate at the time was 0%. (Hint: To use put-call parity, you need to find the market price of a risk-free, zero-coupon bond with a face value equal to the strike price of the options.)

LG4 P13.8 Repeat the analysis of problem 13.7, but this time focus on the Facebook call and put options in Figure 13.1 that have a strike price of $87.50. If you use put-call parity to find the price of Facebook stock at the time those call prices were quoted, would you expect to get the same answer that you found in problem 13.6? Do you in fact get the same answer?

LG4 LG6 P13.9 You believe that oil prices will be rising more than expected and that rising prices will result in lower earnings for industrial companies that use a lot of petroleum-related products in their operations. You also believe that the effects on this sector will be magnified because consumer demand will fall as oil prices rise. You locate an exchange-traded fund, XLB, that represents a basket of industrial companies. You don't want to short the ETF because you don't have enough margin in your account. XLB is currently trading at $23. You decide to buy a put option (for 100 shares) with a strike price of $24, priced at $1.20. It turns out that you are correct. At expiration, XLB is trading at $20. Calculate your profit.

XLB: Materials—$23.00

Calls			Puts		
Strike	Expiration	Price	Strike	Expiration	Price
$20	November	$0.25	$20	November	$1.55
$24	November	$0.25	$24	November	$1.20

LG4 LG6 P13.10 Refer to Problem 13.9. What happens if you are wrong and the price of XLB increases to $25 on the expiration date?

LG6 P13.11 Dorothy Santosuosso does a lot of investing in the stock market and is a frequent user of stock-index options. She is convinced that the market is about to undergo a broad retreat and has decided to buy a put option on the S&P 100 Index. The put option has a strike of 905 and is quoted in the financial press at $14.50. Although the S&P Index of 100 stocks is currently at 900, Dorothy thinks it will drop to 850 by the expiration date on the option. How much profit will she make, and what will be her holding period return if she is right? How much will she lose if the S&P 100 goes up (rather than down) by 25 points and reaches 925 by the date of expiration?

LG3 LG4 P13.12 Myles Houck holds 600 shares of Lubbock Gas and Light. He bought the stock several years ago at $48.50, and the shares are now trading at $75. Myles is concerned that the market is beginning to soften. He doesn't want to sell the stock, but he would like to be able to protect the profit he's made. He decides to hedge his position by buying six puts on Lubbock G&L. The three-month puts carry a strike price of $75 and are currently trading at $2.50.
   a. How much profit or loss will Myles make on this deal if the price of Lubbock G&L does indeed drop to $60 a share by the expiration date on the puts?
   b. How would he do if the stock kept going up in price and reached $90 a share by the expiration date?
   c. What do you see as the major advantages of using puts as hedge vehicles?
   d. Would Myles have been better off using in-the-money puts—that is, puts with an $85 strike price that are trading at $10.50? How about using out-of-the-money puts—say, those with a $70 strike price, trading at $1.00? Explain.

LG4 LG6 **P13.13** Nick Fitzgerald holds a well-diversified portfolio of high-quality, large-cap stocks. The current value of Fitzgerald's portfolio is $735,000, but he is concerned that the market is heading for a big fall (perhaps as much as 20%) over the next three to six months. He doesn't want to sell all his stocks because he feels they all have good long-term potential and should perform nicely once stock prices have bottomed out. As a result, he's thinking about using index options to hedge his portfolio. Assume that the S&P 500 currently stands at 2,200 and among the many put options available on this index are two that have caught his eye: (1) a six-month put with a strike price of 2,150 that's trading at $76, and (2) a six-month put with a strike price of 2,075 that's quoted at $58.

   a. How many S&P 500 puts would Nick have to buy to protect his $735,000 stock portfolio? How much would it cost him to buy the necessary number of puts with a $2,150 strike price? How much would it cost to buy the puts with a $2,075 strike price?

   b. Now, considering the performance of both the put options and Nick's portfolio, determine how much *net* profit (or loss) Nick will earn from each of these put hedges if both the market (as measured by the S&P 500) and Nick's portfolio fall by 15% over the next six months. What if the market and Nick's portfolio fall by only 5%? What if they go up by 10%?

   c. Do you think Nick should set up the put hedge and, if so, using which put option? Explain.

   d. Finally, assume that the DJIA is currently at 17,550 and that a six-month put option on the Dow is available with a strike of 174, and is currently trading at $7.84. How many of these puts would Nick have to buy to protect his portfolio, and what would they cost? Would Nick be better off with the Dow options or the S&P 2,150 puts? Briefly explain.

LG3 LG5 **P13.14** Angelo Martino just purchased 500 shares of AT&E at $61.50, and he has decided to write covered calls against these stocks. Accordingly, he sells five AT&E calls at their current market price of $5.75. The calls have three months to expiration and carry a strike price of $65. The stock pays a quarterly dividend of $0.80 a share (the next dividend to be paid in about a month).

   a. Determine the total profit and holding period return Angelo will generate if the stock rises to $65 a share by the expiration date on the calls.

   b. What happens to Angelo's profit (and return) if the price of the stock rises to more than $65 a share?

   c. Does this covered call position offer any protection (or cushion) against a drop in the price of the stock? Explain.

LG6 **P13.15** Rick owns stock in a retailer that he believes is highly undervalued. Rick expects that the stock will increase in value nicely over the long term. He is concerned, however, that the entire retail industry may fall out of favor with investors as some larger companies report falling sales. There are no options traded on his stock, but Rick would like to hedge against his fears about retail. He locates a symbol RTH, which is a retail exchange-traded fund. Can Rick hedge against the risk he is concerned with by using RTH? Using options?

LG5 LG6 **P13.16** Suppose the DJIA stands at 11,200. You want to set up a long straddle by purchasing 100 calls and an equal number of puts on the index, both of which expire in three months and have a strike of 112. The put price is listed at $1.65 and the call sells for $2.65.

   a. What will it cost you to set up the straddle, and how much profit (or loss) do you stand to make if the market falls by 750 points by the expiration dates on the options? What if it goes up by 750 points by expiration? What if it stays at 11,200?

   b. Repeat part a, but this time assume that you set up a short straddle by selling/writing 100 July 112 puts and calls.

   c. What do you think of the use of option straddles as an investment strategy? What are the risks, and what are the rewards?

LG3 **P13.17** A stock trades for $45 per share. A call option on that stock has a strike price of $50 and an expiration date one year in the future. The volatility of the stock's return is 30%, and the risk-free rate is 2%. What is the Black and Scholes value of this option?

LG3 **P13.18** Repeat the analysis of problem 13.17 assuming that the volatility of the stock's return is 40%. Intuitively, would you expect this to cause the call price to rise or fall? By how much does the call price change?

Visit **http://www.myfinancelab.com** for web exercises, spreadsheets, and other online resources.

Case problem 13.1   The Franciscos' Investment Options

LG3 **LG4**   Hector Francisco is a successful businessman in Atlanta. The box-manufacturing firm he and his wife, Judy, founded several years ago has prospered. Because he is self-employed, Hector is building his own retirement fund. So far, he has accumulated a substantial sum in his investment account, mostly by following an aggressive investment posture. He does this because, as he puts it, "In this business, you never know when the bottom fall out." Hector has been following the stock of Rembrandt Paper Products (RPP), and after conducting extensive analysis, he feels the stock is about ready to move. Specifically, he believes that within the next six months, RPP could go to about $80 per share, from its current level of $57.50. The stock pays annual dividends of $2.40 per share. Hector figures he would receive two quarterly dividend payments over his six-month investment horizon.

In studying RPP, Hector has learned that the company has six-month call options (with $50 and $60 strike prices) listed on the CBOE. The CBOE calls are quoted at $8 for the options with $50 strike prices and at $5 for the $60 options.

Questions

a. How many alternative investments does Hector have if he wants to invest in RPP for no more than six months? What if he has a two-year investment horizon?

b. Using a six-month holding period and assuming the stock does indeed rise to $80 over this time frame:

   1. Find the value of both calls, given that at the end of the holding period neither contains any investment premium.

   2. Determine the holding period return for each of the three investment alternatives open to Hector Francisco.

c. Which course of action would you recommend if Hector simply wants to maximize profit? Would your answer change if other factors (e.g., comparative risk exposure) were considered along with return? Explain.

Case problem 13.2   Luke's Quandary: To Hedge or Not to Hedge

LG3 **LG4**   A little more than 10 months ago, Luke Weaver, a mortgage banker in Phoenix, bought 300 shares of stock at $40 per share. Since then, the price of the stock has risen to $75 per share. It is now near the end of the year, and the market is starting to weaken. Luke feels there is still plenty of play left in the stock but is afraid the tone of the market will be detrimental to his position.

His wife, Denise, is taking an adult education course on the stock market and has just learned about put and call hedges. She suggests that he use puts to hedge his position. Luke is intrigued by the idea, which he discusses with his broker, who advises him that the needed puts are indeed available on his stock. Specifically, he can buy three-month puts, with $75 strike prices, at a cost of $550 each (quoted at $5.50).

Questions

a. Given the circumstances surrounding Luke's current investment position, what benefits could be derived from using the puts as a hedge device? What would be the major drawback?

b. What will Luke's minimum profit be if he buys three puts at the indicated option price? How much would he make if he did not hedge but instead sold his stock immediately at a price of $75 per share?

c. Assuming Luke uses three puts to hedge his position, indicate the amount of profit he will generate if the stock moves to $100 by the expiration date of the puts. What if the stock drops to $50 per share?

d. Should Luke use the puts as a hedge? Explain. Under what conditions would you urge him not to use the puts as a hedge?

Excel@Investing

Excel@Investing

One of the positive attributes of investing in options is the profit potential from the puts or calls. The quoted market price of the option is influenced by the time to expiration, stock volatility, market interest rates, and the behavior of the price of the underlying common stock. The latter variable tends to drive the price movement in options and impacts its potential for profitable returns.

Create a spreadsheet model, similar to that presented below, in order to calculate the profits and/or losses from investing in the option described.

	A	B	C	D	E	F	G	H	I	J
1										
2						Long		100		3-Month Call Option
3						Position		Shares of		on the Stock
4						No		Underlying		Strike Price
5						Option		Common Stock		$$$
6										
7	Today									
8										
9	Market value of stock			$$		$$		$$		
10	Call strike price			$$						
11	Call option premium			$$						
12										
13										
14	Scenario One: 3 months later									
15	Expected market value of stock			$$		$$		$$		
16	Stock value @ strike price			$$						$$
17	Call premium			$$						$$
18	Breakeven point			$$						$$
19										
20	Profit (Loss)					$$		$$		

John has been following the stock market very closely over the past 18 months and has a strong belief that future stock prices will be significantly higher. He has two alternatives that he can follow. The first is to use a long-term strategy—purchase the stock today and sell it sometime in the future at a possibly higher price. The other alternative is to buy a three-month call option. The relevant information needed to analyze these alternatives is presented below:

Current stock price = $49

Desires to buy one round lot = 100 shares

Three-month call option has a strike price of $51 and a call premium of $2

Questions

a. In scenario one, if the stock price three months from now is $58:

   1. What is the long-position profit or loss?

   2. What is the breakeven point of the call option?

   3. Is the option in- or out-of-the-money?

   4. What is the option profit or loss?

b. In scenario two, if the stock price three months from now is $42:

   1. What is the long-position profit or loss?

   2. What is the breakeven point of the call option?

   3. Is the option in- or out-of-the-money?

   4. What is the option profit or loss?

Chapter-Opening Problem

In the beginning of this chapter you read about Neil Dana, who exercised his option to buy six million shares. In that transaction, Mr. Dana spent $3.6 million to acquire stock valued at $229 million. What was the strike price of the options, and what was the market price of GoPro stock at the time that the options were exercised?

Glossary

A

abnormal return The difference between an investment's actual return and its expected return. (Chapter 7)

Accredited investor Investor who is permitted to invest in certain types of higher-risk investments. These investors include wealthy individuals, corporations, endowments, and retirement plans. (Chapter 4)

accrued interest Interest earned (but not yet paid) on a bond since the previous coupon payment. (Chapter 8)

agency bonds Debt securities issued by various agencies and organizations of the U.S. government. (Chapter 2)

American depositary receipts (ADRs) U.S. dollardenominated receipts for the stocks of foreign companies that are held in the vaults of banks in the companies' home countries. Serve as backing for *American depositary shares (ADSs)*. (Chapter 3)

American depositary shares (ADSs) Securities created to permit U.S. investors to hold shares of non-U.S. companies and trade them on U.S. stock exchanges. They are backed by *American depositary receipts (ADRs)*. (Chapter 3)

Amortized loan A loan that is paid off in equal periodic payments. (Chapter 6)

anchoring A phenomenon in which individuals place too much weight on information that they have at hand, even when that information is not particularly relevant. (Chapter 7)

Annual percentage rate (APR) The interest rate paid or earned in one year without compounding. It is calculated as the interest rate per period (for example, per month or week) multiplied by the number of periods during which compounding occurs during the year (m). (Chapter 5)

Annuity A series of equal dollar payments for a specified period of time. (Chapter 6)

annuity A stream of equal cash flows that occur at equal intervals over time. (Chapter 10)

Annuity due An annuity in which the payments occur at the beginning of each period. (Chapter 6)

Annuity future value interest factor The value, $\left[\dfrac{(1 + i)^n - 1}{i}\right]$, used as a multiplier to calculate the future value of an annuity. (Chapter 6)

Annuity present value interest factor The value, $\left[\dfrac{1 - \dfrac{1}{(1 + i)^n}}{i}\right]$, used as a multiplier to calculate the present value of an annuity. (Chapter 6)

arbitrage A transaction in which an investor simultaneously buys and sells identical assets at different prices to earn an instant, risk-free profit. (Chapter 7)

ask price The lowest price offered to sell a security. (Chapter 3)

asset-backed securities (ABSs) Securities similar to mortgagebacked securities that are backed by a pool of bank loans, leases, and other assets. (Chapter 2)

at the money A call or put option is at the money when the strike price of the option and the market price of the underlying stock are equal. (Chapter 13)

B

bear markets Markets normally associated with falling prices, investor pessimism, economic slowdown, and government restraint. (Chapter 3)

behavioral finance The body of research into the role that emotions and other subjective factors play in investment decisions. (Chapter 7)

belief perseverance The tendency to ignore or discount evidence contrary to one's existing beliefs. (Chapter 7)

beta A measure of *undiversifiable*, or *market*, *risk* that indicates how the price of a security responds to market forces. (Chapter 11)

Beta coefficient A measure of the relationship between the returns of a security such as a share of common stock and the returns of the portfolio of all risky assets. (Chapter 12)

bid price The highest price offered to purchase a security. (Chapter 3)

blue-chip stocks Financially strong, high-quality stocks with long and stable records of earnings and dividends. (Chapter 1)

Bond A long-term (10-year or more) promissory note issued by a borrower, promising to pay the owner of the security a predetermined amount of interest each year. (Chapter 4)

bond ladders An investment strategy wherein equal amounts of money are invested in a series of bonds with staggered maturities. (Chapter 8)

bond rating agencies Institutions that perform extensive financial analysis on companies issuing bonds to assess the credit risk associated with a particular bond issue. (Chapter 2)

bond ratings Letter grades that designate investment quality and are assigned to a bond issue by rating agencies. (Chapter 2)

bond swap An investment strategy wherein an investor simultaneously liquidates one bond holding and buys a different issue to take its place. (Chapter 8)

bond-equivalent yield The annual yield on a bond, calculated as twice the semiannual yield. (Chapter 8)

book value The amount of stockholders' equity in a firm; equals the amount of the firm's assets minus the firm's liabilities and preferred stock. (Chapter 1)

broker market The market in which the two sides of a transaction, the buyer and seller, are brought together to execute trades. (Chapter 3)

bull markets Markets normally associated with rising prices, investor optimism, economic recovery, and government stimulus. (Chapter 3)

business risk The degree of uncertainty associated with an investment's earnings and the investment's ability to pay the returns owed to investors. (Chapter 10)

C

call A negotiable instrument that gives the holder the right to buy securities at a stated price within a certain time period. (Chapter 13)

call feature Feature that specifies whether and under what conditions the issuer can retire a bond prior to maturity. (Chapter 2)

call premium The amount added to a bond's par value and paid to investors when a bond is retired prematurely. (Chapter 2)

call price The price the issuer must pay to retire a bond prematurely; equal to par value plus the call premium. (Chapter 2)

Capital Asset Pricing Model (CAPM) A model that describes the theoretical link between the expected rate of return on a risky security such as a share of stock and the security's risk as measured by its beta coefficient. (Chapter 12)

capital asset pricing model (CAPM) Model that formally links the notions of risk and return; it uses beta, the riskfree rate, and the market return to help investors define the required return on an investment. (Chapter 11)

capital market Market in which *long-term* securities (with maturities greater than one year) such as stocks and bonds are bought and sold. (Chapter 3)

Capital market The market for long-term financial instruments. (**Chapter 4**)

cash dividend Payment of a dividend in the form of cash. (Chapter 1)

charting The activity of charting price behavior and other market information and then using the patterns these charts form to make investment decisions. (Chapter 7)

classified common stock Common stock issued by a company in different classes, each of which offers different privileges and benefits to its holders. (Chapter 1)

clean price The price of a bond ignoring any accrued interest. The clean price is the present value of the bond's future cash flows, not including any interest accruing on the next coupon date. (Chapter 8)

collateral trust bonds Senior bonds backed by securities owned by the issuer but held in trust by a third party. (Chapter 2)

collateralized mortgage obligation (CMO) Mortgage-backed bond whose holders are divided into classes based on the length of investment desired; principal is channeled to investors in order of maturity, with short-term classes first. (Chapter 2)

Commercial bank A financial institution that accepts demand deposits, makes loans, and provides other services to the public. (Chapter 4)

Common stock A form of equity security that represents the residual ownership of the firm. (Chapter 4)

common-size income statement A type of financial report that uses a common denominator (net sales) to convert all entries on a normal income statement from dollars to percentages. (Chapter 9)

compound interest Interest paid not only on the initial deposit but also on any interest accumulated from one period to the next. (Chapter 10)

Compound interest The situation in which interest paid on the investment during the first period is added to the principal and, during the second period, interest is earned on the original principal plus the interest earned during the first period. (Chapter 5)

Compounding The process of determining the future value of a payment or series of payments when applying the concept of compound interest. (Chapter 5)

confidence index A ratio of the average yield on high-grade corporate bonds to the average yield on average- or intermediate-grade corporate bonds; a technical indicator based on the theory that market trends usually appear in the bond market before they do in the stock market. (Chapter 7)

continuous compounding Interest calculation in which interest is compounded over the smallest possible interval of time. (Chapter 10)

conventional options Put and call options sold over the counter. (Chapter 13)

conversion equivalent (conversion parity) The price at which the common stock would have to sell in order to make the convertible security worth its present market price. (Chapter 2)

conversion period The time period during which a convertible issue can be converted. (Chapter 2)

conversion price The stated price per share at which common stock will be delivered to the investor in exchange for a convertible issue. (Chapter 2)

conversion privilege The conditions and specific nature of the conversion feature on convertible securities. (Chapter 2)

conversion ratio The number of shares of common stock into which a convertible issue can be converted. (Chapter 2)

conversion value An indication of what a convertible issue would trade for if it were priced to sell on the basis of its stock value. (Chapter 2)

convertible bonds Fixed-income obligations that have a feature permitting the holder to convert the security into a specified number of shares of the issuing company's common stock. (Chapter 2)

correlation A statistical measure of the relationship, if any, between series of numbers representing data of any kind. (Chapter 11)

correlation coefficient A measure of the degree of correlation between two series. (Chapter 11)

Correlation coefficient A measure of the degree to which the variation in one variable is related to the variation in another. The coefficient ranges from −1 for a perfectly negative relationship to +1 for perfectly positive dependence. (Chapter 12)

coupon Feature on a bond that defines the amount of annual interest income. (Chapter 2)

coupon rate A bond's coupon expressed as a percentage of its par value. (Chapter 2)

Coupon rate The amount of interest paid per year expressed as a percent of the face value of the bond. (Chapter 4)

covered options Options written against stock owned (or short-sold) by the writer. (Chapter 13)

Credit default swap An insurance contract that pays off in the event of a credit event such as default or bankruptcy. (Chapter 4)

crossing markets After-hours trading in stocks that involves filling buy and sell orders by matching identical sell and buy orders at the desired price. (Chapter 3)

currency exchange rate The relationship between two currencies on a specified date. (Chapter 3)

currency exchange risk The risk caused by the varying exchange rates between the currencies of two countries. (Chapter 3)

currency options Put and call options written on foreign currencies. (Chapter 13)

current yield Measure of the annual interest income a bond provides relative to its current market price. (Chapter 2)

cyclical stocks Stocks whose earnings and overall market performance are closely linked to the general state of the economy. (Chapter 1)

D

date of record The date on which an investor must be a registered shareholder to be entitled to receive a dividend. (Chapter 1)

dealer market The market in which the buyer and seller are not brought together directly but instead have their orders executed by *dealers* that make markets in the given security. (Chapter 3)

debenture An unsecured (junior) bond. (Chapter 2)

debit balance The amount of money being borrowed in a margin loan. (Chapter 3)

Debt securities Financial instruments that represent loans to corporations. Long-term debt securities are called bonds and can be bought and sold in the bond market. (Chapter 4)

defensive stocks Stocks that tend to hold their own, and even do well, when the economy starts to falter. (Chapter 1)

deferred equity Securities issued in one form and later redeemed or converted into shares of common stock. (Chapter 2)

Defined benefit plans A company retirement plan, such as a pension plan, in which a retired employee receives a specific amount based on his or her salary history and years of service. (Chapter 4)

Defined contribution plans A company retirement plan, such as a 401(k) plan, in which the employee elects to contribute some amount of his or her salary to the plan and the employee takes responsibility for the investment decisions. (Chapter 4)

deflation A period of generally declining prices. (Chapter 10)

designated market maker (DMM) NYSE member who specializes in making transactions in one or more stocks and manages the auction process. (Chapter 3)

dirty price A bond's dirty price equals its clean price plus accrued interest. (Chapter 8)

discount bond A bond with a market value lower than par; occurs when market rates are greater than the coupon rate. (Chapter 2)

discount rate The annual rate of return that could be earned currently on a similar investment; used when finding present value; also called *opportunity cost*. (Chapter 10)

Discount rate The interest rate used in the discounting process. (Chapter 5)

Discounting The inverse of compounding. This process is used to determine the present value of a future cash flow. (Chapter 5)

diversifiable (unsystematic) risk The portion of an investment's risk that results from uncontrollable or random events that are firm-specific; can be eliminated through diversification. (Chapter 11)

Diversifiable risk Risk that can be eliminated through diversification. (Chapter 12)

Diversification The reduction in risk that comes about by combining two or more risky assets into a portfolio where the individual assets are less than perfectly positively correlated. (Chapter 12)

dividend payout ratio The portion of earnings per share (EPS) that a firm pays out as dividends. (Chapter 1)

dividend reinvestment plan (DRIP) Plan in which shareholders have cash dividends automatically reinvested into additional shares of the firm's common stock. (Chapter 1)

dividend valuation model (DVM) A model that values a share of stock on the basis of the future dividend stream it is expected to produce; its three versions are zero-growth, constant-growth, and variable-growth. (Chapter 9)

dividend yield A measure that relates dividends to share price and puts common stock dividends on a relative (percentage) rather than absolute (dollar) basis. (Chapter 1)

dividends-and-earnings (D&E) approach Stock valuation approach that uses projected dividends, EPS, and P/E multiples to value a share of stock; also known as the *DCF approach*. (Chapter 9)

dual listing Listing of a firm's shares on more than one exchange. (Chapter 3)

duration A measure of bond price volatility that captures both price and reinvestment risks and that is used to indicate how a bond will react in different interest rate environments. (Chapter 8)

E

earnings per share (EPS) The amount of annual earnings available to common stockholders, as stated on a pershare basis. (Chapter 1)

Effective annual rate (EAR) The annual compounded rate that produces the same return as the nominal, or stated, rate. (Chapter 5)

efficient frontier The leftmost boundary of the *feasible (attainable) set* of portfolios that includes all *efficient portfolios*—those providing the best attainable tradeoff between risk (measured by the standard deviation) and return. (Chapter 11)

efficient market A market in which securities reflect all possible information quickly and accurately. (Chapter 7)

efficient markets hypothesis (EMH) Basic theory of the behavior of efficient markets, in which there are a large number of knowledgeable investors who react quickly to new information, causing securities prices to adjust quickly and accurately. (Chapter 7)

efficient portfolio A portfolio that provides the highest return for a given level of risk. (Chapter 11)

electronic communications networks (ECNs) Electronic trading networks that automatically match buy and sell orders that customers place electronically. (Chapter 3)

equipment trust certificates Senior bonds secured by specific pieces of equipment; popular with transportation companies such as airlines. (Chapter 2)

equity capital Evidence of ownership position in a firm, in the form of shares of common stock. (Chapter 1)

equity kicker Another name for the conversion feature, giving the holder of a convertible security a deferred claim on the issuer's common stock. (Chapter 2)

Equity securities Financial instruments that represent ownership claims on a business. Equity securities for corporations are called shares of stock and can be bought and sold in the stock market. (Chapter 4)

ethics Standards of conduct or moral judgment. (Chapter 3)

Eurodollar bonds Foreign bonds denominated in dollars but not registered with the SEC, thus restricting sales of new issues. (Chapter 2)

event risk Risk that comes from an unexpected event that has a significant and usually immediate effect on the underlying value of an investment. (Chapter 10)

excess margin More equity than is required in a margin account. (Chapter 3)

Exchange-traded fund (ETF) An investment vehicle traded on stock exchanges much like a share of stock. The entity holds investments in assets that meet the investment objective of the entity (e.g., shares of stock of companies from emerging markets). (Chapter 4)

ex-dividend date Three business days up to the date of record; determines whether one is an official shareholder and thus eligible to receive a declared dividend. (Chapter 1)

expectations hypothesis Theory that the shape of the yield curve reflects investor expectations of future interest rates. (Chapter 8)

expected inflation premium The average rate of inflation expected in the future. (Chapter 10)

expected return The return an investor thinks an investment will earn in the future. (Chapter 10)

expiration date The date at which an option expires. (Chapter 13)

F

face value The value that a bond issuer must pay to the investor when the bond matures. (Chapter 2)

Face, or par value On the face of a bond, the stated amount that the firm is to repay on the maturity date. (Chapter 4)

familiarity bias The tendency to invest in securities simply because they are familiar to the investor. (Chapter 7)

Financial intermediaries Institutions whose business is to bring together individuals and institutions with money to invest or lend with other firms or individuals in need of money. (**Chapter 4**)

financial leverage The use of debt financing to magnify investment returns. (Chapter 3)

financial risk The degree of uncertainty of payment resulting from a firm's mix of debt and equity; the larger the proportion of debt financing, the greater this risk. (Chapter 10)

first and refunding bonds Bonds secured in part with both first and second mortgages. (Chapter 2)

forced conversion The calling in of convertible bonds by the issuing firm. (Chapter 2)

fourth market Transactions made directly between large institutional buyers and sellers of securities. (Chapter 3)

free cash flow The cash flow remaining after a firm has paid all of its expenses and makes necessary investments in working capital and fixed assets. (Chapter 9)

free cash flow to equity method A stock valuation approach that estimates the free cash flow that a company will produce over time and discounts that to the present to estimate the firm's total equity value. (Chapter 9)

fully compounded rate of return The rate of return that includes interest earned on interest. (Chapter 10)

Future value interest factor The value $(1+1i)n$ used as a multiplier to calculate an amount's future value. (Chapter 5)

future value The amount to which a current deposit will grow over a period of time when it is placed in an account paying compound interest. (Chapter 10)

Future value What a cash flow will be worth in the future. (Chapter 5)

G

general obligation bonds Municipal bonds backed by the full faith, credit, and taxing power of the issuer. (Chapter 2)

Growing perpetuity A perpetuity in which the payments grow at a constant rate from period to period over time. (Chapter 6)

growth stocks Stocks that experience high rates of growth in operations and earnings. (Chapter 1)

growth-oriented portfolio A portfolio whose primary objective is long-term price appreciation. (Chapter 11)

H

hedge A combination of two or more securities into a single investment position for the purpose of reducing or eliminating risk. (Chapter 13)

Hedge fund An investment fund that is open to a limited range of investors (accredited investors) and that can undertake a wider range of investment and trading activities than other types of investment funds that are open to the general public (e.g., mutual funds). (Chapter 4)

high-yield bonds Bonds with below investment-grade ratings, also known as junk bonds. (Chapter 2)

holding period return (HPR) The total return earned from holding an investment for a specified *holding period* (*usually one year or less*). (Chapter 10)

holding period The period of time over which one wishes to measure the return on an investment vehicle. (Chapter 10)

I

immunization Bond portfolio strategy that uses duration to offset price and reinvestment effects; a bond portfolio is immunized when its average duration equals the investment horizon. (Chapter 8)

income bonds Unsecured bonds requiring that interest be paid only after a specified amount of income is earned. (Chapter 2)

income stocks Stocks with long and sustained records of paying higher-than-average dividends. (Chapter 1)

income Usually cash or near-cash that is periodically received as a result of owning an investment. (Chapter 10)

income-oriented portfolio A portfolio that is designed to produce regular dividends and interest payments. (Chapter 11)

inflation A period of generally rising prices. (Chapter 10)

initial margin The minimum amount of equity that must be provided by a margin investor at the time of purchase. (Chapter 3)

initial public offering (IPO) The first public sale of a company's stock. (Chapter 3)

insider trading The use of nonpublic information about a company to make profitable securities transactions. (Chapter 3)

interest rate options Put and call options written on fixedincome (debt) securities. (Chapter 13)

interest rate risk The chance that changes in interest rates will adversely affect a security's value. (Chapter 10)

interest The "rent" paid by a borrower for use of the lender's money. (Chapter 10)

in-the-money A call option with a strike price less than the market price of the underlying security; a put option whose strike price is greater than the market price of the underlying security. (Chapter 13)

intrinsic value The underlying or inherent value of a stock, as determined through fundamental analysis. (Chapter 7) Also, the gross amount of money that an investor would receive if he or she chose to exercise an option. (Chapter 13)

Investment bank A financial institution that raises capital, trades in securities, and manages corporate mergers and acquisitions. (Chapter 4)

investment banker Financial intermediary that specializes in assisting companies issue new securities and advising companies with regard to major financial transactions. (Chapter 3)

Investment company A firm that invests the pooled funds of retail investors for a fee. (Chapter 4)

investment grade bonds Bonds with ratings in the three or four highest ratings categories issued by bond rating agencies. (Chapter 2)

investment value The amount that investors believe a security should be trading for, or what they think it's worth. (Chapter 1)

investment value The price at which a convertible would trade if it were nonconvertible and priced at or near the prevailing market yields of comparable nonconvertible issues. (Chapter 2)

J

junior bonds Debt obligations backed only by the promise of the issuer to pay interest and principal on a timely basis. (Chapter 2)

junk bonds High-risk securities that have low ratings but high yields. (Chapter 2)

L

LEAPS Long-term options. (Chapter 13)

Level perpetuity An annuity with a constant level of payments with an infinite life. (Chapter 6)

leverage The ability to obtain a given equity position at a reduced capital investment, thereby magnifying returns. (Chapter 13)

Leveraged buyout fund A private equity firm that raises capital from individual investors and uses these funds along with significant amounts of debt to acquire controlling interests in operating companies. (Chapter 4)

liquidity preference theory Theory that investors tend to prefer the greater liquidity of short-term securities and therefore require a premium to invest in long-term securities. (Chapter 8)

liquidity risk The risk of not being able to liquidate an investment quickly and at a reasonable price. (Chapter 10)

listed options Put and call options listed and traded on organized securities exchanges, such as the CBOE. (Chapter 13)

Load fund A mutual fund that charges investors a sales commission called a "load." (Chapter 4)

Loan amortization schedule A breakdown of the interest and principal payments on an amortized loan. (Chapter 6)

long purchase A transaction in which investors buy securities in the hope that they will increase in value and can be sold at a later date for profit. (Chapter 3)

loss aversion A situation in which the desire to avoid losses is so great that investors who are otherwise risk-averse will exhibit risk-seeking behavior in an attempt to avoid a loss. (Chapter 7)

LYON (liquid yield option note) A zero-coupon bond that carries both a conversion feature and a put option. (Chapter 2)

M

maintenance margin The absolute minimum amount of margin (equity) that an investor must maintain in the margin account at all times. (Chapter 3)

margin call Notification of the need to bring the equity of an account whose margin is below the maintenance level up above the maintenance margin level or to have enough margined holdings sold to reach this standard. (Chapter 3)

margin loan Vehicle through which borrowed funds are made available, at a stated interest rate, in a margin transaction. (Chapter 3)

margin requirement The minimum amount of equity that must be a margin investor's own funds; set by the Federal Reserve Board (the "Fed"). (Chapter 3)

margin trading The use of borrowed funds to purchase securities; magnifies returns by reducing the amount of equity that the investor must put up. (Chapter 3)

market anomalies Irregularities or deviations from the behavior one would expect in an efficient market. (Chapter 7)

market makers *Securities dealers* that "make markets" by offering to buy or sell certain quantities of securities at stated prices. (Chapter 3)

Market portfolio The portfolio of all risky and risk-free assets. (Chapter 12)

market return The average return for all (or a large sample of) stocks, such as those in the *Standard & Poor's 500-Stock Composite Index*. (Chapter 11)

Market risk premium The difference in the expected rate of return on the market portfolio and the risk-free rate of return. (Chapter 12)

market risk Risk of decline in investment returns because of market factors independent of the given investment. (Chapter 10)

market segmentation theory Theory that the market for debt is segmented on the basis of maturity, that supply and demand within each segment determine the prevailing interest rate, and that the slope of the yield curve depends on the relationship between the prevailing rates in each segment. (Chapter 8)

market technicians Analysts who believe it is chiefly (or solely) supply and demand that drive stock prices. (Chapter 7)

market value The prevailing market price of a security. (Chapter 1)

maturity date The date on which a bond matures and the principal must be repaid. (Chapter 2)

Maturity The date when a debt must be repaid. (Chapter 4)

mid-cap stocks Medium-sized stocks, generally with market values of less than $4 or $5 billion but more than $1 billion. (Chapter 1)

mixed stream A stream of returns that, unlike an annuity, exhibits no special pattern. (Chapter 10)

modern portfolio theory (MPT) An approach to portfolio management that uses several basic statistical measures to develop a portfolio plan. (Chapter 11)

money market Market where *short-term* debt securities (with maturities less than one year) are bought and sold. (Chapter 3)

Money market The financial market for short-term debt securities (maturing in one year or less). (Chapter 4)

mortgage bonds Senior bonds secured by real estate. (Chapter 2)

mortgage-backed bond A debt issue secured by a pool of home mortgages; issued primarily by federal agencies. (Chapter 2)

moving average (MA) A mathematical procedure that computes and records the average values of a series of prices, or other data, over time; results in a stream of average values that will act to smooth out a series of data. (Chapter 7)

municipal bond guarantees Guarantees from a party other than the issuer that principal and interest payments will be made in a prompt and timely manner. (Chapter 2)

municipal bonds Debt securities issued by states, counties, cities, and other political subdivisions; most of these bonds are tax-exempt (free of federal income tax on interest income). (Chapter 2)

Mutual fund A professionally managed investment company that pools the investments of many individuals and invests it in stocks, bonds, and other types of securities. (Chapter 4)

N

naked options Options written on securities not owned by the writer. (Chapter 13)

narrow framing Analyzing an investment problem in isolation or in a particularly narrow context rather than looking at all aspects of the problem. (Chapter 7)

Nasdaq market A major segment of the *secondary market* that employs an all-electronic trading platform to execute trades. (Chapter 3)

negatively correlated Describes two series that move in opposite directions. (Chapter 11)

Net asset value (NAV) The difference between the current market value of an entity's (such as a mutual fund) assets and the value of its liabilities. (Chapter 4)

No-load fund A mutual fund that doesn't charge a commission. (Chapter 4)

Nominal or **quoted (stated) interest rate** The interest rate paid on debt securities without an adjustment for any loss in purchasing power. (Chapter 5)

nominal rate of return The actual return earned on an investment expressed in current dollars. (Chapter 10)

Non-diversifiable risk Risk that cannot be eliminated through diversification. (Chapter 12)

note A debt security originally issued with a maturity of from 2 to 10 years. (Chapter 2)

Note Another term used to refer to indebtedness. Notes generally have a maturity between 1 and 10 years when originally issued. (Chapter 4)

O

option chain A list of all options traded on a particular security. An option chain provides the current market prices and trading volumes for all options linked to a particular stock. (Chapter 13)

option premium The quoted price the investor pays to buy a listed put or call option. (Chapter 13)

option Securities that give the holder the right to buy or sell a certain amount of an underlying financial asset at a specified price for a specified period of time. (Chapter 13)

option spreading Combining two or more options with different strike prices and/or expiration dates into a single transaction. (Chapter 13)

option straddle The simultaneous purchase (or sale) of a put and a call on the same underlying common stock (or financial asset). (Chapter 13)

option writer (or seller) The individual or institution that writes/creates put and call options. (Chapter 13)

Ordinary annuity A series of equal dollar payments for a specified number of periods with the payments occurring at the end of each period. (Chapter 6)

ordinary annuity An annuity for which the cash flows occur at the end of each period. (Chapter 10)

Organized security exchanges Security exchanges that physically occupy space (such as a building or part of a building) and trade financial instruments on their premises. (Chapter 4)

out-of-the-money A call option with no real value because the strike price exceeds the market price of the stock; a put option whose market price exceeds the strike price. (Chapter 13)

overconfidence The tendency to overestimate one's ability to perform a particular task. (Chapter 7)

over-the-counter (OTC) market A segment of the *secondary market* that involves trading in smaller, *unlisted securities*. (Chapter 3)

Over-the-counter markets All security markets except the organized exchanges. (Chapter 4)

P

paper return A return that has been achieved but not yet realized by an investor during a given period. (Chapter 10)

par value The stated, or face, value of a stock. (Chapter 1).

par value The stated, or face, value of a stock. (Chapter 6). Also, the value that a bond issuer must pay to the investor when the bond matures. (Chapter 2)

payback period The length of time it takes for the buyer of a convertible to recover the conversion premium from the extra current income earned on the convertible. (Chapter 2)

payment date The actual date on which the company will mail dividend checks to shareholders (also known as the *payable date*). (Chapter 1)

perfectly negatively correlated Describes two negatively correlated series that have a correlation coefficient of −1. (Chapter 11)

perfectly positively correlated Describes two positively correlated series that have a correlation coefficient of 1. (Chapter 11)

Perpetuity An annuity with an infinite life. (Chapter 6)

PIK bond A payment in kind junk bond that gives the issuer the right to make annual interest payments in new bonds rather than in cash. (Chapter 2)

Portfolio beta The beta coefficient of a portfolio of different investments. (Chapter 12)

portfolio beta, bp The beta of a portfolio; calculated as the weighted average of the betas of the individual assets it includes. (Chapter 11)

positively correlated Describes two series that move in the same direction. (Chapter 11)

Preferred stock An equity security that holds preference over common stock in terms of the right to the distribution of cash (dividends) and the right to the distribution of proceeds in the event of the liquidation and sale of the issuing firm. (Chapter 4)

premium bond A bond with a market value in excess of par; occurs when interest rates drop below the coupon rate. (Chapter 2)

Present value interest factor The value [1/(1 1 i)n] used as a multiplier to calculate a future payment's present value. (Chapter 5)

Present value The value in today's dollars of a future payment discounted back to the present at the required rate of return. (Chapter 5)

present value The *value today* of a sum to be received at some future date; the inverse of future value. (Chapter 10)

price/earnings (P/E) approach Stock valuation approach that tries to find the P/E ratio that's most appropriate for the stock; this ratio, along with estimated EPS, is then used to determine a reasonable stock price. (Chapter 9)

Primary market A part of the financial market where new security issues are initially bought and sold. (Chapter 4)

primary market The market in which *new issues* of securities are sold by the issuers to investors. (Chapter 3)

prime rate The lowest interest rate charged to the best business borrowers. (Chapter 3)

principal On a bond, the amount of capital that must be repaid at maturity. (Chapter 2)

Private equity firm A financial intermediary that invests in equities that are not traded on the public capital markets. (Chapter 4)

private placement The sale of new securities directly, without SEC registration, to private investors. (Chapter 3)

promised yield Yield-to-maturity. (Chapter 8)

Proprietary trading Using the bank's capital to make speculative bets on derivatives and securities. (Chapter 4)

prospectus A portion of a security registration statement that describes the key aspects of the issue and issuer. (Chapter 3)

public offering The sale of a firm's securities to public investors. (Chapter 3)

publicly traded issues Shares of stock that are readily available to the general public and are bought and sold in the open market. (Chapter 1)

purchasing power risk The chance that unanticipated changes in price levels (inflation or deflation) will adversely affect investment returns. (Chapter 10)

put A negotiable instrument that enables the holder to sell the underlying security at a specified price over a set period of time. (Chapter 13)

put-call parity A relationship linking the market values of puts and calls of European options written on the same underlying stock and having the same exercise price and expiration date. (Chapter 13)

pyramiding The technique of using paper profits in margin accounts to partly or fully finance the acquisition of additional securities. (Chapter 3)

R

random walk hypothesis The theory that stock price movements are unpredictable, so there's no way to know where prices are headed. (Chapter 7)

rate of growth The compound annual *rate of change* in the value of a stream of income. (Chapter 10)

real rate of return The nominal return minus the inflation rate; a measure of the increase in purchasing power that an investment provides. (Chapter 10)

realized return Current income actually received by an investor during a given period. (Chapter 10)

realized yield Expected return. (Chapter 8)

red herring A preliminary prospectus made available to prospective investors while waiting for the registration statement's SEC approval. (Chapter 3)

refunding provisions Provisions that prohibit the premature retirement of an issue from the proceeds of a lowercoupon refunding bond. (Chapter 2)

reinvestment rate The rate of return earned on interest or other income received from an investment over its investment horizon. (Chapter 10)

relative P/E multiple A measure of how a stock's P/E behaves relative to the average market multiple. (Chapter 9)

relevant risk Risk that is undiversifiable. (Chapter 11)

representativeness Cognitive biases that occur because people have difficulty thinking about randomness in outcomes. (Chapter 7)

required rate of return The rate of return that compensates investors for the risk of a particular investment. The minimum acceptable return on an investment given its risk. (Chapter 9)

required return The rate of return an investor must earn on an investment to be fully compensated for its risk. (Chapter 10)

residual owners Owners/stockholders of a firm, who are entitled to dividend income and a prorated share of the firm's earnings only after all other obligations have been met. (Chapter 1)

restricted account A margin account whose equity is less than the initial margin requirement; the investor may not make further margin purchases and must bring the margin back to the initial level when securities are sold. (Chapter 3)

revenue bonds Municipal bonds that require payment of principal and interest only if sufficient revenue is generated by the issuer. (Chapter 2)

rights offering An offer of new shares of stock to existing stockholders on a pro rata basis. (Chapter 3)

risk premium A return premium that reflects the issue and issuer characteristics associated with a given investment vehicle. (Chapter 10)

risk-averse Describes an investor who requires greater return in exchange for greater risk. (Chapter 10)

risk-free rate The rate of return that can be earned on a riskfree investment; the sum of the real rate of return and the expected inflation premium. (Chapter 10)

risk-indifferent Describes an investor who does not require a change in return as compensation for greater risk. (Chapter 10)

risk-return tradeoff The relationship between risk and return, in which investments with more risk should provide higher returns, and vice versa. (Chapter 10)

risk-seeking Describes an investor who will accept a lower return in exchange for greater risk. (Chapter 10)

Rule of 72 A method for estimating the time it takes for an amount to double in value. To determine the approximate time it takes for an amount to double in value, 72 is divided by the annual interest rate. (Chapter 5)

S

satisfactory investment An investment whose present value of benefits (discounted at the appropriate rate) equals or exceeds the present value of its costs. (Chapter 10)

secondary distributions The public sales of large blocks of previously issued securities held by large investors. (Chapter 3)

Secondary market The financial market where previously issued securities such as stocks and bonds are bought and sold. (Chapter 4)

secondary market The market in which securities are traded *after they have been issued; an aftermarket.* (Chapter 3)

Securities and Exchange Commission (SEC) Federal agency that regulates securities offerings and markets. (Chapter 3)

securities markets Forums that allow suppliers and demanders of *securities* to make financial transactions. (Chapter 3)

securitization The process of transforming lending vehicles such as mortgages into marketable securities. (Chapter 2)

Security A negotiable instrument that represents a financial claim that has value. Securities are broadly classified as debt securities (bonds) and equity securities (shares of common stock). (Chapter 4)

security market line (SML) The graphical depiction of the capital asset pricing model; reflects the investor's required return for each level of undiversifiable risk, measured by beta. (Chapter 11)

Security market line A graphical representation of the Capital Asset Pricing Model. (Chapter 12)

self-attribution bias The tendency to overestimate the role that one's intelligence or skill plays in bringing about a favorable investment result and to underestimate the role of chance in that result. (Chapter 7)

selling group A group of dealers and brokerage firms that join the investment banker(s); each member is responsible for selling a certain portion of a new security issue. (Chapter 3)

semi-strong form (EMH) Form of the EMH holding that abnormally large profits cannot be consistently earned using publicly available information. (Chapter 7)

senior bonds Secured debt obligations, backed by a legal claim on specific property of the issuer. (Chapter 2)

serial bond A bond that has a series of different maturity dates. (Chapter 2)

short interest The number of stocks sold short in the market at any given time; a technical indicator believed to indicate future market demand. (Chapter 7)

short-selling The sale of borrowed securities, their eventual repurchase by the short-seller, and their return to the lender. (Chapter 3)

simple interest Interest paid only on the initial deposit for the amount of time it is held. (Chapter 10)

Simple interest The interest earned on the principal. (Chapter 5)

sinking fund A provision that stipulates the amount of principal that will be retired annually over the life of a bond. (Chapter 2)

small-cap stocks Stocks that generally have market values of less than $1 billion but can offer above-average returns. (Chapter 1)

speculative stocks Stocks that offer the potential for substantial price appreciation, usually because of some special situation, such as new management or the introduction of a promising new product. (Chapter 1)

split ratings Different ratings given to a bond issue by two or more rating agencies. (Chapter 2)

standard deviation, s A statistic used to measure the dispersion (variation) of returns around an asset's average or expected return. (Chapter 10)

stock dividend Payment of a dividend in the form of additional shares of stock. (Chapter 1)

stock spin-off Conversion of one of a firm's subsidiaries to a stand-alone company by distribution of stock in that new company to existing shareholders. (Chapter 1)

stock split A maneuver in which a company increases the number of shares outstanding by exchanging a specified number of new shares of stock for each outstanding share. (Chapter 1)

stock valuation The process by which the underlying value of a stock is established on the basis of its forecasted risk and return performance. (Chapter 9)

stock-index option A put or call option written on a specific stock market index, such as the S&P 500. (Chapter 13)

strike price The stated price at which you can buy a security with a call or sell a security with a put. (Chapter 13)

strong form (EMH) Form of the EMH that holds that there is no information, public or private, that allows investors to consistently earn abnormal profits. (Chapter 7)

subordinated debentures Unsecured bonds whose claim is secondary to other debentures. (Chapter 2)

Systematic risk See Non-diversifiable risk. (Chapter 12)

T

target price The price an analyst expects the stock to reach within a certain period of time, usually a year. (Chapter 9)

tax risk The chance that Congress will make unfavorable changes in tax laws, driving down the after-tax returns and market values of certain investments. (Chapter 10)

tax swap Replacement of a bond that has a capital loss for a similar security; used to offset a gain generated in another part of an investor's portfolio. (Chapter 8)

taxable equivalent yield The return a fully taxable bond would have to provide to match the after-tax return of a lower-yielding, tax-free municipal bond. (Chapter 2)

tech stocks Stocks that represent the technology sector of the market. (Chapter 1)

technical analysis The study of the various forces at work in the marketplace and their effect on stock prices. (Chapter 7)

term bond A bond that has a single, fairly lengthy maturity date. (Chapter 2)

term structure of interest rates The relationship between the interest rate or rate of return (yield) on a bond and its time to maturity. (Chapter 8)

theory of contrary opinion A technical indicator that uses the amount and type of odd-lot trading as an indicator of the current state of the market and pending changes. (Chapter 7)

third market Over-the-counter transactions typically handled by market makers and made in securities listed on the NYSE, the NYSE AMEX, or one of the other exchanges. (Chapter 3)

time value of money The fact that as long as an opportunity exists to earn interest, the value of money is affected by the point in time when the money is received. (Chapter 10)

time value The amount by which the option price exceeds the option's fundamental value. (Chapter 13)

Timeline A linear representation of the timing of cash flows. (Chapter 5)

total return The sum of the current income and the capital gain (or loss) earned on an investment over a specified period of time. (Chapter 10)

total risk The sum of an investment's undiversifiable risk and diversifiable risk. (Chapter 11)

traditional portfolio management An approach to portfolio management that emphasizes "balancing" the portfolio by assembling a wide variety of stocks and/or bonds of companies from a broad range of industries. (Chapter 11)

Treasury bonds U.S. Treasury securities that are issued with 30-year maturities. (Chapter 2)

Treasury inflation-protected securities (TIPS) A type of Treasury security that provides protection against inflation by adjusting investor returns for the annual rate of inflation. (Chapter 2)

Treasury notes U.S. Treasury debt securities that are issued with maturities of 2 to 10 years. (Chapter 2)

treasury stock Shares of stock that have been sold and subsequently repurchased by the issuing firm. (Chapter 1)

Treasury strips Zero-coupon bonds created from U.S. Treasury securities. (Chapter 2)

true rate of interest The actual rate of interest earned. (Chapter 10)

U

uncorrelated Describes two series that lack any relationship or interaction and therefore have a correlation coefficient close to zero. (Chapter 11)

underwriting syndicate A group of investment banks formed by the originating investment banker to share the financial risk associated with *underwriting* new securities. (Chapter 3)

underwriting The role of the *investment banker* in bearing the risk of reselling the securities purchased from an issuing corporation at an agreed-on price. (Chapter 3)

undiversifiable (systematic) risk The risk that remains even in a well-diversified portfolio. Risk that tends to affect all (or nearly all) securities. (Chapter 11)

Unsystematic risk See Diversifiable risk. (Chapter 12)

V

Venture capital firm An investment company that raises money from accredited investors and uses the proceeds to invest in new start-up companies. (Chapter 4)

W

weak form (EMH) Form of the EMH holding that past data on stock prices are of no use in predicting future prices. (Chapter 7)

Y

Yankee bonds U.S. dollar-denominated debt securities issued by foreign governments or corporations and traded in U.S. securities markets. (Chapter 3)

yield (internal rate of return) The compound annual rate of return earned by a long-term investment; the discount rate that produces a present value of the investment's benefits that just equals its cost. (Chapter 10)

yield curve A graph that represents the relationship between a bond's term to maturity and its yield at a given point in time. (Chapter 8)

yield pickup swap Replacement of a low-coupon bond for a comparable higher-coupon bond in order to realize an increase in current yield and yield-to-maturity. (Chapter 8)

yield spreads Differences in interest rates that exist among various sectors of the market. (Chapter 8)

yield-to-call (YTC) The yield on a bond if it remains outstanding only until a specified call date. (Chapter 8)

yield-to-maturity (YTM) The fully compounded rate of return earned by an investor over the life of a bond, including interest income and price appreciation. (Chapter 8)

Z

zero-coupon bonds Bonds with no coupons that are sold at a deep discount from par value. (Chapter 2)

Index

Page numbers in bold type refer to key term definitions;
Page numbers followed by the letters *f, n,* or *t* represent, respectively, figure, note, and table location.